Lecture Notes in Computer Science 6737

Commenced Publication in 1973
Founding and Former Series Editors:
Gerhard Goos, Juris Hartmanis, and Jan van Leeuwen

Abderrahmane Nitaj   David Pointcheval (Eds.)

Progress in Cryptology – AFRICACRYPT 2011

4th International Conference on Cryptology in Africa
Dakar, Senegal, July 5-7, 2011
Proceedings

 Springer

Volume Editors

Abderrahmane Nitaj
Université de Caen
Département de Mathématiques
Campus II, Boulevard Maréchal Juin, BP 5186 - 14032 Caen Cedex, France
E-mail: nitaj@math.unicaen.fr

David Pointcheval
École Normale Supérieure
Département d'Informatique
45 rue d'Ulm, 75230 Paris Cedex 05, France
E-mail: david.pointcheval@ens.fr

ISSN 0302-9743   e-ISSN 1611-3349
ISBN 978-3-642-21968-9   e-ISBN 978-3-642-21969-6
DOI 10.1007/978-3-642-21969-6
Springer Heidelberg Dordrecht London New York

Library of Congress Control Number: 2011929658

CR Subject Classification (1998): E.3, C.2, K.6.5, D.4.6, J.1, H.4

LNCS Sublibrary: SL 4 – Security and Cryptology

Typesetting: Camera-ready by author, data conversion by Scientific Publishing Services, Chennai, India

Printed on acid-free paper

Springer is part of Springer Science+Business Media (www.springer.com)

Preface

AFRICACRYPT 2011, the 4th International Conference on the Theory and Application of Cryptographic Techniques in Africa took place July 5–7, 2011 in Dakar, Senegal. The conference was organized by the LACGAA team of Université Cheikh Anta Diop de Dakar and the STCC team of "Présidence de la République – Service Technique Central des Chiffres et de la Sécurité des Télécommunications" in cooperation with the International Association for Cryptologic Research.

The conference received 76 submissions, and all were reviewed by the Program Committee. Each paper was assigned at least three reviewers, while submissions co-authored by Program Committee members were reviewed by at least five people. The Program Committee, aided by reports from 52 external reviewers, produced a total of 240 reviews in all. After highly interactive discussions and a careful deliberation, the Program Committee selected 23 papers for presentation. The authors of accepted papers were given 3 weeks to prepare final versions for these proceedings. We would like to note that the African paper entitled "On Randomness Extraction in Elliptic Curves" written by Abdoul Aziz Ciss and Djiby Sow was accepted as one of the best papers. The program was completed with invited talks by Jens Groth, Tatsuaki Okamoto and Bart Preneel. We would like to thank everyone who contributed to the success of AFRICACRYPT 2011. We are deeply grateful to the Program Committee for their hard work, enthusiasm, and conscientious efforts to ensure that each paper received a thorough and fair review. These thanks are of course extended to the external reviewers, listed on the following pages, who took the time to help out during the evaluation process. We would also like to thank Thomas Baignères and Matthieu Finiasz for writing the iChair software and Springer for agreeing to an accelerated schedule for printing the proceedings. We also wish to heartily thank Mamadou Sangharé, the General Chair, and Djiby Sow, the General Co-chair, as well as the LAC-GAA and STCC teams, for their efforts in the organization of the conference. Last but not the least, we extend our sincere thanks to all those who contributed to AFRICACRYPT 2011 and especially to the participants, submitters, authors, presenters and invited speakers.

AFRICACRYPT has been emerging as a powerful forum for researchers to interact, share their work and knowledge with others for the overall growth and development of cryptology research in the world, and more specifically in Africa.

July 2011
Abderrahmane Nitaj
David Pointcheval

Organization

General Chairs

Mamadou Sangharé   Université Cheikh Anta Diop de Dakar, Senegal
Djiby Sow   Université Cheikh Anta Diop de Dakar, Senegal

Program Chairs

Abderrahmane Nitaj   Université de Caen, France
David Pointcheval   ENS and CNRS and INRIA, Paris, France

Program Committee

Abdelhak Azhari	University of Casablanca, Morocco
Abdelmalek Azizi	University of Oujda, Morocco
Hatem M. Bahig	Ain Shams University, Cairo, Egypt
Colin Boyd	Queensland University of Technology, Australia
Anne Canteaut	INRIA, France
David Cash	UC San Diego, USA
Dario Catalano	Università di Catania, Italy
Riaal Domingues	South African Communications and Security Agency, South Africa
Eiichiro Fujisaki	NTT Labs, Japan
David Galindo	University of Luxembourg, Luxembourg
Maria Isabel Gonzalez-Vasco	Universidad Rey Juan Carlos, Madrid, Spain
Aline Gouget	CryptoExperts, France
Jens Groth	University College London, UK
Martin Hirt	ETH Zurich, Switzerland
Tetsu Iwata	Nagoya University, Japan
Stanislaw Jarecki	UC Irvine, California, USA
Seny Kamara	Microsoft, Redmond, USA
Fabien Laguillaumie	University of Caen, France
Mark Manulis	TU Darmstadt and CASED, Germany
Bruno Martin	I3S, University of Nice-Sophia Antipolis, France
Keith Martin	Royal Holloway, University of London, UK
Mitsuru Matsui	Mitsubishi Electric, Japan
Kaisa Nyberg	Aalto University and Nokia, Finland
Sami Omar	Tunis University, Tunisia
Ayoub Otmani	University of Caen, France and INRIA, France
Josef Pieprzyk	Macquarie University, Australia
Vincent Rijmen	K.U. Leuven, Belgium and TU Graz, Austria

Magdy Saeb   AST, Alexandria, Egypt
Kazue Sako   NEC, Japan
Palash Sarkar   Indian Statistical Institute, India
Francesco Sica   University of Calgary, Canada
Martijn Stam   EPFL, Switzerland
Christine Swart   University of Cape Town, South Africa
Damien Vergnaud   ENS, Paris, France
Ivan Visconti   University of Salerno, Italy and UCLA, USA
Bogdan Warinschi   Bristol University, UK
Duncan Wong   City University of Hong Kong, China
Scott Yilek   University of St. Thomas, USA
Amr M. Youssef   Concordia University, Montreal, Quebec, Canada

External Reviewers

Divesh Aggarwal   Sebastiaan Indesteege
Ali Akhavi   Toshiyuki Isshiki
Kazumaro Aoki   Kimmo Järvinen
Kfir Barhum   Noboru Kunihiro
Stephanie Bayer   Christoph Lucas
Rishiraj Bhattacharyya   Vadim Lyubashevsky
Joppe W. Bos   Avradip Mandal
Charles Bouillaguet   Nicolas Meloni
Billy Brumley   Shiho Moriai
Stanislav Bulygin   Adam O'Neill
Sébastien Canard   Somindu C Ramanna
Pierre-Louis Cayrel   Robert Rolland
Sandro Coretti   Greg Rose
Claus Diem   Minoru Saeki
Mario Di Raimondo   Subhabrata Samajder
Orr Dunkelman   Juraj Sarinay
Mohamed Elkadi   Alessandra Scafuro
Nadia El Mrabet   Nicolas Sendrier
Martin Franz   Douglas Stebila
Jun Furukawa   Daisuke Suzuki
Xiao-Shan Gao   Isamu Teranishi Stefano Tessaro
Carlos González Guillén   Elmar Tischhauser
Louis Goubin   Yuuki Tokunaga
Jonanthan Hoch   Keita Xagawa
Michal Hojsík   Bin Zhang
Laurent Imbert

Table of Contents

Efficient Implementations

Cryptographic Schemes

Algorithmic Problems

Elliptic Curves

Fault Analysis

Security Proofs

Invited Talks

Secure Outsourced Computation

Jake Loftus and Nigel P. Smart

Dept. Computer Science,
University of Bristol,
Bristol, United Kingdom
{loftus,nigel}@cs.bris.ac.uk

Abstract. The development of multi-party computation was one of the early achievements of theoretical cryptography. Since that time a number of papers have been published which look at specific application scenarios (e-voting, e-auctions), different security guarantees (computational vs unconditional), different adversarial models (active vs passive, static vs adaptive), different communication models (secure channels, broadcast) and different set-up assumptions (CRS, trusted hardware etc). We examine an application scenario in the area of cloud computing which we call *Secure Outsourced Computation*. We show that this variant produces less of a restriction on the allowable adversary structures than full multi-party computation. We also show that if one provides the set of computation engines (or Cloud Computing providers) with a small piece of isolated trusted hardware one can outsource any computation in a manner which requires less security constraints on the underlying communication model and at greater computational/communication efficiency than full multi-party computation. In addition our protocol is highly efficient and thus of greater practicality than previous solutions, our required trusted hardware being particularly simple and with minimal trust requirements.

1 Introduction

One of the crowning achievements in the early days of theoretical cryptography was the result that a set of parties, each with their own secret input, can compute *any* computable function of these inputs securely with polynomial overhead [4,9,20,29,33]. Of course the above statement comes with some caveats, as to what we assume in terms of abilities of any adversaries and what assumptions we make of the underlying infrastructure. However, the concept of general Secure Multi-Party Computation (SMPC) has had considerable theoretical impact on cryptography and has even been deployed in practical applications [6]. One can consider any complex secure computation as an example of SMPC, for example voting, auctions, payment systems etc. Indeed by specialising the application domain one can often obtain protocols which considerably outperform the general SMPC constructions.

CLOUD COMPUTING AND SECURE OUTSOURCED COMPUTATION. In this paper we take a middle approach between general SMPC and specific applications. In particular we examine a realistic application setting for SMPC which we call *Secure Outsourced Computation* (SOC). Below we argue that this is a natural restriction and a practical

A. Nitaj and D. Pointcheval (Eds.): AFRICACRYPT 2011, LNCS 6737, pp. 1–20, 2011.

setting; being particularly suited to the new paradigm of Cloud Computing. We show that by restricting the use of SMPC in this way we can avoid some of the restrictions required for general unconditionally secure SMPC.

Consider the following problem: A data holder wishes to outsource their data storage to a third party, i.e. a cloud computing provider. For example the data holder could be a government health care provider and they wish to store the health records of their population on a third party service. Clearly, there are significant privacy concerns with such a situation and hence the data holder is likely to want to encrypt the data before sending it to the service provider. However, this comes with a significant disadvantage; namely one cannot do anything with the data without downloading it and decrypting it!

This application scenario is in fact close to the common instantiation of practical proposed SMPC applications. Not only does this cover the problem of outsourced data storage, but it also encompasses a number of other applications; for example e-voting can be considered similarly, in that the data holders are now plural (the voters) and e-voting protocols often consist of a number of third parties executing the tallying computation on behalf of the set of voters. As another example the Danish sugar beet auction, in which SMPC was deployed for the first time [6], is also of this form. In the sugar beet auction example the data providers (the buyers and sellers) outsourced the computation of the market clearing price to a number of third party providers.

Essentially SOC consists of a set of entities I called the data providers which provide input, $\mathcal{P}$ the set of players which perform the computation and a set R of receivers which obtain the output of the computation. We assume that I and R may intersect, but we require that $\mathcal{P}$ does not intersect with I or R. The set of input players and receivers are assumed to be honest-but-curious, whereas the set $\mathcal{P}$ may consist of adaptive and/or active adversaries. In this paper we shall concentrate, to simplify the discussion, on the case of where there is a single data provider and receiver, who is outsourcing computation and storage to a set of possibly untrusted third parties. The extension to multiple data providers/receivers is obvious.

PRIOR WORK. This notion of SOC has been considered a number of times in the literature before. From a practical perspective the proposed architecture most closely resembles the architecture behind the Sharemind [5] system. This has notions of "Miner", "Data Doner" and "Client" which have roughly the same functionality as our players, data providers and data receivers. However, Sharemind implements standard SMPC protocols between three players working over the ring $\mathbb{Z}_{2^{32}}$, on the assumption of a single passive adversary. We however use this special application scenario to extend the applicability to different adversary structures and to allow smaller numbers of players.

Theoretically we are now able to perform SOC using only a single server by using the recently discovered homomorphic encryption schemes [15,18,19,32]. However, these are only theoretical solutions and it looks impossible to provide a practical solution based on homomorphic encryption in the near future. In addition using a single server does not on its own protect against active adversaries, unless one requires the server to engage in expensive zero-knowledge proofs for each operation, which in turn will need to be verified by the receiver. An alternative to this approach is given in [17] which combines the use of homomorphic encryption (to obtain confidentiality) with Yao's garbled circuits to protect against malicious servers.

Another (trivial) approach using a single server would be for the data provider to provide the server with a trusted module. The data can then be held encrypted on the server, and the trusted module could be used to perform the computation. (with the server thereby just acting as a storage device). Clearly this means that the trusted module would need to be quite powerful, and would in some sense defeat the objective of the whole outsourcing process.

In [30] another approach using a single server and a trusted module is proposed. Here the trusted module is used to compute a garbled circuit representing the function, with the evaluation of the garbled circuit being computed by the server. Using prior techniques the authors are able to compute the garbled circuit using a small amount of memory. However, this approach requires that the database is itself re-garbled for every query. The authors propose that this is also performed on the trusted module. Whilst this approach is currently deployable, it is not practical and it also requires that the trusted hardware module is relatively complex.

Another approach, and the one we take, to obtain an immediately practical solution to the problem of outsourcing computation, would for the data holder to share his database between more than one cloud provider via a secret sharing scheme. Then to perform some computation the data holder simply instructs the multiple cloud providers to execute an SMPC protocol on the shared database.

OUR CONTRIBUTION. We show that with this restricted notion of SMPC we can relax the necessary conditions for unconditional secure computation to be possible. This essentially arises due to the fact that the people doing the computation have no input to the protocol, and thus the usual impossibility result for general adversary structures does not apply.

However, on its own SOC does not lead to more efficient and hence practical protocols; namely whilst we have relaxed the necessary conditions we have not relaxed the (equivalent) sufficient conditions. To enable the latter we make an additional set up assumption of the existence of small isolated secure trusted modules which are associated/attached to each player in $\mathcal{P}$. This assumptions enables us to significantly improve the performance of protocols compared to general SMPC, at the same time as simplifying the assumptions we require of the underlying communication network. Using additional hardware assumptions to enable SMPC is not new, indeed we discuss the prior work below, but the novelty of our approach is that the additional assumed hardware is relatively simple and cheap to produce. In particular the complexity of the hardware compared to the above approach of [30] is orders of magnitude simpler.

Our work therefore makes two mild simplifying assumptions to the standard SMPC model; this enables much more efficient protocols and reduced network assumptions. Our protocol requires, apart from the isolated trusted modules, only reliable broadcast between the set of players, and secure channels from the data providers to the set of players doing the computation. We also require secure communication from the trusted modules to their associated player, this can either be accomplished via encryption or more probably in practice by physical locality. Before proceeding it is worth stating that we do not claim to make any theoretical contributions or innovations, our methods are to apply existing theoretical tools in a new and novel way so as to obtain greater practically of what has up to now been a generally theoretical tool.

PAPER OVERVIEW. In Section 2 we provide the background details on SMPC based on secret sharing that we will be using. In Section 3 we describe our protocol in the simplified setting where one has a single semi-trusted third party who provides the players with various "random" numbers, giving a UC proof of security in Section 4. We then turn in Section 5 to show how this semi-trusted third party can be implemented using small pieces of trusted hardware. All the previous discussion is done in the context of passive adversaries, so in Section 6 we discuss the case of active and covert adversaries. Finally in Section 7 we briefly discuss two implementation aspects; namely how to perform the transfer of the data from the client to the servers, and we outline the benefits of being able to work over the field $\mathbb{F}_2$ as opposed to having to work over $\mathbb{F}_p$. A key point is that using our trusted hardware, and restricted application domain, we can make use of linear secret sharing schemes over $\mathbb{F}_2$ with a small number of players.

2   Background

We present the necessary background notation and historical notes on standard SMPC.

2.1   Secure Multi-Party Computation

In standard SMPC the goal is for a set of $\mathcal{P} = \{1, \ldots, n\}$ to compute some function $f(x_1, \ldots, x_n)$ of their individual inputs x_i such that the players only learn the output of the function and nothing else.

DEFINITIONS. It is perhaps worth presenting some definitions before we proceed. Adversaries (who are assumed to be one or more of the players) can be given various powers: a *passive* adversary (sometimes called *honest-but-curious*) is one which follows the protocol but who wishes to learn more than they should from the running of the protocol; an *active* adversary (sometimes called *malicious*) is one which can deviate from the protocol description, they also may wish to stop the honest players from completing the computation, or to make the honest players compute the wrong output; a *covert* adversary is one which can deviate from the protocol but they wish to avoid detection when they deviate. We talk of a singular adversary although they may be a set of actual players, such a single adversary can coordinate the operation of a set of adversarial players; this single adversary is often called a *monolithic adversary*. Adversaries can either have unbounded computing power or they can be computationally bounded.

As mentioned above, we also need to consider what communication infrastructure is assumed to be given. In the *secure channels model* we assume perfectly secure channels exist between each player; in the *broadcast model* we assume there exists a broadcast channel linking all players. Use of the broadcast channel model has a minor caveat: we assume not only that when an honest party broadcasts a message to all parties it is received by all parties, but also that a dishonest party cannot send different values to different honest parties as if it was a general broadcast. A broadcast model with both of these properties will be called a *consensus broadcast model*, if only the first property holds we will say we are in a *reliable broadcast model*.

An *adversary structure* Σ is a subset of $2^{\mathcal{P}}$ with the following property, if $A \in \Sigma$ and $B \subset A$ then $B \in \Sigma$. The adversary structure defines which sets of parties the adversary is allowed to corrupt. In early work the adversary structure was a *threshold structure*, i.e. Σ contained all subsets of $\mathcal{P}$ of size less than or equal to some threshold bound t. The set of players which the adversary corrupts can be decided before the protocol runs, in which case we call such an adversary *static*; or it can be decided as the protocol proceeds, in which case we say the adversary is *adaptive*.

HISTORICAL BACKGROUND. The first results were for computationally bounded passive adversaries; the case $n = 2$ is provided by the classical result of Yao [33]. Protocols that obtain security against active adversaries for the case $n = 2$ are feasible but inefficient, the best current proposal being that of [26]; protocols for covert adversaries have only recently been presented [1] (for unbounded adversaries the first work on covert security is even more recent [13]).

For more than two players the first result was for computationally bounded static, active adversaries where [20] showed one could obtain SMPC as long as (for threshold adversaries) we have $t < n/2$. The extension to adaptive adversaries was given in [7], still with a bound of $t < n/2$. If we are prepared to only tolerate passive adversaries then we can obtain a protocol with $t < n$.

It turns out, somewhat surprisingly, that the most efficient and practical protocols for more than two parties are those that give security against unbounded adversaries. Here we obtain (again for the threshold case)

- Passive security, assuming secure channels, if and only if $t < n/2$ [4,9].
- Active security, assuming secure channels, if and only if $t < n/3$ [4,9].
- Active security, assuming secure channels between players and a consensus broadcast channel, if and only if $t < n/2$ [29] (assuming we want statistical security) or $t < n/3$ (if we want perfect security).

All these early protocols are based on the principle of using Shamir secret sharing [31] to derive the underlying secret sharing scheme to implement the above protocols. For general adversary structures we define the following two properties:

- The adversary structure Σ is said to be Q^2 if for all $A, B \in \Sigma$ we have $A \cup B \neq \mathcal{P}$.
- The adversary structure Σ is said to be Q^3 if for all $A, B, C \in \Sigma$ we have $A \cup B \cup C \neq \mathcal{P}$.

We then have the following theorem

Theorem 1 (Hirt and Maurer [23]). *SMPC is possible:*

- *Against adaptive passive adversaries if and only if Σ is Q^2, assuming pairwise secure channels.*
- *Adaptive active adversaries if and only if Σ is Q^3, assuming pairwise secure channels and a consensus broadcast channel.*

The proof of this theorem is via reduction to the threshold case, and is not practical. In [11] the authors show how to perform SMPC by generalising the above constructions using Shamir's secret sharing scheme to an arbitrary Linear Secret Sharing Scheme (LSSS). They define notions of what it means for a LSSS to be multiplicative, and strongly multiplicative. A multiplicative LSSS allows SMPC for passive adversaries, whereas a strongly multiplicative LSSS allows security against active adversaries.

In this paper we shall mainly concentrate on the case of passive adversaries, leaving active adversaries to a discussion at the end. We end this section by examining the above theorem in the case of passive adversaries: That Σ being Q^2 is sufficient to perform unconditional SMPC follows from the work of [11], who show that one can construct for any Q^2 structure a multiplicative LSSS. The multiplicative property enables one to *write down* a protocol to enable SMPC. That Σ being Q^2 is a necessary condition follows from a result first expressed in [4] (see [12] for an explicit proof) which says that unconditional SMPC is impossible if one only has two parties; the non-Q^2 case can then be shown to be reducible to the case of two parties.

Our main result is that by using trusted hardware one can relax the sufficient condition in the above discussion, and that the necessary condition can be relaxed by performing *Secure Outsourced Computation* as opposed to general SMPC. At the same time the protocol we present becomes more efficient and requires less constraints on the overall network assumptions, indeed it is essentially equivalent to the second stage of the asynchronous protocol of [14], which itself is based on Beaver's idea of circuit randomization [2].

2.2   Linear Secret Sharing Schemes

Before going any further it is perhaps instructive to introduce LSSS and how they can be constructed. In this paper we shall be only interested in ideal LSSS, since these provide the most efficient practical protocols with no increase in storage requirements. Note that since our presentation is focused on ideal schemes, to produce non-ideal schemes one needs to slightly adapt the following.

GENERAL LSSS. An ideal LSSS $\mathcal{M}$ over a field $\mathbb{F}_q$ on n-players of dimension k is given by a pair $(M, \mathbf{p})$ where M is a $k \times n$ matrix over $\mathbb{F}_q$ and $\mathbf{p}$ is a k-dimensional column vector over $\mathbb{F}_q$. We write $\mathbf{m}_1, \ldots, \mathbf{m}_n$ for the columns of M. Note that any non-zero vector $\mathbf{p} \in \mathrm{Span}_{\mathbb{F}_q}(\mathbf{m}_1, \ldots, \mathbf{m}_n)$ (the vector space over $\mathbb{F}_q$ spanned by $\mathbf{m}_1, \ldots, \mathbf{m}_n$) can be selected; so one might as well select M and $\mathbf{p}$ such that $\mathbf{p} = (1, \ldots, 1)^\mathsf{T}$; wgere $\mathbf{x}^\mathsf{T}$ denotes the vector-transpose operation. If A is a set of players we let M_A denote the matrix M restricted to the columns in A, and we let $\mathcal{M}_A$ denote the associated LSSS.

To share a secret s one generates a vector $\mathbf{t} \in \mathbb{F}_q^k$ at random such that $\mathbf{t} \cdot \mathbf{p} = s$ and then one computes the shares as $(s_1, \ldots, s_n) = \mathbf{s} = \mathbf{t} \cdot M$. Given a set of shares there is also a vector $\mathbf{r}$ such that $s = \mathbf{r} \cdot (s_1, \ldots, s_n)^\mathsf{T}$, this vector is called the recombination vector. If we set $\mathcal{P} = \{1, \ldots, n\}$ then the access structure $\Gamma(\mathcal{M})$ for the ideal LSSS is given by

$$\left\{ A = \{a_1, \ldots, a_t\} \subset \mathcal{P} : \mathbf{p} \in \mathrm{Span}_{\mathbb{F}_q}(\mathbf{m}_{a_1}, \ldots, \mathbf{m}_{a_t}) \right\}.$$

Since we have assumed that $\mathbf{p} \in \mathrm{Span}_{\mathbb{F}_q}(\mathbf{m}_1, \ldots, \mathbf{m}_n)$ we have that $\mathcal{P} \in \Gamma(\mathcal{M})$, i.e. it is possible for all players to reconstruct the secret. The adversary structure is defined by $\Sigma(\mathcal{M}) = 2^{\mathcal{P}} \setminus \Gamma(\mathcal{M})$. We sometimes write $[s]$ for the sharing of s, $[s]_i = s_i$ for the ith component of the sharing of s, and if $A \subset \mathcal{P}$ we write $[s]_A$ for the vector of shares of s held by the set of players A. We have $H(s|[s]_A) = H(s)$ if $A \in \Sigma(\mathcal{M})$ and $H(s|[s]_A) = 0$ if $A \in \Gamma(\mathcal{M})$.

MULTIPLICATIVE LSSS. The Schur (or Hadamard) product $\mathbf{a} \otimes \mathbf{b}$ of two vectors is defined to be their componentwise product. The LSSS $\mathcal{M}$ is said to be *multiplicative* if there exists a vector $\mathbf{r}_M \in \mathbb{F}_q^k$ such that for two shared values s and s' we have $s \cdot s' = \mathbf{r}_M \cdot ([s] \otimes [s'])$. Note that we may have $\mathbf{r} = \mathbf{r}_M$, which is the case for Shamir secret sharing when $t < n/2$.

A LSSS $\mathcal{M}$ is said to be *strongly multiplicative* if for all $A \in \Gamma(\mathcal{M})$ we have that $\mathcal{M}_A$ is multiplicative. Intuitively multiplicative means that the Schur product of sharings from *all* players is enough to determine the product of two secrets, whereas strongly multiplicative means that this holds even if you only have access to shares from a qualifying set of honest players.

In general SMPC it is not known how to construct ideal LSSS for all possible access structures; the construction in [11] which produces a multiplicative LSSS, from an LSSS with a Q^2 structure, results in a possible doubling of the share sizes and hence results in a non-ideal scheme. In our application we will not need to restrict to Q^2 structures, and so our restriction to ideal LSSS is without loss of generality. This solves a problem with SMPC in that one would prefer to use circuits over $\mathbb{F}_2$, and a reasonably small number of players. Yet no ideal multiplicative LSSS exists over $\mathbb{F}_2$ with less than six players. One can construct schemes with three players but then one loses the ideal nature of the LSSS.

2.3 Trusted Hardware in SMPC

The first mention of the use of trusted modules in the context of secure multiparty computation seems to be [3]. In this paper they assume each party is equipped with a trusted module and each persons trusted module is connected by a secure channel. The set of all trusted modules form what they call a "trusted system". They then reduce the problem of secure MPC to the UIC problem (Uniform Interactive Consistency). The final solution requires $O(n)$ rounds of computation and $O(n^3)$ messages, to compute *any* function as long as at most $t < n/2$ parties are corrupted. The model is such that parties may block communication to and from their trusted modules. Essentially the trusted modules swap their respective inputs and compute the function in the normal way. This solution has a number of major problems, the modules are not simple, they are highly complex, they need to be highly trusted and they need to be able to securely communicate with each other. On the other hand there is a proposed embodiment of this protocol using Java cards in [16]. The question as to who produces and distributes the cards is not addressed.

Most of the recent work on secure hardware modules in SMPC is based on the following observation. We have already remarked that unconditionally secure general SMPC is impossible in the case of Q^2 structures, which includes the case of only two players. However, if we assume oracle access to an ideal functionality such as Oblivious Transfer than unconditionally secure SMPC becomes possible even for two players. Thus the question becomes one of implementing the oracle access to an OT functionality.

Katz [24] looks at how the introduction of tamper proof hardware would enable one to get around various impossibility results in the UC framework. He uses tamper proof hardware to replace standard "set-up" assumptions, such as types of channels, a CRS or a public key infrastructure etc. He assumes that a set of parties want to compute the output of some function which depends on their inputs, and that *each* player can produce their own tamper proof hardware. In addition this hardware when given to another player may not be trusted by the receiving player. Once a player has handed over a token he is unable to send this token any messages. Using this trusted hardware Katz is able to produce a UC commitment functionality which enables him to perform secure MPC. This is very different from our own setup, in particular Katz assumes that *each* player can produce trusted hardware and that we are in the "standard" MPC setting where parties have inputs. In our setting we will have a single data owner who produces (or trusts) a single piece (essentially) of trusted hardware, the players are then computing on behalf of the data owner. This results in our trusted hardware being considerably simpler than the hardware envisaged in Katz's model. However, the restriction on the communication with the trusted module is preserved in our approach.

In [8] Katz's work is extended to include modules for which players do not necessarily "know" the code within the token. This allows for modules to be resettable, and in particular stateless. Again the model of application use is very different from ours, and the modules have a much more complicated functionality (enhanced trapdoor permutations). In [28] the model is extended further, here again one is constructing general UC commitment functionality, but now it is assumed that only one party (Goliath) is able to produce tamper proof modules, where as the other (David) has to ensure that this does not give Goliath an advantage. Again the underlying application is of the parties computing a function of their own inputs, and not ours of the parties computing a function on behalf of someone else.

Katz's work is again extended in [21] where each player constructs a secure token and transmits it to the other player at the start of the protocol. Example protocols requiring both statefull and stateless modules are presented. In the case of statefull modules the authors obtain unconditionally secure protocols, and in the case of stateless modules they require the existence of one-way functions. For statefull modules the trusted modules are use once only modules. In [25] another protocol for performing OT using tamper proof cards is presented.

In [22] the authors examine how standard smart cards can be used to accomplish a number of cryptographic tasks, including ones related to what we discuss. Using their approach they manage to produce protocols which are simulation secure, and they provide some estimated run-times.

Our approach is very different, we do not try to obtain a general OT functionality and do not reduce to the relatively expensive garbled circuit approaches to secure computation. In addition our trusted modules are reusable from one computation to the next, they are only bound to one particular data provider and not to a function or dataset. Our focus is on practicality as opposed to theoretical interest, and so our aim is to use simple trusted modules to enable more efficient and practical protocols.

3   Our Protocol

Focusing on SOC as opposed to general SMPC provides a number of advantages. In this section we present our protocol assuming a semi-trusted third party. The role of this semi-trusted third party is to produce "correlated randomness" to the players who are computing the function, but otherwise takes no part in the protocol. We will then, later on, replace this single semi-trusted third party with multiple simple isolated trusted modules.

Q^2 IS NOT A NECESSARY CONDITION. We first note that our division of players into players who compute $\mathcal{P}$, and players I and R who input data and receive output, removes a major stumbling block to unconditionally secure computation. The standard argument which shows that Q^2 is a necessary condition is that if we did not have a Q^2 access structure, then we could reduce this to the problem of two player secure computation. However, any protocol between two players which was *unconditionally* secure, and for which the two players were trying to compute a function of *their own* inputs could not securely compute the AND functionality of two input bits. This negative result relies crucially on the fact that the function being computed is on two inputs; where one player knows one input and one player the other. In our application this does not hold, the players $\mathcal{P}$ doing the computation only know *shares* of the inputs to the function and not the inputs themselves. Thus SOC might be possible for an arbitrary adversary structure.

REMOVING Q^2 AS A SUFFICIENT CONDITION. Although the above observation might remove the necessary condition of a Q^2 adversary structure,, it does not remove the sufficient condition. Using traditional protocols we still need a multiplicative LSSS to implement the basic SMPC protocol. And since multiplicative LSSS must necessarily have a Q^2 access structure we do not seem to have gained anything. Our protocol gets around this impasse by using an additional assumption, namely a semi-trusted third party.

This assumption might seem like "cheating" but it has a number of practical advantages. Firstly it enables the set of players $\mathcal{P}$ to be reduced to a set of size two if desired (in the passive case). More importantly as we will no longer require multiplicative LSSS, and only a simple LSSS with the required access structure. This enables us to utilize functionality descriptions as arithmetic circuits over $\mathbb{F}_2$ with a small number of players, whilst still using ideal LSSS. This provides greater efficiency and much reduced storage in the case of an application in which a large database is shared between the computation providers. In addition, as we explain later, many practical database operations are best described using $\mathbb{F}_2$-arithmetic (i.e. binary) circuits as opposed to general $\mathbb{F}_p$-arithmetic circuits for some prime $p > 2$.

COMMUNICATION MODEL AND THE SEMI-TRUSTED THIRD PARTY. Our protocol will make use of reliable, but public, broadcast channels between the n servers, however the connection from the data provider to the servers, and the servers to the recipients must be implemented via secure channels. The servers may be adversarially controlled with respect to an adversary structure Σ (which will be the adversary structure of our underlying LSSS). In addition there is a special "server" T who is connected by secure channels to the other servers, this is our semi-trusted third party. The server T is trusted to validly follow its program, but it is assumed not to be trusted (or capable) to deal with any actual data. That the computing players are connected to the semi-trusted third party by secure channels is purely for exposition reasons; in the next section we will show how to replace the global semi-trusted third party with local isolated security modules.

The server T's job will be to perform the first stage of the asynchronous protocol of [14], i.e. the production of the random multiplication triples, leaving the actual servers to compute the second stage. With this set up T never takes any input and simply acts as a source of "correlated" random shared triples to the compute servers. Since T is trusted to come up with the random triples we no longer need a multiplicative LSSS to generate the triples, hence any LSSS will work. Thus we can use a very simple LSSS and cope (in the passive case over $\mathbb{F}_2$) with only two servers.

OUR PROTOCOL. The protocol then proceeds as follows, assuming some fixed ideal LSSS $\mathcal{M} = (M, \mathbf{p})$ is chosen:

Share: Given an input value x the input client generates a vector $\mathbf{t} \in \mathbb{F}_q^k$ such that $\mathbf{t} \cdot \mathbf{p} = x$. Then the input client computes $[x] = \mathbf{t} \cdot M$. The value $[x]_i$ is transmitted (via a secure channel) to server i.

Add Gate: Here the servers can locally compute the addition of their shares, since we are using a LSSS.

Multiplication Gate: The servers wish to compute the sharing of the multiplication of the shares representing x and y. They first poll T who securely provides to each server a random sharing $[a], [b], [c]$ of three random field elements a, b and c such that $c = a \cdot b$. The servers then locally compute the values

$$[d]_i = [x]_i + [a]_i \text{ and } [e]_i = [y]_i + [b]_i.$$

This pair of values $([d]_i, [e]_i)$ is publicly broadcast to each server, so that all servers can reconstruct

$$d = x + a \text{ and } e = y + b.$$

Now each party locally computes

$$[z]_i = [d \cdot e]_i - d \cdot [b]_i - e \cdot [a]_i + [c]_i,$$

where $[d \cdot e]_i$ is a trivial public sharing of the public product $d \cdot e$.

Recombine: Here the servers send the shares $[s]_i$ of the value to be recombined to the recipient. The recipient recovers the shared value by solving the linear equations $\mathbf{t} \cdot M = [s]$ for $\mathbf{t}$ and then uses this to compute $s = \mathbf{t} \cdot \mathbf{p}$.

We reiterate that the above protocol is simply the second stage of the the asynchronous protocol of [14], with the trusted server providing the first stage, mapped over to our SOC application scenario. We now turn to presenting the "code" for our semi-trusted third party T. When T is polled it executes the following steps:

- $\mathbf{t}_1, \mathbf{t}_2 \leftarrow \mathbb{F}_q^k$.
- $a \leftarrow \mathbf{t}_1 \cdot \mathbf{p}$; $b \leftarrow \mathbf{t}_2 \cdot \mathbf{p}$; $c \leftarrow a \cdot b$.
- $\mathbf{t}_3 \leftarrow \mathbb{F}_q^k$ such that $\mathbf{t}_3 \cdot \mathbf{p} = c$.
- $[a] \leftarrow \mathbf{t}_1 \cdot M$; $[b] \leftarrow \mathbf{t}_2 \cdot M$; $[c] \leftarrow \mathbf{t}_3 \cdot M$.
- Send player i the tuple $([a]_i, [b]_i, [c]_i)$.

DISCUSSION. One should ask first what have we gained by introducing a semi-trusted third party? After all we have assumed a semi-trusted third party T, so why do we not just pass the data to T and get T to compute the function? However, this would mean that T if fully trusted as it sees the inputs. In the above protocol the party T does not see any inputs, indeed they do not see anything bar requests to produce random numbers. Thus whilst T is trusted to produce the "correlated randomness" it is not trusted to do anything else.

Note that the semi-trusted third party only needs to be trusted by the person in the SOC who is receiving the data. Although in practice commercial concerns of the $\mathcal{P}$ who are being paid to compute and store the data may require them to also trust the party T. Various standard techniques can be used to provide such trust if needed, all of which would however significantly degrade the performance of the protocol.

A more problematic issue is that T is a single point of failure and needs to communicate with the players via a secure channel. For static adversaries this is not a problem, but could be an issue for adaptive adversaries as it would require a form of non-committing encryption. So whilst we have simplified things somewhat the use of a single semi-trusted third party is not ideal and produces problems of its own. This is why in the next section we replace the centralised semi-trusted third party, with isolated semi-trusted tamper proof modules; one for each server.

4   Security Model and Proof

Our security proof for our protocol is given in the UC framework, and follows from standard arguments. However to emphasise the relationship between SOC and general MPC we present the main details. In general MPC the ideal functionality is given as in Figure 1(a) we have $n+1$ parties all of which have their own input $x_0, \ldots, x_n$ and each of which obtain an output $f_i = F_i(x_0, \ldots, x_n)$ for some agreed functions F_i.

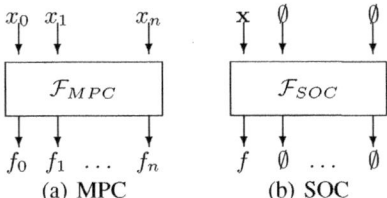

(a) MPC   (b) SOC

Fig. 1. Ideal Functionalities

However for secure outsourced computation the ideal functionality $\mathcal{F}_{SOC}$ is such that there is only one player (the client) I who has any input to the computation, and only they receive the output. The other players(the servers) $P_1, \ldots, P_n$ have no input. Clearly to obtain security only the players P_i can be corruptable, i.e. the special player must be totally honest.

Recall, a protocol π *UC-realises* an ideal functionality $\mathcal{F}$ if for all real world adversaries $\mathcal{A}$ there exists a simulator $\mathcal{S}$ in the ideal world, such that no environment $\mathcal{Z}$ can tell with a non-negligible probability whether it is interacting with $\mathcal{A}$ and parties in the real world running π, or with $\mathcal{S}$ and $\mathcal{F}$ in the ideal world.

We allow the adversary to select the function to be computed, and we also allow it to corrupt a subset of the parties $P_1, \ldots, P_n$ (a subset allowed by the adversary structure). When a player is corrupted passively its past, current and future states are all passed to the adversary; when corrupted actively control of this party passes to the adversary. To describe the function to be computed we assume that the functionality maintains a polynomial sized set of registers.

The ideal functionality $\mathcal{F}_{SOC}$ can then be formally described by the following commands it will accept from the environment:

- **Input**(x_i): On input of a value x_i from I, $\mathcal{F}_{SOC}$ stores the value in a register registers and notifies the adversary that input has been received and the location of where the element was stored.
- **Output**(r): On input of the register location r, $\mathcal{F}_{SOC}$ sends the value stored at position r to I.
- **Linear combination**(z, x, y, λ, μ): On input of register locations x, y, z and field elements λ and μ, $\mathcal{F}_{SOC}$ retrieves the values a and b stored in locations x and y and computes $c = \lambda \cdot a + \mu \cdot b$. The resulting value is stored in the location indexed by z.
- **Multiplication**(z, x, y): On input of register locations x, y, z, $\mathcal{F}_{SOC}$ retrieves the values a and b stored in locations x and y and computes $c = a \cdot b$. The resulting value is stored in the location indexed by z.
- **Corrupt**(i): This command allows the adversary to corrupt player i, where $i \in \{1, \ldots, n\}$. This can only be executed with respect to the allowable adversary structure.

The trivial protocol, in which the distinguished player, actually computes the function for itself is clearly secure in this model. The goal of SOC is to produce protocols in which the only interaction that the distinguished player has in the real protocol is to pass the inputs to the parties. In other words the inputting party performs no computation. Clearly our protocol above has this property, hence all that remains is to show that it is secure.

Theorem 2. *The protocol described unconditionally UC-realises $\mathcal{F}_{SOC}$ for any passive adaptive adversary $\mathcal{A}$ and linear secret sharing scheme $\mathcal{M}$ for which $\mathcal{A}$ corrupts players according to the adversary structure of $\mathcal{M}$.*

Proof. We show that for any adversary $\mathcal{A}$ there exists a simulator $\mathcal{S}$ for which an environment $\mathcal{Z}$ cannot tell the difference between interacting with $\mathcal{A}$ in the real world, or $\mathcal{S}$ in the ideal world. To do this we show how to simulate the output received by the adversary when it executes the above commands.

- **Input**(x_i): The adversary (and the simulator) by definition do not know the value of x_i. The simulator simply stores a random secret sharing of a random element, the environment is informed of the register location which has been used. In the case of corrupt parties the simulator returns the shared values of any corrupt parties, and stores them for uncorrupted parties in case the party is corrupted in the future.
- **Output**(r): The environment is informed that the value of the register at position r has been returned to I.

- **Linear combination**(z, x, y, λ, μ): This is a local computation and so is easily simulated.
- **Multiplication**(z, x, y): Here the simulator needs to simulate the multiplication protocol. This is done by generating a random multiplication triple and executing the real multiplication protocol with respect to the simulated values stored in the locations x and y. Again internal values are returned for any corrupted parties, and stored for later use if a party is corrupted.
- **Corrupt**(i): All prior data for party i is returned to the environment and the party is marked as corrupted.

We need to show that the above simulation is indistinguishable from an execution with an adversary in the real world. The key fact which implies this is that $H(s||[s]_A) = H(s)$ if $A \in \Sigma(\mathcal{M})$ and $H(s||[s]_A) = 0$ if $A \in \Gamma(\mathcal{M})$. This implies that by using sharings of random values in our simulation the output of the simulator is indistinguishable from a protocol run with real values, as long as the set of parties A which are corrupted belongs to the set $\Gamma(\mathcal{M})$[1].

5   Isolated Security Modules

We now notice that the functionality of the semi-trusted party T in our protocol can be localised to each player performing the computation by the use of *isolated tamper proof trusted modules*. In particular we assume a set of trusted modules T_i such that:

- The trusted modules T_i are produced by some third party and distributed to the compute servers, possibly (in the data outsourcing scenario) by the data provider.
- The manufacturer has embedded in each T_i the same long term secret key k_T, which is the index to some pseudorandom function family $\mathsf{PRF}_{k_T}(m)$.
- Each module is tamper proof, and will only supply data to its intended computation server. One could either do this cryptographically (via encryption) or physically (by locality) depending on the application scenario.

Our main protocol is now modified as follows: At the start of the protocol the servers compute a shared one-time nonce N, to which they have all contributed entropy. For example they could all commit to a value N_i, and then after all have committed, they then reveal the N_i and compute $N = N_1 \oplus \cdots \oplus N_n$. The nonce is used to make sure each protocol run uses different randomness. Each multiplication gate is assumed to have a unique number g associated to it.

Now when a server i requires the randomness for a particular gate g in a computation associated with nonce N, it passes the values g and N to the trusted module T_i. As before we write $\mathbf{m}_1, \ldots, \mathbf{m}_n$ for the columns of M, we assume that trusted module T_i has embedded into it $\mathbf{m}_i$ only. The trusted module T_i now executes the following code, where we have assumed that $\mathbf{p} = (1, \ldots, 1)^{\mathsf{T}}$ for simplicity of exposition.

---

[1] We note that we need to use sharings of random values rather than random shares due to the following simple example. Consider the LSSS given by $M = \begin{pmatrix} 1 & 1 & 0 \\ 0 & 0 & 1 \end{pmatrix}$ and $\mathbf{p} = (1, 1)$. The simulator must give an adversary who corrupts player one followed by player two the same randomly generated share if it wishes to remain undetected by the environment.

- $\mathbf{u}\leftarrow\mathsf{PRF}_{k_T}(g\|0\|N)$ where $\mathbf{u}\in\mathbb{F}_q^k$.
- $\mathbf{v}\leftarrow\mathsf{PRF}_{k_T}(g\|1\|N)$ where $\mathbf{v}\in\mathbb{F}_q^k$.
- $a\leftarrow\mathbf{u}\cdot\mathbf{p};\quad b\leftarrow\mathbf{v}\cdot\mathbf{p};\quad c\leftarrow a\cdot b$.
- $\mathbf{w}\leftarrow\mathsf{PRF}_{k_T}(g\|2\|N)$ where $\mathbf{w}\in\mathbb{F}_q^{k-1}$.
- $\mathbf{w}_k\leftarrow c-\sum_{i=1}^{k-1}\mathbf{w}_i$.
- $[a]_i\leftarrow\mathbf{u}\cdot\mathbf{m}_i;\quad [b]_i\leftarrow\mathbf{v}\cdot\mathbf{m}_i;\quad [c]_i\leftarrow\mathbf{w}\cdot\mathbf{m}_i$.
- Output $([a]_i,[b]_i,[c]_i)$.

Note the function PRF can be implemented in practice using any standardized key generation function, for example one based on a cryptographic hash function or a block cipher.

The key observation is that these modules are incredibly simple and easy to implement with only a few gates, especially if one takes $\mathbb{F}_q$ to be the binary field. One may be concerned about protecting them against side channel attacks; for example an adversarial server may try to learn the key k_T embedded within the device. However, such protection can be done using standard defences employed in banking cards etc.

Note that since our main protocol using isolated trusted modules no longer requires secure channels (bar between each trusted modules and the player using it): thus the need for, in the adaptive adversary setting, of using non-committing encryption is removed. Although one would still need this when there is a single semi-trusted third party to secure the channels from this party to the servers.

One caveat is perhaps worth noting at this stage. Whilst our security theorem in the case of having a single semi-trusted third party was for unbounded adversaries we are unable to achieve such security when the semi-trusted party is split into trusted modules as above. This is because an unbounded adversary could simply "learn" the key k_T for the PRF after only a small amount of interaction with a single module. Hence, security in this setting is only provided against computationally bounded adversaries who cannot break the PRF.

6   Active and Covert Adversaries

To deal with active adversaries in the player set $\mathcal{P}$ one needs to have a method to recover from errors introduced by the bad players. The only places where an honest players computation can be affected by a dishonest player are during the broadcast in the multiplication protocol and the recombining step.

To enable the honest player to recover the underlying secret we hence require some form of error correction. To a LSSS we can associate a linear $[n,k,d]$-code as follows, each set of shares $[s]$ becomes an element in the code C. We let $\mathsf{Supp}(\mathbf{x})$ for some vector $\mathbf{x}$ denote the set $\mathsf{Supp}(\mathbf{x})=\{i:\mathbf{x}_i\neq 0\}$. Let $\Sigma'\subset\Sigma$ denote a subset of the adversary structure.

We say that Σ' is "error-decodable" if for all $\mathbf{c}\in\mathbb{F}_q^n$ we have that, for all $(\mathbf{e},\mathbf{e}')\in\mathbb{F}_q^n$ with $\mathsf{Supp}(\mathbf{e}),\mathsf{Supp}(\mathbf{e}')\in\Sigma'$, and for all $\mathbf{t},\mathbf{t}'\in\mathbb{F}_q^k$ with $\mathbf{c}=\mathbf{e}+\mathbf{t}\cdot M=\mathbf{e}'+\mathbf{t}'\cdot M$, we have $\mathbf{t}\cdot\mathbf{p}=\mathbf{t}'\cdot\mathbf{p}$. Note a error-decodable subset Σ' is one for which on receipt of a set of shares $\mathbf{c}$ which may have errors introduced by parties in B for $B\in\Sigma'$, it is "possible" to determine what the underlying secret should have been. For the small values of q and

n we envisage in our application scenario, we can write down the correction algorithm associated to the set Σ' as a trivial enumeration, i.e. list-decoding.

We say that Σ' is "error-detectable" if for all $\mathbf{e} \in \mathbb{F}_q^n$ with $\text{Supp}(\mathbf{e}) \in \Sigma'$ and $\mathbf{e} \neq 0$, and for all $\mathbf{t} \in \mathbb{F}_q^k$ then $\mathbf{e} + \mathbf{t} \cdot M$ is not a code-word. Note a error-detectable subset Σ' is one for which if any errors are introduced by parties in B for $B \in \Sigma'$, we can determine that errors have been introduced but possibly not what the error positions are.

If a set is Σ' is error-detectable then this corresponds to a set of possible adversary structures for which we can tolerate a form of covert corruption. Namely, we are unable to identify exactly which parties are corrupt, but we are able to determine that some parties are trying to interfere with the computation. Note, this is slightly weaker than the standard notion of covert adversary, since we can detect that someone has cheated but not who.

If a set Σ' is error-decodable then in our main protocol, any error introduced by a set parties $B \in \Sigma'$ can be corrected. Thus our protocol can tolerate active adversaries lying in Σ'. For $q = 2$ and $n = 2$ however any error-decodable set must have $\Sigma' = \emptyset$. As a bigger example consider the LSSS $\mathcal{M} = (M, \mathbf{p})$ over $\mathbb{F}_2$ given by

$$M = \begin{pmatrix} 1 1 0 0 \\ 0 0 1 1 \end{pmatrix} \quad \mathbf{p} = \begin{pmatrix} 1 \\ 1 \end{pmatrix}.$$

This has adversary structure $\Sigma(\mathcal{M}) = \{\{1\}, \{2\}, \{3\}, \{4\}, \{1, 2\}, \{3, 4\}\}$. The subset $\Sigma' = \{\{1\}, \{2\}, \{3\}, \{4\}\}$ (and any subset thereof) is a error-detectable set, essentially because the underlying code is the repetition code on two symbols. The following subsets (and any subset thereof) is a error-decodable set

$$\{\{1\}, \{3\}\} \text{ or } \{\{1\}, \{4\}\} \text{ or } \{\{2\}, \{3\}\} \text{ or } \{\{2\}, \{4\}\}.$$

A subset Σ' which is either error-decodable or error-detectable therefore corresponds to a mixed adversary structure.

We end this section with two remarks on how the above discussion differs from prior notions in the literature. Firstly, the notion of error correction used above is not the usual notion in coding theory. We do not require that there is an algorithm which recovers the entire code-word, or equivalently recovers all of the shares, only that there is an algorithm which recovers the underlying shared secret itself. This is a possibly simpler error correction problem, and has been studied before in the context of secret sharing schemes [27]. In [27] it is shown that $\Sigma' \subset \Sigma$ is error-decodable if and only if for all $W_1, W_2 \in \Sigma'$ and all $B \in \Sigma$ we have $W_1 \cup W_2 \cup B \neq \mathcal{P}$, which is a natural extension of the usual Q^3 condition.

Secondly, we associate the secret sharing scheme with the $[k, n, d]$ code consisting of its shares. This is because the parties "see" a code word in this code. Usually in the SMPC literature one associates a secret sharing scheme with the $[k + 1, n, d]$ code in which one also appends the secret to the code-word. In such a situation correction is about recovering the one erased entry in the code word given some errors in the other entries.

7 Implementation Aspects

In this section we outline two implementation aspects which we feel are worth pointing out. However first we discuss why our scheme is more efficient than applying standard SMPC directly to the problem.

7.1 Efficiency Comparison

Our claimed improved efficiency and applicability comes from the following main points:

- We dispense with the costly protocol used to produce multiplication triples in the paper of Damgård et al [14]. This is done by giving each party access to a trusted model. The set of trusted models produce the multiplication triples on behalf of the parties.
- This in turn means our main protocol, in the passive case only, requires access to public channels as opposed to secure channels. In addition requiring security for a subset Σ' of Σ which is error-decodable, in the active adversary case, we only require reliable broadcast channels as opposed to consensus broadcast.
- The removal of the need for secure channels between the parties means that for adaptive security we no longer require any notion of non-committing encryption to secure these channels. Since all known non-committing encryption schemes are not truly practical this provides a major benefit in terms of security analysis.
- Our trusted models are very simple, only requiring the secure evaluation of a PRF. They thus are simpler than existing trusted hardware modules, such as TPMs or Smart Cards. Indeed one could possibly implement our functionality using the APIs on such existing modules, a topic which we leave to future work. One should compare our modules to the modules used in [30], in which the token is used to compute a Yao circuit on-the-fly. Whilst the latter such tokens are relatively inexpensive, they are certainly more complicated than ours and less possible to realise using standard components.
- Our protocol realises a secure system using weaker access structures and hence simpler LSSS. For example we can use two parties and computations over $\mathbb{F}_2$, which is a set of parameters which would be impossible with standard SMPC. Using arithmetic circuits over $\mathbb{F}_2$ implies that existing SMPC protocols for comparison and equality of integers, two common requirements, are significantly simpler than when using SMPC over $\mathbb{F}_p$ for $p > 2$.

However, we should point out that our protocol has two major disadvantages in the context of SOC in a cloud computing environment. Firstly, we require a multitude of cloud providers as opposed to the usual one. Hence, our solution requires a major change in the business model. Without access to practical fully homomorphic encryption, however, this seems unavoidable if we wish to provide some form of security for data holders. Secondly, we require the cloud providers to install a piece of trusted hardware with a shared symmetric key held commonly between the trusted modules. Thus, the cloud model of using off the shelf commodity hardware is broken. This is done however to enable improved efficiency, and the addition trusted hardware has been kept to a minimum. The method of [30] uses a different approach, requiring a single trusted computation party, however this single party is augmented with a more complicated module which implements a functionality less like the commodity functionality which we propose. In addition the proposal of [30] requires a re-garbling of the database on each query.

7.2 Data Transfer from Client to Servers

Up to now we have assumed that the data provider is connected to the servers by pairwise secure channels and that when the data is first transferred to the servers it needs to be sent n times (one distinct transmission for each server). In this section we show a standard trick which enables the data transfer to happen in one-shot, thereby reducing the amount of work for the data provider. The method is a generalisation to arbitrary LSSS of the threshold protocol described in [6], which itself relies on the transform from replicated secret sharing schemes to LSSS schemes presented in [10]. We recap on this technique here for completeness.

Suppose the data provider has input $x_1, \ldots x_t$ which he wishes to share between the servers $P_1 \ldots P_n$ with respect to the LSSS $\mathcal{M} = (M, \mathbf{p})$. Let $\mathcal{U}$ be the collection of maximal unqualified sets U of $\mathcal{M}$. For every set $U \in \mathcal{U}$, let ω_U be a row vector satisfying $\omega_U \cdot M_U = 0$ and $\omega_U \cdot \mathbf{p} = 1$. The vector ω_U is used to construct known valid sharings of 1 which are zero for players in the unqualified set U. We set $[t_U] = \omega_U \cdot M$.

It is not clear that such an ω_U always exists however observe that the set $\mathcal{P} \setminus U$ is minimally qualified and therefore the system of equations $\omega_U \cdot M = \omega_U \cdot (M_U \| M_{\mathcal{P} \setminus U}) = (\mathbf{0} \| \mathbf{v})$ has nontrivial solutions (else we would need an extra contribution from a player $P_i \in U$ so the set $\mathcal{P} \setminus U$ wouldn't be minimally qualified).

To send the data to the servers the client now selects a key K_U, for each $U \in \mathcal{U}$, to a pseudorandom function F. These keys are then distributed such that P_i obtains key K_U if and only if $i \notin U$. This distribution is done once, irrespective of how much data needs to be transmitted, and can be performed in practice by encryption under the public key of each server. The crucial point to observe is that this distribution of values K_T is identical to the distribution of shares with respect to the replicated secret sharing, of the value $\bigoplus_{U \in \mathcal{U}} K_U$ with respect to the access structure defined by our LSSS $\mathcal{M}$. We use an analogue of this fact to distribute the data in one go.

The data provider then computes for each value of x_j

$$y_j = x_j - \sum_{U \in \mathcal{U}} F_{K_U}(j)$$

and broadcasts the values y_j, for $j = 1, \ldots, t$, to all servers. Player i computes his sharing of x_j, namely $[x_j]_i$ as

$$[x_j]_i = y_j \cdot [t_U]_i + \sum_{U \in \mathcal{U}, i \notin U} F_{K_U}(j)$$

Note, due to the construction of the sharings $[t_U]$, namely that $[t_U]_i = 0$ if $i \in U$, we have

$$[x_j]_i = \left(y_j + \sum_{U \in \mathcal{U}} F_{K_U}(j) \right) \cdot [t_U]_i,$$

from which it follows, by linearity, that $[x_j]_i$ is a valid sharing of something with respect to the LSSS $\mathcal{M}$. That $[x_j]$ is a sharing of the value $[y_j]$ follows since $[t_U]$ is a sharing of one.

7.3   LSSS over $\mathbb{F}_2$

A major practical benefit of our combination of application scenario and protocol is that one can use ideal LSSS over $\mathbb{F}_2$ with a small number of players. In most data outsourcing scenarios the major computation is likely to be comparison and equality checks between data as opposed to arithmetic operations. For example most simple SQL queries are simple equality checks, auctions are performed by comparisons, etc. Whilst arithmetic circuits over any finite field can accomplish these tasks, the overhead is more than when using arithmetic circuits over $\mathbb{F}_2$.

For example consider a simple n-bit equality check between two integers x and y. If one uses arithmetic circuits over $\mathbb{F}_p$ with $p > 2^n$ then one can perform this comparison by securely computing $(x - y)^{p-1}$ and applying Fermat's Little Theorem. This requires $O(\log p)$ multiplications, and in particular $(3/2) \log p$ operations on average. Alternatively using an arithmetic circuit over $\mathbb{F}_2$, we hold all the bits x_i and y_i of x and y individually and then compute $z_i = \neg(x_i \oplus y_i)$, which is a linear operation and then $\prod z_i$, which requires n multiplications.

Further benefits occur with this representation when one needs to perform an operation such as $x < y$. Here when working over $\mathbb{F}_p$ one converts the integers to bits, and then performs the standard comparison circuit. But not only is converting between bit and normal representations expensive, the comparison circuit involves a large number of multiplications (due to xor not being a linear operation over $\mathbb{F}_p$). If we work on bits all the time by working over $\mathbb{F}_2$, then both of these problems disappear.

In the following table we present a comparison of our approach of using semi-trusted hardware modules with the approach of using SMPC "out-of-the-box". We focus on the case of honest-but-curious computing parties.

Property	Our Solution	MPC out-of-the-box
Setup Assumptions	Each party has a semi-trusted hardware module	None
Network Assumptions Between Players	None	Pairwise secure channels
Access Structure	Any	Q^2
Production of Multiplication Triples	Requires semi-trusted hardware modules only	Requires an interactive protocol
Assuming threshold LSSS, conditions on q and n	None	$q < n$

Acknowledgments

The first author was partially funded by EPSRC and Trend Micro. The second author was also supported by a Royal Society Wolfson Merit Award. Both authors were partially funded by the eCrypt-2 Network of Excellence through the ICT Programme under Contract ICT-2007-216676 ECRYPT II. Both authors would like to thank Bogdan Warinschi for useful discussions during the writing of this paper.

References

1. Aumann, Y., Lindell, Y.: Security against covert adversaries: Efficient protocols for realistic adversaries. In: Vadhan, S.P. (ed.) TCC 2007. LNCS, vol. 4392, pp. 137–156. Springer, Heidelberg (2007)
2. Beaver, D.: Efficient Multiparty Protocols Using Circuit Randomization. In: Feigenbaum, J. (ed.) CRYPTO 1991. LNCS, vol. 576, pp. 420–432. Springer, Heidelberg (1992)
3. Benenson, Z., Gartner, F.C., Kesdogan, D.: Secure multi-party computation with security modules. In: Proceedings of SICHERHEIT (2004)
4. Ben-Or, M., Goldwasser, S., Wigderson, A.: Completeness theorems for non-cryptographic fault-tolerant distributed computation. In: Symposium on Theory of Computing – STOC 1988, pp. 1–10. ACM, New York (1988)
5. Bogdanov, D., Laur, S., Willemson, J.: Sharemind: A framework for fast privacy-preserving computations. In: Jajodia, S., Lopez, J. (eds.) ESORICS 2008. LNCS, vol. 5283, pp. 192–206. Springer, Heidelberg (2008)
6. Bogetoft, P., Christensen, D.L., Damgård, I., Geisler, M., Jakobsen, T., Kroigaard, M., Nielsen, J.D., Nielsen, J.B., Nielsen, K., Pagter, J., Schwartzbach, M., Toft, T.: Secure multiparty computation goes live. In: Dingledine, R., Golle, P. (eds.) FC 2009. LNCS, vol. 5628, pp. 325–343. Springer, Heidelberg (2009)
7. Canetti, R., Fiege, U., Goldreich, O., Naor, M.: Adaptively secure computation. In: Symposium on Theory of Computing – STOC 1996, pp. 639–648. ACM, New York (1996)
8. Chandran, N., Goyal, V., Sahai, A.: New constructions for UC-secure computation using tamper-proof hardware. In: Smart, N.P. (ed.) EUROCRYPT 2008. LNCS, vol. 4965, pp. 545–562. Springer, Heidelberg (2008)
9. Chaum, D., Crépeau, C., Damgård, I.: Multi-party unconditionally secure protocols. In: Symposium on Theory of Computing – STOC 1988, pp. 11–19. ACM, New York (1988)
10. Cramer, R., Damgård, I., Ishai, Y.: Share conversion, pseudorandom secret-sharing and applications to secure computation. In: Kilian, J. (ed.) TCC 2005. LNCS, vol. 3378, pp. 342–362. Springer, Heidelberg (2005)
11. Cramer, R., Damgård, I., Maurer, U.: Multiparty computations from any linear secret sharing scheme. In: Preneel, B. (ed.) EUROCRYPT 2000. LNCS, vol. 1807, pp. 316–334. Springer, Heidelberg (2000)
12. Cramer, R., Damgård, I., Nielsen, J.B.: Multi-party Computation; An Introduction. Lecture Notes, http://www.daimi.au.dk/~ivan/smc.pdf
13. Damgård, I., Geisler, M., Nielsen, J.B.: From passive to covert security at low cost. In: Micciancio, D. (ed.) TCC 2010. LNCS, vol. 5978, pp. 128–145. Springer, Heidelberg (2010)
14. Damgård, I., Geisler, M., Kroigaard, M., Nielsen, J.B.: Asynchronous multiparty computation: Theory and implementation. In: Jarecki, S., Tsudik, G. (eds.) PKC 2009. LNCS, vol. 5443, pp. 160–170. Springer, Heidelberg (2009)
15. van Dijk, M., Gentry, C., Halevi, S., Vaikuntanathan, V.: Fully homomorphic encryption over the integers. In: Gilbert, H. (ed.) EUROCRYPT 2010. LNCS, vol. 6110, pp. 24–43. Springer, Heidelberg (2010)
16. Fort, M., Freiling, F., Penso, L.D., Benenson, Z., Kesdogan, D.: TrustedPals: Secure multiparty computation implemented with smart cards. In: Gollmann, D., Meier, J., Sabelfeld, A. (eds.) ESORICS 2006. LNCS, vol. 4189, pp. 34–48. Springer, Heidelberg (2006)

17. Gennaro, R., Gentry, C., Parno, B.: Non-interactive verifiable computing: Outsourcing computation to untrusted workers. In: Rabin, T. (ed.) CRYPTO 2010. LNCS, vol. 6223, pp. 465–482. Springer, Heidelberg (2010)
18. Gentry, C.: Fully homomorphic encryption using ideal lattices. In: Symposium on Theory of Computing – STOC 2009, pp. 169–178. ACM, New York (2009)
19. Gentry, C.: A fully homomorphic encryption scheme (2009) (manuscript)
20. Goldreich, O., Micali, S., Wigderson, A.: How to play any mental game or a completeness theorem for protocols with honest majority. In: Symposium on Theory of Computing – STOC 1987, pp. 218–229. ACM, New York (1987)
21. Goyal, V., Ishai, Y., Sahai, A., Venkatesan, R., Wadia, A.: Founding cryptography on tamper-proof hardware tokens. In: Micciancio, D. (ed.) TCC 2010. LNCS, vol. 5978, pp. 308–326. Springer, Heidelberg (2010)
22. Hazay, C., Lindell, Y.: Constructions of truly practical secure protocols using standard smartcards. In: Computer and Communications Security – CCS, pp. 491–500. ACM, New York (2008)
23. Hirt, M., Maurer, U.: Player simulation and general adversary structures in perfect multiparty computation. Journal of Cryptology 13, 31–60 (2000)
24. Katz, J.: Universally composable multi-party computation using tamper-proof hardware. In: Naor, M. (ed.) EUROCRYPT 2007. LNCS, vol. 4515, pp. 115–128. Springer, Heidelberg (2007)
25. Kolesnikov, V.: Truly efficient string oblivious transfer using resettable tamper-proof tokens. In: Micciancio, D. (ed.) TCC 2010. LNCS, vol. 5978, pp. 327–342. Springer, Heidelberg (2010)
26. Lindell, Y., Pinkas, B.: An efficient protocol for secure two-party computation in the presence of malicious adversaries. In: Naor, M. (ed.) EUROCRYPT 2007. LNCS, vol. 4515, pp. 52–78. Springer, Heidelberg (2007)
27. Martin, K.M., Paterson, M.B., Stinson, D.: Error decodable secret sharing and one-round perfectly secure message transmission for general adversary structures. IACR e-print 2009/487
28. Moran, T., Segev, G.: David and Goliath Commitments: UC Computation for Asymmetric Parties Using Tamper-Proof Hardware. In: Smart, N.P. (ed.) EUROCRYPT 2008. LNCS, vol. 4965, pp. 527–544. Springer, Heidelberg (2008)
29. Rabin, T., Ben-Or, M.: Verifiable secret sharing and multiparty protocols with honest majority. In: Symposium on Theory of Computing – STOC 1989, pp. 73–85. ACM, New York (1989)
30. Sadeghi, A.-R., Schneider, T., Winandy, M.: Token-based cloud computing: Secure outsourcing of data and arbitrary computations with lower latency. In: Acquisti, A., Smith, S.W., Sadeghi, A.-R. (eds.) TRUST 2010. LNCS, vol. 6101, pp. 417–429. Springer, Heidelberg (2010)
31. Shamir, A.: How to share a secret. Communications of the ACM 22, 612–613 (1979)
32. Smart, N.P., Vercauteren, F.: Fully homomorphic encryption with relatively small key and ciphertext sizes. In: Nguyen, P.Q., Pointcheval, D. (eds.) PKC 2010. LNCS, vol. 6056, pp. 420–443. Springer, Heidelberg (2010)
33. Yao, A.: Protocols for secure computation. In: Foundations of Computer Science – FoCS 1982, pp. 160–164. ACM, New York (1987)

Fully Simulatable Quantum-Secure Coin-Flipping and Applications

Carolin Lunemann and Jesper Buus Nielsen

Department of Computer Science, Aarhus University, Denmark
{carolin,jbn}@cs.au.dk

Abstract. We propose a coin-flip protocol which yields a string of strong, random coins and is fully simulatable against poly-sized quantum adversaries on both sides. It can be implemented with quantum-computational security without any set-up assumptions, since our construction only assumes mixed commitment schemes which we show how to construct in the given setting. We then show that the interactive generation of random coins at the beginning or during outer protocols allows for quantum-secure realizations of classical schemes, again without any set-up assumptions. As example applications we discuss quantum zero-knowledge proofs of knowledge and quantum-secure two-party function evaluation. Both applications assume only fully simulatable coin-flipping and mixed commitments. Since our framework allows to construct fully simulatable coin-flipping from mixed commitments, this in particular shows that mixed commitments are *complete* for quantum-secure two-party function evaluation. This seems to be the first completeness result for quantum-secure two-party function evaluation from a generic assumption.

1   Introduction

True randomness is a crucial ingredient in many cryptographic applications. Therefore, secure coin-flipping is an essential primitive, which allows two parties to agree on a uniformly random bit in a fair way, such that neither party can influence the value of the coin to his advantage. We investigate coin-flip protocols with classical messages exchange but where the adversary is assumed to be capable of quantum computing. Security of cryptographic protocols in the quantum world means, of course, that quantum computation does not jeopardize the assumption, underlying the protocol construction. However, we encounter additional setbacks in the security proofs, which are mostly due to the fact that some well-known classical proof techniques cannot be applied in a quantum environment.

OUR CONTRIBUTION. We aim at establishing coin-flipping as a stand-alone tool in a model without any setup assumptions. As such, our protocol can be used in several contexts and different generic constructions. One notable application is as subroutine for realizing the theoretical assumption of the common-random-string-model (CRS-model)[1]. Since the generation of a CRS often significantly

---

[1] In the CRS-model the parties are provided with a public common random string CRS before communication, taken from the uniform distribution.

A. Nitaj and D. Pointcheval (Eds.): AFRICACRYPT 2011, LNCS 6737, pp. 21–40, 2011.
© Springer-Verlag Berlin Heidelberg 2011

simplifies the design of (quantum-secure) protocols, this then implies that various interesting applications can be implemented quantum-securely in a simple manner from scratch.

In more detail, we first investigate different degrees of security that a coin-flip protocol can acquire. Then, we propose and prove constructions that allow us to amplify the respective degrees of security such that weaker coins are converted into very strong ones[2]. The amplification only requires mixed commitment schemes, which we know how to construct with quantum security under reasonable assumptions—for instance, based on the quantum hardness of the learning with error problem. Combining our amplification protocols allows to take a very weak notion of coin-flipping and amplify it to a coin-flip protocol which is *fully simulatable against poly-sized quantum adversaries*. By fully simulatable we mean that both sides can be simulated in quantum polynomial time.

Our amplification framework should also be understood as a step towards fully simulatable *constant-round* coin-flipping. To the best of our knowledge, to date there does not exist any fully simulatable protocol which is constant-round and which allows to generate a long random bit-string. In particular, no fully simulatable constant-round coin-flip protocol is known to securely compose in parallel. Since all our amplification protocols work in constant-round, we show that if there exists a constant-round coin-flip protocol of long strings with weak security, then there also exists a constant-round coin-flip protocol of long strings which is fully simulatable. Even though our work leaves fully simulatable constant-round coin-flipping of long strings as a fascinating open problem, we consider it a contribution in itself to define a reasonably weak but sufficient security notion to realize fully simulatable constant-round coin-flipping of long strings.

RELATED WORK. The standard coin-flip protocol of [2] was proven secure in a quantum environment in previous work [7]. In its basic form this protocol yields *one* coin as output. Of greater importance, however, is flipping a string of coins instead of a bit, in particular, when generating a CRS. The basic construction composes in sequence with security classified as medium in our framework here. Parallel composition is possible using an extended construction providing efficient simulations on both sides. This extension, however, requires a CRS as initial assumption, i.e. the CRS-model, and hence, violates our strong requirement of applications, implementable quantum-securely without any set-up assumptions.

As an example application, we discussed in [7] the generation of a CRS in the context of e.g. a quantum zero-knowledge proof. For an overview and more details, see also [14]. To further show the implications of coin-flipping as an implementation of the CRS-model in the quantum setting, we here add the functionalities of a quantum zero-knowledge proof of knowledge and quantum-secure function evaluation. We want to mention the following related work. First, an alternative approach in the context of zero-knowledge was independently investigated by Smith [18]. There, coin-flipping is implemented by a string

---

[2] For clarity, we note that we use the intuitive interpretation of "weak" and "strong" coins related to their security degrees, which differs from the definitions in the quantum literature.

commitment with special openings and validated in subsequent zero-knowledge proofs in sequence, and which therefore has round complexity depending on the security parameter, i.e. how many proofs must be completed to achieve a negligible soundness error. The coin-string is used as key to encode the witness and more zero-knowledge proofs are given to prove that. As encryption scheme, they suggest a scheme with similar properties as in the standard construction for mixed commitments [8,5,4]. To the best of our knowledge, the question of its actual secure implementation was left open, and a formal description and analysis was never published. Second, we want to mention the concurrent and independent work of Hallgren, Smith, and Song, as sketched in [12]. They also prove, among other things, classical protocols for zero-knowledge proofs of knowledge and function evaluation secure in the quantum setting by proposing a composition theorem that allows to use the basic coin-flipping protocol in [7] to generate a CRS. In addition, they give a UC-secure protocol for said tasks in the CRS-model.

Furthermore, the techniques used in our reductions are inspired by techniques used by works in the UC framework (cf. [8]), where rewinding is also a problem. But to the best of our knowledge, all our reductions are novel, and might be also of classical interest.

SECURITY IN THE QUANTUM WORLD. It is well known that bit commitments imply a single coin-flip—in the classical as in the quantum world [2, 7]—in a straightforward way: Alice chooses a random bit a and commits to it, Bob then sends his bit b in plain, then the commitment is opened, and the resulting coin is $a \oplus b$. However, even when basing the embedded commitment scheme on a computational assumption that withstands quantum attacks (for the hiding property), the security proof of the outer coin-flipping (and its integration into other applications) cannot easily be translated from the classical to the quantum world. Typically, security against a classical adversary is argued in this context by rewinding the adversary in a simulation. In brief, it is shown that a run of a protocol between a dishonest Bob and honest Alice can be efficiently simulated without interacting with Alice but with a simulator instead. A simulator basically prepares a valid conversation and tries it on dishonest Bob. Now, in case Bob does not send the expected reply, we need the possibility to rewind him. Then to conclude the proof, we have to show that the expected running time of the simulation is polynomial.

Unfortunately, rewinding as a proof technique can generally not be directly applied in the quantum world, i.e., if the dishonest machine is a quantum computer. First, we cannot trivially copy and store an intermediate state of a quantum system, and second, quantum measurements are in general irreversible. In order to produce a classical transcript, the simulator would have to partially measure the quantum system without copying it beforehand, but then it would become impossible to reconstruct all information necessary for correct rewinding [11]. It is worth mentioning though that rewinding in the quantum world is possible in a limited setting, as shown by Watrous [19]. This technique was also used for proving the quantum security of single coin-flipping based on bit commitments [7].

However, the generation of a string of coin must be based on string commitments. In this setting, the simulator cannot rewind in poly-time. A possible solutions for simulating against a classical Bob is then to let him commit to his message in a way which allows to extract the message in the simulation. Therewith, the message is known to the simulator in any following iteration of rewinding. This technique seems to be doomed to fail in the quantum realm, since it is neither known how to rewind quantumly for string commitments nor can any intermediate status (such as Bob's commitment) be preserved. Moreover, commitment constructions providing flavors of extractability without rewinding require some stronger set-up assumptions. Thus, other techniques such as our method based on mixed commitments, are needed for solutions in this context.

APPLICATIONS. Even though we establish coin-flipping as a stand-alone tool, we highlight again that the generation of a CRS leads to a simple and quantum-secure implementation of various interesting applications without any set-up assumptions. We show two different example applications, in addition to the functionalities already discussed in [7]. First, we propose a *quantum-secure zero-knowledge proof of knowledge* based on a witness encoding scheme, which we define such that it provides a certain degree of extractability and simulatability in the quantum world. Our zero-knowledge construction only requires mixed commitments, which can be implemented with quantum security. This is of particular interest, as the problems of rewinding in the quantum realm complicate implementing proofs of knowledge from scratch. And second, we show that mixed commitment schemes are sufficient for *quantum-secure function evaluation* of *any* classical poly-time function f with security against active quantum adversaries. In more detail, we first show that mixed commitments imply an oblivious transfer protocol with passive security. From that it is straightforward to construct a protocol for any classical poly-time function with security against passive quantum adversaries [13]. As our main result in that context, we then propose a quantum-secure implementation for evaluating any such function with security against active quantum adversaries.

2   Preliminaries

NOTATION. We use $negl\,(n)$ to denote the set of *negligible* functions (in n). For a bit-string $x \in \{0,1\}^n$ and a subset $S \subseteq \{1,\ldots,n\}$ of size s, we define $x|_S \in \{0,1\}^s$ to be the restriction $(x_i)_{i \in S}$. The *probability* of event E is denoted by $\Pr[E]$. For a random variable X we use P_X to denote the *distribution* of X, and for an additional random variable Y we use $P_{X|Y}$ to denote the *conditional distribution* of X given Y. *Statistical indistinguishability* of families of classical random variables is denoted by $\stackrel{s}{\approx}$, and $\stackrel{q}{\approx}$ indicates *quantum poly-time indistinguishability* of families of random variables, i.e., the families cannot be distinguished by poly-sized families of quantum circuits.

DEFINITION OF SECURITY. We are interested in classical two-party protocols secure in a quantum world. We work in the security framework, introduced in [9] and extended in [4]. The definitions are proposed for quantum protocols that implement *classical non-reactive two-party functionalities*, meaning that in- and output must be classical. The framework allows functionalities which behave differently in case of a dishonest player, and it is further shown that any protocol in the framework *composes sequentially* in a classical environment, i.e. within an outer classical protocol. For the sake of simplicity, the framework does not assume additional entities such as e.g. an environment. The original security definitions for unconditional security [9] are phrased in simple information-theoretic conditions, depending on the functionality, which implies strong simulation-based security. In [4], it is then shown that computational security (in the CRS-model) can be defined similarly. In the following, we state the formalism essential for this work[3]. For more details on the framework and notation, we refer to [4,6,9], and to [14] for an overview.

Our protocols run between players Alice (A) and Bob (B) and all definitions are given in the *two-world paradigm* of simulation-based proofs. The *real world* captures the actual protocol Π, consisting of message exchange between the parties and local computations. Real-world players are denoted by honest A, B and are restricted to poly-time classical strategies. Dishonest players A', B' are allowed any *quantum* poly-time strategy. Formally, let $\mathfrak{P}$ denote the set of poly-size quantum circuits, so we assume that A', B' $\in \mathfrak{P}$. The ideal functionality $\mathcal{F}$ models the intended behavior of the protocol in the *ideal world*, where the players interact using $\mathcal{F}$. Honest and dishonest players in the ideal world (a.k.a. simulators) are denoted by Â, B̂ and Â', B̂', respectively. An honest player simply forwards messages to and from $\mathcal{F}$, dishonest players are allowed to change their messages. Again Â', B̂' $\in \mathfrak{P}$. Now, the input-output behavior of $\mathcal{F}$ defines the required input-output behavior of Π. Intuitively, if the executions are indistinguishable, security of the protocol in real life follows. In other words, a dishonest real-world player that attacks protocol Π cannot achieve (significantly) more than an ideal-world adversary that attacks the corresponding functionality $\mathcal{F}$.

The common input state $\rho_{UV} = \sum_{u,v} P_{UV}(u, v)|u\rangle\langle u| \otimes |v\rangle\langle v|$ for some probability distribution P_{UV} is classical, and we understand U, V as random input variables (for Alice and Bob, respectively). The same holds for the classical output state ρ_{XY} with output X, Y for Alice respectively Bob. The input-output behavior of the protocol is uniquely determined by $P_{XY|UV}$, and we write $\Pi(U, V) = (X, Y)$. Then, a general classical ideal functionality $\mathcal{F}$ is given by a conditional probability distribution $P_{\mathcal{F}(U,V)|UV}$ with $\mathcal{F}(U, V)$ denoting the ideal-world execution, where the players forward their inputs U, V to $\mathcal{F}$ and output whatever they obtain from $\mathcal{F}$.

Definition 1 (Correctness). *A protocol* $\Pi(U, V) = (X, Y)$ *correctly implements an ideal classical functionality* $\mathcal{F}$, *if for every distribution of the input values* U *and* V, *the resulting common output* (X, Y) *satisfies* $(U, V, X, Y) \overset{s}{\approx} (U, V, \mathcal{F}(U, V))$.

---

[3] Note that we use a simplified joint output representation in comparison to [9].

We now define computational security against dishonest Alice, the definitions for dishonest Bob are analogue. Let Z and U' denote dishonest Alice's classical and quantum information. We consider a poly-size quantum circuit, called *input sampler*, which takes as input the security parameter and produces the input state $\rho_{U'ZV}$. We require from the input sampler that any $\rho_{U'ZV}$ is restricted to be of form $\rho_{U' \leftrightarrow Z \leftrightarrow V} = \sum_{z,v} P_{ZV}(z,v)|z\rangle\langle z| \otimes |v\rangle\langle v| \otimes \rho_{U'}^z$ (see [6] for notational details), where it holds that[4] $\rho_{U'}^z = \rho_{U'}^{z,v}$. This expresses *conditional independence*, namely that Bob's classical V is independent of Alice's quantum part U' when given Z. In other words, Alice's quantum part U' is correlated with Bob's part only via her classical Z.

Definition 2 (Computational security against dishonest Alice). *A protocol Π implements an ideal classical functionality $\mathcal{F}$ computationally securely against dishonest Alice, if for any real-world adversary $\mathsf{A}' \in \mathfrak{P}$, there exists an ideal-world adversary $\hat{\mathsf{A}}' \in \mathfrak{P}$ such that, for any efficient input sampler with $\rho_{U'ZV} = \rho_{U' \leftrightarrow Z \leftrightarrow V}$, it holds that the outputs are quantum-computationally indistinguishable, i.e., $out^{\Pi}_{\mathsf{A}',\mathsf{B}} \overset{q}{\approx} out^{\mathcal{F}}_{\hat{\mathsf{A}}',\hat{\mathsf{B}}}$.*

We state these output states explicitly as $out^{\Pi}_{\mathsf{A}',\mathsf{B}} = \rho_{UX'ZY}$ and $out^{\mathcal{F}}_{\hat{\mathsf{A}}',\hat{\mathsf{B}}} = \rho_{UX' \leftrightarrow Z \leftrightarrow Y}$, which shows that Alice's possibilities in the ideal world are limited: She can produce some classical input U for $\mathcal{F}$ from her quantum input state U', and then she can obtain a quantum state X' by locally processing U and possibly $\mathcal{F}$'s classical reply X.

3   Security Notions for Coin-Flipping

We denote a generic protocol with a λ-bit coin-string as output by $\Pi^{\lambda-\text{COIN}}_{\mathsf{A},\mathsf{B}}$, corresponding to an ideal functionality $\mathcal{F}_{\lambda-\text{COIN}}$. The outcome of such a protocol is $c \in \{0,1\}^{\lambda} \cup \{\bot\}$, i.e., either an λ-bit-string or an error message. We use several security parameters, indicating the length of coin-strings for different purposes; the length of a coin-flip yielding a key or a challenge are denoted by κ or σ, respectively. The ideal functionality for coin-flipping is defined symmetric such that always the respective dishonest party has an option to abort. We state the ideal functionalities in the case of both players being honest and in the case of dishonest Alice and honest Bob (Fig. 1). Note that the latter then also applies to honest Alice and dishonest Bob by simply switching sides and names.

Recall that the *joint output representation* of a protocol execution is denoted by $out^{\Pi}_{\mathsf{A},\mathsf{B}}$ (with $\Pi = \Pi^{\lambda-\text{COIN}}_{\mathsf{A},\mathsf{B}}$) and given here for the case of honest players. The same notation with $\mathcal{F} = \mathcal{F}_{\lambda-\text{COIN}}$ and $\hat{\mathsf{A}}, \hat{\mathsf{B}}$ applies in the ideal world as $out^{\mathcal{F}}_{\hat{\mathsf{A}},\hat{\mathsf{B}}}$, where the players invoke the ideal functionality $\mathcal{F}_{\lambda-\text{COIN}}$ and output whatever

---

[4] ρ_E^x denotes a state in register E, depending on value $x \in \mathcal{X}$ of random variable X over $\mathcal{X}$ with distribution P_X. Then, from the view of an observer, who holds register E but does not know X, the system is in state $\rho_E = \sum_{x \in \mathcal{X}} P_X(x)\rho_E^x$, where ρ_E depends on X in the sense that E is in state ρ_E^x exactly if $X = x$.

FUNCTIONALITY $\mathcal{F}_{\lambda-\text{COIN}}$ WITH HONEST PLAYERS:

Upon receiving requests start from both Alice and Bob, $\mathcal{F}_{\lambda-\text{COIN}}$ outputs uniformly random $h \in_R \{0,1\}^\lambda$ to Alice and Bob.

FUNCTIONALITY $\mathcal{F}_{\lambda-\text{COIN}}$ WITH DISHONEST ALICE:

1. Upon receiving requests start from both Alice and Bob, $\mathcal{F}_{\lambda-\text{COIN}}$ outputs uniformly random $h \in_R \{0,1\}^\lambda$ to Alice.
2. It then waits to receive her second input $\top$ or $\bot$ and outputs h or $\bot$ to Bob, respectively.

Fig. 1. The Ideal Functionality for λ-bit Coin-Flipping

they obtain from it. We need an additional notation here, describing the *outcome* of a protocol run between e.g. honest A and B, namely $c \leftarrow \Pi_{A,B}^{\lambda-\text{COIN}}$.

We will define three flavors of security for coin-flip protocols, namely *uncontrollable (uncont)*, *random* and *enforceable (force)*. The two sides can have different flavors. Then, if a protocol $\Pi_{A,B}^{\lambda-\text{COIN}}$ is, for instance, enforceable against Alice and random against Bob, we write $\pi^{(\text{force},\text{random})}$, and similarly for the eight other combinations of security. Note that for simplicity of notation, we will then omit the indexed name as well as the length of the coin, as they are clear from the context. Again, we define all three flavors for Alice's side only, as the definitions for Bob are analogue. Recall that U' and Z resp. V denote dishonest Alice's quantum and classical input resp. honest Bob's classical input. As before, we assume a poly-size input sampler, which takes as input the security parameter, and produces a valid input state $\rho_{U'ZV} = \rho_{U' \leftrightarrow Z \leftrightarrow V}$. Note that an honest player's input is empty but models the invocation start. We stress that we require for all three security flavors and for all $c \in \{0,1\}^\lambda$ that

$$\Pr\left[c \leftarrow \Pi_{A,B}^{\lambda-\text{COIN}}\right] = 2^{-\lambda},$$

which implies that when both parties are honest, then the coin is unbiased. Below we only define the extra properties required for each of the three flavors.

We call a coin-flip *uncontrollable* against Alice, if she cannot force the coin to hit some negligible subset, except with negligible probability.

Definition 3 (Uncontrollability against dishonest Alice). *We say that protocol $\Pi_{A,B}^{\lambda-\text{COIN}}$ implements an uncontrollable coin-flip against dishonest Alice, if it holds for any poly-sized adversary $A' \in \mathfrak{P}$ with inputs as specified above and all negligible subsets $Q \subset \{0,1\}^\lambda$ that*

$$\Pr\left[c \leftarrow \Pi_{A',B}^{\lambda-\text{COIN}} : c \in Q\right] \in negl(\kappa).$$

Note that we denote by $Q \subset \{0,1\}^\lambda$ a family of subsets $\{Q(\kappa) \subset \{0,1\}^{\lambda(\kappa)}\}_{\kappa \in \mathbb{N}}$ for security parameter κ. Then we call Q negligible, if $|Q(\kappa)|2^{-\lambda(\kappa)}$ is negligible in κ. In other words, we call a subset negligible, if it contains a negligible fraction of the elements in the set in which it lives.

We call a coin-flip *random* against Alice, if she cannot enforce a non-uniformly random output string in $\{0,1\}^\lambda$, except by making the protocol fail on some chosen runs. That means she can at most lower the probability of certain output strings compared to the uniform case.

Definition 4 (Randomness against dishonest Alice). *We say that protocol* $\Pi_{A,B}^{\lambda-\text{COIN}}$ *implements a* random *coin-flip against dishonest Alice, if it holds for any poly-sized adversary* $A' \in \mathfrak{P}$ *with inputs as specified above that there exists an event E such that* $\Pr[E] \in negl(\kappa)$ *and for all* $x \in \{0,1\}^\lambda$ *it holds that*

$$\Pr\left[c \leftarrow \Pi_{A',B}^{\lambda-\text{COIN}} : c = x \,|\, \bar{E}\right] \leq 2^{-\lambda}.$$

It is obvious that if a coin-flip is random against Alice, then it is also an uncontrollable coin-flip against her. We will later discuss a generic transformation going in the other direction from uncontrollable to random coin-flipping.

We call a coin-flip *enforceable* against Alice, if it is possible, given a uniformly random c, to simulate a run of the protocol hitting exactly the outcome c, though we still allow that the corrupted party forces abort on some outcomes[5].

Definition 5 (Enforceability against dishonest Alice). *We call protocol* $\Pi_{A,B}^{\lambda-\text{COIN}}$ enforceable *against dishonest Alice, if it implements the ideal functionality* $\mathcal{F}_{\lambda-\text{COIN}}$ *against her.*

That means that for any poly-sized adversary $A' \in \mathfrak{P}$, there exists an ideal-world adversary $\hat{A}' \in \mathfrak{P}$ that simulates the protocol with A' as follows. $\hat{A}'$ requests output $h \in \{0,1\}^\lambda$ from $\mathcal{F}_{\lambda-\text{COIN}}$. Then it simulates a run of the coin-flip protocol with A' and tries to enforce output h. If $\hat{A}'$ succeeds, it inputs $\top$ as A''s second input to $\mathcal{F}_{\lambda-\text{COIN}}$. In that case, $\mathcal{F}_{\lambda-\text{COIN}}$ outputs h. Otherwise, $\hat{A}'$ inputs $\bot$ to $\mathcal{F}_{\lambda-\text{COIN}}$ as second input and $\mathcal{F}_{\lambda-\text{COIN}}$ outputs $\bot$. In addition, the simulation is such that the ideal output is quantum-computationally indistinguishable from the output of an actual run of the protocol, i.e., $out_{A',B}^\Pi \stackrel{q}{\approx} out_{\hat{A}',\hat{B}}^\mathcal{F}$, where $\Pi = \Pi_{A',B}^{\lambda-\text{COIN}}$ and $\mathcal{F} = \mathcal{F}_{\lambda-\text{COIN}}$. Enforceability against dishonest Bob is analogously defined. Corollary 1 follows.

Corollary 1. *If* $\Pi_{A,B}^{\lambda-\text{COIN}} \in \pi^{(force,force)}$, *i.e., it is enforceable against both dishonest Alice and dishonest Bob, then* $\Pi_{A,B}^{\lambda-\text{COIN}}$ *is a secure implementation of* $\mathcal{F}_{\lambda-\text{COIN}}$, *according to Definition 2.*

4   Mixed Commitments

We use mixed commitment schemes throughout our constructions—they will indeed be our only computational assumption. Mixed commitment are unconditionally hiding for some public keys and unconditionally binding for others.

---

[5] Note that an enforceable coin-flip is not necessarily a random coin-flip, as it is allowed that the outcome of an enforceable coin-flip is only quantum-computationally indistinguishable from uniformly random, whereas a random coin-flip is required to produce truly random outcomes on the non-aborting runs.

In the following, we introduce mixed commitments, denoted by commit_{pk}, more formally. We also describe a construction of an interactive commitment protocol COMMIT_{pk} with mixed-commitment-scheme-like properties. The reason for presenting the protocol here is to simplify the description of the later protocol in which it is used as a subprotocol.

4.1   Mixed Commitment Schemes

Mixed commitment schemes consists of four poly-time algorithms $\mathcal{G}_{\text{H}}$, $\mathcal{G}_{\text{B}}$, commit, and xtr. The *unconditionally hiding key generator* $\mathcal{G}_{\text{H}}$ outputs public keys $pk \in \{0,1\}^{\kappa}$[6]. The *unconditionally binding key generator* $\mathcal{G}_{\text{B}}$ outputs key pairs (pk, sk), where $pk \in \{0,1\}^{\kappa}$ and where sk is the secret key. The commitment algorithm takes as input a message m, a randomizer r and a public key pk and outputs a commitment $C = \text{commit}_{pk}(m, r)$. The extraction algorithm xtr takes as input a commitment C and a secret key sk and outputs a message m', meant to be the message committed by C. We require the following properties:

Unconditionally hiding: For keys pk generated by $\mathcal{G}_{\text{H}}$ it holds that commit_{pk} is statistically hiding, i.e. $(pk, \text{commit}_{pk}(m_1, r_1)) \overset{s}{\approx} (pk, \text{commit}_{pk}(m_2, r_2))$ for all m_1, m_2 when r_1 and r_2 are uniformly random and independent.

Extractability: It holds for all pairs (pk, sk) generated by $\mathcal{G}_{\text{B}}$ and for all values m, r that $\text{xtr}_{sk}(\text{commit}_{pk}(m, r)) = m$.

Key indistinguishability: A random public key pk_1 generated by $\mathcal{G}_{\text{B}}$ and a random public key pk_2 generated by $\mathcal{G}_{\text{H}}$ are indistinguishable by poly-sized quantum circuits, i.e., $pk_1 \overset{q}{\approx} pk_2$.

We additionally require that random public keys generated by $\mathcal{G}_{\text{H}}$ are statistically close to uniform in $\{0,1\}^{\kappa}$, i.e., almost all keys are unconditionally hiding[7].

As a candidate for instantiating our definition we can, for instance, take the lattice-based public-key encryption scheme of Regev [17] in its multi-bit variant as given in the full version of [16]. Regev's cryptosystem is based on the hardness of the learning with error problem, which can be reduced from worst-case (quantum) hardness of the shortest vector problem (in its decision version). Thus, breaking the scheme implies an efficient algorithm for approximating the lattice problem in the worst-case, which is assumed to be hard even with quantum computing power. A regular public key for Regev's scheme is proven to be quantum-computationally indistinguishable from the case where a public key is chosen from the uniform distribution. In this case, the ciphertext carries

---

[6] For notational simplicity, the length of public keys is assumed to equal security parameter κ.

[7] The definition is a weakening of the original notion of mixed commitments from [8], in that we do not require that unconditionally hiding keys are equipped with an equivocation trapdoor. It is also a strengthening in that we require quantum indistinguishability of the two key flavors.

essentially no information about the message [17, Lemma 5.4]. This proof of semantic security for Regev's cryptosystem is in fact the property we require for our commitment.

4.2 The Protocol COMMIT$_{pk}$

In one of our security amplifications of coin-flip protocols we will need a mixed commitment scheme which also provides *equivocability*, i.e., a simulator can open unconditionally hiding commitments to different values. We add equivocability using an interactive protocol COMMIT$_{pk}$. Instead of equipping unconditionally hiding keys with equivocation trapdoors, we will do it by letting the equivocation trapdoor be the ability of the simulator to force the outcome of a coin-flip protocol in the simulation. The reason for this change, as compared to [8], is that the notion of a mixed commitment scheme in [8] was developed for the CRS-model, where the simulator is free to pick the CRS and hence could pick it to be a unconditionally hiding public key with known equivocation trapdoor. Here we are interested in the bare (CRS devoid) model and hence have to add equivocation in a different manner. This is one of the essential steps in bootstrapping fully simulatable strong coin-flipping from weak coin-flipping.

The protocol COMMIT$_{pk}$ uses a secret sharing scheme sss, described now. Let σ be a secondary security parameter. Given message $m = (m_1, \ldots, m_\sigma) \in \mathbb{F}^\sigma$ and randomizer $s = (s_1, \ldots, s_\sigma) \in \mathbb{F}^\sigma$, let $f_{m,s}(X)$ denote the unique polynomial of degree $2\sigma - 1$, for which $f_{m,s}(-i+1) = m_i$ for $i = 1, \ldots, \sigma$ and $f_{m,s}(i) = s_i$ for $i = 1, \ldots, \sigma$. Furthermore, we "fill up" positions $i = \sigma + 1, \ldots, \Sigma$, where $\Sigma = 4\sigma$, by letting $s_i = f_{m,s}(i)$. The shares are now $s = (s_1, \ldots, s_\Sigma)$.

We stress two simple facts about sss. First, for any message $m \in \mathbb{F}^\sigma$ and any subset $S \subset \{1, \ldots, \Sigma\}$ of size $|S| = \sigma$, the shares $s|_S$ are uniformly random in $\mathbb{F}^\sigma$, when S is chosen uniformly at random in $\mathbb{F}^\sigma$ and independent of m. This aspect is trivial for $S = \{1, \ldots, \sigma\}$, as we defined it that way, and it extends to the other subsets using Lagrange interpolation. And second, if $m^1, m^2 \in \mathbb{F}^\sigma$ are two distinct messages, then $\mathrm{sss}(m^1; s^1)$ and $\mathrm{sss}(m^2; s^2)$ have Hamming distance at least $\Sigma - 2\sigma$. Again, this follows by Lagrange interpolation, since the polynomial $f_{m^1, s^1}(X)$ has degree at most $2\sigma - 1$, and hence, can be computed from any 2σ shares s_i using Lagrange interpolation. The same holds for $f_{m^2, s^2}(X)$. Thus, if 2σ shares are the same, then $f_{m^1, s^1}(X)$ and $f_{m^2, s^2}(X)$ are the same, which implies that the messages $m^1 = f_{m^1, s^1}(-\sigma + 1), \ldots, f_{m^1, s^1}(0)$ and $m^2 = f_{m^2, s^2}(-\sigma + 1), \ldots, f_{m^2, s^2}(0)$ are the same.

In addition to sss, the protocol COMMIT$_{pk}$ uses a mixed commitment scheme commit$_{pk}$. The key generators for COMMIT$_{pk}$ are the same as for commit$_{pk}$. Finally, COMMIT$_{pk}$ uses a coin-flip protocol $\pi^{(\mathrm{random,force})}$ which is random for the committer and which is enforceable against the receiver of the commitment. The details of COMMIT$_{pk}$ are given in Fig. 2.

We first show that when (pk, sk) is generated using $\mathcal{G}_\mathrm{B}$, then COMMIT$_{pk}$ is extractable. Given any commitment $M = (M_1, \ldots, M_\Sigma)$, we extract $\mathrm{xtr}_{sk}(M) = \big(\mathrm{xtr}_{sk}(M_1), \ldots, \mathrm{xtr}_{sk}(M_\Sigma)\big) = (s_1, \ldots, s_\Sigma) = s$. Assume $s' = (s'_1, \ldots, s'_\Sigma)$ is the consistent sharing closest to s. That means that s' is the vector which is

---

COMMITMENT SCHEME COMMIT$_{\text{pk}}$:

COMMITMENT PHASE:

1. Let message $m \in \mathbb{F}^\sigma$ be the message. The committer samples uniformly random $s \in \mathbb{F}^\sigma$ and computes the shares $\texttt{sss}(m; s) = (s_1, \ldots, s_\Sigma)$, where $s_i \in \mathbb{F}$.
2. He computes $\texttt{COMMIT}_{pk}\big(m, (s, r)\big) = \big(M_1, \ldots, M_\Sigma\big)$, where $M_i = \texttt{commit}_{pk}(s_i, r_i)$ for randomness $r = (r_1, \ldots, r_\Sigma)$.
3. The committer sends $(M_1, \ldots, M_\Sigma)$.

OPENING PHASE:

1. The committer sends the shares $s = (s_1, \ldots, s_\Sigma)$ to the receiver.
2. If the shares are not consistent with a polynomial of degree at most $2\sigma - 1$, the receiver aborts.
3. The parties run $\pi^{(\text{random,force})}$ to generate a uniformly random subset $S \subset \{1, \ldots, \Sigma\}$ of size $|S| = \sigma$.
4. The committer sends $r|_S$.
5. The receiver verifies that $M_i = \texttt{commit}_{pk}(s_i, r_i)$ for all $i \in S$. If the test fails, he aborts. Otherwise, he computes the message $m \in \mathbb{F}^\sigma$ consistent with s.

Fig. 2. The Commitment Scheme COMMIT$_{pk}$

SIMULATING COMMIT$_{pk}$ WITH TRAPDOOR S:

1. $\hat{S}$ gets as input a uniformly random subset $S \subset \{1, \ldots, \Sigma\}$ of size σ and an initial message $m \in \mathbb{F}^\sigma$.
2. $\hat{S}$ commits honestly to $m \in \mathbb{F}^\sigma$ by $M = \texttt{COMMIT}_{sk}\big(m, (s, r)\big)$, as specified in the commitment phase.
3. $\hat{S}$ is given an alternative message $\tilde{m} \in \mathbb{F}^\sigma$, i.e., the aim is opening M to $\tilde{m}$.
4. $\hat{S}$ lets $s|_S$ be the σ messages committed to by $M|_S$. Then it interpolates the unique polynomial $f_{\tilde{m},s}$ of degree at most $2\sigma - 1$ for which $f_{\tilde{m},s}(i) = s_i$ for $i \in S$ and for which $f_{\tilde{m},s}(-i+1) = \tilde{m}_i$ for $i = 1, \ldots, \sigma$. Note that this is possible, as we have exactly 2σ points which restrict our choice of $f_{\tilde{m},s}$. $\hat{S}$ sends $s = \big(f_{\tilde{m},s}(1), \ldots, f_{\tilde{m},s}(\Sigma)\big)$ to the receiver.
5. The parties run $\pi^{(\text{random,force})}$ and $\hat{S}$ forces the outcome S.
6. For all $i \in S$, the sender opens M_i to $f_{\tilde{m},s}(i)$. This is possible, since $f_{\tilde{m},s}(i) = s_i$ is exactly the message committed to by M_i when $i \in S$.

Fig. 3. The Ideal-World Simulation of COMMIT$_{pk}$

---

consistent with a polynomial $f_{m',s'}(\mathbf{X})$ of degree at most $2\sigma - 1$ and which at the same time differs from s in the fewest positions. Note that we can find s' in poly-time when using a Reed Solomon code, which has efficient minimal distance decoding. We then interpolate the polynomial $f_{m',s'}(\mathbf{X})$, let $m' = f_{m',s'}(-\sigma + 1), \ldots, f_{m',s'}(0)$, and let $\texttt{xtr}_{sk}(M) = m'$. Any other sharing $s'' = (s''_1, \ldots, s''_\Sigma)$ must have Hamming distance at least 2σ to s'. Now, since s is closer to s' than to any other consistent sharing, it must, in particular, be closer to s' then to s''. This implies that s is at distance at least σ to s''.

We will use this observation for proving soundness of the opening phase. To determine the soundness error, assume that $\texttt{COMMIT}_{pk}$ does not open to the shares s' consistent with s. As observed, this implies that $\left(\texttt{xtr}_{sk}(M_1), \ldots, \texttt{xtr}_{sk}(M_\Sigma)\right)$ has Hamming distance at least σ to s'. However, when $\texttt{commit}_{pk}$ is unconditionally binding, all M_i can only be opened to $\texttt{xtr}_{sk}(M_i)$. From the above two facts, we have that there are at least σ values $i \in \{1, \ldots, \Sigma\}$ such that the receiver cannot open M_i to s_i for $i \in S$. Since $\Sigma = 4\sigma$, these σ bad indices (bad for a dishonest sender) account for a fraction of $\frac{1}{4}$ of all points in $\{1, \ldots, \Sigma\}$. Thus, the probability that none of the σ points in S is a bad index is at most $\left(\frac{3}{4}\right)^\sigma$, which is negligible. Setting $\sigma = \log_{\frac{4}{3}} 2$ gives a negligible error of $\left(\frac{1}{2}\right)^\kappa$, where κ is the security parameter.

We then analyze the equivocability of $\texttt{COMMIT}_{pk}$. We will use the ability of the simulator for the committer to force the challenge S as the simulator's trapdoor. It will simply pick S uniformly at random before the simulation and prepare for this particular challenge. The details are given in Fig. 3. We omit an analysis here but refer to Section 5.2, where the construction will be further discussed.

5 Amplification Theorems for Strong Coin-Flipping

We now propose and prove theorems, which allow us to amplify the security strength of coins. Ultimately, we aim at constructing a strong coin-flip protocol $\pi^{(\texttt{force},\texttt{force})}$ with outcomes of any polynomial length ℓ in λ from a weaker coin-flip protocol $\pi^{(\texttt{force},\texttt{uncont})}$ of κ-bit-strings, where κ is the key length of the mixed commitment scheme. We do this in two steps. We first show how to implement $\pi^{(\texttt{force},\texttt{random})}$ for ℓ-bit-strings (for any polynomial ℓ) given $\pi^{(\texttt{force},\texttt{uncont})}$ for κ-bit-strings, and we then show how to implement $\pi^{(\texttt{force},\texttt{force})}$ for poly-long bit-strings given $\pi^{(\texttt{force},\texttt{random})}$ for poly-long bit-strings.

The ability to amplify $\pi^{(\texttt{force},\texttt{uncont})}$ for κ-bit-strings to $\pi^{(\texttt{force},\texttt{force})}$ for poly-bit-string is of course only interesting, if there exists such a candidate. We do not know of any protocol with flavor $(\texttt{force}, \texttt{uncont})$ but not $(\texttt{force}, \texttt{random})$. However, we consider it as a contribution in itself to find the weakest security notion for coin-flipping that allows to amplify to the final strong $(\texttt{force}, \texttt{force})$ notion using a constant-round reduction.

A candidate for $\pi^{(\texttt{force},\texttt{random})}$ with one-bit outcomes is the protocol in [7], which is—in terms of this context—enforceable against one side in poly-time and random on the other side, with empty event E according to Definition 4, and the randomness guarantee even withstanding an unbounded adversary[8]. The protocol was shown to be sequentially composable [7,14]. Repeating the protocol κ times in sequence gives a protocol $\pi^{(\texttt{force},\texttt{random})}$ for κ-bit-strings. Note that this, in particular, gives a protocol $\pi^{(\texttt{force},\texttt{uncont})}$ for κ-bit-strings.

---

[8] The protocol was described and proven as $\pi^{(\texttt{random},\texttt{force})}$, but due to the symmetric coin-flip definitions here, we can easily switch sides between A and B.

PROTOCOL $\pi^{(\texttt{force},\texttt{random})}$:

1. A and B run $\pi^{(\texttt{force},\texttt{uncont})}$ to produce a public key $pk \in \{0,1\}^\kappa$.
2. A samples $a \in_R \{0,1\}^\ell$, commits to it with $A = \texttt{commit}_{pk}(a, r)$ and randomizer $r \in_R \{0,1\}^\ell$, and sends A to B.
3. B samples $b \in_R \{0,1\}^\ell$ and sends b to A.
4. A opens A towards B.
5. The outcome is $c = a \oplus b$.

Fig. 4. Amplification from $(\texttt{force}, \texttt{uncont})$ to $(\texttt{force}, \texttt{random})$

5.1 From $(\texttt{force}, \texttt{uncont})$ to $(\texttt{force}, \texttt{random})$

Assume that we are given a protocol $\pi^{(\texttt{force},\texttt{uncont})}$, that only guarantees that Bob cannot force the coin to hit a negligible subset (except with negligible probability). We now amplify the security on Bob's side from *uncontrollable* to *random* and therewith obtain a protocol $\pi^{(\texttt{force},\texttt{random})}$, in which Bob cannot enforce a non-uniformly random output string, except by letting the protocol fail on some occasions. The stronger protocol $\pi^{(\texttt{force},\texttt{random})}$ is given in Fig. 4, where $\texttt{commit}_{pk}$ is the basic mixed commitment scheme as described in Section 4.1. Correctness of $\pi^{(\texttt{force},\texttt{random})}$ is obvious by inspection of the protocol.

Theorem 1. *If $\pi^{(force,uncont)}$ is enforceable against Alice and uncontrollable against Bob, then protocol $\pi^{(force,random)}$ is enforceable against Alice and random for Bob.*

We sketch the basic ideas behind the proof, which can be found in greater detail in the full version of the paper [15]. Enforceability against A follows by forcing pk to be a pk generated as $(pk, sk) \leftarrow \mathcal{G}_\mathsf{B}$. The simulator then uses sk to extract a from A and then sends the b which makes $a \oplus b$ hit the desired outcome. Randomness against B follows from the fact that only a negligible fraction of the keys $pk \in \{0,1\}^\kappa$ are not unconditionally hiding keys and the outcome of $\pi^{(\texttt{force},\texttt{uncont})}$ is uncontrollable for B.

5.2 From $(\texttt{force}, \texttt{random})$ to $(\texttt{force}, \texttt{force})$

We now show how to obtain a coin-flip protocol, which is enforceable against both parties. Then, we can also claim by Corollary 1 that this protocol is a strong coin-flip protocol, poly-time simulatable on both sides for the natural ideal functionality $\mathcal{F}_{\ell-\text{COIN}}$. The protocol $\pi^{(\texttt{force},\texttt{force})}$ is described in Fig. 5 and uses the extended commitment construction $\texttt{COMMIT}_{pk}$ from Section 4.2. The protocol makes two calls to a subprotocol with random flavor on one side and enforceability on the other side, but where the sides are interchanged, i.e. $\pi^{(\texttt{force},\texttt{random})}$ and $\pi^{(\texttt{random},\texttt{force})}$, so we simply switch the players' roles. Again, correctness of the protocol can be trivially checked.

Theorem 2. *If $\pi^{(force,random)}$ is enforceable against Alice and random against Bob, then protocol $\pi^{(force,force)}$ is enforceable against both Alice and Bob.*

PROTOCOL $\pi^{(\text{force},\text{force})}$:

1. A and B run $\pi^{(\text{force},\text{random})}$ to produce a random public key $pk \in \{0,1\}^{\kappa}$.
2. A computes and sends commitments $\text{COMMIT}_{pk}(a,(s,r)) = (A_1, \dots, A_{\Sigma})$ to B. In more detail, A samples uniformly random $a, s \in \mathbb{F}^{\sigma}$. She then computes $\text{sss}(a; s) = (a_1, \dots, a_{\Sigma})$ and $A_i = \text{commit}_{pk}(a_i, r_i)$ for $i = 1, \dots, \Sigma$.
3. B samples uniformly random $b \in \{0,1\}^{\ell}$ and sends b to A.
4. A sends secret shares $(a_1, \dots, a_{\Sigma})$ to B. If $(a_1, \dots, a_{\Sigma})$ is not consistent with a polynomial of degree at most $(2\sigma - 1)$, B aborts.
5. A and B run $\pi^{(\text{random},\text{force})}$ to produce a challenge $S \subset \{1, \dots, \Sigma\}$ of length $|S| = \sigma$.
6. A sends $r|_S$ to B.
7. B checks if $A_i = \text{commit}_{pk}(a_i, r_i)$ for all $i \in S$. If that is the case, B computes message $a \in \mathbb{F}^{\sigma}$ consistent with $(a_1, \dots, a_{\Sigma})$ and the outcome of the protocol is $c = a \oplus b$. Otherwise, B aborts and the outcome is $c = \bot$.

Fig. 5. Amplification from (force, random) to (force, force)

We sketch the main ideas behind the proof, which can be found in greater detail in the full version of the paper [15]. Enforceability against A follows by forcing pk to be a key pk generated as $(pk, sk) \leftarrow \mathcal{G}_B$. The simulator then uses sk to extract a from $(A_1, \dots, A_{\Sigma})$. Then it sends the b that makes $a \oplus b$ hit the desired outcome. Enforceability against B follows by letting the simulator sample a uniformly random S and running $\text{COMMIT}_{pk}(a, (s,r)) = (A_1, \dots, A_{\Sigma})$ in the equivocal model with trapdoor S. Then the simulator waits for b and forces the outcome of $\pi^{(\text{random},\text{force})}$ to be S, which allows it to open $(A_1, \dots, A_{\Sigma})$ to the a that makes $a \oplus b$ hit the desired outcome.

6   Application: Zero-Knowledge Proof of Knowledge

The purpose of a zero-knowledge proof of knowledge [10,1] is to verify in classical poly-time in the length of the instance, whether the prover's private input w is a valid witness for the common instance x in relation $\mathcal{R}$, i.e. $(x, w) \in \mathcal{R}$. Here, we propose a quantum-secure construction of a zero-knowledge proof of knowledge based on witness encoding, which we define in the context of a simulation in the quantum world. The protocol is constant-round if the coin-flip protocol is constant-round.

6.1   Simulatable Witness Encodings of $\mathcal{NP}$

We first specify a simulatable encoding scheme for binary relation $\mathcal{R} \subset \{0,1\}^* \times \{0,1\}^*$, which consists of five classical poly-time algorithms $(E, D, S, J, \hat{E})$. Then, we define completeness, extractability and simulatability for such a scheme in terms of the requirements of our zero-knowledge proof of knowledge.

Let $E : \mathcal{R} \times \{0,1\}^m \to \{0,1\}^n$ denote an *encoder*, such that for each $(x, w) \in \mathcal{R}$, the n-bit output $e \leftarrow E(x, w, r')$ is a random encoding of w, with randomness $r' \in \{0,1\}^m$ and polynomials $m(|x|)$ and $n(|x|)$. The corresponding *decoder*

$D : \{0,1\}^* \times \{0,1\}^n \to \{0,1\}^*$ takes as input an instance $x \in \{0,1\}^*$ and an encoding $e \in \{0,1\}^n$ and outputs $w \leftarrow D(x,e)$ with $w \in \{0,1\}^*$. Next, let S denote a *selector* with input $s \in \{0,1\}^\sigma$ (with polynomial $\sigma(|x|)$) specifying a challenge, and output $S(s)$ defining a poly-sized subset of $\{1, \ldots, n\}$ corresponding to challenge s. We will use $S(s)$ to select which bits of an encoding e to reveal to the verifier. For simplicity, we use e_s to denote the collection of bits $e|_{S(s)}$. We denote with J the *judgment* that checks a potential encoding e by inspecting only bits e_s. In more detail, J takes as input instance $x \in \{0,1\}^*$, challenge $s \in \{0,1\}^\sigma$ and the $|S(s)|$ bits e_s, and outputs a judgment $j \leftarrow J(x,s,e_s)$ with $j \in \{\mathsf{abort}, \mathsf{success}\}$. Finally, the *simulator* is called $\hat{E}$. It takes as input instance $x \in \{0,1\}^*$ and challenge $s \in \{0,1\}^\sigma$ and outputs a random collection of bits $t|_{S(s)} \leftarrow \hat{E}(x,s)$. Again for simplicity, we let $t_s = t|_{S(s)}$. Then, if this set has the same distribution as bits of an encoding e in positions $S(s)$, the bits needed for the judgment to check an encoding e can be simulated given just instance x (see Definition 8).

Definition 6 (Completeness). *If an encoding* $e \leftarrow E(x,w,r)$ *is generated correctly, then* $\mathsf{success} \leftarrow J(x,s,e_s)$ *for all* $s \in \{0,1\}^\sigma$.

We will call an encoding e *admissible* for x, if there *exist* two distinct challenges $s,s' \in \{0,1\}^\sigma$ for which $\mathsf{success} \leftarrow J(x,s,e_s)$ and $\mathsf{success} \leftarrow J(x,s',e_{s'})$.

Definition 7 (Extractability). *If an encoding* e *is admissible for* x, *then* $(x, D(x,e)) \in \mathcal{R}$.

We stress that extractability is similarly defined to the special soundness property of a classical Σ-protocol, which allows to extract w from two accepting conversations with distinct challenges. Such a requirement would generally be inapplicable in the quantum setting, as the usual rewinding technique is problematic and in particular in the context here, we cannot measure two accepting conversations during rewinding in the quantum world. Therefore, we define the stronger requirement that if there *exist* two distinct answerable challenges for one encoding e, then w can be extracted given only e. This condition works nicely in the quantum world, since we can obtain e without rewinding, as we demonstrate below.

Definition 8 (Simulatability). *For all* $(x,w) \in \mathcal{R}$ *and all* $s \in_R \{0,1\}^\sigma$, *the distribution of* $e \leftarrow E(x,w,r')$ *restricted to positions* $S(s)$ *is identical to the distribution of* $t_s \leftarrow \hat{E}(x,s)$.

To construct a simulatable witness encoding one can, for instance, start from the commit-and-open protocol for circuit satisfiability in [3], where the bits of the randomized circuit committed to by the sender is easy to see as a simulatable encoding of a witness being a consistent evaluation of the circuit to output 1. The challenge in the protocol is one bit e and the prover replies by showing either the bits corresponding to some positions $S'(0)$ or positions $S'(1)$. The details can be found in [3]. This gives us a simulatable witness encoding for any $\mathcal{NP}$-relation $\mathcal{R}$ with $\sigma = 1$, using a Karp reduction from $\mathcal{NP}$ to circuit simulatability. By

---

FUNCTIONALITY $\mathcal{F}_{\text{ZKPK}(\mathcal{R})}$:
1. On input (x, w) from Alice, $\mathcal{F}_{\text{ZKPK}(\mathcal{R})}$ sets $j = \text{success}$ if $(x, w) \in \mathcal{R}$. Otherwise, it sets $j = \text{abort}$.
2. $\mathcal{F}_{\text{ZKPK}(\mathcal{R})}$ outputs (x, j) to Bob.

Fig. 6. The Ideal Functionality for a Zero-Knowledge Proof of Knowledge

---

PROTOCOL ZKPK($\mathcal{R}$) :
1. A and B invoke $\mathcal{F}_{\kappa-\text{COIN}}$ to get a commitment key $pk \in \{0, 1\}^{\kappa}$.
2. A samples $e \leftarrow E(x, w, r')$ with randomness $r' \in \{0, 1\}^m$ and commits position-wise to all e_i for $i = 1, \ldots, n$, by computing $E_i = \text{commit}_{pk}(e_i, r_i)$ with randomness $r \in \{0, 1\}^n$. She sends x and all E_i to B.
3. A and B invoke $\mathcal{F}_{\sigma-\text{COIN}}$ to flip a challenge $s \in_R \{0, 1\}^{\sigma}$.
4. A opens her commitments to all e_s.
5. If any opening is incorrect, B outputs abort. Otherwise, he outputs $j \leftarrow J(x, s, e_s)$.

Fig. 7. Zero-Knowledge Proof of Knowledge

repeating it σ times in parallel we get a simulatable witness encoding for any σ. For $i = 1, \ldots, \sigma$, compute an encoding e^i of w and let $e = (e^1, \ldots, e^{\sigma})$. Then for $s \in \{0, 1\}^{\sigma}$, let $S(s)$ specify that the bits $S'(s_i)$ should be shown in e^i and check these bits. Note, in particular, that if two distinct s and s' passes this judgment, then there exists i such that $s_i \neq s_i'$, so e^i passes the judgment for both $s_i = 0$ and $s_i = 1$, which by the properties of the protocol for circuit satisfiability allows to compute a witness w for x from e^i. One can find w from e simply by trying to decode each e^j for $j = 1, \ldots, \sigma$ and check if $(x, w_j) \in \mathcal{R}$.

6.2 The Protocol

We now construct a quantum-secure zero-knowledge proof of knowledge from prover A to verifier B. We are interested in the $\mathcal{NP}$-language $\mathcal{L}(\mathcal{R}) = \{x \in \{0, 1\}^* \mid \exists w \text{ s.t. } (x, w) \in \mathcal{R}\}$, where A has input x and w, and both A and B receive positive or negative judgment of the validity of the proof as output. We assume in the following that on input $(x, w) \notin \mathcal{R}$, honest A aborts. Unlike zero-knowledge proofs, proofs of knowledge can be modeled by an ideal functionality, given as $\mathcal{F}_{\text{ZKPK}(\mathcal{R})}$ in Fig. 6. $\mathcal{F}_{\text{ZKPK}(\mathcal{R})}$ can be thought of as a channel which only allows to send messages in the language $\mathcal{L}(\mathcal{R})$. It models *zero-knowledge*, as it only leaks instance x and judgment j but not witness w. Furthermore, it models a *proof of knowledge*, since Alice has to know and input a valid witness w to obtain output $j = \text{success}$.

Protocol ZKPK($\mathcal{R}$) is describe in Fig. 7. It is based on our fully simulatable coin-flip protocol $\pi^{(\text{force}, \text{force})}$, which we analyze here in the hybrid model by invoking the ideal functionality of sequential coin-flipping twice (but with different output lengths)[9]. One call to the ideal functionality $\mathcal{F}_{\kappa-\text{COIN}}$ with output length κ is required to instantiate a mixed bit commitment scheme COMMIT_{pk}. The second call to the functionality $\mathcal{F}_{\sigma-\text{COIN}}$ produces σ-bit challenges for a simulatable witness encoding scheme with $(E, D, S, J, \hat{E})$ as specified in the previous Section 6.1. The formal proof of Theorem 3 can be found in the full version of the paper [15]. Corollary 2 follows immediately.

Theorem 3. *For any simulatable witness encoding scheme $(E, D, S, J, \hat{E})$, satisfying completeness, extractability, and simulatability according to Definitions 6 - 8, and for negligible knowledge error $2^{-\sigma}$, protocol $\text{ZKPK}(\mathcal{R})$ securely implements $\mathcal{F}_{\text{ZKPK}(\mathcal{R})}$.*

Corollary 2. *If there exist mixed commitment schemes, then we can construct a classical zero-knowledge proof of knowledge against any quantum adversary $\mathsf{P}' \in \mathfrak{P}$ without any set-up assumptions.*

7 Application: Two-Party Function Evaluation

Here, we first show that mixed commitments imply a passively secure oblivious transfer protocol. From such a protocol it is straightforward to construct a protocol for *any* classical poly-time function with security against passive quantum adversaries [13]. We then propose a quantum-secure implementation for evaluating any such function with security against active quantum adversaries.

7.1 Oblivious Transfer

In an oblivious transfer protocol (OT), the sender A sends two messages m_0 and m_1 to the selector B. B can choose which message to receive, i.e. m_c according to his choice bit c. B does not learn anything about the other message m_{1-c}, and A does not learn B's choice bit c (see Fig. 8). The protocol is correct, as B knows sk_c and $\text{xtr}_{sk_c}(C_c) = \text{xtr}_{sk_c}(\text{commit}_{pk_c}(m_c, r_c)) = m_c$. Furthermore, it hides the other message m_{1-c} as $\text{commit}_{pk_{1-c}}$ is unconditionally hiding for random pk_{1-c}, except with negligible probability. Last, the choice bit is hidden

---

PROTOCOL OT :
1. B samples two keys pk_0 and pk_1 according to his choice bit c, i.e. he samples pk_c as $(pk_c, sk_c) \leftarrow \mathcal{G}_B$ and pk_{1-c} as $p_{1-c} \leftarrow \mathcal{G}_H$. He sends (pk_0, pk_1) to A.
2. A commits to her messages (m_0, m_1) by computing $C_0 = \text{commit}_{pk_0}(m_0, r_0)$ and $C_1 = \text{commit}_{pk_1}(m_1, r_1)$. She sends (C_0, C_1) to B.
3. B computes $\text{xtr}_{sk_c}(C_c)$.

Fig. 8. Oblivious Transfer based on Mixed Commitments

---

[9] Note that in the hybrid model, a simulator can enforce a particular outcome to hit also when invoking the ideal coin-flip functionality. We then use Definition 5 to replace the ideal functionality by the actual protocol $\pi^{(\text{force,force})}$.

in the sense of quantum-computational indistinguishability between keys for the outer commitments, namely a key produced by $\mathcal{G}_\mathrm{B}$ and a random key by $\mathcal{G}_\mathrm{H}$.

FUNCTIONALITY $\mathcal{F}_\mathrm{SFE}^f$ WITH HONEST PLAYERS:
On input x_1 from Alice and x_2 from Bob, $\mathcal{F}_\mathrm{SFE}^f$ outputs $y = f(x_1, x_2)$ to Alice and Bob.

FUNCTIONALITY $\mathcal{F}_\mathrm{SFE}^f$ WITH DISHONEST ALICE:

1. On input x_1 from Alice and x_2 from Bob, $\mathcal{F}_\mathrm{SFE}^f$ outputs $y = f(x_1, x_2)$ to Alice.
2. It then waits to receive her second input $\top$ or $\bot$ and outputs y or $\bot$ to Bob, respectively.

Fig. 9. The Ideal Functionality for Secure Function Evaluation

---

PROTOCOL $\Pi_\mathrm{A,B}^{\mathrm{SFE}(f)}$:

1. A and B invoke $\mathcal{F}_{\kappa-\mathrm{COIN}}$ to get a commitment key $pk \in \{0,1\}^\kappa$.
2. A sends a random commitment $X_1 = \mathtt{commit}_{pk}(x_1, \tilde{r}_1)$ and B sends a random commitment $X_2 = \mathtt{commit}_{pk}(x_2, \tilde{r}_2)$. Both parties use $\mathcal{F}_{\mathrm{ZKPK}(\mathcal{R})}$ to give a zero-knowledge proof of knowledge that they know the plaintext x_i inside commitments X_i for $i = 1, 2$.
3. A sends random commitment $S_1 = \mathtt{commit}_{pk}(s_1, \hat{r}_1)$ for uniformly random s_1 of length $|s_1| = |r_1|$, where r_1 is the randomness she intends to use in $\Pi_\mathrm{A,B}^f$. Similarly, B sends random commitment $S_2 = \mathtt{commit}_{pk}(s_2, \hat{r}_2)$ for uniformly random s_2 of length $|s_2| = |r_2|$. Again, they use $\mathcal{F}_{\mathrm{ZKPK}(\mathcal{R})}$ to give a zero-knowledge proof of knowledge of s_i in S_i for $i = 1, 2$.
4. A and B invoke $\mathcal{F}_{\sigma-\mathrm{COIN}}$ twice to get uniformly random s_1' and s_2' with $|s_i'| = |s_i|$ for $i = 1, 2$.
5. A lets $r_1 = s_1 \oplus s_1'$ and B lets $r_2 = s_2 \oplus s_2'$.
6. A and B run $\Pi_\mathrm{A,B}^f(x_1, r_1, x_2, r_2)$, i.e. they run the passively secure protocol on inputs and randomness as defined in the previous steps.
7. Whenever A sends a message m in the execution of $\Pi_\mathrm{A,B}^f(x_1, r_1, x_2, r_2)$, she gives a zero-knowledge proof of knowledge of s_1 in S_1 and x_1 in X_1, such that if $\Pi_\mathrm{A,B}^f(x_1, r_1, x_2, r_2)$ is run on x_1, $r_1 = s_1 \oplus s_1'$, and B's messages sent to A so far, then A would indeed send m. This is an $\mathcal{NP}$-statement, so we can use $\mathcal{F}_{\mathrm{ZKPK}(\mathcal{R})}$ for this proof.
8. If $\Pi_\mathrm{A,B}^f(x_1, r_1, x_2, r_2)$ terminates with output y, both parties output y.

Fig. 10. Procedure for Secure Function Evaluation

7.2   The Protocol

Based on protocol OT, we can construct a passively secure protocol for any classical poly-time function f. Let $\Pi_\mathrm{A,B}^f(x_1, r_1, x_2, r_2)$ denote such a protocol between parties A and B with inputs x_1 and x_2 and random strings r_1 and r_2, respectively. We show an implementation of the ideal functionality $\mathcal{F}_\mathrm{SFE}^f$ evaluating—with security against active quantum adversaries—any classical poly-time function f

for which there exists a classical passively secure protocol as described above. Functionality $\mathcal{F}_{\text{SFE}}^f$ is shown in Fig. 9[10]. The implementation $\Pi_{\text{A,B}}^{\text{SFE}(f)}$ of $\mathcal{F}_{\text{SFE}}^f$ is shown in Fig. 10. Corollary 3 is proven in the full version of the paper [15].

Corollary 3. *If there exist mixed commitment schemes, then there exists a classical implementation of $\mathcal{F}_{\text{SFE}}^f$ for all classical poly-time functions f secure, according to Definitions 1 and 2.*

Acknowledgement

Lunemann acknowledges financial support for part of this work by Institut Mittag-Leffler, The Royal Swedish Academy of Sciences. Nielsen acknowledges support from the Danish National Research Foundation and the National Science Foundation of China (under the grant 61061130540) for the Sino-Danish Center for the Theory of Interactive Computation, within which part of this work was performed.

References

1. Bellare, M., Goldreich, O.: On defining proofs of knowledge. In: Brickell, E.F. (ed.) CRYPTO 1992. LNCS, vol. 740, pp. 390–420. Springer, Heidelberg (1993)
2. Blum, M.: Coin flipping by telephone. In: Advances in Cryptology: A Report on CRYPTO 1981, pp. 11–15. U.C. Santa Barbara, Dept. of Elec. and Computer Eng., ECE Report No 82-04 (1981)
3. Brassard, G., Chaum, D., Crépeau, C.: Minimum disclosure proofs of knowledge. Journal of Compututer and System Sciences 37(2), 156–189 (1988)
4. Damgård, I., Fehr, S., Lunemann, C., Salvail, L., Schaffner, C.: Improving the security of quantum protocols via commit-and-open. In: Halevi, S. (ed.) CRYPTO 2009. LNCS, vol. 5677, pp. 408–427. Springer, Heidelberg (2009)
5. Damgård, I.B., Fehr, S., Salvail, L.: Zero-knowledge proofs and string commitments withstanding quantum attacks. In: Franklin, M. (ed.) CRYPTO 2004. LNCS, vol. 3152, pp. 254–272. Springer, Heidelberg (2004)
6. Damgård, I.B., Fehr, S., Salvail, L., Schaffner, C.: Secure identification and QKD in the bounded-quantum-storage model. In: Menezes, A. (ed.) CRYPTO 2007. LNCS, vol. 4622, pp. 342–359. Springer, Heidelberg (2007)
7. Damgård, I.B., Lunemann, C.: Quantum-secure coin-flipping and applications. In: Matsui, M. (ed.) ASIACRYPT 2009. LNCS, vol. 5912, pp. 52–69. Springer, Heidelberg (2009)

---

[10] Note that y does not need to be kept secure against external observers and also allows the adversary to abort depending on the value of y. We stress that it is no restriction that we consider common outputs nor that we leak y to observers. If we want to compute function $g(x_1, x_2) = (y_1, y_2)$ where *only* A (B) learns y_1 (y_2), we evaluate the common output function $y = f((x_1, p_1), (x_2, p_2))$ as follows. Public y contains $y_1 \oplus p_1$ and $y_2 \oplus p_2$, where p_1 and p_2 are A's and B's uniformly random additional input of the same length as y_1 and y_2. Thus, the common outputs are one-time pad encrypted using pads known only to the party who is to learn the result.

8. Damgård, I.B., Nielsen, J.B.: Perfect hiding and perfect binding universally composable commitment schemes with constant expansion factor. In: Yung, M. (ed.) CRYPTO 2002. LNCS, vol. 2442, pp. 581–596. Springer, Heidelberg (2002)

9. Fehr, S., Schaffner, C.: Composing quantum protocols in a classical environment. In: Reingold, O. (ed.) TCC 2009. LNCS, vol. 5444, pp. 350–367. Springer, Heidelberg (2009)

10. Goldwasser, S., Micali, S., Rackoff, C.: The knowledge complexity of interactive proof-systems (extended abstract). In: 17th Annual ACM Symposium on Theory of Computing (STOC), pp. 291–304 (1985)

11. van de Graaf, J.: Towards a formal definition of security for quantum protocols. PhD thesis, Université de Montréal (Canada) (1997)

12. Hallgren, S., Smith, A., Song, F.: Classical cryptographic protocols in a quantum world (2011), Extended abstract available at
qip2011.quantumlah.org/scientificprogramme/abstract/183.pdf

13. Kilian, J.: Founding cryptography on oblivious transfer. In: 20th Annual ACM Symposium on Theory of Computing (STOC), pp. 20–31 (1988)

14. Lunemann, C.: Cryptographic Protocols under Quantum Attacks. PhD thesis, Aarhus University (Denmark) (November 2010), arXiv:1102.0885 [quant-ph]

15. Lunemann, C., Nielsen, J.B.: Fully simulatable quantum-secure coin-flipping and applications (2011), Full version available at eprint.iacr.org/2011/065

16. Peikert, C., Vaikuntanathan, V., Waters, B.: A framework for efficient and composable oblivious transfer. In: Wagner, D. (ed.) CRYPTO 2008. LNCS, vol. 5157, pp. 554–571. Springer, Heidelberg (2008), Full version available at eprint.iacr.org/2007/348.pdf

17. Regev, O.: On lattices, learning with errors, random linear codes, and cryptography. In: 37th Annual ACM Symposium on Theory of Computing (STOC), pp. 84–93 (2005)

18. Smith, A.: Personal communication (2009)

19. Watrous, J.: Zero-knowledge against quantum attacks. SIAM Journal on Computing 39(1), 25–58 (2009); Preliminary version in 38th Annual ACM Symposium on Theory of Computing (STOC), pp. 296–305 (2006)

Efficient and Secure Generalized Pattern Matching via Fast Fourier Transform

Damien Vergnaud

École normale supérieure, C.N.R.S., I.N.R.I.A.
45, Rue d'Ulm, 75230 Paris CEDEX 05, France

Abstract. We present simple protocols for secure two-party computation of generalized pattern matching in the presence of malicious parties. The problem is to determine all positions in a text T where a pattern P occurs (or matches with few mismatches) allowing possibly both T and P to contain single character wildcards. We propose constant-round protocols that exhibit linear communication and quasilinear computational costs with simulation-based security. Our constructions rely on a well-known technique for pattern matching proposed by Fischer and Paterson in 1974 and based on the Fast Fourier Transform. The security of the new schemes is reduced to the semantic security of the ElGamal encryption scheme.

Keywords: Two-party secure computation, Pattern matching, Homomorphic encryption, Fast Fourier Transform.

1 Introduction

We present secure protocols for two-party computation of (exact or approximate) pattern matching which are more efficient and conceptually simpler than previous approaches. Our proposals are constant-round and requires linear communication and quasilinear computational costs.

Prior work. The *pattern matching* problem [9] is to find all the occurrences of a given pattern P of length m in a text T of length n, both being sequences of characters drawn from a finite character set Σ. It is an important problem for many kinds of processes of strings, for instance in molecular biology, information retrieval, pattern recognition, compiling, data compression, program analysis and security. These applications often require more sophisticated forms of searching:

- *approximate pattern matching* [22], where the problem is to find the locations where the Hamming distance of T substrings and P is less than some threshold $k \leq m$;
- *pattern matching with wildcards* (or *"don't cares"*) [11], where the problem is to find all occurrences of a pattern $P \in (\Sigma \cup \{\star\})^m$ in a text $T \in (\Sigma \cup \{\star\})^n$ where the wildcard character $\star \notin \Sigma$ matches any character in Σ.

An intensive research effort since the 1970s has led to the design of several efficient algorithms for generalized pattern matching (see [9]). In 1974, Fischer and Paterson [11] solved the pattern matching with wildcards problem in

A. Nitaj and D. Pointcheval (Eds.): AFRICACRYPT 2011, LNCS 6737, pp. 41–58, 2011.

Table 1. Efficiency Comparison of Secure Generalized Pattern Matching Protocols

	# of Rounds	Communication	Exponentiations
Basic Pattern Matching with alphabet Σ			
Hazay & Toft [17, §3]	$O(1)$	$O(n \log |\Sigma|)$	$O(n \log |\Sigma|)$
§3	$O(1)$	$O(n)$	$O(nm)$
Approximate Binary Pattern Matching with k Mismatches			
Hazay & Toft [17, §5]	$O(1)$	$O(nm)$	$O(nm)$
§5.1	$O(1)$	$O(nk)$	$O(n(\log m + k))$
Binary Pattern Matching with Wildcards			
Hazay & Toft [17, §4]	$O(1)$	$O(nm)$	$O(nm)$
§5.2	$O(1)$	$O(n)$	$O(n \log m)$

$O(n \log m \log(\#\Sigma))$ time using convolution and *Fast Fourier Transform* (FFT). After several improvements, Clifford and Clifford [6] proposed a simple deterministic algorithm that also involves convolutions and runs in time $O(n \log m)$. A more complex algorithm in optimal $O(n)$ time was proposed in [20]. The FFT was also used to propose fast algorithms for the approximate pattern matching problem (*e.g.* [22]).

In the setting of secure *two-party computation*, introduced in 1982 by Yao [25], two parties wish to jointly compute some function of their private inputs while preserving a number of security properties. Troncoso-Pastoriza, Katzenbeisser and Celik [23] were the first to consider (basic) pattern matching in the context of secure computation (in the semi-honest setting). Their protocol implements the well-known Knuth-Morris-Pratt algorithm [19] and is linear in the input length. Hazay and Lindell [15] proposed later a protocol based on oblivious pseudorandom function evaluation which achieves one-sided simulatability security. The first construction for the (basic) pattern matching problem with full simulation-based security in the malicious setting was developed by Gennaro, Hazay and Sorensen in [12]. Their protocol relies on the Knuth-Morris-Pratt algorithm but requires linear round complexity and quadratic communication and computational cost. The first work which addresses the approximate pattern matching problem is [18].

Very recently, Hazay and Toft [17] proposed constant-rounds and efficient protocols for the (basic) pattern matching, the approximate pattern matching and the pattern matching with wildcards problems. Their schemes achieve security against malicious adversaries with (optimal) linear computational cost and bandwidth for the first problem but quadratic communication and computational complexity for the two extended problems.

Contributions of the paper. The main contribution of the paper is to provide protocols for approximate pattern matching (permitting a constant number of mismatches) and pattern matching with wildcards with constant-rounds, linear communication and $O(n \log m)$ computational costs.

The problem we address can be described as follows: let us assume that Alice holds a text $T \in (\Sigma \cup \{\star\})^n$, while Bob has a pattern $P \in (\Sigma \cup \{\star\})^m$. The goal is for Bob to learn where P occurs (or matches with few mismatches) in T while Alice does not gain any information about P from the protocol execution and Bob does not learn anything but the matched text locations. Our approach relies on the classical *homomorphic encryption paradigm* (*e.g.* [16, § 7.2.2.]): Bob will encrypt P bit by bit for an additively homomorphic encryption scheme and Alice will then apply the deterministic algorithm from [6,22] under encryption (using the homomorphic properties of the cryptosystem) and sends back the encrypted result to Bob.

First, we present a protocol for the (basic) pattern matching problem (§ 3) that is secure against malicious adversaries, but for the so-called *one-sided simulatability* weaker security notion. The construction relies on a straightforward observation that permits to perform secure pattern matching independently of the size of the alphabet Σ. Our main goal by presenting this scheme is to illustrate the ideas we will use in the following sections.

The Fast Fourier Transform (FFT) [7] is an algorithm to compute the discrete Fourier transform and its inverse. It leads notably to quasilinear polynomial multiplication algorithms. In order to apply Fischer and Paterson technique to secure two-party generalized pattern matching, one needs to construct a protocol for two-party FFT with quasilinear computational complexity. The idea of using FFT in secure two-party computation is probably not new[1] but we have not been able to locate a reference in the literature. We provide a description (§ 4) in the hope that it may be of independent interest.

Using this tool we provide adaptation of the generalized pattern matching algorithms from [6,22,2] and obtains schemes with overall efficiency summarized in the table Tab. 1 (§ 5.1 and 5.2). As a by-product, we propose a protocol that reports the Hamming distance at every position (irrespective of its value) in $O(n\sqrt{m})$ time.

2 Preliminaries

2.1 Notation

For $n \in \mathbb{N}$, the set of n-bit strings is denoted by $\{0,1\}^n$, the set of integers $\{1, \ldots, n\}$ is denoted $[\![n]\!]$ and the symmetric group on $[\![n]\!]$ is denoted by $\mathfrak{S}_n$. The Hamming distance $d_H(x, y)$ between two words $x, y \in \{0,1\}^n$ is defined as the number of coordinates in which they differ.

We denote the security parameter by κ and input lengths are always assumed to be bounded by some polynomial in κ. A probabilistic algorithm is said to run in polynomial-time (PPT) if it runs in time that is polynomial in κ. Let $\mathcal{A}$ be a PPT algorithm and let x be an input for $\mathcal{A}$. The probability space that assigns to a string σ the probability that $\mathcal{A}$, on input x, outputs σ is denoted by $\mathcal{A}(x)$.

---

[1] An anonymous referee kindly informed us of the recent report [5] in which Cheon, Jarecki and Seo use FFT to speed-up secure set intersection protocols.

Given a probability space S, a PPT algorithm that samples a random element according to S is denoted by $x \xleftarrow{R} S$. For a finite set X, $x \xleftarrow{R} X$ denotes a PPT algorithm that samples a random element uniformly at random from X.

2.2   ElGamal Encryption

For a security parameter κ, the ElGamal encryption scheme [10] operates on a cyclic group $\mathbb{G}$ of κ-bits prime order q and identity element $1_\mathbb{G}$. Let g denote a generator of $\mathbb{G}$. The ElGamal public and secret keys are $(\mathbb{G}, q, g, y)$ and $(\mathbb{G}, q, g, x)$ (respectively) where x is picked uniformly at random in $\mathbb{Z}_q$ and $y = g^x$. A message $m \in \mathbb{G}$ is encrypted by picking r uniformly at random in $\mathbb{Z}_q$ and the ciphertext is $(g^r, y^r \cdot m)$. We will use the notation:

$$(g^r, y^r \cdot m) \xleftarrow{R} \mathsf{Enc}_y(m) \text{ or } (g^r, y^r \cdot m) \leftarrow \mathsf{Enc}_y(m; r)$$

A ciphertext (α, β) is decrypted as $m = \beta/\alpha^x \leftarrow \mathsf{Dec}_x(\alpha, \beta)$. The semantic security of the ElGamal encryption scheme follows from the hardness of Decision Diffie-Hellman (DDH) problem in $\mathbb{G}$ [24].

The ElGamal scheme is homomorphic relative to multiplication. In this paper, we consider a modified version of ElGamal where the encryption is performed in the exponents: one chooses r uniformly at random in $\mathbb{Z}_q$ and computes $(g^r, y^r \cdot g^m)$. Decryption of a ciphertext $c = (\alpha, \beta)$ is performed by computing $g^m = \beta/\alpha^x$. The fact that m cannot be efficiently recovered is not problematic for the way ElGamal is incorporated in our protocols. This variant of ElGamal is additively homomorphic and can be used to perform oblivious linear computations in the exponent: it naturally allows for multiplication with a plaintext constant using repeated doubling and adding.

2.3   Zero-Knowledge

Security in the presence of malicious behavior is usually achieved by forcing the parties to demonstrate that they are well-behaved. In our protocols, we need zero-knowledge proofs of knowledge that some algebraic statement $\mathcal{R}$ holds in a group $\mathbb{G} = \langle g \rangle$ of prime order q with $2^{\kappa-1} < q < 2^\kappa$. We will use Σ-protocols made secure against malicious verifiers (using standard techniques) since they are efficient and achieves constant communication complexity (see [17]):

$\pi_{\mathbf{DL}}$: due to Schnorr [21], this Σ-protocol allows a prover to demonstrate knowledge of the solution to a discrete logarithm problem:

$$\mathcal{R}_{\mathrm{DL}} = \{[h, x] \mid h = g^x\}.$$

$\pi_{\mathbf{eqDL}}$: due to Chaum and Pedersen [4], this Σ-protocol demonstrates equality of two discrete logarithm problems (as well as its knowledge):

$$\mathcal{R}_{\mathrm{eqDL}} = \{[(g_1, g_2, h_1, h_2), x] \mid h_1 = g_1^x \wedge h_2 = g_2^x\}.$$

We will use Σ-protocols for ElGamal ciphertexts for the public key $(\mathbb{G}, q, g, y)$:

$\pi_{\mathbf{Mult}}$: due to Abe, Cramer and Fehr [1], this Σ-protocol demonstrates that a ciphertext is an encryption of the product of the plaintexts of two given ciphertexts:

$$\mathcal{R}_{\mathrm{Mult}} = \{[(c_1, c_2, c_3), (m, r, s)] \,|\, c_1 = \mathsf{Enc}_y(g^m; r) \wedge c_3 = c_2{}^m \cdot \mathsf{Enc}_y(1_{\mathbb{G}}; s)\}.$$

$\pi_{\mathbf{Perm}}$: due to Groth [13], this Σ-protocol demonstrates that a set of ciphertexts is a permutation and rerandomization of another set of ciphertexts:

$$\mathcal{R}_{\mathrm{Perm}} = \left\{ [(c_i, \overline{c_i})_{i \in [\![k]\!]}, (\sigma, (r_i)_{i \in [\![k]\!]})] \,\middle|\, \begin{array}{l} \sigma \in \mathfrak{S}_k \\ \overline{c_i} = c_{\sigma(i)} \cdot \mathsf{Enc}_y(1_{\mathbb{G}}; r_i), \forall i \in [\![k]\!] \end{array} \right\}.$$

$\pi_{\mathbf{nze}}$: this Σ-protocol demonstrates that a ciphertext is a rerandomization of another ciphertext at some *non-zero* power:

$$\mathcal{R}_{\mathrm{nze}} = \left\{ [(c_1, c_2), (R, r)] \,\middle|\, c_1 = c_2^R \cdot \mathsf{Enc}_y(1_{\mathbb{G}}; r) \wedge R \neq 0 \right\}.$$

$\pi_{\mathbf{isBit}}$: this Σ-protocol demonstrates that a ciphertext encrypts 0 or 1:

$$\mathcal{R}_{\mathrm{isBit}} = \{[c, (b, r)] \,|\, c = \mathsf{Enc}_y(g^b; r) \wedge b \in \{0, 1\}\}.$$

$\pi_{\mathbf{isTrit}}$: this Σ-protocol demonstrates that a ciphertext encrypts 0, 1 or 2:

$$\mathcal{R}_{\mathrm{isTrit}} = \{[c, (b, r)] \,|\, c = \mathsf{Enc}_y(g^b; r) \wedge b \in \{0, 1, 2\}\}.$$

The protocol π_{nze} can be otained from π_{Mult} as described in [17] and the protocols π_{isBit} and π_{isTrit} can be obtained from π_{EqDL} using the technique of Cramer, Gennaro and Schoenmakers [8].

We also need a protocol π_{KeyGen} for generation of an ElGamal public key such that two parties hold shares of the secret key and a protocol π_{Dec} for shared decryption of a ciphertext encrypted using a key generated by π_{KeyGen}. We consider a protocol where only one party obtains the decrypted result (see [17, §2.3]). We denote the associated ideal functionalities $\mathcal{F}^{\mathrm{KeyGen}}$ and $\mathcal{F}^{\mathrm{Dec}}$.

2.4   Secure Two-Party Computation

We only provide a brief review of two-party computation definitions and we refer the reader to the recent book [16, Chapter 2] for more details. Let f be a two-argument function and let Alice and Bob be two possibly malicious parties, the first having an input x and the second having an input y. Securely computing f means that Alice and Bob keep turns exchanging message strings so that:

- Bob learns $z = f(x, y)$ but nothing about x (not already implied by y and z);
- Alice learns nothing about y (and nothing about z not already implied by x).

In particular, Alice and Bob wish to ensure that nothing is revealed from the protocol execution to an outsider or the other party (*privacy*) and that the output is computed according to the specified function (*correctness*). In this paper, we do not require the correctness to hold with probability 1 but instead allow negligible probability of error in the value output by the protocol.

The *simulation-based* security definitions formalize the intuition that whatever can be computed by a party can be computed based on its input and output only. This is done by comparing a party's view in a real protocol execution to an "ideal execution", where a trusted party computes the function and sends the output to the parties. In this paper, we consider two flavors of simulation-based security in the presence of malicious adversaries:

- *Full simulation security* [3]: it requires that for every PPT adversary $\mathcal{A}$ in the real world, there exists a corresponding PPT simulator $\mathcal{S}$ in the ideal world such that the view are computationally indistinguishable.
- *One-sided simulation security*: where full simulation is provided for only one of the corruption cases and only privacy is achieved for the other case (guaranteeing that the adversary does not learn anything but the output of the computation).

3   Warm Up: (Basic) Pattern Matching Protocol

In this section, we address the question of how to securely compute the functionality $\mathcal{F}_{\mathrm{PM}}$ defined by

$$((\mathcal{P}, n), (\mathcal{T}, m)) \mapsto \begin{cases} (\{j \in [\![n-m+1]\!], \mathcal{T}_j = \mathcal{P}\}, \bot) & \text{if } \mathcal{P} \in \Sigma^m \wedge \mathcal{T} \in \Sigma^n \\ (\bot, \bot) & \text{otherwise} \end{cases}$$

where $\mathcal{T}_j$ denotes the substring of length m that begins at the j-th position in $\mathcal{T}$. Note that Alice learns nothing about $\mathcal{P}$ and the only thing Bob learns about $\mathcal{T}$ is the locations where $\mathcal{P}$ appears. We assume that $\#\Sigma = \mathsf{poly}(\kappa)$ and $\Sigma \subseteq \mathbb{Z}_q$.

Motivated by the task of constructing a simple protocol for $\mathcal{F}_{\mathrm{PM}}$, we use the straightforward observation that $\mathcal{P} = (p_1, \ldots, p_m)$ occurs at the j-th position in $\mathcal{T} = (t_1, \ldots, t_n)$ if and only if $p_i - t_{i+j-1} = 0$ for all $i \in [\![m]\!]$ and that consequently for random $(s_{1,j}, \ldots, s_{m,j}) \in \mathbb{Z}_q^m$, the equality

$$\sum_{i=1}^{m} s_{i,j}(p_i - t_{i+j-1}) = 0 \tag{1}$$

holds with probability 1 if $\mathcal{P} = \mathcal{T}_j$ and with probability $1/q$ otherwise (where the probability is taken over the random $s_{i,j}$ for $i \in [\![m]\!]$).

This observation results in a simple protocol for $\mathcal{F}_{\mathrm{PM}}$ that can be summarized as follows:

1. Bob picks at random $x \in \mathbb{Z}_q$ and sets $y = g^x$. He sends y to Alice and proves his knowledge of x by running π_{DL} using x.

2. Bob encrypts $\mathcal{P}$ character by character with his own public key y:

$$c_i = (\alpha_i, \beta_i) \xleftarrow{R} \mathsf{Enc}_y(g^{p_i}) \quad \text{for } i \in [\![m]\!]$$

and sends c_i to Alice for $i \in [\![m]\!]$.

3. Using the homomorphic property of ElGamal encryption, Alice computes, for $j \in [\![n-m+1]\!]$, a (uniformly distributed) encryption of the left-hand side of (1) as

$$d_j = \left(g^{r_j} \prod_{i=1}^{m} \alpha_i^{s_{i,j}}, \; y^{r_j} \prod_{i=1}^{m} \left(\beta_i g^{-t_{j+i-1}} \right)^{s_{i,j}} \right)$$

$$= \mathsf{Enc}_y(1_{\mathbb{G}}, r_j) \cdot \prod_{i=1}^{m} \left(c_i \cdot (1_{\mathbb{G}}, g^{-t_{j+i-1}}) \right)^{s_{i,j}}$$

for $r_j, s_{1,j}, \ldots, s_{m,j}$ picked uniformly at random in $\mathbb{Z}_q$. Alice sends d_j for $j \in [\![n-m+1]\!]$ to Bob.

4. Bob decrypts d_j for $j \in [\![n-m+1]\!]$ thanks to his knowledge of x and outputs the set of indices of ciphertexts that encrypt $1_{\mathbb{G}}$.

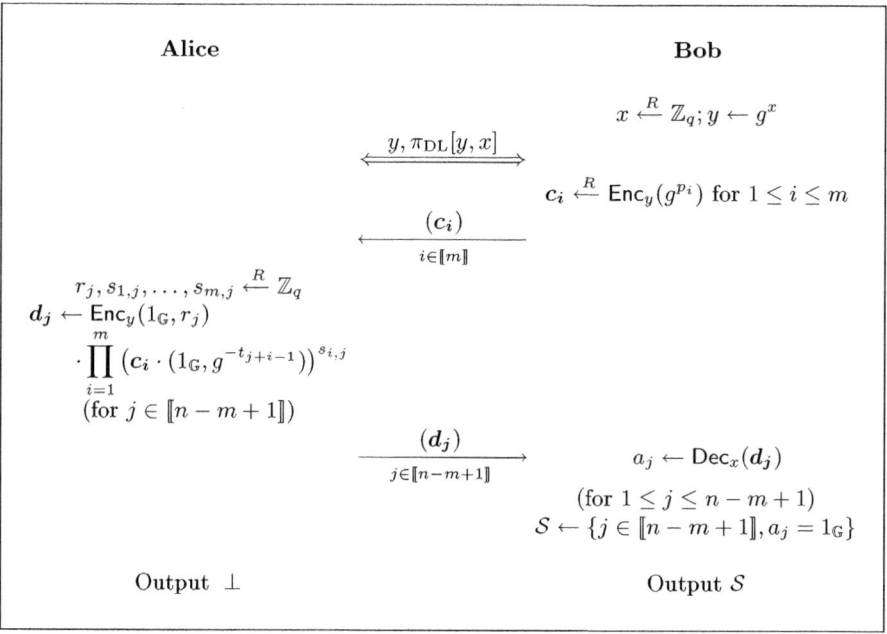

Fig. 1. Secure Basic Pattern Matching

The protocol flow is described in Fig. 1 (where simple arrows indicate data transmission and double arrows stand for interactive protocols). The protocol is less efficient than the scheme from [17] since it exhibits linear communication[2] but quadratic computation costs. However it is simpler and illustrates the ideas we will use in the next sections. It achieves one-sided simulation security against malicious adversaries.

Theorem 1. *If π_{DL} is a zero-knowledge proof of knowledge of a discrete logarithm secure against malicious verifiers and if the ElGamal encryption scheme is semantically secure, then the protocol described in Fig. 1 securely computes $\mathcal{F}_{\mathrm{PM}}$ with one-sided simulation security against malicious adversaries.*

Proof (Sketch). As in [17, Theorem 1], we separately prove the security in the case that Alice is corrupted and the case that Bob is corrupted.

Alice is corrupted: Since Alice does not receive any output from the execution, and we are only proving one-sided simulation security here, all we need to show is that privacy is preserved. This follows readily from the semantic security of the ElGamal encryption scheme.

Bob is corrupted: Let $\mathcal{A}$ denote an adversary controlling Bob. We need to prove that $\mathcal{A}$ does not learn anything but the matching text locations. We construct a simulator $\mathcal{S}$ as follows:

1. $\mathcal{S}$ is given a pattern of length m, an integer n and $\mathcal{A}$'s auxiliary input and invokes $\mathcal{A}$ on these values.
2. $\mathcal{S}$ obtains $\mathcal{A}$'s secret key x from the proof of knowledge extractor for π_{DL}.
3. $\mathcal{S}$ receives from the adversary $\mathcal{A}$ a vector of m ciphertexts c_i for $i \in [\![m]\!]$. Using x, it decrypts each ciphertext and try to compute the discrete log of the corresponding plaintext z_i.
   (a) If $z_i = g^{\sigma_i}$ where $\sigma_i \in \Sigma$ for all $i \in [\![m]\!]$, $\mathcal{S}$ defines the pattern $\mathcal{P}$ as $\mathcal{P} = (\sigma_1, \ldots, \sigma_m)$ and sends it to the trusted party for $\mathcal{F}_{PM}$ and obtains a subset $\mathcal{I} \subseteq [\![n-m+1]\!]$. The simulator $\mathcal{S}$ produces a vector of ciphertexts:

   $$d_j \xleftarrow{R} \left(\mathsf{Enc}_y(g^{b_j})\right)^{\theta_j} \text{ for } j \in [\![n-m+1]\!]$$

   where $b_j \in \{0,1\}$ with $b_j = 0 \iff j \in \mathcal{I}$ and $\theta_j \xleftarrow{R} \mathbb{Z}_q$.
   (b) If there is an $i \in [\![m]\!]$ such $z_i \neq g^{\sigma_i}$ for all $\sigma_i \in \Sigma$, then $\mathcal{S}$ aborts by sending $\perp$ to the trusted party for $\mathcal{F}_{PM}$ and produces a vector of ciphertexts:

   $$d_j \xleftarrow{R} \left(\mathsf{Enc}_y(g)\right)^{\theta_j} \text{ for } j \in [\![n-m+1]\!]$$

   where $\theta_j \xleftarrow{R} \mathbb{Z}_q$.
4. If at any point $\mathcal{A}$ sends an invalid message $\mathcal{S}$ aborts, sending $\perp$ to the trusted party for $\mathcal{F}_{PM}$. Otherwise, it outputs whatever $\mathcal{A}$ does.

---

[2] The round complexity and the communication complexity of our scheme are however smaller by a constant factor and independent of the size of the underlying alphabet.

Since $|\Sigma| = \mathrm{poly}(\kappa)$, the simulator $\mathcal{S}$ runs in polynomial time (the running time of the third step being upper-bounded by $O(m\sqrt{|\Sigma|})$ group operations using generic technique for discrete logarithm computation in short intervals). Our basic observation on (1) shows readily that the adversary's view is statistically close to its view in the real execution of the protocol.   □

Remark 1. Observe that the protocol from Fig. 1 does not achieve correctness when Alice is corrupted. However, it is possible to achieve full simulation security against malicious adversaries by enforcing Alice to use only text symbols t_i in Σ for $i \in [\![n]\!]$ (using for instance generalization of π_{isBit} and π_{isTrit}) and proving consistency of the ciphertexts $(\delta_j, \gamma_j)_{1 \leq j \leq n-m+1}$.

4 Secure Fast Fourier Transform and Polynomial Multiplication

4.1 FFT and Polynomial Multiplication: A Brief Recall

Let q be a prime number, D a divisor of $q - 1$ and ω a primitive D-th root of 1 in $\mathbb{Z}_q^*$ (for simplicity, one can assume that D is a power of two). Suppose we are given two polynomials in $A, B \in \mathbb{Z}_q[X]$ of degree less than $d = D/2$. The FFT is a well-known method to compute the coefficients of $C(X) = A(X)B(X)$ in $O(D \log D)$ multiplications in $\mathbb{Z}_q$:

1. Evaluate A and B at the D points: $1, \omega, \omega^2, \ldots, \omega^{D-1}$ using the Discrete Fourier Transform (DFT):

> **Evaluation of $P \in \mathbb{Z}_q[X]$ at $1, \omega, \omega^2, \ldots, \omega^{D-1}$**
> Write $P(X) = P_0(X^2) + X P_1(X^2)$
> Evaluate (recursively) P_0 and P_1 at $1, \omega^2, \omega^4, \ldots, \omega^{D-1}$
> Write $P(\omega^i) = P_0(\omega^{2i}) + \omega^i P_1(\omega^{2i})$ for $i \in [\![D]\!]$

2. Compute the values of $C(X)$ at these D points $1, \omega, \omega^2, \ldots, \omega^{D-1}$.

3. Interpolate the polynomial C using the inverse DFT:

> **Interpolation of $P \in \mathbb{Z}_q[X]$ given values at $1, \omega, \omega^2, \ldots, \omega^{D-1}$**
> Write $\widetilde{P}(X) = P(1) + P(\omega)X + \cdots + P(\omega^{D-1})X^{D-1}$
> Evaluate (as in **1.**) $\widetilde{P}$ at $1, \omega^{-1}, \omega^{-2}, \ldots, \omega^{1-D}$
> Output $P(X) = \dfrac{1}{D}\left(\widetilde{P}(1) + \widetilde{P}(\omega^{-1})X + \cdots + \widetilde{P}(\omega^{1-D})X^{D-1} \right)$

4.2 Secure Fast Polynomial Multiplication

We now outline a protocol to efficiently and securely compute the encryption of the product of two polynomials (for a given public key y). Let us assume that Alice holds a polynomial $A(X) = \sum_{i=0}^{d-1} a_i X^i \in \mathbb{Z}_q[X]$ and that Bob holds a polynomial $B(X) = \sum_{i=0}^{d-1} b_i X^i \in \mathbb{Z}_q[X]$ both of degree less than d.

1. Alice encrypts the polynomial A coefficient by coefficient (in the exponents):

$$\alpha_0 = \mathsf{Enc}_y(g^{a_0}), \alpha_1 = \mathsf{Enc}_y(g^{a_1}), \ldots, \alpha_{d-1} = \mathsf{Enc}_y(g^{a_{d-1}})$$

   and sends the ciphertexts $(\alpha_0, \alpha_1, \ldots, \alpha_{d-1})$ to Bob.
2. Bob encrypts the polynomial B coefficient by coefficient (in the exponents):

$$\beta_0 = \mathsf{Enc}_y(g^{b_0}), \beta_1 = \mathsf{Enc}_y(g^{b_1}), \ldots, \beta_{d-1} = \mathsf{Enc}_y(g^{b_{d-1}})$$

   and sends the ciphertexts $(\beta_0, \beta_1, \ldots, \beta_{d-1})$ to Alice.
3. Alice and Bob (simultaneously and independently) compute the encrypted value of $g^{A(\omega^i)}$ and $g^{B(\omega^i)}$ for $i \in [\![D]\!]$ using the DFT (Step 1 in the FFT method). Since the encryption scheme is additively homomorphic, it can be used to perform deterministic oblivious linear computations in the exponent. At this step of the protocol, Alice and Bob then share (identical) encryption of $g^{A(\omega^i)}$ and $g^{B(\omega^i)}$ for $i \in [\![D]\!]$ and Alice[3] knows the randomness corresponding to the encryption of $g^{A(\omega^i)}$.
4. Alice computes the encryption of $g^{A(\omega^i)B(\omega^i)}$ for $i \in [\![D]\!]$ knowing $A(\omega^i)$ and the shared encryption of $g^{B(\omega^i)}$ (Step 2 in the FFT method). Alice sends the resulting ciphertexts to Bob and, thanks to her knowledge of the randomness in the shared encryption of $g^{A(\omega^i)}$ she can prove its validity by running the protocol π_{Mult}.
5. Alice and Bob (simultaneously and independently) compute the encrypted coefficients of AB (in the exponents) using the inverse DFT (Step 3 in the FFT method).

The computational complexity of the protocol is $O(D \log D)$ exponentiations in $\mathbb{G}$ and its communication complexity is $O(D)$ (and therefore optimal). In order to use this fast two-party polynomial multiplication protocol in our generalized pattern matching schemes, we will need the encrypted computation to be done under a public-key whose corresponding secret-key is shared between Alice and Bob. The fact that intermediate values are encrypted under a key which neither Alice or Bob know permits the zero-knowledge simulation.

We do not propose any specific application in the realm of polynomial arithmetic for this protocol but we will rather provide applications to the generalized pattern matching problem in the following section.

Remark 2. It is possible to enforce the polynomials coefficients to belong to a specific subset of $\mathbb{Z}_q$ (*e.g.* we will use the set $\{0,1\}$ or $\{0,1,2\}$ in the following and use the protocols π_{isBit} and π_{isTrit} to ensure these properties).

5   Fast Secure Generalized Pattern Matching

The main idea of the algorithm from [6] is to calculate the sum of squared differences between the pattern and the text for every possible alignment. Suppose

---

[3] Of course, Bob knows the randomness corresponding to the encryption of $g^{B(\omega^i)}$ and in the rest of the protocol, one can exchange the role of Alice and Bob.

without loss of generality that $\Sigma \subset \mathbb{N}$. If there are no wildcards then for each location $i \in [\![n - m + 1]\!]$, we can calculate

$$\sum_{j=1}^{m}(p_j - t_{i+j-1})^2 = \sum_{j=1}^{m}\left(p_j{}^2 - 2p_j \cdot t_{i+j-1} + t_{i+j-1}{}^2\right) \tag{2}$$

in $O(n \log n)$ time using FFT. Wherever there is an exact match this sum will be exactly 0. When wildcards are allowed in the pattern and the text we replace the wildcard symbols by 0's (and other symbols by non-negative integers) and then consider the sum

$$\sum_{j=1}^{m}p_j t_{i+j-1}(p_j - t_{i+j-1})^2 = \sum_{j=1}^{m}\left(p_j{}^3 t_{i+j-1} - 2p_j{}^2 \cdot t_{i+j-1}{}^2 + p_j t_{i+j-1}{}^3\right) \tag{3}$$

which equals 0 if and only if there is an exact match with wildcards. The sum (3) can be computed with three convolutions and therefore in $O(n \log n)$ time using FFT.

In order to reduce the time complexity from $O(n \log n)$ to $O(n \log m)$, we will use a standard trick which consists in partitioning $\mathcal{T}$ into n/m overlapping substrings of length $2m$ with the first substring starting at the beginning of the text and each subsequent substring having an overlap of length m with the previous one. The matching algorithm is then performed separately on each substring. Each iteration takes $O(m \log m)$ time giving an overall time complexity of $O((n/m)m \log m) = O(n \log m)$.

In the following, we will use this trick and for simplicity we will assume (without loss of generality) that $n = 2m$ and that $4m$ is a power of 2 dividing $q - 1$. The protocol for (fast) secure polynomial multiplication can be used to securely compute sums of the form (2) or (3) in time $O(m \log m)$. The figure Fig. 2 presents the common opening for our generalized pattern matching protocols. At the end of this subprotocol, Alice and Bob hold

- shares (x_a, x_b) of the secret key corresponding to the public key y.
- encryption $\boldsymbol{a_i}$ of the bit t_i for $i \in [\![2m]\!]$.
- encryption $\boldsymbol{b_i}$ of the bit p_{m-i+1} for $i \in [\![m]\!]$.
- encryption $\boldsymbol{f_{i+m}}$ of the sum $\sum_{j=1}^{m} p_j \cdot t_{i+j-1}$ for $i \in [\![m]\!]$.

Note that we modify the ordering of the pattern bits, in order to compute (2) or (3) as an actual convolution and that we enforce ciphertexts $\boldsymbol{a_i}$ and $\boldsymbol{b_i}$ to encrypt bits using the protocol π_{isBit} (as mentioned above).

5.1   Pattern Matching with Mismatches

Our first algorithm is in fact independent of the bound k and report the Hamming distance at every position irrespective of its value.

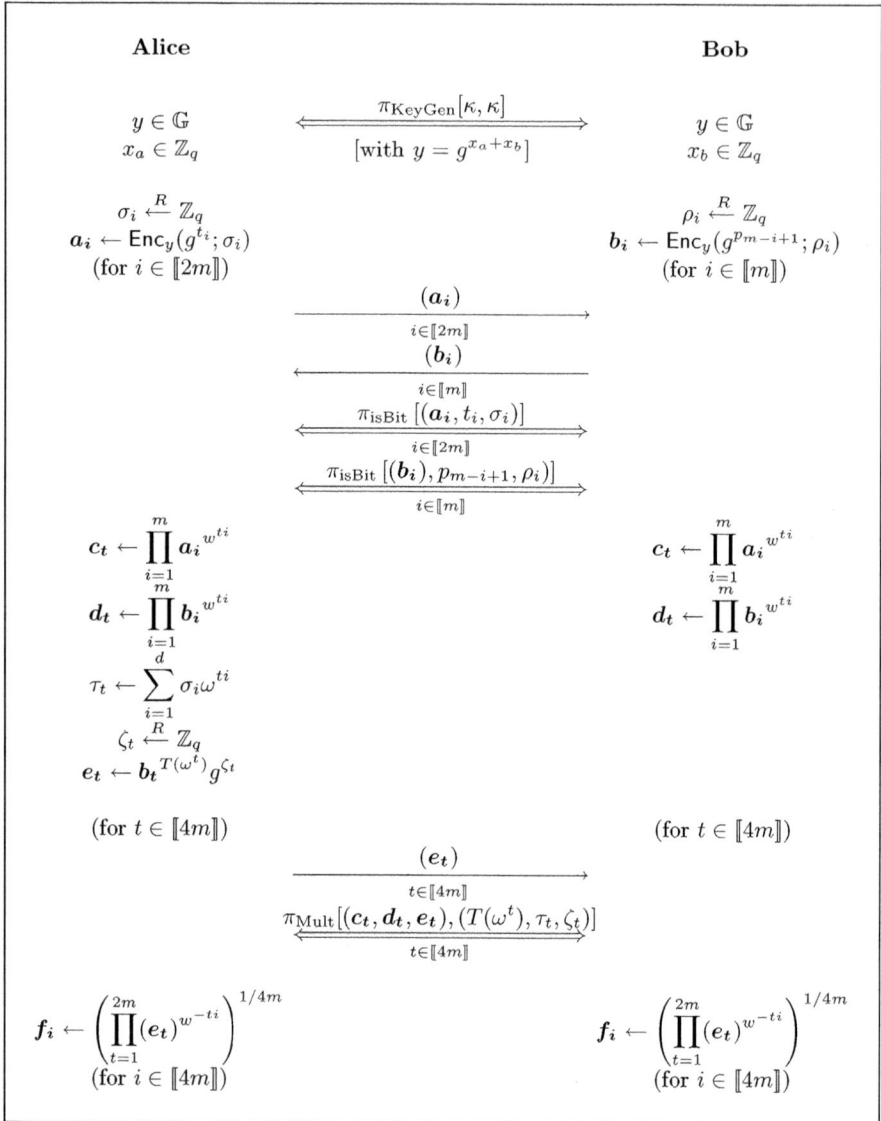

Fig. 2. Basic Protocol for Secure Generalized Pattern Matching

Secure Hamming Distance Computation. The paper [18] examined secure two-party computation of functions which depend only on the Hamming distance of the inputs of the two parties. We revisit this problem in this paragraph and propose an efficient protocol for the following problem: given a binary text $\mathcal{T}$ of length n and a binary pattern $\mathcal{P}$ of length m, compute the Hamming distance between $\mathcal{P}$ and $\mathcal{T}_i$ for $i \in [\![n - m + 1]\!]$, $i.e.$ we consider the question of how to compute the functionality, denoted by $\mathcal{F}_{\mathrm{HD}}$:

$$((\mathcal{P},n),(\mathcal{T},m)) \mapsto \left(\left(d_H(\mathcal{T}_i,\mathcal{P})\right)_{i\in[\![n-m+1]\!]},\perp\right)$$

Again Alice learns nothing about $\mathcal{P}$ and the only thing that Bob learns about $\mathcal{T}$ is the number of matches of $\mathcal{P}$ and $\mathcal{T}_i$ for $i \in [\![n-m+1]\!]$. We denote $\mathrm{HD}(\mathcal{P},\mathcal{T})$ the *Hamming distance vector of* $\mathcal{P}$ *and* $\mathcal{T}$ output by this functionality.

Over a binary alphabet, the sum (2) becomes:

$$d_H(\mathcal{T}_i,\mathcal{P}) = \sum_{j=1}^{m} \left({p_j}^2 - 2p_j \cdot t_{i+j} + {t_{i+j}}^2\right) = \sum_{j=1}^{m} \left(p_j - 2p_j \cdot t_{i+j} + t_{i+j}\right) \quad (4)$$

and therefore, with the previous notation, the product $\prod_{j=1}^{m} \boldsymbol{a_{i+j}} \cdot \boldsymbol{b_j} \cdot \boldsymbol{f_{i+m}}^{-2}$ encrypts the value $d_H(\mathcal{T}_i,\mathcal{P})$ for $i \in [\![n-m+1]\!]$. It is therefore easy to extend the opening of Fig. 2 in order to securely compute the functionality $\mathcal{F}_{\mathrm{HD}}$. The detailed protocol flow is given in Fig. 3.

(follows the protocol described in **Fig. 2**)

Alice		**Bob**
$\boldsymbol{\theta_i} \leftarrow \prod_{j=1}^{m} \boldsymbol{a_{i+j}} \cdot \boldsymbol{b_j} \cdot \boldsymbol{f_{i+m}}^{-2}$ $\psi_i \overset{R}{\leftarrow} \mathbb{Z}_q$ $\overline{\boldsymbol{\theta_i}} \leftarrow \boldsymbol{\theta_i} \cdot \mathsf{Enc}_y(1_{\mathbb{G}};\psi_i)$ (for $i \in [\![n-m+1]\!]$)		$\boldsymbol{\theta_i} \leftarrow \prod_{j=1}^{m} \boldsymbol{a_{i+j}} \cdot \boldsymbol{b_j} \cdot \boldsymbol{f_{i+m}}^{-2}$ (for $i \in [\![n-m+1]\!]$)
	$\xrightarrow{(\overline{\boldsymbol{\theta_i}})_{i\in[\![n-m+1]\!]}}$	
	$\xleftrightarrow{\pi_{\mathrm{eqDL}}[(\overline{\boldsymbol{\theta_i}}/\boldsymbol{\theta_i},g,y),\psi_i]_{i\in[\![n-m+1]\!]}}$	
	$\xleftrightarrow{\pi_{\mathrm{Dec}}[(\overline{\boldsymbol{\theta_i}},x_a)]_{i\in[\![n-m+1]\!]}}$	$(\widetilde{\boldsymbol{\theta_i}})_{1\le i\le n-m+1}$ $h_i \leftarrow \log_g(\mathsf{Dec}_{x_b}(\widetilde{\boldsymbol{\theta_i}}))$ (for $i \in [\![n-m+1]\!]$)
Output $\perp$		Output $(h_1,\ldots,h_{n-m+1})$

Fig. 3. Secure Computation of the Hamming distance vector $\mathrm{HD}(\mathcal{P},\mathcal{T})$

The protocol is constant-round with linear communication complexity and $O(n\sqrt{m})$ time complexity. We can prove that it achieves full simulation security against malicious adversaries.

Theorem 2. *If* π_{eqDL}, π_{Mult}, π_{isBit} *are zero-knowledge proofs of knowledge secure against malicious verifiers for the languages* $\mathcal{R}_{\mathrm{eqDL}}$, $\mathcal{R}_{\mathrm{Mult}}$ *and* $\mathcal{R}_{\mathrm{isBit}}$, *if* π_{KeyGen} *and* π_{Dec} *are protocols secure against malicious verifiers for the functionality* $\mathcal{F}^{\mathrm{KeyGen}}$ *and* $\mathcal{F}^{\mathrm{Dec}}$ *and if the ElGamal encryption scheme is semantically secure, then the protocol described in Fig. 3 securely computes* $\mathcal{F}_{\mathrm{HD}}$ *in the presence of malicious adversaries.*

Proof (Sketch). We consider only the security in the case that Bob is corrupted (the proof in the case that Alice is corrupted follows the same lines).

Bob is corrupted: Let $\mathcal{A}$ denote an adversary controlling Bob. We need to prove that $\mathcal{A}$ does not learn anything but the matching text locations. We construct a simulator $\mathcal{S}$ as follows:

1. $\mathcal{S}$ is given a pattern of length m, an integer n and $\mathcal{A}$'s auxiliary input and invokes $\mathcal{A}$ on these values.
2. $\mathcal{S}$ emulates the trusted party for π_{KeyGen} as follows by choosing two random elements x_A and x_B in $\mathbb{Z}_q$ and hands $\mathcal{A}$, its share x_B and the public key $y = g^{x_A + x_B}$.
3. $\mathcal{S}$ receives from the adversary $\mathcal{A}$ a vector of m ciphertexts (α_i, β_i) for $i \in [\![m]\!]$. If the functionality $\mathcal{F}_{ZK}^{R_{isBit}}$ aborts, then $\mathcal{S}$ aborts, sending $\perp$ to the trusted party for $\mathcal{F}_{HW}$.
4. Otherwise $\mathcal{S}$ defines the pattern $\mathcal{P}$ using the witnesses for π_{isBit} and sends $\mathcal{P}$ to the ideal functionality $\mathcal{F}_{HW}$.
5. The simulator $\mathcal{S}$ sets $T = 1^n \in \Sigma^n$.
6. $\mathcal{S}$ completes the execution as the honest Alice would on input T but simulates the proof in order to be consistent with the vector output by the ideal functionality $\mathcal{F}_{HW}$. If at any point $\mathcal{A}$ sends an invalid message $\mathcal{S}$ aborts, sending $\perp$ to the trusted party for $\mathcal{F}_{PM}$. Otherwise, it outputs whatever $\mathcal{A}$ does.

Following the proof of [17, Theorem 1], it is easy to prove that if there exists a distinguisher $\mathcal{D}$ for these executions, then there exist a PPT adversary breaking the semantic security of ElGamal encryption. $\square$

Secure Pattern Matching with k Mismatches. We now propose an efficient protocol for the following problem: given an integer k, a binary text T of length n and a binary pattern $\mathcal{P}$ of length m, compute the functionality, denoted by $\mathcal{F}_{\text{PM}-k}$:

$$((\mathcal{P}, n), (T, m)) \mapsto (\{i \in [\![n - m + 1]\!], d_H(T_i, \mathcal{P}) \leq k\}, \perp)$$

Again Alice learns nothing about $\mathcal{P}$ and the only thing that Bob learns about T is the locations where $\mathcal{P}$ appears with less than k mismatches.

Let us recall that the protocol of Fig. 3 produces ciphertexts θ_i that encrypt the value $d_H(T_i, \mathcal{P})$ for $i \in [\![n - m + 1]\!]$. Therefore

$$[\theta_i \cdot (1_{\mathbb{G}}, g^{-\ell})]^u \cdot \text{Enc}_y(1_{\mathbb{G}}, v) \tag{5}$$

for random $u \xleftarrow{R} \mathbb{Z}_q^*$ and $v \xleftarrow{R} \mathbb{Z}_q$ is a uniformly distributed encryption of $1_{\mathbb{G}}$ if $d_H(T_i, \mathcal{P}) = \ell$ and of a random element from $\mathbb{G}$ otherwise.

It is therefore easy to extend the opening of Fig. 2 in order to securely compute the functionality $\mathcal{F}_{\text{PM}-k}$: Alice pick, for all $i \in [\![n - m + 1]\!]$, a permutation $\sigma \in \mathfrak{S}_k$ and permute and rerandomize the ciphertexts from (5). She proves for all $i \in [\![n - m + 1]\!]$ the correctness of this operation by running π_{Perm} on k ElGamal ciphertexts. As in the previous protocol, Alice then partially decrypts the permuted ciphertexts for all $i \in [\![n - m + 1]\!]$ by running all π_{Dec} on private

(follows the protocol described in **Fig. 2**)

Alice   **Bob**

$$\mathcal{S} \leftarrow \emptyset$$

$\theta_i \leftarrow \prod_{j=1}^m a_{i+j} \cdot b_j \cdot f_{i+m}^{-2}$ $\theta_i \leftarrow \prod_{j=1}^m a_{i+j} \cdot b_j \cdot f_{i+m}^{-2}$
(for $i \in [\![n-m+1]\!]$)   (for $i \in [\![n-m+1]\!]$)

$u_{1,i}, \ldots, u_{k,i} \xleftarrow{R} \mathbb{Z}_q^*$
$v_{1,i}, \ldots, v_{k,i} \xleftarrow{R} \mathbb{Z}_q$
(for $i \in [\![n-m+1]\!]$)

$\zeta_{i,\ell} \leftarrow [\theta_i \cdot (1_{\mathbb{G}}, g^{-\ell})]^{u_{\ell,i}}$
$\quad \cdot \mathsf{Enc}_y(1_{\mathbb{G}}, v_{\ell,i})$
(for $(i,\ell) \in [\![n-m+1]\!] \times [\![k]\!]$)

$$\xrightarrow[\;(i,\ell) \in [\![n-m+1]\!] \times [\![k]\!]\;]{(\zeta_{i,\ell})}$$

$$\pi_{\mathrm{nze}} \xleftrightarrow[(i,\ell) \in [\![n-m+1]\!] \times [\![k]\!]]{\left[\begin{matrix} (\zeta_{i,\ell}, \theta_i \cdot (1_{\mathbb{G}}, g^{-\ell})) \\ (u_{\ell,i}, v_{\ell,i}) \end{matrix} \right]}$$

$r_{1,i}, \ldots, r_{k,i} \xleftarrow{R} \mathbb{Z}_q$
$\pi_i \xleftarrow{R} \mathfrak{S}_k$
(for $i \in [\![n-m+1]\!]$)
$\gamma_{i,\ell} = \zeta_{i,\pi_i(\ell)} \cdot \mathsf{Enc}_y(1_{\mathbb{G}}, r_{\ell,i})$
(for $(i,\ell) \in [\![n-m+1]\!] \times [\![k]\!]$)

$$\xrightarrow[(i,\ell) \in [\![n-m+1]\!] \times [\![k]\!]]{(\gamma_{i,\ell})}$$

$$\pi_{\mathrm{Perm}} \xleftrightarrow[i \in [\![n-m+1]\!]]{\left[\begin{matrix} (\zeta_{i,\ell}, \gamma_{i,\ell}) \\ (\pi_i, r_{1,i}, \ldots, r_{k,i}) \end{matrix} \right]}$$

$$\xleftrightarrow[i \in [\![n-m+1]\!]]{\pi_{\mathrm{Dec}}[\gamma_{i,\ell}, x_a, x_b]} \qquad h_{\ell,i} \leftarrow \mathsf{Dec}_{x_a+x_b}(\gamma_{i,\ell})$$

(for $(i,\ell) \in [\![n-m+1]\!] \times [\![k]\!]$)

Add i to $\mathcal{S}$ if $1_{\mathbb{G}} \in \{h_{1,i}, \ldots, h_{k,i}\}$
($i \in [\![n-m+1]\!]$)

Output $\perp$ Output $\mathcal{S}$

Fig. 4. End of the Protocol for Secure Pattern Matching with Mismatches

input x_A. Bob then finishes the decryption and outputs the set of $i \in [\![n-m+1]\!]$ such that the vector of (permuted) at location i contains one (and only one) encryption of $1_{\mathbb{G}}$. The detailed protocol flow is given in Fig. 4.

We have the following theorem whose proof will be given in the full version of the paper:

Theorem 3. *If π_{eqDL}, π_{Mult}, π_{Perm}, π_{nze} and π_{isBit} are zero-knowledge proofs of knowledge secure against malicious verifiers for the languages $\mathcal{R}_{\mathrm{eqDL}}$, $\mathcal{R}_{\mathrm{Mult}}$, $\mathcal{R}_{\mathrm{Perm}}$, $\mathcal{R}_{\mathrm{nze}}$ and $\mathcal{R}_{\mathrm{isBit}}$, if π_{KeyGen} and π_{Dec} are protocols secure against malicious verifiers for the functionality $\mathcal{F}^{\mathrm{KeyGen}}$ and $\mathcal{F}^{\mathrm{Dec}}$ and if the ElGamal encryption scheme is semantically secure, then the protocol described in Fig. 4 securely computes $\mathcal{F}_{\mathrm{PM}-k}$ in the presence of malicious adversaries.*

5.2   Pattern Matching with Wildcards

Finally, we consider the secure computation of the functionality $\mathcal{F}_{\mathrm{PM}\star}$ that on input $((\mathcal{P}, n), (\mathcal{T}, m))$ computes

$$\begin{cases} (\{j \in [\![n-m+1]\!] \mid \forall i \in [\![m]\!], p_i = \star \vee t_{i+j-1} = \star \vee p_i = t_{i+j-1}\}, \bot) \\ \qquad\qquad\qquad \text{if } \mathcal{P} \in \{\star, 0, 1\}^m \wedge \mathcal{T} \in \{\star, 0, 1\}^n \\ (\bot, \bot) \qquad\qquad \text{otherwise} \end{cases}$$

Again, Alice learns nothing about $\mathcal{P}$ and the only thing Bob learns about $\mathcal{T}$ is the locations where $\mathcal{P}$ appears (with wildcards).

The protocol is similar to the previous ones and relies on the fact that the sum (3) can be computed with three convolutions and therefore in $O(n \log n)$ time using FFT. Due to space constraints, details will be given in the full version of the paper.

We consider a shifted binary alphabet $\Sigma' = \{1, 2\}$ and identify the wildcard $\star$ with the number 0. Obviously, one needs to replace in the protocol from Fig. 2 the protocol π_{isBit} by π_{isTrit}. In order to compute (3) via FFT, it is also necessary for Alice to provide encryption of $t_i{}^2$ and $t_i{}^3$ for $i \in [\![n]\!]$ and for Bob to provide encryption of $p_j{}^2$ and $p_j{}^3$ for $j \in [\![m]\!]$. They have to prove the consistency of these ciphertexts with a_i for $i \in [\![n]\!]$ and b_j for $j \in [\![m]\!]$ using π_{eqDL}. The algorithm then follows the protocol from Fig. 3 in order to get the Hamming distance (with wildcards) between $\mathcal{P}$ and $\mathcal{T}_i$ for $i \in [\![n-m+1]\!]$. We finally use the technique from Fig. 1 to only reveal to Bob whether this distance is equal to 0 or not.

We can readily prove the security of this protocol (details will be given in the full version of the paper):

Theorem 4. *If π_{eqDL}, π_{Mult}, π_{Perm}, π_{nze} and π_{isTrit} are zero-knowledge proofs of knowledge secure against malicious verifiers for the languages $\mathcal{R}_{\mathrm{eqDL}}$, $\mathcal{R}_{\mathrm{Mult}}$, $\mathcal{R}_{\mathrm{Perm}}$, $\mathcal{R}_{\mathrm{nze}}$ and $\mathcal{R}_{\mathrm{isTrit}}$, if π_{KeyGen} and π_{Dec} are protocols secure against malicious verifiers for the functionality $\mathcal{F}^{\mathrm{KeyGen}}$ and $\mathcal{F}^{\mathrm{Dec}}$ and if the ElGamal encryption scheme is semantically secure, then the protocol outlined above securely computes $\mathcal{F}_{\mathrm{PM}\star}$ in the presence of malicious adversaries.*

6   Conclusion

We presented protocols for secure two-party computation of generalized pattern matching. Our schemes can easily be combined in order to solve, for instance, the approximate pattern matching with wildcards problem. They can be extended in various directions: they can handle larger alphabets, longer pattern, and variants where the length of the pattern or the text remains hidden (as the schemes from [17]). Our technique can also provide round-optimal protocols (with similar efficiency) with universally composable security in the common reference string model (using the Groth-Sahai proof system [14]). Details will be given in the full version of the paper.

Acknowledgements. The author would like to thank Benoît Libert and anonymous referees for their comments and Carmit Hazay for helpful discussions on security models. The author was supported in part by the European Commission through the ICT Program under contract ICT-2007-216676 ECRYPT II.

References

1. Abe, M., Cramer, R., Fehr, S.: Non-interactive distributed-verifier proofs and proving relations among commitments. In: Zheng, Y. (ed.) ASIACRYPT 2002. LNCS, vol. 2501, pp. 206–223. Springer, Heidelberg (2002)
2. Abrahamson, K.R.: Generalized String Matching. SIAM J. Comput. 16(6), 1039–1051 (1987)
3. Canetti, R.: Security and composition of multiparty cryptographic protocols. J. Cryptology 13(1), 143–202 (2000)
4. Chaum, D., Pedersen, T.P.: Wallet databases with observers. In: Brickell, E.F. (ed.) CRYPTO 1992. LNCS, vol. 740, pp. 89–105. Springer, Heidelberg (1993)
5. Cheon, J.H., Jarecki, S., Seo, J.H.: Multi-Party Privacy-Preserving Set Intersection with Quasi-Linear Complexity. IACR ePrint Archive, Report 2010/512 (2010)
6. Clifford, P., Clifford, R.: Simple Deterministic Wildcard Matching. Inf. Process. Lett. 101(2), 53–54 (2007)
7. Cooley, J.W., Tukey, J.W.: An algorithm for the machine calculation of complex fourier series. Math. Comp. 19, 297–301 (1965)
8. Cramer, R., Gennaro, R., Schoenmakers, B.: A secure and optimally efficient multi-authority election scheme. In: Fumy, W. (ed.) EUROCRYPT 1997. LNCS, vol. 1233, pp. 103–118. Springer, Heidelberg (1997)
9. Crochemore, M., Rytter, W.: Jewels of Stringology, p. 310. World Scientific Publishing, Hong-Kong (2002)
10. ElGamal, T.: A Public Key Cryptosystem and a Signature Scheme based on Discrete Logarithms. IEEE Trans. Inf. Theory 31, 469–472 (1985)
11. Fischer, M., Paterson, M.: Paterson, M.: String Matching and Other Products. Complexity of Computation. In: Karp, R. (ed.) Complexity of Computation, SIAM-AMS, vol. 7, pp. 113–125. American Mathematical Society, Providence (1974)
12. Gennaro, R., Hazay, C., Sorensen, J.S.: Text search protocols with simulation based security. In: Nguyen, P.Q., Pointcheval, D. (eds.) PKC 2010. LNCS, vol. 6056, pp. 332–350. Springer, Heidelberg (2010)
13. Groth, J.: A verifiable secret shuffle of homomorphic encryptions. In: Desmedt, Y. (ed.) PKC 2003. LNCS, vol. 2567, pp. 145–160. Springer, Heidelberg (2002)
14. Groth, J., Sahai, A.: Efficient non-interactive proof systems for bilinear groups. In: Smart, N.P. (ed.) EUROCRYPT 2008. LNCS, vol. 4965, pp. 415–432. Springer, Heidelberg (2008)

15. Hazay, C., Lindell, Y.: Efficient Protocols for Set Intersection and Pattern Matching with Security Against Malicious and Covert Adversaries. J. Cryptology 23(3), 422–456 (2010)
16. Hazay, C., Lindell, Y.: Efficient Secure Two-Party Protocols. In: Information Security and Cryptography. Springer, Heidelberg (2010)
17. Hazay, C., Toft, T.: Computationally secure pattern matching in the presence of malicious adversaries. In: Abe, M. (ed.) ASIACRYPT 2010. LNCS, vol. 6477, pp. 195–212. Springer, Heidelberg (2010)
18. Jarrous, A., Pinkas, B.: Secure hamming distance based computation and its applications. In: Abdalla, M., Pointcheval, D., Fouque, P.-A., Vergnaud, D. (eds.) ACNS 2009. LNCS, vol. 5536, pp. 107–124. Springer, Heidelberg (2009)
19. Knuth, D.E., Morris Jr., J.H., Pratt, V.R.: Fast Pattern Matching in Strings. SIAM J. Comput. 6(2), 323–350 (1977)
20. Rahman, M.S., Iliopoulos, C.S.: Pattern Matching Algorithms with Don't Cares. In: van Leeuwen, J., Italiano, G.F., van der Hoek, W., Meinel, C., Sack, H., Plasil, F., Bieliková, M. (eds.) SOFSEM 2007. LNCS, vol. 4362, pp. 116–126. Springer, Heidelberg (2007)
21. Schnorr, C.-P.: Efficient Signature Generation by Smart Cards. J. Cryptology 4(3), 161–174 (1991)
22. Schoenmeyr, T., Zhang, D.Y.: FFT-based algorithms for the string matching with mismatches problem. J. Algorithms 57(2), 130–139 (2005)
23. Troncoso-Pastoriza, J.R., Katzenbeisser, S., Celik, M.: Privacy preserving error resilient dna searching through oblivious automata. In: Ning, P., di Vimercati, S.D.C., Syverson, P.F. (eds.) ACM CCS 2007: 14th Conference on Computer and Communications Security, pp. 519–528. ACM Press, New York (2007)
24. Tsiounis, Y., Yung, M.: On the security of elGamal based encryption. In: Imai, H., Zheng, Y. (eds.) PKC 1998. LNCS, vol. 1431, pp. 117–134. Springer, Heidelberg (1998)
25. Yao, A.C.: Protocols for Secure Computations. In: 23rd Annual Symposium on Foundations of Computer Science, pp. 160–164. IEEE Computer Society Press, Los Alamitos (1982)

Identification Schemes from Key Encapsulation Mechanisms

Hiroaki Anada and Seiko Arita

Institute of Information Security, Yokohama, Japan
hiroaki.anada@gmail.com, arita@iisec.ac.jp

Abstract. We propose a generic way for deriving an identification (ID) scheme secure against concurrent man-in-the-middle attacks from a key encapsulation mechanism (KEM) secure against chosen ciphertext attacks on one-wayness (one-way-CCA). Then we give a concrete one-way-CCA secure KEM based on the Computational Diffie-Hellman (CDH) assumption. In that construction, the Twin Diffie-Hellman technique of Cash, Kiltz and Shoup is essentially employed. We compare efficiency of the ID scheme derived from our KEM with previously known ID schemes and KEMs. It turns out that our KEM-based ID scheme reduces the computation by one exponentiation than the currently most efficient one derived from the Hanaoka-Kurosawa one-way-CCA secure KEM, whose security is based on the same (CDH) assumption.

Keywords: identification scheme, key encapsulation mechanism, one-way-CCA security, concurrent man-in-the-middle attack, the computational Diffie-Hellman assumption.

1 Introduction

An identification (ID) scheme enables a prover to convince a verifier that the prover is indeed itself by proving that it knows some secret information. In the public key framework, a prover holds a secret key and a verifier refers to a matching public key. They interact for some rounds doing necessary computations until the verifier feels certain that the prover has the secret key. The secret key is never revealed directly but hidden in messages through those computations.

Historically, there have been two types of ID schemes. One is challenge-and-response type obtained in a natural way from encryption schemes or signature schemes, and the other is the Σ-protocol type [7] which is a kind of proofs of knowledge [12,4] consisting of 3-round interaction. Most of known traditional ID schemes, such as the Schnorr scheme [24] and the Guillou-Quisquater (GQ) scheme [13], are the Σ-protocol type because they are faster than challenge-and-response type.

Now in the Internet environment where everyone is involved, attacks on ID schemes have become fairly strong. One of the strongest is *concurrent man-in-the-middle attack*. In concurrent man-in-the-middle setting, an adversary stands between a verifier and a prover, and the adversary invokes many instances of the prover application (prover clones), which have independent states and random tapes. Interacting in some cheating

A. Nitaj and D. Pointcheval (Eds.): AFRICACRYPT 2011, LNCS 6737, pp. 59–76, 2011.

way, the adversary collects information of the secret key from the prover clones. At the same time, trying to impersonate the prover, the adversary interacts with the verifier.

Unfortunately, the Schnorr scheme and the GQ scheme are not secure against concurrent man-in-the-middle attacks, hence there have been significant efforts to make ID schemes have tolerance against such concurrent man-in-the-middle attacks based on the Σ-protocol. For example, Katz [16] made an ID scheme of non-malleable proof of knowledge. But the security model is with timing constraint, not against full concurrent man-in-the-middle attacks. Moreover, the protocol utilizes the so-called OR-Proof technique, so it is a little bit costly. Gennaro [11] constructed an ID scheme of (fully) concurrently non-malleable proof of knowledge by employing a multi-trapdoor commitment. But it is no longer so fast as a challenge-and-response ID scheme obtained, for instance, from the Cramer-Shoup encryption scheme [8]. Moreover, the security is based on a strong type of assumption (the Strong Diffie-Hellman (SDH) assumption or the Strong RSA assumption).

One of the reason why it is so difficult to construct an ID scheme secure against concurrent man-in-the-middle attacks seems that we are rooted in the category of Σ-protocols. Let us remember that challenge-and-response ID schemes obtained from IND-CCA secure encryption schemes (see [8] for example) and EUF-CMA secure signature schemes (see [2] for example) are already secure against concurrent man-in-the-middle attacks.

1.1 Our Contribution

In the notion of encryption scheme, key encapsulation mechanism (KEM) is the foundational concept for hybrid construction with data encryption mechanism. As a first contribution in this paper, we propose to use KEM as ID scheme analogous to the usage of encryption scheme. That is, given a KEM, we derive a challenge-and-response ID scheme as follows. A verifier of a KEM-based ID scheme makes a pair of random string and its ciphertext using a public key, and send the ciphertext as a challenge to the prover having the matching secret key. The prover decapsulates the ciphertext and returns the result as a response. The verifier checks whether or not the response is equal to the random string. Although this is a straightforward conversion, it has never been mentioned in the literature, to the best of our knowledge.

As a generic property, KEM-based ID scheme has an advantage over (non-hybrid) encryption-based ID scheme. That is, KEM only has to encapsulate *random* strings and may generate them by itself, while encryption scheme has to encrypt *any* strings given as input. Consequently, KEM-based ID scheme has a possibility to have simpler and more efficient protocol than encryption-based ID scheme.

In addition, as we will show in Section 3, KEM only need to be one-way-CCA secure for derived ID scheme to have security against concurrent man-in-the-middle attacks (cMiM security). In other words, IND-CCA security, which is stronger than one-way-CCA security, is rather excessive for deriving cMiM secure ID scheme. Nonetheless by this time, most known encryption schemes and KEMs have been designed to possess IND-CCA security (because the purpose is not to make up ID schemes, of course).

Hence there arises a need to provide one-way-CCA secure KEMs. As a second contribution, we give a concrete, discrete logarithm-based one-way-CCA secure KEM. It is true that there have already been a few one-way-CCA secure KEMs in discrete log-arithm setting. In contrast to those KEMs, the feature of our KEM is that it needs the smallest amount of computational cost while its security is based on the Computational Diffie-Hellman (CDH) assumption which is weaker than the Decisional Diffie-Hellman (DDH) assumption or the Gap-CDH assumption (see [21] for these assumptions). That feature is achieved by applying the Twin Diffie-Hellman technique [6] to Anada-Arita's scheme [1] to relax the Gap-CDH assumption on which their scheme is based[1].

Finally, we point out a feature that the prover in our generic construction of ID scheme is deterministic, and hence the derived ID scheme is prover-resettable [3]. Moreover, it is also verifier-resettable because it consists of 2-round interaction. This is a remarkable property because, as is discussed by Yilek [27], resettable security is crucially helpful for virtual machine service in the Cloud Computing, for example.

1.2 Related Works

Recently, independently of us, Fujisaki [10] pointed out a fact similar to our generic construction above (that is, the conversion from one-way-CCA secure KEM to cMiM secure ID scheme). We discuss the conversion more precisely than it.

As for concrete constructions, the IND-CCA secure KEM of Shoup [25], which is naturally a one-way-CCA secure KEM, performs comparably efficiently even now, while its security is based on the DDH assumption. Hanaoka-Kurosawa [15] gave a one-way-CCA secure KEM whose assumption is the CDH assumption, which is weaker than the DDH assumption. It is directly comparable with our KEM and our KEM reduces the computation by one exponentiation for encapsulation than the Hanaoka-Kurosawa KEM. While both the Shoup KEM and the Hanaoka-Kurosawa KEM are intended for the hybrid encryption construction, the one-way-CCA secure KEM of Anada-Arita [1] is intended directly for ID scheme. It performs better than Shoup's KEM and its security is based on the Gap-CDH assumption. The Twin Diffie-Hellman technique enables us to relax that gap assumption to lead our one-way-CCA secure KEM.

1.3 Organization of the Paper

In Section 2, we fix some notations and briefly review the notion of ID scheme, KEM and computational hardness assumption. In Section 3, we propose a generic way for deriving a cMiM secure ID scheme from a one-way-CCA secure KEM. In Section 4, we construct a one-way-CCA secure KEM by the Twin Diffie-Hellman technique. In Section 5, we compare our KEM or ID scheme with previously known KEMs or ID schemes. In Section 6, we conclude our work.

2 Preliminaries

The security parameter is denoted k. On input 1^k, a probabilistic polynomial-time (PPT, for short) algorithm Grp runs and outputs (q, g), where q is a prime of length k and g is

---

[1] The strategy to apply the Twin Diffie-Hellman technique was suggested to us by Prof. Kiltz [18].

a generator of a multiplicative cyclic group G_q of order q. Grp specifies elements and group operations of G_q. The ring of exponent domain of G_q, which consists of integers from 0 to $q - 1$ with modulo q operation, is denoted $\mathbf{Z}_q$.

When an algorithm A on input a outputs z, we denote it as $z \leftarrow A(a)$. When A on input a and B on input b interact and B outputs z, we denote it as $z \leftarrow \langle A(a), B(b) \rangle$. When A has oracle-access to $\mathcal{O}$, we denote it as $A^{\mathcal{O}}$. When A has concurrent oracle-access to n oracles $\mathcal{O}_1, \ldots, \mathcal{O}_n$, we denote it as $A^{\mathcal{O}_1|\cdots|\mathcal{O}_n}$. Here "concurrent" means that A accesses to oracles in arbitrarily interleaved order of messages.

A probability of an event X is denoted $\Pr[\mathrm{X}]$. A probability of an event X on conditions $\mathrm{Y}_1, \ldots, \mathrm{Y}_m$ is denoted $\Pr[\mathrm{Y}_1; \cdots ; \mathrm{Y}_m : \mathrm{X}]$.

2.1 Identification Scheme

An *identification scheme* ID is a triple of PPT algorithms (K, P, V). K is a key generator which outputs a pair of a public key and a matching secret key $(\mathrm{pk}, \mathrm{sk})$ on input 1^k. P and V implement a prover and a verifier strategy, respectively. We require ID to satisfy the completeness condition that boolean decision by V(pk) after interaction with P(sk) is TRUE with probability one. We say that V(pk) *accepts* if its boolean decision is TRUE.

Concurrent Man-in-the-Middle Attack on Identification Scheme [3,5]. The aim of an adversary $\mathcal{A}$ that attacks an ID scheme ID is impersonation. We say that $\mathcal{A}$ *wins* when $\mathcal{A}(\mathrm{pk})$ succeeds in making V(pk) accept.

An adversary $\mathcal{A}$ performs a concurrent man-in-the-middle (cMiM, for short) attack in the following way.

Experiment$_{\mathcal{A},\mathrm{ID}}^{\mathrm{imp\text{-}cmim}}(1^k)$

$(\mathrm{pk}, \mathrm{sk}) \leftarrow \mathrm{K}(1^k), \mathrm{decision} \leftarrow \langle \mathcal{A}^{\mathrm{P}_1(\mathrm{sk})|\cdots|\mathrm{P}_n(\mathrm{sk})}(\mathrm{pk}), \mathrm{V}(\mathrm{pk}) \rangle$

If decision $= 1 \wedge \pi^* \notin \{\pi_i\}_{i=1}^n$ then return WIN else return LOSE.

In the above experiment, we denoted a transcript of interaction between $\mathrm{P}_i(\mathrm{sk})$ and $\mathcal{A}(\mathrm{pk})$ as π_i and a transcript between $\mathcal{A}(\mathrm{pk})$ and V(pk) as π^*. As a rule, man-in-the-middle adversary $\mathcal{A}$ is prohibited from relaying a transcript of a whole interaction with some prover clone to the verifier V(pk), as is described $\pi^* \notin \{\pi_i\}_{i=1}^n$ in the experiment. This is a standard and natural constraint to keep man-in-the-middle attack meaningful.

We define $\mathcal{A}$'s *imp-cMiM advantage over* ID as:

$$\mathbf{Adv}_{\mathcal{A},\mathrm{ID}}^{\mathrm{imp\text{-}cmim}}(k) \overset{\mathrm{def}}{=} \Pr[\mathbf{Experiment}_{\mathcal{A},\mathrm{ID}}^{\mathrm{imp\text{-}cmim}}(1^k) \text{ returns WIN}].$$

We say that an ID is secure against concurrent man-in-the-middle attacks (cMiM secure, for short) if, for any PPT algorithm $\mathcal{A}$, $\mathbf{Adv}_{\mathcal{A},\mathrm{ID}}^{\mathrm{imp\text{-}cmim}}(k)$ is negligible in k.

Suppose that an adversary $\mathcal{A}$ consists of two algorithms $\mathcal{A}_1$ and $\mathcal{A}_2$. The following experiment is called a 2-phase concurrent attack.

Experiment$_{\mathcal{A},\mathrm{ID}}^{\mathrm{imp\text{-}2pc}}(1^k)$

$(\mathrm{pk}, \mathrm{sk}) \leftarrow \mathrm{K}(1^k), st \leftarrow \mathcal{A}_1^{\mathrm{P}_1(\mathrm{sk})|\cdots|\mathrm{P}_n(\mathrm{sk})}(\mathrm{pk}), \mathrm{decision} \leftarrow \langle \mathcal{A}_2(st), \mathrm{V}(\mathrm{pk}) \rangle$

If decision $= 1$ then return WIN else return LOSE.

2-phase concurrent attack is a weaker model than cMiM attack because of the constraint that the learning phase of $\mathcal{A}_1$ is limited to before the impersonation phase of $\mathcal{A}_2$.

2-phase concurrent attack and cMiM attack are classified to active attacks. On the contrary, there is a passive attack described below. Let us denote a transcript of a whole interaction between $P(sk)$ and $V(pk)$ as $\pi = |\langle P(sk), V(pk) \rangle|$.

$$\textbf{Experiment}_{\mathcal{A}, \text{ID}}^{\text{imp-pa}}(1^k)$$

$(pk, sk) \leftarrow K(1^k)$

If $\mathcal{A}_1(pk)$ makes a query, reply $\pi_i \leftarrow |\langle P(sk), V(pk) \rangle|$

$st \leftarrow \mathcal{A}_1(\{\pi_i\}_{i=1}^n)$, decision $\leftarrow \langle \mathcal{A}_2(st), V(pk) \rangle$

If decision $= 1$ then return WIN else return LOSE.

Passive attack is a weaker model than 2-phase concurrent attack because of the constraint that $\mathcal{A}$ cannot choose messages in the learning phase.

2.2 Key Encapsulation Mechanism

A *key encapsulation mechanism (KEM) KEM* is a triple of PPT algorithms (K, Enc, Dec). K is a key generator which outputs a pair of a public key and a matching secret key (pk, sk) on input 1^k. Enc is an encapsulation algorithm which, on input pk, outputs a pair (K, ψ), where K is a random string and ψ is a ciphertext of K. Dec is a decapsulation algorithm which, on input (sk, ψ), outputs the decapsulation $\widehat{K}$ of ψ. We require KEM to satisfy the completeness condition that the decapsulation $\widehat{K}$ of a consistently generated ciphertext ψ by Enc is equal to the original random string K with probability one.

Adaptive Chosen Ciphertext Attack on One-Wayness of KEM [22,15]. An adversary $\mathcal{A}$ performs an adaptive chosen ciphertext attack on one-wayness of a KEM (one-way-CCA, for short) in the following way.

$$\textbf{Experiment}_{\mathcal{A}, \text{KEM}}^{\text{ow-cca}}(1^k)$$

$(pk, sk) \leftarrow K(1^k), (K^*, \psi^*) \leftarrow \text{Enc}(pk), \widehat{K^*} \leftarrow \mathcal{A}^{\mathcal{DEC}(sk, \cdot)}(pk, \psi^*)$

If $\widehat{K^*} = K^* \wedge \psi^* \notin \{\psi_i\}_{i=1}^{q_{dec}}$ then return WIN else return LOSE.

In the above experiment, $\psi_i, i = 1, \ldots, q_{dec}$ mean ciphertexts for which $\mathcal{A}$ queries its decapsulation oracle $\mathcal{DEC}(sk, \cdot)$ for the answers. Here the number q_{dec} of queries is polynomial in k. Note that the challenge ciphertext ψ^* itself must not be queried to $\mathcal{DEC}(sk, \cdot)$, as is described $\psi^* \notin \{\psi_i\}_{i=1}^{q_{dec}}$ in the experiment.

We define $\mathcal{A}$'s *one-way-CCA advantage over KEM* as:

$$\textbf{Adv}_{\mathcal{A}, \text{KEM}}^{\text{ow-cca}}(k) \stackrel{\text{def}}{=} \Pr[\textbf{Experiment}_{\mathcal{A}, \text{KEM}}^{\text{ow-cca}}(1^k) \text{ returns WIN}].$$

We say that a KEM is secure against adaptive chosen ciphertext attacks against one-wayness (one-way-CCA secure, for short) if, for any PPT algorithm $\mathcal{A}$, $\textbf{Adv}_{\mathcal{A}, \text{KEM}}^{\text{ow-cca}}(k)$ is negligible in k. Note that if a KEM is IND-CCA secure [8], then it is one-way-CCA secure. So IND-CCA security is a stronger notion than one-way-CCA security.

Suppose that an adversary $\mathcal{A}$ consists of two algorithms $\mathcal{A}_1$ and $\mathcal{A}_2$. The following experiment is called a non-adaptive chosen ciphertext attack on one-wayness of a KEM.

Experiment$_{\mathcal{A},\mathrm{KEM}}^{\mathrm{ow\text{-}cca1}}(1^k)$

$(\mathrm{pk},\mathrm{sk}) \leftarrow \mathrm{K}(1^k),\, st \leftarrow \mathcal{A}_1^{\mathcal{DEC}(\mathrm{sk},\cdot)}(\mathrm{pk}),\, (K^*,\psi^*) \leftarrow \mathrm{Enc}(\mathrm{pk}),\, \widehat{K^*} \leftarrow \mathcal{A}_2(st,\psi^*)$

If $\widehat{K^*} = K^*$ then return WIN else return LOSE.

Non-adaptive chosen ciphertext attack is a weaker model than adaptive one because of the constraint that the learning phase of $\mathcal{A}_1$ is limited to before the solving phase of $\mathcal{A}_2$.

Adaptive and non-adaptive chosen ciphertext attacks are classified to active attacks. On the contrary, there is a passive attack on one-wayness of a KEM described below.

Experiment$_{\mathcal{A},\mathrm{KEM}}^{\mathrm{ow\text{-}pa}}(1^k)$

$(\mathrm{pk},\mathrm{sk}) \leftarrow \mathrm{K}(1^k)$

If $\mathcal{A}_1(\mathrm{pk})$ makes a query, reply $(K_i,\psi_i) \leftarrow \mathrm{Enc}(\mathrm{pk})$

$st \leftarrow \mathcal{A}_1(\{(K_i,\psi_i)\}_{i=1}^n),\, (K^*,\psi^*) \leftarrow \mathrm{Enc}(\mathrm{pk}),\, \widehat{K^*} \leftarrow \mathcal{A}_2(st,\psi^*)$

If $\widehat{K^*} = K^*$ then return WIN else return LOSE.

Passive attack is a weaker model than non-adaptive chosen ciphertext attack because of the constraint that $\mathcal{A}$ cannot choose ciphertexts in the learning phase.

2.3 The Computational Diffie-Hellman Assumption and the Twin Diffie-Hellman Technique

We say a solver $\mathcal{S}$, a PPT algorithm, *wins* when $\mathcal{S}$ succeeds in solving a computational problem instance.

A quadruple (g, X, Y, Z) of elements in G_q is called a *Diffie-Hellman tuple* (DH tuple, for short) if the quadruple is written as (g, g^x, g^y, g^{xy}) for some elements x, y in $\mathbf{Z}_q$. A CDH problem instance is a triple $(g, X = g^x, Y = g^y)$, where the exponents x, y are uniformly random in $\mathbf{Z}_q$. A CDH problem solver is a PPT algorithm which, given a CDH problem instance (g, X, Y) as input, tries to return $Z = g^{xy}$, whose experiment is the following.

Experiment$_{\mathcal{S},\mathrm{Grp}}^{\mathrm{cdh}}(1^k)$

$(q, g) \leftarrow \mathrm{Grp}(1^k),\, x, y \leftarrow \mathbf{Z}_q,\, X := g^x,\, Y := g^y,\, Z \leftarrow \mathcal{S}(g, X, Y)$

If $Z = g^{xy}$ then return WIN else return LOSE.

We define $\mathcal{S}$'s *CDH advantage over* Grp as:

$$\mathbf{Adv}_{\mathcal{S},\mathrm{Grp}}^{\mathrm{cdh}}(k) \stackrel{\mathrm{def}}{=} \Pr[\mathbf{Experiment}_{\mathcal{S},\mathrm{Grp}}^{\mathrm{cdh}}(1^k) \text{ returns WIN}].$$

We say that the CDH assumption [21] holds for Grp if, for any PPT algorithm $\mathcal{S}$, $\mathbf{Adv}_{\mathcal{S},\mathrm{Grp}}^{\mathrm{cdh}}(k)$ is negligible in k.

A 6-tuple $(g, X_1, X_2, Y, Z_1, Z_2)$ of elements in G_q is called a *twin Diffie-Hellman tuple* if the tuple is written as $(g, g^{x_1}, g^{x_2}, g^y, g^{x_1 y}, g^{x_2 y})$ for some elements x_1, x_2, y in $\mathbf{Z}_q$.

The following lemma of Cash, Kiltz and Shoup is used in Section 4 to decide whether or not a tuple is a twin DH tuple in the security proof for our concrete KEM.

Lemma (Cash, Kiltz and Shoup [6] Theorem 2, "Trap Door Test"). *Let X_1, r, s be mutually independent random variables, where X_1 takes values in G_q, and each of r, s is uniformly distributed over $\mathbf{Z}_q$. Define the random variable $X_2 := X_1^{-r} g^s$. Suppose that $\widehat{Y}, \widehat{Z_1}, \widehat{Z_2}$ are random variables taking values in G_q, each of which is defined independently of r. Then the probability that the truth value of $\widehat{Z_1}^r \widehat{Z_2} = \widehat{Y}^s$ does not agree with the truth value of $(g, X_1, X_2, \widehat{Y}, \widehat{Z_1}, \widehat{Z_2})$ being a twin DH tuple is at most $1/q$. Moreover, if $(g, X_1, X_2, \widehat{Y}, \widehat{Z_1}, \widehat{Z_2})$ is a twin DH tuple, then $\widehat{Z_1}^r \widehat{Z_2} = \widehat{Y}^s$ certainly holds.*

3   Identification Scheme from Key Encapsulation Mechanism

In this section, we show a generic way for deriving an ID scheme secure against concurrent man-in-the-middle attacks from a one-way-CCA secure KEM.

3.1   Construction

Let $\texttt{KEM} = (\texttt{K}, \texttt{Enc}, \texttt{Dec})$ be a KEM. Then an ID scheme $\texttt{ID}$ is derived in a natural way as shown in the Fig.1. The key generation algorithm is the same as that of $\texttt{KEM}$. The verifier $\texttt{V}$, given a public key $\texttt{pk}$ as input, invokes the encapsulation algorithm $\texttt{Enc}$ on $\texttt{pk}$ and gets its output (K, ψ). $\texttt{V}$ sends ψ to $\texttt{P}$. The prover $\texttt{P}$, given a secret key $\texttt{sk}$ as input and receiving ψ as input message, invokes the decapsulation algorithm $\texttt{Dec}$ on $(\texttt{sk}, \psi)$ and gets its output $\widehat{K}$. $\texttt{P}$ sends $\widehat{K}$ to $\texttt{V}$. Finally the verifier $\texttt{V}$, receiving $\widehat{K}$ as input message, verifies whether or not $\widehat{K}$ is equal to K. If so, then $\texttt{V}$ returns 1 and otherwise, 0.

It is notable that, if we use an encryption scheme, which is not a KEM, as an ID scheme in a similar way, then we need to *input* a random string into the encryption algorithm. In contrast, in a KEM, an encapsulation algorithm does not need such an input but only has to *output* a random string.

Theorem 1. *If a key encapsulation mechanism KEM is one-way-CCA secure, then the derived identification scheme ID is cMiM secure. More precisely, for any PPT adversary $\mathcal{A}$ that attacks ID in cMiM setting, there exists an PPT adversary $\mathcal{B}$ that attacks KEM in one-way-CCA setting satisfying the following inequality.*

$$\mathbf{Adv}^{\text{imp-cmim}}_{\mathcal{A}, \texttt{ID}}(k) \leqslant \mathbf{Adv}^{\text{ow-cca}}_{\mathcal{B}, \texttt{KEM}}(k).$$

3.2   Proof of Theorem 1

Let $\texttt{KEM}$ be a one-way-CCA secure KEM and $\texttt{ID}$ be the derived ID scheme by the construction above. Let $\mathcal{A}$ be any given cMiM adversary on $\texttt{ID}$. Using $\mathcal{A}$ as subroutine, we construct a PPT one-way-CCA adversary $\mathcal{B}$ that attacks $\texttt{KEM}$ as shown in the Fig.2.

Key Generation
- K: the same as that of KEM

Interaction
- V: given pk as input;
- Invoke Enc on pk: $(K, \psi) \leftarrow \text{Enc}(\text{pk})$
- Send ψ to P
- P: given sk as input and receiving ψ as input message;
- Invoke Dec on (sk, ψ): $\widehat{K} \leftarrow \text{Dec}(\text{sk}, \psi)$
- Send $\widehat{K}$ to V
- V: receiving $\widehat{K}$ as input message;
- If $\widehat{K} = K$ then return 1 else return 0

Fig. 1. An ID scheme ID=(K,P,V) derived from a KEM KEM=(K,Enc,Dec)

Given pk as input;
Initial Setting
- Initialize the inner state
- Invoke $\mathcal{A}$ on pk

Answering $\mathcal{A}$'s Queries
- In case that $\mathcal{A}$ queries V(pk) for the challenge message
- Send ψ^* to $\mathcal{A}$
- In case that $\mathcal{A}$ sends ψ to a prover clone P(sk)
- If $\psi = \psi^*$, then put $K := \perp$
- else Query $\mathcal{DEC}$ for the answer for ψ: $K \leftarrow \mathcal{DEC}(\text{sk}, \psi)$
- Send K to $\mathcal{A}$
- In case that $\mathcal{A}$ sends $\widehat{K^*}$ to V(pk)
- Return $\widehat{K^*}$ as the answer for ψ^*

Fig. 2. A one-way-CCA adversary $\mathcal{B}$ employing a cMiM adversary $\mathcal{A}$ for the proof of Theorem 1

On input pk and the challenge ciphertext ψ^*, $\mathcal{B}$ initializes its inner state and invokes $\mathcal{A}$ on input pk. In case that $\mathcal{A}$ queries V(pk) for the challenge message, $\mathcal{B}$ sends ψ^* to $\mathcal{A}$ as the challenge message. In case that $\mathcal{A}$ sends a challenge message ψ to a prover clone P(sk), $\mathcal{B}$ checks whether or not ψ is equal to ψ^*. If so, then $\mathcal{B}$ puts $K = \perp$. Otherwise, $\mathcal{B}$ queries its decapsulation oracle $\mathcal{DEC}(\text{sk}, \cdot)$ for the answer for the ciphertext ψ and gets K. $\mathcal{B}$ sends K to $\mathcal{A}$ as the response message.

In case that $\mathcal{A}$ sends the response message $\widehat{K^*}$ to V(pk), $\mathcal{B}$ returns $\widehat{K^*}$ as the answer for the challenge ciphertext ψ^*.

The view of $\mathcal{A}$ in $\mathcal{B}$ is the same as the real view of $\mathcal{A}$. This is obvious except the case that ψ is equal to ψ^*. When $\mathcal{A}$ sent $\psi = \psi^*$, the transcript of the interaction between P(sk) and $\mathcal{A}(\text{pk})$ would be wholly equal to that between $\mathcal{A}(\text{pk})$ and V(pk), because the prover P is deterministic. This is ruled out, so $\mathcal{B}$'s response, $K = \perp$, is appropriate.

If $\mathcal{A}$ wins, then $\mathcal{B}$ wins. Hence the inequality in Theorem 1 follows. (*Q.E.D.*)

Remark 1. In analogous ways, we can show the following facts. If a KEM is secure against non-adaptive chosen ciphertext attacks on one-wayness, then the derived ID scheme ID is secure against 2-phase concurrent attacks. If a KEM is secure against passive attacks on one-wayness, then the derived ID scheme ID is secure against passive attacks.

Remark 2. The prover P in the Fig.1 is deterministic. Therefore, the derived ID scheme ID is prover-resettable [3]. Moreover, ID is also verifier-resettable because ID consists of 2-round interaction.

4   A One-Way-CCA Secure KEM Based on the CDH Assumption

In this section, we propose a one-way-CCA secure KEM based on the CDH assumption. The challenge-and-response ID scheme of Anada-Arita [1] can be viewed as a one-way-CCA secure KEM based on the Gap-CDH assumption. Our strategy is to relax the gap assumption by applying the Twin Diffie-Hellman technique of Cash, Kiltz and Shoup [6,18].

In the construction, we employ a target collision resistant (TCR) hash function family. The definition of a TCR hash function family $Hfam(1^k) = \{H_\mu\}_{\mu \in Hkey(1^k)}$ and advantage $\mathbf{Adv}_{CF,Hfam}^{tcr}(k)$ of a PPT collision finder CF over $Hfam$ are in Appendix A.

4.1   Construction

The construction of a KEM KEM1 is shown in the Fig.3.

On input 1^k, the key generator K runs as follows. A group generator Grp outputs (q, g) on input 1^k. In addition, K chooses a hash key μ from a hash key space $Hkey(1^k)$. The hash key μ indicates a specific hash function H_μ with values in $\mathbf{Z}_q$ in a hash function family $Hfam(1^k)$. Then K chooses $x_1, x_2, y_1, y_2 \in \mathbf{Z}_q$ and computes $X_1 = g^{x_1}, X_2 = g^{x_2}, Y_1 = g^{y_1}, Y_2 = g^{y_2}$. K sets pk $= (q, g, X_1, X_2, Y_1, Y_2, \mu)$ and sk $= (q, g, x_1, x_2, y_1, y_2, \mu)$. Then K returns (pk, sk).

On input pk, the encapsulation algorithm Enc runs as follows. Enc chooses $a \in \mathbf{Z}_q$ at random and computes $h = g^a$ and the hash value $\tau \leftarrow H_\mu(h)$. Then Enc computes $d_1 = (X_1^\tau Y_1)^a, d_2 = (X_2^\tau Y_2)^a$ and $K = X_1^a$. The random string is K and the ciphertext is $\psi = (h, d_1, d_2)$. Note here that $(g, X_1^\tau Y_1, X_2^\tau Y_2, h, d_1, d_2)$ is a twin DH tuple. Enc returns the pair (K, ψ).

On input sk and $\psi = (h, d_1, d_2)$, the decapsulation algorithm Dec runs as follows. Dec computes the hash value $\tau \leftarrow H_\mu(h)$. Then Dec verifies whether $\psi = (h, d_1, d_2)$ is a consistent ciphertext, that is, whether $(g, X_1^\tau Y_1, X_2^\tau Y_2, h, d_1, d_2)$ is a twin DH tuple or not. For this sake, Dec checks whether $h^{\tau x_1 + y_1} = d_1$ and $h^{\tau x_2 + y_2} = d_2$ hold. If at least one of them does not hold, then Dec puts $K = \bot$. Otherwise Dec computes the decapsulation $K = h^{x_1}$. Note that (g, X_1, h, K) is a DH tuple. Finally, Dec returns K.

Theorem 2. *The key encapsulation mechanism KEM1 is one-way-CCA secure based on the CDH assumption and the target collision resistance of employed hash function family. More precisely, for any PPT one-way-CCA adversary $\mathcal{A}$ on KEM1 that queries decapsulation oracle at most q_{dec} times, there exist a PPT CDH problem solver $\mathcal{S}$ on Grp and a PPT collision-finder CF on Hfam which satisfy the following tight reduction.*

$$\mathbf{Adv}_{\mathcal{A},KEM1}^{ow\text{-}cca}(k) \leqslant \frac{q_{dec}}{q} + \mathbf{Adv}_{\mathcal{S},Grp}^{cdh}(k) + \mathbf{Adv}_{CF,Hfam}^{tcr}(k).$$

Key Generation

- K: given 1^k as input;
- $(q, g) \leftarrow \texttt{Grp}(1^k), \mu \leftarrow Hkey(1^k)$
- $x_1, x_2, y_1, y_2 \leftarrow \mathbf{Z}_q, X_1 := g^{x_1}, X_2 := g^{x_2}, Y_1 := g^{y_1}, Y_2 := g^{y_2}$
- $\texttt{pk} := (q, g, X_1, X_2, Y_1, Y_2, \mu), \texttt{sk} := (q, g, x_1, x_2, y_1, y_2, \mu)$
- Return $(\texttt{pk}, \texttt{sk})$

Encapsulation

- Enc: given $\texttt{pk}$ as input;
- $a \leftarrow \mathbf{Z}_q, h := g^a, \tau \leftarrow H_\mu(h)$
- $d_1 := (X_1^\tau Y_1)^a, d_2 := (X_2^\tau Y_2)^a, K := X_1^a, \psi = (h, d_1, d_2)$
- Return (K, ψ)

Decapsulation

- Dec: given $\texttt{sk}, \psi = (h, d_1, d_2)$ as input;
- $\tau \leftarrow H_\mu(h)$
- If $h^{\tau x_1 + y_1} \neq d_1$ or $h^{\tau x_2 + y_2} \neq d_2$ then $K := \perp$ else $K := h^{x_1}$
- Return K

Fig. 3. A one-way-CCA secure KEM KEM1

4.2 Proof of Theorem 2

Let $\mathcal{A}$ be any given adversary that attacks KEM1 in one-way-CCA setting. Using $\mathcal{A}$ as subroutine, we construct a PPT CDH problem solver $\mathcal{S}$ as shown in the Fig.4, where an algebraic trick [17] and the Twin Diffie-Hellman technique [6] are essentially used.

$\mathcal{S}$ is given $q, g, X = g^x$ and $Y = g^y$ as input, where x and y are random. $\mathcal{S}$ initializes its inner state. $\mathcal{S}$ chooses $a^* \in \mathbf{Z}_q$ at random and computes $h^* = Y g^{a^*}$. Then $\mathcal{S}$ chooses μ from $Hkey(1^k)$ and computes $\tau^* \leftarrow H_\mu(h^*)$. $\mathcal{S}$ chooses $r, s \in \mathbf{Z}_q$ at random, and puts $X_1 = X, X_2 = X_1^{-r} g^s$. $\mathcal{S}$ chooses $u_1, u_2 \in \mathbf{Z}_q$ at random, and computes $W_1 = X_1^{-\tau^*} g^{u_1}, W_2 = X_2^{-\tau^*} g^{u_2}$. $\mathcal{S}$ computes $d_1^* = (h^*)^{u_1}, d_2^* = (h^*)^{u_2}$. $\mathcal{S}$ sets $\texttt{pk} = (q, g, X_1, X_2, W_1, W_2, \mu), \psi^* = (h^*, d_1^*, d_2^*)$ and invokes $\mathcal{A}$ on input $\texttt{pk}$ and ψ^*. Note that $\texttt{pk}$ is correctly distributed. Note also that $\mathcal{S}$ does not know x_1, x_2, w_1, w_2 at all, where x_1, x_2, w_1, w_2 are the discrete log of X_1, X_2, W_1, W_2, respectively. Especially the followings hold.

$$w_i = \log_g(W_i) = -\tau^* x_i + u_i, \quad i = 1, 2. \tag{1}$$

$\mathcal{S}$ replies to $\mathcal{A}$'s queries as follows.

In case that $\mathcal{A}$ queries its decapsulation oracle $\mathcal{DEC}(\texttt{sk}, \cdot)$ for the answer for $\psi = (h, d_1, d_2)$, $\mathcal{S}$ checks whether ψ is equal to ψ^* or not. If $\psi = \psi^*$, then $\mathcal{S}$ puts $K = \perp$. Otherwise, $\mathcal{S}$ computes $\tau \leftarrow H_\mu(h)$ and verifies whether $\psi = (h, d_1, d_2)$ is consistent or not (call this case CONSISTENCY-CHECK).

That is, $\mathcal{S}$ verifies whether $(g, X_1^\tau W_1, X_2^\tau W_2, h, d_1, d_2)$ is a twin DH tuple as follows. Put $\widehat{Y} = h^{\tau - \tau^*}, \widehat{Z_1} = d_1 / h^{u_1}$ and $\widehat{Z_2} = d_2 / h^{u_2}$. If $\widehat{Z_1}^r \widehat{Z_2} \neq \widehat{Y}^s$, then it is not a twin DH tuple and $\mathcal{S}$ puts $K = \perp$. Otherwise, $\mathcal{S}$ decides that it is a twin DH tuple. Then, if $\tau \neq \tau^*$, $\mathcal{S}$ computes $K = \widehat{Z_1}^{1/(\tau - \tau^*)}$ (call this case SIMDEC). Otherwise ($\tau = \tau^*$), $\mathcal{S}$ aborts (call this case ABORT). $\mathcal{S}$ replies K to $\mathcal{A}$ except the case ABORT.

In case that $\mathcal{A}$ replies $\widehat{K^*}$, $\mathcal{S}$ computes $Z = \widehat{K^*} / X^{a^*}$ and returns Z.

Given $q, g, X = g^x, Y = g^y$ as input;

Initial Setting

  – Initialize the inner state

  – $a^* \leftarrow \mathbf{Z}_q, h^* := Y g^{a^*}$

  – $\mu \leftarrow \text{Hkey}(1^k), \tau^* \leftarrow H_\mu(h^*)$

  – $r, s \leftarrow \mathbf{Z}_q, X_1 := X, X_2 := X_1^{-r} g^s$

  – $u_1, u_2 \leftarrow \mathbf{Z}_q, W_1 := X_1^{-\tau^*} g^{u_1}, W_2 := X_2^{-\tau^*} g^{u_2}$

  – $d_1^* := (h^*)^{u_1}, d_2^* := (h^*)^{u_2}$

  – $\text{pk} := (q, g, X_1, X_2, W_1, W_2, \mu), \psi^* := (h^*, d_1^*, d_2^*)$

  – Invoke $\mathcal{A}$ on pk and ψ^*

Answering $\mathcal{A}$'s Queries

  – In case that $\mathcal{A}$ queries $\mathcal{DEC}(\text{sk}, \cdot)$ for the answer for $\psi = (h, d_1, d_2)$

  • If $\psi = \psi^*$, then put $K := \bot$

  • else (: the case CONSISTENCY-CHECK)

  $\tau \leftarrow H_\mu(h), \widehat{Y} := h^{\tau - \tau^*}, \widehat{Z_1} := d_1/h^{u_1}, \widehat{Z_2} := d_2/h^{u_2}$

  If $\widehat{Z_1}^r \widehat{Z_2} \neq \widehat{Y}^s$, then $K := \bot$

  else

  If $\tau \neq \tau^*$, then $K := \widehat{Z_1}^{1/(\tau - \tau^*)}$ (: the case SIMDEC)

  else abort (: the case ABORT)

  • Reply K to $\mathcal{A}$

  – In case that $\mathcal{A}$ replies $\widehat{K^*}$ as the answer for ψ^*

  • $Z := \widehat{K^*}/X^{a^*}$

  • Return Z

Fig. 4. A CDH problem solver $\mathcal{S}$ employing a one-way-CCA adversary $\mathcal{A}$ for the proof of Theorem 2

$\mathcal{S}$ is able to simulate the real view of $\mathcal{A}$ perfectly until the case ABORT happens except a negligible case, as we see below.

Firstly, the challenge ciphertext $\psi^* = (h^*, d_1^*, d_2^*)$ is consistent and correctly distributed. This is because the distribution of (h^*, d_1^*, d_2^*) is equal to that of the real consistent ciphertext $\psi = (h, d_1, d_2)$. To see it, note that $y + a^*$ is substituted for a:

$$h^* = g^{y+a^*}, \quad d_i^* = (g^{y+a^*})^{u_i} = (g^{u_i})^{y+a^*} = (X_i^{\tau^*} W_i)^{y+a^*}, \quad i = 1, 2.$$

Secondly, $\mathcal{S}$ simulates the decapsulation oracle $\mathcal{DEC}(\text{sk}, \cdot)$ perfectly except a negligible case. To see it, note that the consistency check really works though it may involve a negligible error case, which is explained by the following two claims.

Claim 1. $(g, X_1^\tau W_1, X_2^\tau W_2, h, d_1, d_2)$ is a twin DH tuple if and only if $(g, X_1, X_2, \widehat{Y}, \widehat{Z_1}, \widehat{Z_2})$ is a twin DH tuple for $\widehat{Y} = h^{\tau - \tau^*}, \widehat{Z_1} = d_1/h^{u_1}$ and $\widehat{Z_2} = d_2/h^{u_2}$.

Claim 1 is proven by direct calculations and the proof is noted in Appendix B.

Claim 2. If $\widehat{Z_1}^r \widehat{Z_2} = \widehat{Y}^s$ holds for $\widehat{Y} = h^{\tau - \tau^*}, \widehat{Z_1} = d_1/h^{u_1}$ and $\widehat{Z_2} = d_2/h^{u_2}$, then $(g, X_1, X_2, \widehat{Y}, \widehat{Z_1}, \widehat{Z_2})$ is a twin DH tuple except an error case that occurs at most $1/q$ probability. Conversely, if $(g, X_1, X_2, \widehat{Y}, \widehat{Z_1}, \widehat{Z_2})$ is a twin DH tuple, then $\widehat{Z_1}^r \widehat{Z_2} = \widehat{Y}^s$ certainly holds.

Proof of Claim 2. We observe that each of $\widehat{Y} = h^{\tau-\tau^*}$, $\widehat{Z}_1 = d_1/h^{u_1}$ and $\widehat{Z}_2 = d_2/h^{u_2}$ is given independently of r. So we can apply the Lemma in Section 2. (Q.E.D.)

Let us define the event OVERLOOK as:

$$\text{OVERLOOK} \overset{\text{def}}{=} \begin{cases} \widehat{Z}_1^{\,r}\,\widehat{Z}_2 = \widehat{Y}^s \text{ holds} \\ \text{and} \quad (g, X_1, X_2, \widehat{Y}, \widehat{Z}_1, \widehat{Z}_2) \text{ is not a twin DH tuple.} \end{cases}$$

Then, by the Claim 2, the probability that OVERLOOK occurs is at most $1/q$ for each consistency check. So for at most q_{dec} consistency checks, CONSISTENCY-CHECK$_i$, $i = 1, \ldots, q_{dec}$, the probability that at least one corresponding OVERLOOK$_i$ occurs is at most q_{dec}/q. That is;

$$\Pr[\bigvee_{i=1}^{q_{dec}} \text{OVERLOOK}_i] \leqslant \frac{q_{dec}}{q}. \tag{2}$$

q_{dec} is polynomial and q is exponential in k, so the right hand side is negligible in k.

Suppose $\mathcal{S}$ has confirmed that a decapsulation query $\psi = (h, d_1, d_2)$ passed the consistency check. In that case, $(g, X_1^\tau W_1, X_2^\tau W_2, h, d_1, d_2)$ is a twin DH tuple (except a negligible case OVERLOOK), so $d_1 = h^{\tau x_1 + w_1}$ holds. If, in addition, $\mathcal{S}$ is in the case SIMDEC (that is, $\tau \neq \tau^*$), then the answer $K = \widehat{Z}_1^{\,1/(\tau-\tau^*)}$ of $\mathcal{S}$ to $\mathcal{A}$ is correct. This is because $K = (d_1/h^{u_1})^{1/(\tau-\tau^*)}$ is equal to h^{x_1} by the following equality.

$$d_1/h^{u_1} = h^{\tau x_1 + w_1 - u_1} = h^{(\tau-\tau^*)x_1 + (\tau^* x_1 + w_1 - u_1)} = h^{(\tau-\tau^*)x_1},$$

where we use the equality (1).

As a whole, $\mathcal{S}$ simulates the real view of $\mathcal{A}$ perfectly until the case ABORT happens except the negligible case OVERLOOK.

Now we evaluate the advantage of $\mathcal{S}$. When $\mathcal{A}$ wins, $(g, X, h^*, \widehat{K}^*)$ is a DH tuple, so the following holds.

$$\widehat{K}^* = X^{y+a^*} = g^{x(y+a^*)} = g^{xy + xa^*}.$$

Hence the output Z is equal to $\widehat{K}^*/X^{a^*} = g^{xy}$, which is the correct answer for the input (g, X, Y). That is, $\mathcal{S}$ wins. Therefore, the probability that $\mathcal{S}$ wins is lower bounded by the probability that $\mathcal{A}$ wins, OVERLOOK$_i$ never occurs for $i = 1, \ldots, q_{dec}$ and ABORT does not happen:

$$\Pr[\mathcal{S} \text{ wins}] \geqslant \Pr[\mathcal{A} \text{ wins} \wedge (\bigwedge_{i=1}^{q_{dec}} (\neg \text{OVERLOOK}_i)) \wedge (\neg \text{ABORT})]$$

$$\geqslant \Pr[\mathcal{A} \text{ wins}] - \Pr[(\bigvee_{i=1}^{q_{dec}} \text{OVERLOOK}_i) \vee \text{ABORT}]$$

$$= \Pr[\mathcal{A} \text{ wins}] - (\Pr[\bigvee_{i=1}^{q_{dec}} \text{OVERLOOK}_i] + \Pr[(\bigwedge_{i=1}^{q_{dec}} (\neg \text{OVERLOOK}_i)) \wedge \text{ABORT}]).$$

Using the inequality (2), we get:

$$\mathbf{Adv}^{\mathrm{cdh}}_{\mathcal{S},\mathrm{Grp}}(k) \geqslant \mathbf{Adv}^{\mathrm{ow\text{-}cca}}_{\mathcal{A},\mathrm{KEM1}}(k) - \frac{q_{dec}}{q} - \Pr[(\bigwedge_{i=1}^{q_{dec}}(\neg\mathrm{OVERLOOK}_i)) \wedge \mathrm{ABORT}].$$

So our task being left is to show the following inequality.

Claim 3. $\Pr[(\bigwedge_{i=1}^{q_{dec}}(\neg\mathrm{OVERLOOK}_i)) \wedge \mathrm{ABORT}] \leqslant \mathbf{Adv}^{\mathrm{tcr}}_{\mathcal{CF},\mathit{Hfam}}(k).$

Proof of Claim 3. Using $\mathcal{A}$ as subroutine, we construct a PPT target collision finder $\mathcal{CF}$ on *Hfam* as follows. Given 1^k as input, $\mathcal{CF}$ initializes its inner state. $\mathcal{CF}$ gets (q, g) from $\mathrm{Grp}(1^k)$. $\mathcal{CF}$ chooses $a^* \in \mathbf{Z}_q$ at random, computes $h^* = g^{a^*}$ and outputs h^*. $\mathcal{CF}$ receives a random hash key μ and computes $\tau^* \leftarrow H_\mu(h^*)$. Then $\mathcal{CF}$ makes a secret key and public key honestly by itself : $\mathrm{sk} = (q, g, x_1, x_2, y_1, y_2, \mu), \mathrm{pk} = (q, g, X_1, X_2, Y_1, Y_2, \mu)$. Finally, $\mathcal{CF}$ computes $d_1^* = (X_1^{\tau^*}Y_1)^{a^*}, d_2^* = (X_2^{\tau^*}Y_2)^{a^*}$ and puts $\psi^* = (h^*, d_1^*, d_2^*)$. $\mathcal{CF}$ invokes $\mathcal{A}$ on pk and ψ^*.

In case that $\mathcal{A}$ queries the decapsulation oracle $\mathcal{DEC}(\mathrm{sk}, \cdot)$ for the answer for $\psi = (h, d_1, d_2)$, $\mathcal{CF}$ checks whether ψ is equal to ψ^* or not. If $\psi = \psi^*$, then $\mathcal{CF}$ replies $K =\perp$ to $\mathcal{A}$. Otherwise $(\psi \neq \psi^*)$, $\mathcal{CF}$ computes $\tau \leftarrow H_\mu(h)$ and verifies whether $\psi = (h, d_1, d_2)$ is consistent. $\mathcal{CF}$ can do it in the same way as the Dec does because $\mathcal{CF}$ has the secret key sk. If it is not consistent, $\mathcal{CF}$ replies $K =\perp$ to $\mathcal{A}$. Otherwise, if $\tau \neq \tau^*$, then $\mathcal{CF}$ replies $K = h^{x_1}$ to $\mathcal{A}$. Else if $\tau = \tau^*$, then $\mathcal{CF}$ returns h and stops (call this case COLLISION).

The view of $\mathcal{A}$ in $\mathcal{CF}$ is the same as the real view until the case COLLISION happens.

Observe here the following. If OVERLOOK never occurs in $\mathcal{S}$, then only consistent queries (ψs) have the chance to cause a collision $\tau = \tau^*$ as is the case in $\mathcal{CF}$. Hence we have:

$$\Pr[(\bigwedge_{i=1}^{q_{dec}}(\neg\mathrm{OVERLOOK}_i)) \wedge \mathrm{ABORT}] \leqslant \Pr[\mathrm{COLLISION}]. \tag{3}$$

On the other hand, notice that COLLISION implies the following.

$$\begin{cases} & (g, X_1^{\tau^*}Y_1, X_2^{\tau^*}Y_2, h^*, d_1^*, d_2^*): \text{a twin DH tuple} \\ \text{and} & \exists(g, X_1^{\tau}Y_1, X_2^{\tau}Y_2, h, d_1, d_2): \text{a twin DH tuple} \\ \text{and} & \tau = \tau^*. \end{cases}$$

If, in addition to the above conditions, h were equal to h^*, then (d_1, d_2) would be equal to (d_1^*, d_2^*). This means that ψ is equal to ψ^*, a contradiction. So it must hold that

$$h \neq h^*.$$

Namely, in the case COLLISION, $\mathcal{CF}$ succeeds in making a target collision:

$$\Pr[\mathrm{COLLISION}] = \mathbf{Adv}^{\mathrm{tcr}}_{\mathcal{CF},\mathit{Hfam}}(k). \tag{4}$$

Combining (3) and (4), we get the inequality as claimed. *(Q.E.D.)*

4.3   A Tuning for Efficiency and the Corresponding Identification Scheme

To reduce the length of ciphertext $\psi = (h, d_1, d_2)$, we can replace the term d_2 with its hash value $v_2 := H_\mu(d_2)$. Let us call this KEM KEM2. In KEM2, the ciphertext turns to $\psi = (h, d_1, v_2)$, so the consistency check for index 2 in $\mathrm{Dec}(\mathrm{sk}, \psi)$ becomes $H_\mu(h^{\tau x_2 + y_2}) \overset{?}{=} v_2$. In addition, the trapdoor test in the security proof, $\widehat{Z_1}^r \widehat{Z_2} \overset{?}{=} \widehat{Y}^s$, is deformed as follows.

$$\widehat{Z_1}^r \widehat{Z_2} = \widehat{Y}^s \iff (d_1/h^{u_1})^r (d_2/h^{u_2}) = (h^{\tau - \tau^*})^s$$
$$\iff d_1^{-r} h^{r u_1 + u_2 + s(\tau - \tau^*)} = d_2$$
$$\implies H_\mu(d_1^{-r} h^{r u_1 + u_2 + s(\tau - \tau^*)}) = v_2.$$

The last equality may cause collision, so the security statement for KEM2 needs the collision resistance assumption of employed hash function family $Hfam$ (the name of game "cr" in $\mathbf{Adv}^{\mathrm{cr}}_{\mathcal{CF}', Hfam}(k)$ below means collision resistance).

Corollary of Theorem 2. *The key encapsulation mechanism KEM2 is one-way-CCA secure based on the CDH assumption, the target collision resistance and the collision resistance of employed hash function family. More precisely, for any PPT one-way-CCA adversary $\mathcal{A}$ on KEM2 that queries decapsulation oracle at most q_{dec} times, there exist a PPT CDH problem solver $\mathcal{S}$ on Grp, a PPT collision-finder $\mathcal{CF}$ and $\mathcal{CF}'$ on $Hfam$ which satisfy the following tight reduction.*

$$\mathbf{Adv}^{\mathrm{ow\text{-}cca}}_{\mathcal{A}, \mathrm{KEM2}}(k) \leqslant \frac{q_{dec}}{q} + \mathbf{Adv}^{\mathrm{cdh}}_{\mathcal{S}, \mathrm{Grp}}(k) + \mathbf{Adv}^{\mathrm{tcr}}_{\mathcal{CF}, Hfam}(k) + \mathbf{Adv}^{\mathrm{cr}}_{\mathcal{CF}', Hfam}(k).$$

The ID scheme derived from KEM2 is shown in the Fig.5. The maximum message length of the ID scheme derived from KEM1 (that is, the length of challenge message of V) amounts to three elements in Grp. By the tuning above, the maximum message length reduces to two elements in Grp plus one hash value of H_μ.

5   Efficiency Comparison

In this section, we evaluate the efficiency of our ID schemes comparing with other ID schemes secure against concurrent man-in-the-middle attacks in the standard model. Under the condition that security is based on the CDH assumption, our ID schemes reduce the computation by one exponentiation than the currently most efficient one.

Comparable schemes are divided into four categories. The first category is Σ-protocols, the second category is challenge-and-response ID schemes obtained from EUF-CMA secure signature schemes, the third category is the ones obtained from IND-CCA secure encryption schemes and the fourth category is the ones obtained from one-way-CCA secure KEMs.

In the first category, to the best of our knowledge, the Gennaro scheme is the most efficient but no more efficient than the ID scheme derived from Cramer-Shoup encryption [8,25,9] (the Cramer-Shoup ID scheme, for short). As for the second category, all the known signature schemes in the standard model, including the Short Signature [2] and the Waters Signature [26], are costly than the Cramer-Shoup ID scheme.

Key Generation
- K: given 1^k as input;
  - $(q, g) \leftarrow \texttt{Grp}(1^k), \mu \leftarrow Hkey(1^k)$
  - $x_1, x_2, y_1, y_2 \leftarrow \mathbf{Z}_q, X_1 := g^{x_1}, X_2 := g^{x_2}, Y_1 := g^{y_1}, Y_2 := g^{y_2}$
  - $\text{pk} := (q, g, X_1, X_2, Y_1, Y_2, \mu), \text{sk} := (q, g, x_1, x_2, y_1, y_2, \mu)$
  - Return (pk, sk)

Interaction
- V: given pk as input;
  - $a \leftarrow \mathbf{Z}_q, h := g^a, \tau \leftarrow H_\mu(h)$
  - $d_1 := (X_1^\tau Y_1)^a, v_2 := H_\mu((X_2^\tau Y_2)^a), K := X_1^a, \psi = (h, d_1, v_2)$
  - Send ψ to P
- P: given sk as input and receiving $\psi = (h, d_1, v_2)$ as input message;
  - $\tau \leftarrow H_\mu(h)$
  - If $h^{\tau x_1 + y_1} \neq d_1$ or $H_\mu(h^{\tau x_2 + y_2}) \neq v_2$ then $\widehat{K} := \perp$ else $\widehat{K} := h^{x_1}$
  - Send $\widehat{K}$ to V
- V: receiving $\widehat{K}$ as input message;
  - If $\widehat{K} = K$ then return 1 else return 0

Fig. 5. An ID scheme derived from KEM2

In the third category, the Cramer-Shoup ID scheme is the most efficient. Note that the Cramer-Shoup KEM [25,9] (ShOOKEM) is also usable as a cMiM secure ID scheme, because the KEM is IND-CCA secure and hence one-way-CCA secure. On the contrary, we remark that the KEM part of Kurosawa-Desmedt encryption scheme [19] is not comparable because the KEM is not one-way-CCA secure [14].

In the fourth category the one-way-CCA secure KEM of Hanaoka-Kurosawa [15] (HK08KEM) is vary comparable, as its security is reduced to the CDH assumption. A recently proposed ID scheme of Anada-Arita [1] is also comparable as it can be considered an ID scheme derived from a one-way-CCA secure KEM (AA10KEM)[2].

Table 1 shows comparison of these KEMs with our KEMs KEM1 and KEM2. In the table, we are comparing computational amount by counting the number of exponentiations. We also compares the maximum message length. (For the DDH assumption and the Gap-CDH assumption, see [21].)

Table 1. Efficiency comparison of KEM1 and KEM2 with previous KEMs. G and h mean an element in G_q and a hash value in $\mathbf{Z}_q$, respectively. OW-CCA means one-way-CCA security.

KEM	Security Assump.	Security as KEM	Security as ID scm.	Exponentiation V(Enc) P(Dec)		Max. Msg. Length (Challenge Msg.)
ShOOKEM	DDH	IND-CCA	cMiM	5	3	$3G$
HK08KEM	CDH	OW-CCA	cMiM	7	3	$3G$
AA10KEM	Gap-CDH	OW-CCA	cMiM	4	2	$2G$
Our KEM1	CDH	OW-CCA	cMiM	6	3	$3G$
Our KEM2	CDH	OW-CCA	cMiM	6	3	$2G + 1h$

---

[2] We note that one-time signature in the ID scheme of [1] can be replaced by TCR hash function.

As shown in Table 1, the ID schemes derived from KEM1 and KEM2 reduce the computation by one exponentiation for verifier than the currently most efficient one derived from the Hanaoka-Kurosawa one-way-CCA secure KEM [15], whose security is based on the same (CDH) assumption, which is the weakest in the three assumptions in the table. We can also look at the table as a trade off between strength of security assumptions and computational amounts to execute protocols.

6   Conclusion

We showed a generic way for deriving a cMiM secure ID scheme from a one-way-CCA secure KEM. Then we gave a concrete one-way-CCA secure KEM utilizing the Twin Diffie-Hellman technique. The obtained ID scheme performs better than the currently most efficient one whose security is based on the (same) CDH assumption.

Acknowledgements

We appreciate sincere suggestions offered by Prof. Kiltz [18] and we would like to thank Prof. Kurosawa for inspiring words, both at ProvSec 2010. We also thank anonymous reviewers for careful reading and valuable comments.

References

1. Anada, H., Arita, S.: Identification Schemes of Proofs of Ability Secure against Concurrent Man-in-the-Middle Attacks. In: Heng, S.-H., Kurosawa, K. (eds.) ProvSec 2010. LNCS, vol. 6402, pp. 18–34. Springer, Heidelberg (2010)
2. Boneh, D., Boyen, X.: Short Signatures without Random Oracles. In: Cachin, C., Camenisch, J.L. (eds.) EUROCRYPT 2004. LNCS, vol. 3027, pp. 56–73. Springer, Heidelberg (2004)
3. Bellare, M., Fischlin, M., Goldwasser, S., Micali, S.: Identification Protocols Secure against Reset Attacks. In: Pfitzmann, B. (ed.) EUROCRYPT 2001. LNCS, vol. 2045, pp. 495–511. Springer, Heidelberg (2001)
4. Bellare, M., Goldreich, O.: On Defining Proofs of Knowledge. In: Brickell, E.F. (ed.) CRYPTO 1992. LNCS, vol. 740, pp. 390–420. Springer, Heidelberg (1993)
5. Bellare, M., Palacio, A.: GQ and Schnorr Identification Schemes: Proofs of Security against Impersonation under Active and Concurrent Attacks. In: Yung, M. (ed.) CRYPTO 2002. LNCS, vol. 2442, pp. 162–177. Springer, Heidelberg (2002)
6. Cash, D., Kiltz, E., Shoup, V.: The Twin Diffie-Hellman Problem and Applications. In: Smart, N.P. (ed.) EUROCRYPT 2008. LNCS, vol. 4965, pp. 127–145. Springer, Heidelberg (2008), http://eprint.iacr.org/
7. Cramer, R., Damgård, I., Nielsen, J.B.: Multiparty Computation from Threshold Homomorphic Encryption. In: Pfitzmann, B. (ed.) EUROCRYPT 2001. LNCS, vol. 2045, pp. 280–300. Springer, Heidelberg (2001)
8. Cramer, R., Shoup, V.: A Practical Public Key Cryptosystem Provably Secure against Adaptive Chosen Ciphertext Attack. In: Krawczyk, H. (ed.) CRYPTO 1998. LNCS, vol. 1462, pp. 13–25. Springer, Heidelberg (1998)
9. Cramer, R., Shoup, V.: Design and Analysis of Practical Public-Key Encryption Schemes Secure against Adaptive Chosen Ciphertext Attack. SIAM Journal on Computing 33(1), 167–226 (2003)

10. Fujisaki, E.: New Constructions of Efficient Simulation-Sound Commitments Using Encryption. In: The 2011 Symposium on Cryptography and Information Security, 1A2-3. The Institute of Electronics, Information and Communication Engineers, Tokyo (2011)
11. Gennaro, R.: Multi-trapdoor Commitments and their Applications to Non-Malleable Protocols. In: Franklin, M. (ed.) CRYPTO 2004. LNCS, vol. 3152, pp. 220–236. Springer, Heidelberg (2004)
12. Goldwasser, S., Micali, S., Rackoff, C.: The Knowledge Complexity of Interactive Proof Systems. SIAM Journal on Computing 18(1), 186–208 (1989)
13. Guillou, L., Quisquater, J.J.: A Paradoxical Identity-Based Signature Scheme Resulting from Zero-Knowledge. In: Goldwasser, S. (ed.) CRYPTO 1988. LNCS, vol. 403, pp. 216–231. Springer, Heidelberg (1990)
14. Herranz, J., Hofheinz, D., Kiltz, E.: The Kurosawa-Desmedt Key Encapsulation is not Chosen-Ciphertext Secure. Cryptology ePrint Archive, 2006/207, http://eprint.iacr.org/
15. Hanaoka, G., Kurosawa, K.: Efficient Chosen Ciphertext Secure Public Key Encryption under the Computational Diffie-Hellman Assumption. In: Pieprzyk, J. (ed.) ASIACRYPT 2008. LNCS, vol. 5350, pp. 308–325. Springer, Heidelberg (2008), Full version available at Cryptology eprint Archive, http://eprint.iacr.org/
16. Katz, J.: Efficient Cryptographic Protocols Preventing "Man-in-the-Middle" Attacks. Doctor of Philosophy Dissertation. Columbia University, New York (2002)
17. Kiltz, E.: Chosen-Ciphertext Security from Tag-Based Encryption. In: Halevi, S., Rabin, T. (eds.) TCC 2006. LNCS, vol. 3876, pp. 581–600. Springer, Heidelberg (2006)
18. Kiltz, E.: Personal communication at ProvSec 2010, Malacca (2010)
19. Kurosawa, K., Desmedt, Y.: A New Paradigm of Hybrid Encryption Scheme. In: Franklin, M. K. (ed.) CRYPTO 2004. LNCS, vol. 3152, pp. 426–442. Springer, Heidelberg (2004)
20. Naor, M., Yung, M.: Universal One-Way Hash Functions and their Cryptographic Applications. In: The 21st Symposium on Theory of Computing, pp. 33–43. Association for Computing Machinery, New York (1989)
21. Okamoto, T., Pointcheval, D.: The Gap-Problems: A New Class of Problems for the Security of Cryptographic Schemes. In: Kim, K. (ed.) PKC 2001. LNCS, vol. 1992, pp. 104–118. Springer, Heidelberg (2001)
22. Pointcheval, D.: Chosen-Ciphertext Security for Any One-Way Cryptosystem. In: Imai, H., Zheng, Y. (eds.) PKC 2000. LNCS, vol. 1751, pp. 129–146. Springer, Heidelberg (2000)
23. Rompel, J.: One-Way Functions are Necessary and Sufficient for Secure Signatures. In: The 22nd Annual Symposium on Theory of Computing, pp. 384–387. Association for Computing Machinery, New York (1990)
24. Schnorr, C.P.: Efficient Identification and Signatures for Smart Cards. In: Brassard, G. (ed.) CRYPTO 1989. LNCS, vol. 435, pp. 239–252. Springer, Heidelberg (1990)
25. Shoup, V.: Using Hash Functions as a Hedge against Chosen Ciphertext Attack. In: Preneel, B. (ed.) EUROCRYPT 2000. LNCS, vol. 1807, pp. 275–288. Springer, Heidelberg (2000)
26. Waters, B.: Dual System Encryption: Realizing Fully Secure IBE and HIBE under Simple Assumptions. In: Halevi, S. (ed.) CRYPTO 2009. LNCS, vol. 5677, pp. 619–636. Springer, Heidelberg (2009)
27. Yilek, S.: Resettable Public-Key Encryption: How to Encrypt on a Virtual Machine. In: Pieprzyk, J. (ed.) CT-RSA 2010. LNCS, vol. 5985, pp. 41–56. Springer, Heidelberg (2010)

A   Target Collision Resistant Hash Functions

Target collision resistant (TCR) hash functions [20,23] are treated as a family. Let us denote a function family as $Hfam(1^k) = \{H_\mu\}_{\mu \in Hkey(1^k)}$. Here $Hkey(1^k)$ is a hash key space, $\mu \in Hkey(1^k)$ is a hash key and H_μ is a function from $\{0,1\}^*$ to $\{0,1\}^k$. We may assume that H_μ is from $\{0,1\}^*$ to $\mathbf{Z}_q$, where q is a prime of length k.

Given a PPT algorithm $\mathcal{CF}$, a collision finder, we consider the following experiment.

$\textbf{Experiment}^{\text{tcr}}_{\mathcal{CF},Hfam}(1^k)$

$\quad m \leftarrow \mathcal{CF}(1^k), \mu \leftarrow Hkey(1^k), m' \leftarrow \mathcal{CF}(\mu)$

$\quad$ If $H_\mu(m) = H_\mu(m')$ and $m \neq m'$, then return WIN else return LOSE.

We define $\mathcal{CF}$'s advantage over $Hfam$ in the game of target collision resistance as follows.

$$\textbf{Adv}^{\text{tcr}}_{\mathcal{CF},Hfam}(k) \overset{\text{def}}{=} \Pr[\textbf{Experiment}^{\text{tcr}}_{\mathcal{CF},Hfam}(1^k) \text{ returns WIN}].$$

We say that $Hfam$ is a TCR function family if, for any PPT algorithm $\mathcal{CF}$, $\textbf{Adv}^{\text{tcr}}_{\mathcal{CF},Hfam}(k)$ is negligible in k.

In theory, TCR hash function families can be constructed based on the existence of a one-way function [20,23].

B   Proof of Claim 1

Assume that $(g, X_1^\tau W_1, X_2^\tau W_2, h, d_1, d_2)$ is a twin DH tuple and put

$$X_i^\tau W_i =: g^{\alpha_i}, h =: g^\beta, d_i =: g^{\alpha_i\beta}, \ i = 1, 2.$$

Then $h^{\tau - \tau^*} = g^{\beta(\tau - \tau^*)}$. Note that we have set $W_i := X_i^{-\tau^*} g^{u_i}, \ i = 1, 2$. So $X_i^\tau W_i = X_i^\tau X_i^{-\tau^*} g^{u_i} = X_i^{\tau - \tau^*} g^{u_i}$ and we have $g^{\alpha_i - u_i} = X_i^{\tau - \tau^*}, \ i = 1, 2$. Hence

$$d_i/h^{u_i} = g^{\alpha_i\beta}/g^{\beta u_i} = g^{(\alpha_i - u_i)\beta} = X_i^{\beta(\tau - \tau^*)}, \ i = 1, 2.$$

This means $(g, X_1, X_2, \widehat{Y}, \widehat{Z_1}, \widehat{Z_2})$ is a twin DH tuple for $\widehat{Y} = h^{\tau - \tau^*}, \widehat{Z_1} = d_1/h^{u_1}$ and $\widehat{Z_2} = d_2/h^{u_2}$.

The converse is also verified by setting the goal to be $d_i = g^{\alpha_i\beta}, \ i = 1, 2$ and starting from the assumption that $\widehat{Z_i} = d_i/h^{u_i} = X_i^{\beta(\tau - \tau^*)}, \ i = 1, 2$. (Q.E.D.)

Attacking Bivium and Trivium with the Characteristic Set Method*

Zhenyu Huang and Dongdai Lin

State Key Laboratory of Information Security
Institute of Software, Chinese Academy of Sciences, Beijing, China

Abstract. In this paper we utilize an algebraic method called the characteristic set method to attack Bivium and Trivium in the guess-and-determine way. Our attack focuses on recovering the internal states of these two ciphers. We theoretically analyze the performance of different guessing strategies in the guess-and-determine method and present a good one. We show a large amount of experimental results about these two problems with different parameters. From these experimental data we obtain the following results. For Bivium, with 177-bit keystream the expected attack time by the characteristic set method is about $2^{31.81}$ seconds. And for Trivium, with 288-bit keystream the expected attack time is about $2^{114.27}$ seconds.

Keywords: Stream cipher, Trivium, Bivium, algebraic attack, characteristic set method.

1 Introduction

Trivium [2] is a stream cipher designed in 2005 by C. De Cannière and B. Preneel and submitted to the Profile 2 (hardware) European project eSTREAM [13]. It has an exceptionally simple structure, which leads to very good performance in both hardware and software. Despite Trivium's simplicity, there are no substantial cryptanalytic results against it so far. Due to these outstanding qualities, Trivium was chosen as part of the portfolio for Profile 2 by the eSTREAM project. In [11], Bivium, a reduced version of the cipher Trivium, has been introduced. Our motivation is to find attacks on Bivium and then extend them to Trivium.

Previous works: During the past 5 years, a lot of methods have been used to attack Bivium and Trivium. Some of them focused on finding the 80-bit key[3,6], while others focused on recovering the internal state[4,5,9,11]. In this paper our goal is the second one. There are two reasons for us choosing the second one: 1) The equations generated from the initial 80-bit key are too dense to be solved by algebraic ways. 2) If the length of initial key is extended, the complexity of our

* This work was in part supported by National 973 Program of China under Grant 2011CB302400, the National Natural Science Foundation of China under Grants 60970152 and the Grand Project of Institute of Software under Grant YOCX285056.

A. Nitaj and D. Pointcheval (Eds.): AFRICACRYPT 2011, LNCS 6737, pp. 77–91, 2011.

attack will not increase. The results of previous attacks on Bivium and Trivium for recovering the internal state are summarized below:

- Raddum[11] developed a new algorithm for solving sparse quadratic equations. The results of this method are listed in the following table.

	Bivium-A	Bivium-B	Trivium
time	"about a day"	2^{56} sec	$O(2^{164})$
keystream	177	177	288

- By guessing some key bits and the products of some key bits , Maximov and Biryukov [8] reduced Bivium and Trivium to linear equation systems and obtained the following complexity results:

	Bivium-B	Trivium
time	$c \cdot 2^{36.1}$, where $c \approx 2^{14}$	$c \cdot 2^{83.5}$, where $c \approx 2^{16}$
keystream	$2^{11.7}$	$2^{61.5}$

- By converting the polynomial system into logical expression and using the guess-and-determine method, McDonald, Charnes, and Pieprzyk [9] attacked Bivium with MiniSat. They obtained the following results:

	Bivium-A	Bivium-B	Trivium
time	21 sec	$2^{42.7}$ sec	unknown
keystream	177	177	unknown

- Also based on the guess-and-determine method, Tobias Eibach, Gunnar Völkel and Enrico Pilz used the Gröbner Basis algorithm to attack Bivium-B [5]. They got the best attack result on recovering the internal state of Bivium-B until now.

	Bivium-B	Trivium
time	$2^{35.49}$ sec	unknown
keystream	200	unknown

Our work: We use the guess-and-determine way to recover the internal states of Bivium-B and Trivium. This way is widely used in the previous attacks[4,5,9]. In this paper, we first theoretically analyze the properties of different guessing strategies in this method, and we choose a good one based on our analysis. Then we utilize an algebraic method which is called the characteristic set(CS) method to solve the polynomial systems generated after guessing. In the field of symbolic computation, the CS method is an important tool for studying polynomial, algebraic differential, and algebraic difference equation systems. Its idea is reducing equation systems in general form to equation systems in the form of triangular sets. This method was introduced by Ritt and the recent study of it was inspired by Wu's seminal work on automated geometry theorem proving [12]. In [1], the CS method was firstly extended to solve polynomial equations in boolean ring. In [7], it was further extended to solve polynomial equations in general finite fields, and an efficient variant of the CS method called **MFCS** algorithm was proposed and systematically analyzed. **MFCS** is an algorithm for solving boolean polynomial equations, which has low space consumption and needs small number of equations.

With our guessing strategy and **MFCS** algorithm, the expected attack time for Bivium-B is about $2^{31.81}$ seconds, which is 12.8 times faster than the best known result for recovering the internal state in [5]. The expected attack time for Trivium is about $2^{114.27}$ seconds. This is also a good result. It is only slower than the result $c \cdot 2^{83.5}$ ($c \approx 2^{16}$) in [8]. Comparing to $2^{61.5}$ bits in [8], the keystream we need is much shorter. For Bivium-B and Trivium, the number is 177 and 288 bits respectively. Note that the result of Trivium is worst than $O(2^{80})$ which is the complexity of exhaust searching the 80-bit initial key. However, as mentioned before if the length of initial key is extended, the time complexity of exhaust search will increase while our time complexity will not change.

The rest of this paper is organized as follows. In Section 2, we simply introduce Trivium and Bivium. In Section 3, we propose some analysis about the guessing strategies. In Section 4, we introduce **MFCS** algorithm. In Section 5 and 6, experimental results are shown.

2   Trivium and Bivium

Trivium consists of a non-linear feedback shift register, which operates on a 288-bit state denoted by $(s_1, ..., s_{288})$, coupled with a linear filter function. The initial state of Trivium is initialized by an 80-bit secret key and an 80-bit initial value(IV) which are written into two of the shift registers. The cipher state is updated $4 \times 288 = 1152$ times, and then obtain the initial state. Trivium generates keystream from the initial state by the following pseudo-code:

$$\text{For } i = 1 \text{ to } N \text{ Do}$$
$$t_1 \leftarrow s_{66} + s_{93}$$
$$t_2 \leftarrow s_{162} + s_{177}$$
$$t_3 \leftarrow s_{243} + s_{288}$$
$$z_i \leftarrow t_1 + t_2 + t_3$$
$$t_1 \leftarrow t_1 + s_{91} \cdot s_{92} + s_{171}$$
$$t_2 \leftarrow t_2 + s_{175} \cdot s_{176} + s_{264}$$
$$t_3 \leftarrow t_3 + s_{286} \cdot s_{287} + s_{69}$$
$$(s_1, s_2, \ldots, s_{93}) \leftarrow (t_3, s_1, \ldots, s_{92})$$
$$(s_{94}, s_{95}, \ldots, s_{177}) \leftarrow (t_1, s_{94}, \ldots, s_{176})$$
$$(s_{178}, s_{179}, \ldots, s_{288}) \leftarrow (t_2, s_{178}, \ldots, s_{287})$$

Bivium[11] is a reduced version of Trivium, which has two variants: Bivium-A and Bivium-B. Its internal state is 177-bit which is operated by two registers of length 93 and length 84. It generates keystream by the following pseudo-code:

For $i = 1$ to N do

$$t_1 \leftarrow s_{66} + s_{93}$$
$$t_2 \leftarrow s_{162} + s_{177}$$
$$z_i \leftarrow t_1 + t_2 (\text{Variant B}) \setminus t_2 (\text{Variant A})$$
$$t_1 \leftarrow t_1 + s_{91} \cdot s_{92} + s_{171}$$
$$t_2 \leftarrow t_2 + s_{175} \cdot s_{176} + s_{69}$$
$$(s_1, s_2, \ldots, s_{93}) \leftarrow (t_2, s_1, \ldots, s_{92})$$
$$(s_{94}, s_{95}, \ldots, s_{177}) \leftarrow (t_1, s_{94}, \ldots, s_{176})$$

For Trivium or Bivium, by setting every bit of an internal state to be a variable, we can generate a boolean polynomial system from continuous known keystream. Our purpose is solving this polynomial system in order to reconstruct the internal state. Unless otherwise specified, in the following of this paper the key means the internal state we want to solve, and the initial polynomial equation system means the polynomial equations generated before.

Since directly solving the polynomial system is too hard, most existing attack results are based on the guess-and-determine method. It means we first evaluate some variables with some guessing values and obtain a new polynomial system, then we try to solve this new system. In [4,5,9], the authors used SAT-solver or Gröbner basis algorithm as the tools for solving the new system. By the guess-and-determine method, if we guess k bits of the key and the average attack time for one instant is t, the upper bound of the attack time is $2^k t$ and the expected attack time is $2^{k-1} t$.

3   Guessing Strategy

From the description of guess-and-determine method, we know that finding a good guessing strategy is crucial for optimizing the attack results. In this section, we will analyze some properties of a guessing strategy, and find a good one based on our analysis. Here we are not concerned with the guessing strategy which convert all initial polynomials into linear ones.

In the first phase of the guess-and-determine method, in order to reduce the number of variables we can do the following pre-elimination process: That is after evaluating the guessing values, we do Gauss elimination for the linear polynomials in the new system. And then for every independent linear polynomial $x_c + L$, we substitute x_c with L in other high degree polynomials. If we get new linear ones after substitution, we do the previous operation again until no new linear ones appear. Obviously, by this process we can eliminate variables and will not increase the degree of the polynomial system. Moreover, replacing a variable by a linear polynomial will not significantly increase the density of a polynomial.

After the pre-elimination mentioned before, we will obtain some independent linear equations and some high degree equations. Suppose these high degree equation only involves ℓ variables. Obviously, ℓ essentially influences the running time for solving these high degree equations and also the total running time.

Now let's analyze the value of ℓ for a guessing strategy about Bivium-B. In [8], the authors present a good way to analyze the structure of the initial polynomials. First, denote the key $(s_1, s_2, \ldots, s_{93})$ in the first register as $(p_1, p_2, \ldots, p_{93})$, and denote the key $(s_{94}, s_{95}, \ldots, s_{177})$ in the second register as $(q_1, q_2, \ldots, q_{84})$. Then sort them into three groups:

$$K_0 = K_0^1 \cup K_0^2 = (p_3, p_6, \ldots, p_{93}) \cup (q_3, q_6, \ldots, q_{84})$$
$$K_1 = K_2^1 \cup K_2^2 = (p_2, p_5, \ldots, p_{92}) \cup (q_2, q_5, \ldots, q_{83}) \qquad (1)$$
$$K_2 = K_1^1 \cup K_1^2 = (p_1, p_4, \ldots, p_{91}) \cup (q_1, q_4, \ldots, q_{82})$$

Actually, the classification we did above is coincident with the design of Trivium and Bivium. In the design of Trivium(Bivium), the designer interleave three sub-generator of length $288/3(177/3)$ together and interconnect them through AND-gates. Here each K_i corresponds to each sub-generator.

In the initial polynomials equations there are 66 linear equations. 22 of them only involve the variables of K_0; another 22 ones only involve the variables of K_1; the last 22 ones involve the variables of K_2. For the initial quadratic polynomials, the number of them is 83, and the linear parts of them only involve the variables in one $K_i(i = 1, 2, 3)$. And for a quadratic polynomial, the part of degree two has the form $\sum_r k_{i+1}^r k_{i+2}^r$ where $k_{i+1}^r \in K_{(i+1 \bmod 3)}$ and $k_{i+2}^r \in K_{(i+2 \bmod 3)}$. Note that, the first register outputs quadratic states after 66 clocks, and the second register does it after 69 clocks. Hence there are three quadratic polynomials separately only having one monomial with degree two: $q_{82} \cdot q_{83}, q_{81} \cdot q_{82}, q_{80} \cdot q_{81}$. As mentioned in [8], if we know the values of two bits p_{82}, q_{91} of some internal state, the following two clocks of Bivium-B are linear. Precisely speaking, if we know the values of k $(k \leq 28)$ continuous pairs of variables

$$(q_{82}), (p_{91}, q_{79}), (p_{88}, q_{76}), \ldots, (p_{91-3(k-2)}, q_{79-3(k-2)}) \in K_2, \qquad (2)$$

we can obtain $2k$ new linear equations with variables in K_0, K_1.

If we know the values of k $(k \leq 27)$ continuous pairs of variables

$$(q_{81}), (p_{90}, q_{78}), (p_{87}, q_{75}), \ldots, (p_{90-3(k-2)}, q_{78-3(k-2)}) \in K_0, \qquad (3)$$

we can obtain $2k$ new linear equations with variables in K_1, K_2.

If we know the values of k $(k \leq 28)$ continuous pairs

$$(q_{83}), (p_{92}, q_{80}), (p_{89}, q_{77}), \ldots, (p_{92-3(k-2)}, q_{80-3(k-2)}) \in K_1, \qquad (4)$$

we can obtain $2k - 1$ new linear equations with variables in K_0 and K_2. In the following of this article, when we say a pair we mean it is a variable pair in (2),(3) or (4).

Remark 3.1. *If we guess a large number of variables, some of polynomial with degree≥ 3 will be converted into linear ones. And these cases are very complicated to analyze. Fortunately, for most strategies in [4,5,9] and our choosing one, these complicated cases will not happen. Only the quadratic equations and the first three polynomial equations with degree 3 will be converted into linear ones.*

Here we present the value of ℓ for some guessing strategies in [4,5].

Example 3.2. *In [4], the author concluded that the best strategy for Minisat is guessing the last 48 variables from the end of the second register. That is guessing* $(q_{84}, q_{83}, \ldots, q_{37})$. *Note that every initial linear equation has only four variables. Two of them are in* K_i^1, *and the others are in* K_i^2, $i = 0, 1, 2$. *Moreover, the linear parts of the initial quadratic equations also involve variables both in* K_i^1 *and* K_i^2. *Since the variables guessed in this strategy are only from one register, we will not generate 1 in pre-elimination, and can't derive the value of any other variable from the linear equations. For the pairs in (2) and (3), we just have the values of* (q_{83}) *and* (q_{82}). *Note that* q_{83} *and* q_{82} *occur in a same quadratic term* $q_{83}q_{82}$. *Hence,* $\ell = 177 - 66 - 48 - 2 = 61$.

Example 3.3. *In [5], a strategy called "Ending-halved" is used in their experiment. That is guessing the ends of both register. By this strategy, if we guess 48 variables* $(q_{84}, q_{83}, \ldots, q_{61})$, $(p_{93}, p_{92}, \ldots, p_{70})$, *we can get three groups of pairs:*

$$\{(q_{82}), (p_{91}, q_{79}), \ldots, (p_{73}, q_{61})\} \in K_2,$$

$$\{(q_{81}), (p_{90}, q_{78}), \ldots, (p_{75}, q_{63})\} \in K_1,$$

$$\{(q_{83}), (p_{92}, q_{80}), \ldots, (p_{74}, q_{62})\} \in K_0.$$

From the first group, it is easy to see that 16 new linear equations are generated. Now we consider the following two groups. When we evaluate the variables of the second or third group in an initial quadratic equation, if the terms with degree two of it have elements in K_2, *it has already been converted into a linear equation by evaluating the pairs of the first group. We can conduct that from the pairs of the second and third groups, we can only generate 7 new linear equations. Thus we have* $\ell = 177 - 66 - 48 - 16 - 7 = 40$.

Obviously for most guessing values, we can not obtain the solution. This means a contradiction will occur in some phase of our algorithm. If the contradiction occurs in the pre-elimination process, the running time will be very short. In contrast, if the the contradiction occurs in the process of solving high degree equations, the running time will be much longer. In order to obtain accurate total running time, we expect the running time is smooth for different assignment. Hence, we hope the guessing strategy have a good property that contradiction will not occur in the pre-elimination process. And we say the guessing strategy satisfying this property is *stable*. If we use an unstable strategy, in order to obtain an accurate total running time we need to count how many times our assignment can not pass the pre-elimination process.

Remark 3.4. *Given an unstable strategy, sometimes we can find a corresponding stable one which guesses less variables and has lower time complexity. For example, suppose the contradiction occurs in a linear equation* $x_1 + x_2 + x_3 + x_4 = 0$ *by guessing the values of all* x_i. *We can change the strategy by only guessing* x_1, x_2, x_3, *and solve* x_4 *easily. For the unstable strategy, we exhaust search the* *value of x_4. In contrast, for the stable one we obtain the value of x_4 by solving linear equation. Obviously, the stable one is better. For solving Bivium, the problem are much more complicated than this trivial example. Sometimes in the corresponding stable stretegy we need to solve some higher degree equation with very simple form, and we think solving these equation by an algebraic way is faster than exhaust search. Therefore, we think the corresponding stable strategy is better, and we try to avoid using an unstable strategy.*

From the previous research about solving Bivium with Satsolver or Gröbner Basis, the number for guessing is about 35-55. In this range, we give a nontrivial example which are not stable.

Example 3.5. *For Bivium-B, suppose we guess $(s_{177}, s_{174}, \ldots, s_{96}, s_{93}, s_{90}, \ldots , s_{72})$ and s_{176}. we have an input polynomial $s_{162} + s_{177} + s_{175} \cdot s_{176} + s_{69} + s_{27} + s_{96} + s_{111} + z_{67}$. We can easily get the values of s_{27} and s_{69} from linear equations. If when we set s_{176} to be 0. It is possible that after substitution the above polynomial becomes 1. Consequently, this is not a stable guessing strategy.*

Based on above analysis, we want to find a strategy satisfying the following properties:

- In order to obtain smaller ℓ with less guessing variables, we wish to know the values of continuous pairs in $(2, 3, 4)$ as many as we can.
- From the analysis of Example 3.3, we know the following fact. Assume that we have already obtained the values of k_1 pairs in some K_i. If we know the values of k_2 pairs in $K_{(i+1 \bmod 3)}$ or $K_{(i+2 \bmod 3)}$, the number of new linear ones generated by these k_2 pairs may be less than $2k_2$. The reason is that some quadratic polynomials with the form $L + \sum k_i^j k_{i+1}^j$ or $L + \sum k_i^j k_{i+2}^j$, where $k_i^j \in K_i$, have already been converted into linear ones by evaluating the pairs in K_i. Thus, for getting smaller ℓ with less guessing variables, we need to avoid the above situation. This implies for same number of guessing bits, it is better that all the guessing variables are in a same K_i, $i = 1, 2, 3$.
- It is better to keep the strategy stable.

Now we present a strategy which satisfying the above three properties. That is we guess 37 variables $(p_{93-i}, p_{90-i}, \ldots, p_{69-i})$ and $(q_{84-i}, q_{81-i}, \ldots, q_{3-i})$, for some $i = 0, 1, 2$. From the 22 initial linear equations, we can obtain the values of $(p_{66-i}, p_{63-i}, \ldots, p_{3-i})$. Then we have the values of all the variables in some K_i which containing all the pairs in K_i.

Since we only guess three elements in an initial linear polynomial, we will not obtain contradiction from the initial linear polynomials. Moreover, the variables whose values can be obtained from these linear equations are still in the same K_i. Thus, after we assign these values into quadratic equations, the new linear equations we obtain are with variables in $K_{i+1 \bmod 3}$ and $K_{i+2 \bmod 3}$. And these new linear equations are linear independent with the initial 44 linear ones. Consequently, this strategy is stable.

Here we show the value of ℓ for different i:

1. If $i = 0$, $\ell = 177 - 66 - 37 - 2 \cdot 27 = 20$.
2. If $i = 1$, $\ell = 177 - 66 - 37 - (2 \cdot 28 - 1) = 19$.
3. If $i = 2$, $\ell = 177 - 66 - 37 - 2 \cdot 28 = 18$.

Obviously it is better to guess the 37 variables in K_2 since ℓ is smallest. In [8], this strategy was first mentioned. And in [5], the "Every-3rd" strategy by which they obtained best experimental results is same as our strategy in the case of $i = 0$. However, in [5] the number of their guessing variables is greater than 37, which means they also guess some variables in K_1. Actually if we guess the above 37 variables in some K_i and some other variables in K_{i+1} or K_{i+2}, the strategy will be unstable. For example, let's consider the quadratic polynomial $L_0 + \sum_i k_2^i k_1^i$ where $k_1^i \in K_1$, $k_1^i \in K_2$ and L_0 is a linear one with variables in K_0. If k_1^i are our guessing variables and we set them to be 0. Then we will obtain linear equation $L_0 = 0$. Suppose we already guess 37 variables in K_0 and know the values of all variables in K_0 by solving initial linear equations. If these values do not satisfy $L_0 = 0$, a contradiction will occur in the pre-elimination process. Thus "Every-3rd" is not stable.

4   The Characteristic Set Method

For Bivium-B and Trivium, after the guess and pre-elimination process, we use **MFCS** algorithm to solve the new polynomial system. **MFCS** algorithm is an improved characteristic set algorithm for solving boolean equations [7]. Here we simply introduce it.

For a boolean polynomial $P \in \mathbb{F}_2[x_1, x_2, \ldots, x_n]/(x_1^2 + x_1, x_2^2 + x_2, \ldots, x_n^2 + x_n)$, the *class* of P, denoted as $\mathrm{cls}(P)$, is the largest index c such that x_c occurs in P. If P is a constant, we set $\mathrm{cls}(P)$ to be 0. If $\mathrm{cls}(P) = c > 0$, we call x_c the *leading variable* of P, denoted as $\mathrm{lvar}(P)$. The leading coefficient of P as a univariate polynomial in $\mathrm{lvar}(P)$ is called the *initial* of P, and is denoted as $\mathrm{init}(P)$. Then P can be represented uniquely as the following form: $P = Ix_c + U$, where $I = \mathrm{init}(P)$ and U is a boolean polynomial without variable x_c.

A sequence of nonzero polynomials

$$\mathcal{A}: \quad A_1, A_2, \ldots, A_r \tag{5}$$

is a *triangular set* if either $r = 1$ and $A_1 = 1$ or $0 < \mathrm{cls}(A_1) < \cdots < \mathrm{cls}(A_r)$. A boolean polynomial P is called *monic*, if $\mathrm{init}(P) = 1$. Moreover, if the elements of a triangular set are all monic, we call it a monic triangular set.

With **MFCS** algorithm, we can decompose $\mathrm{Zero}(\mathbb{P})$, the common zero set of a polynomial set $\mathbb{P}$, as $\cup_i \mathrm{Zero}(\mathcal{A}_i)$, the union of the common zero sets of some monic triangular sets $\mathcal{A}_i$. We first convert all polynomials with highest class c in $\mathbb{P}$ into monic ones by the following decomposition formula: $\mathrm{Zero}(Ix_c + U) = \mathrm{Zero}(Ix_c + U, I + 1) \cup \mathrm{Zero}(I, U) = \mathrm{Zero}(x_c + U, I + 1) \cup \mathrm{Zero}(I, U)$. Note that, with decomposition we will generate some new polynomial sets, we call these new polynomial sets to be new components. Then we can choose one monic polynomial $x_c + R$ to eliminate the x_c of other polynomials by doing addition $x_c + R + x_c + R_1 = R + R_1$. Note that $R + R_1$ is a polynomial with lower class. Therefore, we obtain the following group of polynomial sets $\{x_c + R, \mathbb{P}'\}, \mathbb{P}_1, \ldots, \mathbb{P}_t$, where $\mathbb{P}'$ is a set of polynomials with class lower than c and each $\mathbb{P}_i$ is a new generating polynomial set. Then we can recursively do the above operations on the polynomials with highest class in $\mathbb{P}'$. After dealing with all classes, we will obtain a monic triangular set or constant 1, and generate a group of new polynomial sets. Then we recursively do the above operations on every new set. Finally, we will obtain the monic triangular sets we need. Obviously, for a monic triangular set $\{x_1 + c_1, x_2 + f_1(x_1), x_3 + f_2(x_2, x_1), \ldots, x_n + f_{n-1}(x_{n-1}, \ldots, x_1)\}$, we can easily solve it. The precise steps of **MFCS** are shown in Algorithm 1. The proof of correctness and termination can be found in [7]. **MFCS** algorithm has the following properties[7]:

Algorithm 1 — MFCS($\mathbb{P}$)

Input: A finite set of polynomials $\mathbb{P}$.
Output: Monic triangular sets $\{\mathcal{A}_1, \mathcal{A}_2, \ldots, \mathcal{A}_t\}$ such that
            $\text{Zero}(\mathbb{P}) = \cup_{i=1}^{t}\text{Zero}(\mathcal{A}_i)$ and $\text{Zero}(\mathcal{A}_i) \cap \text{Zero}(\mathcal{A}_j) = \emptyset$

1 Set $\mathbb{P}^* = \{\mathbb{P}\}$, $\mathcal{A}^* = \emptyset$ and $\mathcal{C}^* = \emptyset$.
2 While $\mathbb{P}^* \neq \emptyset$ do
   2.1 Choose a polynomial set $\mathbb{Q}$ from $\mathbb{P}^*$.
   2.2 While $\mathbb{Q} \neq \emptyset$ do
      2.2.1 If $1 \in \mathbb{Q}$, $\text{Zero}(\mathbb{Q}) = \emptyset$. Goto Step 2.1.
      2.2.2 Let $\mathbb{Q}_1 \subset \mathbb{Q}$ be the polynomials with the highest class.
      2.2.3 Let $\mathbb{Q}_{monic} = \emptyset$, $\mathbb{Q}_2 = \mathbb{Q} \setminus \mathbb{Q}_1$.
      2.2.4 While $\mathbb{Q}_1 \neq \emptyset$ do
         Let $P = Ix_c + U \in \mathbb{Q}_1$, $\mathbb{Q}_1 = \mathbb{Q}_1 \setminus \{P\}$.
         $\mathbb{P}_1 = \mathbb{Q}_{monic} \cup \mathbb{Q}_2 \cup \mathbb{Q}_1 \cup \{I, U\}$.
         $\mathbb{P}^* = \mathbb{P}^* \cup \{\mathbb{P}_1\}$.
         $\mathbb{Q}_{monic} = \mathbb{Q}_{monic} \cup \{x_c + U\}$, $\mathbb{Q}_2 = \mathbb{Q}_2 \cup \{I + 1\}$.
      2.2.5 Let $Q = x_c + U$ be a polynomial with lowest degree in $\mathbb{Q}_{monic}$.
      2.2.6 $\mathcal{A} = \mathcal{A} \cup \{Q\}$.
      2.2.7 $\mathbb{Q} = \mathbb{Q}_2 \cup \{R \neq 0 | R = Q_i + Q, Q_i \in \mathbb{Q}_{monic}\}$.
   2.3 if $\mathcal{A} \neq \emptyset$, set $\mathcal{A}^* = \mathcal{A}^* \cup \{\mathcal{A}\}$.
3 Return $\mathcal{A}^*$

---

1. The size of polynomials occurring in the whole algorithm can be controlled by that of the input ones. The expansion of the internal result will not happen. Note that in different components most polynomials are same, and the same ones can be shared in the memory with data structure SZDD[10]. For the above reasons, the memory cost of **MFCS** is small.

2. In **MFCS**, solving one component is very fast. The bitsize complexity of solving one component is $O(LMn^{d+2})$, where L is the number of input polynomials, n is the number of variables, d is the highest degree of the input polynomials and M is the maximal number of terms for all input polynomials. Obviously, when d is fixed, this is a polynomial about n.

The reason we utilize **MFCS** algorithm is that the polynomials systems we need to solve have block triangular structure. By block triangular structure, we mean that the polynomial set can be divided into disjoint sets such that each set consists of polynomials with the same leading variable and different sets have different leading variables. Some good experimental results for solving this kind of polynomial system by **MFCS** were presented in [7]. One of the results is that the 177-bit internal state of Bivium-A can be solved in about 49.3 seconds with 700-bit keystream by **MFCS**.

5   Attack Bivium-B by MFCS Algorithm

Now we give our experimental results for attacking Bivium-B by **MFCS**. The computer used in our experiments is a PC with i7 2.8Ghz CPU and 4G memory. The CPU of this computer has four cores, but for our experiment only one was used. All the running times in the following tables are given in seconds. And in our experiments only 160 bits of keystream are needed.

Remark 5.1. *For a polynomial system generated by a stream cipher with n variables and m equations. We found that if $m \approx 1.1n$, the running time for* **MFCS** *is always optimal. In our experiments for Bivium-B, $m = 160 < 177$. However, by guessing 37 variables the system can be seen as one with 197 input polynomials and 177 variables. In our experiments, when our guess is wrong the algorithm always returns no solution. And when our guess is correct, we always obtain a unique solution. Actually, if we can count all 2^{37} instants, the number of solutions maybe greater than 1, since 160 bits of keystream cannot guarantee a unique solution. This means for some wrong guessing values,* **MFCS** *may return some solutions which are not the key. The number of these solutions is so small that we can check their correctness extremely fast by the following bits of keystream. Thus, we can ignore the influence of these redundant solutions to the total running time.*

First in Table 1 we present the results about the strategies of guessing the above 37 variables in different K_i. Here we set $\{p_{93}, q_{84}, p_{92}, q_{83}, p_{91}, q_{82}, \ldots\}$ to be $\{x_1, x_2, x_3, x_4, x_5, x_6, \ldots\}$. With this variable order, the experimental result is best. The running time presented in the following table are from 1000 instants with random keys and random guessing values.

From the results in Table 1, we know that as our analysis in Section 3 the running time for K_2 is shortest and it is quite stable for different instants. In the following other experimental results, the guessing variables are all in K_2.

Table 1. Random keys and random guessing values

Strategy	Bits guessed	Average Time	Max Time	Min Time
K_0	37	0.118	0.302	0.066
K_1	37	0.092	0.154	0.057
K_2	37	0.075	0.156	0.049

Table 2. Random keys and random guessing values

Bits guessed	Average Time	Max Time	Min Time
37	0.075	0.156	0.049
36	0.129	0.254	0.086
35	0.219	0.558	0.120
34	1.114	2.702	0.565

Table 3. The results of different keys

Key	Bits guessed	Average Time	Max Time	Min Time
A fixed random key	35	0.215	0.582	0.120
Key= $\{1, 1 \ldots, 1\}$	35	0.220	0.604	0.116
Key= $\{0, 0, \ldots, 0\}$	35	0.218	0.500	0.117

Although the highest complexity bound of **MFCS** in worst case is exponential, for some problem the experimental results of **MFCS** are much better. Thus we attempt decreasing the number of guessing variables, and observe the results.

- If we guess 36 variables $(p_{91}, p_{88}, \ldots, p_{67})$ and $(q_{82}, q_{79}, \ldots, q_4)$, we have $\ell = 177 - 66 - 36 - 2 \cdot 27 = 21$.
- If we guess 35 variables $(p_{91}, p_{88}, \ldots, p_{67})$ and $(q_{82}, q_{79}, \ldots, q_7)$, we have $\ell = 177 - 66 - 35 - 2 \cdot 26 = 24$.
- If we guess 34 variables $(p_{91}, p_{88}, \ldots, p_{67})$ and $(q_{82}, q_{79}, \ldots, q_{10})$, we have $\ell = 177 - 66 - 34 - 2 \cdot 25 = 27$.

For guessing the above 34, 35 and 36 variables, we also test 1000 instants with random keys and random guessing values. The results are given in the following table. From the results we know that, guessing the above 35 variables is best since $2^{35} \cdot 0.219 < 2^{36} \cdot 0.129 < 2^{37} \cdot 0.075$.

In order to observe the change of the running time for different keys, in Table 3 we fixed the key in three different cases and for each case randomly guessing the above 35 variables for 1000 times. From the results, we know that the influence of the key to the running time is extremely little.

Now let's see the change of the running time for different guessing values. We randomly generated 1000 groups of key, and for each one we test four kinds of guessing values: (a) All the guessing values are 1; (b) All the guessing values are 0; (c) The Hamming-weight of the guessing values is 13. (d) The guessing values are all correct.

From Table 4, we can conclude that the weight of guessing values does not influence the results. However, when the guessing values are correct, the running time is slightly longer[2]. Thus, we think the Hamming distance between the guessing values and the correct values of keys influences the running time.

---

[2] Here we should explain that our comparison is about the average running times. Actually, for a fixed key, the running time for a correct guessing value is not always longer.

Table 4. The results of different guessing values

Guessing values	Bits guessed	Average Time	Max Time	Min Time
$\{1,1,\ldots,1\}$	35	0.218	0.519	0.123
$\{0,0,\ldots,0\}$	35	0.211	0.515	0.116
Weight$= 13$	35	0.220	0.498	0.121
Correct values	35	0.247	0.618	0.130

Table 5. The results of different Hamming distances

$D(g,k)$	1	2	5	10	15	25	30	33	34	35
Average	0.229	0.224	0.219	0.217	0.218	0.221	0.218	0.224	0.230	0.241
Max	0.633	0.597	0.716	0.478	0.525	0.575	0.575	0.546	0.807	0.598
Min	0.124	0.117	0.118	0.120	0.115	0.124	0.123	0.114	0.125	0.120

For a group of guessing values $g = \{g_1, g_2, \ldots, g_m\}$, the *Hamming distance* between g and the correct key values $k = \{k_1, k_2, \ldots, k_m\}$ is defined to be $D(g,k) = \sum_{i=1}^{m}(g_i + k_i \bmod 2)$. In Table 5, we present our results for some different distances, and for every one we test 1000 instances.

From the results we know that only when the Hamming distance is close to 0 or 35 the running time will be a little longer than 0.219. The influence of these cases on the whole attack time can be ignored since $\frac{\sum_{i=0}^{4}\binom{35}{i}+\sum_{j=31}^{35}\binom{35}{j}}{2^{35}} \approx 0$. From the above experimental results, we think choosing 0.219 second as our average running time is suitable. Hence, we have the following attack result: with guessing 35 variables, Bivium-B can be solved by **MFCS** in about $2^{35} \cdot 0.219 = 2^{32.81}$ seconds, and the expected running time is $2^{31.81}$ seconds. Compared to the the expected running time $2^{35.49}$ seconds in [5] which is the best known result for recovering the internal state, our result is about 12.8 times faster.

6   Attacking Trivium by MFCS

Now we extend our attack method to Trivium. We can denote the key of Trivium in three different registers as $\{p_1, p_2, \ldots, p_{93}\}$, $\{q_1, q_2, \ldots, q_{84}\}$, $\{r_1, r_2, \ldots, r_{111}\}$. Then we also sort them into three groups:

$$K_0 = K_0^1 \cup K_0^2 \cup K_0^3 = (p_3, p_6, \ldots, p_{93}) \cup (q_3, q_6, \ldots, q_{84}) \cup (r_3, r_6, \ldots, r_{111})$$
$$K_1 = K_2^1 \cup K_2^2 \cup K_2^3 = (p_2, p_5, \ldots, p_{92}) \cup (q_2, q_5, \ldots, q_{83}) \cup (r_2, r_5, \ldots, r_{110})$$
$$K_2 = K_1^1 \cup K_1^2 \cup K_1^3 = (p_1, p_4, \ldots, p_{91}) \cup (q_1, q_4, \ldots, q_{82}) \cup (r_1, r_4, \ldots, r_{109})$$

The analysis about strategies in Section 3 is still valid. The difference is we need to consider continuous triple-pairs to convert quadratic equations into linear ones. More precisely, if we know $k \leq 28$ continuous triple-pairs:

$$(q_{82}, r_{109}), (p_{91}, q_{79}, r_{107}), \ldots, (p_{97-3k}, q_{85-3k}, r_{112-3k}) \in K_2, \qquad (6)$$

we can obtain $2k$ new linear equations with variables in K_0, K_1.

If we know $k \leq 27$ continuous triple-pairs:

$$(q_{81}, r_{98}), (p_{90}, q_{78}, r_{95}), \ldots, (p_{96-3k}, q_{84-3k}, r_{111-3k}) \in K_0, \qquad (7)$$

we can obtain $2k$ new linear equations with variables in K_1, K_2.

If we know $k \leq 28$ continuous triple-pairs:

$$(q_{83}, r_{110}), (p_{92}, q_{80}, r_{107}), \ldots, (p_{98-3k}), q_{86-3k}, r_{113-3k}) \in K_1, \tag{8}$$

we can obtain $2k - 1$ new linear equations with variables in K_0, K_2. In the following, when we say a triple-pair, we mean a variable set in (6),(7) or (8). We can follow the guessing strategy used in Bivium. That is guessing $m = (288 - 66)/3 = 74$ variables :

$$\{p_{91}, p_{88}, \ldots, p_1\}, \{q_{82}, q_{79}, \ldots, q_1\}, \{r_{109}, r_{106}, \ldots, r_{67}\},$$

here 66 is the number of initial linear equations. Then we can obtain the values of all elements in K_2 which contain 28 continuous triple-pairs. Hence, we have $\ell = 288 - 66 - 74 - 2 \cdot 28 = 92$.

For Trivium, we need to guess more variables in K_0, since ℓ is still too large. As analysis in Bivium, in this case the strategy is unstable. Since this strategy is too complicated to find a corresponding stable one mentioned in Remark 3.4, we have to adopt this unstable one. Hence, we need to count how many instances can pass the pre-elimination process without contradictions.

Let w be the Hamming weight of the guessing values in K_0. Here we call the instance which can not pass the pre-elimination process a trivial one. We found that when w increase the ratio of nontrivial instances will increase. This can be explained as following. Let's consider the initial quadratic polynomials with form $\sum k_2^i + \sum k_1^j k_0^r$, where $k_2^i \in K_2, k_1^j \in K_1$ and $k_0^r \in K_0$. Since we already known the values of all k_2^i, if k_0^r are all 1, then after assignment these quadratic polynomials will become linear ones with variables in K_0. And they are linear independent with the initial linear ones, so no contradiction will occur. If the values of some k_0^r are 0, some of these new linear polynomials will become constants, then contradiction may occur. When all k_0^r is 0, all these new linear ones will become constants. If there are m ones, the probability of an evaluation with all $k_0^r = 0$ passing the pre-elimination process is about $1/2^m$. When m is big enough, this probability is approximate to 0.

Moreover, with w increasing, the average time for solving one nontrivial instance increases too. The reason is that less linear equations will be generated if the weight is bigger. Since we not only guess variables in K_2 but also in K_0, some polynomials with degree ≥ 3 will also be converted into linear ones. It is too complicated to show how many linear ones we can obtain for different w by theoretical analysis. From our experiments, when w is maximal, the corresponding ℓ is also maximal. When w decrease, ℓ will be strictly smaller than this value in most time.

For Trivium, besides 74 variables in K_2, we guess another 41 variables in K_0. In this case, the maximal value of ℓ is 33. The following tables present the experimental results with different w. For each evaluation of w, we test 1000 instances with different keys and guessing values. In order to get the optimal running time, we need 190 bits of keystream. In the following tables, the first row is about the number of nontrivial instances. The second row is about the

Table 6. Results of Trivium with Random keys and Random Guessing values

w	0	5	10	15	20	25	31	36	41
Nontrivial	0	3	35	199	488	769	946	991	1000
Average		3.29	1.01	0.76	1.06	1.87	5.50	16.26	50.79
Minimal		2.88	0.28	0.14	0.18	0.35	1.40	4.59	28.17
Maximal		3.88	3.90	8.69	18.61	19.82	30.88	80.27	336.34

Table 7. Results of Trivium with Random keys and Correct Guessing values

w	0	5	10	15	20	25	31	36	41
Nontrivial	0	3	55	223	520	793	949	993	1000
Average		4.20	1.40	0.90	1.09	2.04	5.73	16.05	49.88
Minimal		3.16	0.28	0.14	0.18	0.35	1.40	4.59	28.17
Maximal		5.07	3.90	8.69	18.61	19.82	30.88	80.27	336.34

average running time over these nontrivial ones. The third and fourth rows are respectively about the maximal and minimal running time.

Table 6 shows the results of Trivium with random guessing values in K_2. Table 7 shows the results when the guessing values in K_2 are correct. We can conclude that comparing to the random cases when the guessing values are correct the running time is slight higher.

We can use the following way to estimate the total running time. For fixed guessing values of variables in K_2 , we set the total running time of solving all instances satisfying $w_1 \leq w \leq w_2$ to be $\sum_{i=w_1}^{w_2} \binom{44}{i} (Nt/1000 + (1 - N/1000)t')$ sec. Here, N is the number of nontrivial instances when $w = w_2$. t is the average running time for these nontrivial ones. And t' is the average running time for solving trivial instances. For Trivium, t' is 0.045 seconds. By this way of estimate, we can induce the following results from the above experimental data:

- The total running time for solving Trivium is about $2^{74} \cdot 2^{41.27} = 2^{115.27}$ seconds, and the expected running time is $2^{114.27}$ seconds.

References

1. Chai, F., Gao, X.S., Yuan, C.: A Characteristic Set Method for Solving Boolean Equations and Applications in Cryptanalysis of Stream Ciphers. Journal of Systems Science and Complexity 21(2), 191–208 (2008)
2. De Cannière, C., Preneel, B.: TRIVIUM - a stream cipher construction inspired by block cipher design principles. eSTREAM, ECRYPT Stream Cipher Project, Report 2005/030 (2005)
3. Dinur, I., Shamir, A.: Cube attacks on tweakable black box polynomials. In: Joux, A. (ed.) EUROCRYPT 2009. LNCS, vol. 5479, pp. 278–299. Springer, Heidelberg (2009)
4. Eibach, T., Pilz, E., Völkel, G.: Attacking Bivium using SAT solvers. In: Kleine Büning, H., Zhao, X. (eds.) SAT 2008. LNCS, vol. 4996, pp. 63–76. Springer, Heidelberg (2008)

5. Eibach, T., Völkel, G.: Optimising Gröbner Bases on Bivium. Mathematics in Computer Science 3(2), 159–172 (2010)
6. Fischer, S., Khazaei, S., Meier, W.: Chosen IV statistical analysis for key recovery attacks on stream ciphers. In: Vaudenay, S. (ed.) AFRICACRYPT 2008. LNCS, vol. 5023, pp. 236–245. Springer, Heidelberg (2008)
7. Gao, X.S., Huang, Z.: Efficient Characteristic Set Algorithms for Equation Solving in Finite Fields and Application in Analysis of Stream Ciphers. Cryptology ePrint Archive, 2009/637; Accepted by Journal of Symbolic Computation
8. Maximov, A., Biryukov, A.: Two Trivial Attacks on Trivium. In: Adams, C., Miri, A., Wiener, M. (eds.) SAC 2007. LNCS, vol. 4876, pp. 36–55. Springer, Heidelberg (2007)
9. McDonald, C., Charnes, C., Pieprzyk, J.: Attacking Bivium with MiniSat. Cryptology ePrint Archive, Report 2007/040 (2007)
10. Minto, S.: Zero-Sppressed BDDs for Set Manipulation in Combinatorial Problems. In: Proc. ACM/IEEE Design Automation, pp. 272–277. ACM Press, New York (1993)
11. Raddum, H.: Cryptanalytic results on TRIVIUM. eSTREAM, ECRYPT Stream Cipher Project, Report 2006/039 (2006)
12. Wu, W.T.: Basic Principles of Mechanical Theorem-proving in Elementary Geometries. Journal Automated Reasoning 2, 221–252 (1986)
13. eSTREAM - The ECRYPT Stream Cipher Project, http://www.ecrypt.eu.org/stream/

Improved Cryptanalysis of the Multi-Prime
Φ-Hiding Assumption

Mathias Herrmann[*]

Horst Görtz Institute for IT-Security
Faculty of Mathematics
Ruhr University Bochum, Germany
mathias.herrmann@rub.de

Abstract. In this paper we investigate the Multi-Prime Φ-Hiding Problem as introduced in a recent construction by Kiltz et al. from Crypto 2010. We are able to improve upon previous cryptanalytic results by making use of the special structure of the polynomial that is derived from the problem instance. Our attack is based on the method of Coppersmith for finding small solutions of modular equations. In particular, we make use of a recent result from Herrmann and May to solve linear equations modulo divisors.

Keywords: Φ-Hiding Assumption, lattices, Coppersmith's algorithm, small roots.

1   Introduction

The Φ-Hiding Assumption has been introduced by Cachin, Micali and Stadler in the context of efficient single database private information retrieval [CMS99]. Since then, it has found a number of applications in various branches of modern cryptography [GR05, HO08, GMR05, CMS99, Cac99]. In its basic form the Φ-Hiding Assumption states that for a given RSA modulus $N = pq$ and a prime e it is hard to decide if e divides $\Phi(N)$ or not, where $\Phi(N) = (p-1)(q-1)$ denotes Euler's totient function. It is well known that by a result of Coppersmith [Cop96, Cop97] the Φ-Hiding Problem is efficiently solvable if $e \geq N^{\frac{1}{4}}$. In detail, suppose e divides $p-1$, then we can write $ex^{(0)}+1 = p$ or more generally $ex^{(0)}+1 = 0 \bmod p$ for an unknown value $x^{(0)}$. Now, if we can find the root $x^{(0)}$ of the polynomial $f(x) := ex + 1$ modulo p, then we in turn have solved the Φ-Hiding Problem. A theorem of Howgrave-Graham [HG97] tells us that for such a polynomial we can efficiently find all small modular roots $x^{(0)}$ if their absolute value is smaller than $N^{\frac{\beta^2}{\delta}}$, where δ is the degree of the polynomial and β denotes the size of the unknown divisor, i.e. $p \geq N^{\beta}$. In the basic Φ-Hiding Problem we have the polynomial $f(x)$ of degree $\delta = 1$ and a divisor $p \geq N^{\frac{1}{2}}$. Thus, we can efficiently find roots of $f(x)$ modulo p that are smaller than $N^{\frac{1}{4}}$. Note that since e divides $p-1$ we have $x^{(0)} < N^{\frac{1}{4}}$ if $e \geq N^{\frac{1}{4}}$.

[*] This research was supported the European Commission through the ICT programme under contract ICT-2007-216676 ECRYPT II.

A. Nitaj and D. Pointcheval (Eds.): AFRICACRYPT 2011, LNCS 6737, pp. 92–99, 2011.
© Springer-Verlag Berlin Heidelberg 2011

Furthermore, at AsiaCrypt 2008 Schridde and Freisleben [SF08] showed that the Φ-Hiding Assumption does not hold for special composite integers of the form $N = pq^{2k}$ for $k > 0$. Such integers are often used in cryptography to speed up certain operations [Tak98].

A particularly interesting application of the Φ-Hiding Assumption has been presented at Crypto 2010 by Kiltz, O'Neill and Smith [KOS10]. In order show the instantiability of RSA-OAEP they constructed a lossy trapdoor permutation from RSA, based on the Φ-Hiding Assumption. To increase the efficiency of their construction, they propose to use multi-prime RSA moduli of the form $N = p_1 \cdots p_m$. In that case, the prime e is chosen to divide $p_1 - 1, \ldots, p_{m-1} - 1$. The lossy trapdoor permutation then relies on the so-called Multi-Prime Φ-Hiding Assumption, which assumes that deciding whether a prime e is a divisor of $p_i - 1$ for all but one of the prime factors or not. Note that if e is chosen such that it divides $p_i - 1$ for all prime factors, then we have a distinguishing algorithm because if e divides all $p_i - 1$ we have $N = 1 \bmod e$, whereas $N \bmod e$ is random if this is not the case.

Kiltz et al. present a cryptanalysis of the Multi-Prime Φ-Hiding Assumption similar to the attack on the Φ-Hiding Assumption based on Coppersmith's algorithm. Say $ex_1 + 1 = 0 \bmod p_1, \ldots, ex_{m-1} + 1 = 0 \bmod p_{m-1}$, then they construct a polynomial equation

$$e^{m-1}(x_1 \cdots x_{m-1}) + e^{m-2}(\cdots) + \ldots + e(\cdots) + 1 = 0 \bmod p_1 \cdots p_{m-1} \quad (1)$$

by multiplying all given equations.

In the next step, they perform a linearization of the left-hand side polynomial, i.e. they introduce one dedicated variable for each sum of monomials that share a common coefficient. This results in a linear polynomial and, in order to solve the Multi-Prime Φ-Hiding Problem the goal is to find a (small) solution modulo the divisor $p_1 \cdots p_{m-1}$ of N. From that point on, Kiltz et al. use a theorem due to Herrmann and May [HM08] which gives upper bounds on the sizes of the unknowns such that the problem can be solved efficiently, depending on the number of variables and the size of the divisor.

Our contribution: We improve the attack of [KOS10] by exploiting the special structure of Equation (1). Namely, the coefficients of the left-hand side polynomial are far from arbitrary, but are all powers of the prime e. This implies that they share a common divisor. This common divisor and the fact that e is not too large allows us to perform different linearizations and thereby reduce the number of variables. The benefit that we obtain comes from the observation that the theorem of Herrmann and May gives much better bounds for a smaller number of variables. Let us exemplify the approach for multi-prime RSA with three prime factors and e that divides $p_1 - 1$ and $p_2 - 1$. Similar to [KOS10] we derive the polynomial equation

$$(ex_1 + 1)(ex_2 + 1) = 0 \bmod p_1 p_2$$
$$\Leftrightarrow e^2(x_1 x_2) + e(x_1 + x_2) + 1 = 0 \bmod p_1 p_2.$$

Because e^2 and e share a common divisor, we can apply a linearization as

$$\underbrace{e\left(e(x_1 x_2) + (x_1 + x_2)\right)}_{u} + 1 = 0 \bmod p_1 p_2,$$

which reduces the number of variables to one. On the negative side, the size of the new variable u is increased by the factor e. Notice that it is sufficient to find the solution $u^{(0)}$ because this reveals a non-trivial factor of the hard to factor integer N. I.e. we do not have to explicitly compute the solutions $x_1^{(0)}, x_2^{(0)}$.

In general, it turns out that performing a linearization to obtain a bivariate polynomial gives the best tradeoff between a decreased number of variables and an increase in the variable size.

Apart from the improvement in the asymptotic bound, our attack also has a great gain in performance. The theorem of Herrmann and May states a running time that is exponential in the number of variables. Thus, limiting the number n of variables to two gives a major speedup in the implementation of the actual attack.

Our attack on the Multi-Prime Φ-Hiding Assumption gives a first approach to make use of a polynomials' coefficients in Coppersmith-type attacks. To the best of our knowledge this topic has not been carefully analyzed before. It is a very interesting task to further improve our result by making even better use of the relations among the coefficients.

2 Preliminaries

In our analysis we will use a theorem of Herrmann and May [HM08] that gives upper bounds on the sizes of the solutions of a linear equation modulo an unknown divisor. As required by most multivariate applications of Coppersmith's algorithm, it relies on an assumption in order to extract the final solutions efficiently.

Assumption 1. *Let $h_1, \ldots, h_n \in \mathbb{Z}[x_1, \ldots, x_n]$ be the polynomials that are found by Coppersmith's algorithm. Then the ideal generated by the polynomial equations $h_1(x_1, \ldots, x_n) = 0, \ldots, h_n(x_1, \ldots, x_n) = 0$ has dimension zero.*

Theorem 1 (Herrmann-May). *Let $\epsilon > 0$ and let N be a sufficiently large composite integer (of unknown factorization) with a divisor $p \geq N^\beta$. Furthermore, let $f(x_1, \ldots, x_n) \in \mathbb{Z}[x_1, \ldots, x_n]$ be a linear polynomial in n variables. Under Assumption 1, we can find all solutions $(x_1^{(0)}, \ldots, x_n^{(0)})$ of the equation $f(x_1, \ldots, x_n) = 0 \bmod p$ with $|x_1^{(0)}| \leq N^{\gamma_1}, \ldots, |x_n^{(0)}| \leq N^{\gamma_n}$ if*

$$\sum_{i=1}^{n} \gamma_i \leq 1 - (1 - \beta)^{\frac{n+1}{n}} - (n+1)(1 - \sqrt[n]{1 - \beta})(1 - \beta) - \epsilon.$$

The time complexity of the algorithm is polynomial in $\log N$ and $(\frac{e}{\epsilon})^n$, where e is Euler's constant.

For completeness we explicitly define the Multi-Prime Φ-Hiding Problem and the Multi-Prime Φ-Hiding Assumption.

Problem 1 (Multi-Prime Φ-Hiding Problem). *Let $N = p_1 \cdots p_m$ be a composite integer (of unknown factorization) with $m \geq 2$ prime factors of equal bit-length. Given N and a prime e, decide whether e divides p_i for $1 \leq i < m$ or not.*

Assumption 2 (Multi-Prime Φ-Hiding Assumption). *There is no efficient algorithm that decides the Multi-Prime Φ-Hiding Problem with non-negligible success probability.*

3   Attacking the Multi-Prime Φ-Hiding Assumption

In this section we will present our new approach in attacking the Multi-Prime Φ-Hiding Assumptionin detail.

To exemplify the benefit obtained by our new approach, consider a modulus N consisting of four primes $p_1, \ldots, p_4$ of equal bitsize. If e is Φ-hidden in N, then e fulfills the following system of equations.

$$ex_1 + 1 = 0 \bmod p_1$$
$$ex_2 + 1 = 0 \bmod p_2$$
$$ex_3 + 1 = 0 \bmod p_3$$

If we multiply all equations we obtain the single equation

$$(ex_1 + 1)(ex_2 + 1)(ex_3 + 1) = 0 \bmod p_1 p_2 p_3$$
$$\Leftrightarrow e^3 x_1 x_2 x_3 + e^2 (x_1 x_2 + x_1 x_3 + x_2 x_3) + e(x_1 + x_2 + x_3) + 1 = 0 \bmod p_1 p_2 p_3. \tag{2}$$

Let $X = N^\delta$ be an upper bound on the solutions $x_i^{(0)}$, i.e. $|x_i^{(0)}| \leq X$ for $i = 1, 2, 3$.

Recall that Kiltz et al. perform a linearization of Equation (2) to get the linear equation $e^3 u_1 + e^2 u_2 + e u_3 + 1 = 0 \bmod p_1 p_2 p_3$, where $u_1 := x_1 x_2 x_3$, $u_2 := x_1 x_2 + x_2 x_3 + x_1 x_3$ and $u_3 := x_1 + x_2 + x_3$. Then for $f(u_1, u_2, u_3) := e^3 u_1 + e^2 u_2 + e u_3 + 1$ they use Theorem 1 to find a small root of $f(u_1, u_2, u_3)$ modulo the divisor $p_1 p_2 p_3$ of N. By the upper bounds on the x_i we are able to derive upper bounds on the u_i, namely $|u_1^{(0)}| \leq N^{3\delta}, |u_2^{(0)}| \leq N^{2\delta}, |u_3^{(0)}| \leq N^\delta$. Furthermore, since the primes of the modulus are balanced, we can lower bound the size of the divisor $p_1 p_2 p_3$ by $\frac{1}{8} N^{\frac{3}{4}}$. We use Theorem 1 with $\beta = \frac{3}{4}$ and let the constant $\frac{1}{8}$ contribute to the error term ϵ to obtain

$$\delta < 0.0787 - \epsilon.$$

For the prime e this means that we can efficiently solve the Multi-Prime Φ-Hiding Problem if $e \geq N^{\left(\frac{1}{4} - 0.0787 + \epsilon\right)} = N^{0.1713 + \epsilon}$.

Our new approach to improve this result is based on two observations. First, the coefficients of the left hand side of Equation (2) are strongly related to one another. In particular, we will exploit the fact that the coefficient e^2 is a divisor of e^3. The second observation is that the bound in Theorem 1 gets worse for an increasing number of variables. Indeed, this degradation happens very fast. Thus, our attack performs a further linearization to decrease the total number of variables.

$$e^2 \underbrace{(ex_1x_2x_3 + x_1x_2 + x_1x_3 + x_2x_3)}_{u_1} + e \underbrace{(x_1 + x_2 + x_3)}_{u_2} + 1 = 0 \bmod p_1p_2p_3.$$

This linearization has two effects. On the one hand, it reduces the number of variables as desired from three to two. However, on the other hand, the variable u_1 is increased by a factor of e since the size of u_1 is dominated by $ex_1x_2x_3$. In the current setting we can estimate the size of the factor e as $N^{\frac{1}{4}-\delta}$. It turns out that the reduced number of variables outweighs the additional cost of the factor e. To be precise, we can upper bound the variables by $|u_1^{(0)}| \le N^{\frac{1}{4}+2\delta}$ and $|u_2^{(0)}| \le N^\delta$, which yields by Theorem 1 with $n = 2$ and $\beta = \frac{3}{4}$

$$\delta < \frac{1}{12} - \epsilon \approx 0.0833 - \epsilon.$$

This means, we can efficiently solve the Multi-Prime Φ-Hiding Problem with a modulus consisting of four balanced primes if $e \ge N^{(\frac{1}{4}-\frac{1}{12}+\epsilon)} = N^{\frac{1}{6}+\epsilon} = N^{0.1667+\epsilon}$.

The generalization to Multi-Prime RSA follows the same idea. Let $N = p_1 \cdots p_m$ be an RSA modulus consisting of m primes of the same bitsize and let e be a prime of size $N^{\frac{1}{m}-\delta}$. To decide if e is Multi-Prime Φ-hidden in N we aim to find a small solution of the system

$$ex_1 + 1 = 0 \bmod p_1$$

$$\vdots$$

$$ex_{m-1} + 1 = 0 \bmod p_{m-1},$$

where the solutions $x_i^{(0)}$ for $i = 1, \dots, m-1$ are upper bounded by $X = N^\delta$. We multiply all equations together to obtain

$$(ex_1 + 1) \cdots (ex_{m-1} + 1) = 0 \bmod p_1 \cdots p_{m-1}. \tag{3}$$

Similar to the example for $m = 3$ we expand Equation (3) and perform a linearization of the $m - 1$ terms with coefficients e^{m-1} to e^2. Thus, we obtain the bivariate equation

$$e^2 \underbrace{(e^{m-3}x_1 \cdots x_{m-1} + e^{m-4}(x_1 \cdots x_{m-2} + \dots + x_2 \cdots x_{m-1}) + \dots + (x_1x_2 + \dots + x_{m-2}x_{m-1}))}_{u_1}$$

$$+ e \underbrace{(x_1 + \dots + x_{m-1})}_{u_2} + 1 = 0 \bmod p_1 \cdots p_{m-1}.$$

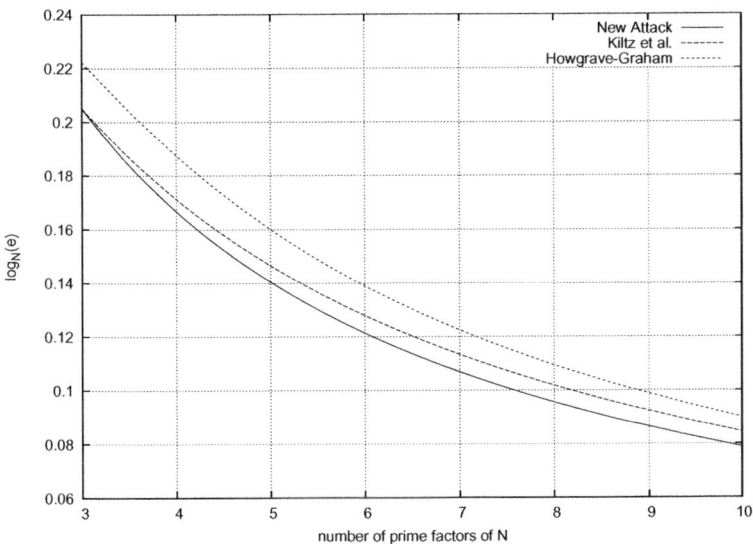

Fig. 1. Comparison of attacks on the Multi-Prime Φ-Hiding Problem

The size of the unknown solution $u_1^{(0)}$ is dominated by the term $e^{m-3}x_1 \cdots x_{m-1}$ which can be upper bounded by

$$|u_1^{(0)}| \leq N^{(m-3)\left(\frac{1}{m}-\delta\right)+(m-1)\delta} = N^{\frac{m-3}{m}+2\delta}.$$

For the solution $u_2^{(0)}$ we have as before $|u_2^{(0)}| \leq N^{\delta}$. Thus, with $n = 2$ and the size $\beta = \frac{m-1}{m}$ of the divisor $p_1 \cdots p_{m-1}$ we obtain by Theorem 1

$$\delta < \frac{2}{3\sqrt{m^3}} - \epsilon.$$

Let us compare this result with previous results on the Multi-Prime Φ-Hiding Problem. As mentioned in [KOS10], a straightforward approach is to restrict our attention to just one equation $ex_1 + 1 = 0 \bmod p_1$. This reveals with the theorem of Howgrave-Graham the bound $\delta < \frac{1}{m^2}$. We will call this *Howgrave-Graham attack*.

By expanding Equation (3) and introducing a dedicated variable for each monomial with coefficient e^i, Kiltz et al. end up with the bound[1]

$$\delta < \frac{2\left(\frac{1}{m}^{\frac{1}{m-1}} - \frac{1}{m}^{\frac{m}{m-1}}\right)}{m(m-1)} - \epsilon.$$

---

[1] Notice that the version from the Crypto 2010 proceedings has a minor mistake in the bound.

Figure 1 compares the resulting values of e for which the Multi-Prime Φ-Hiding Problem is efficiently solvable, i.e. $\log_N e \geq \frac{1}{m} - \delta$ for δ given by the different attacks. Note that all values of e that lie above the respective lines omit a polynomial time factorization attack. It is clearly visible that our new attack solves the Multi-Prime Φ-Hiding Problem for more values of e than the attack of [KOS10].

Thus, any concrete parameters given in [KOS10] for instantiating RSA-OAEP that rely on the Multi-Prime Φ-Hiding Assumption should be appropriately adjusted to withstand our new attack.

Remark 1. *The attack that we described performs a linearization to obtain a bivariate polynomial. Also, the linearization introduces a large variable u_1 and a small variable u_2. A straightforward calculation shows that balancing the variables as well as allowing for more variables worsens the bound.*

4   Future Work and Open Problems

We are convinced that there is still room for improvement in attacking the Multi-Prime Φ-Hiding Problem with Coppersmith-type attacks. One reason for this conjecture is that Theorem 1 is specifically designed for balanced variables, i.e. it is optimized to find solutions that are approximately of the same size. As stated in [HM08] the bound of Theorem 1 can be improved for unbalanced variables if the underlying lattice construction is properly adjusted. Thus, the attack given by [KOS10] can probably be improved by considering this. For an arbitrary number of variables, however, it is quite complicated to derive a general bound including the sizes of the variables. Nevertheless, in the current scenario the bounds on the solutions admit a particular structure. Namely, they form a simple increasing sequence $N^\delta, N^{2\delta}, \ldots$. It might be possible to exploit this relation in the lattice construction in order to find an expression for δ as a function of β and the number of variables n.

Another reason for conjecturing a possible improvement is the fact that the current attack is does not fully exploit the relation between the coefficients of the polynomial. Take for example Equation (2).

$$e^2 \underbrace{(ex_1x_2x_3 + x_1x_2 + x_1x_3 + x_2x_3)}_{u_1} + e \underbrace{(x_1 + x_2 + x_3)}_{u_2} + 1 = 0 \bmod p_1p_2p_3.$$

Our attack is based on the observation that e^3 and e^2 share a large common divisor, but we do not make use of the fact that they are actually both powers of e. Furthermore, the term $(x_1 + x_2 + x_3)$ has also coefficient e which is not used in our attack in any way. Note that the ability to exploit a relation between the coefficients of a polynomial in a Coppersmith-type attack would give an answer to an open question posed in [HM09] concerning RSA-based pseudo random number generators.

References

[Cac99]   Cachin, C.: Efficient private bidding and auctions with an oblivious third party. In: ACM Conference on Computer and Communications Security, pp. 120–127 (1999)

[CMS99]   Cachin, C., Micali, S., Stadler, M.: Computationally Private Information Retrieval with Polylogarithmic Communication. In: Stern, J. (ed.) EURO-CRYPT 1999. LNCS, vol. 1592, pp. 402–414. Springer, Heidelberg (1999)

[Cop96]   Coppersmith, D.: Finding a small root of a bivariate integer equation; factoring with high bits known. In: Maurer, U.M. (ed.) EUROCRYPT 1996. LNCS, vol. 1070, pp. 178–189. Springer, Heidelberg (1996)

[Cop97]   Coppersmith, D.: Small solutions to polynomial equations, and low exponent rsa vulnerabilities. J. Cryptology 10(4), 233–260 (1997)

[GMR05]   Gentry, C., MacKenzie, P.D., Ramzan, Z.: Password authenticated key exchange using hidden smooth subgroups. In: Atluri, V., Meadows, C., Juels, A. (eds.) ACM Conference on Computer and Communications Security, pp. 299–309. ACM, New York (2005)

[GR05]   Gentry, C., Ramzan, Z.: Single-database private information retrieval with constant communication rate. In: Caires, L., Italiano, G.F., Monteiro, L., Palamidessi, C., Yung, M. (eds.) ICALP 2005. LNCS, vol. 3580, pp. 803–815. Springer, Heidelberg (2005)

[HG97]   Howgrave-Graham, N.: Finding small roots of univariate modular equations revisited. In: Darnell, M.J. (ed.) Cryptography and Coding 1997. LNCS, vol. 1355, pp. 131–142. Springer, Heidelberg (1997)

[HM08]   Herrmann, M., May, A.: Solving linear equations modulo divisors: On factoring given any bits. In: Pieprzyk (ed.) (Pie2008), pp. 406–424 (2008)

[HM09]   Herrmann, M., May, A.: Attacking power generators using unravelled linearization: When do we output too much? In: Matsui, M. (ed.) ASIACRYPT 2009. LNCS, vol. 5912, pp. 487–504. Springer, Heidelberg (2009)

[HO08]   Hemenway, B., Ostrovsky, R.: Public-key locally-decodable codes. In: Wagner, D. (ed.) CRYPTO 2008. LNCS, vol. 5157, pp. 126–143. Springer, Heidelberg (2008)

[KOS10]   Kiltz, E., O'Neill, A., Smith, A.: Instantiability of RSA-OAEP under Chosen-Plaintext Attack. In: Rabin, T. (ed.) CRYPTO 2010. LNCS, vol. 6223, pp. 295–313. Springer, Heidelberg (2010)

[Pie08]   Pieprzyk, J. (ed.): ASIACRYPT 2008. LNCS, vol. 5350. Springer, Heidelberg (2008)

[SF08]   Schridde, C., Freisleben, B.: On the validity of the phi-hiding assumption in cryptographic protocols. In: Pieprzyk (ed.) (Pie2008), pp. 344–354 (2008)

[Tak98]   Takagi, T.: Fast RSA-type cryptosystem modulo $p^k q$. In: Krawczyk, H. (ed.) CRYPTO 1998. LNCS, vol. 1462, pp. 318–326. Springer, Heidelberg (1998)

FPGA Implementation of a Statistical Saturation Attack against PRESENT

Stéphanie Kerckhof, Baudoin Collard, and François-Xavier Standaert

UCL Crypto Group, Université catholique de Louvain,
Place du Levant 3, B-1348, Louvain-la-Neuve, Belgium
{stephanie.kerckhof,baudoin.collard,fstandae@uclouvain.be}

Abstract. Statistical attacks against block ciphers usually exploit "characteristics". A characteristic essentially defines a relation between (parts of) the block cipher's inputs, outputs and intermediate values. Intuitively, a good characteristic is one for which the relation between the cipher's inputs and outputs exhibit a significant deviation from the uniform distribution. Due to its intensive computational complexity, the search for good characteristics generally relies on heuristics, e.g. based on a branch-and-bound algorithm. But the use of such heuristics directly raises the question whether these good characteristics remain good, as the number of cipher rounds increases. This question relates to the so-called hull effect, expressing the idea that in a practically secure cipher, only the combination of many characteristics can explain the statistical deviations exploited in cryptanalysis. As characteristics are also a central tool when estimating the data complexities of statistical attacks, determining whether a hull effect can be observed is essential in the security evaluation of a block cipher. Unfortunately, this is again a computationally intensive task, as it ideally requires to sample over the full input space. In this paper, we consequently discuss the interest of hardware assistance, in order to improve the understanding of statistical attacks against block ciphers. More precisely, we propose an FPGA design that allowed us to evaluate a statistical saturation attack against the block cipher PRESENT, for overall complexities up to 2^{50}. Compared to previous software solutions, it corresponds to an increase of the maximum data complexity experimentally reached up to now by a factor 2^{14}. Our experiments confirm that up to 19 rounds of PRESENT can be broken with 2^{48} plaintext/ciphertext pairs. They also serve as a basis for discussing the statistical hull effect and suggest that 31-round PRESENT should be safe against such statistical attacks.

1   Introduction

Since its publication in 2007, PRESENT has been one of the most carefully investigated low cost ciphers. Several papers have analyzed its security against different types of cryptanalysis. Starting in 2008, Wang presented a differential cryptanalysis of reduced round PRESENT, allowing one to attack 16 rounds (out of 31), with 2^{64} chosen plaintexts [23] (these results have been recently re-discussed in an IACR ePrint report [15]). The same year, Z'aba et al. presented a

A. Nitaj and D. Pointcheval (Eds.): AFRICACRYPT 2011, LNCS 6737, pp. 100–116, 2011.
© Springer-Verlag Berlin Heidelberg 2011

bit-pattern integral attack that was able to break up to 7 rounds of PRESENT-128 (the 128-bit key version of the cipher), with 2^{24} chosen plaintexts, and a significant time complexity of 2^{100} partial decryptions [25]. This paper extended previous works on square (aka integral, aka saturation) attacks to ciphers with bit-oriented transforms. Different additional results appeared in 2009. In [19], Nakahara et al. analyzed the security of PRESENT-128 against attacks based on the linear hull effect, claiming to break 25-rounds of PRESENT-128 with the full codebook (again with a time complexity of approximately 2^{100}). They also experimented a purely algebraic attack able to break 5 rounds of PRESENT with 5 known plaintexts (and a few minutes of offline computations). In parallel, Ohkuma presented another linear attack against 24 rounds of PRESENT (80-bit version), with the full codebook, taking advantage of the linear hull effect for a certain class of weak keys [21]. Related-key cryptanalysis of PRESENT was additionally investigated in [22], for 17 rounds. And in a paper from FSE 2009 [1], dedicated to the combination of algebraic and differential cryptanalysis, Albrecht and Cid proposed various attacks against reduced versions of PRESENT. For example, they described a 16-round attack with complexities similar to the ones in [23]. More recently, Cho proposed a multidimensional linear attack, claiming to recover the 80-bit secret key of PRESENT for 25 rounds, with the full codebook [5]. Different empirical evaluations of reduced-round variants (with 6,7,8,9 rounds) were proposed in the paper, allowing to put forward the interest of the multidimensional approach. One can also mention the experiments of Blondeau and Gérard [3], used to confirm their theoretical analysis of differential cryptanalysis. Finally, the statistical saturation attack we experiment in this work has been introduced in [6] and then extended to multiple trails at ACNS 2010 [7].

As usual in cryptanalysis, one limitation shared by most of these previous works is that their estimated data complexity strongly relies on assumptions that may not be fulfilled, as the number of rounds in a block cipher increases. For example, security evaluations against linear cryptanalyses usually exploit Matsui's piling up lemma [18], that simply multiplies the linear biases of single-round linear approximations. A straightforward application of the lemma leads to the counter-intuition that increasing the number of rounds in a cipher may arbitrarily increase its security against linear attacks (as the bias can then be arbitrarily close to zero). In fact, as first explained by Nyberg in 1994 [20], correct estimations of the data complexity in a block cipher require to consider linear hulls (i.e. sets of linear characteristics sharing the same input/output masks). Yet, in practice, the number of characteristics in a hull increases exponentially with the number of rounds, and is rapidly impossible to exploit. Hence, present cipher designs, such as the AES Rijndael, are frequently based on the paradigm of practical security. That is, one assumes that a cipher is secure against linear cryptanalysis if the data complexity determined from the best characteristic in a cipher is prohibitive [14]. And excepted for the investigations of Keliher et al. in [12,13], and the investigations of small scale variants of block ciphers, in [8], few experimental works tackled the problem of determining how many block cipher rounds are actually needed for the linear hull effect to be significant.

In other words, most experiments against real world ciphers consider number of rounds for which the statistical deviations can still be explained by one (or few) characteristics. Such a limitation is typically exemplified by the statistical saturation attack against PRESENT, that can be viewed as a particular case of the multidimensional cryptanalysis described in [11] (see the recent work of Leander [17]). Hence, it is natural to question the validity of the data complexity estimations for large number of rounds, as given in [6].

In this paper, we consequently provide two contributions to the cryptanalysis of the block cipher PRESENT. First, starting from the observation that experimental validation is still a useful step for increasing our understanding of statistical attacks, we investigate the computational power that can be gained by outsourcing parts of the computations to a dedicated hardware platform. For this purpose, we developed a hardware-software co-design, based on an FPGA board, allowing us to accelerate the most consuming tasks of a statistical saturation attack against PRESENT, while keeping the communication rate between the different parts of the system reasonable. We note that the design is generic, and could easily be modified to investigate similar attacks, e.g. linear or differential. Our results include an investigation of different implementation tradeoffs and technologies, together with one fully functional prototype, based on a Xilinx Virtex-5 device. Second, we used our co-design to launch large-scale experimental attacks against 15,16,17 and 18-round PRESENT, with data complexities of up to 2^{48} per attack. These experiments confirmed the previous analyzes from [6], i.e. a data complexity increase by a factor of 2^3 per round, for up to 18 rounds of PRESENT (up to 19 rounds, if a two-round partial decryption is used). By providing a careful investigation of the statistical distributions exploited in the attack, and their key-dependent behavior, our results also allow discussing the apparition of a statistical hull effect in PRESENT on a concrete basis. They suggest that 31 rounds of PRESENT should be safe against statistical attacks. We finally conclude the paper by proposing directions for better selecting the number of rounds in a block cipher.

2   Background

2.1   The Block Cipher PRESENT

PRESENT is an ultra-lightweight block cipher designed for hardware constrained environments, such as RFID tags and sensor networks. It is a 31-round SPN (Substitution Permutation Network), and it was introduced by Bogdanov et al. at CHES 2007 [4]. The block length is 64 bits and the possible key lengths are 80 and 128 bits. Each of the 31 rounds is composed of a XOR operation, a nonlinear substitution layer and a permutation layer, operating as follows. First, the 64-bit input of the round is XORed with the round subkey. The result of that operation is then passed through the substitution layer, which consists of 16 identical 4x4 S-boxes applied in parallel. Finally, the permutation layer performs a bit-by-bit permutation.

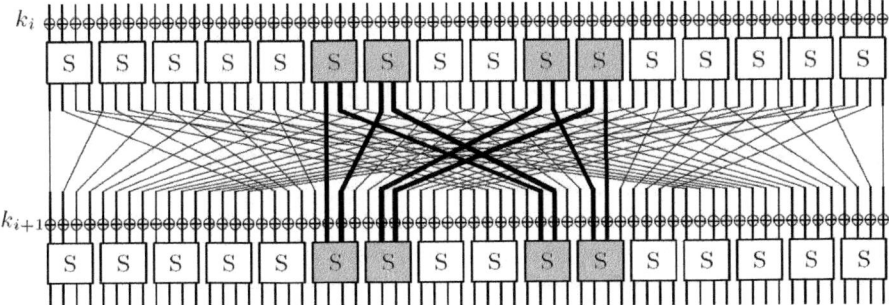

Fig. 1. Weakness of the diffusion property of the PRESENT

2.2 Statistical Saturation Attacks

The statistical saturation attack, originally described in [6], is based on a weakness in the diffusion layer of PRESENT. This weakness can be observed in Figure 1, where it is shown that only 8 out of the 16 output bits of S-boxes 5, 6, 9 and 10 are directed to other S-boxes. Hence, by fixing certain plaintext bits, we are able to observe a non-uniform distribution at the output of the round. Since the input and output bits of the bold trail highlighted in the figure are the same, it is then possible to iterate this weakness for several rounds. In order to turn this weakness into a key recovery attack, one finally assumes that the distribution at the output of the trail remains significantly different from uniform as the number of rounds increases. Hence, by doing a partial decryption through the last encryption round, one can select the key candidate that maximizes the Euclidean distance between the experimental distributions obtained for all the key candidates and the uniform one. If the attack is successful, the key maximizing this distance is the correct one. In the following of the paper, we focus ourselves on two variations of the basic attack, denoted as Extension 1 and Extension 2 in [6]. First, we enlarged the fixed part of the plaintext to 32 bits, in order to increase the non-uniformness of the target distributions. Second, we performed the analysis multiple times, using different values for the 32-bit fixed part of the plaintexts. In other words, we carried out many sub-attacks obtained from sets of 2^{32} varying plaintexts, for different fixed input patterns. Then, for each key candidate, we re-combined the results, by simply taking the sum of the uniform vs. measured distances given by these different 32-bit sub-attacks.

3   Hardware Architecture

As described in the previous section, a statistical saturation attack is composed of three phases. First, a large number of plaintexts are encrypted and the corresponding ciphertexts are collected. Then, a distribution is computed from the resulting ciphertexts. Finally, given this experimental distribution, a partial decryption is processed and the resulting $R-1$-round distributions are tested w.r.t.

uniform. From these three phases, the encryption part is the most time consuming one. On the contrary, the time needed by the partial decryption is not really critical. Therefore, we first decided to implement the PRESENT encryption in hardware, letting the partial decryption task to a software. Next, regarding the distribution generation, we also chose to implement it in hardware, for data rate reasons. As will be clear in section 3.2, our implementation of PRESENT has a huge output bitrate. Implementing the distribution generation in hardware allows us to reduce the output bitrate of our FPGA by a factor of 2^{24} (see section 3.3). Note finally that we did not implement the key schedule in hardware. The keys are generated by a software and provided to the FPGA by an Ethernet port. In the remaining of the section, we will first describe the FPGA technology we used for our implementations. We will then detail the architecture choices we made for the PRESENT encryption and distribution generation. We conclude the section with an overview of the complete system and a description of its performances.

3.1   Hardware Technology

The technologies we used to implement our architecture are Virtex-5 [24] and Virtex-6 FPGAs from Xilinx. The main logic resources of those FPGAs are the CLBs (Configurable Logic Bloc). Those CLBs are divided into two slices which are themselves composed of four logic-function generators (or look-up tables), four storage elements, wide-function multiplexers, and carry logic. These elements are used by all slices to provide logic, arithmetic, and ROM functions. In addition to this, some slices support two additional functions: storing data using distributed RAM and shifting data with 32-bit registers. Slices that support these additional functions are called SLICEM; others are called SLICEL. Figure 2 illustrates a SLICEL. The function generators in Virtex-5 FPGAs are implemented as 6-input look-up tables (LUTs). Each LUT possess 6 independent inputs (A1 to A6) and 2 independent outputs (O5 and O6). It can either implement any arbitrarily defined six-input Boolean function (only O6 is used in this case) or two arbitrarily defined five-input Boolean functions, as long as these two functions share common inputs (both O5 and O6 are used in this case). Signals from the function generators can exit the slice (through A, B, C, D output for O6 or AMUX, BMUX, CMUX, DMUX output for O5), enter the XOR dedicated gate from an O6 output, enter the carry-logic chain from an O5 output, enter the select line of the carry-logic multiplexer from O6 output, feed the D input of the storage element, or go to F7 multiplexers from O6 output. Slices also contain three multiplexers (F7 and F8) that can be used to combine up to four function generators and provide any function of seven or eight inputs in a slice. The storage elements in a slice can be configured as either edge-triggered D-type flip-flops or level-sensitive latches. The D input can be driven directly by a LUT output or by the AX, BX, CX, or DX slice inputs bypassing the function generators. The slices composing a Virtex-6 FPGA are quite similar to those of a Virtex-5. The major difference comes from the possibility to register both LUTs outputs (O5 and O6) in separate flip-flops. Finally, in addition to distributed

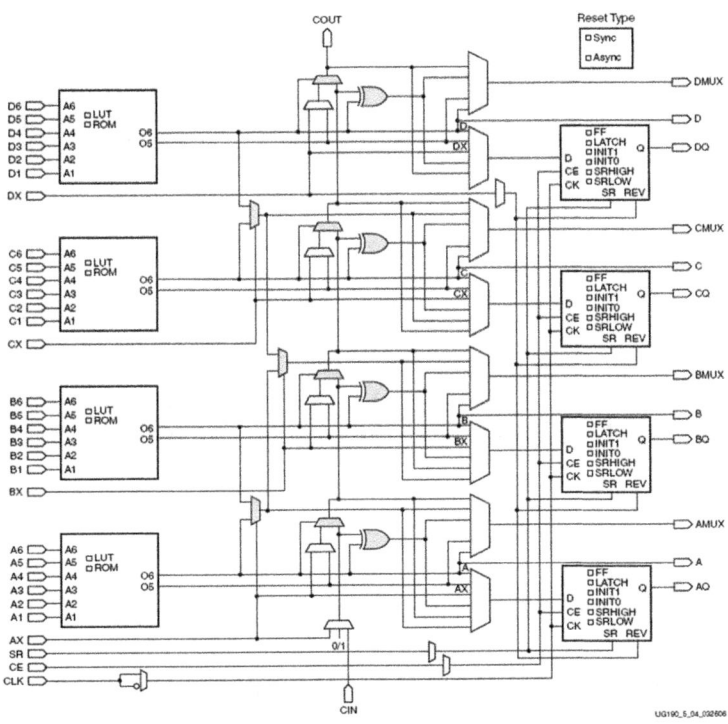

Fig. 2. Diagram of a SLICEL

RAM, Virtex-5 and -6 FPGAs include a large number of 36 Kb block RAMs. Each 36 Kb block RAM contains two independently controlled 18 Kb RAMs.

3.2   PRESENT Architecture

PRESENT was originally designed to be extremely low cost and easy to implement in hardware. Therefore, the resources needed by a round of PRESENT are quite limited. In this section we will focus on the XOR and S-boxes layers, the permutation layer resulting only in routing which is not resource consuming from an FPGA implementation point of view. In order to determine the resources needed by a round of PRESENT, we first detail the resources consumed by the smallest relevant part of a round. This corresponds to one S-box and its corresponding XORed inputs, as depicted in left part of Figure 3.

As previously described, Virtex-5 FPGAs are based on slices composed of four 6-bit LUTs and four 1-bit registers. Therefore, an optimal way to reduce the LUTs used is to regroup all the logical operations in order to obtain a minimum number of blocks that take 6-bit inputs and give 1-bit outputs. Furthermore, in order to be speed efficient, it is also recommended to limit the number of logic levels between two registers (a logic level corresponding to one LUT). The first

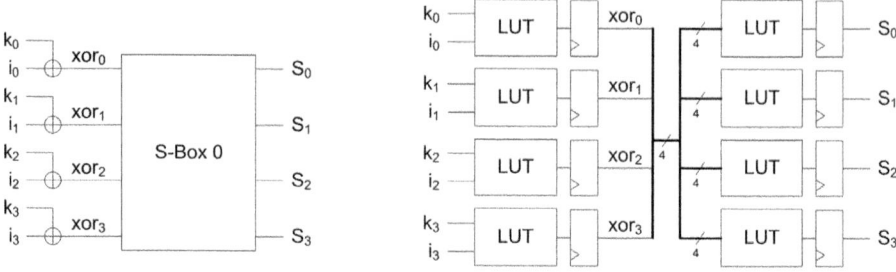

Fig. 3. Diagram of an S-box with its XORed inputs (left), equivalent LUT representation (right)

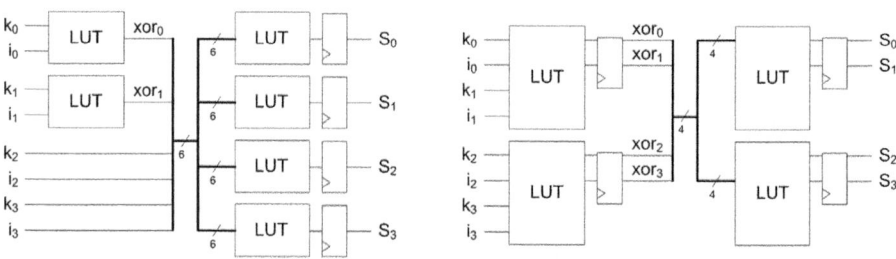

Fig. 4. VIRTEX-5 (left) and VIRTEX-6 (right) LUT representations of a round part

possible way of implementing the combination of one S-box and four XOR operations in hardware is to limit our architecture to only one level of logic between two registers. Here, one LUT is needed per XOR operation and four LUTs are needed for the S-box (see right part of Figure 3). Even if, this architecture is the most speed efficient, it is also the most resource consuming.

A second possibility is to combine some of the XOR operations with the S-box, as illustrated in left part of Figure 4. The number of LUTs needed by this architecture is decreased by two in comparison with the previous one. However, it is now composed of two levels of logic between two consecutive registers.

Finally, Virtex-6 FPGAs have two times more registers than Virtex-5 ones. This gives the possibility to store the two outputs of each LUT. Therefore, to reduce the number of used LUTs, we now need to regroup all logic to either form blocks that takes 6-bit input and 1-bit output, or blocks sharing 5 identical input bits, with 2-bit output. As illustrated in the right part of Figure 4, the number of needed LUTs to implement an S-box and four bitwise XOR is now only four. We indeed combined two XOR operations in a single LUT and the S-box in two of them.

To implement a round of PRESENT, the previous blocks must be repeated 16 times. 64-bit key registers are also needed for each round. In order to be speed efficient, we decided to fully unroll PRESENT, which allows us to encrypt a new plaintext every clock cycle. The implementation results for a 32-round PRESENT are given in Table 1, where V5 - 64 stages is the Virtex-5 design

Table 1. Implementation characteristics of 32-rounds PRESENT

	V5 - 64 stages	V5 - 32 stages	V6 - 64 stages
LUTs	4077	3086	3130
Registers	6177	4162	6177
Slices	1561	1420	819
Max. Frequency	588 MHz	470 MHz	588 MHz
Bitrate	35 Gbps	28 Gbps	35 Gbps

having two levels of registers per round, and V5 - 32 stages is the design having only one such level. These results confirm that the Virtex-5 architecture with 32 stages needs almost 2000 registers less than than the one with 64 stages. The maximum frequency also decreases from one architecture to the other. However, the frequency that can be reached by the 32-stages architecture is more than sufficient as we will later choose to run our complete design at a frequency of 125 MHz (see section 3.4), corresponding to a bitrate of 7,5 Gbps. Results obtained with Virtex-6 FPGAs are even better than those obtained with Virtex-5. The number of slices needed with Virtex-6 is almost half the one needed by the V5 - 64 stages architecture, while the maximum frequency is the same. However, the board on which the experimental tests were performed is a Virtex-5 one and we have therefore decided to use the V5 - 32 stages architecture for our design.

Note finally that the bitrate reachable with these different architectures is anyway far too high to be output by our FPGA interfaces. As previously said, a solution to avoid this interface issue is to compute the distributions on board in order to reduce the data rates, as it will be explained in next section.

3.3   Distribution Generator Architecture

The statistical saturation attack exploits the experimental distributions of a few chosen ciphertext bits. In particular, the trail in Figure 1 involves 16 output bits of which the distribution has to be partially decrypted. In order to decrease the size of the distributions to store in our FPGA implementation, our experiments are based on the analysis of two 8-bit distributions, corresponding to the output of S-boxes 5 and 9 for the first one, and S-boxes 6 and 10 for the second one. This is possible because the partial decryption needed in the key recovery phase can be applied independently for the two sets of S-boxes. A distribution generator was then used to compute those two distributions. Half of this generator is illustrated in Figure 5. It is composed of Virtex RAM blocks of 18 kilobits, an adder, different multiplexers, some additional logic, and essentially works as follows.

We first need 256 counters to compute each distribution and, because we chose to implement Extension 1 of the statistical saturation attack, the distribution has to be computed on 2^{32} ciphertexts, which corresponds to at most 32 bits per counter. Those counters are saved in a Virtex RAM block and are loaded by using the 8-bit ciphertext value as a RAM address. The loaded counter is then incremented and written back in memory. This whole process takes three clock cycles to be performed from the moment a ciphertext is available as RAM

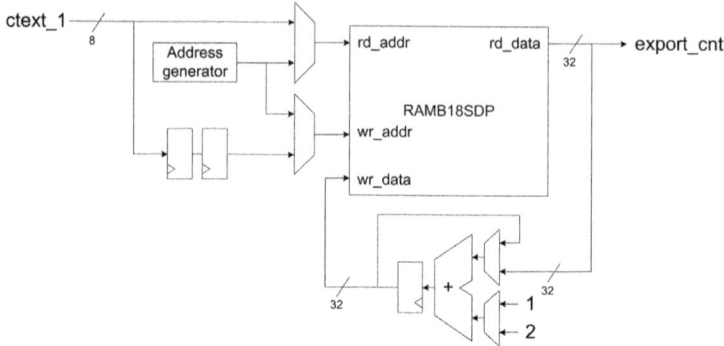

Fig. 5. Hardware architecture of half of the distribution generator

Table 2. Implementation characteristics of two 8-bit distribution computation

	Virtex-5	Virtex-6
LUTs	519	651
Registers	332	269
Slices	205	193
RAM (18 kb)	4	4
Max. Frequency	232 MHz	205 MHz

address to the moment the counter has been updated in RAM. However, to have a continuous flow between PRESENT and the distribution computation, we must be able to update the counters every clock cycle, which means that if at least two out of three consecutive ciphertexts values are identical, the counter in RAM must still be updated properly. For this reason, we added some logic before the adder, which gives us the opportunity to choose between the RAM output and the last incremented counter.

The 256 32-bit counters are exported once every 2^{32} clock cycles which corresponds to a decrease of PRESENT's output bitrate by a factor of 2^{24}. To avoid a loss of time during the exportation, we allocated two RAM blocks per distribution so that the second RAM is used for the computation of a new distribution while the first is being emptied and reset.

The implementation results for the complete distribution generators (composed of two of the illustrated parts) are given in Table 2. The maximum reachable frequency with the distribution generator is lower than the one we had with PRESENT. This is due to a higher number of logic levels between two registers. Indeed, we wanted to limit as much as possible the number of cycles needed to update a counter resulting in longer critical paths.

3.4 Complete Design

The complete design has been implemented on a Xilinx XUPV5 board from which we used the Ethernet port to communicate with a computer. It is

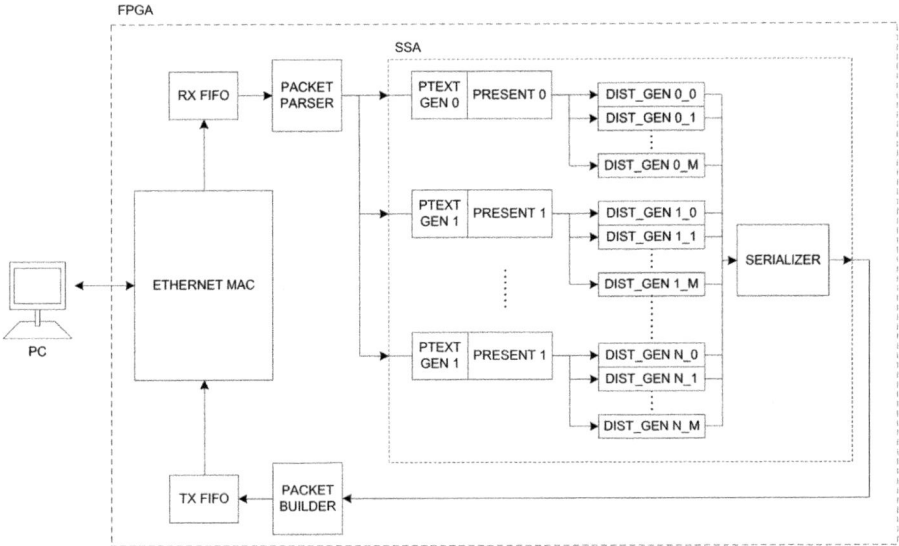

Fig. 6. Block diagram of the complete design

illustrated in Figure 6 and works as follows. First, controls such as round key values, destination MAC address and plaintext initial values are sent to the FPGA board through the Ethernet port. The received Ethernet packets are processed by the Ethernet Media Access Controller (MAC) and sent to an 8-bit width FIFO. A packet parser parallelizes the FIFO's output and sends the relevant information to the statistical saturation attack (SSA) block. The SSA block encrypts a large number of plaintexts and computes the corresponding distributions. The distributions are then sent to the packet builder in order to form Ethernet packets which are finally sent on an Ethernet link.

The FPGA available on our board is a Virtex-5 LX110T FPGA. The number of PRESENT blocks those FPGAs can contain depends on the number of rounds implemented per PRESENT block. For our experimentations, we used 18-round PRESENT and, in order to obtain more experimental results, we computed the distributions for four different rounds simultaneously. With this configuration, we would be able to fit up to 16 PRESENT blocks, and the 64 corresponding distribution generators in a single FPGA. However, due to timing problems during the synthesis of such a huge design, we decided to limit the final implementation to 8 PRESENT blocks and 32 distribution generators. We also decided to have an identical clock frequency for the complete design, which is the same as the one needed by the Ethernet MAC: 125 MHz. At that frequency, the complete design encrypts more than 2^{29} plaintexts per second and outputs 64 distributions (8 per PRESENT block) every 34 seconds.

4   Experimental Results

In this section, we take advantage of the previously described design in order to launch large scale experimental attacks against PRESENT. The goal of these experiments is twofold. First, we aim to challenge the theoretical data complexity estimations of the statistical saturation attack given in [6]. In particular, under some independence assumptions detailed in this previous work, it is expected that the data complexity of an attack exploiting the bold trail in Figure 1 increases by a factor of 2^3 per round. But as for linear cryptanalysis, this estimation should become incorrect as soon as a statistical hull effect starts to have a significant impact on the distributions of the ciphertexts. Next, we note that although the use of an FPGA board allows us to gain a significant computing power compared to previous software-based experiments, our results are still limited. Namely, we performed 5 attacks against 5 independent keys, and each of these attacks was bounded to a data complexity of 2^{48} (which is still far away from the codebook). These limitations are naturally justified by time constraints: each of our 5 attacks corresponds to 3.5 days of computations. It implies a limited sampling, both in terms of keys and plaintexts, that has to be considered in the interpretation of the results. Hence, we aim to take advantage of our experiments to discuss the hull effect in general, and whether it can be detected by experimentally sampling only a part of the plaintext space.

In the following, for each of the two 8-bit distributions exploited in the attack, we consider two main evaluation metrics. We first estimate the gain[1]. That is, if an attack is used to recover an n-bit key and is expected to return the correct key after having checked on the average M candidates, then the gain of the attack, expressed in bits, is defined as:

$$\lambda = -\log_2 \frac{2 \cdot M - 1}{2^n} \tag{1}$$

We provide gains averaged over the 5 experimented keys, for the two 8-bit distributions taken independently (in the left part of Figure 7), and their average (in the right part of the figure). Next, we provide estimates for the Euclidean distance between the partially decrypted output distributions and the uniform distributions. Distances are computed for the correct key candidate, and averaged for all the wrong key candidates, hence allowing to observe if the correct key candidate can be easily distinguished. These distances are again averaged over our 5 experiments. We also plot these distances for each tested key independently, in order to exhibit how their variance compares to the previous mean values. This second metric, computed for data complexities from 2^{32} to 2^{48}, and number of rounds from 15 to 18, is given in Figures 8, 9, 10, 11. We now detail some important observations that can be derived from these plots.

---

[1] Alternative metrics, such as the advantage used by Gérard and Tillich in [10], would allow deriving additional insights on the performances of the attacks, but are harder to estimate in view of our very limited sampling.

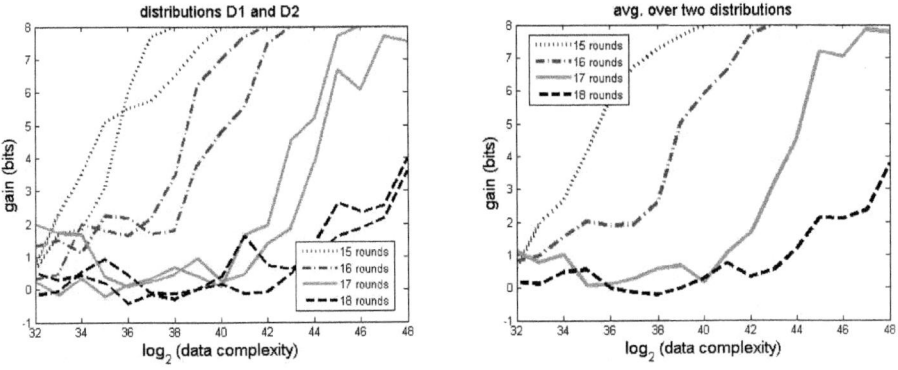

Fig. 7. Gains of the attacks

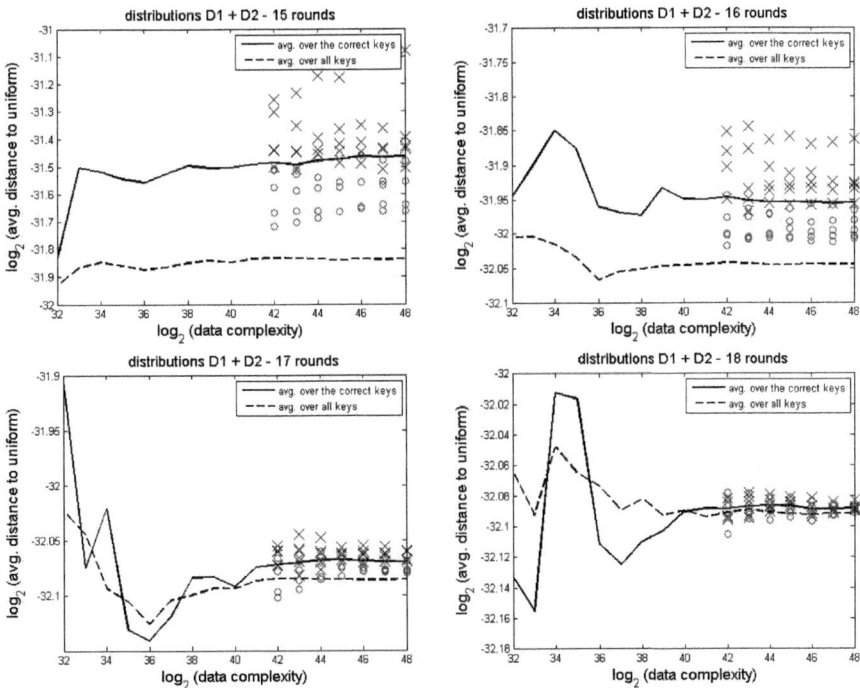

Fig. 8. Distance to uniform of the two distributions

First, regarding the gain pictures (Figure 7), one can see that the 2^3 multiplicative factor is quite accurately observed for up to 17 rounds. We also remark that the two investigated distributions do not behave exactly in the same way (this will be confirmed by the distance to uniform metric). As for the 18th round, a non-negligible gain can still be observed, but more sampling data would be required to analyze this setup with more confidence.

Regarding the distance to uniform metric, we again analyzed the combination of the two distributions (in Figure 8) and these distributions taken separately (see Figures 10 and 11, in appendix). The general observation, also confirming theoretical predictions, is that the distance between the average behavior of the correct key candidate and the average behavior of the wrong key candidates decreases with the number of rounds. In addition, we plotted this metric for the five correct key candidates of our experiments on the figures, for data complexities between 2^{42} and 2^{48} (with blues crosses for distribution D1 and red circles for distribution D2). One can notice that the scattering of these good key candidates becomes more important compared to the distance between the average curves on the plot, as the number of rounds increases. In other words, the problem of recovering the keys by distinguishing these distributions becomes more difficult. For round 18, this scattering even encompasses the two average curves[2].

Eventually, the central question behind these experiments is to know whether these plots indicate the apparition of a non-negligible hull effect for round 18. In other words, is the closeness between the correct and wrong key candidates due to such an effect or is it caused by a too small data complexity (the theoretical data complexity for attacking 18 rounds is 2^{51})? For answering this question, it is most interesting to observe the zoomed pictures of Figure 9. On the left part of the figure (i.e. for round 16), one can clearly see that the distributions D1 and D2 can be distinguished for all key candidates - even before the theoretical data complexity of 2^{45} is reached (this can be further observed from Figures 10 and 11 in appendix). By contrast, in the right part of the figure (i.e. for round 17), there is a significant overlap between the two distributions - in particular when the theoretical data complexity of 2^{48} is not reached. Referring to the small scale experiments in [8], this plot consequently suggests the apparition of a statistical hull effect, with distributions that become harder to distinguish and key dependent. We note again that these observations have to be taken with care, as they are based on visual inspection and not backed up with sufficient statistical confidence (again, due to the computationally intensive nature of our experiments).

5   Conclusion and Open Problems

This paper first highlights the interest of recent reconfigurable devices (FPGAs) in the context of statistical cryptanalysis. Such hardware assistance allowed us increasing the experimental data complexities reached in previous experiments[3], by a factor of 2^{14}. These important gains are due to the very convenient setting of most statistical cryptanalyses, in which one needs huge computing powers, with

---

[2] The average value of the distance to uniform metric is close to 2^{32}, independent of the number of rounds. This directly relates to the use of Extension 2 in our experiments. That is, we evaluate the combination of several sub-attacks of data complexity 2^{32}, where the combination of sub-attacks is performed by a (heuristic) sum of the average distances.

[3] The experiments presented in [6] reached a data complexity of $2^{35.6}$.

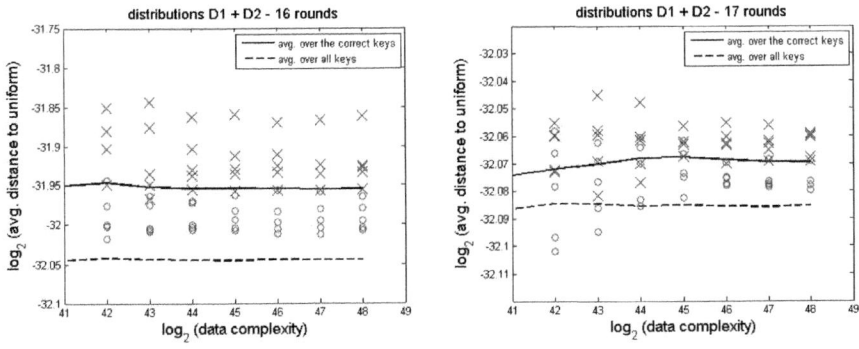

Fig. 9. Distance to uniform of the two distributions (zoom)

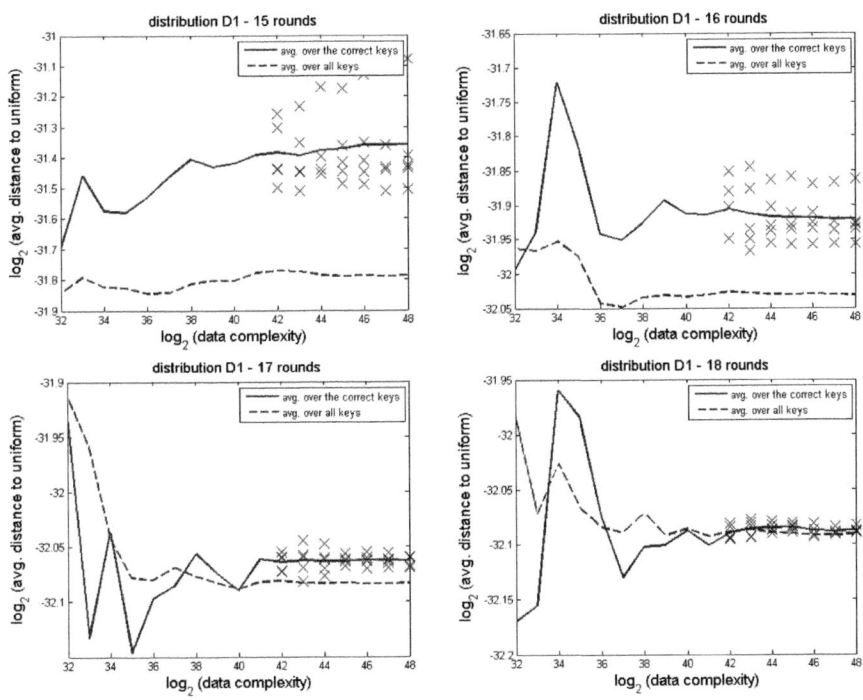

Fig. 10. Distance to uniform of distribution D1

limited connectivity between the hardware and software parts of the system. In this respect, the design proposed in this paper could possibly be improved to gain some (small) additional factors. Focusing our design on only one or two target rounds (rather than four in the present case) and moving to the more recent Virtex-6 technology are typical examples of such improvements. Exploiting

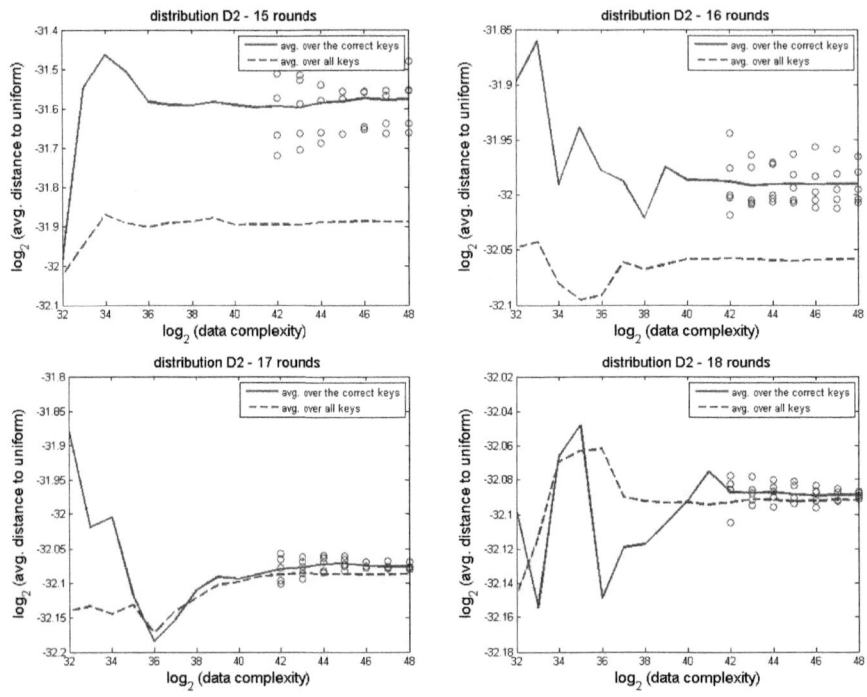

Fig. 11. Distance to uniform of distribution D2

FPGA-based platforms such as COPACOBANA [16] would also be an interesting direction of research. Note that although statistical attacks are well suited for FPGA implementations, other computing platforms could lead to similar speedups. As discussed, e.g. in [2] for the case of elliptic curves, cryptanalysis applications generally benefit from hybrid infrastructures (e.g. based on FPGAs, but also CPUs, GPUs, ASICs, . . .). As far as PRESENT is concerned, optimized implementations on these devices and cost comparisons with the FPGA design we propose in this paper would be another interesting scope for further research.

Next, our experiments confirm the previous theoretical predictions for statistical saturation attacks in [6,7], for up to 18 rounds (and 19 rounds if a two-round partial decryption process was considered). They also provide hints that a statistical hull effect is appearing after 18 rounds of PRESENT. Confirming this effect with more confidence would require analyzing a few more rounds and was not possible within our current computational limits. In particular, extending our experiments for 18 and 19 rounds, and complexities up to 2^{51}, would be interesting. Nevertheless, the evaluations in this paper suggest that assumptions required to theoretically estimate the data complexity of statistical saturation attacks may not be respected beyond 24 rounds. Since the statistical hull effect we consider in this paper is close to the linear hull effect considered in linear cryptanalysis, one should probably question the validity of statistical attacks targeting more than 24-round PRESENT in general. Note that this question also holds for differential cryptanalysis, although the combination of several characteristics always increases the differential probability, because of the key dependencies implied by such a combination.

Finally, in most current block ciphers, the number of rounds needed to resist statistical cryptanalyses is determined based on Knudsen's practical security paradigm. But a more accurate technique would be to determine exactly when the statistical hull effects start to be effective in a cipher. In general, solving this problem is highly computationally intensive. The results in this paper lead to the interesting question whether the hull effect could be detected by sampling less than the full plaintext/key space. In case of a positive answer, a very interesting scope for further research would be to quantify this observation with robust statistics, in order to derive a new criteria for selecting the number of rounds in block ciphers. Analyzing small-scale block ciphers that can be exhaustively evaluated against different attacks could be a first useful step in this direction.

Acknowledgements. Stéphanie Kerckhof is a PhD student funded by a FRIA grant, Belgium. François-Xavier Standaert is a research associate of the Belgian fund for scientific research (FNRS-F.R.S). Work funded in part by the Belgian State's IAP program P6/26 BCRYPT.

References

1. Albrecht, M., Cid, C.: Algebraic techniques in differential cryptanalysis. In: Dunkelman (ed.) [9], pp. 193–208 (2009)
2. Bailey, D.V., Batina, L., Bernstein, D.J., Birkner, P., Bos, J.W., Chen, H.-C., Cheng, C.-M., Damme, G.: v., Meulenaer, G.d., Perez, L.J.D., Fan, J., Güneysu, T., Gurkaynak, F., Kleinjung, T., Lange, T., Mentens, N., Niederhagen, R., Paar, C., Regazzoni, F., Schwabe, P., Uhsadel, L., Herrewege, A.V., Yang, B.-Y.: Breaking ecc2k-130. Cryptology ePrint Archive, Report 2009/541 (2009), http://eprint. iacr.org/
3. Blondeau, C., Gérard, B.: Links between theoretical and effective differential probabilities: Experiments on present. Cryptology ePrint Archive, Report 2010/261 (2010), http://eprint.iacr.org/
4. Bogdanov, A., Knudsen, L.R., Leander, G., Paar, C., Poschmann, A., Robshaw, M.J.B., Seurin, Y., Vikkelsoe, C.: Present: An ultra-lightweight block cipher. In: Paillier, P., Verbauwhede, I. (eds.) CHES 2007. LNCS, vol. 4727, pp. 450–466. Springer, Heidelberg (2007)
5. Cho, J.Y.: Linear cryptanalysis of reduced-round present. In: Pieprzyk, J. (ed.) CT-RSA 2010. LNCS, vol. 5985, pp. 302–317. Springer, Heidelberg (2010)
6. Collard, B., Standaert, F.-X.: A statistical saturation attack against the block cipher present. In: Fischlin, M. (ed.) CT-RSA 2009. LNCS, vol. 5473, pp. 195–210. Springer, Heidelberg (2009)
7. Collard, B., Standaert, F.-X.: Multi-trail statistical saturation attacks. In: Zhou, J., Yung, M. (eds.) ACNS 2010. LNCS, vol. 6123, pp. 123–138. Springer, Heidelberg (2010)
8. Collard, B., Standaert, F.-X.: Experimenting linear cryptanalysis. To appear in Advanced Linear Cryptanalysis (book chapter). IOS Press, Italy (2011)

9. Dunkelman, O. (ed.): FSE 2009. LNCS, vol. 5665. Springer, Heidelberg (2009)
10. Gérard, B., Tillich, J.-P.: On linear cryptanalysis with many linear approximations. In: Parker, M.G. (ed.) Cryptography and Coding 2009. LNCS, vol. 5921, pp. 112–132. Springer, Heidelberg (2009)
11. Hermelin, M., Cho, J.Y., Nyberg, K.: Multidimensional extension of matsui's algorithm 2. In: Dunkelman (ed.) [9], pp. 209–227
12. Keliher, L., Meijer, H., Tavares, S.E.: Improving the upper bound on the maximum average linear hull probability for rijndael. In: Vaudenay, S., Youssef, A.M. (eds.) SAC 2001. LNCS, vol. 2259, pp. 112–128. Springer, Heidelberg (2001)
13. Keliher, L., Meijer, H., Tavares, S.E.: New method for upper bounding the maximum average linear hull probability for spns. In: Pfitzmann, B. (ed.) EUROCRYPT 2001. LNCS, vol. 2045, pp. 420–436. Springer, Heidelberg (2001)
14. Knudsen, L.R.: Practically secure feistel cyphers. In: Anderson, R.J. (ed.) FSE 1993. LNCS, vol. 809, pp. 211–221. Springer, Heidelberg (1994)
15. Kumar, M., Yadav, P., Kumari, M.: Flaws in differential cryptanalysis of reduced round present. Cryptology ePrint Archive, Report 2010/407 (2010), http://eprint.iacr.org/
16. Kumar, S., Paar, C., Pelzl, J., Pfeiffer, G., Schimmler, M.: Breaking ciphers with copacobana - a cost-optimized parallel code breaker. In: Goubin, L., Matsui, M. (eds.) CHES 2006. LNCS, vol. 4249, pp. 101–118. Springer, Heidelberg (2006)
17. Leander, G.: On linear hulls, statistical saturation attacks, present and a cryptanalysis of puffin. To Appear in the Proceedings of Eurocrypt 2011 (2011)
18. Matsui, M.: Linear cryptanalysis method for DES cipher. In: Helleseth, T. (ed.) EUROCRYPT 1993. LNCS, vol. 765, pp. 386–397. Springer, Heidelberg (1994)
19. Nakahara, J., Sepehrdad, P., Zhang, B., Wang, M.: Linear (Hull) and algebraic cryptanalysis of the block cipher PRESENT. In: Garay, J.A., Miyaji, A., Otsuka, A. (eds.) CANS 2009. LNCS, vol. 5888, pp. 58–75. Springer, Heidelberg (2009)
20. Nyberg, K.: Linear approximation of block ciphers. In: De Santis, A. (ed.) EUROCRYPT 1994. LNCS, vol. 950, pp. 439–444. Springer, Heidelberg (1995)
21. Ohkuma, K.: Weak keys of reduced-round present for linear cryptanalysis. In: Jacobson Jr., M.J., Rijmen, V., Safavi-Naini, R. (eds.) SAC 2009. LNCS, vol. 5867, pp. 249–265. Springer, Heidelberg (2009)
22. Özen, O., varaci, K., Tezcan, C., Kocair, Ç.: Lightweight block ciphers revisited: Cryptanalysis of reduced round PRESENT and HIGHT. In: Boyd, C., González Nieto, J.M. (eds.) ACISP 2009. LNCS, vol. 5594, pp. 90–107. Springer, Heidelberg (2009)
23. Wang, M.: Differential cryptanalysis of reduced-round present. In: Vaudenay, S. (ed.) AFRICACRYPT 2008. LNCS, vol. 5023, pp. 40–49. Springer, Heidelberg (2008)
24. Xilinx. Virtex-5 FPGA User Guide (2010), http://www.xilinx.com/support/documentation/user_guides/ug190.pdf
25. Z'aba, M.R., Raddum, H., Henricksen, M., Dawson, E.: Bit-pattern based integral attack. In: Nyberg, K. (ed.) FSE 2008. LNCS, vol. 5086, pp. 363–381. Springer, Heidelberg (2008)

Collisions of MMO-MD5 and Their Impact on Original MD5

Yu Sasaki

NTT Information Sharing Platform Laboratories, NTT Corporation,
3-9-11 Midoricho, Musashino-shi, Tokyo, 180-8585 Japan
sasaki.yu@lab.ntt.co.jp

Abstract. In this paper, we find collisions of MD5 in the Matyas-Meyer-Oseas mode and Miyaguchi-Preneel mode with a complexity of 2^{39} operations, which runs contrary to the cryptographer's belief that these modes are stronger against collision attacks than the Davies-Meyer mode due to the impossibility of the message modification. We then show that, our collision attack for the Matyas-Meyer-Oseas mode can give impact to some collision properties of the Davies-Meyer mode, which we call "free-start given-message collisions" and "NMAC colliding keys". These indicate that collisions of MMO-MD5 give some impacts on the original MD5. The attack is implemented on a PC and we present generated collisions of MMO-MD5.

Keywords: MD5, collision, Matyas-Meyer-Oseas, Davies-Meyer, Miyaguchi-Preneel, PGV, given-message collision, NMAC colliding keys.

1 Introduction

Hash functions are basic symmetric-key primitives widely used to support the security of various cryptographic systems such as digital signatures and digital fingerprintings. One of the most widely used hash functions is MD5 [1], which was designed by Rivest in 1991. There were two outstanding cryptanlayses of MD5 in early days; a free-start collision attack by den Boer and Bosselaers [2] and a semi-free-start collision attack by Dobbertin [3]. The most innovative attack on MD5 was a collision attack by Wang *et al.* in 2005 [4], which showed real collisions of MD5. Since then, many improved collision attacks have been proposed [5,6,7,8,9,10,11,12,13,14]. As far as we know, the most efficient attack by Xie and Feng [13] reports that the complexity for generating a collision is now within 2^{10} MD5 compressions. Xie and Feng also discovered the 1-block collision of MD5 [15,16]. On the other hand, there are many researches that explore other weaknesses of MD5 in applications e.g. attacks on NMAC and HMAC [17,18,19,20,21,22,23], on Challenge-and-Response protocols [24,25], on Certificate Authority in PKI [26,27], on cascaded combiners [28], and so on. In addition, preimage attacks have also been proposed recently [29,30,31,32]. As you can see, although MD5 has already been broken seriously, cryptanalysis of MD5 is still an active research topic even these days. In fact, investigating the

A. Nitaj and D. Pointcheval (Eds.): AFRICACRYPT 2011, LNCS 6737, pp. 117–133, 2011.
© Springer-Verlag Berlin Heidelberg 2011

security of MD5 more is important in order to be prepared for the situation where SHA-1 and SHA-2 [33] suddenly become vulnerable in the future.

Most of hash functions widely used in practice such as MD5, SHA-1, and SHA-2 are composed of block-ciphers. For example, the internal block-cipher of SHA-2 is called SHACAL-2 and was selected as a recommended block-cipher by NESSIE. These block-ciphers are then used to construct compression functions through the PGV mode-of-operations [34]. In PGV, twelve modes were shown to be secure, and which mode we should select is an important issue for the design of hash functions. (Twelve modes are listed in Fig. 2 in Appendix B.)

Among twelve secure PGV modes, three modes have specific names; Davies-Meyer (DM) mode [35, Algorithm 9.42], Matyas-Meyer-Oseas (MMO) mode [35, Algorithm 9.41], and Miyaguchi-Preneel mode [35, Algorithm 9.43]. Let us denote the encryption algorithm by using a block cipher E with a key K by E_K. Each mode constructs the compression function as follows[1].

$$\textbf{DM mode:} \quad CF(H_{N-1}, M_{N-1}) = E_{M_{N-1}}(H_{N-1}) \oplus H_{N-1},$$
$$\textbf{MMO mode:} \quad CF(H_{N-1}, M_{N-1}) = E_{H_{N-1}}(M_{N-1}) \oplus M_{N-1},$$
$$\textbf{Miyaguchi-Preneel:} \quad CF(H_{N-1}, M_{N-1}) = E_{H_{N-1}}(M_{N-1}) \oplus M_{N-1} \oplus H_{N-1}.$$

Many hash functions in practice, including MD5, adopt the DM mode. On the other hand, recently designed hash functions tend to adopt the MMO mode (e.g. Skein [36] and Lesamnta [37]) or Miyaguchi-Preneel mode (e.g. Whirlpool [38]). The followings are examples of the reasons to select the MMO mode or Miyaguchi-Preneel mode rather than the DM mode.

– The DM mode is known to be weak against message modification techniques proposed by Wang et al. [4,39], which adjust message values so that a part of differential path can be satisfied deterministically or with a high probability. In particular, block-ciphers with a weak key-schedule such as internal block-ciphers of the MD-family are weak against the message modification techniques. The MMO and Miyaguchi-Preneel modes can prevent the message modification because there is no input to intermediate steps which is under the full control by attackers.
– In the design of block-ciphers, designers often consider the security against attackers with the access to the plaintext and ciphertext but without the access to the key. Therefore, it is natural to regard a message to be hashed (chosen by attackers) as a plaintext and to regard a chaining variable (uncontrolled by attackers) as a key. Hence, it is natural to use the MMO mode or Miyaguchi-Preneel mode.

From the above discussion, changing the mode-of-operation from the DM mode to the MMO or Miyaguchi-Preneel modes may be a possible countermeasure against the previous collision attacks on the DM mode.

---

[1] In practice, if E is designed to use the modular addition, the feed-forward operation tends to be modular addition instead of XOR. The MD-family is an example of this case.

Our contributions. In this research, firstly, we present collision attacks on variants of MD5 whose mode-of-operation is replaced with the MMO mode and Miyaguchi-Preneel mode. Note that this attack can be performed with a complexity of the birthday attack in generic, hence it takes 2^{64} for MD5. However, for MD5, we observe that it can be performed with a complexity of 2^{48} with a free-start collision attack proposed by den Boer and Bosselaers [2]. We then further improve this complexity by applying a variant of the message modification technique.

In our approach, we first fix 4 consecutive intermediate chaining variables where sufficient conditions for the differential path are most condensed. Then, we compute the other steps, where the conditions are relatively sparse, and check whether all conditions are probabilistically satisfied or not[2]. Moreover, because flipping one bit of a chaining variable only impacts to limited number of bits in other variables within a few steps, we can adjust the values so that conditions in a few steps more are always satisfied. By optimizing the attack by hand, the complexity is reduced to approximately 2^{39} MD5 computations, and real collision values can be generated within a day by a standard PC.

In this research, secondly, we show that our collision attack in the MMO-mode gives some impacts on the security of the DM-mode using the same internal block-cipher. This indicates that the original MD5, which adopts the DM-mode, is also affected by our collision attack on MMO-MD5. The impacts are summarized below.

1. **Free-Start Given-Message Collisions on MD5:** For a given message M, we find a pair of initial values H_1 and H_2 such that $\mathrm{CF}(H_1, M) = \mathrm{CF}(H_2, M)$, where CF is a compression function of MD5. In other words, for a given message, we find a colliding pair by using the freedom of the initial value. Collisions starting from two different initial values are often called *free-start collisions*, and we thus call this attack free-start given-message collision attack.

2. **Given-Message Colliding Keys for NMAC-MD5:** NMAC [41] is a hash function based MAC algorithm using a pair of keys K_1 and K_2. If MD5 (with the DM-mode) is instantiated in NMAC, for any given message M, attackers can generate paired keys $K = (K_1, K_2)$ and $K' = (K'_1, K_2)$ which cause a collision of the NMAC Tag.

Organization. In Section 2, we describe the specification of MD5. In Section 3, we introduce related work. In Section 4, we give details of our collision attack on MD5 in the MMO and Miyaguchi-Preneel modes and the results of the machine experiment. In Section 5, we explain the impact of collisions in the MMO mode to the DM mode. Finally, in Section 6, we conclude this paper.

---

[2] The approach determining the values to satisfy the lowest probability part of the differential path has been taken by the rebound attack proposed by Mendel *et al.* [40].

2   Specifications and Notations

2.1   Description of MD5

MD5 [1] is a 128-bit hash function which adopts the Merkle-Damgård domain extension. At the first, an input message M is padded by the following procedure.

- Append a bit '1' to the end of M.
- Append a necessary number of '0's until the length becomes 448 mod 512.
- Append the 64-bit binary representation of the original length of M.

After that the padded message is divided into 512-bit blocks, M_i ($i = 0, 1, \ldots, N-1$). Then, the hash value is computed as follows:

$$\begin{cases} H_0 \leftarrow \text{IV}, \\ H_{i+1} \leftarrow \text{CF}(H_i, M_i) \qquad \text{for } i = 0, 1, \ldots, N-1, \end{cases}$$

where IV is the initial value defined in the specification, CF: $\{0,1\}^{128} \times \{0,1\}^{512} \rightarrow \{0,1\}^{128}$ is a compression function of MD5 and H_N is the hash value of M.

Compression function CF. The compression function of MD5 adopts the DM-mode of the block-cipher. In the DM-mode, the chaining variable H_i and the message M_i are used as a plaintext and a key of the block-cipher, respectively. Then, CF outputs a combination of a ciphertext and H_i. Let the internal block-cipher of MD5 be md5. In case of MD5, $\text{CF}(H_i, M_i)$ is defined as follows:

$$\text{CF}(H_i, M_i) = H_i + \text{md5}_{M_i}(H_i),$$

where '+' denotes an word-wise addition on modulo 2^{32}.

Block-cipher md5. md5 takes a 128-bit value H_i as a plaintext input and a 512-bit value M_i as a key input. At the first, the key M_i is divided into sixteen 32-bit values $m_0 \| m_1 \| \cdots \| m_{15}$. Then, by using 32-bit variables $Q_j, -3 \le j \le 64$, the ciphertext is computed as follows.

$$Q_{-3} \| Q_0 \| Q_{-1} \| Q_{-2} \leftarrow H_i,$$
$$Q_{j+1} \leftarrow R_j(Q_{j-3} \| Q_j \| Q_{j-1} \| Q_{j-2}, m_{\pi(j)}) \qquad \text{for } j = 0, 1, \ldots, 63,$$
$$\text{md5}_{M_i}(H_i) \leftarrow Q_{61} \| Q_{64} \| Q_{63} \| Q_{62}.$$

R_j is the step function for Step j which computes Q_{j+1} as follows:

$$Q_{j+1} \leftarrow Q_j + (Q_{j-3} + \Phi_j(Q_j, Q_{j-1}, Q_{j-2}) + m_{\pi(j)} + k_j) \lll s_j$$

where Φ_j, k_j, and $\lll s_j$ are the bitwise Boolean function, constant number, and left rotation by s_j-bits defined in the specification, respectively. $\pi(j)$ is a key expansion function. Details of Φ_j, s_j, and $\pi(j)$ are shown in Table 1. Note that, for a fixed message, $R_j^{-1}(Q_{j-2} \| Q_{j+1} \| Q_j \| Q_{j-1}, m_{\pi(j)})$ is computed by $Q_{j-3} \leftarrow ((Q_{j+1} - Q_j) \ggg s_j) - \Phi_j(Q_j, Q_{j-1}, Q_{j-2}) - m_{\pi(j)} - k_j$, where '−' denotes a word-wise subtraction on modulo 2^{32}.

Table 1. Boolean functions, rotation numbers, and key expansion of MD5

$\Phi_0, \Phi_1, \ldots, \Phi_{15}$	$\Phi_j(X,Y,Z) = (X \wedge Y) \vee (\neg X \wedge Z)$			
$\Phi_{16}, \Phi_{17}, \ldots, \Phi_{31}$	$\Phi_j(X,Y,Z) = (X \wedge Z) \vee (Y \wedge \neg Z)$			
$\Phi_{32}, \Phi_{33}, \ldots, \Phi_{47}$	$\Phi_j(X,Y,Z) = X \oplus Y \oplus Z$			
$\Phi_{48}, \Phi_{49}, \ldots, \Phi_{63}$	$\Phi_j(X,Y,Z) = Y \oplus (X \vee \neg Z)$			
$s_0, s_1, \ldots, s_{15}$	7 12 17 22	7 12 17 22	7 12 17 22	7 12 17 22
$s_{16}, s_{17}, \ldots, s_{31}$	5 9 14 20	5 9 14 20	5 9 14 20	5 9 14 20
$s_{32}, s_{33}, \ldots, s_{47}$	4 11 16 23	4 11 16 23	4 11 16 23	4 11 16 23
$s_{48}, s_{49}, \ldots, s_{63}$	6 10 15 21	6 10 15 21	6 10 15 21	6 10 15 21
$\pi(0), \pi(1), \ldots, \pi(15)$	0 1 2 3	4 5 6 7	8 9 10 11	12 13 14 15
$\pi(16), \pi(17), \ldots, \pi(31)$	1 6 11 0	5 10 15 4	9 14 3 8	13 2 7 12
$\pi(32), \pi(33), \ldots, \pi(47)$	5 8 11 14	1 4 7 10	13 0 3 6	9 12 15 2
$\pi(48), \pi(49), \ldots, \pi(63)$	0 7 14 5	12 3 10 1	8 15 6 13	4 11 2 9

2.2 MMO-MD5, Miyaguchi-Preneel-MD5, and Other PGV Modes

The PGV modes are ones for building a compression function. Hence, to define a hash function, we need to define a domain extension. In this research, we assume that the Merkle-Damgård domain extension is used as well as the original MD5.

In the MMO-mode, a chaining variable H_i is used as a key and a message M_i is used as a plaintext. The output is computed by $E_{H_i}(M_i) \oplus M_i$. Note that in the MD-family, the feed-forward operation is often performed in modular addition instead of XOR. To follow the convention, in this research, we assume that the modular addition is used for the feed-forward operation.

To use md5 in the MMO-mode, we need to adjust the length of the compression function's output and the key because the compression function's output is used as the key for the next block. The simplest way is to apply a padding procedure. In this research, we assume the zero-padding, which appends the necessary number of zeros in the end of the compression function's output. For example, the 128-bit IV is padded to the 512-bit message block IV$\|00\cdots 0$, and is used as the key for the first block. Similarly, compression functions based on the Miyaguchi-Preneel mode and the other PGV modes can be defined. In Fig. 2 in Appendix B, we list the all 12 secure PGV constructions.

3 Related Work

3.1 Free-Start Collision Attack on MD5

In 1993, den Boer and Bosselaers [2] showed an example of paired values (H_i, M_i) and (H_i', M_i) such that $\mathrm{CF}(H_i, M_i) = \mathrm{CF}(H_i', M_i)$. In this attack, H_i and H_i' have the following difference:

$$\Delta H_i = H_i \oplus H_i' = (\texttt{0x80000000}, \texttt{0x80000000}, \texttt{0x80000000}, \texttt{0x80000000}).$$

Hereafter, we denote this difference by Δ^{MSB}. To satisfy the differential path, 48 conditions on intermediate chaining variables shown below must be satisfied. (Hereafter, we use the notation $Q_{j,k}, 0 \leq k \leq 31$ to represent the k-th bit of Q_j.)

$$
\begin{aligned}
Q_{j-1,31} &= Q_{j-2,31} & \text{for } 0 \le j \le 15, \\
Q_{j,31} &= Q_{j-1,31} & \text{for } 16 \le j \le 31, \\
Q_{j,31} &= Q_{j-2,31} & \text{for } 48 \le j \le 63.
\end{aligned} \tag{1}
$$

den Boer and Bosselaers chose a message so that the first 16 conditions can be always satisfied, and succeeded in finding colliding pairs in practice.

3.2 Collision Attack on MD5

In 2005, Wang *et al.* proposed a collision attack on MD5 [4]. The overall strategy of their attack is as follows.

1. Identify a good differential path.
2. Identify sufficient conditions on the intermediate variables to satisfy the path.
3. Locate a message that satisfies all conditions by randomly generating messages and adjusting the message by the *message modification (MM)* so that a part of conditions are always satisfied.

In collision attacks, attackers can select the message of their choice, and thus, they can satisfy many sufficient conditions. On the other hand, for given-message collision attacks, attackers cannot choose or modify the message. Hence, MM cannot be used.

4 Collisions of MMO-MD5 and Miyaguchi-Preneel-MD5

In this section, we present collision attacks on variants of MD5 whose mode-of-operation is replaced with the MMO mode and Miyaguchi-Preneel mode. Namely, for a given initial value IV, find a pair of messages M_1 and M_2 such that $\mathrm{md5}_{h_1}(M_1) \boxplus M_1 = \mathrm{md5}_{h_1}(M_2) \boxplus M_2$ for the MMO mode and $\mathrm{md5}_{h_1}(M_1) \boxplus M_1 \boxplus h_1 = \mathrm{md5}_{h_1}(M_2) \boxplus M_2 \boxplus h_1$ for the Miyaguchi-Preneel mode. It is obvious that if collisions in the MMO-mode is obtained, collisions in the Miyaguchi-Preneel mode is also obtained. Hence, in this section, we mainly explain how to obtain collisions in the MMO-mode. A generic attack requires $2^{\frac{n}{2}}$ for an n-bit hash function, which is 2^{64} for MD5. Because computing 2^{64} is hard, we need to reduce the complexity. In this section, we explain how to efficiently obtain this collision.

4.1 Overall Strategy

At the first, we observe that the free-start-collision attack proposed by den Boer and Bosselaers (dBB-attack) [2] can be used to find collisions of MMO-MD5 faster than the brute force attack. Because the differential path of the dBB-attack contains 48 sufficient conditions and each condition is satisfied with a probability of 2^{-1}, the naïve search will require 2^{48} MD5 computations.

Moreover, we can choose the values of 4 consecutive intermediate chaining variables. We call these steps *Ini-steps*. Unfortunately, conditions for the dBB-attack are sparse, and we thus can satisfy up to 3 conditions. After we determine the values in Ini-steps, we compute the other steps in both forward and backward directions and check whether all conditions are satisfied or not. Therefore, at this stage, the complexity is reduced to 2^{45} MD5 computations.

Furthermore, if conditions are not satisfied within a few steps from Ini-steps, we can modify the values in Ini-steps so that these conditions will be satisfied. This idea is principally the same as the original message modification, but we use the freedom degrees of chaining variables and keep the given message unmodified. To make the difference clear, we call this modification *chaining variable modification (CVM)*. Due to CVM, we can guarantee that additional 5 conditions are satisfied with a probability close to 1, and one more condition is satisfied with a probability of 87.5%. In the end, in total 9 conditions can be satisfied with a probability of 87.5%. Because 39 conditions are left, the rough estimation of the attack complexity is 2^{39} MD5 computations.

Note that this is a rough estimation. De Cannière and Rechberger [42] introduced a method to precisely count the work factor of the differential path search algorithm. Briefly speaking, they consider the weight of conditions. Checking the conditions close to Ini-steps is cheaper than the ones far from Ini-steps. Because this evaluation can also be applied to our attack, the complexity of our attack is in fact less than 2^{39} MD5 computations.

4.2   Attack Procedure

In this attack, IV is a 128-bit fixed constant and given to the attacker. As was discussed in Sect. 2.2, IV is padded to be 512 bits, namely, 384-bit '0's are appended to IV. Inside the compression function, this padded IV is divided into sixteen message words $m_0\|m_1\|\cdots\|m_{15}$. The goal of the attack is to find a pair of messages $M_1 = Q_{-3}\|Q_0\|Q_{-1}\|Q_{-2}$ and $M_2 = Q'_{-3}\|Q'_0\|Q'_{-1}\|Q'_{-2}$.

In our attack, we choose Q_5, Q_6, Q_7, and Q_8 as chaining variables fixed in the Ini-step. This strategy is briefly explained in Sect 4.5. The entire attack procedure is described in Algorithm 1. We will explain details of CVM in Sect 4.3.

4.3   Chaining Variable Modification

The goal of CVM is to guarantee that conditions located within a few steps forward or backward from Ini-steps are satisfied with probability 1 or close to 1.

Wang *et al.*'s collision attack [4] can take an advantage of the freedom degrees in the message. Hence, attackers apply the MM, which modifies a few bits of a message so that the impact of the modification can propagate to the target bits and flip its value while other conditions are guaranteed not to be broken. On the other hand, in the given-message attack, attackers cannot modify the given message. Therefore, attackers modify a few bits of the values of Ini-steps and control the propagation of its impact so that only the target bit is flipped but other conditions are not broken. In the following sections, we explain examples of CVM.

Examples of simple CVM.   At Step 1 of Algorithm 1, we choose the values of Q_5, Q_6, Q_7, and Q_8. According to the conditions in equation 1, $Q_{5,31} = Q_{6,31} = Q_{7,31} = Q_{8,31}$. Therefore, we always choose the values which

Algorithm 1. Collision Attack on MMO-MD5

Input: an initial value IV, which also fixes $m_0, m_1, \ldots, m_{15}$.

Output: messages $M_1 = Q_{-3}\|Q_0\|Q_{-1}\|Q_{-2}$ and $M_2 = Q'_{-3}\|Q'_0\|Q'_{-1}\|Q'_{-2}$

1. Randomly choose $Q_5, \ldots, Q_8$ but satisfy all sufficient and extra conditions.
2. Compute $Q_4 \leftarrow R_7^{-1}(Q_5\|Q_8\|Q_7\|Q_6, m_{\pi(7)})$.
3. IF (a condition on Q_4 is not satisfied) { Do the CVM for Q_4.}
4. Compute $Q_9 \leftarrow R_8(Q_5\|Q_8\|Q_7\|Q_6, m_{\pi(8)})$.
5. IF (a condition on Q_9 is not satisfied) { Do the CVM for Q_9.}
6. Compute $Q_3 \leftarrow R_6^{-1}(Q_4\|Q_7\|Q_6\|Q_5, m_{\pi(6)})$.
7. IF (a condition on Q_3 is not satisfied) { Do the CVM for Q_3.}
8. Compute $Q_{10} \leftarrow R_9(Q_6\|Q_9\|Q_8\|Q_7, m_{\pi(9)})$.
9. IF (a condition on Q_{10} is not satisfied) { Do the CVM for Q_{10}.}
10. Compute $Q_2 \leftarrow R_5^{-1}(Q_3\|Q_6\|Q_5\|Q_4, m_{\pi(5)})$.
11. IF (a condition on Q_2 is not satisfied) { Do the CVM for Q_2.}
12. Compute $Q_1 \leftarrow R_4^{-1}(Q_2\|Q_5\|Q_4\|Q_3, m_{\pi(4)})$.
13. IF (a condition on Q_1 is not satisfied) { Do the CVM for Q_1.}
14. FOR ($N = 0$ to -3) DO {
15.   Compute $Q_N \leftarrow R_{N+3}^{-1}(Q_{N+1}\|Q_{N+4}\|Q_{N+3}\|Q_{N+2}, m_{\pi(N+3)})$.
16.   IF (a condition on Q_N is not satisfied) { GOTO Step 1.}
17. } END FOR
18. FOR ($N = 10$ to 63) DO {
19.   Compute $Q_{N+1} \leftarrow R_N(Q_{N-3}\|Q_N\|Q_{N-1}\|Q_{N-2}, m_{\pi(N)})$.
20.   IF (a condition on Q_{N+1} is not satisfied) { GOTO Step 1.}
21. } END FOR
22. Output $M_1 = (Q_{-3}\|Q_0\|Q_{-1}\|Q_{-2})$ and $M_2 = M_1 \oplus \Delta^{MSB}$.

Modification 1.	**Modification 2.**
Target bit: $Q_{4,31}$	Target bit: $Q_{9,31}$
Modifying bit: $Q_{7,21}$	Modifying bit: $Q_{5,24}$
Extra Condition: $Q_{6,21} = Q_{5,21}$	Extra Condition: $Q_{7,24} = 1$
1. IF ($Q_{4,31} \neq Q_{5,31}$) {	1. IF ($Q_{9,31} \neq Q_{8,31}$) {
2. $Q_7 \leftarrow Q_7 \oplus$ 0x00200000	2. $Q_5 \leftarrow Q_5 \oplus$ 0x01000000
3. $Q_4 \leftarrow R_7^{-1}(Q_5\|Q_8\|Q_7\|Q_6, m_{\pi(7)})$	3. $Q_9 \leftarrow R_8(Q_5\|Q_8\|Q_7\|Q_6, m_{\pi(8)})$
4. } END IF	4. } END IF

satisfy these conditions. Besides, later on, we set extra conditions on these variables. Hence, we choose values so that extra conditions are also satisfied.

Then, at Step 3 of Algorithm 1, we apply CVM if the condition $Q_{4,31} = Q_{5,31}$ is not satisfied. Hence, we need to flip the value of $Q_{4,31}$. The procedure to modify $Q_{4,31}$ is described in Modification 1.

In Modification 1, the goal is flipping the value of $Q_{4,31}$. The equation to compute Q_4 is as follows.

$$Q_4 = R_7^{-1}(Q_5\|Q_8\|Q_7\|Q_6, m_{\pi(7)})$$
$$= ((Q_8 - Q_7) \ggg 22) - \Phi_7(Q_7, Q_6, Q_5) - m_{\pi(7)} - k_7 \qquad (2)$$

If the value of $Q_{7,21}$ is modified, the MSB of $((Q_8 - Q_7) \ggg 22)$ will change, and this will flip the value of $Q_{4,31}$. However, it is necessary to consider the possibility where other changes caused by the modification of $Q_{7,21}$ will also propagate to $Q_{4,31}$ and thus the impact of two changes cancel each other. In equation 2, Q_7 also appears inside the function Φ_7. If the modification of $Q_{7,21}$ also changes the 21st bit of Φ_7, it will propagate to $Q_{4,31}$ with a probability of 2^{-10}. To avoid this, we set an extra condition as done in [4]. The property that the change of one input is ignored in Φ is called "absorption property." Refer to [31,4] for details of the absorption property of MD5. By considering this property, we set an extra condition $Q_{6,21} = Q_{5,21}$.

There is another possibility to cancel the impact to $Q_{4,31}$. If $Q_{7,21}$ is modified, the carry (borrow) may occur in the computation of $Q_8 - Q_7$, and thus, 22nd or upper bits of $Q_8 - Q_7$ may change. If so, the changed bits move to the LSB or several upper bits after the right rotation by 22 bits. The change in LSB can propagate $Q_{4,31}$ with a probability of 2^{-31}. In fact, we can prevent this propagation by setting more extra conditions. However, because the probability that the modification succeeds is $1 - 2^{-31} \approx 1$, we ignore this incident.

We show another example of the CVM in Modification 2, which makes the condition on $Q_{9,31}$ be satisfied. The overall concept is the same. A different point is that when we flip the value of $Q_{9,31}$, we need to take care that the already set conditions are not broken. This will increase the number of extra conditions needed. In fact, in Modification 2, the extra condition $Q_{7,24} = 1$ is set to ignore the change of the modifying bit in the computation for Q_4. However, how we set extra conditions is exactly the same as Modification 1, and this is straight-forward unless a contradiction occurs in the same bit position.

An example of complicated CVM. Due to the redundancy, we show the details of similar modifications in Appendix A. Here, we explain the CVM for $Q_{1,31}$, which succeeds only probabilistically. The procedure is shown in Modification 6. The impact of modifying $Q_{5,6}$ is as follows.

$$\underline{Q_1} = ((\underline{Q_5} - Q_4) \ggg 7) - \Phi(Q_4, Q_3, \underline{Q_2}) - m_{\pi(4)} - k_4 \qquad (3)$$

$$\underline{Q_2} = ((Q_6 - \underline{Q_5}) \ggg 12) - \Phi(\underline{Q_5}, Q_4, Q_3) - m_{\pi(5)} - k_5 \qquad (4)$$

$$Q_3 = ((Q_7 - Q_6) \ggg 17) - \Phi(Q_6, \underline{Q_5}, Q_4) - m_{\pi(6)} - k_6 \qquad (5)$$

$$Q_4 = ((Q_8 - Q_7) \ggg 22) - \Phi(Q_7, Q_6, \underline{Q_5}) - m_{\pi(7)} - k_7 \qquad (6)$$

$$\underline{Q_9} = (\underline{Q_5} + \Phi(Q_8, Q_7, Q_6) + m_{\pi(8)} + k_8) \lll 7 + Q_8 \qquad (7)$$

$$\underline{Q_{10}} = (Q_6 + \Phi(\underline{Q_9}, Q_8, Q_7) + m_{\pi(9)}) + k_9) \lll 12 + \underline{Q_9} \qquad (8)$$

In equations 3–8, the underlined variables are the ones influenced by modifying $Q_{5,6}$. For equations 6 and 5, the impact of the change is absorbed in Φ by setting extra conditions $Q_{7,6} = 1$ and $Q_{6,6} = 0$, respectively. In equation 4, modification of $Q_{5,6}$ will cause the change in 26-th or upper bits of Q_2 and may cause the change in 6-th or upper bits through Φ. The latter is not a serious problem because it is far from the MSB. However, the former will cancel the influence to $Q_{1,31}$ if the carry reaches the MSB. This probability is not negligible. On the

---

Modification 6.

Target bit: $Q_{1,31}$

Modifying bit: $Q_{5,6}$

Extra Condition: $Q_{6,6} = 0, Q_{7,6} = 1$

---

1. IF $(Q_{1,31} \neq Q_{2,31})$ {
2. $Q_5 \leftarrow Q_5 \oplus \text{0x00000040}$
3. $Q_2 \leftarrow R_5^{-1}(Q_3\|Q_6\|Q_5\|Q_4, m_{\pi(5)})$
4. $Q_1 \leftarrow R_4^{-1}(Q_2\|Q_5\|Q_4\|Q_3, m_{\pi(4)})$
5. $Q_9 \leftarrow R_8(Q_5\|Q_8\|Q_7\|Q_6, m_{\pi(8)})$
6. $Q_{10} \leftarrow R_9(Q_6\|Q_9\|Q_8\|Q_7, m_{\pi(9)})$
4. } END IF

---

other hand, modification of $Q_{5,6}$ will also cause the change in 13-th or upper bits of Q_9 and this may cause changes in 25-th or upper bits of Q_{10} through Φ. Hence, if the carry reaches the MSB, this will break the condition on $Q_{10,31}$.

We experimentally confirmed the success probability of this modification by running it 10,000 times. As a result, we confirmed that the success probability is almost $87.5\% = \frac{7}{8}$.

4.4 Experiment

We implemented our collision attack on MMO-MD5. The used language is the C-language and the used machine is Intel(R) Core2 CPU 6600 @ 2.40GHz. (2 cores are used for the experiment.) As an initial value IV, we chose 128-bit MD5-IV appended by 384-bit 0 for the first experiment and all 0 for the second experiment. The running time for obtaining a collision was 79589 and 2841 seconds for the first and second experiment, respectively. We show generated collisions in Table 2.

Table 2. Examples of generated collisions (Values with differences are underlined.)

Given IV	m_0=0x67452301 m_1=0xefcdab89 m_2=0x98badcfe m_3=0x10325476			
	$m_4 = m_5 = \cdots = m_{15} =$ 0x00000000			
M_1	0x48ea2fc4	0x8fcad55d	0xc31bb985	0xaafc131c
M_2	0xc8ea2fc4	0x0fcad55d	0x431bb985	0x2afc131c
Hash value	0x633672cc	0xd7e09040	0x0a377ac5	0xed7365bc

Given IV	$m_0 = m_1 = \cdots = m_{15} =$ 0x00000000			
M_1	0x51aa8f55	0x87cca7e8	0xc5fcf975	0xea8b93b4
M_2	0xd1aa8f55	0x07cca7e8	0x45fcf975	0x6a8b93b4
Hash value	0x026e1ddc	0x8f6acd69	0xbd691aab	0x57af28f4

4.5   Remarks

The position of Ini-steps can be chosen from any 4 consecutive steps. Because the conditions close to the Ini-steps can be satisfied with a probability of 1, one of the best strategies is choosing the steps where conditions are most condensed, and leave a sparse part for the probabilistic search. This is not important for the dBB differential path because these exists at most 1 condition in every steps. However, this strategy will be useful for other differential paths in generic. Another strategy is choosing a round where the Φ is easy to control. The last strategy is choosing intermediate 4 steps, not the first or last 4 steps, so that CVM can be applied in both forward and backward directions. Based on our hand-analysis, applying CVM in only one direction is harder than applying it in both directions.

4.6   Collisions in Miyaguchi-Preneel and Other PGV Modes

In this section, we consider attacks in other hashing modes. (We consider secure 12 PGV constructions depicted in Fig 2 in Appendix B.)

In the Miyaguchi-Preneel-mode, chaining variables H_i are used as the key input and messages M_i are used as the plaintext input. Hash values is computed as follows:

$$E_{H_i}(M_i) \oplus M_i \oplus H_i,$$

where only the last feed-forward is different from the MMO-mode. In addition, there are two other PGV constructions, where the message input is not used as a key-input and used in the feed-forward;

$$H_{i+1} \leftarrow E_{h_i}(M_i \oplus h_i) \oplus M_i \oplus h_i,$$
$$H_{i+1} \leftarrow E_{h_i}(M_i \oplus h_i) \oplus M_i.$$

Because XORing/adding a fixed value to the plaintext and ciphertext does not give any impact to our collision attack, similarly to the MMO-mode, collisions in these three modes can also be generated.

Let us consider using md5 in the Miyaguchi-Preneel-mode. We assume the same length adjustment with the MMO-case. Because the difference of the MMO- and Miyaguchi-Preneel-mode is only the feed-forward of H_i, the examples in Table 2 replacing the hash value with the sum (or XOR) of the hash value and $m_0\|m_1\|m_2\|m_3$ is a collision of Miyaguchi-Preneel-md5.

5   Impact of Collisions in MMO Mode to DM Mode

In this section, we show that the collision attack in the MMO-mode explained in Section 4 gives some impacts on the security of the DM-mode using the same internal block-cipher. This indicates that the original MD5, which adopts the DM-mode, is also affected by our collision attack on MMO-MD5.

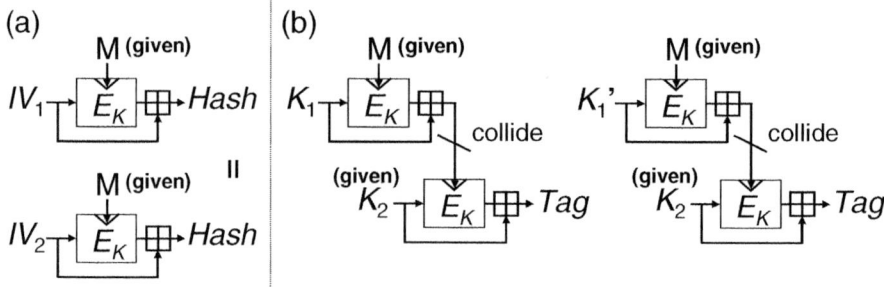

Fig. 1. (a) Given-message free-start collision on Davies-Meyer mode. (b) Given-message colliding keys for NMAC with Davies-Meyer mode.

5.1   Free-Start Given-Message Collisions

The following attack against the MD5 compression function CF with the DM mode is possible:

> *For a given message M, find a pair of initial values H_1 and H_2 such that*
> $\mathrm{CF}(H_1, M) = \mathrm{CF}(H_2, M)$.

The attack is also depicted in the left side of Fig. 1. In this attack, for a given message, we find a colliding pair by using the freedom of the initial value. As far as we know, this attack is the first case which can break a collision property of (compression function of) MD5 for a given message. This is because most of previous attacks used the message modification techniques to efficiently find colliding pairs, while we use CVM and do not modify a message.

The application of free-start given-message collisions is not well-understood. Colliding keys for NMAC in the next section is a possible application.

5.2   Given-Message Colliding Keys for NMAC

In NMAC with the DM-mode, a tag is computed by replacing the initial value H_0 with two secret keys K_1 and K_2 as follows: $E_{E_M(K_1) \boxplus K_1}(K_2) \boxplus K_2$. The computation of NMAC and the attack are illustrated in the right side of Fig. 1. By using the collision attack on the MMO-mode, for any fixed message M, attackers can find a pair of K_1 and K_1' that will collide in the NMAC tag. Hence, for any given message, attackers can find colliding key pairs that result in the same tag regardless of the value of K_2. The attack is different from the forgery attack, but should be avoided. Note that MD5 adopts the DM-mode with md5, and thus, this attack is an application for the original NMAC-MD5.

6   Conclusions and Future Work

In this paper, firstly, we presented a collision attack on MMO-MD5. We used the differential path proposed by den Boer and Bosselaers and applied chaining variable modification CVM to reduce the attack complexity. As a result, the complexity was reduced to 2^{39} MD5 computations, and we found real collisions in practice by implementing the attack on a standard PC. Secondly, we showed that our collision attack on the MMO mode would give some impacts on the DM mode such as the free-start given-message collisions for MD5 and given-message colliding keys for NMAC-MD5.

A possible future direction is finding this type of collisions in other hash functions. For example, in MD4, Yu *et al.* showed a differential path which can be satisfied with a probability of 2^{-62} for a randomly given h_1, h_2, m_1, m_2 [43]. Because this attack requires a difference of the message, the attack will be free-start given-*related*-message collisions. The attack complexity can be reduced by CVM. There are 62 conditions in total [43, Table 4]. Assume that attackers can satisfy conditions on 8 consecutive chaining variables by using CVM. Because the most condition-condensed part contains 22 conditions, 22 conditions can be satisfied and the complexity becomes roughly 2^{40}, which can be generated in practice.

References

1. Rivest, R.L.: Request for Comments 1321: The MD5 Message Digest Algorithm. The Internet Engineering Task Force (1992),
   http://www.ietf.org/rfc/rfc1321.txt
2. den Boer, B., Bosselaers, A.: Collisions for the compression function of MD5. In: Helleseth, T. (ed.) EUROCRYPT 1993. LNCS, vol. 765, pp. 293–304. Springer, Heidelberg (1994)
3. Dobbertin, H.: The status of MD5 after a recent attack. CryptoBytes The Technical Newsletter of RSA Laboratories, a Division of RSA Data Security, Inc. 2(2), (1996) (summer)
4. Wang, X., Yu, H.: How to break MD5 and other hash functions. In: Cramer, R. (ed.) EUROCRYPT 2005. LNCS, vol. 3494, pp. 19–35. Springer, Heidelberg (2005)
5. Black, J., Cochran, M., Highland, T.: A study of the MD5 attacks: Insights and improvements. In: Robshaw, M.J.B. (ed.) FSE 2006. LNCS, vol. 4047, pp. 262–277. Springer, Heidelberg (2006)
6. Klima, V.: Finding MD5 collisions on a notebook PC using multi-message modifications. In: International Scientific Conference Security and Protection of Information (May 2005)
7. Klima, V.: Tunnels in hash functions: MD5 collisions within a minute. In: IACR Cryptology ePrint Archive: Report 2006/105 (2006),
   http://eprint.iacr.org/2006/105.pdf
8. Liang, J., Lai, X.: Improved collision attack on hash function MD5. Cryptology ePrint Archive, Report 2005/425 (2005), http://eprint.iacr.org/2005/425
9. Sasaki, Y., Naito, Y., Kunihiro, N., Ohta, K.: Improved collision attacks on MD4 and MD5. IEICE Transactions on Fundamentals of Electronics, Communications and Computer Sciences E90-A(1), 36–47 (2007)
10. Sasaki, Y., Naito, Y., Yajima, J., Shimoyama, T., Kunihiro, N., Ohta, K.: How to construct sufficient condition in searching collisions of MD5. In: Nguyên, P.Q. (ed.) VIETCRYPT 2006. LNCS, vol. 4341, pp. 243–259. Springer, Heidelberg (2006)

11. Stevens, M.: Fast collision attack on MD5. Cryptology ePrint Archive, Report 2006/104 (2006), http://eprint.iacr.org/2006/104
12. Vábek, J., Joscák, D., Bohácek, M., Tuma, J.: A new type of 2-block collisions in MD5. In: Chowdhury, D.R., Rijmen, V., Das, A. (eds.) INDOCRYPT 2008. LNCS, vol. 5365, pp. 78–90. Springer, Heidelberg (2008)
13. Xie, T., Feng, D.: How to find weak input differences for MD5 collision attacks. Cryptology ePrint Archive, Report 2009/223 Version 20090530:102049 (2009), http://eprint.iacr.org/2009/223
14. Xie, T., Liu, F., Feng, D.: Could the 1-MSB input difference be the fastest collision attack for MD5? Cryptology ePrint Archive, Report 2008/391 (2008), http://eprint.iacr.org/2008/391
15. Xie, T., Feng, D.: Construct MD5 collisions using just a single block of message. Cryptology ePrint Archive, Report 2010/643, Version 20101225:061128 (2010), http://eprint.iacr.org/2010/643
16. Xie, T., Feng, D.: The first 1-block collision attack on MD5 and call for a challedge. Cryptology ePrint Archive, Report 2009/223, Version 20101216:032027 (2010), http://eprint.iacr.org/2009/223
17. Contini, S., Yin, Y.L.: Forgery and Partial Key-Recovery Attacks on HMAC and NMAC Using Hash Collisions. In: Lai, X., Chen, K. (eds.) ASIACRYPT 2006. LNCS, vol. 4284, pp. 37–53. Springer, Heidelberg (2006)
18. Fouque, P.A., Leurent, G., Nguyen, P.: Full key-recovery attacks on HMAC/NMAC-MD4 and NMAC-MD5. In: Menezes, A. (ed.) CRYPTO 2007. LNCS, vol. 4622, pp. 15–30. Springer, Heidelberg (2007)
19. Kim, J., Biryukov, A., Preneel, B., Hong, S.: On the Security of HMAC and NMAC Based on HAVAL, MD4, MD5, SHA-0 and SHA-1. In: De Prisco, R., Yung, M. (eds.) SCN 2006. LNCS, vol. 4116, pp. 242–256. Springer, Heidelberg (2006)
20. Rechberger, C., Rijmen, V.: On Authentication with HMAC and Non-random Properties. In: Dietrich, S., Dhamija, R. (eds.) FC 2007 and USEC 2007. LNCS, vol. 4886, pp. 119–133. Springer, Heidelberg (2007)
21. Rechberger, C., Rijmen, V.: New results on NMAC/HMAC when instantiated with popular hash functions. Journal of Universal Computer Science 14(3), 347–376 (2008)
22. Wang, L., Ohta, K., Kunihiro, N.: New key-recovery attacks on HMAC/NMAC-MD4 and NMAC-MD5. In: Smart, N.P. (ed.) EUROCRYPT 2008. LNCS, vol. 4965, pp. 237–253. Springer, Heidelberg (2008)
23. Wang, X., Yu, H., Wang, W., Zhang, H., Zhan, T.: Cryptanalysis on HMAC/NMAC-MD5 and MD5-MAC. In: Joux, A. (ed.) EUROCRYPT 2009. LNCS, vol. 5479, pp. 121–133. Springer, Heidelberg (2009)
24. Leurent, G.: Message freedom in MD4 and MD5 collisions: Application to APOP. In: Biryukov, A. (ed.) FSE 2007. LNCS, vol. 4593, pp. 309–328. Springer, Heidelberg (2007)
25. Sasaki, Y., Wang, L., Ohta, K., Kunihiro, N.: Security of MD5 challenge and response: Extension of APOP password recovery attack. In: Malkin, T. (ed.) CT-RSA 2008. LNCS, vol. 4964, pp. 1–18. Springer, Heidelberg (2008)
26. Stevens, M., Lenstra, A.K., de Weger, B.: Chosen-prefix collisions for MD5 and colliding X.509 certificates for different identities. In: Naor, M. (ed.) EUROCRYPT 2007. LNCS, vol. 4515, pp. 1–22. Springer, Heidelberg (2007)
27. Stevens, M., Sotirov, A., Appelbaum, J., Lenstra, A.K., Molnar, D., Osvik, D.A., de Weger, B.: Short chosen-prefix collisions for MD5 and the creation of a rogue CA certificate. In: Halevi, S. (ed.) CRYPTO 2009. LNCS, vol. 5677, pp. 55–69. Springer, Heidelberg (2009)

28. Mendel, F., Rechberger, C., Schläffer, M.: MD5 is weaker than weak: Attacks on concatenated combiners. In: Matsui, M. (ed.) ASIACRYPT 2009. LNCS, vol. 5912, pp. 144–161. Springer, Heidelberg (2009)

29. Aoki, K., Sasaki, Y.: Preimage attacks on one-block MD4, 63-step MD5 and more. In: Avanzi, R.M., Keliher, L., Sica, F. (eds.) SAC 2008. LNCS, vol. 5381, pp. 103–119. Springer, Heidelberg (2009)

30. Aumasson, J.P., Meier, W., Mendel, F.: Preimage attacks on 3-pass HAVAL and step-reduced MD5. In: Avanzi, R.M., Keliher, L., Sica, F. (eds.) SAC 2008. LNCS, vol. 5381, pp. 120–135. Springer, Heidelberg (2009)

31. Sasaki, Y., Aoki, K.: Preimage attacks on step-reduced MD5. In: Mu, Y., Susilo, W. (eds.) ACISP 2008. LNCS, vol. 5107, pp. 282–296. Springer, Heidelberg (2008)

32. Sasaki, Y., Aoki, K.: Finding preimages in full MD5 faster than exhaustive search. In: Joux, A. (ed.) EUROCRYPT 2009. LNCS, vol. 5479, pp. 134–152. Springer, Heidelberg (2009)

33. U.S. Department of Commerce, National Institute of Standards and Technology: Secure Hash Standard (SHS) (Federal Information Processing Standards Publication 180-3) (2008),
http://csrc.nist.gov/publications/fips/fips180-3/fips180-3_final.pdf

34. Preneel, B., Govaerts, R., Vandewalle, J.: Hash functions based on block ciphers: A synthetic approach. In: Stinson, D.R. (ed.) CRYPTO 1993. LNCS, vol. 773, pp. 363–378. Springer, Heidelberg (1994)

35. Menezes, A.J., van Oorschot, P.C., Vanstone, S.A.: Handbook of applied cryptography. CRC Press, Boca Raton (1997)

36. Ferguson, N., Lucks, S., Schneier, B., Whiting, D., Bellare, M., Kohno, T., Callas, J., Walker, J.: The Skein hash function family. Submission to NIST, Round 2 (2009)

37. Hirose, S., Kuwakado, H., Yoshida, H.: SHA-3 proposal: Lesamnta. Submission to NIST (2008)

38. Rijmen, V., Barreto, P.S.L.M.: The WHIRLPOOL hashing function. Submitted to NISSIE (September 2000)

39. Wang, X., Yin, Y.L., Yu, H.: Finding collisions in the full SHA-1. In: Shoup, V. (ed.) CRYPTO 2005. LNCS, vol. 3621, pp. 17–36. Springer, Heidelberg (2005)

40. Mendel, F., Rechberger, C., Schläffer, M., Thomsen, S.S.: The rebound attack: Cryptanalysis of reduced whirlpool and grøstl. In: Dunkelman, O. (ed.) FSE 2009. LNCS, vol. 5665, pp. 260–276. Springer, Heidelberg (2009)

41. Bellare, M., Canetti, R., Krawczyk, H.: Keying hash functions for message authentication. In: Koblitz, N. (ed.) CRYPTO 1996. LNCS, vol. 1109, pp. 1–15. Springer, Heidelberg (1996)

42. Cannière, C.D., Rechberger, C.: Finding SHA-1 characteristics: General results and applications. In: Lai, X., Chen, K. (eds.) ASIACRYPT 2006. LNCS, vol. 4284, pp. 1–20. Springer, Heidelberg (2006)

43. Yu, H., Wang, G., Zhang, G., Wang, X.: The second-preimage attack on MD4. In: Desmedt, Y.G., Wang, H., Mu, Y., Li, Y. (eds.) CANS 2005. LNCS, vol. 3810, pp. 1–12. Springer, Heidelberg (2005)

A   Details of Chaining Variable Modifications

Modification 3.

Target bit: $Q_{3,31}$
Modifying bit: $Q_{6,16}$
Extra Condition: $Q_{7,16} = 0, Q_{8,16} = 1$

1. IF $(Q_{3,31} \neq Q_{4,31})$ {
2. $Q_6 \leftarrow Q_6 \oplus$ 0x00010000
3. $Q_3 \leftarrow R_6^{-1}(Q_4\|Q_7\|Q_6|Q_5, m_{\pi(6)})$
4. } END IF

Modification 4.

Target bit: $Q_{10,31}$
Modifying bit: $Q_{6,19}$
Extra Condition: $Q_{8,19} = 1, Q_{7,19} = 0$

1. IF $(Q_{10,31} \neq Q_{9,31})$ {
2. $Q_6 \leftarrow Q_6 \oplus$ 0x00080000
3. $Q_{10} \leftarrow R_9(Q_6\|Q_9\|Q_8\|Q_7, m_{\pi(9)})$
4. $Q_3 \leftarrow R_6^{-1}(Q_4\|Q_7\|Q_6|Q_5, m_{\pi(6)})$
5. } END IF

Modification 5.

Target bit: $Q_{2,31}$
Initialization: $Q_{5,11} = 0, Q_{5,12} = 1$
Modifying bit: $Q_{5,11}$ ($Q_{5,12}$ may also change.)
Extra Condition: $Q_{6,11} = 0, Q_{6,12} = 0, Q_{7,11} = 1, Q_{7,12} = 1, Q_{8,18} = Q_{7,18}$

1. IF $(Q_{2,31} \neq Q_{3,31})$ {
2.   IF $(Q_{9,18} = 1)$ {
3. $Q_5 \leftarrow Q_5 -$ 0x00000800
4.   }ELSE IF $(Q_{9,18} = 0)$ {
5. $Q_5 \leftarrow Q_5 +$ 0x00000800
6.   } END IF
7. $Q_2 \leftarrow R_5^{-1}(Q_3\|Q_6\|Q_5\|Q_4, m_{\pi(5)})$
8. $Q_9 \leftarrow R_8(Q_5\|Q_8\|Q_7\|Q_6, m_{\pi(8)})$
9. $Q_{10} \leftarrow R_9(Q_6\|Q_9\|Q_8\|Q_7, m_{\pi(9)})$
10. } END IF

Modification 5 is complicated. To flip the value of $Q_{2,31}$, we modify $Q_{5,11}$. If we modify $Q_{5,11}$, the impact can propagate to $Q_{9,19}$ with a probability of 2^{-1} by Eq. (9). Then in Eq. (10), this impact always propagates to $Q_{10,31}$ because $Q_{8,19}$ and $Q_{7,19}$ are set to different values by extra conditions for Modification 4.

$$Q_9 = (\underline{Q_5} + \Phi(Q_8, Q_7, Q_6) + m_{\pi(8)}) + k_8) \lll 7 + Q_8 \tag{9}$$

$$Q_{10} = (Q_6 + \Phi(\underline{Q_9}, Q_8, Q_7) + m_{\pi(9)}) + k_9) \lll 12 + \underline{Q_9} \tag{10}$$

Hence, we must guarantee that modifying $Q_{5,11}$ never makes carry on $Q_{9,18}$. Therefore, we do not apply XOR on $Q_{5,11}$, but apply addition or subtraction by looking the value of $Q_{9,18}$. If we set $Q_{5,11} = 0$ and $Q_{5,12} = 1$ in advance, we can guarantee that at most 2 bits of Q_5 are influenced either addition or subtraction on $Q_{5,11}$. Finally, we set extra conditions on Q_6 and Q_7 for the case where both $Q_{5,11}$ and $Q_{5,12}$ change.

B   A List of Twelve Secure PGV Constructions

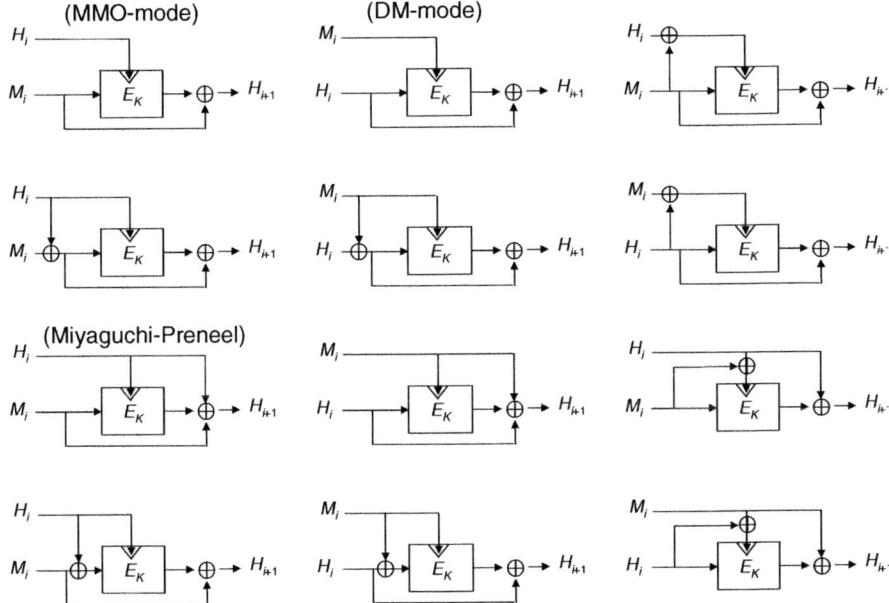

Fig. 2. A list of secure PGV constructions

Really Fast Syndrome-Based Hashing

Daniel J. Bernstein[1], Tanja Lange[2], Christiane Peters[2], and Peter Schwabe[3]

[1] Department of Computer Science
University of Illinois at Chicago, Chicago, IL 60607–7045, USA
djb@cr.yp.to
[2] Department of Mathematics and Computer Science
Technische Universiteit Eindhoven, P.O. Box 513, 5600 MB Eindhoven, Netherlands
tanja@hyperelliptic.org, c.p.peters@tue.nl
[3] Institute of Information Science
Academia Sinica, 128 Section 2 Academia Road, Taipei 115-29, Taiwan
peter@cryptojedi.org

Abstract. The FSB (fast syndrome-based) hash function was submitted to the SHA-3 competition by Augot, Finiasz, Gaborit, Manuel, and Sendrier in 2008, after preliminary designs proposed in 2003, 2005, and 2007. Many FSB parameter choices were broken by Coron and Joux in 2004, Saarinen in 2007, and Fouque and Leurent in 2008, but the basic FSB idea appears to be secure, and the FSB submission remains unbroken. On the other hand, the FSB submission is also quite slow, and was not selected for the second round of the competition.

This paper introduces RFSB, an enhancement to FSB. In particular, this paper introduces the RFSB-509 compression function, RFSB with a particular set of parameters. RFSB-509, like the FSB-256 compression function, is designed to be used inside a 256-bit collision-resistant hash function: all known attack strategies cost more than 2^{128} to find collisions in RFSB-509. However, RFSB-509 is an order of magnitude faster than FSB-256. On a single core of a Core 2 Quad CPU, RFSB-509 runs at 13.62 cycles/byte: faster than SHA-256, faster than 6 of the 14 second-round SHA-3 candidates, and faster than 2 of the 5 SHA-3 finalists.

Keywords: compression functions, collision resistance, linearization, generalized birthday attacks, information-set decoding, tight reduction to L1 cache.

1 Introduction

Finding collisions in a very simple compression function of the form

$$(m_1, m_2, \ldots, m_w) \mapsto c_1[m_1] \oplus c_2[m_2] \oplus \cdots \oplus c_w[m_w]$$

This work was supported by the National Science Foundation under grant 0716498, by the European Commission under Contract ICT-2007-216499 CACE, by the European Commission under Contract ICT-2007-216646 ECRYPT II, and by the National Science Council, National Taiwan University and Intel Corporation under Grant NSC99-2911-I-002-001. Permanent ID of this document: 067a9e99992a54f43b7f859c81b25d16. Date: 2011.04.22.

A. Nitaj and D. Pointcheval (Eds.): AFRICACRYPT 2011, LNCS 6737, pp. 134–152, 2011.
© Springer-Verlag Berlin Heidelberg 2011

turns out to be surprisingly difficult. As an illustration of this difficulty we challenge the reader to break the following parameters:

- w, the weight of the sum, is 112. (Sum here means exclusive-or; we do not bother saying "modulo 2" everywhere.)
- The input chunks $m_1, m_2, \ldots, m_{112}$ range over $\{0, 1, \ldots, 255\}$. The compression function therefore has 896 bits of input.
- Each of the 28672 constants $c_1[0], \ldots, c_1[255], \ldots, c_{112}[0], \ldots, c_{112}[255]$ is an independent uniform random 509-bit vector. The compression function therefore has 509 bits of output.

At first one might think that linear algebra instantaneously finds preimages in this function, with collisions as a trivial side effect. Select 509 of these 28672 constants; there is a good chance that those 509 are linearly independent, guaranteeing that linear algebra modulo 2 will reveal a subset adding up to the target. The reason that this attack does not work is that the resulting subset is extraordinarily unlikely to have the form $c_1[m_1], c_2[m_2], \ldots, c_{112}[m_{112}]$: in particular, the subset will normally have size close to 509/2, much larger than 112. In other words, linear algebra easily finds random codewords in the linear code defined by the matrix of constants, but it does not find *low-weight* codewords, a classic problem in coding theory.

One can also try to find collisions directly, without a detour through preimages. Select, for example, the 510 constants $c_i[j]$ with $j \in \{0, 1, 2, 3\}$ for $1 \leq i \leq 50$ and $c_i[j]$ with $j \in \{0, 1, 2, 3, 4\}$ for $51 \leq i \leq 112$. Use linear algebra to find a nonempty subset adding up to 0, and try to split the subset into 224 constants $c_1[m_1], c_2[m_2], \ldots, c_{112}[m_{112}]$ and $c_1[m'_1], c_2[m'_2], \ldots, c_{112}[m'_{112}]$. Low weight is no longer an obstacle: the subset has about a 2^{-10} chance of having size exactly 224. The reason that this attack does not work is that the subset has chance only about $(6/16)^{50}(10/32)^{62} \approx 2^{-175}$ of containing exactly two $c_1[\cdots]$, exactly two $c_2[\cdots]$, etc.

There is a long history of proposals of compression functions of this type (see Section 2) and also a long history of attacks (see Section 4). Many of the proposals are motivated by speed: the additions are very fast; the structure $c_1[m_1] \oplus c_2[m_2] \oplus \cdots \oplus c_w[m_w]$ also has obvious virtues of incrementality and parallelizability. However, the large matrix of random constants makes small hardware implementations impossible, and software implementations end up spending far longer waiting for memory access than actually performing useful computations. This problem was already highlighted five years ago by Augot, Finiasz, and Sendrier in [2, Section 6].

Obtaining very high speed requires reducing memory-access costs, which in turn requires compressing the matrix. This is impossible for a uniform random matrix, but security does not seem to require a uniform random matrix. Finiasz, Gaborit, and Sendrier in [25] proposed using a quasi-cyclic matrix: each block of the matrix is a block of rotations of a single vector. In [25, Section 4.2] they suggested choosing the vector length r so that the polynomial $(x^r - 1)/(x - 1)$ is irreducible in $\mathbf{F}_2[x]$. They argued, under this assumption on the vector length, that finding a low-weight codeword for a random quasi-cyclic matrix is a well-known hard problem in coding theory, as hard as the generic low-weight-codeword problem.

Most of the specific parameters proposed in [25] were promptly broken in two different ways, showing two mistakes in the parameter selection. The first mistake, exploited by Saarinen in [40], is that [25] chose w too large compared to the vector length r; security against linearization requires w to be considerably smaller than $r/2$. The second mistake, exploited by Fouque and Leurent in [26], is that [25, Section 6] ignored [25, Section 4.2] and chose powers of 2 for r, violating the irreducibility of $(x^r - 1)/(x - 1)$ and allowing the attacker to concentrate on small factors of $(x^r - 1)/(x - 1)$.

Both of these mistakes were fixed in FSB [3], a first-round SHA-3 submission by Augot, Finiasz, Gaborit, Manuel, and Sendrier. FSB resists the previous attack strategies and remains unbroken today. Bernstein, Lange, Niederhagen, Peters, and Schwabe in [9] needed days on an 8-computer cluster (using 64GB of RAM and 5.5TB of disk) to find collisions in the scaled-down FSB-48 compression function by a streamlined generalized birthday attack; for comparison, an unoptimized attack on the FSB-48 *hash* function finds collisions in about a minute on just one core on one of these computers with negligible memory usage. The compression function has vector length $r = 197$ (subsequently truncated to 192 bits, but the rotations are of 197-bit vectors), weight $w = 24$, and 14 bits in each m_i. Scaling the same attack to the 1024-bit FSB-256 compression function would cost far more than 2^{128}, and other attacks also do not seem to pose a threat.

However, FSB is quite slow, and was not selected for the second round of the SHA-3 competition. The best speed reported in eBASH [8] for FSB-256 on an Intel Core 2 Quad Q9550 (10677) (`berlekamp`) is 95.53 cycles/byte (using an assembly-language implementation by Schwabe). SHA-256 takes just 15.26 cycles/byte on the same computer.

Contents of this paper. We introduce the RFSB ("really fast syndrome-based") compression function, an improved version of FSB. In particular, we introduce RFSB-509, a compression function that reaches higher speeds than SHA-256 on a Core 2 Quad CPU, while maintaining higher collision security than SHA-256 against every known attack. See Section 2 for the definitions of RFSB and RFSB-509.

The FSB-to-RFSB improvements come from two sources. First, the design of RFSB pays much closer attention to the efficiency of the computation of $c_1[m_1] \oplus c_2[m_2] \oplus \cdots \oplus c_w[m_w]$. The most important result of this analysis is that RFSB permutes the vectors in the FSB matrix. This permutation has no effect on the best attacks known, and might also seem irrelevant to speed, but we show that it eliminates a critical inefficiency in FSB. See Section 3 for a detailed explanation of our algorithm for computing RFSB.

Second, the design of RFSB pays much closer attention to the cost of attacks. This allows the RFSB parameters to be tuned much more tightly than the FSB parameters were, while still keeping all known attacks safely above our 2^{128}

security target. Our attack survey in Section 4 corrects several algorithm-analysis errors in the literature, and incorporates some new improvements that we found.

Like FSB and earlier designs of this type, RFSB offers incremental hashing and parallelizable hashing. Unlike FSB, RFSB allows fast on-demand matrix generation, making it implementable in very small hardware.

Building a hash function from a compression function. We emphasize that our goal in this paper is the traditional goal of building a collision-resistant compression function F for fixed-length messages. RFSB, specifically RFSB-509, is our proposal for F. Merkle–Damgård iteration then produces a collision-resistant compression function $\overline{F}$ for longer messages; see, e.g., [21, Theorem 3.1]. Our discussion of speed focuses on the speed of this iterated function $\overline{F}$ for long messages.

Many, perhaps most, papers on hash-function design use the iteration mode as an argument for weakening their collision-resistance goals. If the compression function F has input (v, m), where v is the previous chaining value (or initialization vector) and m is an attacker-controlled block, then these papers say that $F(v, m) = F(v', m')$ with $(v, m) \neq (v', m')$ is merely a "pseudo-collision" and that it qualifies as a "collision" only if $v = v'$. However, many papers on hash-function cryptanalysis say that finding a pseudo-collision is a "certificational attack" even if $v \neq v'$. To avoid this debate we have designed RFSB to stop all pseudo-collisions.

One interesting consequence of incrementality is that RFSB can precompute the v-dependent part of its output before m is available. The preliminary FSB designs in [1], [2], and [25] had the same feature, but the FSB SHA-3 submission does not, because it permutes the bits of (v, m). According to [24], this permutation was added in reaction to [26, Section 3], in which Fouque and Leurent object to the following "IV weakness" in the preliminary FSB designs: a collision of the form $\overline{F}(m) = \overline{F}(m')$, where m and m' are distinct single-block messages, implies $\overline{F}(p, m) = \overline{F}(p, m')$ for every prefix p. We do not see why this is any more troubling than the following "weakness" in the compression functions of SHA-1, SHA-2, and every SHA-3 candidate: a collision of the form $\overline{F}(m) = \overline{F}(m')$, where m and m' are distinct identical-length block-aligned messages, implies $\overline{F}(m, q) = \overline{F}(m', q)$ for every suffix q. Our goal is to prevent these collisions from occurring in the first place.

To build a full-fledged cryptographic hash function, suitable for use in message authentication, commitment protocols, etc., we can add any reasonably strong output filter to RFSB-509. One reasonable choice of output filter is SHA-256; of course, the 256-bit output length of SHA-256 then reduces collision resistance to 2^{128}. We emphasize that an output filter adds only a small constant overhead to the cost of hashing; the speed of hashing a long message is the speed of our compression function.

To allow public benchmarking of the RFSB-509 compression function, we implemented a hash function that uses RFSB-509 with Merkle–Damgård iteration, an all-zero initialization vector, and SHA-256 as output filter. The original message is padded to a multiple of 48 bytes as follows: first zero-pad to 40 bytes plus a multiple of 48 bytes; then append 8 bytes containing, in little-endian form, the number of bytes of the message before padding. We have placed the software into the public domain to maximize reusability, and are submitting it to eBASH for benchmarking.

2 Design of RFSB

This section defines the RFSB family of compression functions. In particular, this section defines the RFSB-509 compression function. This section then reviews the literature, showing in particular how RFSB differs from FSB and explaining why we introduced these differences.

Specification of RFSB. There are four RFSB parameters: an odd prime number r, a positive integer b, a positive integer w, and a $2^b \times r$-bit compressed matrix. The prime r is chosen so that 2 has order $r - 1$ in the unit group $\mathbf{F}_r^*$; i.e., so that the cyclotomic polynomial $(x^r - 1)/(x - 1)$ in $\mathbf{F}_2[x]$ is irreducible.

The RFSB output is an r-bit string, represented as a sequence of $\lceil r/8 \rceil$ bytes in little-endian form. The string $(s_0, s_1, \ldots, s_{r-1})$ represents the polynomial $s_0 + s_1 x + \cdots + s_{r-1} x^{r-1}$ in the ring $\mathbf{F}_2[x]/(x^r - 1)$. For example, for $r = 13$, the byte string $(12, 16)$ represents the bit string $(0, 0, 1, 1, 0, 0, 0, 0, 0, 0, 0, 0, 1)$, which in turn represents the polynomial $x^2 + x^3 + x^{12}$ in $\mathbf{F}_2[x]/(x^{13} - 1)$.

The RFSB input is a bw-bit string, represented as a sequence of $\lceil bw/8 \rceil$ bytes in little-endian form. This string represents a sequence $(m_1, m_2, \ldots, m_w)$, where each m_i is an element of $\{0, 1, \ldots, 2^b - 1\}$.

The compressed RFSB matrix is a sequence of r-bit strings $c[0], c[1], \ldots, c[2^b - 1]$. We define $c_i[j] = c[j]x^{128(w-i)}$ in the ring $\mathbf{F}_2[x]/(x^r - 1)$; in other words, $c_i[j]$ is a $128(w - i)$-bit rotation of $c[j]$. This matrix specifies the relationship between the RFSB input and the RFSB output: RFSB is the function

$$(m_1, m_2, \ldots, m_w) \mapsto c_1[m_1] \oplus c_2[m_2] \oplus \cdots \oplus c_w[m_w],$$

i.e., the function that maps an input $(m_1, m_2, \ldots, m_{w-1}, m_w)$ to the output $x^{128(w-1)}c[m_1] \oplus x^{128(w-2)}c[m_2] \oplus \cdots \oplus x^{128}c[m_{w-1}] \oplus c[m_w]$ in $\mathbf{F}_2[x]/(x^r - 1)$.

Sometimes we refer to the uncompressed RFSB matrix. This is a $2^b w \times r$-bit matrix containing the strings $c_i[j]$, for $i \in \{1, 2, \ldots, w\}$ and $j \in \{0, 1, \ldots, 2^b - 1\}$. We do not mean to suggest that implementations are required to compute this matrix.

Specification of RFSB-509. Our RFSB-509 proposal has $r = 509$, $b = 8$, and $w = 112$. In other words, RFSB-509 maps $(m_1, m_2, \ldots, m_{112})$, where each m_i is an 8-bit string, to

$$x^{128(112-1)}c[m_1] \oplus x^{128(112-2)}c[m_2] \oplus \cdots \oplus x^{128}c[m_{111}] \oplus c[m_{112}]$$

in $\mathbf{F}_2[x]/(x^{509} - 1)$. We chose the parameters $(509, 8, 112)$ to maximize the software speed of RFSB (see Section 3) while keeping the cost of all known attacks above 2^{128} (see Section 4).

The compressed RFSB-509 matrix is defined as a concatenation of AES outputs. Specifically, each 509-bit $c[j]$ is obtained by encrypting the four 16-byte strings $(0, j, 0, \ldots, 0, 0)$, $(1, j, 0, \ldots, 0, 0)$, $(2, j, 0, \ldots, 0, 0)$, $(3, j, 0, \ldots, 0, 0)$ with AES, concatenating the 128-bit outputs into a 512-bit string, and reducing modulo $x^{509} - 1$ (i.e., folding the last three bits onto the first three bits). The AES key is a 128-bit all-0 key.

We comment that implementors can trade space for time by computing each $c[j]$ when it is used, rather than precomputing and storing the AES outputs. The hardware area required for RFSB-509 (and an AES-based output filter) is then not much larger than the hardware area required for AES. The regular input structure also allows "counter-mode caching", a sharing of work in the first two rounds of AES; see [11]. We also comment that varying the AES key is a natural way to "salt" RFSB-509, converting RFSB-509 into a keyed compression function.

History and credits.. In a 1970 technical report [46], Zobrist introduced the compression function $(m_1, m_2, \ldots, m_w) \mapsto c_1[m_1] \oplus c_2[m_2] \oplus \cdots \oplus c_w[m_w]$, with random choices of matrix entries $c_i[j]$, as a non-cryptographic hash function. Zobrist's parameter choices were much too small to be of any cryptographic interest.

The same compression function was reintroduced and discarded in a Eurocrypt 1997 paper [6] by Bellare and Micciancio. The only difference between Zobrist's hash and "XHASH" in [6, Section 1] is that $c_i[m_i]$ is replaced by $H(i, m_i)$, allowing much longer input chunks m_i while raising security questions and efficiency questions for the underlying function H. Bellare and Micciancio described "XHASH" as insecure, independently of H, because they were able to find collisions by linearization for large w. They instead proposed various slower alternatives to $\oplus$, such as modular multiplication. They did not consider small values of w.

A very similar compression function with limited w had been introduced a decade earlier by Damgård at Crypto 1989 [21, Section 4.3]. Damgård used addition rather than $\oplus$, took $w = 256$ for 128-bit output (or more generally $w \approx 2r$ for r-bit output), and took $m_i \in \{0, 1\}$. Camion and Patarin introduced generalized birthday attacks (without giving them that name) at Eurocrypt 1991 [16] and showed that Damgård's function is breakable in subexponential time.

As far as we know, the first proposal with limited w and several bits in each m_i was the preliminary version of FSB by Augot, Finiasz, and Sendrier appearing in [1] and [2]. The larger range of m_i appears to allow a security level exponential in r with a polynomial-size matrix, specifically a matrix containing $\Theta(r^2)$ bits. However, the implicit constant in $\Theta(r^2)$ is quite large, and the time to access the matrix is quite troublesome.

FSB with a quasi-cyclic matrix was introduced by Finiasz, Gaborit, and Sendrier in [25]. FSB with a *truncated* quasi-cyclic matrix was introduced by Augot, Finiasz, Gaborit, Manuel, and Sendrier in [3] and submitted to the SHA-3 competition. These proposals appear to allow a security level exponential in r with a compressed matrix containing $\Theta(r)$ bits, although the implicit constant in $\Theta(r)$ is still quite large.

Comparison between FSB and RFSB. The FSB-256 proposal from [3] follows Zobrist's formula $(m_1, m_2, \ldots, m_w) \mapsto c_1[m_1] \oplus c_2[m_2] \oplus \cdots \oplus c_w[m_w]$ with $r = 1061$ bits of output (truncated to 1024 bits), weight $w = 128$ in the sum, and $b = 14$ bits in each input chunk m_i. The uncompressed FSB-256 matrix entries $c_i[0], c_i[1], \ldots, c_i[16383]$ are generated modulo $x^{1061} - 1$ as

$$c_i[0], \qquad c_i[0]x, \qquad c_i[0]x^2, \ldots, \qquad c_i[0]x^{1023},$$
$$c_i[1024], \quad c_i[1024]x, \quad c_i[1024]x^2, \ldots, \quad c_i[1024]x^{1023},$$

$$\vdots$$

$$c_i[15360], c_i[15360]x, c_i[15360]x^2, \ldots, c_i[15360]x^{1023},$$

where $c_i[0], c_i[1024], \ldots, c_i[15360]$ are generated from digits of π.

FSB-256 handles $14 - 1024/128 = 6$ bits of new input for each 1024-bit addition, while RFSB-509 handles $8 - 512/112 \approx 3.43$ bits of new input for each 512-bit addition. We are comfortable with a smaller $r = 509$, and a larger ratio w/r, because of our tighter security analysis; see Section 4. These changes allow the compressed RFSB-509 matrix to fit into just 16384 bytes, comfortably inside L1 cache on typical CPUs.

FSB-256 uses almost r rotations of each vector, while RFSB-509 uses only $w \approx r/4.5$ rotations of each vector. The number of rotations is important because it is the compression factor for the matrix. We could have allowed further compression as an option in RFSB-509 by modifying the definition of the matrix to use $2w$ or $3w$ or $4w$ rotations of each vector; but this option would not help fast software implementations such as ours, and it would slightly complicate implementations that generate matrix entries on the fly.

The most important difference between FSB and RFSB is the order of matrix entries: FSB defines $c_i[j]$ as $c_i[0]x^j$ (at least for a wide range of j), while RFSB defines $c_i[j]$ as $c[j]x^i$ (or rather $c[j]x^{128(w-i)}$), exchanging the roles of i and j. This change is important because j is unpredictable, a chunk of input, while i is a constant, the position of the chunk. The rotation distances in FSB are therefore input-dependent, making them quite expensive. The rotation distances in RFSB are constant, allowing several optimizations that are not available to FSB.

3   Speed of RFSB-509

We implemented RFSB-509 (with Merkle–Damgård iteration) in assembly language, targeting the popular Intel Core 2 Quad line of CPUs. We measured RFSB-509 running at 13.62 cycles/byte on an Intel Core 2 Quad Q9550 (10677) for compressing a 4096-byte message to 64 bytes.

For comparison, eBASH [8] reports SHA-256 running at 15.26 cycles/byte on an Intel Core 2 Quad Q9550 (10677) (berlekamp), using the assembly-language implementation of SHA-256 from Wei Dai's Crypto++ library, and reports that the SPHlib and OpenSSL implementations of SHA-256 are slower.

The algorithm that we use to compute RFSB is explained in this section. This algorithm relies critically on the predictable rotation distances in RFSB; we would not be able to achieve similar speeds for FSB.

This section also describes two additional algorithmic improvements that provide even higher speed for some applications. One improvement, incremental hashing, is well known, while the other improvement, fast batch verification, is less well known. We have not implemented these improvements; we emphasize that RFSB-509 is already quite fast without these improvements. This section concludes by discussing ways to compute RFSB without variable-index table lookups.

How to compute RFSB. Horner's rule computes

$$x^{128(112-1)}c[m_1] \oplus x^{128(112-2)}c[m_2] \oplus \cdots \oplus x^{128}c[m_{111}] \oplus c[m_{112}]$$

by starting with $c[m_1]$, multiplying by x^{128} in $\mathbf{F}_2[x]/(x^{509}-1)$, adding $c[m_2]$, multiplying by x^{128}, etc.

We instead use a 4-way parallel version of Horner's rule. The first step computes the polynomial $x^{384}c[m_1] \oplus x^{256}c[m_2] \oplus x^{128}c[m_3] \oplus c[m_4]$. The second step multiplies by x^{512}, reduces modulo $x^{509}-1$, and adds the polynomial $x^{384}c[m_5] \oplus x^{256}c[m_6] \oplus x^{128}c[m_7] \oplus c[m_8]$. Overall there are 28 steps, each step processing 4 bytes of input.

Each 509-bit vector is represented on the Core 2 Quad as a sequence of 4 128-bit XMM registers in radix x^{128}: for example, the matrix entry $c[m_i]$ is loaded as a sequence of 4 128-bit values $(c[m_i]_0, c[m_i]_1, c[m_i]_2, c[m_i]_3)$, representing $c[m_i]_0 + x^{128}c[m_i]_1 + x^{256}c[m_i]_2 + x^{384}c[m_i]_3$. We use polynomials as large as 893 bits, represented in 7 128-bit registers, before reducing modulo $x^{509}-1$. This representation allows the arithmetic stated above to be decomposed into a small number of 128-bit instructions, as explained in the following paragraphs.

The first step of the compression does the following: Load the matrix column $c[m_4]$ into 4 128-bit XMM register variables $r_0, \ldots, r_3$; load and xor the matrix column $c[m_3]$ into registers $r_1, \ldots, r_4$; load and xor the matrix column $c[m_2]$ into registers $r_2, \ldots, r_5$; and load and xor the matrix column $c[m_1]$ into registers $r_3, \ldots, r_6$. This takes 16 instructions (7 loads and 9 combined xor-load instructions) and results in the following values in registers $r_0, \ldots, r_6$:

$$r_0 = c[m_4]_0$$
$$r_1 = c[m_4]_1 \oplus c[m_3]_0$$
$$r_2 = c[m_4]_2 \oplus c[m_3]_1 \oplus c[m_2]_0$$
$$r_3 = c[m_4]_3 \oplus c[m_3]_2 \oplus c[m_2]_1 \oplus c[m_1]_0$$
$$r_4 = c[m_3]_3 \oplus c[m_2]_2 \oplus c[m_1]_1$$
$$r_5 = c[m_2]_3 \oplus c[m_1]_2$$
$$r_6 = c[m_1]_3$$

We then apply a reduction step. We xor the 125 bits of r_6 into the 125 highest bits of r_2; xor the 3 highest bits of r_5 into the 3 lowest bits of r_2 and the 125 lowest bits of r_5 into the 125 highest bits of r_1; and finally xor the 3 highest bits of r_4 into the 3 lowest bits of r_1 and the 125 lowest bits of r_4 into the 125 highest bits of r_0. We then rename r_i to r_{i+4} for $i = 0, \ldots, 3$. This does not actually consume any instructions; it just means using different registers for the variables $r_0, \ldots, r_3$ in the next step.

The second step loads column $c[m_8]$ into $r_0, \ldots, r_3$; loads and xors $c[m_7]$ into $r_1, \ldots, r_4$; loads and xors $c[m_6]$ into $r_2, \ldots, r_5$; and loads and xors $c[m_5]$ into $r_3, \ldots, r_6$. Then it reduces $r_4, \ldots, r_7$ and again renames r_i to r_{i+4} for $i = 1, \ldots, 3$. Each of the remaining 26 steps proceeds in the same way as the second step.

The reductions described above modulo $x^{509} - 1$ are lazy: they produce polynomials of degree below 512 but not necessarily the unique remainder of degree below 509. At the end of the computation we obtain the unique RFSB output by reducing the highest 3 bits of the highest register, i.e., xoring them into the lowest 3 bits of the lowest register and then setting them to 0.

All but the first step involve 4 128-bit load instructions and 12 128-bit load-and-xor instructions. The reduction of each of the 4 high registers takes another 8 instructions, specifically 1 128-bit register move instruction, 2 packed-64-bit-quadword-shift instructions (psrlq and psllq), 1 128-bit shift instruction (psrldq), 1 128-bit doubleword-shuffle instruction (pshufd), and 3 128-bit xor instructions.

Aside from loading and xoring matrix columns and performing reduction steps we need to load the input bytes and multiply their values by 64 to make them usable offsets for loads from the matrix. The AMD64 architecture allows offsets to be multiplied by a constant as part of the load operation, but this constant must not be larger than 8, which is not enough for 16-byte load operations. We load the input in chunks of 8 bytes into a 64-bit integer register and then extract 8 matrix offsets from these eight bytes using 8 move, 8 shift, and 8 mask instructions.

In total each step (except the first) consists of 60.5 instructions: 16 load and load-xor instructions for the matrix columns, 1 load instruction every second step to retrieve 8 bytes of input, 12 arithmetic instructions to construct matrix offsets from 4 bytes of input, and 32 arithmetic instructions for the reduction.

There are two obvious bottlenecks in this computation. First, each step involves 16.5 load instructions, so each step uses at least 16.5 cycles on all Intel Core 2 and Core i7 processors. Second, each step involves 56 arithmetic instructions, so each step uses at least 18.66 cycles. The second bottleneck implies a lower bound of 522 cycles for 28 steps. With Merkle–Damgård iteration each call to the compression function processes 48 bytes of input (together with the previous output), so these 522 cycles yield a lower bound of 10.89 cycles per byte.

There is enough parallelism in the computation to overcome most latency problems and come close to the lower bound, if instructions are scheduled carefully. Our software actually uses 11.99 cycles per byte on a Xeon X5650 (equivalent to a Core i7), and 13.62 cycles per byte on a Core 2 Quad Q9550.

Extra speed: incremental hashing. Zobrist in [46, page 6] emphasized the incremental nature of his hash, i.e., the ability to quickly update the hash output for a small change to the input: "moves will typically involve two XOR operations." For example, changing m_2 to m'_2 simply adds $c_2[m_2] \oplus c_2[m'_2]$ to the output. Bellare and Micciancio in [6] advertised the same feature, with various generalizations of $\oplus$ and without credit to Zobrist; their paper title was "A new paradigm for collision-free hashing: incrementality at reduced cost."

Chaining an incremental compression function such as RFSB produces a somewhat incremental hash function for long messages. (We say "somewhat" to emphasize, as in [6, Section 1.1], that this requires storage of all intermediate compression-function outputs, not merely the final output.) The block that changes can be recomputed incrementally at very high speed. Each subsequent block must be recomputed, but RFSB allows some of this computation to be skipped, since the only change to the input is in the chaining value. Note that Damgård's tree hash [21, Theorem 3.2] has only a logarithmic number of subsequent blocks for long messages.

Extra speed: fast batch verification. One can compute the sum of many RFSB outputs at higher speed than computing each output separately. The idea is very simple: the number of copies of $c_i[j]$ in the sum is the number of occurrences of j as m_i in the inputs; one can first count this number of occurrences, and then add $c_i[j]$ once if the number is odd. There are $2^b w$ separate counters, and computing all of them requires just one fast pass through all of the inputs. Each b bits require one counter update, which is faster than an r-bit xor for large r. All other steps become negligible as the number of inputs increases, but we nevertheless point out a speedup in those steps for large r: one can combine the $c_i[j]$ additions across i into a convolution, which in turn can be performed in subquadratic time by fast-multiplication techniques.

One can, at almost twice that speed, perform the following simple statistical check of a batch of alleged RFSB outputs: select 50% of the inputs, compute the sum of the RFSB outputs, and see whether the sum matches the sum of alleged outputs. This check cannot be fooled with probability above 50%. This is an example of what Bellare, Garay, and Rabin in [5] call the "atomic random subset test."

To achieve a much higher security level one can compute many independent sums. The cost of this computation grows sublinearly with the number of sums, and therefore sublinearly with the security level, because the sums have large overlaps that can be shared; see generally [5]. For comparison, the cost of separately computing each RFSB output grows linearly with the security level.

Extra security: avoiding variable-index table lookups. Our RFSB software performs a variable-index table lookup $c[m_i]$ for each input chunk m_i. This could be a problem for applications that hash secret data, such as HMAC: table lookups can leak index information through cache-timing attacks, hyperthreading attacks, etc., the same way that conditional branches can leak condition information. See generally [43].

One way to hide indices is to look up *all* table entries, using arithmetic operations to combine the results into each desired $c[m_i]$. RFSB has many table lookups to perform in parallel, and for large tables one can reduce the amount of arithmetic by batching these lookups into a sorting computation, as described in the following two paragraphs.

The inputs to this sorting computation are w vectors $(m_i, 1, i)$ together with 2^b vectors $(j, 0, c[j])$. Sorting brings each j next to all m_i's that are equal to j: first $(0, 0, c[0])$ is followed by all $(m_i, 1, i)$ with $m_i = 0$, then $(1, 0, c[0])$ is followed by all $(m_i, 1, i)$ with $m_i = 1$, etc. A linear-time pass from left to right then replaces each $(m_i, 1, i)$ with $(c[m_i], 1, i)$. A second sorting computation then puts $(c[m_i], 1, i)$ back into order of i.

It is well known that essentially-linear-time sorting does not require variable array indexing, and does not require conditional branches. For example, the Batcher sorting network sorts n items using approximately $(1/2)n(\lg n)^2$ compare-exchange steps, and one can do even better for large n. See [30, Section 5.3.4] for a survey of the extensive literature on sorting networks.

Another way to avoid variable-index table lookups is to compute $c[m_i]$ directly from m_i. The Käsper–Schwabe bitsliced implementation of AES [29] takes only about 7 cycles per byte, and new Intel CPUs support AES instructions taking only about 1.4 cycles per byte in parallelizable modes, i.e., about 90 cycles to compute $c[m_i]$. This is an order of magnitude slower than our software.

We have two suggestions for improving speed in this situation. One suggestion is to replace AES with something much simpler and faster. The full security of AES is certainly not required for RFSB: all that we need is a function generating a few elements of $\mathbf{F}_2[x]/(x^r - 1)$ without any obvious linear structure. The design of such functions is outside the scope of this paper.

The other suggestion, specific to HMAC, is to eliminate the initial keying in HMAC. Normally the HMAC input is public (such as a packet sent through the network), and if no secret key is inserted then RFSB with fast table lookups can be applied to this public input. The second stage of HMAC needs a key but is applied only to a short message; this stage can simply be SHA-256. Eliminating the initial keying allows MAC forgery via offline collision attacks, but we have designed RFSB precisely to make those collision attacks fail.

4   Attacks against RFSB

This section reviews and analyzes three different strategies to find collisions in FSB-type hash functions, including some new attack improvements. All of the strategies cost more than 2^{128} to find collisions in RFSB-509. This section also reviews reducibility, an attack tool that converts many FSB-type hash functions into smaller hash functions that are easier to break, and shows that this tool is inapplicable to RFSB.

We describe each attack for general RFSB parameters r, b, w. We illustrate the scalability of the attacks by considering the special case $b = 8$, $w \approx r/4$. In this case RFSB compresses $\approx 2r$ bits to r bits, using $r/4$ additions of r-bit vectors, i.e., 2 additions of r-bit vectors per byte of input; the compressed RFSB matrix fits into $32r$ bytes; and the cost of each attack is exponential in r.

We make some comments about preimage attacks as a stepping-stone to collision attacks, but we do not systematically analyze preimage attacks. Several modern hash-function designs, such as Keccak [12] and Quark [4], drop the traditional goal of having a preimage exponent twice as large as the best collision exponent; the question of whether RFSB reaches this goal is outside the scope of this paper. We are satisfied knowing that first preimages require breaking an output filter, and that second preimages are even more difficult to find than collisions.

Cost of computation. In this paper, cost means price/performance ratio: the size of the attack machine, multiplied by the time taken by the attack machine. For example, a brute-force k-bit key search can be carried out in time $2^k t$ by a small attack machine, or in time $2^k t/100$ by an attack machine 100 times larger, where t is the time to test a single key; these machines have the same cost.

In a classic paper thirty years ago, Brent and Kung proved that every n-bit multiplication circuit costs at least $n^{3/2}$. Here cost has a precise definition as the circuit area, multiplied by the time taken by the circuit, scaled by a particular constant reflecting the circuit speed, wire size, etc.; see [14, Theorem 3.1]. The same bound applies to other computations such as sorting; what matters is that the computations include n different shifts of one input, where the shift distance depends on the other input. The model of computation in [14] is a very broad class of two-dimensional circuits, including all of the most efficient computer technologies available today.

We use the same definition of cost in this paper. There are some future technologies, notably quantum computers, that cannot be efficiently simulated in this model, but we explicitly disregard those technologies.

We caution the reader that a naive operation count, as used in many cryptanalytic papers, is a poor predictor of cost when the allowed operations include random access to an arbitrarily large array. For example, sorting n keys uses fewer operations than performing n separate hash-function evaluations, even if the hash function is quite fast; but the *cost* of sorting n keys becomes vastly larger than the cost of n separate hash-function evaluations as n grows.

In the real world, sorting 2^{50} keys is a major engineering challenge, while 2^{50} hash-function evaluations are a rather easy computation. The current public sorting record is merely $2^{46.5}$ bytes, sorted by Yahoo's Hadoop in 10380 seconds on 3452 nodes with 13808 disks and 27616 cores. For comparison, readily available software performs 2^{47} separate evaluations of SHA-1 in 10380 seconds on just 20 PCs, each equipped with two GTX 295 graphics cards. We see overwhelming evidence that naive operation counts exaggerate the threat posed by communication-intensive cryptanalytic algorithms, and that this exaggeration grows with the size of the problem being solved. We see no evidence of similar problems with the cost model in [14].

Linearization. The following preimage attack was introduced by Bellare and Micciancio in [6, Appendix A]. First choose $m_1, m_2, \ldots, m_w$ and compute the difference $\Delta = h \oplus c_1[m_1] \oplus c_2[m_2] \oplus \cdots \oplus c_w[m_w]$, where h is the target hash. Then, for each i, choose $m_i' \neq m_i$ and compute the difference $\delta_i = c_i[m_i] \oplus c_i[m_i']$. Use linear algebra to find a subset of $\delta_1, \ldots, \delta_w$ with sum Δ, i.e., a linear relation $\epsilon_1 \delta_1 \oplus \cdots \oplus \epsilon_w \delta_w = \Delta$, if a linear relation exists. Then $c_1[m_1 \oplus \epsilon_1(m_1' \oplus m_1)] \oplus \ldots \oplus c_w[m_w \oplus \epsilon_w(m_w' \oplus m_w)] = h$ as desired. If no linear relation exists, try again with new choices of m_i and m_i'.

The main obstacle to this attack is that if $w < r$ then $\delta_1, \ldots, \delta_w$ generate a linear space of dimension at most w (and sometimes less), so under suitable randomness assumptions the desired linear relation exists with probability at most $2^w/2^r$. The expected number of iterations is therefore at least $2^r/2^w$; e.g., approximately $2^{0.75r}$ if $w \approx r/4$.

Saarinen in [40, Section 5] suggested doubling the number of generators for $w \leq r/2$ by computing two differences for each i, say $\delta_i = c_i[m_i] \oplus c_i[m_i']$ and $\delta_i' = c_i[m_i] \oplus c_i[m_i'']$. There are two obstacles to this attack: first, if $2w < r$ then a linear relation exists with probability at most $2^{2w}/2^r$; second, a relation is useful with probability only $(3/4)^w$, since a relation involving both δ_i and δ_i' is useless. The expected number of iterations is therefore at least $2^r/3^w$; e.g., approximately $2^{0.60r}$ if $w \approx r/4$.

More generally, for $k \geq 1$ and $w \leq r/k$, Saarinen suggested computing k differences $c_i[m_i] \oplus c_i[m_i'], c_i[m_i] \oplus c_i[m_i''], \ldots$ for each i. Then there are kw generators, so a linear relation exists with probability at most $2^{kw}/2^r$. A relation is useful with probability $((k+1)/2^k)^w$, so the expected number of iterations is slightly above $2^r/(k+1)^w$; e.g., approximately $2^{0.42r}$ if $w \approx r/4$ and $k = 4$.

Saarinen in [40, Section 4] suggested a different way to double the number of generators for collision attacks: compute $\delta_i = c_i[m_i] \oplus c_i[m_i']$ and $\delta_i' = c_i[n_i] \oplus c_i[n_i']$, and use linear algebra to find a subset of $\delta_1, \delta_1', \ldots, \delta_w, \delta_w'$ with sum $\Delta = c_1[m_1] \oplus c_1[n_1] \oplus c_2[m_2] \oplus c_2[n_2] \oplus \cdots \oplus c_w[m_w] \oplus c_w[n_w]$. The expected number of iterations here is at least $2^r/4^w$; e.g., approximately $2^{0.50r}$ if $w \approx r/4$.

More generally, for $w \leq r/(2k)$, one can take $2k$ generators for each i, with the first k generators of the form $c_i[m_i] \oplus c_i[m_i'], c_i[m_i] \oplus c_i[m_i''], \ldots$ and the second k generators of the form $c_i[n_i] \oplus c_i[n_i'], c_i[n_i] \oplus c_i[n_i''], \ldots$. A subset of these generators has sum $\Delta = c_1[m_1] \oplus c_1[n_1] \oplus c_2[m_2] \oplus c_2[n_2] \oplus \cdots \oplus c_w[m_w] \oplus c_w[n_w]$ with probability at most $2^{2kw}/2^r$. This subset is useful, revealing a collision, with probability $((k+1)^2/4^k)^w$, so the expected number of iterations is slightly above $2^r/(k+1)^{2w}$; e.g., approximately $2^{0.21r}$ if $w \approx r/4$ and $k = 2$.

A hybrid approach is to take $2k + 2$ generators for v values of i and $2k$ generators for $w - v$ values of i, assuming that $2kw + 2v \leq r$ and $0 \leq v \leq w$. The expected number of iterations is then slightly above $2^r/((k+1)^{2w}((k+2)/(k+1))^{2v})$. For $k = 1$ this approach appears in [40, Section 5.2].

For RFSB-509 the optimal attack parameters are $k = 2$ and $v = 30$, and the expected number of iterations is slightly above $2^{509}/(9^{112}(16/9)^{30}) > 2^{129}$. Since our security target is 2^{128}, we do not need to assess the cost of each iteration, but we make one comment on this cost: namely, taking more than r generators allows the cost of linear algebra to be amortized across several relations.

Note that [26, page 2] claims a simpler formula for the number of iterations for linearization, namely $(4/3)^{r-2w}$ whenever $w \leq r/2$. This claim is correct for $r/4 \leq w \leq r/2$ (take $k = 1$ in the hybrid approach above), but understates the number of iterations for $w < r/4$. The problem is that for $r/4 \leq w \leq r/2$ one can reach r generators by taking at most 4 generators for each i, but for $w < r/4$ this is no longer true. For the same reason, we disagree with the comment in [40, Section 5] that large values of k do not have "cryptanalytic advantages."

In the opposite direction, [24, Section 3.3] states that linearization is applicable only for $w \geq r/4$. Our RFSB-509 example disproves this statement. As a more extreme example, for the case $w = r/8$ used in [3], linearization finds collisions in time approximately $2^{0.41r}$. The time grows rapidly as w/r drops.

Generalized birthday attacks. The k-sum problem is to find $x_1 \in L_1, \ldots, x_k \in L_k$ such that $x_1 \oplus x_2 \oplus \cdots \oplus x_k = 0$, given k lists $L_1, \ldots, L_k$ of r-bit strings drawn uniformly and independently at random.

If $k = 2^{i-1}$ and each list has $2^{r/i}$ elements then generalized birthday attacks solve this problem using $O(k \cdot 2^{r/i})$ operations. In the next three paragraphs we review Wagner's single-modulus generalized birthday attack from [44], which is slightly simpler and faster than the original multiple-modulus generalized birthday attack introduced by Camion and Patarin in [16].

Merge lists L_1 and L_2 to find all sums of elements $u \oplus v$ with $u \in L_1$ and $v \in L_2$ that are 0 on their first r/i bits. Store these sums in a new list $L_{1,2}$. The expected number of elements in $L_{1,2}$ is again $2^{r/i}$. In the same way build a list $L_{3,4}$ from lists L_3 and L_4 and so on and a list $L_{k-1,k}$ from lists L_{k-1} and L_k. This first level of operations thus generates 2^{i-2} lists of expected length $2^{r/i}$ containing r-bit strings with their first r/i bits zero.

On the next level merge lists $L_{1,2}$ and lists $L_{3,4}$ to find all sums of elements $u \oplus v$ with $u \in L_{1,2}$ and $v \in L_{3,4}$ that are 0 on their first $2r/i$ bits. Store these sums in a new list $L_{1,2,3,4}$. As r/i bits are already known to be zero, the expected size of this list is again $2^{r/i}$. Similarly build lists $L_{5,6,7,8}$ and so on to list $L_{k-3,k-2,k-1,k}$.

Continue for $i - 2$ levels to build lists in the same way to obtain two lists $L_{1,\ldots,k/2}$ and $L_{k/2+1,\ldots,k}$, each containing an expected number of $2^{r/i}$ strings that are 0 on their first $(i-2)r/i$ bits. Compute all sums $u \oplus v$ with $u \in L_{1,\ldots,k/2}$ and $v \in L_{k/2+1,\ldots,k}$ to see, on average, one element with all r bits zero.

Applying this attack to an FSB-type hash function, and taking $k = w$, runs into an obstacle: there are only 2^b entries in each of the w input lists. The attack needs $2^{r/(1+\lfloor \lg k \rfloor)}$ entries. Usually b is much smaller than $r/(1 + \lfloor \lg k \rfloor)$, drastically reducing the success probability of the attack.

However, Coron and Joux in [20] used generalized birthday attacks to break many instances of the preliminary version of FSB presented in [1]. The idea is to take k smaller than w and to build the starting lists $L_1, \ldots, L_k$ by considering all possible xors of columns from one block. To build fewer but larger lists one can also consider xors of columns from multiple blocks, two columns per block. The solution of Wagner's tree algorithm is then the xor of $2w$ columns, exactly 2 per block. For extensions see [2], [7], and [36].

In the case of RFSB-509 the number of operations is minimized for $k = 16$. There are $\binom{256}{2} \approx 2^{15}$ possible 2-column combinations $c_1[m_1] \oplus c_1[m_1']$, and therefore 2^{105} possible 14-column combinations involving $c_1, c_1, c_2, c_2, \ldots, c_7, c_7$. Generate all of these combinations, and build a list containing the combinations that have their first 4 bits equal to 0, leaving 505 bits uncontrolled; this list has approximately 2^{101} elements. Build 16 lists from $c_1, c_2, \ldots, c_{112}$ by repeating this procedure. Then apply the generalized birthday attack, zeroing $5 \cdot 101 = 505$ bits. Overall this takes 15 merging steps on lists of size 2^{101}.

The cost of a single merging step is more than 2^{150} by [14, Theorem 3.1]; see the "Cost of computation" subsection above. Reducing the list size to 2^{82} would bring the merging cost down to approximately 2^{128}; but then 5 rounds clear only 410 bits, leaving 99 bits uncontrolled. At most $105 - 82 = 23$ bits can be controlled through precomputation, so the algorithm must be repeated 2^{76} times on average, bringing the cost above 2^{200}. We have considered several further variants of Wagner's attack, including the "Pollard" variant in [9, Section 2.2], and all of them cost far more than 2^{128}.

Information-set decoding. Augot, Finiasz, and Sendrier in [1, Section 4.2] presented an algorithm that uses roughly

$$\min\left\{ 2^r \Big/ \left(\binom{r/w_0}{2} + 1 \right)^{w_0} : w_0 \in \{1, 2, \ldots, w\} \right\}$$

iterations to find a collision $c_1[m_1] \oplus \cdots \oplus c_w[m_w] = c_1[m_1'] \oplus \cdots \oplus c_w[m_w']$. For $w \approx r/4$ this number of iterations is roughly $2^{0.3r}$. Each iteration uses some linear algebra, inverting an $r \times r$ matrix.

The second attack stated in Section 1 is a simplified version of the attack from [1]; the main difference is that their algorithm also allows having 0 columns in one block. For RFSB-509, with $r = 509$ and $w = 112$, the expected number of iterations is $(2^{510}/((\binom{4}{2} + \binom{4}{0})^{50}(\binom{5}{2} + \binom{5}{0})^{62}) \approx 2^{155}$.

Our new paper [10] presents a generalized version of the attack from [1]. The generalization combines ideas from various improved versions of information-set decoding, and restructures those ideas to fit the more complicated context of useful codewords having exactly two $c_1[\cdots]$, exactly two $c_2[\cdots]$, etc. In particular, the attack uses the ideas of Lee-Brickell [31], Leon [32], and Stern [42] to increase the chance of success per iteration at the expense of more effort, and more memory, per iteration. These generalized attack parameters allow the number of bit operations to be reduced below 2^{145}; but this is still far above 2^{128}, and the cost is even larger than the number of bit operations.

Reducibility. As mentioned in Section 1, the preliminary quasi-cyclic FSB proposals in [25] used powers of 2 for r, specifically $r = 512$ and $r = 1024$. Fouque and Leurent broke these proposals in [26].

To understand the Fouque–Leurent idea, consider transforming RFSB-509 into a smaller compression function f that works as follows. Take a string $(m_1, m_2, m_3, m_4, m_5)$ as input. Apply RFSB-509 to the repeated input

$$(m_1, m_2, m_3, m_4, m_5, \ldots, m_1, m_2, m_3, m_4, m_5, 0, 0).$$

Note that the output in $\mathbf{F}_2[x]/(x^{509} - 1)$ is a constant (for the $(0,0)$) plus a multiple of $\varphi = 1 + x^{128\cdot5} + x^{128\cdot10} + \cdots + x^{128\cdot105}$. Subtract the constant and divide by $g = \gcd\{x^{509} - 1, \varphi\}$, obtaining an element of $\mathbf{F}_2[x]/((x^{509} - 1)/g)$. The output of f is this element.

Observe that f is another Zobrist-type hash: $f(m_1, m_2, m_3, m_4, m_5)$ has the shape $f_1[m_1]\oplus f_2[m_2]\oplus f_3[m_3]\oplus f_4[m_4]\oplus f_5[m_5]$. The difficulty of finding collisions in this hash depends on how long its output is, i.e., on the degree of $(x^{509} - 1)/g$. If this output is short then one can easily find collisions in f, and therefore collisions in RFSB-509.

This attack does not work because the output is actually very long: g turns out to be $x - 1$, so $(x^{509} - 1)/g$ has degree 508. Attacks might marginally benefit from this change in degree, but not enough to compensate for the restricted set of inputs to f.

Modifying the attack to construct multiples of other polynomials φ also cannot work. The only divisors of $x^{509} - 1$ are $x^{509} - 1$, $(x^{509} - 1)/(x - 1)$, $x - 1$, and 1, corresponding to finding multiples of 1, $x - 1$, $(x^{509} - 1)/(x - 1)$, and $x^{509} - 1$ respectively. Finding multiples of 1 or $x - 1$ is trivial but useless, as in the $(m_1, m_2, m_3, m_4, m_5)$ example. Finding multiples of $(x^{509} - 1)/(x - 1)$ or $x^{509} - 1$ is a very hard preimage problem, preventing the attack from even getting started; an attacker able to solve that preimage problem would not have any need to transform RFSB-509 into a smaller function.

All RFSB parameters, and all parameters in the FSB SHA-3 submission [3], are protected in the same way against the Fouque–Leurent attack: r is chosen so that $(x^r - 1)/(x - 1)$ is irreducible. We are not aware of attacks against primes r with reducible $(x^r - 1)/(x - 1)$, but insisting on irreducibility does not severely restrict the choice of r.

References

[1] Augot, D., Finiasz, M., Sendrier, N.: A fast provably secure cryptographic hash function (2003), http://eprint.iacr.org/2003/230 Citations in this document: §1, §2, §4, §4, §4, §4

[2] Augot, D., Finiasz, M., Sendrier, N.: A family of fast syndrome based cryptographic hash functions. In: Mycrypt 2005 [23], pp. 64–83 (2005), http://lasecwww.epfl.ch/pub/lasec/doc/AFS05.pdf Citations in this document: §1, §1, §2, §4

[3] Augot, D., Finiasz, M., Gaborit, P., Manuel, S., Sendrier, N.: SHA-3 proposal: FSB (2008), http://www-rocq.inria.fr/secret/CBCrypto/fsbdoc.pdf Citations in this document: §1, §2, §2, §4, §4

[4] Aumasson, J.-P., Henzen, L., Meier, W., Naya-Plasencia, M.: QUARK: A lightweight hash. In: CHES 2010 [34], pp. 1–15 (2010), http://131002.net/quark/quark_full.pdf Citations in this document: §4

[5] Bellare, M., Garay, J.A., Rabin, T.: Fast batch verification for modular exponentiation and digital signatures. In: EUROCRYPT '98 [37], pp. 236–250 (1998), http://cseweb.ucsd.edu/~mihir/papers/batch.html Citations in this document: §3, §3

[6] Bellare, M., Micciancio, D.: A new paradigm for collision-free hashing: Incrementality at reduced cost. In: EUROCRYPT '97 [27], pp. 163–192 (1997), http://www-cse.ucsd.edu/~mihir/papers/incremental.html Citations in this document: §2, §2, §3, §3, §4

[7] Bernstein, D.J.: Better price-performance ratios for generalized birthday attacks. In: Workshop Record of SHARCS '07: Special-purpose Hardware for Attacking Cryptographic Systems (2007), http://cr.yp.to/papers.html#genbday Citations in this document: §4

[8] Bernstein, D.J., Lange, T. (eds.): eBASH: ECRYPT Benchmarking of All Submitted Hashes (2011), http://bench.cr.yp.to (accessed April 21, 2011) Citations in this document: §1, §3

[9] Bernstein, D.J., Lange, T., Niederhagen, R., Peters, C., Schwabe, P.: FSBday: implementing Wagner's generalized birthday attack against the SHA–3 round–1 candidate FSB. In: INDOCRYPT 2009 [39], pp. 18–38 (2009), http://eprint.iacr.org/2009/292 Citations in this document: §1, §4

[10] Bernstein, D.J., Lange, T., Peters, C., Schwabe, P.: Faster 2-regular information-set decoding. In: IWCC 2011 [17], pp. 81–98 (2011), http://eprint.iacr.org/2011/120 Citations in this document: §4

[11] Bernstein, D.J., Schwabe, P.: New AES software speed records. In: INDOCRYPT 2008 [38], pp. 322–336 (2008), http://cr.yp.to/papers.html#aesspeed Citations in this document: §2

[12] Bertoni, G., Daemen, J., Peeters, M., Van Assche, G.: Note on Keccak parameters and usage (2010), http://keccak.noekeon.org/NoteOnKeccakParametersAndUsage.pdf Citations in this document: §4

[13] Brassard, G. (ed.): CRYPTO '89. LNCS, vol. 435. Springer, Heidelberg (1990) See [21]

[14] Brent, R.P., Kung, H.T.: The area-time complexity of binary multiplication. Journal of the ACM 28, 521–534 (1981), http://wwwmaths.anu.edu.au/~brent/pub/pub055.html Citations in this document: §4, §4, §4, §4

[15] Buchmann, J., Ding, J. (eds.): PQCrypto 2008. LNCS, vol. 5299. Springer, Heidelberg (2008) See [24]

[16] Camion, P., Patarin, J.: The knapsack hash function proposed at Crypto'89 can be broken. In: EUROCRYPT '91 [22], pp. 39–53 (1991), http://hal.inria.fr/inria-00075097/en/ Citations in this document: §2, §4

[17] Chee, Y.M., Guo, Z., Ling, S., Shao, F., Tang, Y., Wang, H., Xing, C. (eds.): IWCC 2011. LNCS, vol. 6639. Springer, Heidelberg (2011) See [10]

[18] Clavier, C., Gaj, K. (eds.): CHES 2009. LNCS, vol. 5747. Springer, Heidelberg (2009) See [29]

[19] Cohen, G.D., Wolfmann, J. (eds.): Coding Theory and Applications, 3rd international colloquium, Toulon, France, November 2–4, 1988, proceedings. LNCS, vol. 388. Springer, Heidelberg (1989) See [42]

[20] Coron, J.-S., Joux, A.: Cryptanalysis of a provably secure cryptographic hash function (2004), http://eprint.iacr.org/2004/013 Citations in this document: §4

[21] Damgård, I.B.: A design principle for hash functions. In: CRYPTO '89 [13], pp. 416–427 (1990) Citations in this document: §1, §2, §3

[22] Davies, D.W. (ed.): EUROCRYPT '91. LNCS, vol. 547, pp. 3–540. Springer, Heidelberg (1991) See [16]

[23] Dawson, E., Vaudenay, S. (eds.): Mycrypt 2005. LNCS, vol. 3715. Springer, Heidelberg (2005) See [2]

[24] Finiasz, M.: Syndrome based collision resistant hashing. In: PQCrypto 2008 [15], pp. 137–147 (2008), http://www-rocq.inria.fr/secret/Matthieu.Finiasz/research/2008/finiasz-pqcrypto08.pdf Citations in this document: §1, §4

[25] Finiasz, M., Gaborit, P., Sendrier, N.: Improved fast syndrome based cryptographic hash functions. In: Proceedings of ECRYPT Hash Workshop (2007), http://www-roc.inria.fr/secret/Matthieu.Finiasz/research/2007/finiasz-gaborit-sendrier-ecrypt-hash-workshop07.pdf Citations in this document: §1, §1, §1, §1, §1, §1, §1, §2, §4

[26] Fouque, P.-A., Leurent, G.: Cryptanalysis of a hash function based on quasi-cyclic codes. In: CT-RSA 2008 [33], pp. 19–35 (2008) Citations in this document: §1, §1, §4, §4

[27] Fumy, W. (ed.): EUROCRYPT '97. LNCS, vol. 1233. Springer, Heidelberg (1997) See [6]

[28] Günther, C.G. (ed.): EUROCRYPT '88. LNCS, vol. 330. Springer, Heidelberg (1988) See [31]

[29] Käsper, E., Schwabe, P.: Faster and timing-attack resistant AES-GCM. In: CHES 2009 [18], pp. 1–17 (2009), http://eprint.iacr.org/2009/129 Citations in this document: §3

[30] Knuth, D.E.: The art of computer programming, vol. 3, Sorting and Searching, 2nd edn. Addison-Wesley, Reading (1998) Citations in this document: §3

[31] Lee, P.J., Brickell, E.F.: An observation on the security of McEliece's public-key cryptosystem. In: EUROCRYPT '88 [28], pp. 275–280 (1988) Citations in this document: §4

[32] Leon, J.S.: A probabilistic algorithm for computing minimum weights of large error-correcting codes. IEEE Transactions on Information Theory 34, 1354–1359 (1988) Citations in this document: §4

[33] Malkin, T. (ed.): CT-RSA 2008. LNCS, vol. 4964. Springer, Heidelberg (2008) See [26]

[34] Mangard, S., Standaert, F.-X. (eds.): CHES 2010. LNCS, vol. 6225. Springer, Heidelberg (2010) See [4]

[35] Mathieu, C. (ed.): Proceedings of the twentieth annual ACM-SIAM symposium on discrete algorithms, SODA 2009, New York, January 4–6, 2009. SIAM, Philadelphia (2009) See [36]

[36] Minder, L., Sinclair, A.: The extended k-tree algorithm. In: SODA 2009 [35], pp. 586–595 (2009), http://www.cs.berkeley.edu/~sinclair/ktree.pdf Citations in this document: §4

[37] Nyberg, K. (ed.): EUROCRYPT '98. LNCS, vol. 1403. Springer, Heidelberg (1998) See [5]

[38] Chowdhury, D.R., Rijmen, V., Das, A. (eds.): INDOCRYPT 2008. LNCS, vol. 5365. Springer, Heidelberg (2008) See [11]

[39] Roy, B., Sendrier, N. (eds.): INDOCRYPT 2009. LNCS, vol. 5922. Springer, Heidelberg (2009) See [9]

[40] Saarinen, M.-J.O.: Linearization attacks against syndrome based hashes. In: INDOCRYPT 2007 [41], pp. 1–9 (2007) Citations in this document: §1, §4, §4, §4, §4

[41] Srinathan, K., Rangan, C.P., Yung, M. (eds.): INDOCRYPT 2007. LNCS, vol. 4859. Springer, Heidelberg (2007) See [40]

[42] Stern, J.: A method for finding codewords of small weight. In: [19], pp. 106–113 (1989) Citations in this document: §4

[43] Tromer, E., Osvik, D.A., Shamir, A.: Efficient cache attacks on AES, and countermeasures. Journal of Cryptology 23, 37–71 (2010), http://people.csail.mit.edu/tromer/papers/cache-joc-official.pdf Citations in this document: §3

[44] Wagner, D.: A generalized birthday problem. In: CRYPTO 2002 [45], pp. 288–304 (2002), http://www.cs.berkeley.edu/~daw/papers/genbday.html Citations in this document: §4

[45] Yung, M. (ed.): CRYPTO 2002. LNCS, vol. 2442. Springer, Heidelberg (2002) See [44]

[46] Zobrist, A.L.: A new hashing method with application for game playing. Technical Report 88, Computer Sciences Department, University of Wisconsin (1970), https://www.cs.wisc.edu/techreports/1970/TR88.pdf Citations in this document: §2, §3

Montgomery's Trick and Fast Implementation of Masked AES

Laurie Genelle[1], Emmanuel Prouff[1], and Michaël Quisquater[2]

[1] Oberthur Technologies
{l.genelle,e.prouff}@oberthur.com
[2] University of Versailles
michael.quisquater@prism.uvsq.fr

Abstract. Side Channel Analysis (SCA) is a class of attacks that exploit leakage of information from a cryptographic implementation during execution. To thwart it, masking is a common strategy that aims at hiding correlation between the manipulated secret key and the physical measures. Even though the soundness of masking has often been argued, its application is very time consuming, especially when so-called higher-order SCA (HO-SCA) are considered. Reducing this overhead at the cost of limited RAM consumption increase is a hot topic for the embedded security industry. In this paper, we introduce such an improvement in the particular case of the AES. Our approach consists in adapting a trick introduced by Montgomery to efficiently compute several inversions in a multiplicative group. For such a purpose, and to achieve security against HO-SCA, recent works published at CHES 2010 and ACNS 2010 are involved. In particular, the secure dirac computation scheme introduced by Genelle *et al.* at ACNS is extended to achieve security against SCA at any order. As argued in the second part of this paper, our approach improves in time complexity all previous masking methods requiring little RAM .

Keywords: Montgomery's Trick, Side Channel Analysis, Secret Sharing, AES.

1 Introduction

In the nineties, a new family of attacks against implementations of cryptographic algorithms in embedded devices has been introduced. The idea of those attacks, called *Side Channel Analysis*, is to take advantage of the correlation between the manipulated secret data (*e.g.* secret keys) and physical measures such as the power consumption of the device. During the last two decades, the development of the smart card industry has urged the cryptographic research community to carry on with SCA and many papers describing either countermeasures or attacks developments have been published. In particular, the original attacks in [2, 9] have been improved and the concept of higher-order SCA (HO-SCA) has been introduced [11]. It consists in targeting the manipulation of several (and not only one) intermediate values at different times or different locations during

A. Nitaj and D. Pointcheval (Eds.): AFRICACRYPT 2011, LNCS 6737, pp. 153–169, 2011.
© Springer-Verlag Berlin Heidelberg 2011

the algorithm processing to reveal information on secret-dependent data called *sensitive data*. A HO-SCA targeting d intermediate values is usually named d^{th}-*order SCA*.

A common countermeasure against SCA is to randomize any sensitive variable appearing during the algorithm processing by *masking* techniques (also known as *secret sharing*)[1, 5, 7, 10, 17, 18, 22]. The principle is to randomly split each sensitive variable into several shares which will be manipulated separately. The shares propagate throughout the algorithm in such a way that no intermediate variable is sensitive. An advantage of dth-*order masking* schemes, for which the number of shares per sensitive variable is $d + 1$, is that they perfectly thwart d^{th}-order SCA. Moreover, whatever the kind of attacks (HO-SCA of any order or template attacks [15]), their soundness as a countermeasure has been argued for realistic leakage models in [3], where it is proved that the difficulty of recovering information on a variable shared into several parts grows exponentially with the number of shares. Resistance against HO-SCA is of importance since their effectiveness has been demonstrated against some family of devices [11, 16, 25]. Nowadays it must therefore be possible to easily scale the security of an implementation, starting from a resistance against 1st-order SCA and possibly going to resistance against d^{th}-order SCA for any d. In the case of block ciphers such as AES, the most critical part to protect when applying masking is the non-linear layer. The latter one involves 16 times a same non-linear function, called *s-box*. Several methods have been proposed in the literature to deal with this issue. We list in the next section those that are privileged, to the best of our knowledge, by the embedded device industry.

1.1 Related Work

State-of-the-art methods to protect the AES non-linear layer can be split into two categories. In one part we have methods that involve pre-computed look-up tables in RAM[1] to achieve good timing performances [5, 10, 19]. They are moreover particularly dedicated to 1st-order SCA. A few attempts have been done to extend these methods to deal with HO-SCA [22, 24]. However the approach did not permit to thwart SCA at order 3 or higher. Moreover, security against 2nd-order SCA is only achieved at the cost of a prohibitive memory overhead which excludes its use in low-cost devices. In brief, countermeasures that use pre-computed tables cannot be used to protect algorithms at order $d > 1$ in a RAM constrained environment. In a second part, we have methods that achieve SCA security at the cost of a limited amount of RAM memory (*e.g.* less than 100 bytes), which is particularly relevant for the smart cards industry [1, 17, 18, 20]. They have in common to exploit the simple algebraic structure of the AES s-box, which is affinely equivalent to a field inversion extended in 0 by setting $0^{-1} = 0$. They are less efficient in terms of timing than the methods in the first category, but can be embedded in constrained devices. Moreover, in contrast with the

---

[1] RAM is a volatile memory. It can be accessed in read/write mode and is usually used to store local or global variables used by the programs.

schemes in the first category, they are more suitable for the extension of the security at order d, since they do not rely on the table re-computation principle. Actually a scheme has been proposed in this category that achieves d^{th}-order SCA resistance whatever d [23]. It moreover turns out that even for $d = 2$ this scheme is much more efficient (around 3 times) than the methods based on table re-computations [22, 24].

1.2   Our Results

State-of-the-art methods secure the overall AES non-linear layer by separately securing each of the 16 s-boxes computation. Their complexity is hence merely equal to that of securing the AES s-box processing, or equivalently the field inversion over $GF(2^8)$. In this paper a different approach is introduced, where the masking of the whole non-linear layer is considered at once. This is accomplished by applying Montgomery's trick [13]. The latter one can be applied in any multiplicative group and enables to compute say n multiplicative inverses at the cost of $3(n - 1)$ field multiplications and one single inversion. It is relevant when the inversion processing is much more costly than that of a multiplication (*i.e.* at least around 3 times more costly) which is often the case in the context where the inversion includes SCA countermeasures. Even if the context of AES secure implementation seems to be a natural outlet for Montgomery's trick, its application is not straightforward. First, the field multiplications must be secured such that their use in the non-linear layer computation does not decrease the security of the implementation against (HO-)SCA. In other terms, if the inversions were resistant against d^{th}-order SCA, then the multiplications replacing them in the new process must also resist to those attacks. Secondly, since the elements of the AES state are defined over $GF(2^8)$ whereas Montgomery's trick applies on $GF(2^8)^\star$, a pre-processing must be defined to map the state elements up to the multiplicative group without modifying the functional behavior of the AES. Moreover, the mapping must not introduce any flaw w.r.t. d^{th}-order SCA. This paper deals with the two issues by using memory as little as possible for any SCA resistance order d. First, we suggest to use the multiplication algorithm proposed in [23] which can be specified to thwart HO-SCA of any order at the cost of acceptable timings and without extra large RAM memory consumption. To deal with the second issue, we base our approach on the technique suggested in [5], that reduces the problematic to that of securing a Dirac function (which is a function that maps zero values into non-zero ones). We improve the method to use less RAM memory than in the original method and we extend it to get a Dirac computation secure at any order d. The use of such solutions results in a secure and efficient adaptation of Montgomery's trick in the context of SCA-resistant AES implementations. Since our approach is only relevant when the ratio between the cost of a secure inversion and that of secure multiplication is lower than some threshold, it is not suitable when both functions are tabulated once per algorithm execution. In the other cases (which include all the proposed countermeasures against HO-SCA), our proposal improves the timing performance at the cost of a small RAM overhead: 1st-order secure methods not based on table re-computation are improved by at least 21% and we have a timing gain of at least 13% and 9% for 2nd-order and 3rd-order secure methods respectively.

1.3 Paper Organization

The paper is organized as follows. We briefly introduce in Sect. 2 some basics on AES and SCA. Section 3 describes Montgomery's trick in the context of a SCA-resistant AES implementation. Section 4 presents the different tools required for the new generic scheme. Section 5 reports on the efficiency of several implementations of our method in combination with state-of-the-art secure implementations of AES. Eventually Sect. 6 concludes the paper.

2　Notations and Basics on AES and SCA

We briefly introduce here the AES algorithm, and we give some notations and definitions used to describe our proposal and to analyze its security.

The AES block cipher algorithm is the composition of several rounds that operate on an internal *state* denoted by $\mathbf{s} = (s_i)_{i \leq 15}$ and viewed in the following either as a (16×1)-matrix over GF(2^8) or as a (16×8)-binary matrix (in this case each s_i is considered as a vector in GF$(2)^8$ whose bit-coordinates are denoted by $s_i[j]$). Field multiplication will be denoted by $\otimes$, whereas field addition will be denoted by $\oplus$. The latter exactly corresponds to the bitwise addition in GF$(2)^8$. Eventually the bitwise multiplication (AND) will be denoted by $\odot$. Each AES round is the composition of a round-key addition, a linear layer and a non-linear layer. The latter one consists in a single AES s-box that is applied to each state element s_i separately. It is defined as the composition of an affine function with the multiplicative inverse function in GF(2^8), i.e. $s \mapsto s^{-1}$, extended in 0 by setting $0^{-1} = 0$. We call the latter function *extended inversion* and we denote it Inv. The global transformation $(s_i)_{i \leq 15} \mapsto (s_i^{-1})_{i \leq 15}$ is denoted by Inv-Layer. In this paper, we focus on protecting the processing of Inv-Layer against (HO-)SCA, the round-key addition, the linear layer and the affine transformation being straightforward to secure (see for instance [10]). We moreover assume that the masking strategy is followed to protect the overall AES. When such a scheme is specified at order d, the state $\mathbf{s}$ is randomly split into $d + 1$ shares $(\mathbf{s}^0, \cdots, \mathbf{s}^d)$ such that $\mathbf{s} = \bigoplus_{i=0}^{d} \mathbf{s}^i$. We shall say that $(\mathbf{s}^0, \cdots, \mathbf{s}^d)$ is a $(d + 1)$-*sharing* of $\mathbf{s}$. After denoting by s_i^j the ith line of the jth share, we can check that $(s_i^0, ..., s_i^d)$ is a $(d + 1)$-sharing of the state element s_i. In the following, we shall say that a variable is sensitive if it can be expressed as a deterministic function of the plaintext and the secret key and which is not constant with respect to the secret key. Additionally, we shall say that an algorithm achieves d^{th}-*order SCA security* if every d-tuple of its intermediate variables is independent of any sensitive variable.

In the next section we give the core principle of our proposal to improve the timing efficiency of the state-of-the-art d^{th}-order SCA-secure AES implementations.

3   Montgomery's Trick to Secure the AES Inv-Layer: Core Idea

This section is organized as follows: first we introduce the classical approach when masking is involved, secondly we describe Montgomery's trick as introduced in [13] and eventually we show the adaption of the latter to SCA-secure AES implementations.

3.1   Classical Approach

Usual implementations of Inv-Layer are protected against d^{th}-order SCA by following a divide-and-conquer approach. The global security is deduced from the local security of each of the sixteen processings of Inv. To achieve local security, a scheme Sec-Inv$(d, \cdot)$ is involved. It applies on the $(d + 1)$-sharing $(s_i^0, \cdots, s_i^d)$ of each state element s_i and outputs a $(d+1)$-sharing $(r_i^0, \cdots, r_i^d)$ of the inverse Inv(s_i). Eventually the secure version of Inv-Layer outputs a $(d+1)$-sharing $(\mathbf{r}^0, \cdots, \mathbf{r}^d)$ of Inv-Layer$(\mathbf{s})$. For $d = 1$, the secure inversion algorithm Sec-Inv$(d, \cdot)$ can be chosen among the numerous ones proposed in the literature [1, 5, 7, 10, 17, 18, 22]. For $d > 1$, the choice is much more reduced and the secure inversion algorithm must be one of those proposed in [22, 23, 24].

In the next section we introduce an alternative to the classical approach which starts from a trick introduced by Montgomery[13].

3.2   Approach with Montgomery's Trick

The principle of Montgomery's trick is to reduce the total number of field inversions by using field multiplications. Let us consider n field elements s_i. With Montgomery's trick the n inverses $(s_i^{-1})_{0 \leq i \leq n-1}$ are computed by performing two separate passes through the data. In the forward pass, a variable Prod$_0$ is initialized with s_0 and then the following product is computed for $i = 1, \ldots, n-1$:

$$\text{Prod}_i = \text{Prod}_{i-1} \otimes s_i \ .$$

The last product Prod$_{n-1}$ satisfies Prod$_{n-1} = \prod_{i=0}^{n-1} \text{Prod}_i$. Then a single field inversion

$$I = (\text{Prod}_{n-1})^{-1}$$

is computed. Next, in the backward pass, t_{n-1} is initialized by I and then for $i = n - 1, \ldots, 1$, the two following products are computed

$$s_i^{-1} = t_i \otimes \text{Prod}_{i-1} \qquad \text{and} \qquad t_{i-1} = t_i \otimes s_i \ .$$

To finish s_0^{-1} is set to t_0. In total the algorithm requires a single field inverse, and $3(n - 1)$ field multiplications.

Montgomery's trick has been applied in many contexts [6, 12, 14]. This paper investigates its application to improve the secure AES Inv-Layer computation. Clearly this application cannot be done directly and we have to deal with two main issues. The first issue is that the inverse I cannot be computed directly from the product of the AES state elements since the latter ones may equal zero. The second issue is that the application of the trick must be secure against SCA of any order d. We propose hereafter a modification of Montgomery's trick that circumvents the first issue. Then, in Sect. 3.3, we explain how it can be efficiently secured at any order.

To deal with the first issue we propose to first transform the elements of the state in such way that their image is always non-zero and to keep track of this transformation. More precisely, prior to the forward pass, we add each state element s_i with its Dirac value $\delta_0(s_i)$ defined by $\delta_0(s_i) = 1$ if $s_i = 0$ and $\delta_0(s_i) = 0$ otherwise. The computation of the products $(\mathrm{Prod}_i)_{0 \leq i \leq 15}$ is let unchanged except that it applies on $(s_i \oplus \delta_0(s_i))_{i \leq 15}$ instead of $(s_i)_{i \leq 15}$. Eventually the potential modification is corrected by adding $\delta_0(s_i)$ to $(s_i \oplus \delta_0(s_i))_{i \leq 15}^{-1}$ after having computed $(t_i)_{i \leq 15}$. The completeness of this treatment holds from $(s_i \oplus \delta_0(s_i))^{-1} = s_i^{-1} \oplus \delta_0(s_i)$. The sequence of those different steps is presented in Alg. 1.

Algorithm 1. Montgomery's Trick Applied on AES State Elements

---

INPUT(S): The AES state $\mathbf{s} = (s_i)_{i \leq 15}$ in $\mathrm{GF}(2^8)^{16}$
OUTPUT(S): $(s_i^{-1})_{i \leq 15} = \texttt{Inv-Layer}(\mathbf{s})$

** *Mapping of the state elements from $\mathrm{GF}(2^8)$ to $\mathrm{GF}(2^8)^\star$.*
1. **for** $i = 0$ **to** 15 **do**
   $\delta_0(s_i) \leftarrow \texttt{Dirac}(s_i)$
   $s_i \leftarrow s_i \oplus \delta_0(s_i)$

** *Computation of intermediate products used for the inverses extraction.*
2. $\mathrm{Prod}_0 \leftarrow s_0$
3. **for** $i = 1$ **to** 15 **do**
   $\mathrm{Prod}_i \leftarrow \mathrm{Prod}_{i-1} \otimes s_i$

** *Computation of the single inverse.*
4. $I \leftarrow (\mathrm{Prod}_{15})^{-1}$

** *Extraction of s_i^{-1} for every $i \leq 15$.*
5. **from** $i = 15$ **down to** 1 **do**
   $s_i^{-1} \leftarrow I \otimes \mathrm{Prod}_{i-1}$
   $I \leftarrow I \otimes s_i$
6. $s_0^{-1} \leftarrow I$

** *Mapping of the state elements from $\mathrm{GF}(2^8)^\star$ to $\mathrm{GF}(2^8)$.*
7. **for** $i = 0$ **to** 15 **do**
   $s_i^{-1} \leftarrow s_i^{-1} \oplus \delta_0(s_i)$

8. **return** $(s_0^{-1}, \ldots, s_{15}^{-1})$

The operation $\texttt{Dirac}(s_i)$ computes the Dirac value of s_i. Algorithm 1 could be optimized by doing the calls to $\texttt{Dirac}(\cdot)$ inside the loops in Steps 3, but for a better comprehension of our proposal we described intentionally the different steps separately.

3.3 Secure Computation

The application of Alg. 1 in a context where all the sensitive data are represented by a $(d+1)$-sharing requires two modifications. First any intermediate result (including the input and output) must be replaced by a $(d+1)$-sharing representing it. Additionally, operations $\texttt{Dirac}(\cdot)$ and $\otimes$ shall be replaced by secure versions of them, called $\texttt{Secure-Dirac}(d, \cdot)$ and $\texttt{Secure-MUL}(d, \cdot, \cdot)$ and satisfying the following properties:

- $\texttt{Secure-Dirac}(d, \cdot)$ must output a $(d+1)$-sharing $(\Delta^0, \cdots, \Delta^d)$ of $\Delta = (\delta_0(s_0), \cdots, \delta_0(s_{15}))$ from the $(d+1)$-sharing $(\mathbf{s}^0, \cdots, \mathbf{s}^d)$ of $\mathbf{s}$. The processing must moreover be d^{th}-order secure.
- $\texttt{Secure-MUL}(d, \cdot, \cdot)$ must output the $(d+1)$-sharing $(p^0, \ldots, p^d)$ of $p = s_i \otimes s_j$ from the $(d+1)$-sharing $(s_i^0, \cdots, s_i^d)$ and $(s_j^0, \cdots, s_j^d)$ of s_i and s_j.

We shall moreover also need a function $\texttt{Add-Dirac}(\cdot, \cdot)$ that applies on the $(d+1)$-sharing of Δ and $\mathbf{s}$ and simply replaces the first column of each matrix share $\mathbf{s}^i$ by the bitwise addition of this column with the binary column vector Δ^i. Its cost $\mathsf{C}_{\text{A-D}}$ in terms of logical operations is therefore $16(d+1) \times \mathsf{c}_\oplus$, where $\mathsf{c}_\oplus$ denotes the cost of a bitwise addition over $\mathrm{GF}(2^8)$.

We sum-up hereafter the main steps of our new proposal to implement the AES $\texttt{Inv-Layer}$ in a dth-order SCA-secure way.

Completeness. Step 1 computes the $(d+1)$-sharing of the Dirac of each state element s_i, the shares of same index being grouped to form the 16-bit vectors Δ^0, ..., Δ^d. It is viewed as a $(16 \times (d+1))$-binary matrix whose bit-coordinates are denoted by $\Delta^j[i]$. The second step transforms the $(d+1)$-sharing $(s_i^0, \cdots, s_i^d)$ of each state element s_i into a new one $(s_i^0 \oplus \Delta^0[i], \cdots, s_i^d \oplus \Delta^d[i])$. Since the sum $\bigoplus_j \Delta^j[i]$ (resp. $\bigoplus_j s_i^j$) equals $\delta_0(s_i)$ (resp. s_i), this step outputs a $(d+1)$-sharing of $s_i \oplus \delta_0(s_i)$. Steps 3 to 7 simply implement the SCA-secure Montgomery's Trick, where each elementary operation is performed thanks to a dth-order secure algorithm. Eventually, the 8th step reverses the mapping (if it has occurred) of a state element $r_i = 0$ into 1. Namely, it processes in a secure way the $(d+1)$-sharing of $(r_i + \delta_0(s_i))^{-1} \oplus \delta_0(s_i)$ which equals r_i^{-1}, since $1^{-1} = 1$ and 0^{-1} equals 0 by assumption.

Algorithm 2 involves four procedures: $\texttt{Sec-Inv}(d, \cdot)$, $\texttt{Add-Dirac}(\cdot, \cdot)$, $\texttt{Secure-Dirac}(d, \cdot)$ and $\texttt{Secure-MUL}(d, \cdot, \cdot)$. The different ways how to choose the function $\texttt{Sec-Inv}(d, \cdot)$ have been presented in Sect. 3.1. Additionally, we have shown in

---

Algorithm 2. Secure Inv-Layer with Montgomery's Trick

INPUT(S): The AES state s split into $d+1$ shares $(s^0, \cdots, s^d)$
OUTPUT(S): A new $(d+1)$-sharing $(r^0, \cdots, r^d)$ of the AES state r such that $r = $ Inv-Layer(s)

** *Mapping of the state elements from* $GF(2^8)$ *to* $GF(2^8)^\star$.
1. $(\Delta^0, \cdots, \Delta^d) \leftarrow$ Secure-Dirac$(d, (s^0, \cdots, s^d))$
2. $(s^0, \cdots, s^d) \leftarrow$ Add-Dirac$((s^0, \cdots, s^d), (\Delta^0, \cdots, \Delta^d))$

** *Computation of the* $(d+1)$-*sharing* $(\mathrm{Prod}_i^0, \cdots, \mathrm{Prod}_i^d)$ *of the intermediate products* Prod_i *used for the inverses extraction.*
3. $(\mathrm{Prod}_0^0, \cdots, \mathrm{Prod}_0^d) \leftarrow (s_0^0, \cdots, s_0^d)$
4. **for** $i = 1$ **to** 15 **do**
  $(\mathrm{Prod}_i^0, \cdots, \mathrm{Prod}_i^d) \leftarrow$ Secure-MUL$(d, (\mathrm{Prod}_{i-1}^0, \cdots, \mathrm{Prod}_{i-1}^d), (s_i^0, \cdots, s_i^d))$
** *Secure computation of the* $(d+1)$-*sharing of* $(\mathrm{Prod}_{15})^{-1}$ *from its sharing*
$(\mathrm{Prod}_{15}^0, \cdots, \mathrm{Prod}_{15}^d)$.
5. $(\mathrm{Inv}^0, \cdots, \mathrm{Inv}^d) \leftarrow$ Sec-Inv$(d, (\mathrm{Prod}_{15}^0, \cdots, \mathrm{Prod}_{15}^d))$

** *Extraction of the* $(d+1)$-*sharing* $(r_i^0, \cdots, r_i^d)$ *of* s_i^{-1} *for every* $i \leq 15$.
6. **from** $i = 15$ **down to** 1 **do**
  $(r_i^0, \cdots, r_i^d) \leftarrow$ Secure-MUL$(d, (\mathrm{Prod}_{i-1}^0, \cdots, \mathrm{Prod}_{i-1}^d), (\mathrm{Inv}^0, \cdots, \mathrm{Inv}^d))$
  $(\mathrm{Inv}^0, \cdots, \mathrm{Inv}^d) \leftarrow$ Secure-MUL$(d, (\mathrm{Inv}^0, \cdots, \mathrm{Inv}^d), (s_i^0, \cdots, s_i^d))$
7. $(r_0^0, \cdots, r_0^d) \leftarrow (\mathrm{Inv}^0, \cdots, \mathrm{Inv}^d)$

** *Mapping of the state elements from* $GF(2^8)^\star$ *to* $GF(2^8)$.
8. $(r^0, \cdots, r^d) \leftarrow$ Add-Dirac$((r^0, \cdots, r^d), (\Delta^0, \cdots, \Delta^d))$

9. **return** $(r^0, \cdots, r^d)$

---

this section how to simply process Add-Dirac$(\cdot, \cdot)$. For our presentation to be consistent, procedures Secure-MUL$(d, \cdot, \cdot)$ and Secure-Dirac$(d, \cdot)$ still need to be described and they are actually the most tricky parts of our proposal. The purpose of the following section is to present them. Eventually, the analysis of the complexity and security of the overall proposal (Alg. 2) is done in Sect. 4.3.

4   Secure and Efficient Implementations of the Primitives

4.1   Field and Logical Multiplications Secure at Any Order

Let ℓ be a positive integer and let a and b be two elements of the field $GF(2^\ell)$ with multiplication law $\otimes$. We denote by p the product $a \otimes b$. In Sect. 3, we have promoted the need for a secure multiplication Secure-MUL$(d, \cdot, \cdot)$ that securely constructs a $(d+1)$-sharing $(p^0, \cdots, p^d)$ of p from the $(d+1)$-sharings $(a^0, \cdots, a^d)$ and $(b^0, \cdots, b^d)$ of a and b respectively. An algorithm to process such a secure multiplication has been proposed in [23] as an extension of Ishaï *et al.* 's work [7]. The main steps of this algorithm are recalled hereafter.

Algorithm 3. Secure-MUL$(d, \cdot, \cdot)$

INPUT(S): A masking order d and two $(d+1)$-sharings $(a^0, \cdots, a^d)$ and $(b^0, \cdots, b^d)$ of a and b respectively.

OUTPUT(S): A $(d+1)$-sharing $(p^0, \cdots, p^d)$ such that $p = a \otimes b$.

---

1. Compute the $((d+1) \times (d+1))$-matrix $\mathbf{M} = (a^0, \cdots, a^d)^\mathsf{T} \times (b^0, \cdots, b^d)$, where $\times$ denotes the matrix product and where the matrix coordinates are multiplied with the law $\otimes$.
2. Split $\mathbf{M}$ into an upper triangular matrix $\mathbf{M}_1$ and a strictly lower triangular matrix $\mathbf{M}_2$ such that $\mathbf{M} = \mathbf{M}_1 \oplus \mathbf{M}_2$.
3. Generate a strictly upper triangular random matrix $\mathbf{R}_1 = (r_{ij})_{i,j}$ (i.e. $j \leq i$ implies $r_{ij} = 0$).
4. Compute $\mathbf{U} = \mathbf{M}_1 \oplus \mathbf{R} \oplus \mathbf{M}_2^\mathsf{T}$ from left to right, where $\mathbf{R}$ denotes $\mathbf{R}_1 \oplus \mathbf{R}_1^\mathsf{T}$.
5. Return $(p^0, \cdots, p^d) = \mathbf{1} \times \mathbf{U}$, where $\mathbf{1}$ denotes the line vector whose $d+1$ coordinates are all equal to 1.

In the three following paragraphs we discuss the completeness, the security and the complexity of Alg. 3.

Completeness. By construction, the sum p of the output shares p^i satisfies $\bigoplus_{i \leq d} p^i = \mathbf{1} \times \mathbf{U} \times \mathbf{1}^\mathsf{T}$. On the other hand, we have:

$$\mathbf{1} \times \mathbf{U} \times \mathbf{1}^\mathsf{T} = \mathbf{1} \times (\mathbf{M_1} \oplus \mathbf{R} \oplus \mathbf{M_2}^\mathsf{T}) \times \mathbf{1}^\mathsf{T} \ ,$$
$$= \mathbf{1} \times (\mathbf{M_1} \oplus \mathbf{R_1} \oplus \mathbf{M_2}^\mathsf{T} \oplus \mathbf{R_1}^\mathsf{T}) \times \mathbf{1}^\mathsf{T} \ ,$$
$$= \mathbf{1} \times (\mathbf{M_1} \oplus \mathbf{R_1} \oplus (\mathbf{M_2} \oplus \mathbf{R_1})^\mathsf{T}) \times \mathbf{1}^\mathsf{T} \ ,$$
$$= \mathbf{1} \times (\mathbf{M_1} \oplus \mathbf{R_1}) \times \mathbf{1}^\mathsf{T} \oplus \mathbf{1} \times (\mathbf{M_2} \oplus \mathbf{R_1}) \times \mathbf{1}^\mathsf{T} \ ,$$
$$= \mathbf{1} \times (\mathbf{M_1}) \times \mathbf{1}^\mathsf{T} \oplus \mathbf{1} \times (\mathbf{M_2}) \times \mathbf{1}^\mathsf{T} \oplus \mathbf{1} \times (\mathbf{R_1}) \times \mathbf{1}^\mathsf{T} \oplus \mathbf{1} \times (\mathbf{R_1}) \times \mathbf{1}^\mathsf{T},$$
$$= \mathbf{1} \times \mathbf{M} \times \mathbf{1}^\mathsf{T} = \mathbf{1} \times (a^0, \cdots, a^d)^\mathsf{T} \times (b^0, \cdots, b^d) \times \mathbf{1}^\mathsf{T} \ .$$

Since $(a^0, \cdots, a^d)$ and $(b^0, \cdots, b^d)$ are respectively a $(d+1)$-sharing of a and b, we have $a = \mathbf{1} \times (a^0, \cdots, a^d)^\mathsf{T}$ and $b = \mathbf{1} \times (b^0, \cdots, b^d)^\mathsf{T}$. We thus deduce that $\mathbf{1} \times \mathbf{U} \times \mathbf{1}^\mathsf{T}$ equals $p = a \otimes b$ which states the completeness of Alg. **??**.

Security. The security of Secure-MUL$(d, \cdot, \cdot)$ against d^{th}-order SCA has been proved in [23].

Complexity. Let us denote by $\mathsf{c}_\otimes$ (resp. $\mathsf{c}_\oplus$) the cost of a field multiplication $\otimes$ (resp. bitwise addition $\oplus$) in terms of logical operations. In [23], it is argued that Secure-MUL$(d, \cdot, \cdot)$ algorithm can be processed with $(d+1)^2$ field multiplications $\otimes$ and $2d(d+1)$ bitwise additions $\oplus$. Its cost, denoted by $\mathsf{C}_{\text{S-M}}$, therefore satisfies:

$$\mathsf{C}_{\text{S-M}} = (d+1)^2 \times \mathsf{c}_\otimes + 2d(d+1) \times \mathsf{c}_\oplus \ . \tag{1}$$

It moreover requires the generation of $d(d + 1)/2$ random bytes. As an illustration, securing a field multiplication $\otimes$ over $\mathrm{GF}(2^8)$ thanks to Secure-MUL$(d, \cdot, \cdot)$ requires $C_{\text{S-M}} = 4 \times c_\otimes + 4 \times c_\oplus$ for $d = 1$, and $C_{\text{S-M}} = 9 \times c_\otimes + 12 \times c_\oplus$ for $d = 2$, and $C_{\text{S-M}} = 16 \times c_\otimes + 24 \times c_\oplus$ for $d = 3$.

In the following, we shall also need a slightly modified version of Secure-MUL$(d, \cdot, \cdot)$ called Secure-AND$(d, \ell, \cdot, \cdot)$ and enabling to securely process the bitwise multiplication $\odot^\ell$ of two ℓ-bit vectors a and b (*i.e.* a bitwise AND). It applies exactly the same steps as Secure-MUL$(d, \cdot, \cdot)$ algorithm except that the operation $\otimes$ is replaced by $\odot^\ell$. It moreover obviously inherits its dth-order SCA security and its complexity from that of Secure-MUL$(d, \cdot, \cdot)$. To be absolutely clear in our argument in the next sections, we shall denote by $\odot^\ell_{\text{sec}}$ the operation $\odot^\ell$ when it is processed by applying Secure-AND$(d, \ell, \cdot, \cdot)$.

4.2   Dirac Computation Secure at Any Order

In [5], a 1st-order secure implementation of the Dirac function is proposed. It involves a look-up table in RAM whose size (32 or 256 bytes) is chosen according to an expected timing/memory trade-off. This method has two drawbacks in our context. First, it consumes RAM whereas we are looking for a secure AES implementation that uses memory as little as possible. Secondly, the method is only resistant to 1st-order SCA and its extension to achieve higher-order security seems to be an issue. Indeed, it inherits from the same drawbacks w.r.t higher-order SCA than all the methods based on table re-computations techniques [4].

In order to define a Dirac implementation secure at any order, we chose to start from the description of this function in terms of logical instructions.

Dirac Computation. Let $\overline{x}$ denote the bitwise complement of a word (or a matrix) x and let $\odot$ be the logical binary AND. The Dirac $\delta_0(s)$ of a ℓ-bit vector $s = (s[0], \cdots, s[\ell - 1])$ satisfies:

$$\delta_0(s) = (\overline{s}[0]) \odot (\overline{s}[1]) \odot \cdots \odot (\overline{s}[\ell - 1]) \ . \tag{2}$$

The computation of the Dirac of ℓ elements $s_0,..., s_{\ell-1}$ in $\mathrm{GF}(2)^\ell$ can be performed by using a bit-slicing approach (see *e.g.* [8])[2]. The elements are first represented as a $(\ell \times \ell)$-binary matrix $\mathbf{s}$ whose lines are the s_i. Denoting by $\mathbf{t}$ the transpose of $\mathbf{s}$, the line t_j of $\mathbf{t}$ satisfies $t_j = (s_0[j], \cdots, s_{\ell-1}[j])$.

The Dirac values of the s_i are then computed by applying the operation $\odot^\ell$ on the bitwise complement of the t_j, leading to the following analogous of (2):

$$\Delta = (\delta_0(s_0), \cdots, \delta_0(s_{\ell-1})) = \overline{t}_0 \odot^\ell \overline{t}_1 \odot^\ell \cdots \odot^\ell \overline{t}_{\ell-1} \ . \tag{3}$$

The cost of the Dirac computation (3) per ℓ-bit vector s_i is around $(\ell - 1)/\ell$ computation of $\odot^\ell$ plus 1 bitwise complement, to which we have to add the cost of a $(\ell \times \ell)$-matrix transposition over $\mathrm{GF}(2)$ (to get $\mathbf{t}$ from $\mathbf{s}$).

---

[2] To easy the description of the method we assume that there are ℓ elements s_i of size ℓ. This is needed to have a square matrix in the following. The generalization of the method for $n > \ell$ is given at the end of the section.

Secure Dirac Computation. In the context of a dth-order masking scheme, (3) must be modified to no longer operate on $\mathbf{t}$ but on a $(d+1)$-sharing $(\mathbf{t}^0, \ldots, \mathbf{t}^d)$ of it (each share $\mathbf{t}^i$ being a binary $(\ell \times \ell)$-matrix). Moreover the computations of the operation $\odot^\ell$ must be secured thanks to the algorithm $\texttt{Secure-AND}(d, \ell, \cdot, \cdot)$ introduced in Sect. 4.1. By applying the latter algorithm to the lines of the $\mathbf{t}^i$, we can construct a $(d+1)$-sharing $(\Delta^0, \cdots, \Delta^d)$ of the ℓ-bit vector Δ defined in (3). Actually, if we denote by t_j^i the jth line of $\mathbf{t}^i$, the algorithm we present in this section aims at processing the following computation:

$$(\Delta^0, \cdots, \Delta^d) = (\bar{t}_0^0, \cdots, t_0^d) \underset{\text{sec}}{\odot^\ell} (\bar{t}_1^0, \cdots, t_1^d) \underset{\text{sec}}{\odot^\ell} \cdots \underset{\text{sec}}{\odot^\ell} (\bar{t}_{\ell-1}^0, \cdots, t_{\ell-1}^d) \ . \quad (4)$$

Comparing (3) and (4), we can observe that each $\bar{t}_i$ has been replaced by its $(d+1)$-sharing, and that the operation $\odot^\ell$ has been replaced by its secure version $\underset{\text{sec}}{\odot^\ell}$. We give hereafter a formal description of $\texttt{Secure-Dirac}(d, \cdot)$.

Algorithm 4. $\texttt{Secure-Dirac}(d, \cdot)$

INPUT(S): An order d, a length ℓ and a $(d+1)$-sharing $(s^0, \cdots, s^d)$ of a binary $(\ell \times \ell)$-matrix s whose lines are the s_i.
OUTPUT(S): A $(d+1)$-sharing $(\Delta^0, \cdots, \Delta^d)$ of the ℓ-bit vector $\Delta = (\delta_0(s_0), \cdots, \delta_0(s_{\ell-1}))$

** *Compute the bitwise complement $\bar{s}^0$ of the $(\ell \times \ell)$-matrix s^0.*
1. $s^0 \longleftarrow \bar{s}^0$.

** *Transpose the $(\ell \times \ell)$ matrices s^i for every $i \leq d$.*
2. **for** $i = 0$ to d
       do $t^i \longleftarrow (s^i)^{\mathsf{T}}$.

** *Process the Dirac computations.*
3. $(\Delta^0, \cdots, \Delta^d) \longleftarrow (t_0^0, \cdots, t_0^d)$
4. **for** $i = 1$ to $\ell - 1$
       do $(\Delta^0, \cdots, \Delta^d) \longleftarrow \texttt{Secure-AND}(d, \ell, (\Delta^0, \cdots, \Delta^d), (t_i^0, \cdots, t_i^d))$

5. **return** $(\Delta^0, \cdots, \Delta^d)$

The ith call to $\texttt{Secure-AND}(d, \ell, \cdot, \cdot)$ outputs $\bar{t}_0 \odot^\ell \bar{t}_1 \odot^\ell \cdots \odot^\ell \bar{t}_{i-1}$, the operation being performed in a secure way from the $(d+1)$-sharings $(\Delta^0, \cdots, \Delta^d)$ and $(t_{i-1}^0, \cdots, t_{i-1}^d)$ which represent Δ and $\bar{t}_{i-1}$ respectively.

Security (Sketch of Proof). The dth-order security of $\texttt{Secure-AND}(d, \ell, \cdot, \cdot)$ implies that of each iteration of the loop. Moreover, the d random values used to construct the $(d+1)$-sharing of the $\texttt{Secure-AND}(d, \ell, \cdot, \cdot)$ output are randomly regenerated at each call. We thus deduce that the local d^{th}-order security implies that of the overall algorithm.

Complexity. Let us denote by c_{T} (resp. $c_\odot$) the cost of a $(\ell \times \ell)$-matrix transposition (resp. bitwise multiplication $\odot$). The dth-order secure processing of the Dirac of ℓ elements in $GF(2)^\ell$ costs $(d+1) \times c_T + (\ell-1)(d+1)^2 \times c_\odot + 2(\ell-1)d(d+1) \times c_\oplus$ (which corresponds to $d+1$ matrix transpositions and $\ell-1$ calls to Secure-AND$(d, \ell, \cdot, \cdot)$). We experimented that the cost c_T is of around 150 logical operations on a ℓ-bit architecture with bit-addressable memory (see Sect. 5)[3].

Let n be a multiple of ℓ. Algorithm 4 can be simply extended to compute the $(d+1)$-sharings of the Dirac's of n elements $s_0, \ldots, s_{n-1}$ in $GF(2^\ell)$. In this case, the matrix $\mathbf{s}$ is a binary $(n \times \ell)$-matrix and its $(d+1)$-sharing is also composed of binary $(n \times \ell)$-matrices. Thus, before applying Alg. 4 the elements of the $(d+1)$-sharing $(\mathbf{s}^0, \cdots, \mathbf{s}^d)$ of $\mathbf{s}$ are split into n/ℓ sub-matrices of ℓ lines and ℓ columns. This results in the definition of a splitting of $(\mathbf{s}^0, \cdots, \mathbf{s}^d)$ into n/ℓ sharings $(\mathbf{s}^0_{j(\ell)}, \cdots, \mathbf{s}^d_{j(\ell)})$, each corresponding to the sub-matrix $\mathbf{s}_{j(\ell)}$ composed of the jth block of ℓ lines of $\mathbf{s}$. Once this splitting has been done, Alg. 4 is applied to each $(d+1)$-sharing $(\mathbf{s}^0_{j(\ell)}, \cdots, \mathbf{s}^d_{j(\ell)})$ separately to output a $(d+1)$-sharing of the Dirac values corresponding to the state elements $s_{j\ell}, \ldots, s_{(j+1)\ell-1}$. The overall procedure is denoted by Secure-Dirac$(d, (\mathbf{s}^0, \cdots, \mathbf{s}^d))$ in the following. It inherits its dth-order security from that of Secure-AND$(d, \ell, \cdot, \cdot)$ and its cost in terms of elementary operations, denoted by $C_{\text{S-D}}$, is exactly n/ℓ times that of Alg. 4. For instance, in the case of the AES ($n = 16$ and $\ell = 8$) we have:

$$C_{\text{S-D}} = 2(d+1) \times c_T + 14(d+1)^2 \times c_\odot + 28d(d+1) \times c_\oplus . \qquad (5)$$

4.3   Security and Complexity Analysis of the Proposal

Based on the analysis conducted in the two previous sections, we study hereafter the security and the complexity of our proposal presented in Alg. 2 to secure the AES Inv-Layer.

Security (Sketch of Proof). Add-Dirac$(\cdot, \cdot)$ is a linear function operating on two data masked with independent d-tuples of masks. It operates on each share independently. For those two reasons it is d^{th}-order secure. Except the memory allocations (Steps 3 and 7) which are obviously d^{th}-order secure since they always manipulate the shares separately, the other steps process operations (Secure-Dirac$(d, \cdot)$, Sec-MUL$(d, \cdot, \cdot)$ and Sec-Inv$(d, \cdot)$) that have been proved to be d^{th}-order secure either in previous works [23] or in the present paper (see Sect. 4.2). The fact that all operations in Alg. 2 are d^{th}-order SCA-secure straightforwardly implies that Alg. 2 is at least 1st-order SCA secure. Actually, we claim here that it is also d^{th}-order SCA-secure. The precise formalization of the dth-order security of Alg. 2 can be done by following the outlines of the proof of [23, Theorem 2] and may possibly require some *mask-refreshing* procedure (such as involved in [23]) to change the $(d+1)$-sharing of an internal state into a new one.

Complexity. Algorithm 2 involves 2 calls to the function Add-Dirac$(\cdot, \cdot)$, $3 \times (16-1)$ calls to Secure-MUL$(d, \cdot, \cdot)$, 1 call to Sec-Dirac$(d, \cdot)$ and 1 call to Sec-Inv$(d, \cdot)$.

---

[3] Note that we did not took into account the cost of the bitwise complement which is negligible compared to the other costs.

Its complexity C_{S-L} therefore satisfies:

$$C_{S-L} = 2 \times C_{A-D} + 45 \times C_{S-M} + C_{S-D} + C_{Inv} \ .$$

From the complexity analysis conducted in previous sections we hence deduce that the cost C_{S-L} of our proposal in terms of elementary operations satisfies:

$$C_{S-L} = (d+1)[2 \times c_T + (32 + 118d) \times c_\oplus + 14(d+1) \times c_\odot + 45(d+1) \times c_\otimes] + C_{Inv} \ .$$

The cost of a classical processing of Inv-layer is around 16 times the cost C_{Inv} of the secure processing of a field inversion. Hence, our method improves the classical approach if and only if C_{Inv} satisfies:

$$C_{Inv} \geq \frac{(d+1)[2 \times c_T + (32 + 118d) \times c_\oplus + 14(d+1) \times c_\odot + 45(d+1) \times c_\otimes]}{15} \ . \tag{6}$$

For our implementations reported in Sect. 5, we experimented $c_\oplus = c_\odot = 1, c_T = 148$ and $c_\otimes = 22$. In this particular case, (6) becomes $C_{Inv} \geq \frac{1122d^2 + 2454d + 1332}{15}$. For $d = 1$, $d = 2$ and $d = 3$ the lower bound respectively equals 328, 717 and 1256.

5   Experimentations

The purpose of this section is twofold. First, we experimentally validate the relevance of the SCA-secure Montgomery's trick by improving many methods of literature. Secondly, we quantify in practice the efficiency gain provided by our proposal. Even if this section reports on AES implementation in mode 128, the main conclusions stay valid in all the other modus operandi. Our AES implementations involve the same code to process the round-key addition and the linear/affine steps. Actually, they only differ in the code part dedicated to the processing of Inv-Layer. To protect the linear/affine AES steps against (HO-) SCA, the masking scheme (a.k.a secret sharing scheme) presented in [11] for order 1 and extended in [23] to any order has been applied. To secure the AES Inv-Layer, we first implemented some 1st-order SCA-secure methods, then all the existing 2nd-order SCA-secure methods, and eventually the single 3rd-order SCA-secure method existing in the literature (see Sect. 1.1 for an argumentation of the choices). In what follows, we give more details about the methods we chose in each category.

For $d = 1$, we chose to only consider methods requiring a limited amount of RAM memory, which excludes the methods proposed in [11] and [19]. Indeed, as mentioned in the introduction, our purpose is to improve the timing efficiency of 1st-order SCA-secure implementations in contexts where a limited amount of RAM is available. Moreover, we experimented that usually our proposal does not improve 1st-order methods optimized by involving RAM look-up tables precomputed with part of (or all) the masking material (as *e.g.* in [11] and [19]). In this case indeed, C_{Inv} does not satisfy (6). Eventually, we chose to implement the methods in [17, 18, 20, 21, 23].

- In [17, 18], the field $GF(2^8)$ is represented as an extension of $GF(2^2)$. Thanks to linear isomorphisms, the AES s-box is evaluated with operations in $GF(2^2)$ where the extended inversion is linear.
- In [20], the extended inversion over $GF(2^8)$ is essentially performed by going down to $GF(2^4)^2$ and by computing a Fourier transform on $GF(2^4)$.
- In [21], the authors perform the extended inversion by going down to $(GF(2^4))^2$ and by bitwisely adding 15 elements of a ROM look-up table representing a permutation over $GF(2^4)$.
- In [23], the extended inversion is represented as the power function $x \mapsto x^{254}$ and the evaluation of this function is essentially secured against SCA by decomposing the exponentiation into a minimum number of multiplications which are not squaring and by securing those multiplications. The latter step is done by calling the function $\texttt{Secure-MUL}(1, \cdot, \cdot)$ recalled in Sect. 4.

For $d = 2$, only a few methods exist that are perfectly SCA-secure. Actually, only the works [24], [22] and [23] propose such kind of schemes (the two first ones working for any s-box and the third one being dedicated to the AES s-box). The method in [24] can be viewed as a generalization of the re-computation table method proposed in [10]. Each time a s-box must be evaluated, a new pair of input/output masks is generated and two new look-up tables in RAM are generated from both those masks and a ROM look-up table representing the AES s-box. The method [22] is a generalization of [21]. Eventually, the method [23] applied for $d = 2$ protects the evaluation of the power function $x \mapsto x^{254}$ by securing the linear steps in a straightforward way (by applying the computations on each share separately) and by securing the multiplications thanks to $\texttt{Secure-}$$\texttt{MUL}(2, \cdot, \cdot)$.

For $d = 3$, only [23] proposes a solution. It involves $\texttt{Secure-MUL}(3, \cdot, \cdot)$ to secure the non-linear steps of the exponentiation $x \mapsto x^{254}$.

Table 1 lists the timing/memory performances of the different implementations. Memory performances correspond to the number of bytes allocations and cycles numbers correspond to multiple of 10^3. The right-hand column gives the performance gain achieved by applying the SCA-secure Montgomery's trick (*e.g.* a gain of 60% signifies that the new timing equals 40% of the timings of the original code). Codes have been written in assembly language for a 8051-based 8-bit architecture with bit-addressable memory. RAM consumption related to implementation choices (*e.g.* use of some local variables, use of pre-computed values to speed-up some computations, etc.) are not taken into account in the performances reporting. Also, ROM consumptions (*i.e.* code sizes) are not listed since they always were lower than 5 K-bytes which is acceptable in almost all current embedded devices (for comparison a software secure implementation of RSA usually uses more than 10 K-bytes). Eventually, for $d = 1$ (Implementations 2 to 5) improvements have been added to the original proposals. They essentially amount to preprocess a part of the masking material, which is possible since the latter one does not need to be changed during the algorithm processing when

Table 1. Comparison of AES implementations

Method to secure the s-box		Without trick		With trick		Timing Gain
		Cycles	RAM	Cycles	RAM	
Unprotected Implementation						
1.	No Masking	2	0	Na.	Na.	Na.
First-Order SCA						
2.	Tower Field in $GF(2^4)$ [17, 18]	77	0	55	56	29%
3.	Masking *on-the-fly* [21]	82	0	55	56	33%
4.	Fourier Transform [20]	122	0	58	56	52%
5.	Secure Exponentiation [23]	73	24	58	24 + 32	21%
Second-Order SCA						
6.	Double Recomputations [24]	594	512	190	512 + 96	68%
7.	Single Recomputation [22]	672	256	195	256 + 96	70%
8.	Secure Exponentiation [23]	189	48	165	48 + 48	13%
Third-Order SCA						
9.	Secure Exponentiation [23]	326	72	292	72 + 64	9%

only first-order SCA are considered (*e.g.* the same input/output mask can be used for all the s-box evaluations).

As it can be seen in the last column of Table 1, SCA-secure Montgomery's trick always improves the timing efficiency of the method on which it is applied to. At every order, this gain has been obtained at the cost of a small RAM overhead: $24d$ bytes to implement Secure-MUL$(d, \cdot, \cdot)$ and $14(d + 1) + 2(d + 1)$ bytes dedicated to Montgomery's trick. For $d = 1$, this overhead is acceptable, even in a very constrained context (we indeed still have a consumption lower than 100 bytes). For $d > 1$, the RAM overhead is either negligible for methods which already consumed a lot of RAM [22, 24] or acceptable for [23] since the total amount of RAM allocation (96 bytes) is not prohibitive in view of the security level ($d = 2, 3$).

For $d = 1$, it can be observed that the timing performances of the methods become very close when the SCA-secure Montgomery's trick is applied. In view of (6), this result was expected since the performances of the inversion method has a small impact on performances of the global algorithm when the trick is involved. Indeed, in this case only 10 secure inversions for the overall AES-128 calculation are performed instead of 160. So, when the trick is involved the timings performances essentially correspond to the cost of 10 applications of Alg. 2 and the cost of Step 5 (the secure inversion) is negligible. For $d = 2$, this remark is less pertinent. This is a consequence of the huge difference between the timings of the secure inversion methods proposed in [22, 24] and in [23] (the latter one being at least 2.2 times faster). In this case, the impact of the method used to protect the inversion (Step 5 in Alg. 2) is still measurable. For $d = 3$, the SCA-secure Montgomery's trick continues to improve the efficiency of the inner method but its impact is less significant than for $d = 1, 2$. Actually, the method used in [23] to secure the inversion involves 4 calls to Secure-MUL$(d, \cdot, \cdot)$ and when d grows the timing efficiency of the method essentially corresponds to the cost of those 4 calls. When applied, the SCA-secure Montgomery's trick merely replaces 4 calls to Secure-MUL$(d, \cdot, \cdot)$ by 3 calls to Secure-MUL$(d, \cdot, \cdot)$ plus a dth-order secure Dirac computation. The gain in efficiency thus essentially relies on the difference of performances between one execution of Secure-MUL$(d, \cdot, \cdot)$ and the cost per byte of the dth-order secure Dirac computation described in Alg. 4.

6 Conclusion

In this paper, we have proposed a different approach for the masking of the non-linear layer of the AES. Instead of sequentially computing the image of masked data through each s-box, we have proposed to evaluate them globally. Our approach is based on Montgomery's trick combined with the use of masked Dirac functions. Our solution allows us to improve significantly in time complexity all previous masking methods requiring a small amount of RAM at the cost of a little memory overhead.

References

1. Blömer, J., Merchan, J.G., Krummel, V.: Provably Secure Masking of AES. In: Matsui, M., Zuccherato, R. (eds.) SAC 2004. LNCS, vol. 3357, pp. 69–83. Springer, Heidelberg (2004)
2. Brier, É., Olivier, F., Clavier, C.: Correlation Power Analysis with a Leakage Model. In: Joye, M., Quisquater, J.-J. (eds.) CHES 2004. LNCS, vol. 3156, pp. 16–29. Springer, Heidelberg (2004)
3. Chari, S., Jutla, C.S., Rao, J.R., Rohatgi, P.: Towards Sound Approaches to Counteract Power-Analysis Attacks. In: Wiener, M.J. (ed.) CRYPTO 1999. LNCS, vol. 1666, pp. 398–412. Springer, Heidelberg (1999)
4. Coron, J.-S., Prouff, E., Rivain, M.: Side Channel Cryptanalysis of a Higher Order Masking Scheme. In: Paillier, P., Verbauwhede, I. (eds.) CHES 2007. LNCS, vol. 4727, pp. 28–44. Springer, Heidelberg (2007)
5. Genelle, L., Prouff, E., Quisquater, M.: Secure Multiplicative Masking of Power Functions. In: Zhou, J., Yung, M. (eds.) ACNS 2010. LNCS, vol. 6123, pp. 200–217. Springer, Heidelberg (2010)
6. Harris, D. G.: Simultaneous field divisions: an extension of montgomery's trick. Cryptology ePrint Archive, Report 2008/199 (2008), http://eprint.iacr.org/
7. Ishai, Y., Sahai, A., Wagner, D.: Private Circuits: Securing Hardware against Probing Attacks. In: Boneh, D. (ed.) CRYPTO 2003. LNCS, vol. 2729, pp. 463–481. Springer, Heidelberg (2003)
8. Matsui, M., Fukuda, S.: How to Maximize Software Performance of Symmetric Primitives on Pentium III and 4 Processors. In: Handschuh, H., Gilbert, H. (eds.) FSE 2005. LNCS, vol. 3557, pp. 398–412. Springer, Heidelberg (2005)
9. Messerges, T.S.: Power Analysis Attacks and Countermeasures for Cryptographic Algorithms. PhD thesis, University of Illinois (2000)

10. Messerges, T.S.: Securing the AES Finalists against Power Analysis Attacks. In: Schneier, B. (ed.) FSE 2000. LNCS, vol. 1978, pp. 150–164. Springer, Heidelberg (2001)
11. Messerges, T.S.: Using Second-order Power Analysis to Attack DPA Resistant Software. In: Koç, Ç.K., Paar, C. (eds.) CHES 2000. LNCS, vol. 1965, pp. 238–251. Springer, Heidelberg (2000)
12. Mishra, P.K., Sarkar, P.: Application of Montgomery's Trick to Scalar Multiplication for Elliptic and Hyperelliptic Curves Using a Fixed Base Point. In: Bao, F., Deng, R.H., Zhou, J. (eds.) PKC 2004. LNCS, vol. 2947, pp. 41–54. Springer, Heidelberg (2004)
13. Montgomery, P.L.: Modular multiplication without trial division. Mathematics of Computation 54, 839–854 (1990)
14. Okeya, K., Kurumatani, H., Sakurai, K.: Elliptic Curves with the Montgomery-Form and Their Cryptographic Applications. In: Imai, H., Zheng, Y. (eds.) PKC 2000. LNCS, vol. 1751, pp. 238–257. Springer, Heidelberg (2000)
15. Oswald, E., Mangard, S.: Template Attacks on Masking—Resistance Is Futile. In: Abe, M. (ed.) CT-RSA 2007. LNCS, vol. 4377, pp. 243–256. Springer, Heidelberg (2006)
16. Oswald, E., Mangard, S., Herbst, C., Tillich, S.: Practical Second-Order DPA Attacks for Masked Smart Card Implementations of Block Ciphers. In: Pointcheval, D. (ed.) CT-RSA 2006. LNCS, vol. 3860, pp. 192–207. Springer, Heidelberg (2006)
17. Oswald, E., Mangard, S., Pramstaller, N.: Secure and Efficient Masking of AES – A Mission Impossible? Cryptology ePrint Archive, Report 2004/134 (2004)
18. Oswald, E., Mangard, S., Pramstaller, N., Rijmen, V.: A Side-Channel Analysis Resistant Description of the AES S-box. In: Handschuh, H., Gilbert, H. (eds.) FSE 2005. LNCS, vol. 3557, pp. 413–423. Springer, Heidelberg (2005)
19. Oswald, E., Schramm, K.: An Efficient Masking Scheme for AES Software Implementations. In: Song, J., Kwon, T., Yung, M. (eds.) WISA 2005. LNCS, vol. 3786, pp. 292–305. Springer, Heidelberg (2006)
20. Prouff, E., Giraud, C., Aumônier, S.: Provably Secure S-Box Implementation Based on Fourier Transform. In: Goubin, L., Matsui, M. (eds.) CHES 2006. LNCS, vol. 4249, pp. 216–230. Springer, Heidelberg (2006)
21. Prouff, E., Rivain, M.: A Generic Method for Secure SBox Implementation. In: Kim, S., Yung, M., Lee, H.-W. (eds.) WISA 2007. LNCS, vol. 4867, pp. 227–244. Springer, Heidelberg (2008)
22. Rivain, M., Dottax, E., Prouff, E.: Block Ciphers Implementations Provably Secure Against Second Order Side Channel Analysis. In: Baignères, T., Vaudenay, S. (eds.) FSE 2008. LNCS, vol. 5086, pp. 127–143. Springer, Heidelberg (2008)
23. Rivain, M., Prouff, E.: Provably Secure Higher-Order Masking of AES. In: Mangard, S., Standaert, F.-X. (eds.) CHES 2010. LNCS, vol. 6225, pp. 413–427. Springer, Heidelberg (2010)
24. Schramm, K., Paar, C.: Higher Order Masking of the AES. In: Pointcheval, D. (ed.) CT-RSA 2006. LNCS, vol. 3860, pp. 208–225. Springer, Heidelberg (2006)
25. Tillich, S., Herbst, C.: Attacking State-of-the-Art Software Countermeasures—A Case Study for AES. In: Oswald, E., Rohatgi, P. (eds.) CHES 2008. LNCS, vol. 5154, pp. 228–243. Springer, Heidelberg (2008)

Memory-Constrained Implementations of Elliptic Curve Cryptography in Co-*Z* Coordinate Representation

Michael Hutter[1], Marc Joye[2], and Yannick Sierra[3]

[1] TU Graz, Institute for Applied Information Processing and Communications
Inffeldgasse 16a, 8010 Graz, Austria
michael.hutter@iaik.tugraz.at
[2] Technicolor, Security & Content Protection Labs
1 avenue de Belle Fontaine, 35576 Cesson-Sévigné Cedex, France
marc.joye@technicolor.com
[3] Oberthur Technologies
71-73 rue des Hautes Pâtures, 92726 Nanterre Cedex, France
y.sierra@oberthur.com

Abstract. It has been recently shown that sharing a common coordinate in elliptic curve cryptography implementations improves the performance of scalar multiplication. This paper presents new formulæ for elliptic curves over prime fields that provide efficient point addition and doubling using the Montgomery ladder. All computations are performed in a common projective *Z*-coordinate representation to reduce the memory requirements of low-resource implementations. In addition, all given formulæ make only use of *out-of-place* operations therefore insuring that it requires no additional memory for any implementation of the underlying finite-field operations whatsoever. Our results outperform existing solutions in terms of memory and speed and allow a fast and secure implementation suitable for low-resource devices and embedded systems.

Keywords: Public-key cryptography, elliptic curves, co-*Z* coordinates, out-of-place formulæ, Montgomery ladder, embedded systems.

1 Introduction

Elliptic curve cryptography (ECC) [17,27] has gained much importance in the field of low-resource devices such as smart cards and Radio Frequency Identification (RFID) devices. The main benefits of ECC compared to traditional cryptographic primitives like RSA [30] are the significant improvements in terms of speed and memory. In fact, memory is one of the most expensive resources in the design of embedded systems which encourages the use of ECC on such platforms. In this paper, we present new formulæ for ECC implementations that allow very efficient (speed-wise and memory-wise) computations especially applicable to resource-constrained devices.

Among the most resource-consuming operation in ECC implementations is the scalar multiplication. A secret scalar k is multiplied with a point P on an

A. Nitaj and D. Pointcheval (Eds.): AFRICACRYPT 2011, LNCS 6737, pp. 170–187, 2011.

elliptic curve $E(\mathbb{F}_q)$ resulting in the point $\boldsymbol{Q}$. This operation is used in many cryptographic primitives which rely on the intractability of solving the elliptic curve discrete logarithm problem (ECDLP), *i.e.* finding the discrete logarithm for $\boldsymbol{Q}$ with respect to the elliptic curve point $\boldsymbol{P}$.

In view of embedded systems, where memory and computational power are scarce resources, there exist many proposals to improve the scalar multiplication. One of the most prominent methods is the so-called Montgomery ladder [28]. First, it allows one to omit the y-coordinate of the involved elliptic curve points which lowers the memory requirements for low-resource designs. Second, it implicitly provides resistance against certain implementation attacks [16,20,24] which encourages its use in security-related applications.

Another improvement was proposed by Meloni [25] in 2007. He showed that points on an elliptic curve can be added quickly when they share a common co-ordinate, *e.g.* the projective Z-coordinate. Meloni applied the formula to specific Euclid addition chains to perform a scalar multiplication. However, the observation not only improves the speed of ECC implementations but reduces even the memory requirements by one coordinate as practically shown by Lee and Verbauwhede [22] over binary fields.

Recently, Goundar *et al.* [10] extended the idea of Meloni and provided formulæ over prime fields that can be even applied to classical binary scalar multiplication methods. They introduced a new operation (*conjugate co-Z addition*) that can be used together with the addition formula of Meloni to perform fast computations with points sharing the same Z-coordinate (co-Z arithmetic). However, the method has not been applied to the x-coordinate only version of the Montgomery ladder so far.

In this paper, we present new formulæ for elliptic curves over finite fields of characteristic $q \neq 2, 3$ that apply the co-Z method to the Montgomery ladder scalar multiplication. The given formulæ perform a differential addition-and-doubling operation of elliptic curve points using x-coordinates only, *i.e.* two projective X-coordinates of the involved points and a common Z-coordinate. It shows that the formulæ lead to very efficient scalar multiplications especially suitable to low-resource devices. In addition, we consider the practical constraint imposed by the implementations of both the modular multiplication and the modular squaring which may not support the result to be written *in-place*, that is overwriting one of the operands. This constraint is common in practice since it allows to save memory with many efficient implementations of those operations as discussed later and it can be imposed by the hardware accelerator when one is available. Unfortunately this typically implies the need of more memory than claimed in order to implement formulæ which have been designed with *in-place* operations. To our best knowledge, it is indeed the first paper that provides formulæ that use *out-of-place* operations guaranteing that no additional memory is necessary even when the finite-field arithmetic computations do not support *in-place* results. Our outcomes improve the state of the art in low-resource ECC implementations in terms of both memory and speed.

The rest of this paper is organized as follows. In Section 2, we briefly introduce elliptic curve cryptography. Section 3 describes different scalar-multiplication methods including the Montgomery ladder. Section 4 presents new formulæ for (differential) addition-and-doubling and projective coordinate recovery in co-Z coordinates. Section 5 discusses the difference between *in-place* versus *out-of-place* formulæ for ECC. In Section 6, the results are discussed in terms of security and performance. Conclusions are drawn in Section 7.

2   Preliminaries

This section introduces some elementary background on elliptic curves. We refer the reader to e.g. [11] for further details.

An elliptic curve E over a finite field $\mathbb{F}_q$ of characteristic $\neq 2, 3$ can be defined by the short Weierstraß equation

$$E : y^2 = x^3 + ax + b \,,$$

where $a, b \in \mathbb{F}_q$ are curve parameters satisfying $4a^3 + 27b^2 \neq 0$ and $(x, y) \in \mathbb{F}_q \times \mathbb{F}_q$ represents a point on the elliptic curve. The set of all points on the elliptic curve together with the point at infinity O is denoted by $E(\mathbb{F}_q)$. It forms an (additively written) abelian group with the point at infinity O as the identity element.

Scalar multiplication. The main operation in elliptic curve cryptography (ECC) is the scalar multiplication, $Q = kP$, where P and Q are points on the curve E and k is a scalar such that $0 \leq k < \mathrm{ord}_E(P)$. The security of ECC primitives relies on the intractability to solve the elliptic curve discrete logarithm problem (ECDLP), *i.e.* determining k from P and Q.

Point representation. The scalar multiplication uses two basic operations that are addition and doubling of points. The points can be represented in several coordinate systems. Points in affine coordinates are represented by two coordinates x and y but involve the computation of inversions in $\mathbb{F}_q$ which are relatively expensive operations. Due to these reasons, most implementations represent the points in projective coordinates. In homogeneous projective coordinates, each affine point (x, y) is represented by three coordinates (X, Y, Z) where $x = X/Z$ and $y = Y/Z$. Another coordinate system that is widely used in practice is the Jacobian projective coordinate system. There, the relation $x = X/Z^2$ and $y = Y/Z^3$ is used to represent the points. The curve equation in Jacobian coordinates becomes $E : Y^2 = X^3 + aXZ^4 + bZ^6$.

Point addition. Let $P_1 = (X_1, Y_1, Z_1)$ and $P_2 = (X_2, Y_2, 1)$ be two points represented in Jacobian projective coordinates on the curve. Then the sum $P_1 + P_2 = (X_3, Y_3, Z_3)$ (also known as *mixed* sum since $Z_2 = 1$), is given by

$$\begin{cases} X_3 = (Y_2 Z_1{}^3 - Y_1)^2 - (X_2 Z_1{}^2 - X_1)^2 (X_1 + X_2 Z_1^2) \\ Y_3 = (Y_2 Z_1{}^3 - Y_1)(X_1(X_2 Z_1{}^2 - X_1)^2 - X_3) - Y_1(X_2 Z_1{}^2 - X_1)^3 \\ Z_3 = (X_2 Z_1{}^2 - X_1)Z_1 \end{cases} \quad . \quad (1)$$

The formula for point doubling, $2\boldsymbol{P_1} = (X_4, Y_4, Z_4)$, is given by

$$\begin{cases} X_4 = (3X_1{}^2 + aZ_1{}^4)^2 - 8X_1Y_1{}^2 \\ Y_4 = (3X_1{}^2 + aZ_1{}^4)(4X_1Y_1{}^2 - X_3) - 8Y_1{}^4 \\ Z_4 = 2Y_1Z_1 \end{cases} . \qquad (2)$$

To evaluate the costs of the given formulæ we denote by M the cost of a field multiplication and by S the cost of a field squaring. For multiplications with fixed parameters such as the curve parameters, we use the notation $\mathsf{M}_\star$ (e.g. M_a, M_b). Additions and subtractions are later assumed to have the same complexity and are represented by add.

Evaluating formulæ (1) and (2) in terms of computational cost shows that a point addition needs 7M + 4S if $Z_2 = 1$ [11]. Point doubling can be performed with 4M + 4S or 1M + 8S + 1M_a. For comparability reasons, we use the same performance metric as in the dedicated website Explicit Formulas Database (EFD) [6].

Co-Z arithmetic. In 2007, Meloni proposed new point addition and doubling formulæ in Jacobian coordinates where the two involved points share the same Z-coordinate [25]. We refer to this coordinate system as the *co-Z coordinate system*. When the two points satisfy this condition, the addition of two points can be evaluated much faster than an addition in Jacobian coordinates (actually even faster than a doubling operation in Jacobian coordinates). Let $\boldsymbol{P_1} = (X_1, Y_1, Z)$ and $\boldsymbol{P_2} = (X_2, Y_2, Z)$ the two points that share the same Z-coordinate, then the sum of the two points, $\boldsymbol{P_1} + \boldsymbol{P_2} = \boldsymbol{P_3} = (X_3, Y_3, Z_3)$, is given by

$$\begin{cases} X_3 = (Y_2 - Y_1)^2 - X_2(X_2 - X_1)^2 - X_1(X_2 - X_1)^2 \\ Y_3 = (Y_2 - Y_1)[X_1(X_2 - X_1)^2 - X_3] - Y_1(X_2 - X_1)^3 \\ Z_3 = Z(X_2 - X_1) \end{cases} . \qquad (3)$$

This addition only requires 5M + 2S. As observed in [25], the given formulæ have the advantage of providing an equivalent representation $\boldsymbol{P_1'}$ of the point $\boldsymbol{P_1} = (X_1, Y_1, Z)$ such that the points $\boldsymbol{P1'}$ and $\boldsymbol{P3}$ have the same Z-coordinate value. Namely $\boldsymbol{P_1'} = (X_1\lambda^2, Y_1\lambda^3, Z\lambda)$ with $\lambda = (X_2 - X_1)$, is calculated without any additional cost since the coordinates are already computed as intermediate values in the addition formula (cf. Eq. (3)).

3   Scalar Multiplication Methods

There exist several algorithms to perform the scalar multiplication.

One of the most common methods is the *double-and-add* algorithm (a.k.a. left-to-right binary method), shown in Algorithm 1. It takes the binary representation of the scalar k as an input and processes the bits from left to right. A point doubling operation is performed at every iteration whereas point addition is only performed if the bit value, k_i, is 1.

Algorithm 1. Double-and-add

Input: $P \in E(\mathbb{F}_q)$ and $k = (k_{n-1}, \ldots, k_0)_2 \in \mathbb{N}$, with $k_{n-1} \neq 0$
Output: $Q = kP$

1: $R_0 \leftarrow P$
2: **for** $i = n - 2$ downto 0 **do**
3:     $R_0 \leftarrow 2R_0$
4:     **if** $(k_i = 1)$ **then** $R_0 \leftarrow R_0 + P$
5: **end for**
6: **return** R_0

The method has the advantage that it provides a very efficient point multiplication but suffers from that it may leak information about the secret scalar k via physical side-channels [20,24]. In Simple Power Analysis (SPA) attacks, an adversary tries to recover the scalar k by measuring the power-consumption traces during scalar multiplication. If a difference between the operations of point addition and point doubling can be observed in the traces, then the scalar k is revealed bit-by-bit.

In [4], Coron proposes a simple countermeasure that involves a dummy point addition operation if the scalar bit is set to 0. The so-called *double-and-add always* method actually prevents SPA attacks but becomes vulnerable to safe-error attacks, as shown in [35]. A fault can be induced during the computation and an adversary can check whether the final result is correct or not. If the fault is injected during a dummy addition, the result is still correct and the corresponding bit of the scalar is 0. If the result is incorrect, the scalar bit is 1.

Another scalar-multiplication method that is commonly used is known as the *Montgomery ladder* [28] and is depicted in Algorithm 2. The method presents several advantages for cryptographic applications.

Algorithm 2. Montgomery ladder

Input: $P \in E(\mathbb{F}_q)$ and $k = (k_{n-1}, \ldots, k_0)_2 \in \mathbb{N}$, with $k_{n-1} \neq 0$
Output: $Q = kP$

1: $R_0 \leftarrow P$; $R_1 \leftarrow 2P$
2: **for** $i = n - 2$ downto 0 **do**
3:     $b \leftarrow k_i$; $R_{1-b} \leftarrow R_{1-b} + R_b$
4:     $R_b \leftarrow 2R_b$
5: **end for**
6: **return** R_0

First, the Montgomery ladder implicitly offers security against implementation attacks [16]. Since it performs the same curve operations in every loop iteration, an attacker cannot distinguish individual bits of the secret scalar by simply observing a side-channel trace and so prevents SPA-type attacks. Furthermore, the Montgomery ladder has a very regular structure and does not use dummy operations. This prevents fault-injection based safe-error attacks.

Second, group operations can be performed without the need of y-coordinates. Montgomery originally applied the technique to special (Montgomery form) elliptic curves as a way to speed up the elliptic curve factoring method. The technique was subsequently generalized to Weierstraß form curves [2,7,15,14].

Let $P_1 = (x_1, y_1)$ and $P_2 = (x_2, y_2)$ be two points on the elliptic curve E : $y^2 = x^3 + ax + b$ and x_D the x-coordinate of their difference $D = P_2 - P_1$. Then the x-coordinate of the sum $P_1 + P_2$, say x_3, is given by

$$x_3 = \frac{2(x_1 + x_2)(x_1 x_2 + a) + 4b}{(x_1 - x_2)^2} - x_D \ . \tag{4}$$

Alternatively, the x-coordinate of $P_1 + P_2$ can be obtained in a multiplicative way as

$$x_3 = \frac{-4b(x_1 + x_2)(x_1 x_2 - a)^2}{x_D (x_1 - x_2)^2} \ . \tag{4'}$$

The x-coordinate of $2P_2$, say x_4, can be expressed from the x-coordinate of P_2 as

$$x_4 = \frac{(x_2{}^2 - a)^2 - 8bx_2}{4(x_2{}^3 + ax_2 + b)} \ . \tag{5}$$

It is worth noticing that the Montgomery ladder keeps invariant the difference of the involved points throughout the entire scalar multiplication. Indeed, from the description in Algorithm 2, it is easily seen that $R_1 - R_0 = (R_1 + R_0) - 2R_0$ when $b = 0$, and $R_1 - R_0 = 2R_1 - (R_0 + R_1)$ when $b = 1$. Hence, $D := R_1 - R_0 = P$. Consequently, R_1 will contain the value of $(k + 1)P$ at the end of the algorithm. When the calculation is performed using x-coordinates only, this allows one to recover the y-coordinate of kP. Letting (x_1, y_1) the coordinates of $Q = kP$, (x_D, y_D) the coordinates of P and x_2 the x-coordinate of $(k+1)P$, one has

$$y_1 = \frac{2b + (a + x_D x_1)(x_D + x_1) - x_2(x_D - x_1)^2}{2y_D} \ . \tag{6}$$

This is useful for cryptographic schemes needing the y-coordinate of the resulting point; for example, in the verification of an ECDSA digital signature [29].

4   New x-Coordinate Only Formulæ

This section presents new x-coordinate only formulæ for Weierstraß elliptic curves. We first provide the formulæ for addition and doubling of points in the co-Z coordinate representation. Second, we give formulæ for efficient differential addition-and-doubling in the same coordinate representation. Third, we discuss optimizations when applying dynamic ECC parameters and give appropriate formulæ to recover the full coordinates of the output point.

Let $P_1 = (X_1, Y_1, Z)$ and $P_2 = (X_2, Y_2, Z)$ be two points on the Weierstraß elliptic curve $E : Y^2 Z = X^3 + aXZ^2 + bZ^3$ in *homogeneous*[1] projective

---

[1] Previous works considered Jacobian coordinates when applying co-Z arithmetic on elliptic curves over fields of characteristic $\neq 2, 3$.

coordinates that share the same Z-coordinate. Then, the x-coordinate of the addition of the two points, $\mathrm{x}(P_1 + P_2) = (X_3, Z_3)$, can be evaluated as

$$\begin{cases} X_3 = 2(X_1 + X_2)(X_1 X_2 + aZ^2) + 4bZ^3 - x_D Z(X_1 - X_2)^2 \\ Z_3 = Z(X_1 - X_2)^2 \end{cases} , \qquad (7)$$

where $D = P_2 - P_1 = (x_D, y_D)$ is the difference of the points P_1 and P_2 in affine coordinates. Note that the formula performs the point addition with x-coordinates only, thus no Y-coordinate is used. The point addition needs $5\mathsf{M} + 2\mathsf{S} + 1\mathsf{M}_a + 1\mathsf{M}_{4b}$ to get the resulting x-coordinate $\mathrm{x}(P_1 + P_2)$.

The x-coordinate of a point doubling operation, $\mathrm{x}(2P_2) = (X_4, Z_4)$, needs $4\mathsf{M} + 3\mathsf{S} + 1\mathsf{M}_a + 1\mathsf{M}_{4b}$ and can be evaluated as

$$\begin{cases} X_4 = (X_2{}^2 - aZ^2)^2 - 8bZ^3 X_2 \\ Z_4 = Z[4X_2(X_2{}^2 + aZ^2) + 4bZ^3] \end{cases} . \qquad (8)$$

Applying formulæ (7) and (8) to the Montgomery ladder needs three additional multiplications to project the resulting x-coordinates $\mathrm{x}(R_0) = (X_3, Z_3)$ and $\mathrm{x}(R_1) = (X_4, Z_4)$ to a common Z-coordinate. An equivalent representation for R_0 and R_1 can be obtained by evaluating

$$X_1' = X_3 Z_4, \quad X_2' = X_4 Z_3, \quad \text{and} \quad Z' = Z_3 Z_4,$$

resulting in $R_0 \cong (X_1', Z')$ and $R_1 \cong (X_2', Z')$ sharing the same Z-coordinate. The total complexity for one Montgomery ladder loop iteration is therefore $12\mathsf{M} + 5\mathsf{S} + 2\mathsf{M}_a + 2\mathsf{M}_{4b}$. In the following, we show how to reduce the complexity for differential addition-and-doubling to only $9\mathsf{M} + 5\mathsf{S} + 1\mathsf{M}_a + 1\mathsf{M}_{4b}$.

4.1   Differential Addition-And-Doubling

By combining the projective formulæ given by Eqs. (7) and (8) and class equivalences to have the same Z-coordinate, we obtain

$$\begin{cases} X_1' = V[2(X_1 + X_2)(X_1 X_2 + aZ^2) + 4bZ^3 - x_D ZU] \\ X_2' = U[(X_2{}^2 - aZ^2)^2 - 8bZ^3 X_2] \\ Z' = UVZ \end{cases} , \qquad (9)$$

where $U = (X_1 - X_2)^2$ and $V = 4X_2(X_2{}^2 + aZ^2) + 4bZ^3$. The points $\mathrm{x}(R_0) = (X_1, Z)$ and $\mathrm{x}(R_1) = (X_2, Z)$ get added and doubled resulting in the points $\mathrm{x}(R_0') = (X_1', Z')$ and $\mathrm{x}(R_1') = (X_2', Z')$. The formula reduces the complexity to $10\mathsf{M} + 4\mathsf{S} + 1\mathsf{M}_a + 1\mathsf{M}_{4b}$.

This can be further optimized by replacing the multiplication $X_1 X_2$ involved in the previous formula with the equivalent expression $(X_1{}^2 + X_2{}^2 - (X_1 - X_2)^2)/2$. The term can be multiplied with the leading factor 2 so that we finally obtain

$$\begin{cases} X_1' = V[(X_1 + X_2)(X_1{}^2 + X_2{}^2 - U + 2aZ^2) + 4bZ^3 - x_D ZU] \\ X_2' = U[(X_2{}^2 - aZ^2)^2 - 8bZ^3 X_2] \\ Z' = UVZ \end{cases} . \qquad (10)$$

This latter formula can be evaluated with $9M + 5S + 1M_a + 1M_{4b}$. Note that the formula overwrites the input coordinates X_1, X_2, and Z with the output variables X_1', X_2', and Z'. This avoids additional memory allocations for the output variables and avoids variable copying since the output variables serve as input variables for the next Montgomery loop iteration. Furthermore, the resulting points $\mathrm{x}(\boldsymbol{R_0}) = (X_1', Z')$ and $\mathrm{x}(\boldsymbol{R_1}) = (X_2', Z')$ share the same Z-coordinate and do not need any further updates. A detailed implementation is provided in Algorithm 5 (Appendix A).

4.2 (X, Y, Z) Recovery

We now give the formula for the recovery of the full projective coordinates for output point $\boldsymbol{Q} = k\boldsymbol{P}$, from the x-coordinates $\boldsymbol{R_0} = (X_1, Z)$ and $\boldsymbol{R_1} = (X_2, Z)$ in co-Z representation available in memory at the end of the Montgomery ladder. First, we transform Eq. (6) from affine to projective coordinates and set $x_i = X_i/Z$ and $y_i = Y_i/Z$ ($i \in \{1, 2\}$). Then, we can calculate the representation of output point $\boldsymbol{Q}$ in the projective coordinates $\boldsymbol{Q} \cong (X_1', Y_1', Z_1')$ with

$$
\begin{cases}
X_1' = DX_1 A \\
Y_1' = 2[(CX_1 + aA)(C + X_1) - X_2(C - X_1)^2] + 4bB \\
Z_1' = DB
\end{cases}
\quad , \quad (11)
$$

where $A = Z^2$, $B = ZA$, $C = x_D Z$, $D = 4y_D$. X_1, X_2, and Z are the coordinates of the elliptic curve points after scalar multiplication and $\boldsymbol{D} = (x_D, y_D)$ represents the invariant of the Montgomery ladder in affine coordinates (namely, input point $\boldsymbol{P}$). The given formula needs $8M + 2S + 1M_a + 1M_{4b}$. The affine coordinates of output point $\boldsymbol{Q}$ can then be calculated by one inversion and two multiplications, i.e., $\boldsymbol{Q} = (x_1, y_1) = (X_1' \cdot Z_1'^{-1}, Y_1' \cdot Z_1'^{-1})$. See Algorithm 7 (Appendix A) for a detailed implementation.

4.3 Optimizations for Dynamic ECC Parameters

If the curve parameters such as a, b are not fixed by the implementation and are chosen dynamically, the formula given in Eq. (10) can be optimized. In this case, the curve parameters have to be handled in RAM and their memory allocation can therefore be re-used as working space as soon as they are not needed. The following formulæ allows to save one register compared to the implementation of Eq. (10) with a and b permanently occupying a full register in RAM. By initializing three additional coordinates $T_a = aZ^2$, $T_b = 4bZ^3$, and $T_D = x_D Z$, we can evaluate

$$
\begin{cases}
T_D' = T_D W \\
T_a' = T_a W^2 \\
T_b' = T_b W^3 \\
X_1' = V[(X_1 + X_2)(X_1^2 + X_2^2 - U + 2T_a) + T_b] - T_D' \\
X_2' = U[(X_2^2 - T_a)^2 - 2X_2 T_b]
\end{cases}
\quad (12)
$$

to perform a differential addition-and-doubling operation, where $U = (X_1 - X_2)^2$, $V = 4X_2(X_2{}^2 + T_a) + T_b$, and $W = UV$. The given formula reduces the memory requirements by one working register and increases the performance by 1M if the relation $\mathsf{M}_a = \mathsf{M}_b = 1\mathrm{M}$ is given (however, in practice, one has usually the relation $\mathsf{M}_a + \mathsf{M}_b = 1\mathrm{M}$; see § 6.2) . Note that the formula does not involve either a, b, or x_D nor an explicit Z-coordinate throughout the scalar multiplication. See Algorithm 6 (Appendix A) for a detailed implementation.

The full coordinates (X_1', Y_1', Z_1') can be recovered with 10M+3S by evaluating

$$\begin{cases} X_1' = 4y_D x_D T_D{}^2 X_1 \\ Y_1' = x_D{}^3 [T_b + 2(T_D X_1 + T_a)(X_1 + T_D) - 2X_2(X_1 - T_D)^2] \\ Z_1' = 4y_D T_D{}^3 \end{cases} \qquad . \qquad (13)$$

See Algorithm 8 (Appendix A) for a detailed implementation.

5   In-Place vs. Out-of-Place Formulæ

Most descriptions of the elliptic-curve operations presented in the literature have claims of memory requirements and performances that assume that the finite-field operations can be performed *in-place*. That means that one source operand of the operation may be overwritten by the resulting value during the execution, e.g.

$$R_1 \leftarrow R_1 \circ R_2 \,,$$

where $R_1 \in \mathbb{F}_p$ and $R_2 \in \mathbb{F}_p$ are variables that store the source operands and R_1 is overwritten by the resulting value after execution of an operation $\circ$. In contrast, operations that do not overwrite the input operands are referred to as *out-of-place* operations, e.g.

$$R_3 \leftarrow R_1 \circ R_2 \,,$$

where $R_3 \in \mathbb{F}_p$ is an additional variable that stores the result of the operation.

In general, there exist several ways to implement modular operations in software and hardware. Most implementations use multi-precision arithmetic to process the large integer operands. That means that each operand is represented as a multiple-word data structure, *i.e.* $a = (a_{t-1}, \ldots, a_1, a_0)$ and $b = (b_{t-1}, \ldots, b_1, b_0)$, where t denotes the number of words. A 160-bit addition operation, for instance, that runs on a 16-bit processor, performs therefore ten additions by loading the input operands from memory, adding the two operands, and storing the result back to the memory. A subtraction is done in the same way, performing machine word subtractions instead of additions. However, during the computation both operations process each word of the operands sequentially and can thus perform the operation *in-place* at no cost in terms of memory or computational efficiency [11].

In contrast, modular multiplication (and squaring) can be implemented in several ways. Basically, we can distinguish between *separated* and *integrated* modular multiplication [19,18]. Separated modular multiplications perform the multiplication first and apply the reduction afterwards. In this approach, the result of the multiplication is stored in a temporary variable R_m which is then reduced in a separated step, e.g.

$$R_m \leftarrow R_1 \times R_2,$$
$$R_1 \leftarrow R_m \pmod{p}.$$

This approach needs additional memory to store the temporary variable $R_m \in [0, 2^{2Wt})$, where W denotes the number of bits of a word (i.e. typically 8, 16, 32, or 64 bits).

The integrated (or interleaved) modular multiplication approach alternates between multiplication and reduction. There, partial products get reduced during the multiplication which avoids storing the double-sized result R_m and thus reduces the memory requirements significantly to the size of about the modulus $p \in [0, 2^{Wt})$ [1,33,34,19,12,21]. However, for both multiplication types, the input operands cannot be overwritten with the resulting words because they are used not only once but multiple times throughout the algorithm. Therefore, implementations that allow *in-place* multiplications (and squarings) may need either an extra buffer to store the intermediate result $2^{Wt} \leq R_m < 2^{2Wt}$ or save the input operand to be overwritten during the computation. Formulæ for point operations in elliptic curves that involve *in-place* operations are thus very likely to require more memory in practice than claimed.

In this work, we propose *out-of-place* formulæ that use different source and destination variables to perform the modular multiplication and squaring operations. This guarantees that no additional memory is needed to perform the computation neither for software nor hardware implementations and that our formulæ will therefore meet our claims in all contexts.

6   Discussion

6.1   Security Analysis

The resistance to side-channel attacks and fault attacks is essential for the implementation of cryptographic applications in embedded device. The given formulæ allow the use of traditional countermeasures against such attacks without disadvantages. As described in Section 3, the Montgomery ladder is well suited to the implementation of the scalar-multiplication method since it is resistant against SPA attacks [20,24] as well as safe-error attacks [35].

In addition, there exist several proposals to protect the Montgomery ladder against statistical attacks such as Differential Power Analysis (DPA) [20,24]. One cheap but effective countermeasure against these attacks is the use of Randomized Projective Coordinates (RPC) as proposed by Coron [4]. In our context, this countermeasure can be implemented by randomizing the intermediate points of the Montgomery ladder since they are represented in projective-coordinate representation as seen in Section 4. This can be done in Algorithm 2 at the cost of only two multiplications by randomizing the initial coordinates of the points R_0 and R_1 which are represented by the triplet $\{X_1, X_2, Z\}$ such that $\mathrm{x}(R_0) = (X_1, Z)$ and $\mathrm{x}(R_1) = (X_2, Z)$. Then, given a random value λ, the point $\mathrm{x}(P) = (x_P, 1)$ is randomized to $\mathrm{x}(P') = (\lambda x_P, \lambda)$ for the initialization of $\mathrm{x}(R_0)$ and $\mathrm{x}(R_1)$ as follows:

$$\begin{cases} \mathrm{x}(R_1) \leftarrow (\lambda x_P, \lambda) = \mathrm{x}(P') \\ \mathrm{x}(R_1) \leftarrow \mathrm{doubling}(R_1) = \mathrm{x}(2P') \\ \mathrm{x}(R_0) \leftarrow (Z x_P, Z) = \mathrm{x}(P') \end{cases} . \tag{14}$$

This effectively randomizes every intermediate value during scalar multiplication and makes therefore DPA attacks ineffective. Note that the doubling can computed using the differential algorithms 4, 5, and 6 to save the need for a dedicated function.

In order to thwart fault injections during the scalar multiplication [32,31] a countermeasure that checks the resulting point can be applied. Checking that $x^3 + ax + b$ is a square may seem conceivable, unfortunately that may not detect if the point belongs to the twist curve instead of the original curve and would leave the implementation vulnerable to attacks such as the one introduced by Fouque *et al.* [8]. Another check consists in verifying that the coordinates of the resulting point satisfy the curve equation, in which case the recovery of the y-coordinate is required. However that can be done in an efficient way with projective coordinates *i.e.* $Z(Y^2 - bZ^2) = X(X^2 + aZ^2)$ [5]. This countermeasure effectively protects against fault attacks on the Montgomery ladder even when implemented with x-coordinate only formulæ [8].

Algorithm 3 shows the proposed Montgomery ladder in projective co-Z coordinate system using RPC [4] and Point-Validity Check [5]. AddDblCoZ denotes the implemented differential addition-and-doubling operation using Algorithms 4, 5, or 6. RecoverFullCoordinatesCoZ recovers the coordinates using Algorithm 7 or 8.

Algorithm 3. Montgomery ladder in projective co-Z coordinate system using RPC [4] and Point-Validity Check [5].

Input: $P \in E(\mathbb{F}_q)$ and $k = (k_{n-1}, \ldots, k_0)_2 \in \mathbb{N}$, with $k_{n-1} \neq 0$
Output: $Q = kP$

1: $\{X_1, X_2, Z\} \leftarrow \mathtt{AddDblCoZ}(\{0, \lambda x_P, \lambda\})$
2: $X_1 \leftarrow x_P \cdot Z$
3: **for** $i = n - 2$ downto 0 **do**
4:     $b \leftarrow k_i;$
5:         $\{X_{2-b}, X_{1+b}, Z\} \leftarrow \mathtt{AddDblCoZ}(\{X_{2-b}, X_{1+b}, Z\})$
6: **end for**
7: $\{X, Y, Z\} \leftarrow \mathtt{RecoverFullCoordinatesCoZ}(\{X_1, X_2, Z\})$
8: $Z(Y^2 - bZ^2) \overset{?}{=} X(X^2 + aZ^2)$
9: **return** $\{X, Y, Z\}$

Table 1. Complexity of scalar multiplications per bit of scalar

Method	Costs[a]	M/bit[b]	M/bit[c]
Algorithm 6	**10M + 5S + 13add**	**14**	**17.9**
Algorithm 5	**9M + 5S + 1M_a + 1M_{4b} + 14add**	**14**	**18.8**
Izu et al. [14]	10M + 4S + 2M_a + 1M_b + 18add	14.2	20.8
Goundar et al. [10]	8M + 7S + 3M_a + 1M_b + 18add	14.6	21.8
Algorithm 4	**11M + 4S + 1M_a + 1M_{4b} + 14add**	**15.2**	**20.0**
Fischer et al. [7]	10M + 5S + 2M_a + 2M_b + 14add	16	21.4

[a] The explicit formulæ are given in Appendix A.
[b] $M_b = 1M$; $S = 0.8M$; $1M_a \simeq 0$; $1add \simeq 0$ (negligible)
[c] $M_b = 1M$; $S = 0.8M$; $1M_a = 2add$; $1add = 0.3M$

6.2   Performance Analysis

We now compare our formulæ with existing differential addition-and-doubling formulæ. Comparing one formula with another is not straightforward because the complexity ratio of the field-arithmetic operations involved may vary according to the underlying implementation as well as the usage context. Hence we provide the global complexity of each algorithm along with figures corresponding to some assumptions that are made based on on-the-field experience and previous works.

Thus, we first adopt the common assumption that the squaring operation is faster than a multiplication with the weighting $1S = 0.8M$ [11,6]. The cost of additions and subtractions are usually neglected when evaluating the complexity of the formulæ. However, according to several previous works [23,26,9] it may be relevant to take these operations into account since in practice they have reported ratios from $1add = 0.1M$ up to $1add = 0.3M$. Hence, in the following we will consider both cases, by first considering additions negligible and then the worst case where $1add = 0.3M$. Besides, a special case can also be made for the multiplications involving the curve parameters and especially the parameter a because several standardized curves have a set to -3. In any case, this assumption can be applied without loss of generality because a curve isomorphism can be used to reduce a to a small relative integer [13, §§ A.9.5 and A.10.4] (see also [3]). Subsequently, we will assume that a multiplication with a takes 2 additions, i.e. $1M_a = 2add$. Rescaling a curve to reduce the value of a also modifies the value b in a way that it is unlikely in the general case to have both a and b small. Therefore a multiplication with b (or any fixed pre-computed multiple e.g. $4b$ denoted M_{4b}) is considered as a regular modular multiplication of cost $M_b = 1M$.

In the following, we compare different low-memory scalar multiplication formulæ first sorted by performances in Table 1 and then sorted by memory requirements in Table 2.

Table 1 shows the efficiency of the formulæ we proposed in Section 4. Algorithm 5 is more efficient than any previous works found in literature since $1S \geq 0.5M$ [26, §§ 14.18]. In practice, Algorithm 6 is also more efficient because

Table 2. Memory requirements of scalar multiplications

Method	Working registers	In-place[a] memory	Constants	Total
Algorithm 4	**7 reg.**	-	$\{x_D, a, 4b\}$	**10 reg.**
Izu et al. [14]	7 reg.	+1 reg.	$\{x_D, a, b\}$	11 reg.
Goundar et al. [10]	7 reg.	+1 reg.	$\{x_D, a, b\}$	11 reg.
Algorithm 5	**8 reg.**	-	$\{x_D, a, 4b\}$	**11 reg.**
Fischer et al. [7]	8 reg.	+1 reg.	$\{x_D, a, 4b\}$	12 reg.
Algorithm 6	**10 reg.**	-	-	**10 reg.**

[a] In-place operations require additional memory to perform multiple-precision arithmetic operations (see Section 5).

rescaling general curves implies at best $1M_a + 1M_b \geq 1M$. The performance improvement is significant (up to 14 % less multiplications per bit) when adopting the usual assumption that $1S \geq 0.8M$ (cf [11,6]) and $1M_b = 1M$. One can also remark that the benefits of our approach increases when the squaring is performed using the multiplication instead of a dedicated implementation (for program or hardware saving) as well as when the secondary operations such as additions and subtractions are not negligible (as observed in practice).

Table 2 lists the memory requirements of the scalar multiplication methods. For constrained devices where the elliptic-curve parameters x_D, a, b or $4b$ are hard-coded or stored in read-only memory, Algorithm 4 provides the lowest memory requirements. It allows to implement the scalar multiplication with only 7 working registers combined with the memory gain offered by the implementation of *out-of-place* field operations as described in Section 5.

In a context where the curve parameters cannot be set during the design-time of the device or if they can not be processed directly from the read-only memory as it is in the case with most cryptographic accelerators, Algorithm 6 becomes equivalent in terms of memory requirement to Algorithm 4 while being faster as shown in Table 1.

7   Conclusion

In this paper, we presented new formulæ for fast and memory-wise scalar multiplication on elliptic curves over prime fields. The proposed formulæ use *out-of-place* operations, namely the source and destination variables of finite-field multiplications are always different. This guarantees that neither additional memory is needed nor additional operations have to be executed to perform multiple-precision arithmetic operations in both software or hardware implementations. Furthermore, the given formulæ outperform existing solutions by using a co-Z coordinate representation. The formulæ can be applied on general elliptic curves and allow the integration of conventional countermeasures against implementation attacks. They can be efficiently applied in low-resource implementations of RFIDs, smart cards, and other embedded systems.

Acknowledgements. The work has been supported in part by the European Commission through the ICT program under contract ICT-2007-216646 (European Network of Excellence in Cryptology - ECRYPT II).

References

1. Blakely, G.R.: A computer algorithm for calculating the product ab modulo m. IEEE Transactions on Computers 32(5), 497–500 (1983)
2. Brier, E., Joye, M.: Weierstraß elliptic curves and side-channel attacks. In: Naccache, D., Paillier, P. (eds.) PKC 2002. LNCS, vol. 2274, pp. 335–345. Springer, Heidelberg (2002)
3. Brier, E., Joye, M.: Fast point multiplication on elliptic curves through isogenies. In: Fossorier, M., Høholdt, T., Poli, A. (eds.) AAECC 2003. LNCS, vol. 2643, pp. 43–50. Springer, Heidelberg (2003)
4. Coron, J.-S.: Resistance against differential power analysis for elliptic curve cryptosystems. In: Koç, Ç.K., Paar, C. (eds.) CHES 1999. LNCS, vol. 1717, pp. 292–302. Springer, Heidelberg (1999)
5. Ebeid, N.M., Lambert, R.: Securing the elliptic curve Montgomery ladder against fault attacks. In: Breveglieri, L., et al. (eds.) Fault Diagnosis and Tolerance in Cryptography (FDTC 2009), pp. 46–50. IEEE Computer Society, Los Alamitos (2009)
6. Explicit-formulas database (EFD), http://www.hyperelliptic.org/EFD/
7. Fischer, W., Giraud, C., Knudsen, E.W., Seifert, J.-P.: Parallel scalar multiplication on general elliptic curves over $\mathbb{F}_p$ hedged against non-differential side-channel attacks. Cryptology ePrint Archive, Report 2002/007 (2002)
8. Fouque, P.-A., Lercier, R., Réal, D., Valette, F.: Fault attack on elliptic curve Montgomery ladder implementation. In: Breveglieri, L., et al. (eds.) Fault Diagnosis and Tolerance in Cryptography (FDTC 2008), pp. 92–98. IEEE Computer Society, Los Alamitos (2008)
9. Giraud, C., Verneuil, V.: Atomicity improvement for elliptic curve scalar multiplication. In: Gollmann, D., Lanet, J.-L., Iguchi-Cartigny, J. (eds.) CARDIS 2010. LNCS, vol. 6035, pp. 80–101. Springer, Heidelberg (2010)
10. Goundar, R.R., Joye, M., Miyaji, A.: Co-Z addition formulæ and binary ladders on elliptic curves. In: Mangard, S., Standaert, F.-X. (eds.) CHES 2010. LNCS, vol. 6225, pp. 65–79. Springer, Heidelberg (2010)
11. Hankerson, D., Menezes, A., Vanstone, S.: Guide to Elliptic Curve Cryptography. Springer, Heidelberg (2004)
12. Hein, D., Wolkerstorfer, J., Felber, N.: ECC is ready for RFID – A proof in silicon. In: 4th Workshop on RFID Security 2008 (RFIDsec 2008), July 9–11 (2008)
13. IEEE Std 1363-2000. IEEE Standard Specifications for Public-Key Cryptography. IEEE Computer Society (August 2000)
14. Izu, T., Möller, B., Takagi, T.: Improved elliptic curve multiplication methods resistant against side channel attacks. In: Menezes, A., Sarkar, P. (eds.) INDOCRYPT 2002. LNCS, vol. 2551, pp. 296–313. Springer, Heidelberg (2002)
15. Izu, T., Takagi, T.: A fast parallel elliptic curve multiplication resistant against side channel attacks. In: Naccache, D., Paillier, P. (eds.) PKC 2002. LNCS, vol. 2274, pp. 280–296. Springer, Heidelberg (2002)
16. Joye, M., Yen, S.-M.: The Montgomery powering ladder. In: Kaliski Jr., B.S., Koç, Ç.K., Paar, C. (eds.) CHES 2002. LNCS, vol. 2523, pp. 291–302. Springer, Heidelberg (2003)

17. Koblitz, N.: Elliptic curve cryptosystems. Mathematics of Computation 48, 203–209 (1987)
18. Koç, Ç.K.: RSA Hardware Implementation. Technical report, RSA Laboratories, RSA Data Security, Inc. 100 Marine Parkway, Suite 500 Redwood City, CA 94065-1031 (1995)
19. Koç, Ç.K., Acar, T., Kaliski Jr., B.S.: Analyzing and comparing Montgomery multiplication algorithms. IEEE Micro. 16, 26–33 (1996)
20. Kocher, P., Jaffe, J., Jun, B.: Differential power analysis. In: Wiener, M. (ed.) CRYPTO 1999. LNCS, vol. 1666, pp. 388–397. Springer, Heidelberg (1999)
21. Lee, Y.K., Sakiyama, K., Batina, L., Verbauwhede, I.: Elliptic-curve-based security processor for RFID. IEEE Transactions on Computers 57(11), 1514–1527 (2008)
22. Lee, Y.K., Verbauwhede, I.: A compact architecture for montgomery elliptic curve scalar multiplication processor. In: Kim, S., Yung, M., Lee, H.-W. (eds.) WISA 2007. LNCS, vol. 4867, pp. 115–127. Springer, Heidelberg (2008)
23. Lim, C.H., Hwang, H.S.: Fast implementation of elliptic curve arithmetic in $GF(p^n)$. In: Imai, H., Zheng, Y. (eds.) PKC 2000. LNCS, vol. 1751, pp. 405–421. Springer, Heidelberg (2000)
24. Mangard, S., Oswald, E., Popp, T.: Power Analysis Attacks – Revealing the Secrets of Smartcards. Springer, Heidelberg (2007)
25. Meloni, N.: New point addition formulae for ECC applications. In: Carlet, C., Sunar, B. (eds.) WAIFI 2007. LNCS, vol. 4547, pp. 189–201. Springer, Heidelberg (2007)
26. Menezes, A.J., van Oorschot, P.C., Vanstone, S.A.: Handbook of Applied Cryptography. CRC Press, Boca Raton (1997)
27. Miller, V.S.: Use of elliptic curves in cryptography. In: Williams, H.C. (ed.) CRYPTO 1985. LNCS, vol. 218, pp. 417–426. Springer, Heidelberg (1986)
28. Montgomery, P.L.: Speeding up the Pollard and elliptic curve methods of factorization. Mathematics of Computation 48(177), 243–264 (1987)
29. National Institute of Standards and Technology. FIPS 186-3 – Digital Signature Standard (DSS) (June 2009),
http://csrc.nist.gov/publications/fips/fips186-3/fips_186-3.pdf
30. Rivest, R.L., Shamir, A., Adleman, L.: A method for obtaining digital signatures and public-key cryptosystems. Communications of the ACM 21, 120–126 (1978)
31. Schmidt, J.-M.: Implementation Attacks – Manipulating Devices to Reveal Their Secrets. PhD thesis, Graz University of Technology (2009)
32. Skorobogatov, S.P.: Semi-Invasive Attacks – A New Approach to Hardware Security Analysis. PhD thesis, University of Cambridge (2005),
http://www.cl.cam.ac.uk/techreports/UCAM-CL-TR-630.pdf
33. Sloan, K.R.: Comments on "A computer algorithm for calculating the product AB modulo M". IEEE Transactions on Computers 34, 290–292 (1985)
34. Wolkerstorfer, J.: Dual-field arithmetic unit for $GF(p)$ and $GF(2^m)$. In: Kaliski Jr., B.S., Koç, Ç.K., Paar, C. (eds.) CHES 2002. LNCS, vol. 2523, pp. 500–514. Springer, Heidelberg (2003)
35. Yen, S.-M., Joye, M.: Checking before output may not be enough against fault-based cryptanalysis. IEEE Transactions on Computers 49(9), 967–970 (2000)

A   Appendix

In the following, the explicit formulæ for differential addition-and-doubling and full projective coordinate recovery in co-Z coordinates are given. Algorithm 4 gives the formulæ for differential addition-and-doubling using $11M + 4S + 14add + 1M_a + 1M_{4b}$ and $7 + \{x_D, a, 4b\}$ registers. Algorithm 5 show the formulæ using $9M + 5S + 14add + 1M_a + 1M_{4b}$ and $8 + \{x_D, a, 4b\}$ registers. Algorithm 6 gives the formulae using $10M + 5S + 13add$ and 10 registers (without involving curve parameters). The recovery of the full projective coordinates is given in Algorithm 7 and Algorithm 8. All given formulæ provide the *out-of-place* property so that input operands are not overwritten by output operands of squaring and multiplication operations. Furthermore, the elliptic curve parameter b is always used in a quadruple representation so that it can be pre-computed and pre-stored as $4b$. In addition, all formulae update the input variables with the resulting values using the same memory location. This avoids memory copies or pointer manipulations in hardware or software implementations. Finite field operations are denoted by $\times$ for multiplication, $\cdot^2$ for squaring, $+$ for addition, and $-$ for subtraction.

Algorithm 4. Out-of-place differential addition-and-doubling in projective co-Z coordinate system using $11M + 4S + 14add + 1M_a + 1M_{4b}$ and $7 + \{x_D, a, 4b\}$ registers.

Require: $X_1, X_2, Z, x_D, a, 4b$
Ensure: X_1, X_2, Z

1:
1. $R_1 \leftarrow X_1 \times X_2$
2. $R_3 \leftarrow Z^2$
3. $R_4 \leftarrow Z \times R_3$
4. $R_2 \leftarrow a \times R_3$
5. $R_1 \leftarrow R_1 + R_2$
6. $X_1 \leftarrow X_1 + X_2$
7. $R_3 \leftarrow X_1 \times R_1$
8. $X_1 \leftarrow X_1 - X_2$
9. $X_1 \leftarrow X_1 - X_2$
10. $R_1 \leftarrow 4b \times R_4$
11. $R_4 \leftarrow X_1{}^2$
12. $X_1 \leftarrow R_4 \times Z$
13. $R_3 \leftarrow R_3 + R_3$
14. $R_3 \leftarrow R_3 + R_1$
15. $Z \leftarrow X_2 \times R_4$

16. $R_4 \leftarrow R_1 \times X_2$
17. $R_1 \leftarrow X_2{}^2$
18. $R_2 \leftarrow R_1 + R_2$
19. $R_1 \leftarrow R_1 + R_1$
20. $X_2 \leftarrow x_D \times X_1$
21. $R_3 \leftarrow R_3 - X_2$
22. $X_2 \leftarrow R_1 \times R_2$
23. $X_2 \leftarrow X_2 + X_2$
24. $R_2 \leftarrow R_2 - R_1$
25. $R_1 \leftarrow R_4 + R_4$
26. $R_4 \leftarrow X_2 + R_4$
27. $X_2 \leftarrow R_2{}^2$
28. $R_1 \leftarrow X_2 - R_1$
29. $X_2 \leftarrow R_1 \times Z$
30. $Z \leftarrow X_1 \times R_4$
31. $X_1 \leftarrow R_3 \times R_4$

2: **return** (X_1, X_2, Z)

Algorithm 5. Out-of-place differential addition-and-doubling in projective co-Z coordinate system using $9M + 5S + 14\text{add} + 1M_a + 1M_{4b}$ and $8 + \{x_D, a, 4b\}$ registers.

Require: $X_1, X_2, Z, x_D, a, 4b$
Ensure: X_1, X_2, Z

1:

1. $R_2 \leftarrow Z^2$	16. $X_1 \leftarrow X_1 - X_2$
2. $R_3 \leftarrow a \times R_2$	17. $X_2 \leftarrow X_2 + X_2$
3. $R_1 \leftarrow Z \times R_2$	18. $R_3 \leftarrow X_2 \times R_2$
4. $R_2 \leftarrow 4b \times R_1$	19. $R_4 \leftarrow R_4 - R_3$
5. $R_1 \leftarrow X_2{}^2$	20. $R_3 \leftarrow X_1{}^2$
6. $R_5 \leftarrow R_1 - R_3$	21. $R_1 \leftarrow R_1 - R_3$
7. $R_4 \leftarrow R_5{}^2$	22. $X_1 \leftarrow X_1 + X_2$
8. $R_1 \leftarrow R_1 + R_3$	23. $X_2 \leftarrow X_1 \times R_1$
9. $R_5 \leftarrow X_2 \times R_1$	24. $X_2 \leftarrow X_2 + R_2$
10. $R_5 \leftarrow R_5 + R_5$	25. $R_2 \leftarrow Z \times R_3$
11. $R_5 \leftarrow R_5 + R_5$	26. $Z \leftarrow x_D \times R_2$
12. $R_5 \leftarrow R_5 + R_2$	27. $X_2 \leftarrow X_2 - Z$
13. $R_1 \leftarrow R_1 + R_3$	28. $X_1 \leftarrow R_5 \times X_2$
14. $R_3 \leftarrow X_1{}^2$	29. $X_2 \leftarrow R_3 \times R_4$
15. $R_1 \leftarrow R_1 + R_3$	30. $Z \leftarrow R_2 \times R_5$

2: **return** (X_1, X_2, Z)

Algorithm 6. Out-of-place differential addition-and-doubling in projective co-Z coordinate system using $10M + 5S + 13\text{add}$ and 10 registers.

Require: $X_1, X_2, T_D = x_D Z, T_a = aZ^2, T_b = 4bZ^3$
Ensure: X_1, X_2, T_D, T_a, T_b

1:

1. $R_2 \leftarrow X_1 - X_2$	16. $X_2 \leftarrow X_1{}^2$
2. $R_1 \leftarrow R_2{}^2$	17. $R_2 \leftarrow R_2 + X_2$
3. $R_2 \leftarrow X_2{}^2$	18. $X_2 \leftarrow R_5 \times R_2$
4. $R_3 \leftarrow R_2 - T_a$	19. $X_2 \leftarrow X_2 + T_b$
5. $R_4 \leftarrow R_3^2$	20. $X_1 \leftarrow R_3 \times X_2$
6. $R_5 \leftarrow X_2 + X_2$	21. $X_2' \leftarrow R_1 \times R_4$
7. $R_3 \leftarrow R_5 \times T_b$	22. $R_2 \leftarrow R_1 \times R_3$
8. $R_4 \leftarrow R_4 - R_3$	23. $R_3 \leftarrow R_2 \times T_b$
9. $R_5 \leftarrow R_5 + R_5$	24. $R_4 \leftarrow R_2{}^2$
10. $R_2 \leftarrow R_2 + T_a$	25. $R_1 \leftarrow T_D \times R_2$
11. $R_3 \leftarrow R_5 \times R_2$	26. $R_2 \leftarrow T_a \times R_4$
12. $R_3 \leftarrow R_3 + T_b$	27. $T_b \leftarrow R_3 \times R_4$
13. $R_5 \leftarrow X_1 + X_2$	28. $X_1 \leftarrow X_1 - R_1$
14. $R_2 \leftarrow R_2 + T_a$	29. $T_D \leftarrow R_1$
15. $R_2 \leftarrow R_2 - R_1$	30. $T_a \leftarrow R_2$

2: **return** $(X_1, X_2, T_D, T_a, T_b)$

Algorithm 7. Out-of-place (X, Y, Z)-recovery in projective co-Z coordinate system using $8M + 2S + 8add + 1M_a + 1M_{4b}$ and $7 + \{x_D, y_D, a, 4b\}$ registers.

Require: X_1, X_2, Z, x_D, y_D, a, $4b$
Ensure: X_1, X_2, Z

1:
  1. $R_1 \leftarrow x_D \times Z$
  2. $R_2 \leftarrow X_1 - R_1$
  3. $R_3 \leftarrow R_2{}^2$
  4. $R_4 \leftarrow R_3 \times X_2$
  5. $R_2 \leftarrow R_1 \times X_1$
  6. $R_1 \leftarrow X_1 + R_1$
  7. $X_2 \leftarrow Z^2$

  8. $R_3 \leftarrow a \times X_2$
  9. $R_2 \leftarrow R_2 + R_3$
 10. $R_3 \leftarrow R_2 \times R_1$
 11. $R_3 \leftarrow R_3 - R_4$
 12. $R_3 \leftarrow R_3 + R_3$
 13. $R_1 \leftarrow y_D + y_D$
 14. $R_1 \leftarrow R_1 + R_1$

 15. $R_2 \leftarrow R_1 \times X_1$
 16. $X_1 \leftarrow R_2 \times X_2$
 17. $R_2 \leftarrow X_2 \times Z$
 18. $Z \leftarrow R_2 \times R_1$
 19. $R_4 \leftarrow 4b \times R_2$
 20. $X_2 \leftarrow R_4 + R_3$

2: **return** (X_1, X_2, Z)

Algorithm 8. Out-of-place (X, Y, Z)-recovery in projective co-Z coordinate system using $10M + 3S + 8add$ and $9 + \{x_D, y_D, a, 4b\}$ registers.

Require: X_1, X_2, $T_D = x_D Z$, $T_a = aZ^2$, $T_b = 4bZ^3$, x_D, y_D
Ensure: X_1, X_2, Z

1:
  1. $R_1 \leftarrow T_D \times X_1$
  2. $R_2 \leftarrow R_1 + T_a$
  3. $R_3 \leftarrow X_1 + T_D$
  4. $R_4 \leftarrow R_2 \times R_3$
  5. $R_3 \leftarrow X_1 - T_D$
  6. $R_2 \leftarrow R_3^2$
  7. $R_3 \leftarrow R_2 \times X_2$

  8. $R_4 \leftarrow R_4 - R3$
  9. $R_4 \leftarrow R_4 + R_4$
 10. $R_4 \leftarrow R_4 + T_b$
 11. $R_2 \leftarrow T_D^2$
 12. $R_3 \leftarrow X_1 \times R_2$
 13. $R_1 \leftarrow x_D \times R_3$
 14. $R_3 \leftarrow y_D + y_D$

 15. $R_3 \leftarrow R_3 + R_3$
 16. $X_1 \leftarrow R_3 \times R_1$
 17. $R_1 \leftarrow R_2 \times T_D$
 18. $Z \leftarrow R_3 \times R_1$
 19. $R_2 \leftarrow x_D^2$
 20. $R_3 \leftarrow R_2 \times x_D$
 21. $X_2 \leftarrow R_3 \times R_4$

2: **return** (X_1, X_2, Z)

Efficient Multiplication in
Finite Field Extensions of Degree 5

Nadia El Mrabet[1], Aurore Guillevic[2,3], and Sorina Ionica[4]

[1] LIASD - Université Paris 8, France
nelmrabe@mime.univ-paris8.fr
[2] Laboratoire Chiffre, Thales Communications S.A.,
160 bd de Valmy BP 82, 92704 Colombes Cedex France
[3] Équipe crypto DI/LIENS, École Normale Supérieure, France
aurore.guillevic@fr.thalesgroup.com
[4] TANC, Inria Saclay and LIX, École Polytechnique, France
sorina.ionica@m4x.org

Abstract. Small degree extensions of finite fields are commonly used for cryptographic purposes. For extension fields of degree 2 and 3, the Karatsuba and Toom Cook formulæ perform a multiplication in the extension field using 3 and 5 multiplications in the base field, respectively. For degree 5 extensions, Montgomery has given a method to multiply two elements in the extension field with 13 base field multiplications. We propose a faster algorithm, which requires only 9 base field multiplications. Our method, based on Newton's interpolation, uses a larger number of additions than Montgomery's one but our implementation of the two methods shows that for cryptographic sizes, our algorithm is much faster.

Keywords: finite field arithmetic, implementation, interpolation.

1 Introduction

Efficient implementation of a cryptosystem often relies on high performance arithmetic in a finite field $\mathbb{F}_q$ or over some extension field of small degree. In view of recent proposals for torus-based cryptography [6] and pairing-based cryptography [7], we propose a method to implement the arithmetic of the finite field $\mathbb{F}_{q^5}$, if the characteristic of $\mathbb{F}_q$ is greater than 11. Our method, based on Newton's interpolation method for multiplying two polynomials, is faster than previously known methods to perform multiplication in such fields.

We begin by enumerating several uses of degree five extension fields in cryptography. Firstly, Rubin and Silverberg [16] considered the problem of compression (i.e. representing elements in a finite field subgroup with fewer bits than classical algorithms) for extension fields in terms of *algebraic tori* $T_n(\mathbb{F}_q)$ (i.e. the elements of $\mathbb{F}_{q^n}^*$ whose norm is one down to every proper subfield of $\mathbb{F}_{q^n}/\mathbb{F}_q$). Rubin and Silverberg developed the CEILIDH cryptosystem based on $T_6(\mathbb{F}_q)$. In [6], van Dijk et al. gave applications based on $T_{30}(\mathbb{F}_q)$, such as El Gamal encryption,

A. Nitaj and D. Pointcheval (Eds.): AFRICACRYPT 2011, LNCS 6737, pp. 188–205, 2011.

El Gamal signatures and voting schemes. Van Dijk et al. proposed an implementation of $T_{30}(\mathbb{F}_q)$, based on some techniques used to implement CEILIDH. More precisely, they implemented $\mathbb{F}_{q^5}$ by using a degree 5 subfield of the degree 10 extension $\mathbb{F}_q[X]/\Phi_{11}(X)$, with $\Phi_{11}(X)$ the eleventh cyclotomic polynomial. Their operation count shows that multiplication in $\mathbb{F}_{q^5}$ requires $15M_q + 75A_q$, where M_q and A_q denote the costs of multiplication and addition in $\mathbb{F}_q$.

Secondly, we note that several families of elliptic curves having embedding degree 10, 15, 30 or 35 have been proposed for pairing-based cryptography [7,8]. These families are recommended for implementations at high security levels, i.e. 192 and 256. On such curves, we need an efficient implementation of an extension field whose degree is divisible by 5. This is generally done by using tower fields and thus requires an efficient arithmetic of $\mathbb{F}_{q^5}$. Moreover, note that the pairing values can be represented in compressed form by using algebraic tori. Up to the present, such implementations were done for supersingular curves in characteristic 3 (see [9]) and for Barreto-Naehrig curves (see [15]). The arithmetic of $T_{30}(\mathbb{F}_q)$ may be used for compressible pairings on curves with embedding degree 30, for example.

Bodrato [4] proposed a method to speed up the Toom Cook algorithm for degree 5 extension fields with characteristic 2. In [2], the multiplication in $\mathbb{F}_{q^5}$ is computed with two applications of the Karatsuba method and requires $14M_q + 34A_q$. To the best of our knowledge, the fastest known formula for computing multiplication over $\mathbb{F}_{q^5}$ with $\mathrm{char}(\mathbb{F}_q) > 5$ can be derived from Montgomery's method to multiply two five-term polynomials [14]. The complexity of his method is $13M_q + 62A_q$.

We propose a method to perform multiplication over $\mathbb{F}_{q^5}$ which relies on Newton's interpolation method. Interpolation methods require performing a certain number of divisions. Divisions are generally expensive, but we show that with Newton's interpolation, it is possible to choose the interpolation values such that we only need to perform a small number of divisions by small constants. Our operation count gives a total cost of $9M_q + 137A_q$ for a multiplication in $\mathbb{F}_{q^5}$. In order to apply Montgomery's method to multiplication in $\mathbb{F}_{q^5}$, some extra additions are needed. Even though our algorithm performs a great number of additions, our method is faster than Montgomery's one if $M_q > 18A_q$. Our method can be adapted for degree 6 and 7 extension fields. Our operation count shows that we need $11M_q + 196A_q$ for a multiplication in $\mathbb{F}_{q^6}$ and $13M_q + 271A_q$ for a multiplication in $\mathbb{F}_{q^7}$.

This paper is organized as follows: in Sect. 2 we describe Montgomery's method and estimate the number of additions in $\mathbb{F}_q$ that this method performs. In Sect. 3 we describe an efficient multiplication based on the interpolation for the field $\mathbb{F}_{p^5}$. Section 4 describes our implementation and gives experimental results. In Sect. 5 we show that our idea can be used to optimize the arithmetic of degree 6 and 7 extension fields. Finally, Sect. 6 shows that our method applies for implementations in pairing-based and torus-based cryptography, for high levels of security. In Appendix A we display the complete formula for inversion in $\mathbb{F}_{q^5}$.

2   Montgomery's Approach

Let $\mathbb{F}_q$ be a finite field of characteristic greater than 5. Usually, an extension of degree k of $\mathbb{F}_q$ is defined by $\mathbb{F}_{q^k} = \mathbb{F}_q[X]/(P(X)\mathbb{F}_q[X])$ where $P(X) \in \mathbb{F}_q[X]$ is an irreducible polynomial of degree k. Consequently, elements of $\mathbb{F}_{q^k}$ are represented by polynomials in X, of degree at most $k - 1$ and with coefficients in $\mathbb{F}_q$. Montgomery [14] proposed a Karatsuba-like formula for 5-term polynomials. We recall here his method. Let $A = a_0 + a_1 X + a_2 X^2 + a_3 X^3 + a_4 X^4$ and $B = b_0 + b_1 X + b_2 X^2 + b_3 X^3 + b_4 X^4$ in $\mathbb{F}_{q^5}$ with coefficients over $\mathbb{F}_q$.

Montgomery constructs the polynomial $C(X) = A(X) \cdot B(X)$ using the following formula

$$
\begin{aligned}
C &= (a_0 + a_1 X + a_2 X^2 + a_3 X^3 + a_4 X^4)(b_0 + b_1 X + b_2 X^2 + b_3 X^3 + b_4 X^4) \\
&= (a_0 + a_1 + a_2 + a_3 + a_4)(b_0 + b_1 + b_2 + b_3 + b_4)(X^5 - X^4 + X^3) \\
&\quad + (a_0 - a_2 - a_3 - a_4)(b_0 - b_2 - b_3 - b_4)(X^6 - 2X^5 + 2X^4 - X^3) \\
&\quad + (a_0 + a_1 + a_2 - a_4)(b_0 + b_1 + b_2 - b_4)(-X^5 + 2X^4 - 2X^3 + X^2) \\
&\quad + (a_0 + a_1 - a_3 - a_4)(b_0 + b_1 - b_3 - b_4)(X^5 - 2X^4 + X^3) \\
&\quad + (a_0 - a_2 - a_3)(b_0 - b_2 - b_3)(-X^6 + 2X^5 - X^4) \\
&\quad + (a_1 + a_2 - a_4)(b_1 + b_2 - b_4)(-X^4 + 2X^3 - X^2) \\
&\quad + (a_3 + a_4)(b_3 + b_4)(X^7 - X^6 + X^4 - X^3) \\
&\quad + (a_0 + a_1)(b_0 + b_1)(-X^5 + X^4 - X^2 + X) \\
&\quad + (a_0 - a_4)(b_0 - b_4)(-X^6 + 3X^5 - 4X^4 + 3X^3 - X^2) \\
&\quad + a_4 b_4 (X^8 - X^7 + X^6 - 2X^5 + 3X^4 - 3X^3 + X^2) \\
&\quad + a_3 b_3 (-X^7 + 2X^6 - 2X^5 + X^4) \\
&\quad + a_1 b_1 (X^4 - 2X^3 + 2X^2 - X) \\
&\quad + a_0 b_0 (X^6 - 3X^5 + 3X^4 - 2X^3 + X^2 - X + 1).
\end{aligned}
$$

The cost of these computations is $13M_q + 22A_q$. Note that in order to recover the final expression of the polynomial of degree 8, we have to re-organize the 13 lines to find its coefficients. We denote the products on each of the 13 lines by u_i, $0 \leq i \leq 12$ (i.e. $u_{12} = (a_0 + a_1 + a_2 + a_3 + a_4)(b_0 + b_1 + b_2 + b_3 + b_4)$, $u_{11} = (a_0 - a_2 - a_3 - a_4)(b_0 - b_2 - b_3 - b_4)$ etc.) By re-arranging the formula in function of the degree of X, we obtain the following expression for C

$$
\begin{aligned}
C = {}& u_3 X^8 \\
&+ (-u_2 - u_3 + u_6) X^7 \\
&+ (u_0 + 2u_2 + u_3 - u_4 - u_6 - u_8 + u_{11}) X^6 \\
&+ (-3u_0 - 2u_2 - 2u_3 + 3u_4 - u_5 + 2u_8 + u_9 - u_{10} - 2u_{11} + u_{12}) X^5 \\
&+ (3u_0 + u_1 + u_2 + 3u_3 - 4u_4 + u_5 + u_6 - u_7 - u_8 - 2u_9 + 2u_{10} + 2u_{11} - u_{12}) X^4 \\
&+ (-2u_0 - 2u_1 - 3u_3 + 3u_4 - u_6 + 2u_7 + u_9 - 2u_{10} - u_{11} + u_{12}) X^3 \\
&+ (u_0 + 2u_1 + u_3 - u_4 - u_5 - u_7 + u_{10}) X^2 \\
&+ (-u_0 - u_1 + u_5) X \\
&+ u_0.
\end{aligned}
$$

Considering this expression, we can easily count hidden additions in Montgomery's formula. We have taken into account that some operations are repetitive and simplified the expression of C very carefully by hand. We obtain the following formula

$C = u_3 X^8$
$+ (-u_2 + u_6 - u_3) X^7$
$+ ((u_0 + u_3 - u_4) - (u_6 - u_2) + (u_2 - u_8 + u_{11})) X^6$
$+ (u_3 - u_5 + u_9 - u_{10} + u_{12} - 2(u_2 - u_8 + u_{11}) - 3(u_0 + u_3 - u_4)) X^5$
$+ (u_1 + u_2 - u_4 + u_5 + u_6 - u_7 - u_8 - u_{12} - 2(u_9 - u_{10} - u_{11}) + 3(u_0 + u_3 - u_4)) X^4$
$+ (u_0 - u_6 + u_9 - u_{11} + u_{12} - 2(u_1 - u_7 + u_{10}) - 3(u_0 + u_3 - u_4)) X^3$
$+ ((u_0 + u_3 - u_4) + u_1 - u_5 + (u_1 - u_7 + u_{10})) X^2$
$+ (-u_0 - u_1 + u_5) X$
$+ u_0$

We consider that a multiplication by 3 costs one addition. This is due to the fact that $3U = 2U + U$ and that the product by 2 is only a shift in the binary decomposition (see Sect. 4.2). Our operation count shows that we need to perform 40 extra additions in order to get C. To sum up, Montgomery's method costs $13M_q + 62A_q$. Finally, in order to compute $C \mod P(X)$, we need some extra operations. Since the reduction technique is similar to the one for the multiplication method we propose, we detail it in Sect. 3.

3   Our Approach

In extensions of degree 2 and 3 Karatsuba and Toom Cook multiplications are the most efficient known. For composite degree extensions (i.e. $2^i 3^j$, for $i, j > 0$) one can use tower field extensions [11] and apply Karatsuba and Toom Cook methods [18]. If the degree of the extension is not composite, one may use the FFT method [18].

In this paper, we are interested in efficiently computing multiplications in extension fields of degree 5. Note that the use of FFT is not interesting in this case. Indeed, during a FFT multiplication, we have to multiply by roots of unity. In the general case, q is a large random prime number and the roots of unity over $\mathbb{F}_q$ do not necessarily have a sparse representation, even after recoding. Hence multiplications by these roots are expensive.

Finally, we may use Lagrange or Newton's interpolation method to implement the multiplication in $\mathbb{F}_{q^5}$. Generally, interpolation methods have the drawback to increase the number of additions during a multiplication. Moreover, with interpolation methods we need to perform several divisions. Bajard et al. [3] study these methods and replace divisions by multiplications by large numbers. In this paper, we study Newton's interpolation and by carefully choosing our interpolation points, we perform divisions by small constants. While multiplication by large constants uses a general multiplier, we explain that divisions by small constants can be handled as 2 additions.

Note that Karatsuba and Toom Cook's formulæ can be found using Newton's interpolation by applying Newton's forward difference formula. We use the same approach for a degree five extension, and we show that the number of extra additions is not large.

3.1   Newton's Interpolation

We denote by $A(X) = a_0 + a_1 X + \ldots + a_{k-1} X^{k-1}$ and $B(X) = b_0 + b_1 X + \ldots + b_{k-1} X^{k-1}$ the expressions of A and B in $\mathbb{F}_{q^k}$. The interpolation method for the multiplication follows this steps

- Find $2k - 1$ different values in $\mathbb{F}_q$ $\{\alpha_0, \alpha_1, \ldots, \alpha_{2k-2}\}$.
- Evaluate the polynomials $A(X)$ and $B(X)$ at these $2k - 1$ values: $A(\alpha_0), \ldots, A(\alpha_{2k-2}), B(\alpha_0), \ldots, B(\alpha_{2k-2})$.
- Compute $C(X) = A(X) \times B(X)$ at these $2k - 1$ values $C(\alpha_i) = A(\alpha_i)B(\alpha_i)$.
- Interpolate the polynomial $C(X)$ of degree $2k - 2$ (with Newton's method).

Newton's interpolation constructs the polynomial $C(X)$ in the following way

$$c'_0 = C(\alpha_0)$$
$$c'_1 = (C(\alpha_1) - c'_0) \frac{1}{(\alpha_1 - \alpha_0)}$$
$$c'_2 = \left((C(\alpha_2) - c'_0) \frac{1}{(\alpha_2 - \alpha_0)} - c'_1 \right) \frac{1}{(\alpha_2 - \alpha_1)}$$
$$\vdots$$

The reconstruction of $C(X)$ is done by

$$C(X) = c'_0 + c'_1(X - \alpha_0) + c'_2(X - \alpha_0)(X - \alpha_1) + \cdots$$
$$+ c'_{2k-2}(X - \alpha_0)(X - \alpha_1) \ldots (X - \alpha_{2k-2}).$$

This can be computed using Horner's scheme

$$C(X) = c'_0 + (X - \alpha_0) \left[c'_1 + (X - \alpha_1) \left(c'_2 + (X - \alpha_2) \langle \ldots \rangle \right) \right].$$

The global complexity of Newton's interpolation is the sum of the following operations:

1. the evaluations at α_i of $A(X)$ and $B(X)$
2. the $2k - 1$ multiplications in $\mathbb{F}_q$ ($A(\alpha_i) \times B(\alpha_i)$)
3. the computation of the c'_i
4. Horner's scheme to find the expression of $C(X) = A(X) \times B(X)$ of degree $2k - 2$.

3.2   Simplifying Operations in Newton's Interpolation

Since we want to multiply two polynomials of degree 4, we choose 9 values for the interpolation

$$\alpha_0 = 0, \alpha_1 = 1, \alpha_2 = -1, \alpha_3 = 2, \alpha_4 = -2, \alpha_5 = 4, \alpha_6 = -4, \alpha_7 = 3, \alpha_8 = \infty.$$

These values were chosen in order to minimize both the number of additions during the evaluation step and the costs of divisions by constants.

Complexity of the evaluations in α_i of A and B. For the first step, we have to evaluate $A(X)$ and $B(X)$ in the α_i. With the chosen values, evaluations of $A(X)$ and $B(X)$ are done using only additions and shifts in $\mathbb{F}_q$. Indeed, a product by a power of 2 is composed of shifts in binary base. In order to evaluate $A(X)$ at 2^j, we compute the products $a_i \times (2^j)^i$ which are shifts, and then the additions $\sum_{i=0}^{k-1} a_i (2^j)^i$ using a FFT scheme. For example, we describe the FFT scheme for the evaluation of $A(2)$ and $A(-2)$. First, we compute evaluations for even indices and odd indices, separately. Let $A_e = a_0 + a_2 \times 2^2 + (a_4 \times 2^2) \times 2^2$ and $A_o = a_1 \times 2 + (a_3 \times 2^2) \times 2$. The evaluations are then $A(2) = A_e + A_o$ and $A(-2) = A_e - A_o$.

As explained in [3], by writing down $3 = 2+1$ and $3^2 = 2^3 + 1$, the evaluation at 3 of $A(X)$ and $B(X)$ is composed only of shifts and additions. In practice, it is more efficient to design a direct procedure to multiply by 3 which is equivalent to one addition. This will be detailed in Sect. 4.

Adding the different costs, the evaluations of $A(X)$ and $B(X)$ have a total complexity of $48A_q$. Once we have performed the evaluations, we are able to compute the 9 multiplications $A(\alpha_i) \times B(\alpha_i)$, which are obtained with $9M_q$. The complexity of steps 1 and 2 is then $9M_q + 48A_q$.

Complexity of the computations of c'_j. The complete formulæ for computing the c'_j are

$$c_0 = u_0$$
$$c_1 = u_1 - c_0$$
$$c_2 = (u_2 - c_0 + c_1)/2$$
$$c_3 = ((u_3 - c_0)/2 - c_1 - c_2)/3$$
$$c_4 = (((u_4 - c_0)/2 + c_1)/3 - c_2 + c_3)/4$$
$$c_5 = (((((u_5 - c_0)/4 - c_1)/3 - c_2)/5 - c_3)/2 - c_4)/6$$
$$c_6 = ((((((u_6 - c_0)/4 + c_1)/5 - c_2)/3 + c_3)/6 - c_4)/2 + c_5)/8$$
$$c_7 = (((((-u_7 + c_0)/3 + c_1)/2 + c_2)/4 + c_3 + c_4)/5 + c_5 - c_6)/7.$$

In order to compute the coefficients c'_j during Newton's interpolation, one has to compute divisions by differences of α_i. In a binary basis, divisions by a power of 2 are rather simple, since they are equivalent to shifts to the right, plus sometimes an addition (see below). We approximate a division by a power of 2 by $1A_q$. Among all the differences of the α_i we choose, eleven are not a power of 2. They are given in Table 1. In Sect. 4.2, our analysis of divisions by 3, 5, 7 shows that the complexity of these divisions is equivalent to $2A_q$. In order to compute the c'_j, we need $28A_q$, 11 divisions by 2, 4 or 8, and 11 divisions by 3, 5 or 7. Consequently, the complexity of computing the c'_j is $61A_q$.

Cost of the polynomial interpolation. We use Horner's scheme to find the expression of the product polynomial $C = A \times B$. More precisely, we have to compute

Table 1. The problematic differences

$\alpha_3 - \alpha_2 = 3$	$\alpha_4 - \alpha_1 = -3$	$\alpha_5 - \alpha_1 = 3$	$\alpha_5 - \alpha_2 = 5$
$\alpha_5 - \alpha_4 = 6$	$\alpha_6 - \alpha_1 = -5$	$\alpha_6 - \alpha_2 = -3$	$\alpha_6 - \alpha_3 = -6$
$\alpha_7 - \alpha_0 = 3$	$\alpha_7 - \alpha_4 = 5$	$\alpha_7 - \alpha_6 = 7$	

$$C(X) = ((((c_8'(X - \alpha_7) + c_7')(X - \alpha_6) + c_6')(X - \alpha_5) + c_5') \dots$$

$$+ c_1')(X - \alpha_0) + c_0'.$$

We begin to compute from the inside to the outside. First, we compute the parenthesis $(c_8'(X - \alpha_7) + c_7')$, next $((c_8'(X - \alpha_7) + c_7')(X - \alpha_6) + c_6')$, and so on.

Horner's scheme for the chosen values of α_is is composed only of shifts and additions. The total complexity of the polynomial reconstruction is $28A_q$.

Complexity of the polynomial reduction. We may use the same technique for polynomial reduction in both Montgomery's method and our interpolation method. Indeed, we may represent the finite field $\mathbb{F}_{q^5}$ using an irreducible reduction polynomial of the form $X^5 - \alpha$.

We consider q such that $q \equiv 1 \mod 5$. Then the following result [12, Theorem 3.75] guarantees that such polynomials exist over $\mathbb{F}_q$.

Theorem 1. *[12, Theorem 3.75] Let $\mathbb{F}_{q^5}$ be a finite field, and let α be an element of $\mathbb{F}_q$. Then the binomial $X^5 - \alpha$ is irreducible in $\mathbb{F}_q[X]$ if and only if 5 divides the order e of $\alpha \in \mathbb{F}_q$, but not $(q-1)/e$.*

Moreover, in practice we may take α a small integer (such as 2 or 3). The reduction step needs 4 operations which are multiplications by α, but in practice they are computed as shifts and additions.

Table 2. Details of the operation count

Operation	Complexity
evaluation	$9M_q + 48A_q$
computation of c_j'	$61A_q$
interpolation	$28A_q$
Total	$9M_q + 137A_q$

3.3   Results and Comparison

Table 3 gives the complexity of a multiplication with Montgomery's formulæ and with our interpolation formulæ.

Table 3. Cost of multiplication in $\mathbb{F}_{q^5}$

Montgomery	This work
$13M_q + 62A_q$	$9M_q + 137A_q$

We save 4 multiplications in $\mathbb{F}_q$ using interpolation whereas we add 75 additions considering Montgomery's formula. The method we propose is more efficient if a multiplication in $\mathbb{F}_q$ has a cost greater than 18 additions in $\mathbb{F}_q$. The benchmarks of the library we used show that for q prime, the ratio M_q/A_q depends on the size of q. Consequently, our method is more efficient than Montgomery's formula if $\log q > 512$. Our benchmarks are given in Sect. 4.

4 Technical Details and Implementation

If q is a prime power, then $a \in \mathbb{F}_q$ can be represented as a polynomial of degree k with coefficients $a_0, a_1, \ldots, a_{k-1} \in \mathbb{F}_p$ such that $p^k = q$. Then additions and divisions by small constants are performed on every coefficient. Hence in the remainder of this section, we assume that q is prime.

4.1 Cost of Additions and Shifts in C Language

Our implementation is written in the C language. Over $\mathbb{F}_q$ with a and b of w 32-bit words, at each word addition, a carry must be taken into account. Indeed in C, an assembly instruction such as Add With Carry is not available. Algorithm 1 explains the processor behavior when performing an addition.

When computing a shift to the left written as $a \ll s$ in C, no carry appears. Hence this procedure is cheaper than an addition in $\mathbb{F}_q$. At each 32-bit word state ℓ, the instruction $r_\ell \leftarrow (a_\ell \ll s)\mathsf{Xor}(a_{\ell-1} \gg (32 - s))$ is enough. It needs 1 reading because $a_{\ell-1}$ was already loaded in a register at the preceding state, 3 instructions and 1 writing, plus 2 counter imcrementations for the word a_ℓ and r_ℓ memory address. The total count is then about $8w$ instructions. To conclude, with a C implementation, the ratio Shift/Add = $8/12 \approx 0.66$ is obtained. To improve the performance, a function which computes $a + (b \ll s)$ is provided. See details in Algorithm 2.

For the procedure in Algorithm 2 the ratio (Add with Shift)/Add is about $15/12 \approx 1.25$.

Finally, a direct multiplication by 3 is also used. As $3a = a + 2a$, this is performed as an Add with Shift, but neither the memory access for b_ℓ nor the counter incrementation for its address is needed. Hence the ratio Mult By 3 / Add is $13/12 \approx 1.08$. Practical results are given in Table 4. The benchmarks are close to the theoretical results. The compiler and processor type do not influence too much the timing results.

Algorithm 1. Addition in a prime field $\mathbb{F}_q$

INPUT : $a = a_{w-1}a_{w-2}\ldots a_0 \in \mathbb{F}_q$ and $b = b_{w-1}b_{w-2}\ldots b_0 \in \mathbb{F}_q$ of w 32-bit words
OUTPUT : $r = a + b = r_w r_{w-1} r_{w-2} \ldots r_0$ not reduced $\mod q$
1: $r_0 \leftarrow a_0 + b_0$
2: set carry
3: **for** $\ell \leftarrow 1, \ldots, w-1$ **do**
4:     $\mathsf{tmp} \leftarrow a_\ell + b_\ell$ ▷ 2 readings, 1 instruction
5:     $r_\ell \leftarrow \mathsf{tmp} + \mathsf{carry}$ ▷ 1 instruction, 1 writing
6:     carry update   ▷ 3 instructions
7:                              ▷ 3 counter imcrementations for memory address of a_ℓ, b_ℓ, r_ℓ
8: **end for**   ▷ 1 instruction
9: $a_w \leftarrow$ carry   ▷ overflow bit
10: **return** r ▷ $\approx 12w$ instructions

Algorithm 2. Shift to the left with addition in a prime field $\mathbb{F}_q$

INPUT : $a = a_{w-1}a_{w-2}\ldots a_0 \in \mathbb{F}_q$ and $b = b_{w-1}b_{w-2}\ldots b_0 \in \mathbb{F}_q$ of w 32-bit words, $0 < s < 32$
OUTPUT : $r = a + b2^s = a + (b \ll s) = r_w r_{w-1} r_{w-2} \ldots r_0$ not reduced $\mod q$
1: $r_0 \leftarrow a_0 + (b_0 \ll s)$
2: set carry
3: **for** $\ell \leftarrow 1, \ldots, w-1$ **do**
4:     $\mathsf{tmp} \leftarrow a_\ell + (b_\ell \ll s)\mathsf{Xor}(b_{\ell-1} \gg (32-s))$ ▷ 2 readings, 4 instructions
5:     $r_\ell \leftarrow \mathsf{tmp} + \mathsf{carry}$ ▷ 1 instruction, 1 writing
6:     carry update   ▷ 3 instructions
7:   ▷ 3 counter incrementations
8: **end for**   ▷ 1 instruction
9: $a_w \leftarrow$ carry $+ (b_{w-1} \gg (32-s))$ ▷ overflow bit
10: **return** r ▷ $\approx 15w$ instructions

4.2   Division by Small Constants

Division by 2, 4 and 8 in a prime field $\mathbb{F}_q$. Let $a \in \mathbb{F}_q$. If the last significant bit of a is 0, a is even and computing $a/2$ is just a shift to the right. Otherwise, a is odd but as q is a large prime, q is odd; hence $a+q$ is even and $a/2 = (a+q)/2$ with a shift. There remains a slight detail : $a + q$ may induce a bit overflow. Indeed, the modular integers are normally smaller than q. If q is of $32w$ bits, $a+q$ may be of $32w+1$ bits. To avoid that, we shift a and q before adding them. To finish we add the carry loss in the shift. Writing $a = 2a' + 1$, $q = 2q' + 1$, a' is a shifted of one bit to the right, q' is the same for q. The result is obtained as $a/2 = (a + q)/2 = a' + q' + 1$.

Following the same idea, division by 4 or 8 is a shift with sometimes an addition. We write $a = 4a' + r_a$, $r_a \in \{0, 1, 2, 3\}$ and $q = 4q' + r_q$, $r_q \in \{1, 3\}$. If $r_a = 0$, then the shift of two bits is enough; otherwise the value of $a/4$ is given in Table 5.

Note that a', q' are just shifts of two bits of a and q, respectively. Moreover, $q', 2q'$ and $3q'$ can be precomputed. For division by 8, we follow the same method,

Table 4. Theoretical and practical ratio Operation/Addition without modular reduction

Operation	Ratio Operation/Add								
	Theoretical	Our implementation in a prime field $\mathbb{F}_q$							
$\log q$		160	192	256	384	512	768	1024	1536
Shift to the left	0.66	0.50	0.50	0.50	0.48	0.46	0.42	0.47	0.42
Shift and Add	1.25	1.11	1.13	1.18	1.32	1.23	1.26	1.34	1.33
Multiplication by 3	1.08	0.88	0.89	1.02	0.97	1.00	1.00	1.08	1.09

Table 5. Division by 4

	$r_a = 1$	$r_a = 2$	$r_a = 3$
$r_q = 1$	$a' + 3q' + 1$	$a' + 2q' + 1$	$a' + q' + 1$
$r_q = 3$	$a' + q' + 1$	$a' + 2q' + 2$	$a' + 3q' + 3$

considering that $a = 8a' + r_a$, $r_a \in \{0, 1, \ldots, 7\}$ and $q = 8q' + r_q$, $r_q \in \{1, 3, 5, 7\}$. Benchmarks are given in Table 7.

Divisions by 3, 5 and 7 in a prime field $\mathbb{F}_q$. For these cases, shifts are not possible. We present a detailed division by 3, and give the main idea for 5 and 7.

We write a basic division of a by 3, considering that a is composed of 32-bit words. For each word, the possible remainders are 0, 1 or 2 (10 in binary base). This leads to a 33 or 34 bit word to the next state if the remainder is not zero. Fortunately, we know that $2^{32} = 3 \cdot 0x55555555 + 1$ and $2 \cdot 2^{32} = 3 \cdot 0xaaaaaaaa + 2$. This leads to Algorithm 3.

Now $a = 3a' + r_a$. If $r_a = 0$ then $a/3 = a'$. If not, write $q = 3q' + r_q$ (which can be precomputed). The result of the division is computed as explained in Table 6.

Table 6. Division by 3

	$r_a = 1$	$r_a = 2$
$r_q = 1$	$a' + 2q' + 1$	$a' + q' + 1$
$r_q = 2$	$a' + q' + 1$	$a' + 2q' + 2$

Cost of the divisions by small constants. Division by 3 is is carefully detailed in Algorithm 3. Our counting shows that in Algorithm 3 we perform around $15w$ processor instructions. Since in $\frac{2}{3}$ of cases we have to add p' (as explained in Table 6), we have on average the ratio

$$\text{Div}_q/A_q \simeq 2.$$

where Div_q denotes the cost of division by 3, 5 or 7. However, this number is just an approximation since the exact costs depends on

Algorithm 3. Division by 3 in a prime field $\mathbb{F}_q$

INPUT : $a = a_{w-1}a_{w-2}\ldots a_0 \in \mathbb{F}_q$ of w 32-bit words
OUTPUT : $a' = a/3 = a'_{w-1}a'_{w-2}\ldots a'_0$ and r such that $a = 3a' + r$

1: $a'_{w-1} \leftarrow a_{w-1}$ div 3; carry $\leftarrow a_{w-1}$ mod 3
2: **for** $\ell \leftarrow w - 2, \ldots, 0$ **do**
3:     **if** carry $= 0$ **then**   ▷ 1
4:         $a'_\ell \leftarrow a_\ell$ div 3; carry $\leftarrow a_\ell$ mod 3   ▷ $\frac{1}{3}$ 3
5:     **else**   ▷ 1
6:         **if** carry $= 1$ **then**   ▷ $\frac{2}{3}$ 1
7:             $a'_\ell \leftarrow$ 0x55555555 $+ (a_\ell$ div 3$)$ ▷ $\frac{1}{3}$ 4
8:             carry $\leftarrow$ carry $+ (a_\ell$ mod 3$)$ ▷ $\frac{1}{3}$ 2
9:         **else**   ▷ $\frac{2}{3}$ 1
10:             $a'_\ell \leftarrow$ 0xaaaaaaaa $+ (a_\ell$ div 3$)$ ▷ $\frac{1}{3}$ 4
11:             carry $\leftarrow$ carry $+ (a_\ell$ mod 3$)$ ▷ $\frac{1}{3}$ 2
12:         **end if**
13:         **if** carry $\geqslant 3$ **then**   ▷ $\frac{2}{3}$ 1
14:             carry $\leftarrow$ carry -3; $a'_\ell \leftarrow a'_\ell + 1$ ▷ $\frac{2}{3}$ 4
15:         **end if**
16:     **end if**
17: **end for**   ▷ 2 counter imcrementations $+ 1$
18: **return** (a', carry) ▷ $\approx 15w$ instructions

- the type of the compiler,
- the compiler directives,
- the number of cycles required for each processor instruction,
- the pipeline depth into the processor,
- the cache memory, etc.

Moreover, there are some conditional jumps in Algorithm 3. In an implementation, they may be replaced by access to a table indexed by the remainder's value. Table 7 gives a practical estimation of the ratio division/addition.

Table 7. Theoretical and practical ratio Division by a small constant/Add

Operation	Ratio Operation/Add						
	Theoretical	Our implementation in a prime field $\mathbb{F}_q$					
$\log q$		160	192	256	384	512	768	1024
Division by 2	1	1.00	0.82	0.85	0.84	1.01	0.62	0.76
Division by 3	2	1.57	1.10	1.37	1.42	1.44	1.60	1.59
Division by 4	1	1.00	1.00	0.79	0.92	0.88	1.03	1.07
Division by 5	2	1.69	1.41	1.47	1.58	1.74	1.62	2.01
Division by 6	2	2.76	2.15	2.00	2.14	2.34	2.14	2.36
Division by 7	2	2.15	1.52	1.89	1.62	1.76	1.88	1.96
Division by 8	1	1.36	1.05	1.04	1.01	1.04	0.89	1.21

The idea for division by 5 or 7 is the same, except that computing a'_ℓ needs different values (see Table 8).

Table 8. Constants for division by 5 and 7

division by 5	division by 7
$2^{32} = 5 \cdot \text{0x33333333} + 1$	$2^{32} = 7 \cdot \text{0x24924924} + 4$
$2 \cdot 2^{32} = 5 \cdot \text{0x66666666} + 2$	$2 \cdot 2^{32} = 7 \cdot \text{0x49249249} + 1$
$3 \cdot 2^{32} = 5 \cdot \text{0x99999999} + 3$	$3 \cdot 2^{32} = 7 \cdot \text{0x6db6db6d} + 5$
$4 \cdot 2^{32} = 5 \cdot \text{0xcccccccc} + 4$	$4 \cdot 2^{32} = 7 \cdot \text{0x92492492} + 2$
	$5 \cdot 2^{32} = 7 \cdot \text{0xb6db6db6} + 6$
	$6 \cdot 2^{32} = 7 \cdot \text{0xdb6db6db} + 3$

4.3   Implementation Results

We implemented Montgomery's formula and our multiplication in C in order to compare them. The subfield $\mathbb{F}_q$ is simply built with $q \equiv 1 \mod 5$ a large random prime number of cryptographic size, from 160 to 1536 bits. Our benchmarks on Montgomery's algorithm and our method use the same prime numbers q. The modular library implementing the arithmetic of $\mathbb{F}_q$ is LIBCRYPTOLCH [17] and uses the Montgomery representation to perform a modular multiplication (see chapter 14 of [13]). This library is also written in C. Parameters such as maximum moduli size and size of words are set at compilation. We used a gcc compiler with -O2 optimization directive. The code was running on a Pentium 64 bits 3GHz under Linux, Ubuntu 10.10. The reduction step (mod $X^5 - \alpha$) is done at each multiplication. Degree 5 extensions $\mathbb{F}_q[X]/(X^5 - \alpha)$ with very small α such as $\alpha = 2$ were found.

Depending on the size of q, the cost of a M_q in terms of A_q increases as shown in Table 9.

Table 9. Ratio M_q/A_q for different sizes of q

$\log q$	160	256	384	512	768	1024	1536
32 bits	5.2	7.1	12.1	16.1	26.6	36.3	50.0
64 bits	3.9	5.7	6.9	9.3	16.6	19.4	32.1

On this 64 bit processor, our formula is better than Montgomery's one for $\log q$ greater than 512, as shown in Figure 1. Implementation of additions in the base field library is not optimized, so the ratio M_q/A_q takes quite small values for small sizes of q. The timing ratio between Montgomery's method and our algorithm is shown in Table 10.

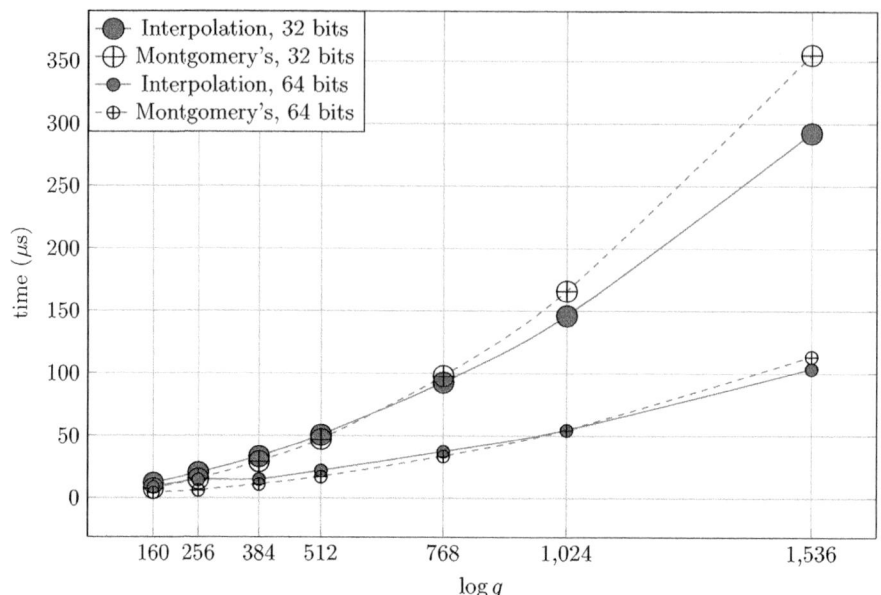

Fig. 1. Implementation results

Table 10. Timing ratio: Montgomery's formula results/ our's

$\log q$	160	256	384	512	768	1024	1536
32-bit words, theory	0.70	0.76	0.89	0.96	**1.08**	**1.15**	**1.21**
32-bit words, practice	0.64	0.75	0.88	0.93	**1.05**	**1.13**	**1.21**
64 bit words, theory	0.65	0.72	0.76	0.82	**1.00**	**1.01**	**1.12**
64 bit words, practice	0.49	0.31	0.73	0.77	0.90	**1.00**	**1.09**

5   Results and Comparison for Quintic and Sextic Polynomials

We use the same approach by interpolation to compute multiplication in extension fields of degree 6 and 7. Our results for an extension of degree 6 are the following

- the complexity of the evaluation step is $11M_q + 80A_q$,
- the complexity of the computation of the c'_i is $36A_q + 22\text{Div}_q$, where Div_q denotes the cost of division by 3, 5 or 7,
- the complexity of the Horner's scheme is $39A_q$.

As explained in Sect. 3.2, we count a division by 3, 5, 7 and 11 as $2A_q$. We perform 21 divisions by 2, 13 by 3, 6 by 5 and 3 by 7. Thus the total complexity of our multiplication is $11M_q + 199A_q$. We compare our results to Devegili et al. [5] most efficient result, and to Montgomery's one. The comparison is given in Table 11, where $M_{\mathbb{Z}}$ denotes the cost of multiplication by a small constant. Our method needs a smaller number of additions than Devegili et al.'s one.

Our results for an extension of degree 7 are the following

- the complexity of the evaluation step is $13M_q + 89A_q$,
- the complexity of the computation of the c_i' is $55A_q + 36\mathrm{Div}_q$,
- the complexity of the Horner's scheme is $65A_q$.

Estimating the cost of a division by 3, 5, 7 and 11 by $2A_q$, the total complexity of our multiplication is $13M_q + 281A_q$. We perform here 31 divisions by 2 or power of 2, 21 divisions by 3, 9 by 5, 5 by 7 and one by 11. The comparison is given in Table 11. Our method is more efficient than Mongomery's one if the ratio M_q/A_q is greater than 8.5.

Table 11. Complexity of different method of 6-term and 7-term multiplications

Method	Devegili et al. [5]	Montgomery	this work
6-term	$11M_q + 93M_{\mathbb{Z}} + 236A_q$	$17M_q + 161A_q$	$11M_q + 199A_q$
7-term	—	$22M_q + 205A_q$	$13M_q + 281A_q$

6   Cryptographic Use

We claim that our method is useful for cryptographic use in pairing-based cryptography and torus-based cryptography. We give in Tables 12 and 13 recommended security levels and the corresponding sizes of the field $\mathbb{F}_q$ for these applications.

Table 12. Pairing-based cryptography

Embedding degree	ρ-value	Security level	Size of q	Extension field
10	1.5	192	800	$\mathbb{F}_{q^{10}}$ (8000 bits)
15	1.5	192	576	$\mathbb{F}_{q^{15}}$ (8640 bits)
15	1.5	256	768	$\mathbb{F}_{q^{15}}$ (11520 bits)
20	1.375	256	704	$\mathbb{F}_{q^{20}}$ (14080 bits)
30	1.5	256	768	$\mathbb{F}_{q^{30}}$ (23040 bits)

Note that in order to achieve the 192 and 256 bit security levels, the size of the extension field $\mathbb{F}_{q^k}$ has to be within the range 8000-10000 and 14000-18000, respectively. The parameters given in Table 12 correspond to known families of pairing-friendly elliptic curves and the choices were made taking into account recommendations in [8]. Since our method is faster than Montgomery's formula if $\log q > 512$, our algorithm is interesting for implementations on these curves.

For torus-based cryptography, our method may be interesting for example when implementing $T_{30}(\mathbb{F}_q)$ for applications suggested in [6]. The choice of parameters in Table 13 is done according to recommendations [1,6]. We suppose that the following tower of extensions is chosen when implementing $\mathbb{F}_{q^{30}}$

$$\mathbb{F}_{q^2} \subset \mathbb{F}_{q^6} \subset \mathbb{F}_{q^{30}}.$$

Table 13. Torus-based cryptography

Security level	Torus	Size of $\mathbb{F}_q$	Size of extension field
128	$T_{30}(\mathbb{F}_q)$	102	$\mathbb{F}_{q^{30}}$ (3072 bits)
256	$T_{30}(\mathbb{F}_q)$	512	$\mathbb{F}_{q^{30}}$ (15360 bits)

Then the cost of a multiplication in $\mathbb{F}_{q^6}$ is $15M_q + 72A_q$ using Karatsuba and Toom Cook algorithms, while the cost of an addition is $6A_q$. Our method is efficient if $M_{q^6}/A_{q^6} > 18$. This ratio depends on the value of M_q/A_q, which obviously depends on the type of the processor chosen. For example, using data in Table 9, we obtain $M_{q^6}/A_{q^6} \simeq 53.66$ for an implementation at 256 bit security level using a 32 bit architecture.

Finally, note that the arithmetic of $T_{30}(\mathbb{F}_q) \subset \mathbb{F}_{q^{30}}$ may be used to compress pairing values for curves with embedding degree 30. The size of q for such curves is given in Table 12.

7   Conclusion

We proposed an efficient arithmetic for the field $\mathbb{F}_{q^5}$, using a multiplication by interpolation. Our idea to use Newton's method of interpolation requires some divisions by small constants which are not a power of two but we have shown that these divisions have a slight cost. Our method can be applied to 6 and 7 degree extensions. In each case, the number of multiplications over the base field is smaller than the one in other known methods. The number of additions is larger but for cryptographic sizes of q, as shown in our implementation, our method is faster.

Acknowledgments

This work was supported in part by the French ANR-09-VERS-016 BEST Project. The authors express their gratitude to Jean Claude Bajard, Renaud Dubois and Damien Vergnaud for helpful comments and careful proofreading and to Nicolas Guillermin for giving hints on the implementation part. The authors thank the anonymous reviewers of the Africacrypt conference for their useful comments.

References

1. Recommendations for Key Management, Special Publication 800-57 Part 1 (2007)
2. Avanzi, R., Cesena, E.: Trace Zero Varieties over Fields of Characteristic 2 for Cryptographic Applications. In: Hromkovič, J., Královič, R., Nunkesser, M., Widmayer, P. (eds.) SAGA 2007. LNCS, vol. 4665, Springer, Heidelberg (2007)
3. Bajard, J.C., Imbert, L., Negre, C.: Arithmetic operations in finite fields of medium prime characteristic using the Lagrange representation. IEEE Transactions on Computers 55(9), 1167–1177 (2006)

4. Bodrato, M.: Towards Optimal Toom-Cook Multiplication for Univariate and Multivariate Polynomials in Characteristic 2 and 0. In: Carlet, C., Sunar, B. (eds.) WAIFI 2007. LNCS, vol. 4547, pp. 116–133. Springer, Heidelberg (2007)
5. Devegili, A.J., Ó hÉigeartaigh, C., Scott, M., Dahab, R.: Multiplication and squaring on pairing-friendly fields. Cryptology ePrint Archive, Report 2006/471 (2006), http://eprint.iacr.org/
6. van Dijk, M., Granger, R., Page, D., Rubin, K., Silverberg, A., Stam, M., Woodruff, D.: Practical cryptography in high dimensional tori. In: Cramer, R. (ed.) EUROCRYPT 2005. LNCS, vol. 3494, pp. 234–250. Springer, Heidelberg (2005)
7. Freeman, D.: Constructing pairing-friendly elliptic curves with embedding degree 10. In: Hess, F., Pauli, S., Pohst, M. (eds.) ANTS 2006. LNCS, vol. 4076, pp. 452–465. Springer, Heidelberg (2006)
8. Freeman, D., Scott, M., Teske, E.: A taxonomy of pairing-friendly elliptic curves. Journal of Cryptology 23, 224–280 (2010)
9. Granger, R., Page, D., Smart, N.: On small characteristic algebraic tori in pairing based cryptography. LMS Journal of Computation and Mathematics (9), 64–85 (2006)
10. Itoh, T., Tsujii, S.: A Fast Algorithm for Computing Multiplicative Inverses in $GF(2^m)$ Using Normal Bases. Info. and Comp. 78(3), 171–177 (1988)
11. Koblitz, N., Menezes, A.: Pairing-based cryptography at high security levels. In: Smart, N.P. (ed.) Cryptography and Coding 2005. LNCS, vol. 3796, pp. 13–36. Springer, Heidelberg (2005)
12. Lidl, R., Niederreiter, H.: Finite Fields, 2nd edn. Cambridge University Press, Cambridge (1997)
13. Menezes, A., van Oorschot, P., Vanstone, S.: Handbook of Applied Cryptology. CRC Press, Boca Raton (2001)
14. Montgomery, P.L.: Five, six, and seven-term Karatsuba-like formulae. IEEE Transactions on Computers 54(3), 362–369 (2005)
15. Naehrig, M., Barreto, P., Schwabe, P.: On compressible pairings and their computation. In: Vaudenay, S. (ed.) AFRICACRYPT 2008. LNCS, vol. 5023, pp. 371–388. Springer, Heidelberg (2008)
16. Rubin, K., Silverberg, A.: Torus-based cryptography. In: Boneh, D. (ed.) CRYPTO 2003. LNCS, vol. 2729, pp. 349–365. Springer, Heidelberg (2003)
17. Thales Communications. LibCryptoLCH Librairie cryptographique du Laboratoire Chiffre (2011)
18. Von ZurGathen, J., Gerhard, J.: Modern Computer Algebra. Cambridge University Press, New York (2003)

Appendix: Details for Inversion

We have also counted the number of M_q for and inversion in $\mathbb{F}_{q^5}$. We consider that $5 \mid q - 1$ and $\mathbb{F}_{p^5}$ is built as $\mathbb{F}_q[X]/(X^5 - \alpha)$. Following the idea of T. Itoh and S. Tsujii [10] we perform an inversion in $\mathbb{F}_{q^5}$ as

$$a^{-1} = \frac{a^q \ a^{q^2} a^{q^3} a^{q^4}}{a \ a^q \ a^{q^2} a^{q^3} a^{q^4}} = \frac{\bar{a}}{\mathrm{Norm}_{\mathbb{F}_{q^5}/\mathbb{F}_q}(a)}$$

In order to compute a^{q^i}, we need the values of X^{q^i}, $1 \leqslant i \leqslant 4$. We have $X^{q^i} = X^{q^i-1}X = X^{5\frac{q^i-1}{5}}X = X^{5\frac{q-1}{5}(1+q+\ldots+q^{i-1})}X = \alpha^{\frac{q-1}{5}(1+q+\ldots+q^{i-1})}X$. Let $\mu = \alpha^{(q-1)/5}$. Note that $\mu^5 = 1$ and that $\mu \neq 1$. Hence μ is a root of the polynomial $1 + T + T^2 + T^3 + T^4$. Since $\mu \in \mathbb{F}_q$, we have $\mu^{q^i} = \mu$ and $\mu^{1+q+\ldots+q^{i-1}} = \mu^i$. So $X^{q^i} = \mu^i X$. Finally, for $1 \leqslant j \leqslant 4$, we have $(X^{q^i})^j = \mu^{ij \mod 5} X^j$. By writing $a = a_0 + a_1 X + a_2 X^2 + a_3 X^3 + a_4 X^4$, we obtain

$$a^{q^i} = a_0 + a_1 \mu X + a_2 \mu^{2i \mod 5} X^2 + a_3 \mu^{3i \mod 5} X^3 + a_4 \mu^{4i \mod 5} X^4, \ 1 \leqslant i \leqslant 4$$

Then we compute the numerator of the expression a^{-1} above.

$a^q \ a^{q^2} a^{q^3} a^{q^4} \mod 1 + \mu + \mu^2 + \mu^3 + \mu^4 =$
$a_4^4 X^{16}$
$- a_3 a_4^3 X^{15}$
$+ (-a_2 a_4^3 + a_3^2 a_4^2) X^{14}$
$+ (-a_1 a_4^3 + 2a_2 a_3 a_4^2 - a_3^3 a_4) X^{13}$
$+ (-a_0 a_4^3 + 2a_1 a_3 a_4^2 + a_2^2 a_4^2 - 3a_2 a_3^2 a_4 + a_3^4) X^{12}$
$+ (-3a_0 a_3 a_4^2 - 3a_1 a_2 a_4^2 + 2a_1 a_3^2 a_4 + 2a_2^2 a_3 a_4 - a_2 a_3^3) X^{11}$
$+ (2a_0 a_2 a_4^2 + 2a_0 a_3^2 a_4 + a_1^2 a_4^2 - a_1 a_2 a_3 a_4 - a_1 a_3^3 - a_2^3 a_4 + a_2^2 a_3^2) X^{10}$
$+ (2a_0 a_1 a_4^2 - a_0 a_2 a_3 a_4 - a_0 a_3^3 - 3a_1^2 a_3 a_4 + 2a_1 a_2^2 a_4 + 2a_1 a_2 a_3^2 - a_2^3 a_3) X^9$
$+ (a_0^2 a_4^2 - a_0 a_1 a_3 a_4 - 3a_0 a_2^2 a_4 + 2a_0 a_2 a_3^2 + 2a_1^2 a_2 a_4 + a_1^2 a_3^2 - 3a_1 a_2^2 a_3 + a_2^4) X^8$
$+ (2a_0^2 a_3 a_4 - a_0 a_1 a_2 a_4 - 3a_0 a_1 a_3^2 + 2a_0 a_2^2 a_3 - a_1^3 a_4 + 2a_1^2 a_2 a_3 - a_1 a_2^3) X^7$
$+ (2a_0^2 a_2 a_4 + a_0^2 a_3^2 + 2a_0 a_1^2 a_4 - a_0 a_1 a_2 a_3 - a_0 a_2^3 - a_1^3 a_3 + a_1^2 a_2^2) X^6$
$+ (-3a_0^2 a_1 a_4 - 3a_0^2 a_2 a_3 + 2a_0 a_1^2 a_3 + 2a_0 a_1 a_2^2 - a_1^3 a_2) X^5$
$+ (-a_0^3 a_4 + 2a_0^2 a_1 a_3 + a_0^2 a_2^2 - 3a_0 a_1^2 a_2 + a_1^4) X^4$
$+ (-a_0^3 a_3 + 2a_0^2 a_1 a_2 - a_0 a_1^3) X^3$
$+ (-a_0^3 a_2 + a_0^2 a_1^2) X^2$
$- a_0^3 a_1 X$
$+ a_0^4$

We simplify this formula as follows

$$
\begin{aligned}
\bar{a} = &\ (a_0^2(2a_1a_3 - a_0a_4 + a_2^2) + a_1^2(a_1^2 - 3a_0a_2 - 3a_3a_4\alpha) + a_2^2(2a_1a_4 - a_2a_3)\alpha \\
&+ a_3^2(2a_1a_2 - a_0a_3)\alpha + a_4^2(2a_0a_1 + \alpha(a_3^2 - a_2a_4))\alpha - a_0a_2a_3a_4\alpha)X^4 \\
+ &\ (a_0^2(2a_1a_2 - a_0a_3) + a_1^2(-a_0a_1 + 2a_2a_4\alpha) + a_2^2(a_2^2 - 3a_0a_4 - 3a_1a_3)\alpha \\
&+ a_3^2(a_1^2 + 2a_0a_2 - a_3a_4\alpha)\alpha + a_4^2(a_0^2 + (2a_2a_3 - a_1a_4)\alpha)\alpha - a0a_1a_3a_4\alpha)X^3 \\
+ &\ (a_0^2(a_1^2 - a_0a_2 + 2a_3a_4\alpha) + a_1^2(2a_2a_3 - a_1a_4)\alpha + a_2^2(2a_0a_3 - a_1a_2)\alpha \\
&+ a_3^2(-3a_0a_1 + (a_3^2 - 3a_2a_4\alpha)\alpha) + a_4^2(a_2^2 - a_0a_4 + 2a_1a_3)\alpha^2 - a_0a_1a_2a_4\alpha)X^2 \\
+ &\ (a_0^2(-a_0a_1 + (2a_2a_4 + a_3^2)\alpha) + a_1^2(2a_0a_4 - a_1a_3 + a_2^2)\alpha + a_2^2(-a_0a_2 + 2a_3a_4\alpha)\alpha \\
&+ a_3^2(2a_1a_4 - a_2a_3)\alpha^2 + a_4^2(-3a_0a_3 - 3a_1a_2 + a_4^2\alpha)\alpha^2 - a_0a_1a_2a_3\alpha)X \\
+ &\ (a_0^2(a_0^2 + (-3a_1a_4 - 3a_2a_3)\alpha) + a_1^2(2a_0a_3 - a_1a_2)\alpha + a_2^2(2a_0a_1 - a_2a_4\alpha)\alpha \\
&+ a_3^2(2a_0a_4 - a_1a_3 + a_2^2)\alpha^2 + a_4^2(2a_0a_2 + a_1^2 - a_3a_4\alpha)\alpha^2 - a_1a_2a_3a_4\alpha^2)
\end{aligned}
$$

We precompute $a_0^2, a_1^2, a_2^2, a_3^2, a_4^2$ and a_0a_1, a_0a_2, a_0a_3, a_0a_4, a_1a_2, a_1a_3, a_1a_4, a_2a_3, a_2a_4, a_3a_4. This leads to $5S_q + 10M_q$. With this method, computing $\bar{a}$ needs $6M_q$ for each coefficient, hence $30M_q$ altogether. To compute the norm as $a \cdot \bar{a}$, we need an extra cost of $5M_q$. Indeed, by writing $\bar{a} = \bar{a}_0 + \bar{a}_1 X + \bar{a}_2 X^2 + \bar{a}_3 X^3 + \bar{a}_4 X^4$, we have $a \cdot \bar{a} = a_0\bar{a}_0 + \alpha(a_1\bar{a}_4 + a_2\bar{a}_3 + a_3\bar{a}_2 + a_4\bar{a}_1)$. The total count is $I_{q^5} = 45M_q + 5S_q + I_q$. In [2], Avanzi and Cesena report a cost of $50M_q + I_q$.

Achieving Optimal Anonymity in Transferable E-Cash with a Judge[*]

Olivier Blazy[1], Sébastien Canard[2], Georg Fuchsbauer[3],
Aline Gouget[4], Hervé Sibert[5], and Jacques Traoré[2]

[1] École Normale Supérieure – CNRS – INRIA, Paris, France
[2] Orange Labs – Applied Crypto Group, Caen, France
[3] University of Bristol – Dept. Computer Science, UK
[4] Gemalto – Security Lab, Meudon, France
[5] ST-Ericsson, Le Mans, France

Abstract. Electronic cash (e-cash) refers to money exchanged electronically. The main features of traditional cash are usually considered desirable also in the context of e-cash. One such property is *off-line transferability*, meaning the recipient of a coin in a transaction can transfer it in a later payment transaction to a third person without contacting a central authority. Among security properties, the anonymity of the payer in such transactions has been widely studied. This paper proposes the first efficient and secure transferable e-cash scheme with the strongest achievable anonymity properties, introduced by Canard and Gouget. In particular, it should not be possible for adversaries who receive a coin to decide whether they have owned that coin before. Our proposal is based on two recent cryptographic primitives: the proof system by Groth and Sahai, whose randomizability enables strong anonymity, and the commuting signatures by Fuchsbauer, which allow one to sign values that are only given as encryptions.

Keywords: Transferable e-cash, anonymity, Groth-Sahai proofs, commuting signatures.

1   Introduction

While electronic cash has long been one of the most challenging problems in cryptography, its use in practice remains rare. Indeed, despite the numerous benefits it may provide, e-cash still has many significant disadvantages. These include susceptibility to fraud, failure of technology and possible surveillance of individuals. With the recent emergence of new communication means and the availability of many applications for smart phones, the interest of the cryptographic community in electronic money has returned. Recent technologies provide the foundations for novel and desirable features such as, among others, the

---

[*] This work has been supported by the French Agence Nationale de la Recherche under the PACE 07 TCOM Project, the European Commission through the ICT Program under Contract ICT-2007-216676 ECRYPT II and EPSRC Grant EP/H043454/1. Work done while the third author was at École normale supérieure, Paris, France.

A. Nitaj and D. Pointcheval (Eds.): AFRICACRYPT 2011, LNCS 6737, pp. 206–223, 2011.

transferability of digital money. The desired security properties for e-cash are today well-known and for transferable e-cash systems anonymity is a particularly delicate issue.

Anonymity properties in transferable e-cash. The traditional properties of anonymous electronic cash are called *weak anonymity* and *strong anonymity*. The former means that it is infeasible for an attacker to identify the spender or the recipient in a transaction, and the latter states that it is infeasible for an attacker to decide whether two transactions are done by the same user or not. In [4] Canard and Gouget give a complete taxonomy of anonymity properties for transferable e-cash systems. They observe that in the transferability setting the attacker may recognize a coin that he has already observed during previous transfers. Thus, in addition to the two above traditional properties, they introduce *full anonymity* (FA), which means that an attacker is not able to recognize a coin he has already observed during a transaction between two honest users (*"observe then receive"*). They also introduce *perfect anonymity* (PA), defined as an attacker's inability to decide whether he has already owned a coin he is receiving.

Chaum and Pedersen [6] showed that a payer with unlimited computing power can always recognize his own money if he sees it later being spent; thus, the PA property cannot be achieved against unbounded adversaries. But even when his power is limited, an adversary impersonating the bank can still win the anonymity game, as shown in [4]. Perfect anonymity can therefore not be achieved by a transferable e-cash scheme. Due to this impossibility result, Canard and Gouget [4] introduce two additional anonymity notions called PA_1 and PA_2. In order to break PA_1, the adversary is given a coin and must decide whether he has already (passively) seen it in a past transaction (*"spend then observe"*). For PA_2, the bank is trusted and the adversary should not be able to decide whether or not he has already owned a coin he is receiving (*"spend then receive"*). It is shown in [4] that both properties PA_1 and PA_2 are satisfiable and that a transferable e-cash scheme should satisfy full anonymity, PA_1 and PA_2 in order to achieve "optimal" anonymity guarantees. In this paper we maintain these anonymity notions but slightly modify the used terminologies to improve readability.

Related work. Many transferable e-cash schemes have been proposed, but most of them only provide weak [10,11] or strong anonymity [13,6,5,3]. A generic construction of a transferable e-cash system with FA and PA_1 security from a one satisfying strongly anonymity is shown in [4]. PA_2 remains thus the property that is hardest to achieve.

The first proposal of a transferable e-cash scheme satisfying PA_2 is a theoretical scheme in [4] that cannot be implemented effectively. This is due to its use of complex meta-proofs [12] which allow the blinding of previous transfers of a coin, even w.r.t. a previous owner of that coin.

Subsequently, Fuchsbauer et al. [8] proposed the first practical PA_2-secure scheme. However, their scheme has the important drawbacks that (i) each user has to keep in memory the data associated to all past transactions to prove her innocence in case of a fraud and (ii) the anonymity of all subsequent owners of a double-spent coin must be revoked in order to trace the defrauder, which constitutes a serous breach of anonymity.

In conclusion, the remaining open problem is an *efficient* transferable e-cash scheme that satisfies all anonymity properties including PA$_2$.

Our contribution. In this paper, we propose such a scheme. More precisely, we describe a new transferable e-cash scheme based on the work on randomization of Groth-Sahai proofs [9,2] and on the recent primitive of commuting signatures [7] based on them. This yields a new way to efficiently blind previous transfers of a coin and permits to achieve the PA$_2$ property, without requiring the users to store anything. We moreover believe that the use of Groth-Sahai proofs and commuting signatures in concrete cryptographic applications is technically interesting.

There is a lot of concern regarding anonymity for electronic cash with respect to illegal activities, such as money laundering or financing of terrorism. A possible compromise between user privacy and the prevention of its abuse is to provide the opportunity to appeal to a judge either in case of double-spending or in a court case. In our proposal we introduce a trusted authority called *judge*, which retrieves the identity of the defrauder after detection of a double-spending (while detection can be performed locally by the bank). Although we do not consider this explicitly, the judge could additionally trace coins and users, as required for *fair e-cash* [14]. We argue that the use of Groth-Sahai proofs—which, besides not relying on the random-oracle heuristic and being efficient, are the only randomizable proofs known to date—requires a common reference string (CRS). Therefore, instead of assuming the existence of a trusted CRS "in the sky", we entrust the judge with its setup and let him use the contained trapdoor constructively rather than "forgetting" it.

The paper is now organized as follows. In Section 2 we present the procedures constituting a transferable e-cash scheme with a judge, and we detail its security properties in Section 3. In Section 4 we give the main cryptographic tools used to instantiate our scheme, which we describe in Section 5.

2   Definitions for Transferable E-Cash with Judge

In this section, we first describe the algorithms for transferable e-cash, involving a bank $\mathcal{B}$, users $\mathcal{U}$ and a judge $\mathcal{J}$. We extend the model given in [4] to include the judge authority. Moreover, in accordance with [4], the bank $\mathcal{B}$ may be divided into two entities: $\mathcal{W}$ for the withdrawal phase and $\mathcal{D}$ for the deposit phase.

2.1   Algorithms

For simplicity and contrary to [4], we represent a coin simply as a value c, while its *identifier Id* is the value that the bank retrieves during a deposit to check for double-spending. Formally, a transferable e-cash system with judge, denoted Π, is composed of the following procedures, where λ is a security parameter.

- ParamGen(1^λ) is a probabilistic algorithm that outputs the parameters of the system par. In the following, we assume that par contains λ and that it is a default input of all the other algorithms.
- BKeyGen(), JKeyGen() and UKeyGen() are probabilistic algorithms executed respectively by $\mathcal{B}$, $\mathcal{J}$ or $\mathcal{U}$, that output a key pair. When BKeyGen() is executed by $\mathcal{B}$, the output is $(\mathsf{sk}_\mathcal{B}, \mathsf{pk}_\mathcal{B})$. The secret key $\mathsf{sk}_\mathcal{B}$ may be divided into two parts: $\mathsf{sk}_\mathcal{W}$ for the withdrawal phase and $\mathsf{sk}_\mathcal{D}$ for the deposit phase. Consequently, we define separate algorithms WKeyGen() and DKeyGen() for the bank's key generation. The output of JKeyGen() is a keypair $(\mathsf{sk}_\mathcal{J}, \mathsf{pk}_\mathcal{J})$ for the judge, and UKeyGen() outputs $(\mathsf{sk}_\mathcal{U}, \mathsf{pk}_\mathcal{U})$.
  As a convention, we assume that each secret key contains the corresponding public key.
- Withdraw($\mathcal{W}[\mathsf{sk}_\mathcal{W}, \mathsf{pk}_\mathcal{U}], \mathcal{U}[\mathsf{sk}_\mathcal{U}, \mathsf{pk}_\mathcal{B}]$) is an interactive protocol where $\mathcal{U}$ withdraws one transferable coin from $\mathcal{B}$. At the end, $\mathcal{U}$ either gets a coin c and outputs ok, or it outputs $\perp$. The output of $\mathcal{B}$ is either its view $\mathcal{V}_\mathcal{B}^\mathsf{W}$ of the protocol (including $pk_\mathcal{U}$), or $\perp$ in case of error.
- Spend($\mathcal{U}_1[c, \mathsf{sk}_{\mathcal{U}_1}, \mathsf{pk}_\mathcal{B}, \mathsf{pk}_\mathcal{J}], \mathcal{U}_2[\mathsf{sk}_{\mathcal{U}_2}, \mathsf{pk}_\mathcal{B}, \mathsf{pk}_\mathcal{J}]$) is an interactive protocol in which $\mathcal{U}_1$ spends/transfers the coin c to $\mathcal{U}_2$. At the end, $\mathcal{U}_2$ outputs either a coin c' or $\perp$, and $\mathcal{U}_1$ either tags the coin c as spent and outputs ok, or outputs $\perp$.
- Deposit($\mathcal{U}[c, \mathsf{sk}_\mathcal{U}, \mathsf{pk}_\mathcal{B}], \mathcal{D}[\mathsf{sk}_\mathcal{D}, \mathsf{pk}_\mathcal{U}, \mathcal{L}]$) is an interactive protocol where $\mathcal{U}$ deposits a coin c at the bank $\mathcal{B}$. If c is not consistent, then $\mathcal{B}$ outputs $\perp_1$. Else, $\mathcal{B}$ computes the identifier Id of the deposited coin. If $\mathcal{L}$, the list of spent coins, contains an entry (Id, c'), for some c', then $\mathcal{B}$ outputs $(\perp_2, Id, c, c')$. Else, $\mathcal{B}$ adds (Id, c) to its list $\mathcal{L}$, credits $\mathcal{U}$'s account, and returns $\mathcal{L}$. $\mathcal{U}$'s output is ok or $\perp$.
- Identify($Id, c, c', \mathsf{sk}_\mathcal{J}$) is a deterministic algorithm executed by the judge $\mathcal{J}$ that outputs a key $\mathsf{pk}_\mathcal{U}$ and a proof τ_G. If the users who had submitted c and c' are not malicious, then τ_G is a proof that $\mathsf{pk}_\mathcal{U}$ is the registered key of a user that double-spent a coin. If $Id = 0$, this signifies that the judge cannot conclude.
- VerifyGuilt($\mathsf{pk}_\mathcal{U}, \tau_G$) is a deterministic algorithm that can be executed by anyone. It outputs 1 if τ_G is correct and 0 otherwise.

The main differences between these algorithms and those described in [4] is the additional key generation algorithm JKeyGen() and the modification of the procedure to identify a defrauder in case of a double-spending detection.

2.2 Global Variables and Oracles

Before formalizing the security properties, we first define the adversary's means of interaction with his challenger in the security experiments of a transferable e-cash system: we introduce global variables (in accordance with to [4]) and oracles[1].

---

[1] By convention, the name of an oracle corresponds to the action done by this oracle.

Global variables. The set of public (resp. secret) user keys is denoted by $\mathcal{PK} = \{(i, \mathsf{pk}_i) : i \in \mathbb{N}\}$ (resp. $\mathcal{SK} = \{(i, \mathsf{sk}_i) : i \in \mathbb{N}\}$ with $sk_i = \perp$ if user i is corrupted). The set of views by the bank of the withdrawals done by the adversary is denoted by $\mathcal{SC}$ (for supplied coins) and the set of all coins owned by the oracles is denoted by $\mathcal{OC}$ (for obtained coins). The set of deposited electronic cash (corresponding to $\mathcal{L}$) is denoted by $\mathcal{DC}$ (for deposited coins). In addition, we define the set of users who have received a coin from the adversary, denoted by $\mathcal{RU}$; and the set of users who have spent a coin to the adversary, denoted by $\mathcal{SU}$. These modifications should improve the understanding of the original description of oracles provided in [4].

Creation and corruption of users. The oracle $\mathsf{Create}(i)$ executes $(\mathsf{sk}_i, \mathsf{pk}_i) \leftarrow \mathsf{UKeyGen}()$, defines $\mathcal{PK}[i] = \mathsf{pk}_i$ and $\mathcal{SK}[i] = \mathsf{sk}_i$, and outputs pk_i. The oracle $\mathsf{Corrupt}(i, \mathsf{pk}_i)$ defines $\mathcal{PK}[i] = \mathsf{pk}_i$ and $\mathcal{SK}[i] = \perp$, and outputs ok. If the adversary calls $\mathsf{Corrupt}(i, \perp)$ then the oracle outputs $\mathcal{SK}[i]$ and then sets $\mathcal{SK}[i] = \perp$. In all cases, the coins belonging to user i, stored in $\mathcal{OC}$, are also given to $\mathcal{A}$.

Withdrawal protocol. We define three oracles relating to withdrawal.

- The oracle $\mathsf{BWith}()$ plays the bank side of a $\mathsf{Withdraw}$ protocol. It updates $\mathcal{SC}$ by adding $\mathcal{V}_\mathcal{B}^\mathsf{W}$ with bit 1 to flag it as a corrupted coin.
- The oracle $\mathsf{UWith}(i)$ plays the user i in a $\mathsf{Withdraw}$ protocol. It updates $\mathcal{OC}$ by adding the value (i, j, c) with flag 1, where j is the first empty entry of $\mathcal{OC}$ (independently of the user i to which it belongs).
- The oracle $\mathsf{With}(i)$ simulates a complete $\mathsf{Withdraw}$ protocol, playing the role of both $\mathcal{B}$ and user i, updates $\mathcal{OC}$ as for $\mathsf{UWith}(i)$ and updates $\mathcal{SC}$ by adding $\mathcal{V}_\mathcal{B}^\mathsf{W}$ both with flag 0. It outputs the communications between $\mathcal{B}$ and $\mathcal{U}$.

Spending protocol. Here we take into account that during a Spend protocol the adversary can play the role of the payer, the receiver, or can only be a passive observer. This will be relevant for the anonymity experiments in Section 3.4.

- The oracle $\mathsf{Rcv}(i)$ allows $\mathcal{A}$ to spend a coin to user i. The oracle plays the role of $\mathcal{U}_2$ with the secret key of user i in the Spend protocol. It updates the set $\mathcal{OC}$ by adding a new entry (i, j, c) and adds i to the set $\mathcal{RU}$.
- The oracle $\mathsf{Spd}(i, j)$ enables $\mathcal{A}$ to receive either the coin j or a coin transferred from user i. Either i or j can be undetermined (equal to $\perp$). The owner i of the spent coin j is then added to $\mathcal{SU}$. The oracle plays the role of user $\mathcal{U}_1$ in the Spend protocol with the secret key of the owner i of the coin j in $\mathcal{OC}$. It uses the entry (i, j, c) of $\mathcal{OC}$ as the Spend protocol describes it. It finally updates this entry by changing the flag to 1.
- The oracle $\mathsf{S\&R}$ (spend-and-receive) permits $\mathcal{A}$ to observe the spending of a coin j between users i_1 (in the role of $\mathcal{U}_1$) and i_2 (in the role of $\mathcal{U}_2$), who are both played by the oracle. It updates $\mathcal{OC}$ by adding (i_2, j', c) and by flagging the coin j as spent by i_1. It outputs all the (external) communications of the spending.

Deposit protocol. Depending on who the adversary impersonates there are several oracles for deposit.[2]

- The oracle BDepo() plays the role of the bank during a Deposit protocol and interacts with the adversary. The oracle gives the output of a Deposit procedure and updates the set $\mathcal{DC}$.
- The oracle UDepo(i, c) plays the role of the user i during a Deposit protocol for the coin c. The adversary is in this case the bank. If $c = \perp$ then the oracle randomly chooses one coin belonging to user i and deposits it.
- The oracle Depo(i, c) plays the role of both the bank and the user i in the Deposit protocol of the coin c. If $c = \perp$, then the oracle randomly chooses the coin to be deposited.
- The oracle Idt(Id, c, c') plays the role of the judge in the Identify procedure, with the same outputs.

A consequence of the result by Chaum and Pedersen [6], who showed that a transferred coin necessarily grows in size, is that an adversary may easily break anonymity by checking the number of times a given coin has been transferred. In the following, we say that two users i_0 and i_1 are *compatible*, and write comp(i_0, i_1) = 1, if they both own at least one coin with the same size.

3 Security Properties

In this section, we define the security notions for an e-cash system with a judge, adapting those from Canard and Gouget [4]. In every security game the challenger first generates the parameters and the keys for the bank and the judge; we denote this by AllGen. The challenger then gives the adversary the keys corresponding to the parties he is allowed to impersonate.

3.1 Unforgeability

Unforgeability is a notion protecting the bank, meaning that no collection of users can ever spend more coins than they withdrew, even by corrupting the judge. Formally, we have the following definition based on the experiment given below.

Definition 1 (Unforgeability). *Let Π be a transferable e-cash system with a judge. For an adversary $\mathcal{A}$ and $\lambda \in \mathbb{N}$, we let $\boldsymbol{Succ}_{\Pi,\mathcal{A}}^{unfor}(\lambda) = \Pr[\boldsymbol{Exp}_{\Pi,\mathcal{A}}^{unfor}(\lambda) = 1]$. Π is said to be* unforgeable *if the function $\boldsymbol{Succ}_{\Pi,\mathcal{A}}^{unfor}(\cdot)$ is negligible for any polynomial-time adversary $\mathcal{A}$.*

---

[2] The main difference between these oracles and those described in [4] is the modification of the oracle BDepo() and the definition of the new oracle Idt(Id, c, c'). In [4] there is a single oracle CreditAccount(), which executes both BDepo() and Ident(Id, c, c'). This modification is necessitated by the inclusion of the judge.

$$\mathbf{Exp}_{\Pi,\mathcal{A}}^{\mathsf{unfor}}(\lambda)$$

- $(\mathsf{par}, \mathsf{sk}_\mathcal{B}, \mathsf{pk}_\mathcal{B}, \mathsf{sk}_\mathcal{J}, \mathsf{pk}_\mathcal{J}) \leftarrow \mathsf{AllGen}(1^\lambda);\ \ cont \leftarrow \mathsf{true};\ st \leftarrow \emptyset;$
- While $(cont = \mathsf{true})$ do {
    - $(cont, st)$
        $\leftarrow \mathcal{A}^{\mathsf{Create},\mathsf{Corrupt},\mathsf{BWith},\mathsf{With},\mathsf{Rcv},\mathsf{Spd},\mathsf{S\&R},\mathsf{BDepo},\mathsf{Depo}}(st, \mathsf{par}, \mathsf{sk}_\mathcal{J}, \mathsf{pk}_\mathcal{B});$
        Let q_W be the number of successful calls to BWith and With;
        let q_D denote the number of successful calls to BDepo and Depo;
    - If $q_W < q_D$ then return 1; }
- Return $\perp$.

3.2 Identification of Double-Spenders

This notion guarantees the bank that no collection of users, collaborating with the judge, can spend a coin twice (double-spend) without revealing one of their identities. Formally, we have the following experiment and definition.

$$\mathbf{Exp}_{\Pi,\mathcal{A}}^{\mathsf{ident}}(\lambda)$$

- $(\mathsf{par}, \mathsf{sk}_\mathcal{B}, \mathsf{pk}_\mathcal{B}, \mathsf{sk}_\mathcal{J}, \mathsf{pk}_\mathcal{J}) \leftarrow \mathsf{AllGen}(1^\lambda);\ \ cont \leftarrow \mathsf{true};\ st \leftarrow \emptyset;$
- While $(cont = \mathsf{true})$ do {
    - $st \leftarrow \mathcal{A}^{\mathsf{Create},\mathsf{Corrupt},\mathsf{BWith},\mathsf{With},\mathsf{Rcv},\mathsf{Spd},\mathsf{S\&R},\mathsf{BDepo},\mathsf{Depo},\mathsf{Idt}}(st, \mathsf{par}, \mathsf{sk}_\mathcal{J}, \mathsf{pk}_\mathcal{B});$
    - If a call to BDepo outputs $(\perp_2, Id, c, c')$ then $cont \leftarrow \mathsf{false};$ }
- $(i^*, \tau_G) \leftarrow \mathsf{Identify}(Id, c, c', \mathsf{sk}_\mathcal{J});$
- If $\mathsf{VerifyGuilt}(\mathsf{pk}_{i^*}, \tau_G) = 0$ or $i^* = 0$ then return 1;
- Return $\perp$.

Definition 2 (Double-Spender Identification). *Let Π be a transferable e-cash system with a judge. For any adversary $\mathcal{A}$ and $\lambda \in \mathbb{N}$, we let $\boldsymbol{Succ}_{\Pi,\mathcal{A}}^{ident}(\lambda) = \Pr[\boldsymbol{Exp}_{\Pi,\mathcal{A}}^{ident}(\lambda) = 1]$. Π identifies double spenders if the function $\boldsymbol{Succ}_{\Pi,\mathcal{A}}^{ident}(\cdot)$ is negligible for any polynomial-time adversary $\mathcal{A}$.*

3.3 Exculpability

This notion protects honest users in that the bank, even when colluding with a collection of malicious users and possibly the judge, cannot falsely accuse (with a proof) honest users of having double-spent a coin. Formally, we have the following experiment and definition.

$$\mathbf{Exp}_{\Pi,\mathcal{A}}^{\mathsf{excul}}(\lambda)$$

- $(\mathsf{par}, \mathsf{sk}_\mathcal{B}, \mathsf{pk}_\mathcal{B}, \mathsf{sk}_\mathcal{J}, \mathsf{pk}_\mathcal{J}) \leftarrow \mathsf{AllGen}(1^\lambda);$
- $(Id^*, c_1^*, c_2^*, i^*, \tau^*)$
    $\leftarrow \mathcal{A}^{\mathsf{Create},\mathsf{Corrupt},\mathsf{UWith},\mathsf{Rcv},\mathsf{Spd},\mathsf{S\&R},\mathsf{UDepo},\mathsf{Idt}}(st, \mathsf{par}, \mathsf{sk}_\mathcal{J}, \mathsf{sk}_\mathcal{B});$
- If $\mathsf{VerifyGuilt}(\mathsf{pk}_{i^*}, \tau^*) = 1$ and $\mathsf{sk}_{i^*} \neq \perp$, return 1;
- Return $\perp$.

Definition 3 (Exculpability). *Let Π be a transferable e-cash system with judge. For an adversary $\mathcal{A}$ and $\lambda \in \mathbb{N}$, we let $\boldsymbol{Succ}_{\Pi,\mathcal{A}}^{excul}(\lambda) = \Pr[\boldsymbol{Exp}_{\Pi,\mathcal{A}}^{excul}(\lambda) = 1]$. Π is said to be exculpable if the function $\boldsymbol{Succ}_{\Pi,\mathcal{A}}^{excul}(\cdot)$ is negligible for any polynomial-time adversary $\mathcal{A}$.*

3.4 Anonymity Properties in Transferable E-Cash

Regarding anonymity, Canard and Gouget [4] distinguish between five different notions: weak anonymity (WA), strong anonymity (SA), full anonymity (FA), and two types of restricted perfect anonymity (PA$_1$ and PA$_2$). They show that FA implies SA, which implies WA, and that FA, PA$_1$ and PA$_2$ are all incomparable. We say the anonymity for a transferable e-cash scheme is *optimal* when it satisfies the latter 3 properties. We work with the formal definitions of [4] but slightly modify the terminology[3].

- *Observe-then-Receive Full Anonymity* (OtR-FA, previously FA): the adversary, impersonating the bank, cannot link a coin he receives as "legitimate" user to a previously (passively) observed transfer between honest users.
- *Spend-then-Observe Full Anonymity* (StO-FA, previously PA$_1$): the adversary, impersonating the bank, cannot link a (passively) observed coin transferred between two honest users to a coin he has already owned as a "legitimate" user.
- *Spend-then-Receive Full Anonymity* (StR-FA, previously PA$_2$): when the bank is honest, the adversary cannot link two transactions involving the same coin, i.e. make the link between two coins he has received.

In the following, we say that a transferable e-cash scheme achieves *optimal anonymity* if it satisfies at the same time OtR-FA, StO-FA and StR-FA, which are incomparable, according to [4]. These anonymity notions are formally defined below, based on the corresponding experiments given in Figure 1.

Definition 4 (Anonymity Properties). *Let Π be a transferable e-cash system with judge and let $c \in \{otr\text{-}fa, sto\text{-}fa, str\text{-}fa\}$. For an adversary $\mathcal{A}$ and $\lambda \in \mathbb{N}$, we let $\boldsymbol{Adv}_{\Pi,\mathcal{A}}^{c}(\lambda) = \Pr[\boldsymbol{Exp}_{\Pi,\mathcal{A}}^{c\text{-}1}(\lambda) = 1] - \Pr[\boldsymbol{Exp}_{\Pi,\mathcal{A}}^{c\text{-}0}(\lambda) = 1]$. Π is said to be Observe-then-Receive fully anonymous (resp. Spend-then-Observe fully anonymous, Spend-then-Receive fully anonymous) if the function $\boldsymbol{Adv}_{\Pi,\mathcal{A}}^{otr\text{-}fa}(\cdot)$ (resp. $\boldsymbol{Adv}_{\Pi,\mathcal{A}}^{sto\text{-}fa}(\cdot)$, $\boldsymbol{Adv}_{\Pi,\mathcal{A}}^{str\text{-}fa}(\cdot)$) is negligible for any polynomial-time adversary $\mathcal{A}$.*

4 Cryptographic Tools

In this section we give the main tools we need to construct our new transferable e-cash system with judge. For each of them, we introduce the concept, give the underlying procedures and formally describe the main security characteristics.

---

[3] In particular, the notion of "perfect" anonymity in [4] is not based on the indistinguishability of distributions, which may be confusing as we only achieve computational security.

$\mathbf{Exp}_{\Pi,\mathcal{A}}^{\text{otr-fa-}b}(\lambda)$ // $b \in \{0,1\}$, $\mathcal{A} = (\mathcal{A}_{ch}, \mathcal{A}_c, \mathcal{A}_{gu})$

- $(\text{par}, \text{sk}_{\mathcal{B}}, \text{pk}_{\mathcal{B}}, \text{sk}_{\mathcal{J}}, \text{pk}_{\mathcal{J}}) \leftarrow \text{AllGen}(1^{\lambda})$;
- $(i_0^*, i_1^*, st) \leftarrow \mathcal{A}_{ch}^{\text{Create,Corrupt,UWith,Rcv,Spd,S\&R,UDepo,Idt}}(\text{par}, \text{sk}_{\mathcal{B}}, \text{pk}_{\mathcal{J}})$;
- If $\text{sk}_{i_0^*} = \perp \vee \text{sk}_{i_1^*} = \perp \vee \text{comp}(i_0^*, i_1^*) = 0 \vee i_0^* \in \mathcal{RU} \vee i_1^* \in \mathcal{RU}$
  then return $\perp$;
- Choose j^* such that coin number j^* belongs to i_b^* and i_{1-b}^* owns a
  coin of equal size. Simulate $\text{Spd}(i_b^*, j^*)$ to $\mathcal{A}_c$, which outputs st_c;
- $b^* \leftarrow \mathcal{A}_{gu}^{\text{Create,Corrupt,UWith,Rcv,Spd,S\&R,UDepo,Idt}}(st_c)$;
- Return b^*.

$\mathbf{Exp}_{\Pi,\mathcal{A}}^{\text{sto-fa-}b}(\lambda)$ // $b \in \{0,1\}$, $\mathcal{A} = (\mathcal{A}_{ch}, \mathcal{A}_{gu})$

- $(\text{par}, \text{sk}_{\mathcal{B}}, \text{pk}_{\mathcal{B}}, \text{sk}_{\mathcal{J}}, \text{pk}_{\mathcal{J}}) \leftarrow \text{AllGen}(1^{\lambda})$;
- $(i_0^*, i_1^*, i_2^*, st) \leftarrow \mathcal{A}_{ch}^{\text{Create,Corrupt,UWith,Rcv,Spd,S\&R,UDepo,Idt}}(\text{par}, \text{sk}_{\mathcal{B}}, \text{pk}_{\mathcal{J}})$;
- If $\text{sk}_{i_0^*} = \perp \vee \text{sk}_{i_1^*} = \perp \vee \text{sk}_{i_2^*} = \perp \vee \text{comp}(i_0^*, i_1^*) = 0$, return $\perp$;
- Choose j^* such that coin number j^* belongs to i_b^*, and i_{1-b}^* owns a
  coin of equal size; run $out \leftarrow \text{S\&R}(j^*, i_b^*, i_2^*)$;
- $b^* \leftarrow \mathcal{A}_{gu}^{\text{Create,Corrupt,UWith,Rcv,Spd,S\&R,UDepo,Idt}}(out, st_c)$;
- If an oracle call involved the coin used in S&R then return $\perp$;
- Return b^*.

$\mathbf{Exp}_{\Pi,\mathcal{A}}^{\text{str-fa-}b}(\lambda)$ // $b \in \{0,1\}$, $\mathcal{A} = (\mathcal{A}_{ch}, \mathcal{A}_c, \mathcal{A}_{gu})$

- $(\text{par}, \text{sk}_{\mathcal{B}} = (\text{sk}_{\mathcal{W}}, \text{sk}_{\mathcal{D}}), \text{pk}_{\mathcal{B}} = (\text{pk}_{\mathcal{W}}, \text{pk}_{\mathcal{D}}), \text{sk}_{\mathcal{J}}, \text{pk}_{\mathcal{J}}) \leftarrow \text{AllGen}(1^{\lambda})$;
- (i_0^*, i_1^*, st)
  $\leftarrow \mathcal{A}_{ch}^{\text{Create,Corrupt,UWith,Rcv,Spd,S\&R,Depo,Idt}}(\text{par}, \text{sk}_{\mathcal{W}}, \text{pk}_{\mathcal{D}}, \text{pk}_{\mathcal{J}})$;
- If $\text{sk}_{i_0^*} = \perp \vee \text{sk}_{i_1^*} = \perp \vee \text{comp}(i_0^*, i_1^*) = 0$ then return $\perp$;
- Choose j^* such that coin number j^* belongs to i_b^*, and i_{1-b}^* owns a
  coin of equal size. Simulate $\text{Spd}(i_b^*, j^*)$ to $\mathcal{A}_c$, which outputs st_c;
- $b^* \leftarrow \mathcal{A}_{gu}^{\text{Create,Corrupt,UWith,Rcv,Spd,S\&R,Depo,Idt}}(st_c)$;
- If the oracle Depo is called on input either i_0^* or i_1^*, return $\perp$;
- Return b^*.

Fig. 1. Experiments for full-anonymity notions

4.1 Assumptions

Our construction will rely on two cryptographic assumptions: the *symmetric external Diffie-Hellman (DH) assumption* and the *asymmetric double hidden strong DH assumption*, a "q-type" assumption introduced in [1].

Definition 5 ((SXDH)). *Let $\mathbb{G}_1, \mathbb{G}_2$ be cyclic groups of prime order generated by g_1 and g_2, respectively, and let $e: \mathbb{G}_1 \times \mathbb{G}_2 \to \mathbb{G}_T$ be a bilinear map. The*

SXDH assumption states that for $i = 1, 2$, given g_i, g_i^a, g_i^b, for random a, b, it is hard to distinguish g_i^{ab} from a random element from $\mathbb{G}_i$.

Definition 6 (q-ADHSDH). *Given* $(g, f, k, g^{\xi}, h, h^{\xi}) \in \mathbb{G}_1^4 \times \mathbb{G}_2^2$ *and*

$$\left(a_i = (k \cdot g^{\nu_i})^{\frac{1}{\xi + \gamma_i}}, b_i = f^{\gamma_i}, v_i = g^{\nu_i}, d_i = h^{\gamma_i}, w_i = h^{\nu_i} \right)_{i=1}^{q-1}$$

for random $g, f, k \leftarrow \mathbb{G}_1$, $h \leftarrow \mathbb{G}_2$, $\xi, \gamma_i, \nu_i \leftarrow \mathbb{Z}_p$, *it is hard to output a new such tuple* $(a, b, v, d, w) \in \mathbb{G}_1^3 \times \mathbb{G}_2^2$, *i.e., one that satisfies*

$$e(a, h^{\xi} \cdot d) = e(k \cdot v, h) \qquad e(b, h) = e(f, d) \qquad e(v, h) = e(g, w)$$

4.2   Groth-Sahai Proofs

Groth and Sahai [9] proposed the first efficient non-interactive proof system for a large class of statements over bilinear groups in the standard model. Those proofs fit our purpose perfectly: their witness indistinguishability guarantees the anonymity of the users that withdraw, transfer and spend coins, and their randomizability provides unlinkability of transferred coins.

We use SXDH-based Groth-Sahai commitments and proofs in a pairing-friendly setting in order to commit to elements and prove relations satisfied by the associated plaintexts. The commitment key is: $\mathbf{u} \in \mathbb{G}_1^{2 \times 2}$, $\mathbf{v} = \in \mathbb{G}_2^{2 \times 2}$. Depending on whether the commitments should be perfectly binding or perfectly hiding (for simulations in security proofs), the initialization of the parameters will vary between: $\mathbf{u}_1 = (g_1, u)$ with $u = g_1^{\mu}$ and $\mathbf{u}_2 = \mathbf{u}_1^{\nu}$ with $\mu, \nu \overset{\$}{\leftarrow} \mathbb{Z}_p^*$ (which makes $\mathbf{u}$ a Diffie-Hellman tuple in $\mathbb{G}_1$) for the binding setting, and for the hiding setting $\mathbf{u}_2 = \mathbf{u}_1^{\nu} \odot (1, g_1)^{-1} = (g_1^{\nu}, g_1^{\mu\nu-1})$. Similarly, we define key pairs $\mathbf{v}_1$ and $\mathbf{v}_2$ in $\mathbb{G}_2^2$ with independent randomness.

Commitments to group elements. To commit to $X \in \mathbb{G}_1$ with random values $s_1, s_2 \in \mathbb{Z}_p$, we set $\mathcal{C}(X) = (1, X) \odot \mathbf{u}_1^{s_1} \odot \mathbf{u}_2^{s_2} = (u_{1,1}^{s_1} \cdot u_{2,1}^{s_2}, X \cdot u_{1,2}^{s_1} \cdot u_{2,2}^{s_2})$.

- Perfectly binding setting: We have $\mathcal{C}(X) = (g_1^a, X \cdot u^a)$, with $a = s_1 + \nu s_2$. A simulator that knows μ can extract X as this is an ElGamal encryption of X under (g_1, g_1^{μ}). The key μ is called the extraction key for such an *extractable commitment*.
- Perfectly hiding setting: We have $\mathcal{C}(X) = (g_1^a, X \cdot g_1^b \cdot u^a)$, for $a = s_1 + \nu s_2$ and $b = -s_2$, two independent random values. $\mathcal{C}(X)$ is thus an encryption of $X \cdot g_1^b$, for a random b, so it blinds X.

Analogously, one commits to elements from $\mathbb{G}_2$ by replacing $\mathbf{u}$ by $\mathbf{v}$ and g_1 by g_2 in the above.

Proofs. Under the SXDH assumption, the two initializations of the commitment key are indistinguishable. Groth and Sahai [9] show how to construct proofs that a set of committed values satisfies an equation of a certain type. A proof is in $\mathbb{G}_2^{2 \times 2} \times \mathbb{G}_1^{2 \times 2}$; it can be constructed using the committed values satisfying the equation and their randomness, and it is verified w.r.t. the commitments and the commitment key. If the key is set up as perfectly hiding then the proof does not reveal more than the fact that the values satisfy the equation.

Randomization. The commitments can easily be randomized. Given, e.g., a commitment $c \in \mathbb{G}_1^2$, one chooses two random values s'_1, s'_2 and computes the randomization as $c' = (c_1 \cdot u_{1,1}^{s'_1} \cdot u_{2,1}^{s'_2}, c_2 \cdot u_{1,2}^{s'_1} \cdot u_{2,2}^{s'_2})$. In [2] it is shown how to randomize and adapt a proof (π, θ) for a vector of commitments $(c_i)_i$ to their randomizations $(c'_i)_i$.

4.3   Commuting Signatures

Commuting signatures and verifiable encryption [7] is a primitive combining a signature scheme (the automorphic signature from [1], whose messages are group elements) with Groth-Sahai (GS) proofs. This allows one to commit to a message, a verification key, or a corresponding signature (or arbitrary combinations of them), and prove that the committed values are valid (i.e. the signature is valid on the message under the key), via the GS methodology.

Commuting signatures provide several additional functionalities, of which we use the following two.

SigCom: This allows a signer, who is given a commitment $\mathbf{C}$ to a message, to make a commitment $\mathbf{c}_\Sigma$ to a signature (under his secret key) on that message (without knowing it though) and a proof that $\mathbf{c}_\Sigma$ contains a valid signature on the value committed in $\mathbf{C}$.

AdC$_\mathcal{K}$: Given a commitment to a message, a commitment to a signature and a proof of validity w.r.t. to a verification key, this algorithm allows anyone to commit to that key and adapt the proof; more precisely, AdC$_\mathcal{K}$ outputs a proof asserting that a commitment contains a valid signature on a committed message under a committed verification key.

Security states that the output of SigCom is the same as if the signer had known the message, signed it, made commitments to the message and the signature and had given a GS proof of validity w.r.t. his signature-verification key. Analogously, the output of AdC$_\mathcal{K}$ is the same as a proof constructed for the known committed values.

In our e-cash scheme commuting signatures will enable users to produce signatures on values that are only available as commitments and make a proof of validity under their verification key, which is also given as a commitment.

5   A Tranferable E-Cash System with Judge

Based on the cryptographic building blocks introduced in the last section, we are now in a position to describe our transferable e-cash system with judge. In our solution the withdrawer is anonymous towards the bank, a feature that previous schemes do not offer. This is motivated by the fact that our withdrawal is very similar to the spending protocol and it is easy to make the withdrawer non-anonymous, should one wish to. A possible application of our scheme is the anonymous purchase of tickets which can then be transferred to other users. Another scenario could be e-cash which can be purchased in exchange for actual cash.

5.1 Overview of Our Solution

A coin is represented by a unique chain of nonces $n = n_0 \| n_1 \| n_2 \| \cdots$, where each n_i is randomly chosen by a consecutive owner of the coin. Thus, n_0 is chosen by the bank, n_1 by the withdrawer, n_2 by the one who receives this coin from the withdrawer, and so on.

A double-spending has occurred when two coins n and n' are deposited which both begin with $n_0 = n'_0$. Note that the minimum value i such that $n_i \neq n'_i$ corresponds to the transfer of the coin where it was double-spent. If we oblige every user to commit to her identity during a transfer and include this commitment in the coin then a judge holding an extraction key can trace the defrauder.

When a coin is transferred from $\mathcal{U}_i$ to $\mathcal{U}_{i+1}$, the spender $\mathcal{U}_i$ signs the following: (i) the nonce she chose when receiving the coin (during a spending or withdrawal), (ii) the nonce chosen by the receiver $\mathcal{U}_{i+1}$, and (iii) $\mathcal{U}_{i+1}$'s verification key. The latter binds this transfer to the next one, where $\mathcal{U}_{i+1}$ will use her signing key. In fact, since only $\mathcal{U}_{i+1}$ knows the secret key corresponding to the signed public key, she is the only one able to spend the coin.

However, to remain anonymous, $\mathcal{U}_{i+1}$ cannot let the spender know her verification key. This is where commuting signatures come into play: they allow the signer to make (a commitment to) a signature on the receiver's key, even when it is only given to the signer as a commitment. Since SigCom additionally outputs a proof, validity of the committed signature is publicly verifiable.

When a coin is spent, its entire history (i.e. committed nonces, keys, signatures and proofs of their validity from previous transfers) is transmitted. This will guarantee unforgeability, identification of double-spending and non-frameability, without requiring data to be stored by the user and provided later on demand to prove innocence (as was the case in the relaxed model in [8]). Every time a coin is transferred, its history (consisting of commitments and Groth-Sahai proofs) can be completely randomized. Thus, a previous owner of a coin cannot recognize it at a later moment; this is how our scheme achieves strong anonymity notions.

5.2 Key-Generation Algorithms

During the generation phase, the judge $\mathcal{J}$ generates two pairs of commitment/extraction keys, which will enable identification of double spenders. Similarly, the double-spending detector $\mathcal{D}$ also generates such a key pair.

We denote a commitment under $\mathcal{J}$'s keys by either c (first key) or $\tilde{c}$ (second key) and a commitment under $\mathcal{D}$'s key by d. Using their secret extraction keys, the judge and the detector can open commitments under their respective keys using $\mathsf{Open}_{\mathcal{J}}$ and $\mathsf{Open}_{\mathcal{D}}$.

The judge also generates a key pair for a commuting signature scheme; in the following, a signature on m from $\mathcal{J}$ is denoted $\mathsf{Sign}_{\mathcal{J}}(m)$. Moreover, the bank $\mathcal{B}$ and each user $\mathcal{U}$ generate key pairs $(\mathsf{bsk}, \mathsf{bpk})$ and $(\mathsf{usk}, \mathsf{upk})$ for the commuting signature scheme. When registering, a user $\mathcal{U}$ obtains from the judge $\mathcal{J}$ a signature on her verification key as membership certificate: $\mathsf{cert} = \mathsf{Sign}_{\mathcal{J}}(\mathsf{upk})$. In the following, we differentiate the users by different indices: $\mathcal{U}_1, \mathcal{U}_2$, etc.

5.3 Withdrawal Protocol

The withdrawal protocol involves a user $\mathcal{U}_1$ and the bank $\mathcal{B}$. In a nutshell, the bank $\mathcal{B}$ generates a random nonce n_0 and the user a random nonce n_1, which together will be the beginning of the serial number of the coin. The bank then signs these nonces and the user's public key upk_1, which will bind the user's identity to the coin and enable tracing in case of double spending.

However, to guarantee anonymity, rather than sending these values in the clear, the user sends *commitments* to them. She also adds a commitment to her certificate and a proof of validity, which convinces the bank that she is registered. This can be done since the certificate is an *automorphic* signature [1], for which GS proofs can be used to prove that a committed value is a signature on another committed value, in this case upk_1, valid under the judge's verification key.

The bank now has to construct a committed signature on the values n_0, n_1 and upk_1, which are only given in the form of commitments. This is where we take advantage of the functionality SigCom of the commuting-signature scheme introduced in Section 4.3: given commitments, a signer can produce a commitment to a signature on the values contained in them, together with a proof of validity of the signature.

All these commitments will be done w.r.t. the judge's commitment key. To enable the double-spending detector $\mathcal{D}$ to *detect* a double-spending (however without breaking the user's anonymity), we do the following: in addition to committing to the nonces w.r.t. the judge's key, the user and the bank make another commitment d_{n_i} to n_i under $\mathcal{D}$'s key. In order to show that this was done correctly, we require a proof that two commitments w.r.t. different keys contain the same value. This can be done by using two instances of Groth-Sahai proofs on top of each other, as was done in [8]. The outer layer is the one corresponding to c, which will enable us to simulate such a proof when the commitment key for c is set up as hiding, but the key for d is still binding.

We formalize the above in the following protocol:

$\mathcal{U}_1$ picks at random a nonce n_1 and makes two extractable commitments (for $\mathcal{J}$ and $\mathcal{D}$) to n_1 denoted respectively by c_{n_1} and d_{n_1}, and a proof π_{n_1} that the two committed values are equal.

  Moreover, $\mathcal{U}_1$ makes commitments $c_{u_1}, \tilde{c}_{u_1}$ and c_{c_1} to its public key upk_1 and its certificate cert_1, respectively, together with a proof π_{c_1} that the value in c_{c_1} is a valid signature on the value in c_{u_1}, i.e. $\mathsf{cert}_1 = \mathsf{Sign}_{\mathcal{J}}(\mathsf{upk}_1)$, and a proof $\tilde{\pi}_{u_1}$ that the committed values on c_{u_1} and $\tilde{c}_{u_1}$ are equal.

  $\mathcal{U}_1$ sends the following values to the bank: $(c_{n_1}, c_{u_1}, c_{c_1}, \pi_{c_1})$.

$\mathcal{B}$ after verifying π_{c_1} now also generates a random nonce n_0 and makes two commitments (for $\mathcal{J}$ and $\mathcal{D}$) to n_0 denoted by c_{n_0} and d_{n_0}, and a proof π_{n_0} that the two committed values are equal.

  $\mathcal{B}$ produces a committed signature c_{s_1} on the values n_0, n_1 and upk_1 by running SigCom on c_{n_0}, c_{n_1} and c_{u_1}; this also outputs a proof π_{s_1} of validity of c_{s_1} w.r.t. c_{n_0}, c_{n_1} and c_{u_1} and the bank's verification key (which is public). The bank sends all these values, from which the user forms the coin

$$\mathsf{coin}_1 = (c_{n_0}, d_{n_0}, \pi_{n_0},\ c_{n_1}, d_{n_1}, \pi_{n_1},\ c_{u_1}, \tilde{c}_{u_1}, \tilde{\pi}_{u_1},\ c_{c_1}, \pi_{c_1},\ c_{s_1}, \pi_{s_1})\ . \quad (1)$$

In the sequel, this coin will be randomized before being spent. The result of randomizing coin_1 is denoted $\text{coin}_1^{(1)}$ and consists of randomizing all its components, i.e. commitments and proofs, as described in [2]. After randomization, we have thus $\text{coin}_1^{(1)} = (c_{n_0}^{(1)}, d_{n_0}^{(1)}, \pi_{n_0}^{(1)}, c_{n_1}^{(1)}, d_{n_1}^{(1)}, \pi_{n_1}^{(1)}, c_{u_1}^{(1)}, \tilde{c}_{u_1}^{(1)}, \tilde{\pi}_{u_1}^{(1)}, c_{c_1}^{(1)}, \pi_{c_1}^{(1)}, c_{s_1}^{(1)}, \pi_{s_1}^{(1)})$.

5.4   Spending Protocol

This is a protocol between a user $\mathcal{U}_1$ holding a coin as in (1) and a user $\mathcal{U}_2$ playing the role of the receiver. The protocol is very similar to the withdrawal protocol, except for two points. First, $\mathcal{U}_1$ has to randomize the coin, which prevents a later linking of the coin. Note that, due to the contained proofs, the validity of a coin is publicly verifiable.

Second, while the bank's verification key is public, $\mathcal{U}_1$'s key must remain hidden. Thus, after $\mathcal{U}_1$ produces a commitment to a signature on the values n_1, n_2 (the nonce chosen by $\mathcal{U}_2$), and $\mathcal{U}_2$'s public key upk_2, and a proof that verifies w.r.t. her public key upk_1, $\mathcal{U}_1$ does the following: using the functionality $\text{AdC}_{\mathcal{K}}$ (described in Section 4.3), she converts the proof into one asserting that the committed signature is valid under the value committed in $c_{u_1}^{(1)}$ (i.e. the randomization of the commitment to upk_1).

$\mathcal{U}_2$ picks at random a nonce n_2 and commits to it as c_{n_2} and d_{n_2} (for $\mathcal{J}$ and $\mathcal{D}$) and makes a proof π_{n_2} of equality of the committed values.

$\quad\quad$ $\mathcal{U}_2$ makes further commitments c_{u_2}, $\tilde{c}_{u_2}$ and c_{c_2} to her public key upk_2 and her certificate cert_2, together with a proof π_{c_2} that c_{c_2} contains a valid certificate and a proof $\tilde{\pi}_{u_2}$ that the committed values in c_{u_2} and $\tilde{c}_{u_2}$ are equal. She sends $(c_{n_2}, c_{u_2}, c_{c_2}, \pi_{c_2})$ to $\mathcal{U}_1$

$\mathcal{U}_1$ checks the proof sent by $\mathcal{U}_2$ and randomizes coin_1 to $\text{coin}_1^{(1)}$. $\mathcal{U}_1$ then produces a committed signature on the values committed in $c_{n_1}^{(1)}, c_{n_2}$ and c_{u_2} using SigCom: this generates a commitment c_{s_2} to a signature on the values n_1, n_2 and upk_2, as well as a proof π_{s_2}' of validity of c_{s_2} on $c_{n_1}, c_{n_2}, c_{u_2}$ w.r.t. upk_1. Running $\text{AdC}_{\mathcal{K}}$, $\mathcal{U}_1$ converts π_{s_2}' to a proof π_{s_2} asserting validity w.r.t. the key committed in $c_{u_2}^{(1)}$. Note that this works since c_{u_1} was produced and randomized to $c_{u_1}^{(1)}$ by $\mathcal{U}_1$, who therefore knows its randomness. Finally, $\mathcal{U}_1$ sends $\mathcal{U}_2$ the following: $(\text{coin}_1^{(1)}, c_{s_2}, \pi_{s_2})$.

$\quad\quad$ $\mathcal{U}_2$ checks the proofs contained in $\text{coin}_1^{(1)}$ and π_{s_2} and defines the transferred coin as

$$\text{coin}_2 := (\text{coin}_1^{(1)}, \ c_{n_2}, d_{n_2}, \pi_{n_2}, \ c_{u_2}, \tilde{c}_{u_2}, \tilde{\pi}_{u_2}, \ c_{c_2}, \pi_{c_2}, \ c_{s_2}, \pi_{s_2}) \ .$$

5.5   Deposit and Identify Procedures

To deposit a coin, a user spends it to the bank, that is, she runs the protocol from the last section with the bank playing the role of $\mathcal{U}_2$. In order to detect a double-spending given a coin, the detector $\mathcal{D}$ opens all the commitments $d_{n_0}^{(\ell)}, d_{n_1}^{(\ell)}, d_{n_2}^{(\ell-1)}, \cdots, d_{n_\ell}^{(1)}$ contained in it, using her extraction key. She thus obtains the serial number $n = n_0 \| n_1 \| \cdots \| n_\ell$ of this coin, which allows her to check whether the coin was double-spent.

To do so, $\mathcal{D}$ checks whether n_0 already exists in her database. If this is not the case then the Deposit is validated and the list $\mathcal{L}$ is updated by adding $n = n_0\|n_1\|\cdots\|n_\ell$. Otherwise, if a serial number $\tilde{n}$ beginning with n_0 already exists in her database then with overwhelming probability the coin was double-spent and $\mathcal{D}$ outputs $\perp_1$. She compares the two serial numbers $n = n_0\|n_1\|n_2\|\cdots\|n_\ell$ and $\tilde{n} = n_0\|\tilde{n}_1\|\tilde{n}_2\|\cdots\|\tilde{n}_\ell$ and stops at the last i_0 such that $n_{i_0} = \tilde{n}_{i_0}$. She finally asks for the execution of the Identify procedure by the Judge on input the two related spendings and i_0.

To identify the double spender, the judge extracts the value committed in $c_{u_{i_0}}$ using her extraction key, which reveals the public key upk_{i_0} of the defrauder. The proof τ_G of identification is a proof of correct opening of the commitment, as done in [8].

5.6 Security Considerations

We now sketch how to prove that our scheme is secure. We have to show that it fulfills all the security requirements given in Section 3.

Claim 1. *Our transferable e-cash system with a judge is secure under the following assumptions: unforgeability of the commuting signature scheme and soundness and witness indistinguishability of Groth-Sahai proofs.*

Unforgeability. Let us assume that an adversary is able to break the unforgeability of our transferable e-cash scheme. We use it as a black box to design a machine which breaks commuting signatures, i.e. their unforgeability under chosen-message attacks.

Given a challenge public key by our challenger, we use it as the bank's public key and generate the remaining parameters as described in our e-cash scheme (without any modifications), and send it to the adversary. We answer all oracle queries by the adversary either by using the appropriate key or by querying the signing oracle provided by our challenger (for BWith and With calls).

Suppose the adversary wins the game. For each of the q_D successfully deposited coins, using the judge's extraction key we open the commitments c_{s_1}, c_{n_0}, c_{n_1} and c_{u_1}. By soundness of π_{s_1}, the extracted signature s_1 is valid on $(n_0, n_1, \mathsf{upk}_1)$, the other extracted values, under the bank's public key. Since every deposit was successful, none of the q_D coins was double-spent, which means that their n_0 components are all different. We have thus q_D signatures on different triples $(n_0, n_1, \mathsf{upk}_1)$. On the other hand, there were fewer calls (q_W) to withdraw oracles, and thus fewer calls to our signing oracle. There must thus be a signature on a message which was not queried to the signing oracle. We output that signature/message pair as a forgery and win thus the unforgeability game with the same probability as the adversary.

Identification of double-spender. As for unforgeability, we use a successful adversary to break unforgeability of the commuting signature scheme. This time we use the public key given by our challenger as the judge's public key and set up the remaining parameters as described in our scheme. We can therefore answer any oracle call by the adversary, except for the certification of a new user in the system (oracle Create), for which we use our signing oracle.

At some point the adversary makes a call to the BDepot oracle that is answered as $(\perp_2, Id, c, c')$, i.e. a double-spending is detected. If the adversary is successful then Identify outputs (i^*, τ_G) such that either VerifyGuilt$(\mathsf{pk}_{i^*}, \tau_G) = 0$ or $i^* = 0$. Since each valid coin must contain a valid certificate for the public key corresponding to each transfer, by soundness of the proofs, the adversary must have forged the certificate. Otherwise Identify would have output an existing user key.

Exculpability. This is shown similarly to unforgeability, except that here we focus on signatures issued by an honest user rather than the bank.

A user with public key upk is accused of double-spending when there are two coins c and c' with serial numbers n and n', such that for some index i, we have $n_0 = n'_0, \ldots, n_i = n'_i$ and $n_{i+1} \neq n'_{i+1}$, and moreover c_{u_i} contains the user's public key upk. Since both coins are valid, by the soundness of the proofs, they contain signatures on $(n_i, n_{i+1}, \mathsf{upk}_{i+1})$ and $(n_i, n'_{i+1}, \mathsf{upk}'_{i+1})$, respectively.

Since an honest user does not transfer or spend one of his coins twice, and it only happens with negligible probability that she chooses twice the same nonce n_i when receiving two different coins, one of the signatures must be a forgery.

The adversary we build against unforgeability of the commuting signature scheme receives the challenge public key and sets it as the public key of a randomly chosen user. It uses the signing oracle to simulate this user, whenever the adversary asks her to spend/transfer a coin. If the probability that the e-cash adversary wins the exculpability game is non-negligible then so is the probability that he wins by framing the user chosen by the simulator. We break thus unforgeability of the commuting signature.

Anonymity properties

- To achieve Spend-the-Observe Full Anonymity, it suffices to encrypt the messages sent between the users when transferring a coin; this was shown in [4].
- Spend-then-Receive Full Anonymity (formerly known as PA$_2$) is harder to achieve, since the adversary is given the challenge coin, which he could already have owned before; the adversary therefore must not know the key to detect double-spendings.

   Groth-Sahai proofs are witness indistinguishable in the following sense: if the commitment key is set up as perfectly hiding then the commitments are random values independent of the committed values and the proofs are distributed equally for any such values—as long as they satisfy the equations. Thus, if we set up all commitment keys (the two for the judge and one for the double-spending detector), a coin would not reveal anything about the chosen nonces, the public keys and certificates of its owners and their signatures. Moreover, after being transferred, the coins are perfectly unlinkable, since a randomization transforms one set of random values into an independent set of random values (conditioned on the fact that the values that could have been committed satisfy the equations).

However, if the coins do not contain any information, we cannot correctly simulate the experiment for StR-FA. In particular, we cannot simulate the deposit and identification oracles, which rely on the detector's and the judge's extraction keys. This is the reason why we introduced the commitments d and $\tilde{c}$, which double some of the values committed in the c's, namely the nonces and the user public keys.

The anonymity properties are shown by a sequence of game hops. The first game is the original game, and in the second we extract from the commitments d and $\tilde{c}$ to detect and trace double-spendings. In a third game, we set up the judge's key for the commitments c as perfectly hiding. Under SXDH this changes the adversary's behavior only negligibly. In a forth game we simulate the proofs π_{n_i} and $\tilde{\pi}_{u_i}$ of equality of commitments under different keys. This can be done using the trapdoor information for the key for the c-commitments.

Finally, we mentioned in Section 4.2 that commitments under binding keys are actually ElGamal encryptions of the committed value. Under SXDH we can thus replace such encryptions by random pairs of elements from the corresponding group. When we perform the challenge spending via Spd in the experiment, we replace the commitments/encryptions d_{n_i} and $\tilde{c}_{u_i}$ by random values. This is done by a sequence of hybrid games, replacing one value after the other.

In the final game now the challenge coin is perfectly random, and does thus not contain any information about the bit b. The adversary's probability of winning the game is thus $\frac{1}{2}$. This concludes the proof for StR-FA as the final game is indistinguishable from the original game.
- The remaining notion, OtR-FA, is proved similarly, but here we cannot replace values d by random ones, as the adversary gets the corresponding extraction key, contained in sk_B. However, we can simply leave the values d in the challenge coin unchanged, as the adversary has never seen them before: he has never owned the coin and does not get the value d_{n_1} when impersonating the bank during a withdraw.

References

1. Abe, M., Fuchsbauer, G., Groth, J., Haralambiev, K., Ohkubo, M.: Structure-preserving signatures and commitments to group elements. In: Rabin, T. (ed.) CRYPTO 2010. LNCS, vol. 6223, pp. 209–236. Springer, Heidelberg (2010)
2. Belenkiy, M., Camenisch, J., Chase, M., Kohlweiss, M., Lysyanskaya, A., Shacham, H.: Randomizable proofs and delegatable anonymous credentials. In: Halevi, S. (ed.) CRYPTO 2009. LNCS, vol. 5677, pp. 108–125. Springer, Heidelberg (2009)
3. Blanton, M.: Improved conditional e-payments. In: Bellovin, S.M., Gennaro, R., Keromytis, A.D., Yung, M. (eds.) ACNS 2008. LNCS, vol. 5037, pp. 188–206. Springer, Heidelberg (2008)

4. Canard, S., Gouget, A.: Anonymity in transferable e-cash. In: Bellovin, S.M., Gennaro, R., Keromytis, A.D., Yung, M. (eds.) ACNS 2008. LNCS, vol. 5037, pp. 207–223. Springer, Heidelberg (2008)
5. Canard, S., Gouget, A., Traoré, J.: Improvement of efficiency in (unconditional) anonymous transferable e-cash. In: Tsudik, G. (ed.) FC 2008. LNCS, vol. 5143, pp. 202–214. Springer, Heidelberg (2008)
6. Chaum, D., Pedersen, T.P.: Transferred cash grows in size. In: Rueppel, R.A. (ed.) EUROCRYPT 1992. LNCS, vol. 658, pp. 390–407. Springer, Heidelberg (1993)
7. Fuchsbauer, G.: Commuting signatures and verifiable encryption. In: Paterson, K.G. (ed.) EUROCRYPT 2011. LNCS, vol. 6632, Springer, Heidelberg (2011)
8. Fuchsbauer, G., Pointcheval, D., Vergnaud, D.: Transferable anonymous constant-size fair e-cash. In: Garay, J.A., Miyaji, A., Otsuka, A. (eds.) CANS 2009. LNCS, vol. 5888, pp. 226–247. Springer, Heidelberg (2009)
9. Groth, J., Sahai, A.: Efficient non-interactive proof systems for bilinear groups. In: Smart, N.P. (ed.) EUROCRYPT 2008. LNCS, vol. 4965, pp. 415–432. Springer, Heidelberg (2008)
10. Okamoto, T., Ohta, K.: Disposable zero-knowledge authentications and their applications to untraceable electronic cash. In: Brassard, G. (ed.) CRYPTO 1989. LNCS, vol. 435, pp. 481–496. Springer, Heidelberg (1990)
11. Okamoto, T., Ohta, K.: Universal electronic cash. In: Feigenbaum, J. (ed.) CRYPTO 1991. LNCS, vol. 576, pp. 324–337. Springer, Heidelberg (1992)
12. De Santis, A., Yung, M.: Cryptographic applications of the non-interactive metaproof and many-prover systems. In: Menezes, A., Vanstone, S.A. (eds.) CRYPTO 1990. LNCS, vol. 537, pp. 366–377. Springer, Heidelberg (1991)
13. van Antwerpen, H.: Electronic Cash. PhD thesis, CWI (1990)
14. von Solms, S.H., Naccache, D.: On blind signatures and perfect crimes. Computers & Security 11(6), 581–583 (1992)

Revocable Attribute-Based Signatures
with Adaptive Security in the Standard Model

Alex Escala[1], Javier Herranz[2], and Paz Morillo[2]

[1] Dept. Computer Science, University College London,
Gower Street, WC1E 6BT, London, United Kingdom
alex.escala.10@ucl.ac.uk
[2] Dept. Matemàtica Aplicada IV, Universitat Politècnica de Catalunya,
C. Jordi Girona 1-3, Mòdul C3, 08034, Barcelona, Spain
{jherranz,paz}@ma4.upc.edu

Abstract. An attribute-based signature with respect to a signing policy, chosen ad-hoc by the signer, convinces the verifier that the signer holds a subset of attributes satisfying that signing policy. The verifier must obtain no other information about the identity of the signer or the attributes he holds. This primitive has many applications in real scenarios requiring both authentication and anonymity/privacy properties.

We propose in this paper the first attribute-based signature scheme satisfying at the same time the following properties: (1) it admits general signing policies, (2) it is proved secure against fully adaptive adversaries, in the standard model, and (3) the number of elements in a signature depends only on the size of the signing policy. Furthermore, our scheme enjoys the additional property of revocability: an external judge can break the anonymity of a signature, when necessary. This property may be very interesting in real applications where authorities are unwilling to allow full anonymity of users.

Keywords: attribute-based signatures, Groth-Sahai proofs, unforgeability, non-linkability, revocability.

1 Introduction

Attribute-based cryptography has emerged in the last years as a very interesting and powerful paradigm [3,2,8]. In an attribute-based cryptosystem, the secret operation (signing or decrypting) can be performed only by users who hold a subset of attributes that satisfy some policy. A successful execution of the secret operation should leak no information about the identity of the user or the attributes he holds, other than the fact that these attributes satisfy the given policy. Thanks to that property, attribute-based cryptography has a lot of applications in real-life scenarios where users want to preserve some level of privacy. Attribute-based cryptosystems must satisfy a collusion-resistance property: if a set of users, each of them holding attributes that do not satisfy the given policy, collude and try to perform the secret operation, they must fail to do so, even if the union of all their attributes satisfies the policy.

A. Nitaj and D. Pointcheval (Eds.): AFRICACRYPT 2011, LNCS 6737, pp. 224–241, 2011.

Attribute-based signatures were introduced explicitly in the first version of [12]. In an attribute-based signature (we will use sometimes ABS, for short) scheme, users receive from a master entity a secret key which depends on the attributes that they hold. Later, a user can choose a signing policy (a monotone increasing family of subsets of attributes) satisfied by his attributes, and use his secret key to compute a signature on a message, for this signing policy. The verifier of the signature is convinced that some user holding a set of attributes satisfying the signing policy is the author of the signature, but does not obtain any other information about the actual identity of the signer or the attributes he holds. Besides the general applications of any attribute-based cryptosystem (such as private access control), this kind of signatures have many applications in specific scenarios where both authentication and privacy properties are desired. A typical example is the leakage of secrets; see [12] for other applications.

All the attribute-based signature schemes that have been proposed up to date have some drawback in their efficiency, functionality or security analysis [12,14,9]. We propose in this paper a new attribute-based signature scheme which overcomes these drawbacks. Namely, our scheme is the first one[1] enjoying at the same time the following properties: (1) it admits general signing policies, (2) its security against adaptive adversaries is proved in the standard model, (3) the number of elements in a signature depends linearly on the size of the signing policy.

Table 1 summarizes the state of the art in attribute-based signatures, and the contribution of our new scheme. In the table, λ denotes a security parameter (the size of the underlying mathematical groups), and $|\Gamma|$ denotes the size of the mathematical object used to represent the signing policy. For example, in the case of (ℓ, n)-threshold signing policies, containing all subsets of at least ℓ attributes among a set of n attributes, we have $|\Gamma| = n$. Note that the difference between λ and $|\Gamma|$ can be quite significant; for example, in typical threshold scenarios the number of involved attributes can be $|\Gamma| = n \approx 20$, whereas $\lambda \geq 160$. Selective adversaries are those who choose the signing policy they want to attack at the very beginning, before having access to secret key or signing queries. In contrast, adaptive adversaries are more powerful: they can choose the attacked signing policy much later. Proving security against adaptive adversaries is obviously much better than proving security against selective adversaries.

Table 1. Comparison between existing attribute-based signature schemes

ABS scheme	#elements in a signature	admitted policies	considered adversaries	model for the security proof
Instantiations 1,2 in [12]	$\mathcal{O}(\lambda)$	general	adaptive	standard
Instantiation 3 in [12]	$\mathcal{O}(|\Gamma|)$	general	adaptive	generic group
[14,9]	$\mathcal{O}(|\Gamma|)$	threshold	selective	standard
Our scheme, [11]	$\mathcal{O}(|\Gamma|)$	general	adaptive	standard

---

[1] A scheme with the same properties has been independently proposed, in [11].

We construct our scheme in different steps. First we concentrate on the case of threshold signing policies, and we start with a basic scheme which produces linkable signatures. The design of this first scheme is inspired by the ring signature scheme of Shacham-Waters [13]. Then we add more technical tools to provide non-linkability and anonymity to the signatures. Specifically, we use Groth-Ostrovsky-Sahai [5] and Groth-Sahai [6] proofs. Such proofs have been proved very useful in the design of signature schemes with some anonymity properties, such as ring signatures [13] and group signatures [4]. Our second scheme can be proved secure in the random oracle model. Finally, we explain which modifications have to be applied to this second scheme in order to admit more general signing policies (possibly at the cost of an increase in the length of the signatures) and to achieve provable security in the standard model (at the cost of an increase in the length of the public parameters).

Interestingly, our schemes enjoy the additional property of revocability: the master entity can send some secret information to some special user, for example a judge. This user may then revoke the anonymity of an attribute-based signature, when needed, by tracing this signature to the user who computed it. To the best of our knowledge, previous attribute-based signature schemes do not satisfy this property. Revocability can be really useful when implementing the primitive of attribute-based signatures in real-life scenarios, because authorities do not usually like the idea of full anonymity.

2   Preliminaries

In this section we review some concepts, hardness assumptions and cryptographic primitives that will appear in the description and analysis of our schemes.

2.1   Symmetric Bilinear Groups and Hardness Assumptions

A symmetric bilinear group is a tuple $(n, \mathbb{G}, \mathbb{G}_T, e, g)$ where $\mathbb{G}$ and $\mathbb{G}_T$ are cyclic groups of order n (which can be prime or composite), g generates $\mathbb{G}$ and $e : \mathbb{G} \times \mathbb{G} \to \mathbb{G}_T$ is a pairing, i.e., an efficiently computable non-degenerate bilinear map.

The security of our schemes is based on different assumptions. Given a prime order symmetric bilinear group $(p, \mathbb{G}, \mathbb{G}_T, e, g)$, the *CDH assumption* states that any probabilistic polynomial time algorithm that takes as input $(g, g^a, g^b) \in \mathbb{G}^3$ outputs $g^{ab} \in \mathbb{G}$ only with negligible probability. We will use the CDH assumption in the subgroup of order p of a composite order symmetric bilinear group $\mathbb{G}$ to prove the unforgeability of our scheme.

Given a composite order symmetric bilinear group $(n, \mathbb{G}, \mathbb{G}_T, e, g)$ with $n = pq$ the product of two large primes, the *subgroup decision assumption* states that it is hard to distinguish an element in $\mathbb{G}$ from an element in $\mathbb{G}_q$, the subgroup of order q of $\mathbb{G}$. This assumption is needed to construct non-interactive witness indistinguishable proofs to provide anonymity to our scheme.

Finally, an automorphic signature scheme will be used in the design of the schemes, and the hardness assumptions ensuring the security of such automorphic signature scheme will be inherited by our scheme.

2.2 Automorphic Signatures

An automorphic signature scheme is a signature scheme that satisfies the following properties: the verification keys lie in the message space, messages and signatures consist of elements of a bilinear group, and verification is done by evaluating a set of pairing-product equations. We will use an automorphic signature in the design of our scheme, essentially as a black-box.

Instantiations of automorphic signature schemes can be found in [1]. Therein, automorphic signature schemes using either symmetric or asymmetric bilinear groups are presented. For the symmetric case (the one that we consider here), the security of the scheme is based on the *q-DHSDH* (q-Double Hidden Symmetric Diffie-Hellman) and *WFCDH* (Weak Flexible Computational Diffie-Hellman) assumptions. These are non-standard but reasonable assumptions: under the Knowledge of the Exponent Assumption, the first assumption is equivalent to the *q-SDH-III* (q-Strong Diffie-Hellman III) assumption, which is a bit weaker than the quite standard *q-SDH* assumption. Under the same Knowledge of the Exponent Assumption, the asymmetric version of the *WFCDH* assumption is equivalent to the standard discrete logarithm assumption.

2.3 NIWI Proofs for Pairing Product Equations

Groth, Ostrovsky and Sahai [5] and Groth and Sahai [6] propose two different methodologies to construct non-interactive witness indistinguishable (NIWI) proofs for different statements. In our scheme we will use both kinds of proofs.

First, Groth,Ostrovsky and Sahai [5] propose a construction of NIWI proofs for all NP languages. More specifically, they constructed proofs for circuit satisfiability. We are just interested in a particular step of the construction: a NIWI proof that a commitment contains 0 or 1. The setup algorithm outputs a bilinear group $(n, \mathbb{G}, \mathbb{G}_T, e, g)$, where g is a generator of $\mathbb{G}$ and $n = pq$ is the product of two large primes, and also an element $h \in \mathbb{G}$ of order q. The commitment to $m \in \{0, 1\}$ is $c = g^m h^r$, the NIWI proof is computed as $\pi = (g^{2m-1}h^r)^r$ and the verifier must check if $e(c, c/g) = e(h, \pi)$. As proved in [5], this proof is correct, sound and witness indistinguishable. Instead of using a unique value g, we will use different values (the hash of some attributes).

Groth and Sahai [6] propose a construction of NIWI proofs of the satisfiability of equations in bilinear groups. They give three instantiations of their methodology based on three different assumptions. In our scheme, we will mainly use the instantiation based on the subgroup decision assumption. The methodology of Groth-Sahai applies to different kinds of equations, but we are only interested in pairing product equations, that is, those of the form

$$\prod_{i=1}^{r} e(g_i, X_i) \cdot \prod_{i=1}^{r} \prod_{j=1}^{s} e(X_i, X_j)^{\gamma_{ij}} = t_T$$

where g_i, t_T and γ_{ij} are public constants in $\mathbb{G}$, G_T and $\mathbb{Z}_n$ respectively, and X_i are secret variables in $\mathbb{G}$.

The setup algorithm outputs a bilinear group $(n, \mathbb{G}, \mathbb{G}_T, e, g)$, where g is a generator of $\mathbb{G}$ and $n = pq$ is the product of two large primes, and an element h of order q. To construct a NIWI proof, first all secret variables should be committed computing $\mathsf{Com}(X_i, \rho_i) = X_i h^{\rho_i}$. After that, the proof π is computed using a protocol $Proof(ck, E, \{X_i, \rho_i\})$, where E is the equation to be satisfied and ck is the commitment key. Finally, the verifier must check that

$$\prod_{i=1}^{r} e(g_i, \mathsf{Com}(X_i)) \cdot \prod_{i=1}^{r} \prod_{j=1}^{s} e(\mathsf{Com}(X_i), \mathsf{Com}(X_j))^{\gamma_{ij}} = t_T e(h, \pi).$$

The correctness, soundness and witness indistinguishability of these proof systems are proved in [6].

3   Revocable Attribute-Based Signatures: Protocols and Security

In this section we describe the protocols that form an attribute-based signature scheme, as well as the security properties that must be required to such a scheme. A difference with respect to previous definitions for this primitive (such as the one in [12]) is that we deal explicitly with the identity of the users, because of the revocability property of our scheme. An attribute-based signature is linked to a determined *signing policy* $(\mathcal{P}, \Gamma)$: a set $\mathcal{P}$ of attributes and a monotone increasing family $\Gamma \subset 2^{\mathcal{P}}$ of subsets of $\mathcal{P}$. A valid signature means that a signer possessing all the attributes of some of the subsets in Γ is the author of the signature. The monotonicity property ensures that $A_1 \subset A_2, A_1 \in \Gamma \Rightarrow A_2 \in \Gamma$. The most common and simple example of such a monotone increasing family of subsets is the threshold case: in a (ℓ, n)-threshold signing policy, the set $\mathcal{P}$ contains n attributes, and $\Gamma = \{A \subset \mathcal{P} : |A| \geq \ell\}$. That is, by verifying a threshold attribute-based signature, the verifier is convinced that the author of the signature holds at least ℓ of the attributes included in the set $\mathcal{P}$.

3.1   Syntactic Definition

A revocable attribute-based signature scheme consists of four probabilistic polynomial-time algorithms:

- Setup(1^λ). The setup algorithm takes as input a security parameter λ and outputs some public parameters params, a master secret key msk and a revocation key rk. The public parameters contain the possible universe of attributes $\tilde{\mathcal{P}} = \{\mathsf{at}_1, \ldots, \mathsf{at}_m\}$.
- KeyGen(id, A, msk, params). The key generation algorithm takes as input the master secret key msk, the public parameters params and then an identity id and a set of attributes $A \subset \tilde{\mathcal{P}}$ satisfied by the user with identity id. The output is a private key $\mathsf{sk}_{\mathsf{id}, A}$. The master entity may store some information (for example, a table) relating the executions of this protocol with the identities id of the users. We refer to this information as st.

- Sign($M, \mathcal{P}, \Gamma, \mathsf{sk}_{\mathsf{id},A}, \mathsf{params}$). The signing algorithm takes as input a message M, a signing policy $(\mathcal{P}, \Gamma)$ where $\mathcal{P} \subset \tilde{\mathcal{P}}$ and $\Gamma \subset 2^{\mathcal{P}}$, a secret key $\mathsf{sk}_{\mathsf{id},A}$ and the public parameters params, and outputs a signature σ.
- Verify($\sigma, M, \mathcal{P}, \Gamma, \mathsf{params}$). The verification algorithm takes as input the signature σ, the message M, the signing policy $(\mathcal{P}, \Gamma)$ and the public parameters params, and outputs accept or reject, depending on the validity of the signature.
- Revoke($\sigma, \mathsf{rk}, \mathsf{params}, \mathsf{st}$). The revocation algorithm takes as input a signature σ, the revocation key rk, the public parameters params and possibly the information st stored by the master entity during the executions of KeyGen, and outputs an identity id or the special symbol $\perp$.

Of course, the usual properties of correctness for the verification and revocation algorithms must be required. Intuitively, a signature for a signing policy $(\mathcal{P}, \Gamma)$ that is computed by using $\mathsf{sk}_{\mathsf{id},A}$ such that $A \in \Gamma$ must be always accepted by the verification protocol and must be always revoked to identity id.

We stress that we have chosen the expression *revocable* to denote the property of opening the anonymity of an attribute-based signature, instead of *traceable*, to avoid confusion with the (different) notion of traceable signature [10].

3.2 Security Definitions

Unforgeability. An attribute-based signature scheme must satisfy the property of existential unforgeability against chosen message and signing policy attacks. Such property is defined by the following game between a challenger $\mathcal{C}$ and an adversary $\mathcal{F}$.

Setup. $\mathcal{C}$ runs the setup algorithm and keeps the master secret key msk and the revocation key rk to itself, then gives the public parameters params to $\mathcal{F}$.

Queries. Adaptively, $\mathcal{F}$ can request any queries described below.

- Secret key query: $\mathcal{F}$ requests a private key on an identity id and a set of attributes $B \subset \tilde{\mathcal{P}}$.
- Signature query: $\mathcal{F}$ requests a signature for a message M and a signing policy $(\mathcal{P}, \Gamma)$, where $\mathcal{P} \subset \tilde{\mathcal{P}}$ and $\Gamma \subset 2^{\mathcal{P}}$.
- Revocation query: $\mathcal{F}$ sends a tuple $(M, \sigma, \mathcal{P}, \Gamma)$. If the signature is valid, then $\mathcal{F}$ expects to receive as answer an identity id for the author of the signature σ.

Output. Finally, $\mathcal{F}$ outputs a tuple $(\sigma^*, M^*, \mathcal{P}^*, \Gamma^*)$ and wins the game if (1) the signature is valid, (2) $\mathcal{F}$ has not made any secret key query for a set of attributes $A \subset \tilde{\mathcal{P}}$ such that $A \in \Gamma^*$, and (3) $\mathcal{F}$ has not made any signature query for the tuple $(M^*, \mathcal{P}^*, \Gamma^*)$.

Definition 1. *An attribute-based signature scheme is unforgeable if, for any adversary $\mathcal{F}$ that runs in polynomial time, the probability that $\mathcal{F}$ wins the above game is negligible in the security parameter λ.*

The above definition of unforgeability guarantees collusion resistance: a group of colluding users that pull their secret keys together will not be able to sign messages for a signing policy that none of the attribute sets of these users satisfies. The definition is in the *adaptive* setting where the attacker chooses the target signing policy $(\mathcal{P}^*, \Gamma^*)$ after making some queries. This is in contrast to the *selective* setting where the attacker must choose the target signing policy at the very beginning of the attack.

Non-Linkability and Anonymity. Intuitively, non-linkability means that an observer cannot distinguish if two valid signatures for the same signing policy have been computed by the same user. Non-linkability is defined via the following game between a challenger $\mathcal{C}$ and an adversary $\mathcal{A}$.

Setup. The setup is the same as the setup of the unforgeability game.

Queries. $\mathcal{A}$ can make the same queries as $\mathcal{F}$ in the unforgeability game.

Challenge. $\mathcal{A}$ submits a challenge tuple $(\mathsf{id}_0, M_0, \sigma_0, M_1, \mathcal{P}, \Gamma)$. If some of the following conditions fails, the challenger aborts:

- $\mathcal{A}$ has asked for a secret key for (id_0, A_0) such that $A_0 \cap \mathcal{P} \in \Gamma$,
- $\mathsf{Verify}(\sigma_0, M_0, \mathcal{P}, \Gamma, \mathsf{params}) = \mathsf{accept}$,
- $\mathsf{Revoke}(\sigma_0, \mathsf{rk}, \mathsf{params}) = \mathsf{id}_0$.

Otherwise, the challenger $\mathcal{C}$ recovers the secret key $\mathsf{sk}_{\mathsf{id}_0, A_0}$ that has been delivered to $\mathcal{A}$, chooses at random a different identity $\mathsf{id}_1 \neq \mathsf{id}_0$ and a subset of attributes $A_1 \in \Gamma$ and runs $\mathsf{sk}_{\mathsf{id}_1, A_1} \leftarrow \mathsf{KeyGen}(\mathsf{id}_1, A_1, \mathsf{msk}, \mathsf{params})$. Then $\mathcal{C}$ flips a random coin $b \in \{0, 1\}$ and computes $\sigma_1 \leftarrow \mathsf{Sign}(M_1, \mathcal{P}, \Gamma, \mathsf{sk}_{\mathsf{id}_b, A_b}, \mathsf{params})$. The values $\sigma_1, \mathsf{id}_1, A_1, \mathsf{sk}_{\mathsf{id}_1, A_1}$ are returned to $\mathcal{A}$.

Queries. $\mathcal{A}$ can make more queries, with the restriction that the signature σ_1 cannot be queried to the revocation oracle.

Output. Finally, $\mathcal{A}$ outputs a guess b' of b and wins the game if $b = b'$.

Definition 2. *An attribute-based signature scheme is non-linkable if, for any adversary $\mathcal{A}$ that runs in polynomial time, the difference between the probability that $\mathcal{A}$ wins the above game and $1/2$ is negligible in the security parameter λ.*

The more standard property of signer's anonymity can be defined in a very similar way. Since in both definitions the adversary can obtain secret keys for all identities of his choice, it is easy to see that non-linkability implies signer's anonymity.

Non-Frameability. Our schemes will enjoy the interesting property of revocability, which means that there exists an authority that can break the anonymity of a signature, when needed. This property brings new possibilities for an adversary to cheat the system, that must be dealt with by our security model. Specifically, we must consider *framing* attacks where an adversary tries to produce a signature that is later revoked to the identity of some honest user. This intuition is formalized by considering the following game, between a challenger $\mathcal{C}$ and a framing attacker $\mathcal{T}$.

Setup. The setup is similar to the setup of the unforgeability game, but now even the revocation key rk is given to the adversary $\mathcal{T}$.

Queries. $\mathcal{A}$ can make the same queries as $\mathcal{F}$ in the unforgeability game. Note that revocation queries make no sense now, since $\mathcal{T}$ knows the revocation key. Let $\mathcal{M} = \{M$ s.t. $(M, \mathcal{P}, \Gamma)$ is a signing query$\}$ be the set of messages queried to the signing oracle, and let $\mathcal{ID} = \{$id s.t. (id, B) is a secret key query$\}$ be the set of identities for which $\mathcal{T}$ obtains secret keys.

Output. At some point, $\mathcal{T}$ outputs a tuple $(\sigma^*, M^*, \mathcal{P}^*, \Gamma^*)$ and wins the game if (1) the signature is valid, (2) $M^* \notin \mathcal{M}$, and (3) Revoke$(\sigma^*, \mathsf{rk}, \mathsf{params}) \notin \mathcal{ID}$.

Definition 3. *A revocable attribute-based signature scheme is non-frameable if, for any adversary $\mathcal{T}$ that runs in polynomial time, the probability that $\mathcal{T}$ wins the above game is negligible in the security parameter λ.*

4   The New Scheme

In this section, we construct our attribute-based signature scheme. We proceed in different steps. First, we construct a linkable scheme which works for threshold signing policies. Then we will introduce some changes in order to achieve non-linkability. The security of the resulting scheme will be proved in the random oracle model. After that, we will modify the scheme to admit more general signing policies. And finally, we will explain how to achieve security in the standard model.

4.1   The Intuition: A Linkable Scheme

Our basic construction is inspired by the ring signature scheme of Shacham-Waters [13].

Setup(1^λ). The setup algorithm first generates a symmetric bilinear group $(n, \mathbb{G}, \mathbb{G}_T, e, g)$ of composite order $n = pq$, where p and q are primes of bit size $\Theta(\lambda)$. Next, it chooses random $w \in \mathbb{G}$, $h \in \mathbb{G}_q$, where $\mathbb{G}_q$ is the subgroup of $\mathbb{G}$ of order q, $s \in \mathbb{Z}_n$ and cryptographic hash functions $H_1, H_2 : \{0,1\}^* \to \mathbb{G}$. It also generates a value $\delta_p \in \mathbb{Z}_n$ such that $\delta_p = 0 \mod q$ and $\delta_p = 1 \mod p$. An automorphic signature scheme is chosen, with public key $\mathsf{pk_{aut}}$ and secret key $\mathsf{sk_{aut}}$. Finally, a universe of attributes $\tilde{\mathcal{P}}$ is chosen. Then, the public parameters params, the master secret key msk and the revocation key rk are defined as

$$\mathsf{params} = (n, \mathbb{G}, \mathbb{G}_T, e, g, g_1 = g^s, h, h_1 = h^s, w, H_1, H_2, \mathsf{pk_{aut}}, \tilde{\mathcal{P}})$$

$$\mathsf{msk} = (s, \mathsf{sk_{aut}}) \qquad\qquad \mathsf{rk} = \delta_p$$

The master entity can erase the values (p, q, δ_p), because they are not needed to answer key generation queries.

KeyGen(id, A, msk, params). The key generation algorithm takes as input an identity id, a subset of attributes $A \subset \tilde{\mathcal{P}}$ satisfied by id, the master secret key msk and the public parameters params. The master entity chooses a random element $K_{id} \in \mathbb{G}$ and signs this value with the automorphic signature, obtaining $\sigma_{K_{id}}$. For each attribute $at_i \in A$, the algorithm chooses a random $r_i \in \mathbb{Z}_n$ and defines the attribute secret key as $sk_i = (E_i, G_i) = (H_1(at_i)^s K_{id}^{r_i}, g^{r_i})$. Finally, the global secret key is $sk_{id,A} = (K_{id}, \sigma_{K_{id}}, \{sk_i\}_{at_i \in A})$. The master entity secretly stores the relation between id and K_{id} in a table st, that can be sent to the revocation judge.

Sign$(M, \mathcal{P}, \ell, sk_{id,A}, params)$. The signing algorithm takes as input a message M, a set of attributes $\mathcal{P} \subset \tilde{\mathcal{P}}$, a threshold ℓ, a secret key $sk_{id,A}$ and the public parameters params. The algorithm selects a minimal authorized set A', this is, a subset of $A \cap \mathcal{P}$ of cardinality exactly ℓ. To generate the signature, it proceeds as follows:

1. First, for each $at_i \in \mathcal{P}$ it chooses a random $z_i \in \mathbb{Z}_n$ and computes the commitment C_i of f_i and the corresponding proof π_i as

$$C_i = (H_1(at_i)/w)^{f_i} h^{z_i} \text{ and } \pi_i = ((H_1(at_i)/w)^{2f_i - 1} h^{z_i})^{z_i}$$

where $f_i = 1$ if $at_i \in A'$ and $f_i = 0$ otherwise.
2. Then, it computes $H_m = H_2(M, \mathcal{P}, \ell)$. It also chooses a random $t \in \mathbb{Z}_n$ and computes $\sigma_1 = \left(\prod_{at_i \in A'} E_i\right) H_m^t h_1^z$, $\sigma_2 = g^t$ and $\sigma_3 = \prod_{at_i \in A'} G_i$, where $z = \sum_{at_i \in \mathcal{P}} z_i$.
3. Finally, the signature is $\sigma = (\sigma_1, \sigma_2, \sigma_3, \{(C_i, \pi_i)\}_{at_i \in \mathcal{P}}, K_{id}, \sigma_{K_{id}})$.

Verify$(\sigma, M, \mathcal{P}, \ell, params)$. The verification algorithm takes as input a message M, the signature σ on M, the threshold signing policy $(\mathcal{P}, \ell)$ and the public parameters params. It proceeds as follows:

1. For all $at_i \in \mathcal{P}$, check if $e(C_i, C_i/(H_1(at_i)/w)) \overset{?}{=} e(h, \pi_i)$.
2. Compute $H_m = H_2(M, \mathcal{P}, \ell)$ and check if $e(\sigma_1, g) \overset{?}{=}$
$$e(w^\ell \prod_{at_i \in \mathcal{P}} C_i, g_1)e(H_m, \sigma_2)e(K, \sigma_3).$$
3. Check that $\sigma_{K_{id}}$ is a valid automorphic signature on K_{id}.
4. Output accept if all the tests are successful, and reject otherwise.

Revoke$(\sigma, rk, params, st)$. Since the value K_{id} is included in the signature σ, the judge only needs to recover the relation (id, K_{id}) from the secret table st.

4.2   Achieving Non-linkability

It is easy to see that the scheme described in the previous section works correctly. However, the values σ_3, K_{id} and $\sigma_{K_{id}}$ allow any verifier to link two signatures issued by the same signer, even if the relation between K_{id} and the identity of the signer is unknown. To solve this drawback, we will use Groth-Sahai proofs to commit to K_{id} and $\sigma_{K_{id}}$, and we will randomize σ_3.

Let $\mathsf{Com}(K_{\mathsf{id}})$ and $\mathsf{Com}(\sigma_{K_{\mathsf{id}}})$ be the commitments to K_{id} and $\sigma_{K_{\mathsf{id}}}$ respectively. Let π_σ be the NIWI proof of the satisfiability of the second verification equation, and $\pi_{K_{\mathsf{id}}}$ the NIWI proof of the satisfiability of the verification equation of the automorphic signature of K_{id}. We remind the reader that the verification of an automorphic signature is done by evaluating a set of pairing-product equations, so we can build Groth-Sahai proofs of satisfiability for these equations.

In addition, we randomize the value σ_3 by choosing a random $r' \in \mathbb{Z}_n$ and multiplying σ_3 with $g^{r'}$. We will also need to multiply σ_1 with $K_{\mathsf{id}}^{r'}$ in order to satisfy the verification equation. So, we redefine $\sigma_3 = \prod_{\mathsf{at}_i \in A'} G_i g^{r'}$ and $\sigma_1 = $

$$\left(\prod_{\mathsf{at}_i \in A'} E_i \right) K_{\mathsf{id}}^{r'} H_m^t h_1^z.$$

Now, the signature will be the tuple $\sigma = (\sigma_1, \sigma_2, \sigma_3, \{(C_i, \pi_i)\}_{\mathsf{at}_i \in \mathcal{P}}, \mathsf{Com}(K_{\mathsf{id}}),$ $\mathsf{Com}(\sigma_{K_{\mathsf{id}}}), \pi_{K_{\mathsf{id}}}, \pi_\sigma)$. The verification algorithm $\mathsf{Verify}(\sigma, M, \mathcal{P}, \ell, \mathsf{params})$ proceeds now as follows:

1. For all $\mathsf{at}_i \in \mathcal{P}$, check if $e(C_i, C_i/(H_1(\mathsf{at}_i)/w)) \overset{?}{=} e(h, \pi_i)$.
2. Check if $e(\sigma_1, g) \overset{?}{=} e(w^l \prod_{\mathsf{at}_i \in \mathcal{P}} C_i, g_1) e(H_m, \sigma_2) e(\mathsf{Com}(K_{\mathsf{id}}), \sigma_3) e(h, \pi_\sigma)$
3. Checks that $\sigma_{K_{\mathsf{id}}}$ is a valid signature on K_{id} using the proof $\pi_{K_{\mathsf{id}}}$ and the commitments $\mathsf{Com}(K_{\mathsf{id}}), \mathsf{Com}(\sigma_{K_{\mathsf{id}}})$.
4. Outputs accept if all the tests are successful, and reject otherwise.

Finally, the revocation algorithm must be modified in the following way.

$\mathsf{Revoke}(\sigma, \mathsf{rk}, \mathsf{params}, \mathsf{st})$. The revocation algorithm takes as input the revocation key $\mathsf{rk} = \delta_p$, a valid signature σ, the public parameters params and the table st. It computes $\mathsf{Com}(K_{\mathsf{id}})^{\delta_p} = K_{\mathsf{id}}^{\delta_p}$. This value $K_{\mathsf{id}}^{\delta_p}$ can be detected in the secret table st, in order to obtain the identity id of the signer. Note that this process can be made more efficient if a third value $K_{\mathsf{id}}^{\delta_p}$ is added to each entry $(\mathsf{id}, K_{\mathsf{id}})$ in the table st.

Security Analysis. Now we prove that the scheme described in this section achieves the properties of non-linkability, non-frameability and unforgeability. The proofs for the first two property are just sketched.

Theorem 1. *If the subgroup decision assumption holds in $\mathbb{G}$, then our threshold attribute-based signature scheme is non-linkable.*

Proof (sketch). The challenger can use the Setup algorithm to choose the parameters of the security game. As he knows the secret and revocation keys, he can answer all the queries made by the adversary using the algorithms KeyGen, Sign and Revoke.

The advantage of $\mathcal{A}$ is negligible because σ_1, σ_2 and σ_3 are randomized elements. All the commitments and proofs to the attributes $\{(C_i, \pi_i)\}$ and the commitments $\mathsf{Com}(K_{\mathsf{id}}), \mathsf{Com}(\sigma_{K_{\mathsf{id}}})$, and the proofs $\pi_{K_{\mathsf{id}}}, \pi_\sigma$ do not reveal any information about f_i or K_{id} because they are commitments and NIWI proofs.   □

It is easy to see that our scheme also enjoys non-linkability (and anonymity) with respect to the subset of attributes employed to compute a signature.

Theorem 2. *Assuming that the underlying automorphic signature scheme is secure, our threshold attribute-based signature scheme is non-frameable.*

Proof (sketch). The challenger can use the knowledge of all the elements in msk and rk, excepting sk_{aut}, and also its access to a signing oracle for the automorphic signature scheme, to answer the different queries that a framing adversary $\mathcal{T}$ makes.

If $\mathcal{T}$ succeeds in forging a signature σ^* for which $Com(K^*)^{\delta_p} \neq K_{id}^{\delta_p}$ for all the values K_{id} that have been generated in the secret key queries, then the values in the forged attribute-based signature can be used to obtain a valid forgery against the automorphic signature scheme. $\square$

Theorem 3. *If the CDH assumption holds in $\mathbb{G}_p$ and the subgroup decision assumption holds in $\mathbb{G}$, then our threshold attribute-based signature scheme is existentially unforgeable under chosen message and signing policy attacks.*

Proof. We construct an algorithm $\mathcal{B}$ that solves the CDH problem in $\mathbb{G}_p$ running an adversary $\mathcal{F}$ attacking the unforgeability of our scheme. Note that each proof (C_i, π_i) in a forged signature $(\sigma^*, M^*, \mathcal{P}^*, \ell^*)$ generated by $\mathcal{F}$ must pass the verification equation $e(C_i, C_i/(H(at_i))/w)) = e(h, \pi_i)$. This implies that C_i has the form $(H_1(at_i)/w)^{f_i}h^{z_i}$ for some $f_i \in \{0,1\}$ and $z_i \in \mathbb{Z}_n$. According to the value of $\sum_{at_i \in \mathcal{P}^*} f_i$, we consider two types of adversaries as follows.

1. A type-1 adversary $\mathcal{F}_1$ is one such that $\sum_{at_i \in \mathcal{P}^*} f_i \neq \ell^*$, where ℓ^* is the threshold defining the signing policy of the forged signature.
2. A type-2 adversary $\mathcal{F}_2$ is one such that $\sum_{at_i \in \mathcal{P}^*} f_i = \ell^*$.

For each type of adversary $\mathcal{F}_1$ and $\mathcal{F}_2$, we will construct algorithms $\mathcal{B}_1$ and $\mathcal{B}_2$, respectively, to solve the CDH problem in $\mathbb{G}_p$. We do this in the following two lemmas, which complete the proof of the theorem.

Lemma 1. *Assume that the inherent automorphic signature scheme is secure. If there exists a type-1 adversary $\mathcal{F}_1$ against our threshold attribute-based signature scheme, then there exists an algorithm $\mathcal{B}_1$ that solves the CDH problem in $\mathbb{G}_p$.*

Proof. Suppose there exists a type-1 adversary $\mathcal{F}_1$ that breaks unforgeability of our scheme. Let us construct an algorithm $\mathcal{B}_1$ that solves the CDH problem in $\mathbb{G}_p$. $\mathcal{B}_1$ is given the description of the bilinear group $\mathbb{G}$, the factorization p, q of n, which is the order of $\mathbb{G}$, and a random CDH challenge $(g_p, g_p^\alpha, g_p^\beta) \in \mathbb{G}_p^3$, where g_p is a generator of $\mathbb{G}_p$. Its goal is to compute $g_p^{\alpha\beta}$. The algorithm $\mathcal{B}_1$ interacts with $\mathcal{F}_1$ as follows:

Setup. $\mathcal{B}_1$ selects a generator $h \in \mathbb{G}_q$ and chooses random values $r_1 \in \mathbb{Z}_q^*, r_2, r_3 \in \mathbb{Z}_q$. It also chooses the keys (sk_{aut}, pk_{aut}) of an automorphic signature scheme and a universe of attributes $\tilde{\mathcal{P}}$. Next it defines the public parameters as params $= (n, \mathbb{G}, \mathbb{G}_T, e, g = g_p h^{r_1}, g_1 = g_p^\alpha h^{r_2}, h, h_1 = h^{r_2/r_1}, w = g_p^\beta h^{r_3}, H_1, H_2, pk_{aut}, \tilde{\mathcal{P}})$

and gives params to $\mathcal{A}_1$. The public parameters are correctly distributed because $e(g_1, h) = e(g_p^\alpha h^{r_2}, h) = e(h^{r_1}, h^{r_2/r_1}) = e(g_p h^{r_1}, h^{r_2/r_1}) = e(g, h_1)$. This is because $g_p \in \mathbb{G}_p$ and $h \in \mathbb{G}_q$ imply that $e(g_p^\alpha, h) = 1$.

Queries. Adaptively, $\mathcal{F}_1$ can make H_1-hash queries, H_2-hash queries, secret key queries, signature queries or revocation queries at any time. For hash queries, $\mathcal{B}_1$ creates and maintains two lists H_1-list and H_2-list storing the information of all the queries; these lists are consulted before answering any new query, for consistency.

For a H_1-hash query on at_i, $\mathcal{B}_1$ generates a random $c_i \in \mathbb{Z}_n$ and responds with $H_1(\mathsf{at}_i) = g^{c_i}$. For a H_2-hash query on a message M, a set of attributes $\mathcal{P}$ and a threshold ℓ, $\mathcal{B}_1$ generates a random $d \in \mathbb{Z}_n$ and responds with $H_2(M, \mathcal{P}, \ell) = g^d$. For a secret key query for an identity id and attribute set $A \subset \tilde{\mathcal{P}}$, $\mathcal{B}_1$ generates a random $e_j \in \mathbb{Z}_n$, computes $K_{\mathsf{id}} = g^{e_j}$ and the signature $\sigma_{K_{\mathsf{id}}}$ and for each $\mathsf{at}_i \in A$ computes $\mathsf{sk}_i = (g_1^{c_i} K_{\mathsf{id}}^{r_i}, g^{r_i})$, where r_i is chosen at random in $\mathbb{Z}_n$. It responds with $\mathsf{sk}_{\mathsf{id},A} = (K_{\mathsf{id}}, \{\mathsf{sk}_i\}_{\mathsf{at}_i \in A})$. Using these secret keys, $\mathcal{B}_1$ can answer signature queries properly, as well. Since $\mathcal{B}_1$ knows p, q, it can easily answer revocation queries, as well.

Output. Finally, $\mathcal{F}_1$ outputs a signature $(\sigma^*, M^*, \mathcal{P}^*, \ell^*)$, where

$$\sigma^* = (\sigma_1, \sigma_2, \sigma_3, \{(C_i, \pi_i)\}_{\mathsf{at}_i \in \mathcal{P}^*}, \mathsf{Com}(K_{\mathsf{id}^*}), \mathsf{Com}(\sigma_{K_{\mathsf{id}^*}}), \pi_{K_{\mathsf{id}^*}}, \pi_\sigma).$$

If (1) $\mathcal{F}_1$ did request a private key $\mathsf{sk}_{\mathsf{id},A}$ such that $A \cap \mathcal{P}^*$ has cardinality at least ℓ^*, or (2) $\mathcal{F}_1$ did request a signature on the tuple $(M^*, \mathcal{P}^*, \ell^*)$, or (3) if the forged signature is not valid; then $\mathcal{B}_1$ stops the simulation because $\mathcal{F}_1$ has not been successful.

Otherwise, $\mathcal{B}_1$ solves the given instance of the CDH problem as follows: let δ_p be such that $\delta_p = 0 \mod q$ and $\delta_p = 1 \mod p$. We have $u^{\delta_p} = 1$ if, and only if, $u \in \mathbb{G}_q$. We obtain $C_i^{\delta_p} = (H_1(\mathsf{at}_i)^{\delta_p}/w^{\delta_p})^{f_i} = (g_p^{c_i}/g_p^\beta)^{f_i}$ for all $\mathsf{at}_i \in \mathcal{P}^*$, and so $C^{\delta_p} = \prod_{\mathsf{at}_i \in \mathcal{P}^*} C_i^{\delta_p} = g_p^c/(g_p^\beta)^f$, where $c = \sum_{\mathsf{at}_i \in \mathcal{P}^*} c_i f_i$ and $f = \sum_{\mathsf{at}_i \in \mathcal{P}^*} f_i$. From the second verification equation of the scheme (see Section 4.2), we obtain $e(g_p, \sigma_1^{\delta_p}) = e(g_p^\alpha, (g_p^\beta)^{\ell^*} g_p^c/(g_p^\beta)^f) e(\sigma_2^{\delta_p}, g_p^d) e(\sigma_3^{\delta_p}, g_p^e)$, where $H_2(M^*, \mathcal{P}^*, \ell^*)^{\delta_p} = g_p^d$ and $K^{\delta_p} = g_p^e$. This equation comes from the fact that $\mathsf{Com}(K_{\mathsf{id}^*})^{\delta_p} = K_{\mathsf{id}^*}^{\delta_p}$ and $e(h, \pi_\sigma)^{\delta_p} = 1$. By rewriting this equation, we have $e(g_p^\alpha, g_p^\beta)^{\ell^*-f} = e(g_p, \sigma_1^{\delta_p}(\sigma_2^{\delta_p})^{-d}(\sigma_3^{\delta_p})^{-e}(g_p^\alpha)^{-c})$. $\mathcal{B}_1$ recovers from H_1-list the values c_i corresponding to all the attributes in $\mathcal{P}^*$ and the value d corresponding to the H_2-query $(M^*, \mathcal{P}^*, \ell^*)$. It also recovers the value e corresponding to K_{id^*}. As the automorphic signature scheme is secure, we can be sure that the value of K_{id^*} used in the forgery comes from a query, so it is known to $\mathcal{B}_1$. Finally, $\mathcal{B}_1$ recovers $\{f_i\}_{i \in \mathcal{P}^*}$ using that $C_i^{\delta_p} = 1$ if, and only if, $f_i = 0$. By assumption $f = \sum_{\mathsf{at}_i \in \mathcal{P}^*} f_i \neq \ell^*$, and so the value $(\ell^* - f)^{-1} \mod p$ exists. Therefore, $\mathcal{B}_1$ can solve the CDH problem as $g_p^{\alpha\beta} = [(\sigma_1 \sigma_2^{-d} \sigma_3^{-e})^{\delta_p} g_p^{-\alpha c}]^{\frac{1}{\ell^*-f}}$. $\qquad\square$

Lemma 2. *If there exists a type-2 adversary $\mathcal{F}_2$ against our threshold attribute-based signature scheme, then there exists an algorithm $\mathcal{B}_2$ that solves the CDH problem in $\mathbb{G}_p$.*

Proof. Suppose there exists a type-2 adversary $\mathcal{F}_2$ that breaks the unforgeability of our scheme. We construct an algorithm $\mathcal{B}_2$ that solves the CDH problem in $\mathbb{G}_p$. $\mathcal{B}_2$ is given the description of the bilinear group $\mathbb{G}$, the factorization p, q of n, which is the order of $\mathbb{G}$, and a random CDH challenge $(g_p, g_p^\alpha, g_p^\beta) \in \mathbb{G}_p^3$, where g_p is a generator of $\mathbb{G}_p$. Its goal is to compute $g_p^{\alpha\beta}$. The algorithm $\mathcal{B}_2$ interacts with $\mathcal{F}_2$ as follows:

Setup. $\mathcal{B}_2$ selects a generator $h \in \mathbb{G}_q$ and chooses random values $r_1 \in \mathbb{Z}_q^*, r_2, r_3, r_4 \in \mathbb{Z}_q, r_5 \in \mathbb{Z}_p$. It also chooses keys $(\mathsf{sk}_{\mathsf{aut}}, \mathsf{pk}_{\mathsf{aut}})$ of an automorphic signature scheme and a universe of attributes $\tilde{\mathcal{P}}$. Next it sets the public parameters $\mathsf{params} = (n, \mathbb{G}, \mathbb{G}_T, e, g = g_p h^{r_1}, g_1 = g_p^\alpha h^{r_2}, h, h_1 = h^{r_2/r_1}, w = g_p^{r_5} h^{r_3}, H_1, H_2, \mathsf{pk}_{\mathsf{aut}}, \tilde{\mathcal{P}})$, defines $g_2 = g_p^\beta h^{r_4}$ and gives params to $\mathcal{F}_2$. The public parameters are correctly distributed because $e(g_1, h) = e(g_p^\alpha h^{r_2}, h) = e(h^{r_1}, h^{r_2/r_1}) = e(g_p h^{r_1}, h^{r_2/r_1}) = e(g, h_1)$. These equalities hold because $g_p \in \mathbb{G}_p$ and $h \in \mathbb{G}_q$ imply that $e(g_p^\alpha, h) = 1$. With these parameters, $s = \log_g g_1$ is implicitly defined.

Queries. Adaptively, $\mathcal{F}_1$ can make H_1-hash queries, H_2-hash queries, secret key queries, signature queries or revocation queries at any time. $\mathcal{B}_2$ creates and maintains lists H_1-list, H_2-list and K-list, for consistency. Again, since $\mathcal{B}_2$ knows p, q, it can easily answer revocation queries.

For a H_1-hash query on at_i, $\mathcal{B}_2$ responds as follows: if at_i was in a previous H_1-hash query, it recovers $(\mathsf{at}_i, H_1\text{-coin}_i, c_i)$ from H_1-list; otherwise, it generates a random $H_1\text{-coin}_i \in \{0, 1\}$ so that $\Pr[H_1\text{-coin}_i = 1] = \rho_1$, for ρ_1 to be determined later. It generates a random $c_i \in \mathbb{Z}_n^*$ and stores $(\mathsf{at}_i, H_1\text{-coin}_i, c_i)$ in H_1-list. If $H_1\text{-coin}_i = 0$, then it responds with $H_1(\mathsf{at}_i) = g^{c_i}$; otherwise, it responds with $H_1(\mathsf{at}_i) = g_2^{c_i}$.

For a H_2-hash query on a tuple $(M, \mathcal{P}, \ell)$, $\mathcal{B}_2$ responds as follows: if $(M, \mathcal{P}, \ell)$ already exists in H_2-list, $\mathcal{B}_2$ recovers $(M, \mathcal{P}, \ell, d)$ from its H_2-list; otherwise, it generates a random $d \in \mathbb{Z}_n$, stores $(M, \mathcal{P}, \ell, d)$ in H_2-list and responds with $H_2(M, \mathcal{P}, \ell) = g^d$.

For a secret key query for an identity id and a set of attributes $A \subset \tilde{\mathcal{P}}$, $\mathcal{B}_2$ responds as follows: it generates a random $K_{\mathsf{id}}\text{-coin} \in \{0, 1\}$ so that $\Pr[K_{\mathsf{id}}\text{-coin} = 1] = \rho_2$, for ρ_2 to be determined later. If $K_{\mathsf{id}}\text{-coin} = 0$, $\mathcal{B}_2$ generates a random $e \in \mathbb{Z}_n$ and sets $e' = 0$; otherwise, it generates two random elements $e, e' \in \mathbb{Z}_n^*$. It defines $K_{\mathsf{id}} = g^e g_1^{e'}$ and stores $(K_{\mathsf{id}}\text{-coin}, e, e', K_{\mathsf{id}})$ in K-list. Next, for each attribute $\mathsf{at}_i \in A$, it recovers $(\mathsf{at}_i, H_1\text{-coin}_i, c_i)$ from H_1-list.

- If $H_1\text{-coin}_i = 0$, then it generates a random $r_i \in \mathbb{Z}_n$ and defines $\mathsf{sk}_i = (g_1^{c_i} K_{\mathsf{id}}^{r_i}, g^{r_i})$.
- If $H_1\text{-coin}_i = 1$ and $K\text{-coin} = 1$, it generates a random $r_i \in \mathbb{Z}_n$ and sets $\mathsf{sk}_i = ((g_2^{c_i})^{-\frac{e}{e'}} (g^e g_1^{e'})^{r_i}, g^{r_i} g_2^{-\frac{c_i}{e'}})$. The secret key is correctly distributed (we denote by β^* the value $\log_g g_2$) because: $E_i = (g_2^{c_i})^{-\frac{e}{e'}} (g^e g_1^{e'})^{r_i} = (g_2^{c_i})^s (g^e g_1^{e'})^{(r_i - \frac{c_i}{e'} \beta^*)} = H(\mathsf{at}_i)^s K_{\mathsf{id}}^{r_i'}$ and, on the other hand, $G_i = g^{r_i} g_2^{-\frac{c_i}{e'}} = g^{(r_i - \frac{c_i}{e'} \beta^*)} = g^{r_i'}$.
- Otherwise, if $H_1\text{-coin}_i = 1$ and $K_{\mathsf{id}}\text{-coin}_j = 0$, then $\mathcal{B}_2$ cannot create sk_i.

If $\mathcal{B}_2$ can create sk_i for all $\mathsf{at}_i \in A$, then it uses $\mathsf{sk}_{\mathsf{aut}}$ to compute an automorphic signature $\sigma_{K_{\mathsf{id}}}$ on K_{id} and responds to $\mathcal{F}_2$'s query with $\mathsf{sk}_{\mathsf{id},A} = (K_{\mathsf{id}}, \sigma_{K_{\mathsf{id}}}, \{\mathsf{sk}_i\}_{\mathsf{at}_i \in A})$. Otherwise, it aborts.

For a signature query for the tuple $(M, \mathcal{P}, \ell)$, $\mathcal{B}_2$ acts as follows. It recovers $(M, \mathcal{P}, \ell, d)$ from H_2-list and recovers $(H(\mathsf{at}_i), H_1\text{-coin}_i, c_i)$ from H_1-list, for all the attributes $\mathsf{at}_i \in \mathcal{P}$. $\mathcal{B}_2$ creates a K value by generating at random $e, e' \in \mathbb{Z}_n$ and computing $K = g^e g_1^{e'}$. With this value of K, $\mathcal{B}_2$ can create secret keys for any attribute at, so a secret key $\mathsf{sk}_{\mathcal{P}}$ can be generated and used to sign the message M, by following the algorithm Sign of the scheme. Note that the adversary $\mathcal{F}_2$ cannot distinguish which value of K has been used in the signature (due to the anonymity properties of the scheme).

Output. Finally, $\mathcal{F}_2$ outputs a signature $(\sigma^*, M^*, \mathcal{P}^*, \ell^*)$ where

$$\sigma^* = (\sigma_1, \sigma_2, \sigma_3, \{(C_i, \pi_i)\}_{\mathsf{at}_i \in \mathcal{P}^*}, \mathsf{Com}(K_{\mathsf{id}^*}), \mathsf{Com}(\sigma_{K_{\mathsf{id}^*}}), \pi_{K_{\mathsf{id}^*}}, \pi_\sigma).$$

If (1) $\mathcal{F}_2$ did request a private key $\mathsf{sk}_{\mathsf{id},A}$ such that $A \cap \mathcal{P}^*$ has cardinality at least ℓ^*, or (2) $\mathcal{F}_2$ did request a signature for the tuple $(M^*, \mathcal{P}^*, \ell^*)$, or (3) if the forged signature is not valid; then $\mathcal{B}_2$ stops the simulation because $\mathcal{F}_2$ has not been successful.

Otherwise, $\mathcal{B}_2$ solves the given instance of the CDH problem as follows: let δ_p be such that $\delta_p = 0 \mod q$ and $\delta_p = 1 \mod p$. Computing $C_i^{\delta_p}$ for all $\mathsf{at}_i \in \mathcal{P}^*$, $\mathcal{B}_2$ recovers $\{f_i\}_{\mathsf{at}_i \in \mathcal{P}^*}$, so it recovers the subset A' of attributes that has been used in the forged signature. Next it recovers $(M^*, \mathcal{P}^*, \ell^*, d^*)$ from H_2-list and $(\mathsf{at}_i, H_1\text{-coin}_i, c_i)$ from H_1-list, for every attribute $\mathsf{at}_i \in A'$. On the other hand, it computes $\mathsf{Com}(K_{\mathsf{id}^*})^{\delta_p} = K_{\mathsf{id}^*}^{\delta_p}$. Since the automorphic signature scheme is secure, we can be sure that the value of K_{id^*} used in the forgery has been obtained in a secret key query, so K_{id^*} is known to $\mathcal{B}_2$, that can recover $(K_{\mathsf{id}^*}\text{-coin}, e, e', K_{\mathsf{id}^*})$ from K-list. If $K_{\mathsf{id}^*}\text{-coin} = 1$, then $\mathcal{B}_2$ aborts. Otherwise, let B_0 be the set of indices $i \in A'$ such that $H_1\text{-coin}_i = 0$ and let B_1 be the set of indices i such that $H_1\text{-coin}_i = 1$. We have $A' = B_0 \cup B_1$. Due to the non-malleability properties of the employed hash functions, σ_1 must be of the form

$$\sigma_1 = \left(\prod_{\mathsf{at}_i \in A'} (H(\mathsf{at}_i))^s \right) K_{\mathsf{id}^*}^r H_m^t h_1^z = \left(\prod_{i \in B_0} (H(\mathsf{at}_i))^s \prod_{i \in B_1} (H(\mathsf{at}_i))^s \right) (g^e)^r (g^{d^*})^t h_1^z$$

$$= \left(\prod_{i \in B_0} (g^{c_i})^s \prod_{i \in B_1} (g_2^{c_i})^s \right) \sigma_3^e \sigma_2^{d^*} h_1^z = g_1^{\sum_{i \in B_0} c_i} (g_2^s)^{\sum_{i \in B_1} c_i} \sigma_3^e \sigma_2^{d^*} h_1^z$$

Let $c_{B_0} = \sum_{i \in B_0} c_i$ and $c_{B_1} = \sum_{i \in B_1} c_i$. If $c_{B_1} \mod p = 0$, $\mathcal{B}_2$ aborts because it cannot solve the CDH problem. Otherwise, we have $g_2^s = (\sigma_1 \sigma_2^{-d^*} \sigma_3^{-e} g_1^{-c_{B_0}} h_1^{-z})^{1/c_{B_1}}$. We also have $(g_2^s)^{\delta_p} = g_p^{\alpha\beta}$, that comes from the fact that $g_p^\alpha = g_1^{\delta_p} = (g^s)^{\delta_p}$. Using that $\mathsf{Com}(\sigma_3)^{\delta_p} = \sigma_3^{\delta_p}$, we have that $\mathcal{B}_2$ can solve the CDH problem as follows:

$$g_p^{\alpha\beta} = (g_2^s)^{\delta_p} = \left[\sigma_1^{\delta_p} (\sigma_2^{\delta_p})^{-d^*} (\sigma_3^{\delta_p})^{-e} (g_p^\alpha)^{-c_{B_0}} \right]^{\frac{1}{c_{B_1}}}$$

Analysis. Let abort be the event that $\mathcal{B}_2$ aborts during the simulation and let forge be the event that $\mathcal{F}_2$ produces a valid forgery according to the definition of the unforgeability game. We have

$$\text{Adv}_{\mathcal{B}_2}^{\text{CDH}} \geq \Pr[\text{forge} \wedge \neg\text{abort}] = \Pr[\text{forge}|\neg\text{abort}]\Pr[\neg\text{abort}] = \text{Adv}_{\mathcal{F}_2}^{\text{ABS}}\Pr[\neg\text{abort}]$$

The last equality comes from the fact that, if abort does not occur, then $\mathcal{B}_2$ simulates perfectly the environment of $\mathcal{F}_2$. Let abort_E be the event that $\mathcal{B}_2$ aborts at a secret key query, let abort_K be the event that $K_{\text{id}^*}\text{-coin} = 1$ when $\mathcal{F}_2$ outputs a forgery, and let abort_C be the event that $c_{B_1} \mod p = 0$.

$$\begin{aligned}
\Pr[\neg\text{abort}] &= \Pr[\neg\text{abort}_E \wedge \neg\text{abort}_K \wedge \neg\text{abort}_C] \\
&= \Pr[\neg\text{abort}_E]\Pr[\neg\text{abort}_K \wedge \neg\text{abort}_C|\neg\text{abort}_E] \\
&= \Pr[\neg\text{abort}_E]\Pr[\neg\text{abort}_K|\neg\text{abort}_E]\Pr[\neg\text{abort}_C|\neg\text{abort}_E] \\
&\geq \left[((1-\rho_2)(1-\rho_1)^{q_E} + \rho_2)\right] \cdot \left[(1-\rho_2)(1-\rho_1)^{q_E}\right] \cdot \\
&\quad \cdot \left[(1-1/p)(1-(1-\rho_1)^{q_E})\rho_2\right]
\end{aligned}$$

The third equality follows from the fact that the events abort_K and abort_C are independent. We note that $F(\rho_1, \rho_2) = ((1-\rho_2)(1-\rho_1)^{q_E} + \rho_2)(1-\rho_2)(1-\rho_1)^{q_E}(1-1/p)(1-(1-\rho_1)^{q_E})\rho_2$ is greater than 0 except when $\rho_1 = 0, \rho_1 = 1, \rho_2 = 0$ or $\rho_2 = 1$. Therefore, by choosing appropriate values for ρ_1 and ρ_2, we obtain $\text{Adv}_{\mathcal{B}_2}^{\text{CDH}} \geq \text{Adv}_{\mathcal{F}_2}^{\text{ABS}} \cdot \Omega(1)$, as desired. □

4.3   Admitting more General Signing Policies

The previous scheme admits only threshold signing policies. Let us consider now more general signing policies, not necessarily defined by any threshold. We consider $\mathbb{Z}_n$-monotone span programs [7]. A signing policy $(\mathcal{P}, \Gamma)$ is a $\mathbb{Z}_n$-monotone span program if there exist a $m_1 \times m_2$ matrix Ψ with entries in $\mathbb{Z}_n$, being $m_1 \geq |\mathcal{P}|$, and a function $\tau : \{1, \ldots, m_1\} \rightarrow \{1, \ldots, |\mathcal{P}|\}$ that associates each row of Ψ to an attribute in $\mathcal{P}$, such that

$$A \in \Gamma \iff \left(\exists \boldsymbol{\lambda} \in (\mathbb{Z}_n)^{m_1} : \boldsymbol{\lambda}\Psi = (1, 0, \ldots, 0)\right) \text{ and } \left(\forall j = 1, \ldots, m_1, \text{at}_{\tau(j)} \notin A \Rightarrow \lambda_j = 0\right)$$

An ℓ-threshold policy can be represented as a $\mathbb{Z}_n$-monotone span program if $\ell < p, \ell < q$, by considering Vandermonde-type matrices. We have to modify the Sign and Verify protocols of our threshold scheme in order to admit $\mathbb{Z}_n$-monotone span program signing policies. The signer has to convince the verifier that he possesses a secret key for a set A of authorized attributes, i.e., that there exists a vector $\boldsymbol{\lambda} \in (\mathbb{Z}_n)^{m_1}$ such that $\boldsymbol{\lambda}\Psi = (1, 0, \ldots, 0)$ and such that $\lambda_j = 0$ for any index $j \in \{1, \ldots, m_1\}$ for which $\text{at}_{\tau(j)} \notin A$. In order to guarantee the anonymity of the attributes, the signer will commit to the components λ_j of this vector $\boldsymbol{\lambda}$. In addition, NIWI proofs will be added in the signature to convince the verifier that the commitments are well-formed.

Namely, the signer will prove for all $at_i \in \mathcal{P}$ that there exist a value $\tilde{\lambda}_i \neq 0$ and an index $j \in \tau^{-1}(i)$ satisfying the equality $\lambda_j = \tilde{\lambda}_i f_i$. Remember that $f_i = 1$ if $at_i \in A$ and $f_i = 0$ otherwise, being A the authorized subset of attributes held by the signer. On the one hand, if $f_i = 1$, then $\lambda_j \neq 0$ for some $j \in \tau^{-1}(i)$ (we can assume this without loss of generality; otherwise, the attribute $at_i \in A$ would be useless, and $A - \{at_i\} \in \Gamma$). In this case, $\tilde{\lambda}_i = \lambda_j$ satisfies the previous equality. On the other hand, if $f_i = 0$ then $\lambda_j = 0$ for all $j \in \tau^{-1}(i)$, and any value $\tilde{\lambda}_i \in \mathbb{Z}_n^*$ satisfies the desired equality. Note that commitments $\mathsf{Com}(f_i)$ to the values f_i will have to be added to the signature, as well.

To prove that these values $\tilde{\lambda}_i$ are different to 0, the signer will prove that they are invertible. That is, he will prove that there exists $\mu_i \in \mathbb{Z}_n^*$ such that $\mu_i \tilde{\lambda}_i = 1$, for all $at_i \in \mathcal{P}$. The probability that $\tilde{\lambda}_i$ is different to zero but is not invertible is very small because n is the product of two large primes. Note that it would be more efficient to prove and check that the product of all the values $\tilde{\lambda}_i$ is invertible; this is not possible to do by using Groth-Sahai proofs, because they only apply to quadratic equations.

Summing up, given the monotone span program (Ψ, τ) defining the signing policy $(\mathcal{P}, \Gamma)$, and given the commitments $C_i = (H_1(at_i))^{f_i} h^{z_i}$ and $\mathsf{Com}(f_i)$, for each $at_i \in \mathcal{P}$, the signer makes NIWI proofs to convince the verifier that:

1. $\exists \boldsymbol{\lambda} \in (\mathbb{Z}_n)^{m_1}$ such that $\boldsymbol{\lambda}\Psi = (1, 0, \ldots, 0)$. Note that this means m_2 NIWI proofs, one for each component in this vector equality. We denote such proofs as $\{\pi_{\boldsymbol{\lambda},k}\}_{k=1}^{m_2}$.
2. $\exists \tilde{\lambda}_i \in \mathbb{Z}_n, \exists j \in \tau^{-1}(i)$ such that $\lambda_j = \tilde{\lambda}_i f_i$ for all $at_i \in \mathcal{P}$. We denote such proofs as $\{\pi_{\tilde{\lambda}_i}\}_{at_i \in \mathcal{P}}$, whose global length is linear in m_1.
3. $\exists \mu_i \in \mathbb{Z}_n^*$ such that $\mu_i \tilde{\lambda}_i = 1 \mod n$, for all $at_i \in \mathcal{P}$. We denote such proofs as $\{\pi_{\mu_i}\}_{at_i \in \mathcal{P}}$.
4. The commitment $\mathsf{Com}(f_i)$ and C_i commit to the same value, for all $at_i \in \mathcal{P}$. We denote such proofs as $\{\pi_{f_i}\}_{at_i \in \mathcal{P}}$.

The signatures that result from this process have the form

$$\sigma = \Big(\{C_i, \pi_i, \mathsf{Com}(f_i), \mathsf{Com}(\tilde{\lambda}_i), \mathsf{Com}(\lambda_i), \pi_{f_i}, \pi_{\lambda_i}, \pi_{\mu_i}\}_{at_i \in \mathcal{P}},$$

$$\{\pi_{\boldsymbol{\lambda},k}\}_{k=1}^{m_2}, \sigma_1, \sigma_2, \sigma_3, \mathsf{Com}(K_{id}), \mathsf{Com}(\sigma_{K_{id}}), \pi_{K_{id}}, \pi_\sigma \Big)$$

Therefore, the length of the signature depends linearly on the size $m_1 + m_2$ of the monotone span program Ψ. Using analogous arguments to those used for the threshold case, one can prove that the resulting attribute-based signature scheme enjoys the properties of unforgeability and non-linkability.

4.4   Security in the Standard Model

We have proved the security properties of our schemes in the random oracle model, but there are well-known techniques that can be applied to our schemes so that security can be proved in the standard model. The hash function H_1 is used to transform attributes into elements in $\mathbb{G}$. Since the universe of attributes $\tilde{\mathcal{P}}$ is chosen in the Setup algorithm, a different element $Q_i \in \mathbb{G}$ can be chosen at random and associated to each attribute $at_i \in \tilde{\mathcal{P}}$. These elements will be included in the public parameters params. In the security proofs, we would define $Q_i = g^{c_i}$ with some probability ρ and $Q_i = g_2^{c_i}$ with probability $1 - \rho$, for some random value $c_i \in \mathbb{Z}_n$ (as it is done in the proof of Lemma 2). The other hash function, H_2, is used to transform tuples $(M, \mathcal{P}, \Gamma)$ into elements of $\mathbb{G}$. A well-known solution to avoid the random oracle in this case, proposed by Waters in [15], is to consider a collusion resistant hash function $H : \{0,1\}^* \rightarrow \{0,1\}^m$ and elements $v_1, v_2, \ldots, v_m \in \mathbb{G}$, which are included in params. Then the value of $H_2(M, \mathcal{P}, \Gamma)$ is replaced with $\prod_{j=1}^{m} v_j^{H(M,\mathcal{P},\Gamma)_j}$, where $H(M, \mathcal{P}, \Gamma)_j$ denotes the j-th bit of $H(M, \mathcal{P}, \Gamma)$. In the security proof the elements $v_1, v_2, \ldots, v_m$ are chosen by algorithm $\mathcal{B}$ so that $\mathcal{B}$ knows their discrete logarithm with respect to g.

4.5 Prime Order Bilinear Groups

Our scheme uses composite order groups and the security is based (among others) on the subgroup decision assumption. Alternatively, we can consider a prime order symmetric bilinear group $(p, \mathbb{G}, \mathbb{G}_T, e, g)$, because Groth-Sahai proofs can be implemented there and revocation keys rk can be defined in this case, as well. The underlying hardness assumption is then the *decisional linear assumption*: given $(g^\alpha, g^\beta, g^{r\alpha}, g^{s\beta}, g^t)$ for random $\alpha, \beta, r, s \in \mathbb{Z}_p$ it is hard to tell whether $t = r + s$ or t is random. However, whereas in the composite order group setting both commitments and proofs consist of a single element, in the prime order group setting commitments and proofs consist of multiple elements (1 element for each variable, and 6 or 9 elements for each equation). Anyway, considering that computing a pairing has complexity of $O(n^3)$ in time, and that the size of composite order groups is about ten times larger than the size of prime order groups, the scheme in the prime order group setting might be more efficient. We have described our constructions in the setting of composite order groups, though, because this simplifies notation and understandability.

References

1. Abe, M., Fuchsbauer, G., Groth, J., Haralambiev, K., Ohkubo, M.: Structure-preserving signatures and commitments to group elements. In: Rabin, T. (ed.) CRYPTO 2010. LNCS, vol. 6223, pp. 209–236. Springer, Heidelberg (2010)
2. Bethencourt, J., Sahai, A., Waters, B.: Ciphertext-policy attribute-based encryption. In: Proc. of IEEE Symposium on Security and Privacy, pp. 321–334. IEEE Society Press, Los Alamitos (2007)
3. Goyal, V., Pandey, O., Sahai, A., Waters, B.: Attribute-based encryption for fine-grained access control of encrypted data. In: Proc. of Computer and Communications Security, CCS 2006, pp. 89–98. ACM Press, New York (2006)

4. Groth, J.: Fully anonymous group signatures without random oracles. In: Kurosawa, K. (ed.) ASIACRYPT 2007. LNCS, vol. 4833, pp. 164–180. Springer, Heidelberg (2007)

5. Groth, J., Ostrovsky, R., Sahai, A.: Perfect non-interactive zero knowledge for NP. In: Vaudenay, S. (ed.) EUROCRYPT 2006. LNCS, vol. 4004, pp. 339–358. Springer, Heidelberg (2006)

6. Groth, J., Sahai, A.: Efficient non-interactive proof systems for bilinear groups. In: Smart, N.P. (ed.) EUROCRYPT 2008. LNCS, vol. 4965, pp. 415–432. Springer, Heidelberg (2008)

7. Karchmer, M., Wigderson, A.: On span programs. In: Proc. of SCTC 1993, pp. 102–111. IEEE Computer Society Press, Los Alamitos (1993)

8. Lewko, A., Okamoto, T., Sahai, A., Takashima, K., Waters, B.: Fully secure functional encryption: Attribute-based encryption and (Hierarchical) inner product encryption. In: Gilbert, H. (ed.) EUROCRYPT 2010. LNCS, vol. 6110, pp. 62–91. Springer, Heidelberg (2010)

9. Li, J., Au, M.H., Susilo, W., Xie, D., Ren, K.: Attribute-based signature and its applications. In: Proc. of ASIACCS 2010, pp. 60–69. ACM Press, New York (2010)

10. Libert, B., Yung, M.: Efficient traceable signatures in the standard model. Theoretical Computer Science 412(12-14), 1220–1242 (2011)

11. Okamoto, T., Takashima, K.: Efficient attribute-based signatures for non-monotone predicates in the standard model. In: Catalano, D., Fazio, N., Gennaro, R., Nicolosi, A. (eds.) PKC 2011. LNCS, vol. 6571, pp. 35–52. Springer, Heidelberg (2011)

12. Maji, H.K., Prabhakaran, M., Rosulek, M.: Attribute-based signatures. In: Kiayias, A. (ed.) CT-RSA 2011. LNCS, vol. 6558, pp. 376–392. Springer, Heidelberg (2011)

13. Shacham, H., Waters, B.: Efficient ring signatures without random oracles. In: Okamoto, T., Wang, X. (eds.) PKC 2007. LNCS, vol. 4450, pp. 166–180. Springer, Heidelberg (2007)

14. Shahandashti, S.F., Safavi-Naini, R.: Threshold attribute-based signatures and their application to anonymous credential systems. In: Preneel, B. (ed.) AFRICACRYPT 2009. LNCS, vol. 5580, pp. 198–216. Springer, Heidelberg (2009)

15. Waters, B.: Efficient identity-based encryption without random oracles. In: Cramer, R. (ed.) EUROCRYPT 2005. LNCS, vol. 3494, pp. 114–127. Springer, Heidelberg (2005)

Using the Inhomogeneous Simultaneous Approximation Problem for Cryptographic Design

Frederik Armknecht[1], Carsten Elsner[2], and Martin Schmidt[3]

[1] Group for Theoretical Computer Science and Data Security,
Universität Mannheim, Germany
[2] FHDW Hannover, Germany
[3] Leibniz Universität Hannover, Institute of Applied Mathematics, Germany

Abstract. We introduce the Inhomogeneous Simultaneous Approximation Problem (ISAP), an old problem from the field of analytic number theory. Although the Simultaneous Approximation Problem (SAP) is already known in cryptography, it has mainly been considered in its *homogeneous* instantiation for *attacking* schemes. We take a look at the hardness and applicability of ISAP, i. e., the *inhomogeneous* variant, for *designing* schemes.

More precisely, we define a decisional problem related to ISAP, called DISAP, and show that it is NP-complete. With respect to its hardness, we review existing approaches for solving related problems and give suggestions for the efficient generation of hard instances. Regarding the applicability, we describe as a proof of concept a bit commitment scheme where the hiding property is directly reducible to DISAP. An implementation confirms its usability in principle (e. g., size of one commitment is 6273 bits and execution time is in the milliseconds).

1 Introduction

Motivation. The concept of provable security is one cornerstone of modern cryptography. The approach is to prove the security of a cryptographic scheme by reducing its security (in the sense of complexity theory) to another presumably hard problem. Consequently, there is a huge interest on finding appropriate problems. Although a variety of problems[1] have been considered in the recent decades, only few of them turned out to be useful for cryptographic design and to allow for an easy generation of hard instances. Mainly these are connected to factorization, discrete logarithm, lattices, pairings, or error-correcting codes. Here, we would like to advert to *analytic* number theory, more precisely to the field of diophantine analysis. The adjective "diophantine" means that one is interested in integral or rational solutions. This field emerged around 250 A. D. and had

---

[1] See the website
`www.ecrypt.eu.org/wiki/index.php/Hard_Problems_in_Cryptography` for an overview.

A. Nitaj and D. Pointcheval (Eds.): AFRICACRYPT 2011, LNCS 6737, pp. 242–259, 2011.

since then attracted the interest of many important and influential mathematicians like Gauss or the Fields medal winners Roth, Baker, and Faltings. Despite the enormous progress, diophantine analysis is still full of open (computational) problems. As a representative, we investigate the Simultaneous Approximation Problem or more precisely its inhomogeneous variant: Given rational numbers α_i and η_i, $i = 1, \ldots, n$, find integer values q and p_i such that $|q\alpha_i - p_i - \eta_i| < \varepsilon$. The most common variant is the homogeneous one, i.e., $\eta_i = 0$ for all i, whereas our contribution is to consider for the first time the inhomogeneous variant, i.e., $\eta_i \neq 0$, for cryptographic design. To be in compliance with established notation, we refer to the homogenous Simultaneous Approximation Problem simply by SAP and denote the inhomogenous variant by ISAP.

Related Work. SAP is known in cryptography, but has mainly been considered for *attacking* cryptosystems, e.g., knapsack systems (e.g., Shamir [28], Estes et al. [12]), factorization and discrete logarithm (e.g., see Schnorr [23], Seifert [27]), and RSA (e.g., see Wiener [32]).

Regarding the *design* of cryptosystems, we are only aware of very few works that base their security on SAP or related problems. Isselhorst [9] presented a public-key scheme based on fractions. He showed that the scheme could be broken in principle by solving an appropriate simultaneous approximation problem. He proposed parameters for which he suspected that the algorithm of Lagarias [13] is not capable of finding a solution. Nonetheless, the scheme was broken soon after by Stern and Toffin [29] using the LLL algorithm [14] instead. Elsner and Schmidt [4] used continued fractions to design new S-boxes. In both cases, there was no direct reduction of the security of the scheme to the hardness of solving (I)SAP.

Regev [19] presented a public key cryptosystem where the public key contains rational numbers a_i that are close to integer multiples of N/h where N and h are some integers and h is the secret key. Obviously, the ability of solving SAP would allow for breaking the scheme. Indeed, it seems that the scheme uses special SAP instances: the public key includes explicitly an index i_0 such that a_{i_0} is an *odd* multiple of N/h.

Van Dijk et al. [31] used the Approximate Greatest Common Divisor (approximate GCD) Problem for constructing a fully homomorphic encryption scheme. This problem is related to SAP in the following sense. In SAP, a set of rational numbers α_i and some bound $B < 1$ is given and the task is to find integers q and p_i such that $|q \cdot \alpha_i - p_i| < B$ for all i. In approximate GCD, a set of *integer* values α_i and some *integer* bound $1 \leq B$ is given and the task is to find integers q and p_i such that $|\alpha_i - q \cdot p_i| < B$ for all i. The authors pointed out that their scheme could be attacked by solving an appropriate SAP instance.

Both works seem to be related to (probably special instances) of SAP, that is the homogenous approximation problem. To the best of our knowledge the usage of ISAP, i.e., the inhomogeneous variant, for cryptographic design has not been considered so far. Here, we have to stress that our contribution is not the design of a specific scheme but rather to show up the general *hardness* and *applicability* of ISAP.

Contribution. In this paper, we put for the first time ISAP into the heart of a cryptosystem. Our contributions are as follows:

Problem Description: We formalize the Decisional Inhomogeneous Simultaneous Approximation Problem (DISAP) and show that it is NP-complete. Furthermore, we explain that while SAP represents in principle the shortest vector problem (SVP) in certain lattices, the inhomogeneous variant ISAP is equivalent to the closest vector problem (CVP).

Instance Generation: We investigate a related computational problem and deduce the conjecture that increasing/decreasing certain parameters will probably increase the hardness of the problem and formulate an accordant assumption. With respect to the connection to lattices, a possibly interesting fact is that besides the dimension another parameter exists for adjusting the hardness. In certain cases, this might provide a higher flexibility for creating hard instances and eventually more efficient solutions. Furthermore, we derive suggestions for concrete parameter ranges.

Cryptographic Application: We demonstrate the usefulness of DISAP for cryptographic applications by constructing a bit commitment scheme on it. The scheme is perfectly binding and computationally hiding if hard DISAP instances are used. An implementation confirms its usability in principle (e. g., size of one commitment is 6273 bits and execution time is in the milliseconds).

Summing up, we demonstrate that DISAP might be a valuable addition to the existing set of established problems in cryptography and hope to encourage further research on problems from analytic number theory in general and DISAP in particular.

Organization. In Sec. 2, we present DISAP and discuss its hardness. In addition, we define and motivate an appropriate hardness assumption, named DISAP hardness assumption. In Sec. 3, we describe a bit commitment scheme based on DISAP. The binding property is proven in Sec. 4 and the hiding property is proven in Sec. 5 under the DISAP hardness assumption. In Sec. 6, we present a concrete instantiation and give implementation results. Sec. 7 concludes the paper.

2   The (Inhomogeneous) Simultaneous Approximation Problem

2.1   Motivation

In this section we give a short introduction to the main terms of rational diophantine approximation and motivate and define the Inhomogeneous Simultaneous Approximation Problem (ISAP) and variants.

In the following, $\mathbb{N}$ will denote the set of positive integers, $\mathbb{Z}$ the ring of integers, $\mathbb{Q}$ the field of rational numbers, and $\mathbb{R}$ the field of real numbers. We will distinguish between single values and vectors by putting the latter in bold.

In diophantine analysis the approximation of numbers $\alpha \in \mathbb{R}$ by rationals $p/q \in \mathbb{Q}$ is a main topic.[2] One of the most basic results is the approximation theorem of Dirichlet (1805–1859) [8, Theorem 185], which states that for any $\alpha \in \mathbb{R} \setminus \mathbb{Q}$ there exist infinitely many co-prime numbers p and q such that

$$\left| \alpha - \frac{p}{q} \right| < \frac{1}{q^2} \iff |q\alpha - p| < \frac{1}{q}. \tag{1}$$

If $\alpha \in \mathbb{Q}$, the number of solutions might be finite only. A theorem of Hurwitz (1859–1919) [8, Theorem 193] states that for every $\alpha \in \mathbb{R} \setminus \mathbb{Q}$ there exist infinitely many co-prime numbers p and q such that

$$\left| \alpha - \frac{p}{q} \right| < \frac{1}{\sqrt{5}q^2} \tag{2}$$

holds and that for any stronger approximation quality, the number of solutions might be finite only. Interestingly, such approximations can be efficiently computed, using *continued fractions*

$$a_0 + \cfrac{1}{a_1 + \cfrac{1}{a_2 + \cfrac{1}{\cdots + \cfrac{1}{a_N}}}} \tag{3}$$

where the leading coefficient a_0 is an integer and all *partial quotients* a_i ($i = 1, \ldots, N$) are positive integers. It can be shown that for $N \to \infty$ the above given expression converges to some real number α depending on all partial quotients a_i. In that case we call the expression an *infinite continued fraction*, or simply *continued fraction*. For $\alpha \in \mathbb{Q}$, the corresponding continued fraction is *finite* like in (3).

An important term is a *convergent*, which is a rational number. Given the partial quotients of the continued fraction, the corresponding convergents can easily be computed using the recurrence formulas (see [8, Theorem 149])

$$p_0 = a_0, \quad p_1 = a_1 a_0 + 1, \quad p_n = a_n p_{n-1} + p_{n-2} \quad (n \geq 2), \tag{4}$$
$$q_0 = 1, \quad q_1 = a_1, \quad q_n = a_n q_{n-1} + q_{n-2} \quad (n \geq 2). \tag{5}$$

p_n/q_n is called the n-th convergent of the continued fraction. Observe that computing the n-th convergent requires $2n$ additions and multiplications of integers. It can be shown that (for irrational α or, if $\alpha \in \mathbb{Q}$, $n < N$)

$$\frac{1}{q_n(q_n + q_{n+1})} \leq \left| \alpha - \frac{p_n}{q_n} \right| \leq \frac{1}{q_n q_{n+1}} \leq \frac{1}{q_n^2} \tag{6}$$

holds (see [16, Chapter 10.2]). We note that from (6) it follows that the convergents satisfy inequality (1) of Dirichlet's theorem. Furthermore, it is proven

---

[2] Nice introductions to this discipline can be found in [8,16].

that the convergents are the best rational approximations with a bounded denominator, e. g., for $\alpha \in \mathbb{R}, n > 1, 0 < q \le q_n$ and $p_n/q_n \ne p/q$ it holds (see [8, Theorem 181])

$$\left| \alpha - \frac{p_n}{q_n} \right| < \left| \alpha - \frac{p}{q} \right| . \tag{7}$$

It is useful to know that p_n and q_n are co-prime for all convergents.

The type of approximation in (1) is called *homogeneous* in contrast to the inhomogeneous case, for which Kronecker (1823–1891) proved the following theorem (see [20, Chapter 10, Theorem 2.6]).

Theorem 1 (Kronecker's Approximation Theorem). *For each $\alpha \in \mathbb{R} \setminus \mathbb{Q}$, $\eta \in \mathbb{R}$, $n > 0$ and $\delta \in \mathbb{R}$ with $\delta > 0$ there are integers p, q with $q > n$ such that*

$$|q\alpha - p - \eta| < \left(\frac{1}{2} + \frac{1}{\sqrt{5}} + \delta \right) \frac{1}{q} . \tag{8}$$

Thereby η is called the *inhomogeneity*.

In the field of *simultaneous* diophantine approximation one considers more than one diophantine inequality at once and tries to approximate the given numbers α_i with fractions p_i/q sharing a common denominator. Again, the most basic result was proved by Dirichlet (see [8, Theorem 200]): There are infinitely many solutions $(q, p_1, \ldots, p_n)$ to the system

$$\left| \alpha_i - \frac{p_i}{q} \right| < \frac{1}{q^{1+1/n}} , \quad \forall i \in \{1, \ldots, n\} , \tag{9}$$

in positive integers q and integers $p_1, \ldots, p_n$ if at least one of the real numbers $\alpha_1, \ldots, \alpha_n$ is irrational. An inhomogeneous generalization about the existence of simultaneous approximations was also proved by Kronecker (see [8, Theorem 442]):

Theorem 2 (Kronecker's Simultaneous Approximation Theorem). *Let $1, \alpha_1, \ldots, \alpha_n$ be real numbers that are linearly independent over $\mathbb{Q}$. Furthermore, let $\eta_1, \ldots, \eta_n$ be arbitrary real numbers, $\varepsilon > 0$ and $N \in \mathbb{N}$. Then there exists integers $p_1, \ldots, p_n$ and a natural number q with $q > N$ and*

$$|q\alpha_i - p_i - \eta_i| < \varepsilon \quad \forall i \in \{1, \ldots, n\} . \tag{10}$$

2.2   Definition

We remark that the one-dimensional theorems from the previous subsection can all be proved in a constructive manner by using continued fractions and convergents. However, as opposed to the one-dimensional case, no constructive proofs are known for the multi-dimensional versions. This has lead to the formulation of a variety of related problems, e. g. [13], for some it has been proven that they are NP-complete. Nevertheless, some of them have never been successfully used for cryptographic applications. The main goal of this paper is to actually remind of these and to choose one concrete problem formulation, termed decisional inhomogenous approximation problem (DISAP), and demonstrate a possible cryptographic application.

Next, we make DISAP (and variants) precise. Although our focus will be on DISAP, the consideration of other variants is helpful for assessing the hardness and generation of DISAP instances.

Definition 1 ((Inhomogeneous) Simultaneous Approximation Problem).
An instance I of the Inhomogeneous Simultaneous Approximation Problem *(ISAP) consists of a vector $\boldsymbol{\alpha} := (\alpha_1, \ldots, \alpha_n) \in (\mathbb{Q}^*)^n$ of non-zero rational values, a vector $\boldsymbol{\eta} := (\eta_1, \ldots, \eta_n) \in \mathbb{Q}^n$, a positive real value $\varepsilon \in \mathbb{R}_{>0}$, and a positive integer $N \in \mathbb{N}$.*

A tuple $(q, \boldsymbol{p})$ where $q \in \mathbb{N}_{>0}$ and $\boldsymbol{p} = (p_1, \ldots, p_n) \in \mathbb{Z}^n$ is a solution to I if

$$|q\alpha_i - p_i - \eta_i| < \varepsilon \quad \forall i \in \{1, \ldots, n\} \quad and \quad q \leq N. \tag{11}$$

The value n is called the dimension, *and ε the* approximation quality. *In the case that $\eta_i = 0$ for all i, that is in the homogeneous case, we call the problem simply the* Simultaneous Approximation Problem *(SAP).*

A variant of (I)SAP is where the approximation quality is not fixed but depends on the solution q. To distinguish these variants, we refer to the latter by (I)SAP*. More precisely, an instance I of ISAP* consists of a vector $\boldsymbol{\alpha} := (\alpha_1, \ldots, \alpha_n) \in (\mathbb{Q}^*)^n$ of non-zero rational values, a vector $\boldsymbol{\eta} := (\eta_1, \ldots, \eta_n) \in \mathbb{Q}^n$, a positive real value $\Delta \in \mathbb{R}_{>0}$, and a positive integer $N \in \mathbb{N}$.

A tuple $(q, \boldsymbol{p})$ where $q \in \mathbb{N}_{>0}$ and $\boldsymbol{p} = (p_1, \ldots, p_n) \in \mathbb{Z}^n$ is a solution to I if

$$\left| \alpha_i - \frac{p_i + \eta_i}{q} \right| < \frac{1}{q^\Delta} \quad \forall i \in \{1, \ldots, n\} \quad and \quad q \leq N. \tag{12}$$

The value Δ is called the approximation order.

As customary, we will consider computational *and* decisional *variants of the above problems. In the computational variant, the goal is to compute a solution while in the decisional variant, the task is to decide whether at least one solution does exist. We indicate these problems by prepending the letter "C" or "D", respectively. For example, CISAP and DISAP refer to the computational and decisional variants of ISAP, respectively. Analoguesly, we will define CSAP, DSAP, CISAP*, DISAP*, CSAP*, and DSAP*.*

Although the dimension n is implicitly given by the dimension of the vectors $\boldsymbol{\alpha}$ and $\boldsymbol{\eta}$, we note it explicitly for reasons of clarity. Observe that we restrict to rational and integer values on purpose: Working in practice with irrational numbers effectively means in most cases to approximate them anyway by rational numbers.

Before we formulate and investigate an appropriate hardness assumption, we point out some similarities between the (inhomogeneous) approximation problem and known problems from lattice theory. Recall that a lattice $\mathcal{L}$ is a discrete subgroup of $\mathbb{R}^n$ which can be expressed by

$$\mathcal{L} = \left\{ \sum_{i=1}^d \lambda_i \cdot \boldsymbol{b_i} \mid \{\lambda_1, \ldots, \lambda_d\} \subset \mathbb{Z} \right\} \tag{13}$$

for an appropriate (non-unique) basis $\{\boldsymbol{b_1}, \ldots, \boldsymbol{b_d}\} \subset \mathbb{R}^n$. Consider the $\|\cdot\|_\infty$ norm, that is $\|\boldsymbol{x}\|_\infty = \max_i |x_i|$ for a vector $\boldsymbol{x} = (x_1, \ldots, x_n) \in \mathbb{R}^n$. Two famous problems in the context of a lattice $\mathcal{L}$ are the *shortest vector problem* (SVP) and the *closest vector problem* (CVP). Informally, the SVP is to find a vector $\boldsymbol{v} \in \mathcal{L}$ such that $\|\boldsymbol{v}\|_\infty$ is minimal (or beyond a certain bound). Similarly, for the CVP a target vector $\boldsymbol{w} \in \mathbb{R}^n$ is given and the task is to find a vector $\boldsymbol{v} \in \mathcal{L}$ such that $\|\boldsymbol{w} - \boldsymbol{v}\|_\infty$ is minimal (or beyond a certain bound). Goldreich, Micciancio, Safra and Seifert [7] showed that any algorithm to efficiently approximate CVP can be used to efficiently approximate SVP within the same approximation factor and with essentially the same computational effort, formalizing the intuition that CVP is not an easier (and is a possibly harder) problem than SVP.

Now let an ISAP instance $I := (\boldsymbol{\alpha}, \boldsymbol{\eta}, N, n, \varepsilon)$ be given. We define the vectors $\boldsymbol{b_1} := (\varepsilon/N, \alpha_1, \ldots, \alpha_n)^t \in \mathbb{R}^{n+1}$ and for $i = 2, \ldots, n+1$ the vector $\boldsymbol{b_i}$ to be the i-th negative unit vector which is zero everywhere except of position i where the entry is equal to -1. As $\varepsilon \neq 0$, the vectors $\boldsymbol{b_i}$ are linearly independent. Let $\mathcal{L}$ be the lattice defined from $\boldsymbol{b_1}, \ldots, \boldsymbol{b_{n+1}}$ as specified in Eq. (13).

Furthermore, we define a matrix $M := (\boldsymbol{b_1}|\ldots|\boldsymbol{b_{n+1}}) \in \mathbb{R}^{n+1 \times n+1}$. Let $\boldsymbol{s} := (q, p_1, \ldots, p_n) \in \mathbb{Z}^{n+1}$ where $q \in \mathbb{N}_{>0}$ and $(p_1, \ldots, p_n) \in \mathbb{Z}^n$ and define $\boldsymbol{v} := M\boldsymbol{s}$. Obviously, it holds that $\boldsymbol{v} \in \mathcal{L}$.

Consider first the homogeneous case, that is $\boldsymbol{\eta} = \boldsymbol{0}$. One can easily compute that $\|\boldsymbol{v}\|_\infty < \varepsilon$ if and only if $\boldsymbol{s}$ is a solution to SAP. In other words, solving the SAP is equivalent to solving the SVP with a fixed bound ε in $\mathcal{L}$. Similar holds for the imhomogeneous case, i.e., $\boldsymbol{\eta} \neq \boldsymbol{0}$. At this end, we define $\boldsymbol{w} := (0, \eta_1, \ldots, \eta_n)$. Then it holds that $\boldsymbol{s}$ is a solution to ISAP if and only if it is a solution to the CVP within $\mathcal{L}$ with respect to the target vector $\boldsymbol{w}$.

Summing up, SAP resp. ISAP can be interpreted as the SVP resp. CVP in specific lattices. As CVP seems to be harder than SVP and as generating ISAP instances allows for a higher degree of freedom than generating SAP instances (because of the η_i values), it is a natural question if and how ISAP can be used for constructing cryptographic schemes.

2.3   Hardness Assumption

Next, we show that the problem class of DISAP contains indeed hard instances, i.e., instances where no efficient solving algorithms are known so far.

Theorem 3 (NP-Completeness). *DISAP is NP-complete.*

Proof. We have to show that (i) DISAP is in NP, and (ii) every problem in NP is reducible to DISAP in polynomial time. The first claim is trivial. Given an DISAP instance $(\boldsymbol{\alpha}, \boldsymbol{\eta}, N, n, \varepsilon)$ and a possible solution $(q, \boldsymbol{p})$, one can check in polynomial time (i.e., polynomial in the length of the input) whether (11) is fulfilled. For the second claim, we make use of Lagarias' result [13]. He showed that DSAP is NP-complete (the problem was named "Good Simultaneous Approximation Problem (GSA)" there). That is, any NP problem can be reduced (in polynomial time) to an instance of DSAP. As any instance of DSAP is an instance of DISAP as well, it follows directly that any NP problem can be reduced in polynomial time to an instance of DISAP.   □

Still, it remains to clarify how to generate hard instances. For this purpose, we review existing work on one problem variant: CSAP*. There are several algorithms in the literature to solve CSAP*. In the case of real algebraic and over $\mathbb{Q}$ linear independent numbers $1, \alpha_1, \ldots, \alpha_n$ and $\delta^* > 0$ arbitrary, W. Schmidt shows in [22] that there are at most finitely many $(q, \boldsymbol{p}) \in \mathbb{N} \times \mathbb{Z}^n$ with

$$\left| \alpha_i - \frac{p_i}{q} \right| < \frac{1}{q^{1+1/n+\delta^*}} \quad \forall i \in \{1, \ldots, n\} . \tag{14}$$

Furthermore, with $\delta^* = 0$, under these conditions the approximation order $\Delta = 1 + 1/n$ is the best possible.

There are a lot of generalizations of continued fractions for the simultaneous case, starting with the work of Jacobi [10] which lead to the Jacobi-Perron-Algorithm (JPA) [18,26,24,2,6]. However, the JPA is not able to compute solutions to such approximation quality as we will require in our proposed commitment scheme (cf. Sec. 3). For example, in the case $n = 2$ only a system with an approximation quality of $2/q^{3/2}$ is attackable with the JPA (cf. [26]). In [26] it is also mentioned that the JPA is only able to solve systems with significantly larger ε in the arbitrary case ($n \geq 3$). In particular, the best affordable approximation quality ε increases with the dimension n. Additionally, we want to mention Baldwin's numerical experiments [1] in which he computes the approximation order of the JPA in two dimensions – with $\Delta = 1.374$ it is significantly below the upper bound $1 + 1/2 = 1.5$ from theory.

There are some other relevant algorithms based on continued fraction generalizations, namely the ones of Güting, Brun, and Selmer (cf. [26]), and Just [11]. The first three ones have comparable properties like the JPA (see [26,3,25,30]). Just's algorithm is much more worse concerning the approximation order ($\Delta = 1 + 1/(2n(n+1))$) [11]. Thus, the above given considerations about the JPA can also be applied to these algorithms.

Another well known algorithm for solving simultaneous diophantine approximation problems is the lattice-based LLL algorithm presented by Lenstra, Lenstra Jr. and Lovasz in [14]. The LLL algorithm is able to find solutions nearly as good as the best possible. Indeed, they can compute solutions $(q, \boldsymbol{p})$ such that

$$\left| \alpha_i - \frac{p_i}{q} \right| \leq \frac{c(n)}{q^{1+1/n}} \quad \forall i \in \{1, \ldots, n\} , \tag{15}$$

whereas the α_i have to be rationals and $c(n) \in \mathcal{O}(2^n)$ (see [14], [17, Chapter 6, Theorem 8]). Thus, by choosing small enumerators for the upper bound, e. g., $= 1$ in our construction, one can construct instances that fall outside of the parameter ranges that can be solved by LLL.

We conclude with the theoretical work of Lagarias. In [13] he proved that the problem of computing a denominator q such that

$$|q\alpha_i - p_i| \leq s_1/s_2 , \quad 1 \leq q \leq N , \quad \forall i \in \{1, \ldots, n\} , \tag{16}$$

for given positive integers N, s_1, s_2 and rational numbers $\alpha_i = a_i/b_i$ is in P for fixed dimension n. We remark that this technique has an exponential runtime in the dimension n. Thus, increasing n is a simple method for excluding the applicability of Lagarias' algorithm.

Summing up, no efficient algorithms are known for solving CSAP* with an approximation order of $\Delta \geq 1 + 1/n$ if the dimension is high enough. Motivated by this observation, we introduce the according assumption: increasing the dimension n and/or chosing a sharper approximation quality ε, i.e., decreasing this value, can make the problem only harder:

Definition 2 ($\mathcal{P}$ Hardness Assumption). *Let $\mathcal{P}$ denote one of the problems defined in Def. 1. W.l.o.g., we focus on a problem with a fixed approximation quality.[3] Consider a probabilistic polynomial-time (PPT) algorithm* Gen *that on input $N \in \mathbb{N}_{>0}$, $n \in \mathbb{N}_{>0}$, and $\varepsilon \in \mathbb{R}_{>0}$ generates a $\mathcal{P}$ instance I.*

Let $\mathcal{I}$ denote the set of all possible $\mathcal{P}$ instances that can be generated by Gen *and let $\mathcal{A}$ denote a PPT algorithm that on input of $I \in \mathcal{I}$ outputs a solution. We define by $\mathsf{Adv}_{\mathsf{Gen},\mathcal{A}}(N, n, \varepsilon)$ the advantage of $\mathcal{A}$, being the difference between the probabilities that $\mathcal{A}$ outputs a correct solution and that it outputs a wrong solution.[4]*

The $\mathcal{P}$ hardness assumption (with respect to Gen*) states that for any positive integer $s \in \mathbb{N}_{>0}$, being the security parameter, there exist thresholds $N^* = N^*(s) \in \mathbb{N}_{>0}$, $n^* = n^*(s) \in \mathbb{N}_{>0}$ and $\varepsilon^* = \varepsilon^*(s) \in \mathbb{R}_{>0}$ such that $\mathsf{Adv}_{\mathsf{Gen},\mathcal{A}}(N, n, \varepsilon)$ is negligible in s for all PPT $\mathcal{A}$ if $N \geq N^*$, $n \geq n^*$, and $0 < \varepsilon \leq \varepsilon^*$.*

Remark 1. Observe that most strategies for creating hard lattice instances involve only one parameter for increasing the hardness: the dimension n. Here, the situation is different as the hardness can be increased by increasing the dimension and/or the approximation quality/order. This gives more freedom in selecting suitable instances and possibly allows for more efficient implementations. Indeed, we will show later that it is in fact possible to generate problem instances with an *arbitrary* approximation quality where the solution is known to the generator. At this end, we will make use of the inhomogenous variant.

3   A Bit Commitment Scheme Based on DISAP

In this section, we present a bit commitment scheme based on DISAP. In the commitment phase, the committer generates an instance of DISAP with a given dimension and approximation quality. The crucial aspect here is that the problem instance is constructed *backwards*. That is the committer first starts with

---

[3] The adaptation of the hardness assumption for the variant using an approximation order is straightforward.

[4] More precisely, in the case of a computational problem $\mathcal{P}$, $\mathcal{A}$ outputs a possible solution, while in the case of a decision problem the output is one bit. For the sake of brevity, we omit a full-formal definition here as these notions are standard by now.

the solution (q, p) that is connected to the message and then generates a problem instance (α, η) from it where (q, p) is the unique solution. For this purpose, we strongly make use of the inhomogeneity η. Observe that the generation procedure allows for choosing the parameters outside the range that is feasible for the algorithms described in Sec. 2.3 in the *normal* direction and ensures that the instances are of the form as required in the security proofs in Sec. 4 and 5. Regarding the security, as only one solution exists, the scheme is perfectly binding. Furthermore, the commitment scheme is computationally hiding if the DISAP assumption holds.

Setup Phase. In the setup phase, an algorithm

$$\mathcal{P} := (N, \varepsilon, n, \mu) \leftarrow \mathsf{Setup}(s) \tag{17}$$

is executed. The purpose of this algorithm is to fix in dependence of a security parameter s the bound N, the approximation quality ε, the dimension n, and an upper bound[5] μ on the denominators of η for DISAP instances that will be used in the other phases of the commitment scheme. Starting from the DISAP assumption (Def. 2), these are chosen such that $N \geq N^*(s)$, $\varepsilon \leq \varepsilon^*(s)$ and $n \geq n^*(s)$ where $N^*(s)$, $\varepsilon^*(s)$, and $n^*(s)$ are the thresholds conjectured in the DISAP assumption. We will discuss concrete parameter choices later in Sec. 6. For example, we will fix $N := 2^s$ to avoid brute force guessing attacks.

Commitment Phase. In this phase, the committer generates a commitment for a message $m \in \{0, 1\}$. The commitment algorithm has the following format:

$$((\alpha, \eta), (q, p)) \leftarrow \mathsf{Commit}_{\mathcal{P}}(m) \tag{18}$$

where $(\alpha, \eta, N, n, \varepsilon)$ specifies an instance of DISAP as defined in Def. 1 and (q, p) is a solution to this instance. The tuple (α, η) represents the commitment to the message m which is made public. The tuple (q, p) represents the opening information and is kept secret. The value q is constructed in such a way that its least significant bit (LSB) is equal to the message m.

The commitment algorithm is depicted in Alg. 1. During an execution, a series of values are generated that have to fulfill certain conditions. For the sake of clarity, we separated in the description of Alg. 1 the value generation and the testing of the parameters. In real implementations, one would group this steps together to reduce the number of trials. For example, if parameter generation fails for one index i, one could retry other values for this index but still use the values generated for indices $j < i$. We have to point out that it is not mathematically guaranteed that all conditions can be met. However, this was straightaway the case in almost all of our simulations (see Sec. 6 for details). Furthermore, in all other cases a small number of repetitions was sufficient to find values that fulfill the conditions.

---

[5] The reason for the upper bound on the denominators will be explained later in the context of the security proofs.

Finally, some words on the conditions themselves. The condition $\frac{1}{\sqrt{\varepsilon}} < d_i$ (Eq. (19)) is introduced to achieve the claimed approximation quality with the given solution. The other part of the same inequality, $d_i < b_i$, is used to guarantee that the approximation c_i/d_i does not give $q \cdot a_i/b_i$ again. The last conditions, given in Eq. (20), ensures that the value q is uniquely determined, making the scheme perfectly binding.

Opening Phase. To open the commitment, the committer sends the solution $(q, \boldsymbol{p})$ to the verifier. The verifier runs the algorithm

$$\text{out} \leftarrow \text{Verify}_{\mathcal{P}}\left((\boldsymbol{\alpha}, \boldsymbol{\eta}), (q, \boldsymbol{p})\right) \tag{21}$$

where $\text{out} \in \{\text{accept}, \perp\}$. The verifier accepts if $\text{out} = \text{accept}$ and rejects otherwise. The algorithm $\text{Verify}_{\mathcal{P}}$ outputs accept if and only if

1. $q \leq N$
2. $|q\alpha_i - p_i - \eta_i| < \varepsilon$ for all $i \in \{1, \ldots, n\}$
3. There exists an index $i^* \in \{1, \ldots, n\}$ such that $N < b_{i^*}$ and $\sqrt{2b_{i^*}} < d_{i^*}$ (see Eq. (20)). Observe that the values b_i are part of the commitment and the values d_i can be computed from η_i and p_i by using that c_i and d_i are co-prime (see Sec. 2.1).

Correctness. The correctness of the scheme follows directly from condition $\frac{1}{\sqrt{\varepsilon}} < d_i$ (see Eq. (19)) given in Alg. 1. For any $i \in \{1, \ldots, n\}$, it holds that

$$|q\alpha_i - p_i - \eta_i| = \left|q\alpha_i - p_i - \left(\frac{c_i}{d_i} - p_i\right)\right| = \left|q\alpha_i - \frac{c_i}{d_i}\right| \overset{(6)}{\leq} \frac{1}{d_i^2} \overset{(19)}{<} \varepsilon. \tag{22}$$

4   Binding Property

In this section, we prove that q is uniquely determined by the commitment $(\boldsymbol{\alpha}, \boldsymbol{\eta})$. Thus, the scheme is perfectly binding.

Theorem 4 (Binding). *The commitment scheme is perfectly binding.*

Proof. Assume two solutions $(q, \boldsymbol{p})$ and $(q', \boldsymbol{p}')$. (20) ensures the existence of an index i^* such that $N < b_{i^*}$ and $\sqrt{2b_{i^*}} < d_{i^*}$. We omit the index i^* in the following. By definition it holds that $\eta = \frac{c}{d} - p$ and $\eta = \frac{c'}{d'} - p'$ for some appropriate integers c, d, c', d' and in particular $\frac{c}{d} - \frac{c'}{d'} \in \mathbb{Z}$. Therefore, there exists an integer $z \in \mathbb{Z}$ such that

$$\frac{c}{d} - \frac{c'}{d'} = z \iff cd' - c'd = zdd'. \tag{23}$$

It follows that $cd' - c'd \equiv 0 \pmod{d}$, $cd' \equiv 0 \pmod{d}$, and $d' \equiv 0 \pmod{d}$. The latter holds as c and d are co-prime (see Sec. 2.1). Analogously, one shows that $d \equiv 0 \pmod{d'}$. As both d and d' are positive, we get $d = d'$. Now recall that the fractions $\frac{c}{d}$ and $\frac{c'}{d}$ are both approximations of $q \cdot \frac{a}{b}$ and $q' \cdot \frac{a}{b}$, respectively, stemming from continued fractions. With (6) we have

---

Algorithm 1. The commitment algorithm $\mathsf{Commit}_{\mathcal{P}}$

Input: $\mathcal{P} = (N, \varepsilon, n, \mu)$ with approximation quality ε, dimension n, and upper bound μ; a message $m \in \{0, 1\}$

Output: A commitment on m

1: //**Map the message**

2: Extend $m \in \{0, 1\}$ to a s-bit value q, that is $[q]_2 = (r_{s-1}, \ldots, r_1, m)$ with $r_i \xleftarrow{\$} \{0, 1\}$. $[q]_2$ denotes the bit representation of q. This implies $0 \leq q < 2^s =: N$.

3: //**Generate rational numbers** $\alpha_i := \frac{a_i}{b_i}$

4: **for** $i = 1, \ldots, n$ **do**

5:     Choose co-prime integers a_i and b_i where b_i is odd, co-prime to q, and less than or equal to μ.

6:     Set $\alpha_i := \frac{a_i}{b_i}$.

7: **end for**

8: //**Generate approximations** $\frac{c_i}{d_i}$ **of** $q \cdot \frac{a_i}{b_i}$

9: **for** $i = 1, \ldots, n$ **do**

10:    Use continued fractions to find an approximation of $\frac{c_i}{d_i}$ of $q \cdot \frac{a_i}{b_i}$ such that

$$\frac{1}{\sqrt{\varepsilon}} < d_i < b_i . \qquad (19)$$

11:    If (19) is not satisfiable, restart at line 3.

12: **end for**

13: //**Check additional condition**

14: Beside the conditions given above, we require the existence of an index $i^* \in \{1, \ldots, n\}$ with

$$N < b_{i^*} \quad \text{and} \quad \sqrt{2b_{i^*}} < d_{i^*} . \qquad (20)$$

15: If (20) is not satisfiable, restart at line 3.

16: //**Generate** p **and** η

17: **for** $i = 1, \ldots, n$ **do**

18:    Choose $p_i \in \mathbb{Z}$ arbitrary

19:    Set $\eta_i := \frac{c_i}{d_i} - p_i$

20: **end for**

21: **return**   A (public) commitment $(\boldsymbol{\alpha}, \boldsymbol{\eta})$ to m and (secret) opening information $(q, \boldsymbol{p})$

$$\left| q \cdot \frac{a}{b} - \frac{c}{d} \right| < \frac{1}{d^2} \quad \text{and} \quad \left| q' \cdot \frac{a}{b} - \frac{c'}{d} \right| < \frac{1}{d^2} \tag{24}$$

and in particular

$$\left| (q - q') \frac{a}{b} - z \right| < \frac{2}{d^2} \iff \left| (q - q') a - z \cdot b \right| < \frac{2b}{d^2}. \tag{25}$$

Recall that $\sqrt{2b} < d$ by Eq. (20). Thus, the right hand side of (25) is strictly less than 1 while the left hand side is an integer value. This immediately implies that $(q - q')a - z \cdot b = 0$. As a and b are co-prime, it follows that

$$q - q' \equiv 0 \pmod{b}. \tag{26}$$

With $0 \le q, q' < N$, we have $-N < q - q' < N$. By Eq. (20), it holds that $b > N$. Thus, (26) actually implies $q - q' = 0 \Leftrightarrow q = q'$.   □

5   Hiding Property

5.1   Proof

In this section, we prove that the commitment scheme is computationally hiding. Recall that this means that no efficient algorithm exists that can decide for a given commitment $(\boldsymbol{\alpha}, \boldsymbol{\eta})$ if it commits to $m = 0$ or to $m = 1$.

Theorem 5 (Hiding). *Let* Gen *denote the algorithm that generates DISAP instances as explained in Alg. 1 and let* Gen* *denote the algorithm that first invokes* Gen *and then replaces* $\boldsymbol{\alpha}$ *by* $2\boldsymbol{\alpha}$. *If the DISAP hardness assumption (Def. 2) holds with respect to* Gen*, *the commitment scheme is computationally hiding.*

Proof. Recall that the DISAP assumption tells that it is hard to decide whether a given instance has a solution or not. Furthermore, by definition the committed message equals to the least significant bit of q, for short: LSB(q). Thus, breaking the hiding property is equivalent to deciding the LSB of q. Let $I^* := (2\boldsymbol{\alpha}, \boldsymbol{\eta}, N, n, \varepsilon)$ where $I := (\boldsymbol{\alpha}, \boldsymbol{\eta}, N, n, \varepsilon)$ is the instance generated by Gen. We show now that the LSB of q is equal to 0 if and only if I^* has a solution.

Assume that LSB of q is zero. That is we can write $q = 2q^*$ and one sees easily that it holds for all $i = 1, \ldots, n$:

$$|q \cdot \alpha_i - p_i - \eta_i| < \varepsilon \Leftrightarrow |(2q^*) \cdot \alpha_i - p_i - \eta_i| < \varepsilon \Leftrightarrow |q^* \cdot (2\alpha_i) - p_i - \eta_i| < \varepsilon. \tag{27}$$

Thus, if q is a solution to I with LSB$(q) = 0$, then there exists a solution to I^*.

Contrariwise, assume that I^* has a solution q^*. Then, with (27) it follows that $q' = 2q^*$ is a solution to I. Moreover, as we have shown in Theorem 4, I has one unique solution q. Thus, $q' = q$. Thus, the existence of a solution q^* for I^* implies that the LSB of the solution of I is equal to zero.

Summing up, we showed that $\text{LSB}(q) = 0$ if and only if I^* has a solution. This implies that the advantage of a hiding attacker is upper bounded by the advantage of a DISAP attacker. Thus, if the DISAP hardness assumption holds, the advantage of a hiding attacker is negligible, showing the hiding property of the scheme. □

Remark 2. It may occur that the fraction $\eta_i = c_i/d_i - p_i$ cannot be cancelled down. In this case, η_i has denominator d_i and c_i is known up to an integer multiple of p_i. This may be used to mount a naive attack running over all possible c_i using the fact that $\alpha_i = a_i/b_i$ as well c_i/d_i are known. However, by choosing p_i from the same range as q_i it can be seen that this attack has the same complexity as a brute force attack on q.

5.2 On the Underlying Assumption

In this section, we investigate the assumption the security proof is based on. Recall that according to the overview given in Sec. 2.3, the current state of knowledge states that the hardness assumption holds for multidimensional CSAP*, i.e., the *computational homogenous* problem with a *non-fixed* approximation order and $n \geq 2$, is hard for an approximation order of $\Delta \geq 1 + 1/n$. We will argue how and to what extent this indicates that certain instances of DISAP, i.e., the *decisional imhomogenous* problem with a *fixed* approximation quality, are hard as well.

The first step is to relate the CSAP* hardness assumption to a special set of CISAP instances, that is the computational variant of DISAP:

Theorem 6. *Assume an algorithm $\mathcal{A}$ that is able to efficiently compute solutions (if existent) to CISAP-instances $(\boldsymbol{\alpha}, \boldsymbol{\eta}, N, n, N^{-\delta})$ where $\eta_i = \frac{\lambda_i}{\mu_i}$ with $0 < \mu_i \leq N^{\delta'}$ and $0 < \delta' \leq \delta$. Then, there exists another algorithm $\mathcal{B}$ with the following property: Given $(\boldsymbol{\beta}, N, n)$ with $\boldsymbol{\beta} \in \mathbb{Q}^n$, invoke $\mathcal{A}$ such that any solution $(q, \boldsymbol{p})$ returned by $\mathcal{A}$ implies values $\tilde{q} \in \mathbb{N}_{>0}$ and $\tilde{\boldsymbol{p}} = (\tilde{p}_1, \ldots, \tilde{p}_n) \in \mathbb{Q}^n$ such that*

$$\left| \beta_i - \frac{\tilde{p}_i}{\tilde{q}} \right| < \frac{1}{\tilde{q}^{1+(\delta-\delta')}} \quad \forall i \in \{1, \ldots, n\}. \tag{28}$$

That is, $\mathcal{B}$ solves a CSAP* instance for an approximation order of $1 + (\delta - \delta')$.

Proof. Let $(\boldsymbol{\beta}, N, n)$ be given as defined above. At first, $\mathcal{B}$ chooses some values $0 < \mu_i \leq N^{\delta'}$ and sets $\alpha_i := \beta_i/\mu_i \in \mathbb{Q}$. Furthermore, some positive integers $\lambda_i \in \mathbb{N}_{>0}$ are sampled according to some arbitrary distribution and $\eta_i := \lambda_i/\mu_i$ are defined. Then, $\mathcal{B}$ hands the ISAP-instance $(\boldsymbol{\alpha}, \boldsymbol{\eta}, N, n, N^{-\delta})$ to $\mathcal{A}$. Assume that $\mathcal{A}$ returns a solution $(q, \boldsymbol{p})$. $\mathcal{B}$ sets $\tilde{q} := q$ and $\tilde{p}_i := p_i \cdot \mu_i + \lambda_i$ and outputs $(\tilde{q}, \tilde{\boldsymbol{p}})$.

We show now that $(\tilde{q}, \tilde{\boldsymbol{p}})$ meets condition (28). By assumption, the response $(q, \boldsymbol{p})$ of $\mathcal{A}$ is a solution to the ISAP instance, i.e., $|q\alpha_i - p_i - \eta_i| < N^{-\delta}$ for $i = 1, \ldots, n$. Because of $\mu_i \leq N^{\delta'}$ and $q \leq N$, we have $\frac{1}{N^\delta} = \frac{1}{N^{\delta-\delta'} \cdot N^{\delta'}} \leq \frac{1}{q^{\delta-\delta'} \cdot \mu_i}$. Thus, one can show that

$$\left| q\alpha_i - \frac{\tilde{p}_i}{\mu_i} \right| = |q\alpha_i - p_i - \eta_i| < \frac{1}{N^\delta} \le \frac{1}{q^{(\delta-\delta')} \cdot \mu_i} \overset{\tilde{q}=q}{\Longrightarrow} \left| \beta_i - \frac{\tilde{p}_i}{\tilde{q}} \right| < \frac{1}{\tilde{q}^{1+\delta-\delta'}} .$$

Therefore, the output of $\mathcal{B}$ represents a solution to (28).   □

Remark that the ISAP instances generated according to Gen* as explained in Th. 5 meet the conditions given in Th. 6. Thus, if the CSAP* assumption holds (as we conjecture in Sec. 2.3), then choosing CISAP instances such that $\delta - \delta' \ge 1/n$ is a sufficient condition for getting hard CISAP instances. We will make use of this observation for choosing concrete parameters in Sec. 6.

We have to stress that our analysis leaves a gap between CISAP and DISAP, that is the computational and the decisional variant. Unfortunately, as for most mathematical problems, only the computational variant has been investigated. Therefore, we have to leave the analysis of the decisional variant as an open problem. Observe that the proof of Th. 5 tells in principle that in certain cases, the decisional and computational problem are equally hard. More precisely, given an algorithm $\mathcal{A}$ that decides for certain DISAP instances with success probability 1 whether a solution exists or not, one can construct another algorithm $\mathcal{B}$ that actually computes the solution for related CISAP instances. The idea is that once the LSB of a DISAP solution is known, it is easy to transfrom the instance into a new one which shares almost the same solution but where the LSB is removed. That is, by iteratively applying this technique, one can eventually compute the solution.

6   A Concrete Instantiation and Implementation

The hardness assumption states that a promising strategy for creating hard instances is to choose values N, n and ε which are beyond certain thresholds. In this section, we will construct instances as explained in Th. 6 where the approximation quality and the dimension are too high for all algorithms mentioned in Sec. 2.3. Regarding the upper bound N, one has to take care that it is big enough for excluding brute force approaches. We will set $N := 2^s$ in our construction where s represents the security parameter. Observe that in our scheme, we construct instances that have only one unique solution. Hence, it will not be possible to look for other solutions that might be easier to find. In this context we would like to refer to the results by Rössner and Seifert [21]: They showed that approximating the best solution is almost NP-hard. Thus, approximating the unique solution q seems to be not an option either.

In this section we want to fix some values for the thresholds ε^* and n^*. Due to our discussion of the algorithmic landscape in Sec. 2.3 and because of $q^{-(1+1/2)} \le q^{-(1+1/n)}$ for all $n \ge 2$, we know that there exists no algorithm with a runtime polynomial in n that given (β, N, n), finds integers $\tilde{q}$ and $\tilde{p}$ such that

$$\left| \beta_i - \frac{\tilde{p}_i}{\tilde{q}} \right| < \frac{1}{\tilde{q}^{1+\delta-\delta'}} \tag{29}$$

with $\delta - \delta' = 1/2$. We set $\varepsilon^* := N^{-\delta} = 2^{-\delta s}$ and mention the upper bound on μ_i of $\mu^* := N^{\delta'} = 2^{\delta's}$. In [13] it is stated that the used algorithm of Lenstra Jr. [15]

has a runtime that grows exponentially in the dimension. This motivates us to set $n^* := \log(s)$. Observe that the effort of the commitment scheme grows linearly with n. Thus, increasing n in the case of need induces only a linear overhead.

Looking back to Alg. 1, we set $\varepsilon := \varepsilon^*$ and $n := n^*$ in the following as concrete parameters. Next, we compute the size of a commitment and thereby get a hint how to choose δ'. Due to the fact that the sizes of a_i and p_i do not effect the proofs of binding and hiding we are free in the choice of their bounds. Thus, we choose a_i and p_i equally distributed from the same interval as q, namely $[0, 2^s)$. Only for the b_i we have to pay attention that $b_i \leq \mu$ holds.

The commitment consists of the quantities $\boldsymbol{\alpha}$ and $\boldsymbol{\eta}$. The $\alpha_i := a_i/b_i$ require $s + \delta's$ bits because $a_i \in [0, 2^s)$ and $b_i \in [0, \mu) = \left[0, 2^{\delta's}\right)$. Moreover, the denominators d_i of the second part $\boldsymbol{\eta}$ of the commitment require $\delta's$ bits due to $0 < d_i < b_i < 2^{\delta's}$ (see condition (19) in Alg. 1). Finally we consider the expanded numerators $c_i - p_i d_i \in [-p_i d_i, c_i]$ and note that we need $s + \delta's$ bits for the negative range because $p_i d_i < 2^s b_i < 2^{s+\delta's}$ and $2s$ bits for the positive range ($c_i < q a_i < 2^{2s}$). Subsuming η_i requires $3s + 2\delta's$ bits leading to a complete commitment size of

$$|(\boldsymbol{\alpha}, \boldsymbol{\eta})|_2 = n(s + \delta's) + n(3s + 2\delta's) = ns(4 + 3\delta').$$

Because of $\delta' > 1$ we have the lower bound of $7ns$ bits for the commitment size. We see that we minimize the commitment size by minimizing δ' with respect to $\delta' > 1$. By setting $\delta' := 1 + \delta''$ with $\delta'' > 0$ we get $|(\boldsymbol{\alpha}, \boldsymbol{\eta})|_2 = 7ns + 3ns\delta''$, leading to $(3ns)^{-1}$ as a minimal choice for δ''.

We implemented the scheme[6] and made about 10^6 test runs on a AMD Athlon X2 Dual-Core QL-62 with $2\,\mathrm{GHz}$ per core with $n = 7, s = 128$ and minimal $\delta'' = (3 \cdot 128 \cdot 7)^{-1}$. This gives a commitment size of 6273 bit. The algorithm restarts the computation of the commitment on an average of 3.0579 times in order to satisfy (20) (cf. line 15 in Alg. 1). The maximal number of restarts to compute a single commitment was 23. Condition (19) was always fulfilled. Furthermore, all operations are really cheap in software – leading to running times in the milliseconds not measurable in seconds.

7   Future Work and Conclusions

In this work, we focused on one particular problem from analytic number theory, namely the Decisional Inhomogeneous Simultaneous Approximation Problem (DISAP). The problem is NP-complete and one can efficiently generate presumably hard instances. Observe that the difficulty can be easily increased, e. g., by raising the dimension n. As a proof of concept, we constructed a bit commitment scheme on DISAP.

However, other schemes could have been imaginable. For example, it might be possible to construct DISAP instances in such a way that the addition or multiplication of several instances yield a new instance. In the positive case, it would

---

[6] We used the GNU MP (http://gmplib.org/) and MPFR [5] library for arbitrary large integers and arbitrary precise floating point arithmetic. Our C++ implementation can be downloaded from http://www.ifam.uni-hannover.de/~mschmidt/

be interesting to explore whether one can adapt the approach by Van Dijk et al. [31] for constructing a full-homomorphic encryption scheme. Also with respect to DISAP itself, several questions remain open. To begin with the gap between the decisional and computational variants needs to be examined further. Moreover, the connection to lattices might turn out to be very fruitful. In the best case, DISAP (and variants) might give an alternative approach for constructing hard lattice instances.

Despite DISAP, other problems and results from analytic number theory might be worth to be investigated as well. For example, one can easily transform a rational number from its binary representation to continued fractions and vice versa. But only little is known on the relations between changes in one representation and the corresponding changes in the other representation. This "fragility" might be used to construct a collision-resistant compression function. Furthermore, several results exist on the periodicity of certain representations. The construction of bitstream generators based on these might be an interesting question.

Concluding, we think that the established discipline of analytic number theory contains many interesting open problems and results that only wait to be (re-)discovered for cryptographic applications. We hope to encourage further research into this direction.

References

1. Baldwin, P.R.: A convergence exponent for multidimensional continued-fraction algorithms. Journal of Statistical Physics 66(5/6), 1507–1526 (1992)
2. Bernstein, L.: The Jacobi-Perron algorithm, it's theory and application. Lecture Notes in Mathematics, vol. 207. Springer, Heidelberg (1971)
3. Brentjes, A.J.: Multi-dimensional continued fraction algorithms. Mathematical Centre Tracts 145 (1981)
4. Elsner, C., Schmidt, M.: KronCrypt - a new symmetric cryptosystem based on Kronecker's approximation theorem. Cryptology ePrint Archive, Report 2009/416 (2009), http://eprint.iacr.org/
5. Fousse, L., Hanrot, G., Lefèvre, V., Pélissier, P., Zimmermann, P.: MPFR: A multiple-precision binary floating-point library with correct rounding. ACM Trans. Math. Softw. 33(2), 13 (2007)
6. Gärtner, R.: Zur Geometrie des Jacobi-Perron Algorithmus. Arch. Math. 39, 134–146 (1982)
7. Goldreich, O., Micciancio, D., Safra, S., Seifert, J.-P.: Approximating shortest lattice vectors is not harder than approximating closest lattice vectors. Information Processing Letters 71(2), 55–61 (1999)
8. Hardy, G.H., Wright, E.M.: An introduction to the theory of numbers, 3rd edn. Clarendon Press, Oxford (1954)
9. Isselhorst, H.: The use of fractions in public-key cryptosystems. In: Quisquater, J.-J., Vandewalle, J. (eds.) EUROCRYPT 1989. LNCS, vol. 434, pp. 47–55. Springer, Heidelberg (1990)
10. Jacobi, C.G.J.: Allgemeine Theorie der kettenbruchähnlichen Algorithmen, in welchen jede Zahl aus drei vorhergehenden gebildet wird. Journal Für Die Reine und Angewandte Mathematik (Crelle's Journal) 69, 29–64 (1868)

11. Just, B.: Generalizing the continued fraction algorithm to arbitrary dimensions. SIAM Journal on Computing 21, 909–926 (1992)
12. Estes, D., Adleman, L.M., Kompella, K., McCurley, K.S., Miller, G.L.: Breaking the Ong-Schnorr-Shamir signature scheme for quadratic number fields. In: Williams, H.C. (ed.) CRYPTO 1985. LNCS, vol. 218, pp. 3–13. Springer, Heidelberg (1986)
13. Lagarias, J.C.: The computational complexity of simultaneous diophantine approximation problems. SIAM J. Comput. 14(1), 196–209 (1985)
14. Lenstra, A.K., Lenstra Jr., H.W., Lovasz, L.: Factoring polynomials with rational coefficients. Mathematische Annalen 261, 515–534 (1982)
15. Lenstra Jr., H.W.: Integer programming with a fixed number of variables. Mathematics of Operations Research 8(4), 538–548 (1983)
16. Keng, H.L.: Introduction to number theory, 5th edn. Springer, Heidelberg (1982)
17. Nguyen, P.Q., Valle, B.: The LLL Algorithm. Survey and Applications. In: Information Security and Cryptography, Springer, Heidelberg (2010)
18. Perron, O.: Grundlagen für eine Theorie des Jacobischen Kettenbruchalgorithmus. Math. Ann. 64, 1–76 (1907)
19. Regev, O.: New lattice-based cryptographic constructions. J. ACM 51(6), 899–942 (2004)
20. Rieger, G.J.: Zahlentheorie. Vandenhoeck & Ruprecht, Göttingen (1976)
21. Rössner, C., Seifert, J.-P.: Approximating good simultaneous diophantine approximations is almost NP-hard. In: Penczek, W., Szałas, A. (eds.) MFCS 1996. LNCS, vol. 1113, pp. 494–505. Springer, Heidelberg (1996)
22. Schmidt, W.: Diophantine approximations. Springer, Berlin (1980)
23. Schnorr, C.-P.: Factoring integers and computing discrete logarithms via diophantine approximation. In: Davies, D.W. (ed.) EUROCRYPT 1991. LNCS, vol. 547, pp. 281–293. Springer, Heidelberg (1991)
24. Schweiger, F.: The metrical theory of Jacobi-Perron algorithm. Lecture Notes in Mathematics, vol. 334. Springer, Heidelberg (1973)
25. Schweiger, F.: Multidimensional continued fractions. Oxford University Press, Oxford (2000)
26. Schweiger, F.: Was leisten mehrdimensionale Kettenbrüche? Mathematische Semesterberichte 53, 231–244 (2006)
27. Seifert, J.-P.: Using fewer qubits in Shor's factorization algorithm via simultaneous diophantine approximation. In: Naccache, D. (ed.) CT-RSA 2001. LNCS, vol. 2020, pp. 319–327. Springer, Heidelberg (2001)
28. Shamir, A.: A polynomial time algorithm for breaking the basic Merkle-Hellman cryptosystem. In: SFCS 1982: Proceedings of the 23rd Annual Symposium on Foundations of Computer Science, pp. 145–152. IEEE Computer Society, Washington, DC, USA (1982)
29. Stern, J., Toffin, P.: Cryptanalysis of a public-key cryptosystem based on approximations by rational numbers. In: Damgård, I.B. (ed.) EUROCRYPT 1990. LNCS, vol. 473, pp. 313–317. Springer, Heidelberg (1991)
30. Szekeres, C.: Multidimensional continued fractions. Ann. Univ. Sci. Budap. Eötös, Sect. Math. 13, 113–140 (1980)
31. van Dijk, M., Gentry, C., Halevi, S., Vaikuntanathan, V.: Fully homomorphic encryption over the integers. In: Gilbert, H. (ed.) EUROCRYPT 2010. LNCS, vol. 6110, pp. 24–43. Springer, Heidelberg (2010)
32. Wiener, M.J.: Cryptanalysis of short RSA secret exponents. IEEE Transactions on Information Theory 36, 553–558 (1990)

Analyzing Standards for RSA Integers

Daniel Loebenberger and Michael Nüsken

b-it, University of Bonn
{daniel,nuesken}@bit.uni-bonn.de

Abstract. The key-generation algorithm for the RSA cryptosystem is specified in several standards, such as PKCS#1, IEEE 1363-2000, FIPS 186-3, ANSI X9.44, or ISO/IEC 18033-2. All of them substantially differ in their requirements. This indicates that for computing a "secure" RSA modulus it does not matter how exactly one generates RSA integers. In this work we show that this is indeed the case to a large extend: First, we give a theoretical framework that will enable us to easily compute the entropy of the output distribution of the considered standards and show that it is comparatively high. To do so, we compute for each standard the number of integers they define (up to an error of very small order) and discuss different methods of generating integers of a specific form. Second, we show that factoring such integers is hard, provided factoring a product of two primes of similar size is hard.

Keywords: RSA integer, output entropy, reduction. ANSI X9.44, FIPS 186-3, IEEE 1363-2000, ISO/IEC 18033-2, NESSIE, PKCS#1.

1 Introduction

An *RSA integer* is an integer that is suitable as a modulus for the RSA cryptosystem as proposed by Rivest, Shamir & Adleman (1977, 1978):

> "You first compute n as the product of two primes p and q:
>
> $$n = p \cdot q.$$
>
> These primes are very large, 'random' primes. Although you will make n public, the factors p and q will be effectively hidden from everyone else due to the enormous difficulty of factoring n."

Also in earlier literature such as Ellis (1970) or Cocks (1973) one does not find any further restrictions. In subsequent literature people define RSA integers similarly to Rivest, Shamir & Adleman, while sometimes additional safety tests are performed. Real world implementations, however, require *concrete algorithms* that specify in detail how to generate RSA integers. This has led to a variety of standards, notably the standards PKCS#1 (Jonsson & Kaliski 2003), ISO 18033-2 (International Organization for Standards 2006), IEEE 1363-2000 (IEEE working group 2000), ANSI X9.44 (Accredited Standards Committee X9 2007), FIPS 186-3 (Information Technology Laboratory 2009), the standard of the RSA foundation

A. Nitaj and D. Pointcheval (Eds.): AFRICACRYPT 2011, LNCS 6737, pp. 260–277, 2011.

(RSA Laboratories 2000), the standard set by the German Bundesnetzagentur (Wohlmacher 2009), and the standard resulting from the European NESSIE project (NESSIE working group 2003). All of those standards define more or less precisely how to generate RSA integers and all of them have substantially different requirements. This reflects the intuition that it does not really matter how one selects the prime factors in detail, the resulting RSA modulus will do its job. But what is needed to show that this is really the case?

Following Brandt & Damgård (1993) a quality measure of a generator is the entropy of its output distribution. In abuse of language we will most of the time talk about the *output entropy* of an algorithm. To compute it, we need estimates of the probability that a certain outcome is produced. This in turn needs a thorough analysis of how one generates RSA integers of a specific form. If we can show that the outcome of the algorithm is roughly uniformly distributed, the output entropy is closely related to the count of RSA integers it can produce. It will turn out that in all reasonable setups this count is essentially determined by the desired length of the output. For primality tests there are several results in this direction (see for example Joye & Paillier 2006) but we are not aware of any related work analyzing the output entropy of algorithms for generating RSA integers.

Another requirement for the algorithm is that the output should be 'hard to factor'. Since this statement does not even make sense for a single integer, this means that one has to show that the restrictions on the shape of the integers the algorithm produces do not introduce any further possibilities for an attacker. To prove this, a *reduction* has to be given that reduces the problem of factoring the output to the problem of factoring a product of two primes of similar size, see Section 7. Also there it is necessary to have results on the count of RSA integers of a specific form to make the reduction work. As for the entropy estimations, we do not know any related work on this.

In the following section we will develop a formal framework that can handle all possible definitions for RSA integers. After discussing the necessary number theoretic tools in Section 3, we give explicit formulæ for the count of such integers which will be used later for entropy estimations of the various standards for RSA integers. In Section 4 we show how our general framework can be instantiated, yielding natural definitions for several types of RSA integers (as used later in the standards). Section 5 gives a short overview on generic constructions for fast algorithms that generate such integers almost uniformly. At this point we will have described all necessary techniques to compute the output entropy, which we discuss in Section 6. The following section resolves the second question described above by giving a reduction from factoring special types of RSA integers to factoring a product of two primes of similar size. We finish by applying our results to various standards for RSA integers in Section 8.

We omitted here most of the number theoretic details. For the proofs of those theorems see Loebenberger & Nüsken (2011). Note that for ease of comparison, we have retained the numbering of the extended version.

2   RSA Integers in General

If one generates an RSA integer it is necessary to select for each choice of the security parameter the prime factors from a certain region. This security parameter is typically an integer k that specifies (roughly) the size of the output. We use a more general definition by asking for integers from the interval $]x/r, x]$, given a *real* bound x and a parameter r (possibly depending on x). Clearly, this can also be used to model the former selection process by setting $x = 2^k - 1$ and $r = 2$. Let us in general introduce a *notion of RSA integers with tolerance r* as a family

$$\mathcal{A} := \langle \mathcal{A}_x \rangle_{x \in \mathbb{R}_{>1}}$$

of subsets of the positive quadrant $\mathbb{R}^2_{>1}$, where for every $x \in \mathbb{R}_{>1}$

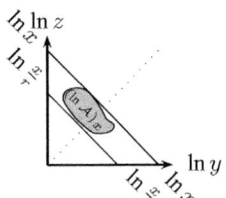

$$\mathcal{A}_x \subseteq \left\{ (y, z) \in \mathbb{R}^2_{>1} \,\middle|\, \frac{x}{r} < yz \leq x \right\}.$$

The tolerance r shall always be larger than 1. We allow here that r varies (slightly) with x, which of course includes the case that r is a constant. Typical values used for RSA are $r = 2$ or $r = 4$ which fix the bit-length of the modulus more or less. We can — for a fixed choice of parameters — easily visualize any notion of RSA integers by the corresponding region $\mathcal{A}_x$ in the (y, z)-plane. It is favorable to look at these regions in logarithmic scale. We write $y = e^v$ and $z = e^\zeta$ and denote by $(\ln \mathcal{A})_x$ the region in the (v, ζ)-plane corresponding to the region $\mathcal{A}_x$ in the (y, z)-plane, formally $(v, \zeta) \in (\ln \mathcal{A})_x :\Leftrightarrow (y, z) \in \mathcal{A}_x$. Now an *$\mathcal{A}$-integer n of size x* — for use as a modulus in RSA — is a product $n = pq$ of a prime pair $(p, q) \in \mathcal{A}_x \cap (\mathbb{P} \times \mathbb{P})$, where $\mathbb{P}$ denotes the set of primes. They are counted by the associated *prime pair counting function* $\#\mathcal{A}$ for the notion $\mathcal{A}$:

$$\#\mathcal{A} \colon \begin{array}{l} \mathbb{R}_{>1} \longrightarrow \mathbb{N}, \\ x \longmapsto \# \left\{ (p, q) \in \mathbb{P} \times \mathbb{P} \,\middle|\, (p, q) \in \mathcal{A}_x \right\}. \end{array}$$

Thus every $\mathcal{A}$-integer $n = pq$ is counted once or twice in $\#\mathcal{A}(x)$ depending on whether only $(p, q) \in \mathcal{A}_x$ or also $(q, p) \in \mathcal{A}_x$, respectively. We call a notion *symmetric* if for all choices of the parameters the corresponding area in the (y, z)-plane is symmetric with respect to the main diagonal, i.e. that $(y, z) \in \mathcal{A}_x$ implies also $(z, y) \in \mathcal{A}_x$. If to the contrary $(y, z) \in \mathcal{A}_x$ implies $(z, y) \notin \mathcal{A}_x$ we call the notion *antisymmetric*. If we are only interested in RSA integers we can always require symmetry or antisymmetry, yet many algorithms proceed in an asymmetric way.

Certainly, we will also need restrictions on the shape of the area we are analyzing: If one considers any notion of RSA integers and throws out exactly the prime pairs one would be left with a prime-pair-free region and any approximation for the count of such a notion based on the area would necessarily have a tremendously large error term. However, for practical applications it turns out that it is enough to consider regions of a very specific form. Actually, we will most of the time have regions whose boundary can be described by graphs of certain smooth functions. In the following, we call notions having such boundaries *monotone*. A more detailed explanation of the restrictions we have to impose to make the number-theoretic work sound can be found in the extended version Loebenberger & Nüsken (2011).

For RSA, people usually prefer two prime factors of roughly the same size, where size is understood as bit length. Accordingly, we call a notion of RSA integers $[c_1, c_2]$-*balanced* iff additionally for every $x \in \mathbb{R}_{>1}$

$$\mathcal{A}_x \subseteq \left\{ (y,z) \in \mathbb{R}^2_{>1} \,\middle|\, y, z \in [x^{c_1}, x^{c_2}] \right\},$$

where $0 < c_1 \leq c_2$ can be thought of as constants or — more generally — as smooth functions in x defining the amount of allowed divergence subject to the side condition that x^{c_1} tends to infinity when x grows. If $c_1 > \frac{1}{2}$ then $\mathcal{A}_x$ is empty, so we will usually assume $c_1 \leq \frac{1}{2}$. In order to prevent trial division from being a successful attacker it would be sufficient to require $y, z \in \Omega\left(\ln^k x\right)$ for every $k \in \mathbb{N}$. Our stronger requirement still seems reasonable and indeed equals the condition Maurer (1995) required for secure RSA moduli, as the supposedly most difficult factoring challenges stay within the range of our attention. As a side-effect this greatly simplifies our approximations later. The German Bundesnetzagentur (see Wohlmacher 2009) uses a very similar restriction in their algorithm catalog. There it is additionally required that the primes p and q are not too close to each other. We ignore this issue here, since the probability that two primes are *very close* to each other would be tiny if the notion from which (p, q) was selected is sufficiently large. If necessary, we are able to modify our notions such that also this requirement is met.

Often the considered integers $n = pq$ are also subject to further side conditions, like $\gcd((p-1)(q-1), e) = 1$ for some fixed public RSA exponent e. Most of the number theoretic work below can easily be adapted, but for simplicity of exposition we will often present our results without those further restrictions and just point out when necessary how to incorporate such additional properties.

As we usually deal with balanced notions the considered regions are somewhat centered around the main diagonal. We will show in Section 7 that if factoring products of two primes is hard then it is also hard to factor integers generated from such notions.

3 Toolbox

We will now develop the necessary number theoretic concepts to obtain formulæ for the count of RSA integers that will later help us to estimate the output entropy of the various standards for RSA integers. In related articles, like Decker & Moree (2008) one finds counts for *one particular* definition of RSA integers. We believe that in the work presented here for the first time a sufficiently general theorem is established that allows to compute the number of RSA integers for *all* reasonable definitions.

We assume the Riemann hypothesis throughout the entire paper. The main terms are the same without this assumption, but the error bounds one obtains are then much weaker. We skip intermediate results here and just summarize the number theoretic work (to ease later comparison we have retained the numbering of the extended version Loebenberger & Nüsken 2011). The following lemma covers all the estimation work.

Lemma 3.6 (Two-dimensional prime sum approximation for monotone notions).
Assume that we have a monotone $[c_1, c_2]$-balanced notion $\mathcal{A}$ of RSA integers with tolerance r, where $0 < c_1 \leq c_2$. (The values r, c_1, c_2 are allowed to vary with x.) Then under the Riemann hypothesis there is a value $\tilde{a}(x) \in \left[\frac{1}{4c_2^2}, \frac{1}{4c_1^2}\right]$ such that

$$\#\mathcal{A}(x) \in \tilde{a}(x) \cdot \frac{4\,\mathrm{area}(\mathcal{A}_x)}{\ln^2 x} + \mathcal{O}\left(c_1^{-1} x^{\frac{3+c}{4}}\right),$$

where $c = \max(2c_2 - 1, 1 - 2c_1)$.   □

Note that the omitted proof gives a precise expression for $\widetilde{a}(x)$, namely

$$\widetilde{a}(x) = \frac{\iint_{\mathcal{A}_x} \frac{1}{\ln p \ln q} \, dp \, dq}{4 \iint_{\mathcal{A}_x} \frac{1}{\ln^2 x} \, dp \, dq}.$$

It turns out that we can only evaluate $\widetilde{a}(x)$ numerically in our case and so we tend to estimate also this term. Then we often obtain $\widetilde{a}(x) \in 1 + o(1)$. Admittedly, this mostly eats up the advantage obtained by using the Riemann hypothesis. However, we accept this because it still leaves the option of going through that difficult evaluation and obtain a much more precise answer. If we do not use the Riemann hypothesis we need to replace $\mathcal{O}\left(c_1^{-1} x^{\frac{3+c}{4}}\right)$ with $\mathcal{O}\left(\frac{x}{\ln^k x}\right)$ for any $k > 2$ of your choice.

As mentioned before, in many standards the selection of the primes p and q is additionally subject to the side condition that $\gcd((p-1)(q-1), e) = 1$ for some fixed public exponent e of the RSA cryptosystem. To handle these restrictions, we state a theorem from the extended version.

Theorem 3.11. *Let $e \in \mathbb{N}_{>2}$ be a public RSA exponent and $x \in \mathbb{R}$. Then we have for the number $\pi_e(x)$ of primes $p \leq x$ with $\gcd(p-1, e) = 1$ that*

$$\pi_e(x) \in \frac{\varphi_1(e)}{\varphi(e)} \cdot \mathrm{Li}(x) + \mathcal{O}\left(\sqrt{x} \ln x\right),$$

where $\mathrm{Li}(x) = \int_2^x \frac{1}{\ln t} \, dt$ is the integral logarithm, $\varphi(e)$ is Euler's totient function and

$$\frac{\varphi_1(e)}{\varphi(e)} = \prod_{\substack{\ell \mid e \\ \ell \text{ prime}}} \left(1 - \frac{1}{\ell - 1}\right). \tag{3.12}$$

□

This theorem shows that the prime pair approximation in Lemma 3.6 can be easily adapted to RSA integers whose prime factors satisfy the conditions of Theorem 3.11, since the density of such primes differs for every fixed e just by a constant.

4   Some Common Definitions for RSA Integers

We will now give formal definitions of two specific notions of RSA integers. In particular, we consider the following example definitions within our framework:

- The simple construction given by just choosing two primes in given intervals. This construction occurs in several standards, like the standard of the RSA foundation (RSA Laboratories 2000), the standard resulting from the European NESSIE project (NESSIE working group 2003) and the FIPS 186-3 standard (Information Technology Laboratory 2009). Also open source implementations of OpenSSL (Cox *et al.* 2009), GnuPG (Skala *et al.* 2009) and the GNU crypto library GNU Crypto (Free Software Foundation 2009) use some variant of this construction.

– An algorithmically inspired construction which allows one prime being chosen arbitrarily and the second is chosen such that the product is in the desired interval. This was for example specified as the IEEE standard 1363 (IEEE working group 2000), Annex A.16.11. However, we could not find any implementations following this standard.

4.1   A Fixed Bound Notion

We consider the number of integers smaller than a real positive bound x that have exactly two prime factors p and q, both lying in a fixed interval $]B, C]$, in formulæ:

$$\pi^2_{B,C}(x) := \# \left\{ n \in \mathbb{N} \; \middle| \; \begin{array}{c} \exists p, q \in \mathbb{P} \cap]B, C] : \\ n = pq \; \wedge \; n \leq x \end{array} \right\}.$$

To avoid problems with rare prime squares, which are also not interesting when talking about RSA integers, we instead count

$$\kappa^2_{B,C}(x) := \# \left\{ (p, q) \in (\mathbb{P} \cap]B, C])^2 \; \middle| \; pq \leq x \right\}.$$

Such functions are treated in Loebenberger & Nüsken (2010) . In the context of RSA integers we consider the notion

$$\mathcal{A}^{\mathrm{FB}(r,\sigma)} := \left\langle \left\{ (y, z) \in \mathbb{R}^2_{>1} \; \middle| \; \sqrt{\frac{x}{r}} < y, z \leq \sqrt{r^\sigma x} \; \wedge \; yz \leq x \right\} \right\rangle_{x \in \mathbb{R}_{>1}}$$

with $\sigma \in [0, 1]$. The parameter σ describes the (relative) distance of the restriction $yz \leq x$ to the center of the rectangle in which y and z are allowed. The next theorem follows directly from Loebenberger & Nüsken (2010) but we can also derive it from Lemma 3.6:

Theorem 4.6. *We have for* $\ln r \in o(\ln x)$ *under the Riemann hypothesis*

$$\# \mathcal{A}^{\mathrm{FB}(r,\sigma)}(x) \in \widetilde{a}(x) \frac{4x}{\ln^2 x} \left(\sigma \ln r + 1 - \frac{2}{r^{\frac{1-\sigma}{2}}} + \frac{1}{r} \right) + \mathcal{O}\left(x^{\frac{3}{4}} r^{\frac{1}{4}} \right)$$

with $\widetilde{a}(x) \in \left[\left(1 - \frac{\sigma \ln r}{\ln x + \sigma \ln r} \right)^2, \left(1 + \frac{\ln r}{\ln x - \ln r} \right)^2 \right] \subseteq 1 + o(1).$

$\square$

4.2   An Algorithmically Inspired Notion

A second option to define RSA integers is the following notion: Assume you wish to generate an RSA integer between $\frac{x}{r}$ and x, which has two prime factors of roughly equal size. Then algorithmically we might first generate the prime p and afterward select the prime q such that the product is in the correct interval. As we will see later, this procedure does — however — not produce every number with the same probability, see Section 5. Formally, we consider the notion

$$\mathcal{A}^{\mathrm{ALG}(r,\sigma)}(x) := \left\langle \left\{ (y,z) \in \mathbb{R}_{>1}^2 \;\middle|\; \begin{array}{c} r^{\sigma-1}\sqrt{x} < y \le r^\sigma \sqrt{x} \;\wedge\; \frac{x}{ry} < z \le \frac{x}{y} \\ \frac{x}{r} < yz \le x \end{array} \right\} \right\rangle_{x \in \mathbb{R}_{>1}},$$

with $\sigma \in [0,1]$. The parameter σ describes here the (relative) position of the defining area of the notion with respect to the diagonal. Write $\sigma' := \max(\sigma, 1-\sigma)$. Similar to the theorem above we obtain

Theorem 4.11. *Assuming* $\ln r \in o(\ln x)$ *we have under the Riemann hypothesis*

$$\#\mathcal{A}^{\mathrm{ALG}(r,\sigma)}(x) \in \tilde{a}(x) \frac{4x}{\ln^2 x}\left(\ln r - \frac{\ln r}{r}\right) + \mathcal{O}\left(x^{\frac{3}{4}} r^{\frac{1}{4}}\right),$$

with $\tilde{a}(x) \in \left[\left(1 - \frac{2\sigma' \ln r}{\ln x + 2\sigma' \ln r}\right)^2, \left(1 + \frac{2(1+\sigma)\ln r}{\ln x - 2(1+\sigma)\ln r}\right)^2\right] \subseteq 1 + o(1).$ □

As we see both notions open a slightly different view. However the outcome is not that different, at least the numbers of described RSA integers are quite close to each other. The proof that this is the case for *all* reasonable notions can be found in the extended version Loebenberger & Nüsken (2011).

Current standards and implementations of various crypto packages mostly use the notions $\mathcal{A}^{\mathrm{FB}(4,0)}$, $\mathcal{A}^{\mathrm{FB}(4,1)}$, $\mathcal{A}^{\mathrm{FB}(2,0)}$ or $\mathcal{A}^{\mathrm{ALG}(2,1/2)}$. For details see Section 8.

5   Generating RSA Integers Properly

In this section we analyze how to generate RSA integers properly. It completes the picture and we found several implementations overlooking this kind of arguments. We wish that all the algorithms generate integers with the following properties:

– If we fix x we should with overwhelming probability generate integers that are a product of a prime pair in $\mathcal{A}_x$.
– These integers (not the pairs) should be selected roughly uniformly at random.
– The algorithm should be efficient. In particular, it should need only few primality tests.

5.1   Rejection Sampling

Assume that $\mathcal{A}$ is a $[c_1, c_2]$-balanced notion of RSA integers with tolerance r. The easiest approach for generating a pair from $\mathcal{A}$ is based on von Neumann's rejection sampling method. Let $\mathcal{B}_x := x^{[c_1,c_2]} \times x^{[c_1,c_2]}$. There may be better ways for choosing $\mathcal{B}_x \supseteq \mathcal{A}_x$, but we skip this here. We obtain the following straightforward Las Vegas algorithm:

Algorithm 5.2. Generating an RSA integer (Las Vegas version).
Input: A notion $\mathcal{A}$, a bound $x \in \mathbb{R}_{>1}$.
Output: An integer $n = pq$ with $(p,q) \in \mathcal{A}_x$.

1. Repeat 2–4
2.   Repeat

3.   Select (y, z) at random from $\mathcal{B}_x \cap \mathbb{N}^2$.
4.   Until $(y, z) \in \mathcal{A}_x$.
5. Until y prime and z prime.
6. $p \leftarrow y, q \leftarrow z$.
7. Return pq.

The expected repetition count of the inner loop is roughly $\frac{\text{area}(\mathcal{B}_x)}{\text{area}(\mathcal{A}_x)}$. The expected number of primality tests is about $\frac{\text{area}(\mathcal{A}_x)}{\#\mathcal{A}(x)}$. This is for many notions in $\mathcal{O}\left(\ln^2 x\right)$. We have seen implementations (for example the one of GnuPG) where the inner and outer loop have been exchanged. This increases the number of primality tests by the repetition count of the inner loop. Also easily checkable additional conditions, like $\gcd((p-1)(q-1), e) = 1$, should be checked before the primality tests to improve the efficiency.

5.2   Inverse Transform Sampling

Actually we would like to avoid generating out-of-bound pairs completely. To retain uniform selection, we need to select the primes p non-uniformly with the following distribution:

Definition 5.4. *Let $\mathcal{A}$ be a notion of RSA integers with tolerance r. For every $x \in \mathbb{R}_{>1}$ the associated cumulative distribution function of $\mathcal{A}_x$ is defined as*

$$F_{\mathcal{A}_x} : \begin{array}{l} \mathbb{R} \longrightarrow [0, 1], \\ y \longmapsto \frac{\text{area}(\mathcal{A}_x \cap ([1,y] \times \mathbb{R}))}{\text{area}(\mathcal{A}_x)}. \end{array}$$

In fact we should use the function $G_{\mathcal{A}_x} : \mathbb{R} \to [0, 1]$, $y \mapsto \frac{\#(\mathcal{A}_x \cap (([1,y] \cap \mathbb{P}) \times \mathbb{P}))}{\#\mathcal{A}_x}$, in order to compute the density but computing $G_{\mathcal{A}_x}$ (or its inverse) is tremendously expensive. Fortunately, by virtue of Lemma 3.6 we know that $F_{\mathcal{A}_x}$ approximates $G_{\mathcal{A}_x}$ for monotone, $[c_1, c_2]$-balanced notions $\mathcal{A}$ quite well. So we use the function $F_{\mathcal{A}_x}$ to capture the distribution properties of a given notion of RSA integers. As can be seen by inspection, in practically relevant examples this function is sufficiently easy to handle. We obtain the following algorithm:

Algorithm 5.5. Generating an RSA integer.
Input: A notion $\mathcal{A}$, a bound $x \in \mathbb{R}_{>1}$.
Output: An integer $n = pq$ with $(p, q) \in \mathcal{A}_x$.

1. Repeat
2.   Select y with distribution $F_{\mathcal{A}_x}$ from $\{y \in \mathbb{R} \mid \exists z \colon (y, z) \in \mathcal{A}_x\} \cap \mathbb{N}$.
3. Until y prime.
4. $p \leftarrow y$.
5. Repeat
6.   Select z uniformly at random from $\{z \in \mathbb{R} \mid (p, z) \in \mathcal{A}_x\} \cap \mathbb{N}$.
7. Until z prime.
8. $q \leftarrow z$.
9. Return pq.

As desired, this algorithm generates any pair $(p, q) \in \mathcal{A}_x \cap (\mathbb{P} \times \mathbb{P})$ with almost the same probability. In order to generate y with distribution $F_{\mathcal{A}_x}$ one can use inverse transform sampling, see for example Knuth (1998). The expected number of primality tests now is in $\mathcal{O}(\ln x)$. Of course we have to take into account that for each trial y the inverse $F_{\mathcal{A}_x}^{-1}(y)$ has to be computed — at least approximately —, yet this cost is usually negligible compared to a primality test.

5.3   Other Constructions

There are variants around, where the primes are selected differently: Take an integer randomly from a suitable interval and increase the result until the first prime is found. This has the advantage that the amount of randomness needed is considerably lower and by optimizing the resulting algorithm can also be made much faster. The price one has to pay is that the produced primes will not be selected uniformly at random: Primes p for which $p - 2$ is also prime will be selected with a much lower probability than randomly selected primes of a given length. As shown in Brandt & Damgård (1993) the output entropy of such algorithms is still almost maximal and also generators based on these kind of prime-generators might be used in practice.

5.4   Summary

We have seen that Algorithm 5.2 and Algorithm 5.5 are practical uniform generators for any symmetric or antisymmetric notion.

Note that Algorithm 5.2 and Algorithm 5.5 may, however, still produce numbers in a non-uniform fashion: In the last step of both algorithms a product is computed that corresponds to either one pair or two pairs in $\mathcal{A}_x$. To solve this problem we have two choices: Either we replace $\mathcal{A}$ by its symmetric version $\mathcal{S}$ which we define as $\mathcal{S}_x :=$ $\left\{ (y, z) \in \mathbb{R}_{>1}^2 \mid (y, z) \in \mathcal{A}_x \vee (z, y) \in \mathcal{A}_x \right\}$, or by its, say, top half $\mathcal{T}$ given by $\mathcal{T}_x :=$ $\{(y, z) \in \mathcal{S}_x \mid z \geq y\}$ before anything else.

6   Output Entropy

The entropy of the output distribution is one important quality measure of a generator. For primality tests several analyses where performed, see for example Brandt & Damgård (1993) or Joye & Paillier (2006). For generators of RSA integers we are not aware of any work in this direction.

Let $\mathcal{A}_x$ be any monotone notion. Consider a generator G_ϱ that produces a pair of primes $(p, q) \in \mathcal{A}_x$ with distribution ϱ. Seen as random variables, G_ϱ induces two random variables P and Q by its first and the second coordinate, respectively. The entropy of the generator G_ϱ is given by

$$H(G_\varrho) = H(P \times Q) = H(P) + H(Q \mid P),$$

where H denotes the binary entropy and $H(Q \mid P)$ denotes the conditional entropy. If ϱ is the uniform distribution U we obtain by Lemma 3.6 maximal entropy

$$H(G_U) = \log_2(\#\mathcal{A}(x)) \approx \log_2(\mathrm{area}(\mathcal{A}_x)) - \log_2(\ln x) + 1,$$

with an error of very small order. The algorithms from Section 5, however, return the product $P \cdot Q$. The entropy of this random variable can be estimated as

$$
\begin{aligned}
H(P \cdot Q) &= - \sum_{\substack{n=pq \in \mathbb{N} \\ (p,q) \in \mathcal{A}_x}} \mathrm{prob}(P \cdot Q = n) \log_2(\mathrm{prob}(P \cdot Q = n)) \\
&\geq - \sum_{(p,q) \in \mathcal{A}_x} \mathrm{prob}(P \times Q = (p,q)) \log_2(2\,\mathrm{prob}(P \times Q = (p,q))) \\
&= H(P \times Q) - 1.
\end{aligned}
$$

Some of the standards and implementations in Section 8 (like the standard IEEE 1363-2000 or the implementation of GNU Crypto) *do not* generate every possible outcome with the same probability. All of them have in common that the prime p is selected uniformly at random and afterwards the prime q is selected uniformly at random from an appropriate interval. This is a non-uniform selection process since for some choices of p there might be less choices for q.

If in general the probability distribution ϱ is close to the uniform distribution, say $\varrho(p,q) \in [2^{-\varepsilon}, 2^{\varepsilon}] \frac{1}{\#\mathcal{A}(x)}$ for some fixed $\varepsilon \in \mathbb{R}_{>0}$, then the entropy of the resulting generator G_ϱ can be estimated as

$$
H(G_U) - \varepsilon \leq H(G_\varrho).
$$

7   Complexity Theoretic Considerations

We are about to reduce factoring products of two comparatively equally sized primes to the problem of factoring integers generated from a sufficiently large notion. As far as we know there are no similar reductions in the literature.

We consider finite sets $M \subset \mathbb{N} \times \mathbb{N}$, in our situation we actually have only prime pairs. The multiplication map μ_M is defined on M and merely multiplies, that is, $\mu_M : M \to \mathbb{N}$, $(y, z) \mapsto y \cdot z$. The random variable U_M outputs uniformly distributed values from M. An attacking algorithm F gets a natural number $\mu_M(U_M)$ and attempts to find factors inside M. Its success probability

$$
\mathrm{succ}_F(M) = \mathrm{prob}\left(\ F(\mu_M(U_M)) \in \mu_M^{-1}(\mu_M(U_M)) \ \right) \tag{7.1}
$$

measures its quality in any fixed-size scenario. Integers generated from a notion $\mathcal{A}$ are *hard to factor* iff for all probabilistic polynomial time machines F, all $s \in \mathbb{N}$, there exists a value $x_0 \in \mathbb{R}_{>1}$ such that for any $x > x_0$ we have $\mathrm{succ}_F(\mathcal{A}_x) \leq \ln^{-s} x$.

For any polynomial f we define the set $R_f = \{(m, n) \in \mathbb{N} \mid m \leq f(n) \wedge n \leq f(m)\}$ of f-related positive integer pairs. Denote by $\mathbb{P}^{(m)}$ the set of m-bit primes. We can now formulate the basic assumption:

Assumption 7.2 (Intractability of factoring). *For any unbounded positive polynomial f integers from the f-related prime pair family $(\mathbb{P}^{(m)} \times \mathbb{P}^{(n)})_{(m,n) \in R_f}$ are hard to factor.*

This is exactly the definition given by Goldreich (2001). Note that this assumption implies that factoring in general is hard, and it covers the supposedly hardest factoring instances. Now we are ready to state that integers from all relevant notions are hard to factor.

Theorem 7.3. *Let* $\ln r \in \Omega\left(\frac{1-2c_1}{\ln^\ell x}\right)$ *and* $\mathcal{A}$ *be a monotone,* $[c_1, c_2]$-*balanced notion for RSA integers of tolerance* r *with large area, namely, for some* k *and large* x *we have area* $\mathcal{A}_x \geq \frac{x}{\ln^k x}$. *Assume that factoring is difficult in the sense of Assumption 7.2 (or if only integers from the family of linearly related prime pairs are hard to factor). Then integers from the notion* $\mathcal{A}$ *are hard to factor.*   □

Proof. Assume that we have an algorithm F that factors integers generated uniformly from the notion $\mathcal{A}$. Our goal is to prove that this algorithm also factors polynomially related prime pairs successfully. In other words: its existence contradicts the assumption that factoring in the form of Assumption 7.2 is difficult.

By assumption, there is an exponent s so that for any x_0 there is $x > x_0$ such that the assumed algorithm F has success probability $\mathrm{succ}_F(\mathcal{A}_x) \geq \ln^{-s} x$ on inputs from $\mathcal{A}_x$. We are going to prove that for each such x there exists a pair (m_0, n_0), both in the interval $[c_1 \ln x - \ln 2, c_2 \ln x + \ln 2]$, such that F executed with an input from image $\mu_{\mathbb{P}^{m_0}, \mathbb{P}^{n_0}}$ still has success probability at least $\ln^{-(s+k)} x$. By the interval restriction, m_0 and n_0 are polynomially (even linearly) related, namely $m_0 < \frac{2c_2}{c_1} n_0$ and $n_0 < \frac{2c_2}{c_1} m_0$ for large x. So that contradicts Assumption 7.2.

First, we cover the set $\mathcal{A}_x$ with small rectangles. Let $S_{m,n} := \mathbb{P}^{(m)} \times \mathbb{P}^{(n)}$ and $I_x := \{(m,n) \in \mathbb{N}^2 \mid S_{m,n} \cap \mathcal{A}_x \neq \emptyset\}$ then

$$\mathcal{A}_x \cap \mathbb{P}^2 \subseteq \biguplus_{(m,n) \in I_x} S_{m,n} =: S_x. \tag{7.4}$$

Next we give an upper bound on the number $\#S_x$ of prime pairs in the set S_x in terms of the number $\#\mathcal{A}(x)$ of prime pairs in the original notion: First, since each rectangle $S_{m,n}$ extends by a factor 2 along each axis we overshoot by at most that factor in each direction, that is, we have for $c_1' = c_1 - (1 + 2c_1)\frac{\ln 2}{\ln x}$ and all $x \in \mathbb{R}_{>1}$

$$S_x \subset \mathcal{M}_{4x}^{16r, c_1'} = \left\{(y,z) \in \mathbb{R}^2 \,\middle|\, y, z \geq \frac{1}{2}x^{c_1} \wedge \frac{x}{4r} < yz \leq 4x\right\}.$$

Provided x is large enough we can guarantee by Theorem 5.2 from the extended version (similar to Lemma 3.6) that

$$\#S_x \leq \#\mathcal{M}^{16r, c_1'}(4x) \leq \frac{8x}{c_1'^2 \ln x}.$$

On the other hand side we apply Lemma 3.6 for the notion $\mathcal{A}_x$ and use that $\mathcal{A}_x$ is large by assumption. Let $c = \max(2c_2 - 1, 1 - 2c_1)$. Then we obtain for large x with some $e_{\mathcal{A}}(x) \in \mathcal{O}\left(x^{\frac{3+c}{4}}\right)$.

$$\#\mathcal{A}(x) \geq \frac{\mathrm{area}(\mathcal{A}_x)}{c_2^2 \ln^2 x} - e_{\mathcal{A}}(x) \geq \frac{x}{2c_2^2 \ln^{k+2} x}.$$

Together we obtain

$$\frac{\#\mathcal{A}(x)}{\#S_x} \geq \frac{c_1'^2}{16c_2^2 \ln^{k+1} x} \geq \ln^{-(k+2)} x \tag{7.5}$$

By assumption we have $\mathrm{succ}_F(\mathcal{A}_x) \geq \ln^{-s} x$ for infinitely many values x. Thus F on an input from S_x still has large success even if we ignore that F might be successful for elements on $S_x \setminus \mathcal{A}_x$,

$$\mathrm{succ}_F(S_x) \geq \mathrm{succ}_F(\mathcal{A}_x)\frac{\#\mathcal{A}(x)}{\#S_x} \geq \ln^{-(k+s+2)} x.$$

Finally choose $(m_0, n_0) \in I_x$ for which the success of F on S_{m_0,n_0} is maximal. Then $\mathrm{succ}_F(S_{m_0,n_0}) \geq \mathrm{succ}_F(S_x)$. Combining with the previous we obtain that for infinitely many x there is a pair (m_0, n_0) where the success $\mathrm{succ}_F(S_{m_0,n_0})$ of F on inputs from S_{m_0,n_0} is still larger than inverse polynomial: $\mathrm{succ}_F(S_{m_0,n_0}) \geq \ln^{-(k+s+2)} x$.

For these infinitely many pairs (m_0, n_0) the success probability of the algorithm F on S_{m_0,n_0} is at least $\ln^{-(k+s+2)} x$ contradicting the hypothesis. $\qquad\Box$

All the specific notions that we have found in the literature fulfill the criterion of Theorem 7.3. Thus if factoring is difficult in the stated sense then each of them is invulnerable to factoring attacks. Note that the above reduction still works if the primes p, q are due to the side condition $\gcd((p-1)(q-1), e) = 1$ for a fixed integer e (see Theorem 3.11). We suspect that this is also the case if p and q are strong primes. Yet, this needs further investigation.

8   Impact on Standards and Implementations

In order to get an understanding of the common implementations, it is necessary to consult the main standard on RSA integers, namely the standard PKCS#1 (Jonsson & Kaliski 2003). However, one cannot find any requirements on the shape of RSA integers. Interestingly, they even allow more than two factors for an RSA modulus. Also the standard ISO 18033-2 (International Organization for Standards 2006) does not give any details besides the fact that it requires the RSA integer to be a product of two different primes of similar length.

8.1   RSA-OAEP

The RSA Laboratories (2000) describe the following variant:

Algorithm 8.1. Generating an RSA number for RSA-OAEP and variants.

Input: A number of bits k, the public exponent e.
Output: A number $n = pq$.

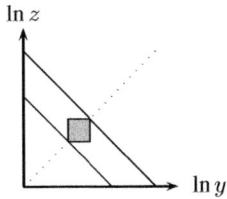

1. Pick p from $\left[\lfloor 2^{(k-1)/2}\rfloor + 1, \lceil 2^{k/2}\rceil - 1\right] \cap \mathbb{P}$ such that $\gcd(e, p-1) = 1$.
2. Pick q from $\left[\lfloor 2^{(k-1)/2}\rfloor + 1, \lceil 2^{k/2}\rceil - 1\right] \cap \mathbb{P}$ such that $\gcd(e, q-1) = 1$.
3. Return pq.

This will produce uniformly at random a number from the interval $[2^{k-1} + 1, 2^k - 1]$ and no cutting off. The output entropy is thus maximal. So this corresponds to the notion $\mathcal{A}^{\mathrm{FB}(2,0)}$ generated by Algorithm 5.5. The standard requires an expected number of $k \ln 2$ primality tests if the gcd condition is checked first. Otherwise the expected number of primality tests increases to $\frac{\varphi(e)}{\varphi_1(e)} \cdot k \ln 2$ (see 3.12). We will in the following always mean by the above notation that the second condition is checked first and afterwards the number is tested for primality. For the security Theorem 7.3 applies.

8.2   IEEE

IEEE standard 1363-2000, Annex A.16.11 (IEEE working group 2000) introduces our algorithmic proposal:

Algorithm 8.2. Generating an RSA number, IEEE 1363-2000.
Input: A number of bits k, the odd public exponent e.
Output: A number $n = pq$.

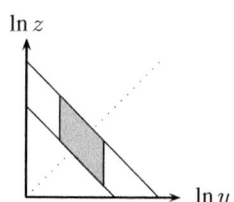

1. Pick p from $\left[2^{\lfloor \frac{k-1}{2} \rfloor}, 2^{\lfloor \frac{k+1}{2} \rfloor} - 1\right] \cap \mathbb{P}$ such that $\gcd(e, p - 1) = 1$.
2. Pick q from $\left[\left\lfloor \frac{2^{k-1}}{p} + 1 \right\rfloor, \left\lfloor \frac{2^k}{p} \right\rfloor\right] \cap \mathbb{P}$ such that $\gcd(e, q - 1) = 1$.
3. Return pq.

Since the resulting integers are in the interval $[2^{k-1}, 2^k - 1]$ this standard follows $\mathcal{A}^{\text{ALG}(2,1/2)}$ generated by a corrupted variant of Algorithm 5.5 using an expected number of $k \ln 2$ primality tests like the RSA-OAEP standard. The notion it implements is neither symmetric nor antisymmetric. The selection of the integers is *not* done in a uniform way, since the number of possible q for the largest possible p is roughly half of the corresponding number for the smallest possible p. Since the distribution of the outputs is close to uniform, we can use the techniques from Section 6 to estimate the output entropy to find that the entropy-loss is less than 0.69 bit. The (numerically approximated) values in Table 8.1 gave an actual entropy-loss of approximately 0.03 bit.

8.3   NIST

We will now analyze the standard FIPS 186-3 Information Technology Laboratory (2009). In Appendix B.3.1 of the standard one finds the following algorithm:

Algorithm 8.3. Generating an RSA number, FIPS186-3.
Input: A number of bits k, a number of bits $\ell < k$, the odd
       public exponent $2^{16} < e < 2^{256}$.
Output: A number $n = pq$.

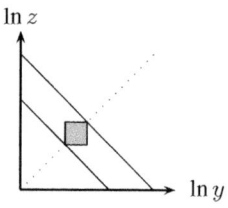

1. Pick p from $\left[\sqrt{2}2^{k/2-1}, 2^{k/2} - 1\right] \cap \mathbb{P}$ such that $\gcd(e, p - 1) = 1$ and $p \pm 1$ has a prime factor with at least ℓ bits.
2. Pick q from $\left[\sqrt{2}2^{k/2-1}, 2^{k/2} - 1\right] \cap \mathbb{P}$ such that $\gcd(e, p - 1) = 1$ and $q \pm 1$ has a prime factor with at least ℓ bits and $|p - q| > 2^{k/2-100}$.
3. Return pq.

In the standard it is required that the primes p and q shall be either provable prime or at least probable primes. The (at least ℓ-bit) prime factors of $p \pm 1$ and $q \pm 1$ have to be provable primes. We observe that also in this standard a variant of the notion $\mathcal{A}^{FB(2,0)}$ generated by Algorithm 5.5 is used. The output entropy is thus maximal. However, we do not have any restriction on the parity of k, such that the value $k/2$ is not necessarily an integer. Another interesting point is the restriction on the prime factors of $p \pm 1, q \pm 1$. Our notions cannot directly handle such requirements, but we are confident that this can be achieved by appropriately modifying the densities in Lemma 3.6.

The standard requires an expected number of slightly more than $k \ln 2$ primality tests. It is thus slightly less efficient than the RSA-OAEP standard. For the security the remarks from the end of Section 7 apply.

8.4   ANSI

The ANSI X9.44 standard (Accredited Standards Committee X9 2007), formerly part of ANSI X9.31, requires strong primes for an RSA modulus. Unfortunately, we could not access ANSI X9.44 directly and are therefore referring to ANSI X9.31-1998. Section 4.1.2 of the standard requires that

- $p - 1$, $p + 1$, $q - 1$, $q + 1$ each should have prime factors p_1, p_2, q_1, q_2 that are randomly selected primes in the range 2^{100} to 2^{120},
- p and q shall be the first primes that meet the above, found in an appropriate interval, starting from a random point,
- p and q shall be different in at least one of their first 100 bits.

The additional restrictions are similar to the ones required by NIST. This procedure will have an output entropy that is close to maximal (see Section 6).

8.5   OpenSSL

We now turn to implementations: For OpenSSL (Cox *et al.* 2009), we refer to the file rsa_gen.c. Note that in the configuration the routine used for RSA integer generation can be changed, while the algorithm given below is the standard one. OpenSSH (de Raadt *et al.* 2009) uses the same library. Refer to the file rsa.c. We have the following algorithm:

Algorithm 8.5. Generating an RSA number in OpenSSL.

Input: A number of bits k.

Output: A number $n = pq$.

1. Pick p from $\left[2^{\lfloor \frac{k-1}{2} \rfloor}, 2^{\lfloor \frac{k+1}{2} \rfloor} - 1 \right] \cap \mathbb{P}$.
2. Pick q from $\left[2^{\lfloor \frac{k-3}{2} \rfloor}, 2^{\lfloor \frac{k-1}{2} \rfloor} - 1 \right] \cap \mathbb{P}$.
3. Return pq.

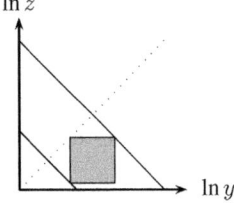

This is nothing but a rejection-sampling method of a notion similar to the fixed-bound notion $\mathcal{A}^{FB(4,0)}$ generated by Algorithm 5.2. The output entropy is thus maximal. The result the algorithm produces is always in $[2^{k-2}, 2^k - 1]$. It is clear that this notion is antisymmetric and the factors are on average a factor 2 apart of each other. The implementation runs in an expected number of $k \ln 2$ primality tests. The public exponent e is afterwards selected such that $\gcd((p-1)(q-1), e) = 1$. It is thus slightly more efficient than the RSA-OAEP standard. For the security Theorem 7.3 applies.

8.6   GnuPG

Also GnuPG (Skala *et al.* 2009) uses rejection-sampling of the fixed-bound notion $\mathcal{A}^{\mathrm{FB}(2,1)}$ generated by a variant of Algorithm 5.2, implying that the entropy of its output distribution is maximal.

Algorithm 8.7. Generating an RSA number in GnuPG.

Input: A number of bits k.
Output: A number $n = pq$.

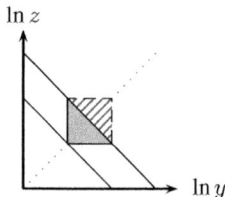

1. Repeat 2–3
2.   Pick p from $\left[2^{\lfloor \frac{k-1}{2} \rfloor}, 2^{\lfloor \frac{k+1}{2} \rfloor} - 1\right] \cap \mathbb{P}$.
3.   Pick q from $\left[2^{\lfloor \frac{k-1}{2} \rfloor}, 2^{\lfloor \frac{k+1}{2} \rfloor} - 1\right] \cap \mathbb{P}$.
4. Until $\operatorname{len}(pq) = 2 \lceil k/2 \rceil$
5. Return pq.

The hatched region in the picture above shows the possible outcomes that are discarded. We refer here to the file rsa.c. The algorithm is given in the function generate_std and produces always numbers with either k or $k+1$ bits depending on the parity of k. Note that the generation procedure indeed first selects primes before checking the validity of the range. This is of course a waste of resources, see Section 5.

The implementation runs in an expected number of roughly $2.589 \cdot (k+1) \ln 2$ primality tests. It is thus less efficient than the RSA OAEP standards. Like in the other so far considered implementations, the public exponent e is afterwards selected such that $\gcd((p-1)(q-1), e) = 1$. For the security Theorem 7.3 applies.

8.7   GNU Crypto

The GNU Crypto library (Free Software Foundation 2009) generates RSA integers the following way. Refer here in the file RSAKeyPairGenerator.java to the function generate.

Algorithm 8.8. Generating an RSA number in GNU Crypto.

Input: A number of bits k.
Output: A number $n = pq$.

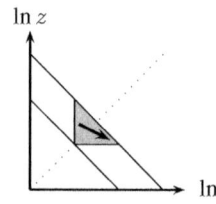

1. Pick p from $\left[2^{\lfloor \frac{k-1}{2} \rfloor}, 2^{\lfloor \frac{k+1}{2} \rfloor} - 1\right] \cap \mathbb{P}$.
2. Repeat
3.   Pick q from $\left[2^{\lfloor \frac{k-1}{2} \rfloor}, 2^{\lfloor \frac{k+1}{2} \rfloor} - 1\right]$.

Table 8.1. Overview of various standards and implementations. The entropies given there are always above 99.89% of the maximal entropy. As explained in the text, the entropy of the standards is sightly smaller than the values given due to the fixed public exponent e. Additionally there is a small entropy loss for the standard FIPS 186-3 due to the fact that it requires strong primes.

Standard	Notion	Entropy for specific k			Remarks
Implementation		768	1024	2048	
PKCS#1					
ISO 18033-2	Undefined	—	—	—	— — —
ANSI X9.44					
FIPS 186-3	$\mathcal{A}^{\mathrm{FB}(2,0)}$	$\lesssim 747.34$	$\lesssim 1002.51$	$\lesssim 2024.51$	strong primes
RSA-OAEP	$\mathcal{A}^{\mathrm{FB}(2,0)}$	747.34	1002.51	2024.51	—
IEEE 1363-2000	$\mathcal{A}^{\mathrm{ALG}(2,\frac{1}{2})}$	749.33	1004.50	2026.50	non-uniform
GNU Crypto	$\mathcal{A}^{\mathrm{FB}(2,1)}$	747.89	1003.06	2025.06	non-uniform
GnuPG	$\mathcal{A}^{\mathrm{FB}(2,1)}$	748.52	1003.69	2025.69	—
OpenSSL	$\cong \mathcal{A}^{\mathrm{FB}(4,0)}$	749.89	1005.06	2027.06	—

4. Until $\mathrm{len}(pq) = k$ and $q \in \mathbb{P}$.
5. Return pq.

The arrow in the picture above points to the results that will occur with higher probability. Also here the notion $\mathcal{A}^{\mathrm{FB}(2,1)}$ is used, but the generated numbers will not be uniformly distributed, since for a larger p we have much less choices for q. Since the distribution of the outputs is not close to uniform, we could only compute the entropy for real-world parameter choices numerically (see Table 8.1). For all choices the loss was less than 0.63 bit. The implementation is as efficient as the RSA-OAEP standard.

9   Conclusion

We have seen that there are various definitions for RSA integers, which result in substantially differing standards. We have shown that the concrete specification does not essentially affect the (cryptographic) properties of the generated integers: The entropy of the output distribution is always almost maximal, generating those integers can be done efficiently, and the outputs are hard to factor if factoring in general is hard. It remains open to incorporate strong primes into our model. Also a tight bound for the entropy of non-uniform selection is missing if the distribution is not close to uniform.

Acknowledgements

This work was funded by the B-IT foundation and the state of North Rhine-Westphalia.

References

1. Accredited Standards Committee X9, ANSI X9.44-2007: Public Key Cryptography Using Reversible Algorithms for the Financial Services Industry: Transport of Symmetric Algorithm Keys Using RSA. Technical report, American National Standards Institute, American Bankers Association (2007)

2. Brandt, J., Damgård, I.B.: On generation of probable primes by incremental search. In: Brickell, E.F. (ed.) CRYPTO 1992. LNCS, vol. 740, pp. 358–370. Springer, Heidelberg (1992), http://dx.doi.org/10.1007/3-540-48071-4_26

3. Cocks, C.C.: A note on 'non-secret encryption'. CESG Memo (1973) http://www.cesg.gov.uk/publications/media/notense.pdf (last download May 12, 2009)

4. Cox, M.J., Engelschall, R., Henson, S., Laurie, B.: OpenSSL 0.9.8j. Open source implementation (2009), http://www.openssl.org/ Refer to, http://www.openssl.org/ (last download April 21, 2009)

5. Decker, A., Moree, P.: Counting RSA-integers. Results in Mathematics 52, 35–39 (2008), http://dx.doi.org/10.1007/s00025-008-0285-5

6. Ellis, J.H.: The possibility of secure non-secret digital encryption (1970), http://cryptocellar.web.cern.ch/cryptocellar/cesg/possnse.pdf (last download May 12, 2009)

7. Free Software Foundation, GNU Crypto. Open source implementation (2009), http://www.gnu.org/software/gnu-crypto/ Refer to gnu-crypto-2.0.1.tar.bz2 (last download April 21,2009)

8. Goldreich, O.: Foundations of Cryptography: Basic Tools, vol. 1. Cambridge University Press, Cambridge (2001) ISBN 0-521-79172-3

9. IEEE working group 2000. IEEE 1363-2000: Standard Specifications For Public Key Cryptography. IEEE standard, IEEE, New York, NY 10017, http://grouper.ieee.org/groups/1363/P1363/

10. Information Technology Laboratory, FIPS 186-3: Digital Signature Standard (DSS). Technical report, National Institute of Standards and Technology (2009)

11. International Organization for Standards, ISO/IEC 18033-2, Encryption algorithms — Part 2: Asymmetric ciphers. Technical report, International Organization for Standards (2006)

12. Jonsson, J., Kaliski, B.: Public-Key Cryptography Standards (PKCS) #1: RSA Cryptography Specifications Version 2.1 (2003), http://tools.ietf.org/html/rfc3447 RFC 3447

13. Joye, M., Paillier, P.: Fast generation of prime numbers on portable devices: An update. In: Goubin, L., Matsui, M. (eds.) CHES 2006. LNCS, vol. 4249, pp. 160–173. Springer, Heidelberg (2006) ISBN 978-3-540-46559-1. ISSN 0302-9743, http://dx.doi.org/10.1007/11894063_13

14. Knuth, D.E.: The Art of Computer Programming, Seminumerical Algorithms, 3rd edn., vol. 2. Addison-Wesley, Reading (1998) ISBN 0-201-89684-2, 1st edn. (1969)

15. Loebenberger, D., Nüsken, M.: Coarse-grained integers e-print arXiv:1003.2165v1 (2010), http://arxiv.org/abs/1003.2165

16. Loebenberger, D., Nüsken, M.: Analyzing standards for RSA integers – extended version. e-print arXiv:1104.4356v2 (2011), http://www.arxiv.org/abs/1104.4356

17. Maurer, U.M.: Fast Generation of Prime Numbers and Secure Public-Key Cryptographic Parameters. Journal of Cryptology 8(3), 123–155 (1995), http://dx.doi.org/10.1007/BF00202269

18. NESSIE working group, NESSIE D20 - NESSIE security report. Technical report, NESSIE (2003)

19. von Neumann, J.: Various techniques used in connection with random digits. Monte Carlo methods. National Bureau of Standards, Applied Mathematics Series, vol. 12, pp. 36–38 (1951)

20. de Raadt, T., Provos, N., Friedl, M., Beck, B., Campbell, A., Song, D.: OpenSSH 2.1.1. Open source implementation (2009), http://www.openssh.org/, Refer to openssh-2.1.1p4.tar.gz (last download April 21,2009)

21. Rivest, R.L., Shamir, A., Adleman, L.M.: A Method for Obtaining Digital Signatures and Public-Key Cryptosystems. Technical Report MIT/LCS/TM-82, Massachusetts Institute of Technology, Laboratory for Computer Science, Cambridge, Massachusetts (1977)
22. Rivest, R.L., Shamir, A., Adleman, L.M.: A Method for Obtaining Digital Signatures and Public-Key Cryptosystems. Communications of the ACM 21(2), 120–126 (1978)
23. RSA Laboratories :RSAES-OAEP Encryption Scheme. Algorithm specification and supporting documentation, RSA Security Inc., Bedford, MA 01730 USA (2000),ftp://ftp.rsasecurity.com/pub/rsalabs/rsa_algorithm/rsa-oaep_spec.pdf.
24. Skala, M., Roth, M., Hernaeus, N., Guyomarch, R., Koch, W.: GnuPG. Open source implementation (2009), http://www.gnupg.org Refer to gnupg-2.0.9.tar.bz2 (last download April 21, 2009)
25. Wohlmacher, P.: Bekanntmachung zur elektronischen Signatur nach dem Signaturgesetz und der Signaturverordnung (Übersicht über geeignete Algorithmen). Bundesanzeiger 13, 346–350 (2009), http://www.bundesnetzagentur.de/media/archive/14953.pdf

Hashing into Hessian Curves

Reza Rezaeian Farashahi

Department of Computing,
Macquarie University,
Sydney, NSW 2109, Australia
reza.farashahi@mq.edu.au

Abstract. We describe a hashing function from the elements of the finite field $\mathbb{F}_q$ into points on a Hessian curve. Our function features the uniform and smaller size for the cardinalities of almost all fibers compared with the other known hashing functions for elliptic curves. For ordinary Hessian curves, this function is $2:1$ for almost all points. More precisely, for odd q, the cardinality of the image set of the function is exactly given by $(q+i+2)/2$ for some $i = -1, 1$.

Next, we present an injective hashing function from the elements of $\mathbb{Z}_m$ into points on a Hessian curve over $\mathbb{F}_q$ with odd q and $m = (q+i)/2$ for some $i = -1, 1, 3$.

Keywords: Elliptic curve cryptography, Hessian curve, hashing.

1 Introduction

It is well-known that many cryptographic schemes based on elliptic curves (especially pairing-based) require efficient hashing of finite field elements into points on a given elliptic curve. Examples are the Boneh- Franklin identity based encryption scheme [1], the SPEKE (Simple Password Exponential Key Exchange) [16] and the PAK (Password Authenticated Key exchange) [3].

For instance, in the Boneh- Franklin identity based encryption scheme [1], they use a particular supersingular elliptic curve over the finite field $\mathbb{F}_p$ endowed with a one-to-one mapping f from elements of $\mathbb{F}_p$ into the points on the curve. This enables to hash using $f(h(m))$ where h is a classical hash function.

For hashing into an ordinary elliptic curve, the classical approach is the probabilistic try and increment method. We note that designing a deterministic efficient hash function from field elements to points on an elliptic curve has been an open problem for quite a long time. Recently, two constructions have appeared. The first one is that of Shallue and van de Woestijne [20] which has been later simplified and extended to hyperelliptic curves by Ulas in [24]. The second one is by Icart [15]. Furthermore, the properties of the Icart's function have been studied in [9,10]. Also, several new ones have been presented recently [4,18] both for elliptic and hyperelliptic curves.

Moreover, designing an efficient injective hashing from the elements of $\mathbb{Z}_m$, for some integer m, into the points of a given elliptic curve is a challenging open

A. Nitaj and D. Pointcheval (Eds.): AFRICACRYPT 2011, LNCS 6737, pp. 278–289, 2011.

problem. Such functions will have several applications in many cryptographic schemes based on elliptic curves and in designing cryptographically secure pseudorandom generators with elliptic curves.

In this paper, we describe a function from fields element into the points on a Hessian curve. The use of Hessian curves in cryptography has been studied in [5,17,21,13,14]. Moreover, recently very efficient and fast unified addition formulas for Hessian curves have provided, see [8,2]. Our technique to obtain a hash function for Hessian curves is similar to that of Icart's technique [15] which is based on computing the cubic root of a field element. Moreover, for ordinary Hessian curves, our function is $2 : 1$ at almost all points, which gives the uniform and small size 2 for the cardinalities of the fibers. Furthermore, the cardinality of the image set of the function is exactly given by $m = (q + i + 2)/2$, for some $i = -1, 1$, if q is odd.

We also describe how to extract random integers in $\mathbb{Z}_m$ from the elements of the image set of the Hessian hash function. This leads us to describe an injective hashing function from $\mathbb{Z}_m$ into points of the Hessian curve. This perfect hashing function is the first known injective hashing into points of ordinary elliptic curves over finite fields.

Throughout the paper, we use

$$\mathbb{N}_\ell = \{1, 2, \dots, \ell\} \qquad \text{and} \qquad \mathbb{Z}_m = \{0, 1, \dots, m - 1\}.$$

The cardinality of a finite set $\mathcal{S}$ is denoted by $\#\mathcal{S}$.

For a field $\mathbb{F}$, we denote its algebraic closure by $\overline{\mathbb{F}}$ and its multiplicative subgroup by $\mathbb{F}^*$. The letter p always denotes an odd prime number and the letter q always denotes a prime power. As usual, $\mathbb{F}_q$ is a finite field of size q. We note that the $\mathbb{F}_q$ is of odd characteristic p.

For the odd prime p, let χ be the quadratic character in $\mathbb{F}_q$. So, for $x \in \mathbb{F}_q$, we have $\chi(x) = 0, 1$ or -1, if $x = 0$, $x = w^2$ for some $w \neq 0$ or $x \neq w^2$ for all $w \in \mathbb{F}_q$, respectively.

2   Background on Hessian Curves

A Hessian curve H_d over a finite field $\mathbb{F}_q$ is given by the equation

$$\mathrm{H}_d \; : \; x^3 + y^3 + 1 = 3dxy, \tag{1}$$

where $d \in \mathbb{F}_q$ with $d^3 \neq 1$, see [12].

We recall that the set of $\mathbb{F}_q$-rational points of H_d denoted by $\mathrm{H}_d(\mathbb{F}_q)$ forms an Abelian group. For $q \equiv 2 \pmod 3$, the Hessian curve H_d has one $\mathbb{F}_q$-rational point at infinity $\mathcal{O}$ which is the neutral element of the group. For an affine point P of H_d, the x-coordinate of P is denoted by $x(P)$.

Let π_d be the projection map

$$\pi_d : \mathrm{H}_d(\mathbb{F}_q) \longrightarrow \mathbb{F}_q \bigcup \{\infty\} \tag{2}$$

defined by $\pi_d(P) = x(P)$ if $P \neq \mathcal{O}$ and $\pi_d(P) = \infty$ if $P = \mathcal{O}$.

For $i = 1, 2$, let $\mathcal{X}_{i,d}$ be the subset of $\mathbb{F}_q$ given by

$$\mathcal{X}_{i,d} = \left\{ x \in \mathbb{F}_q : \#\pi_d^{-1}(x) = i \right\} \tag{3}$$

and let

$$\mathcal{X}_d = \mathcal{X}_{1,d} \cup \mathcal{X}_{2,d}. \tag{4}$$

In other words, $\mathcal{X}_d$ is the the set of elements $x \in \mathbb{F}_q$ so that there exist only one or two affine points P in $\mathrm{H}_d(\mathbb{F}_q)$ with $x(P) = x$.

For an element $x \in \mathbb{F}_q$, let g_x be the polynomial in $\mathbb{F}_q[Y]$ given by

$$g_x = Y^3 - 3dxY + x^3 + 1.$$

Then, the number of distinct roots of g_x in $\mathbb{F}_q$ is equal to $\#\pi_d^{-1}(x)$. For $x \in \mathbb{F}_q$, let Δ_x be the discriminant of g_x, that is

$$\Delta_x = -27(x^6 + 2(1 - 2d^3)x^3 + 1). \tag{5}$$

Remark 1. For all $d \in \mathbb{F}_q$ with $d^4 - d \neq 0$ and $p > 3$, we have

$$\mathcal{X}_{2,d} = \left\{ x \in \mathbb{F}_q : \Delta_x = 0 \right\}.$$

Proposition 1. *Let $q \equiv 2 \pmod 3$ and let H_d be a Hessian curve over $\mathbb{F}_q$ defined by the equation (1) with $d \neq 1$. For the cardinality of the set $\mathcal{X}_d$, given by equation (4), we have*

$$\#\mathcal{X}_d = \begin{cases} q, & \text{if } d = 0, \\ \left(q + \chi(d^4 - d) \right)/2, & \text{if } d \neq 0. \end{cases}$$

Proof. We note that the map $\kappa : \mathbb{F}_q \to \mathbb{F}_q$ by $\kappa(x) = x^3$ is a bijection, since $q \equiv 2 \pmod 3$. For an element $x \in \mathbb{F}_q$, let Δ_x be the discriminant of the polynomial g_x given by (5).

If $d = 0$, for all $x \in \mathbb{F}_q$ the polynomial g_x has only one root in $\mathbb{F}_q$, since κ is a bijection over $\mathbb{F}_q$. So, $\mathcal{X}_d = \mathbb{F}_q$.

Next, we assume that $d \neq 0$. If $\Delta_x \neq 0$, then the number of irreducible factors of g_x over $\mathbb{F}_q$ equals 2 if and only if Δ_x is a quadratic non-residue element of $\mathbb{F}_q$ (see [6,22] or [23, Corollary 1]). Therefore, we have

$$\mathcal{X}_{1,d} = \left\{ x \in \mathbb{F}_q : \chi(\Delta_x) = -1 \right\}.$$

Recall from Remark 1 that $\mathcal{X}_{2,d} = \left\{ x \in \mathbb{F}_q : \chi(\Delta_x) = 0 \right\}$. Hence,

$$\mathcal{X}_d = \left\{ x \in \mathbb{F}_q : \chi(\Delta_x) \neq 1 \right\},$$

and

$$\#\mathcal{X}_d = \sum_{x \in \mathbb{F}_q, \chi(\Delta_x) \neq 1} 1.$$

We recall that the map κ is a bijection over $\mathbb{F}_q$. For $x \in \mathbb{F}_q$, let

$$D_x = x^2 + 2(1 - 2d^3)x + 1.$$

For $q \equiv 2 \pmod 3$, we have $\chi(-3) = -1$. Therefore, we obtain

$$\#\mathcal{X}_d = \sum_{x \in \mathbb{F}_q, \chi(\mathcal{D}_x) \neq -1} 1 = \sum_{x \in \mathbb{F}_q} \frac{1 + \chi(\mathcal{D}_x)}{2} + \sum_{x \in \mathbb{F}_q, \mathcal{D}_x = 0} \frac{1}{2}.$$

We note that $\sum_{x \in \mathbb{F}_q} \chi(\mathcal{D}_x) = -1$ if $d^4 - d \neq 0$ (see [19, Theorem 5.48]). Moreover, there are two distinct values of $x \in \mathbb{F}_q$ with $\mathcal{D}_x = 0$ if and only if $\chi(d^4 - d) = 1$. Hence, for $d \neq 0$, we have

$$\#\mathcal{X}_d = \frac{q-1}{2} + \frac{1 + \chi(d^4 - d)}{2} = \frac{q + \chi(d^4 - d)}{2}.$$

So, the proof of Proposition 1 is complete. $\square$

3   The Encoding Map

Let $\mathbb{F}_q$ be the finite field with $q \equiv 2 \pmod 3$ and let H_d be the Hessian curve over $\mathbb{F}_q$ defined by the equation (1), with $d \neq 1$. In this section, we define an encoding map from the elements of $\mathbb{F}_q$ to the $\mathbb{F}_q$-rational points of H_d. We also describe a bijection between the set of affine points of the image set of this map and the set $\mathcal{X}_d$, given by equation (4). Then, we obtain the cardinality of the image set of the map.

3.1   The Encoding Map from $\mathbb{F}_q$ to $H_d(\mathbb{F}_q)$

For $q \equiv 2 \pmod 3$, we consider the map

$$h_d : \mathbb{F}_q \longrightarrow H_d(\mathbb{F}_q) \tag{6}$$

defined by $h_d(u) = (x, y)$ if $u \neq -1$, where

$$x = -u \left(\frac{d^3 u^3 + 1}{u^3 + 1} \right)^{1/3} , \quad y = - \left(\frac{d^3 u^3 + 1}{u^3 + 1} \right)^{1/3} + du \tag{7}$$

and $h_d(u) = \mathcal{O}$ if $u = -1$.

We note that the map $\kappa : \mathbb{F}_q \to \mathbb{F}_q$ by $\kappa(x) = x^3$ is a bijection, since $q \equiv 2 \pmod 3$. Moreover, for $u \in \mathbb{F}_q$, the point $(x, y) = h_d(u)$ satisfies the equation (1). So, the map h_d is well defined. We let

$$\mathcal{H}_d = h_d(\mathbb{F}_q), \tag{8}$$

that is the image set of the map h_d. We also note that, for a point $P = (x, y) \in H_d(\mathbb{F}_q)$, we have $P \in \mathcal{H}_d$ if and only if there exists an element $u \in \mathbb{F}_q$ satisfying

$$du^2 - uy + x = 0. \tag{9}$$

Notice that if $d = 0$, the Hessian curve H_d is a supersingular elliptic curve with $q + 1$ $\mathbb{F}_q$-rational points. Furthermore, the corresponding map h_d is injective.

3.2   Size of the Image Set $\mathcal{H}_d$

The following theorem gives the explicit formulas for the cardinality of the image set $\mathcal{H}_d = h_d(\mathbb{F}_q)$.

Theorem 1. *Let $q \equiv 2$ (mod 3) and let H_d be a Hessian curve over $\mathbb{F}_q$ defined by the equation (1) with $d \neq 1$. Let h_d be the map defined by the equation (6). For the cardinality of the image set $\mathcal{H}_d = h_d(\mathbb{F}_q)$, we have*

$$\#\mathcal{H}_d = \begin{cases} q, & \text{if } d = 0, \\ (q + \chi(d^4 - d) + 2)\,/2, & \text{if } d \neq 0. \end{cases}$$

Proof. Let

$$N_k = \# \left\{ P : P \in \mathcal{H}_d,\ \#h_d^{-1}(P) = k \right\}, \qquad k = 1, 2, \dots.$$

From the definition of the map h_d, we have $\#h_d^{-1}(P) = 1$ if $P = \mathcal{O}$. Moreover, from equation (9), for a point $P = (x, y) \in H_d(\mathbb{F}_q)$, we have $P \in \mathcal{H}_d$ if and only if the equation

$$dU^2 - yU + x = 0 \qquad (10)$$

has a solution $u \in \mathbb{F}_q$. Furthermore, the number of distinct roots of the equation (10) equals $\#h_d^{-1}(P)$. We see that, for $P \in \mathcal{H}_d$, $\#h_d^{-1}(P) = 1$ or 2. Therefore, $N_k = 0$ for $k > 2$. Notice that $N_1 + 2N_2 = q$. So, we have

$$\#\mathcal{H}_d = \sum_{k=1}^{2} N_k = \frac{q + N_1}{2}. \qquad (11)$$

As we noticed before, the value $N_1 - 1$ is equal to the number of points $P = (x, y) \in H_d(\mathbb{F}_q)$ where the equation (10) has exactly one root in $\mathbb{F}_q$. To compute the value of N_1, we distinguish the following possibilities for d.

- If $d = 0$, then for all points $P \in \mathcal{H}_d$ we have $\#h_d^{-1}(P) = 1$. In other words, the map h_d is injective. So, $N_1 = q$.
- If $d \neq 0$, for a point $(x, y) \in H_d(\mathbb{F}_q)$, the equation (10) has only one root in $\mathbb{F}_q$ if and only if $y^2 - 4dx = 0$. This implies that $z^2 + 16d^3z + 64d^3 = 0$ with $z = y^3$. The discriminant of the latter quadratic equation is $4^4 d^3 (d^3 - 1)$. Since $q \equiv 2$ (mod 3), we have $N_1 = 1$ if $\chi(d^4 - d) = -1$ and $N_1 = 3$ if $\chi(d^4 - d) = 1$.

So, we have $N_1 = q$ if $d = 0$ and $N_1 = 2 + \chi(d^4 - d)$ if $d \neq 0$. Then, using (11), we obtain the explicit formulas for the cardinality of $\mathcal{H}_d$.   □

3.3   Correspondence between the Sets $\mathcal{X}_d$ and $\mathcal{H}_d$

Here, we show the correspondence between the sets $\mathcal{X}_d$ and $\mathcal{H}_d$, given by (4) and (8) respectively.

We consider the restriction of the projection map π_d, given by (2), to the set $\mathcal{H}_d$, that is the map

$$\pi_d : \mathcal{H}_d \longrightarrow \mathcal{X}_d \bigcup \{\infty\} \tag{12}$$

defined by $\pi_d(P) = x(P)$ if $P \neq \mathcal{O}$ and $\pi_d(P) = \infty$ if $P = \mathcal{O}$. In the following lemma we shall show the map π_d is well defined.

For $d = 0$, we have $\mathcal{X}_d = \mathbb{F}_q$. Furthermore, the map π_d is injective and

$$\pi_d(\mathcal{H}_d) = (\mathcal{X}_d \setminus \{-1\}) \bigcup \{\infty\}.$$

Moreover, in the following Proposition we will see the map π_d, for $d \neq 0, 1$, is bijective.

Lemma 1. *Let $q \equiv 2 \pmod 3$ and let H_d be a Hessian curve over $\mathbb{F}_q$ defined by the equation (1) with $d \neq 0, 1$. Let π_d be the map defined by (12). Then, the map π_d is well defined.*

Proof. We note only the point $\mathcal{O}$ is mapped to ∞. Then, let P be an affine point of $\mathcal{H}_d$. We have

$$x(P) = -u \left(\frac{d^3 u^3 + 1}{u^3 + 1} \right)^{1/3}$$

for some $u \in \mathbb{F}_q$.

Recall from the proof of Proposition 1 that $x(P) \in \mathcal{X}_d$ if and only if $\chi(\Delta_{x(P)}) \neq 1$, where Δ_x, for $x \in \mathbb{F}_q$, is given by (5). We have,

$$\Delta_{x(P)} = -27 \left(x(P)^6 + 2 \left(1 - 2d^3 \right) x(P)^3 + 1 \right).$$

Then, we obtain

$$\Delta_{x(P)} = -27 \left(\frac{d^3 u^6 + 2d^3 u^3 + 1}{u^3 + 1} \right)^2.$$

Therefore, we have $\chi(\Delta_{x(P)}) \neq 1$, since $\chi(-3) \neq 1$. Hence, $x(P) \in \mathcal{X}_d$, which shows that the map π_d is well defined. $\qquad\square$

Here, we describe the inverse image of the set $\mathcal{X}_{2,d}$, given by (3), under the map π_d. Let $\mathcal{H}_{2,d}$ be the subset of $\mathcal{H}_d$ given by

$$\mathcal{H}_{2,d} = \#\pi_d^{-1}(\mathcal{X}_{2,d}). \tag{13}$$

Lemma 2. *Let $q \equiv 2 \pmod 3$. For the set $\mathcal{H}_{2,d}$, given by (13), we have*

$$\mathcal{H}_{2,d} = \left\{ (x, y) : x = (2d^3 - 1 + 2ds)^{1/3}, \ y = 2(s - d^2)x^2, \ s^2 = d^4 - d \right\}$$

if $\chi(d^4 - d) = 1$ and $\mathcal{H}_{2,d} = \{\}$ if $\chi(d^4 - d) \neq 1$.

Proof. Let $x \in \mathcal{X}_{2,d}$. Recall from the Remark 1 that $\Delta_x = 0$. Then, $x^3 = 2d^3 - 1 + 2ds$, where s is a square root of $d^4 - d$ in $\mathbb{F}_q$. Next, the points (x, y_1), (x, y_2) with $y_1 = (d^2 - s)x^2$, $y_2 = 2(s - d^2)x^2$ are the only points of $H_d(\mathbb{F}_q)$

with the x-coordinate equal to x. Moreover, from equation (9), for a point $P = (x, y) \in H_d(\mathbb{F}_q)$, we have $P \in \mathcal{H}_d$ if and only if $\chi(y^2 - 4dx) \neq -1$. We have

$$y_1^2 - 4dx = -3dx = -3y_1^2.$$

Since $\chi(-3) = -1$ and $d \neq 0$, we see that $(x, y_1) \notin \mathcal{H}_d$. But, we have $y_2^2 - 4dx = 0$. So, (x, y_2) is a point of $\mathcal{H}_d$ and $\#\pi_d^{-1}(x) = 1$. $\square$

Proposition 2. *Let $q \equiv 2 \pmod{3}$ and let H_d be a Hessian curve over $\mathbb{F}_q$ defined by the equation (1) with $d \neq 0, 1$. Let π_d be the map defined by (12). Then, the map π_d is a bijection.*

Proof. Lemma 1 shows that the map π_d is well defined. Next, we shall prove that the map π_d is injective, i.e., for all elements x in $\mathcal{X}_d$, we have $\#\pi_d^{-1}(x) \leq 1$.

Let $x \in \mathcal{X}_d$. By the definition of the set $\mathcal{X}_d$, given by (4), we have $x \in \mathcal{X}_{1,d} \cup \mathcal{X}_{2,d}$. Recall from the proof of Proposition 1 that $x \in \mathcal{X}_{1,d}$ if and only if $\Delta_x \neq 0$ and $x \in \mathcal{X}_{2,d}$ if and only if $\Delta_x = 0$. So, we have the following cases.

- If $x \in \mathcal{X}_{1,d}$ then from the definition of $\mathcal{X}_{1,d}$, given by (3), there is only one point on $H_d(\mathbb{F}_q)$ with $x(P) = x$. Hence, $\#\pi_d^{-1}(x) \leq 1$.
- If $x \in \mathcal{X}_{2,d}$, then form Lemma 2 we see that $\#\pi_d^{-1}(x) = 1$.

Therefore for all $x \in \mathcal{X}_d$, we have $\#\pi_d^{-1}(x) \leq 1$, i.e., the map π_d is injective. We note that the point $\mathcal{O}$ is mapped to ∞. From Proposition 1 and Theorem 1, we have $\#\mathcal{H}_d = 1 + \#\mathcal{X}_d$. Hence, the map π_d is a bijection, which completes the proof of this lemma. $\square$

4   Randomness of the Encoding Map h_d

Here, we study how to extract random bits from the point $h_d(u)$ of $H_d(\mathbb{F}_q)$ where u is chosen uniformly at random in $\mathbb{F}_q$.

Let num be a bijective encoding map

$$\text{num} : \mathbb{F}_q \longrightarrow \{-(q-1)/2, \cdots, -1, 0, 1, \cdots, (q-1)/2\}, \qquad (14)$$

with $\text{num}(-x) = -\text{num}(x)$. Moreover, let

$$\text{sgn} : \mathbb{F}_q \to \{-1, 1\}$$

be the sign function given by $\text{sgn}(x) = -1, 1$, if $\text{num}(x)$ is a negative or non-negative integer, respectively.

Let $q = 2\ell + 1$ and let ext_d be the map defined by

$$\text{ext}_d : \mathcal{X}_d \longrightarrow \mathbb{N}_\ell$$
$$\text{ext}_d(x) = |\text{num}(s)|, \qquad (15)$$

where $s = x^3 + w + 1 - 2d^3$ with $w^2 = x^6 + 2(1 - 2d^3)x^3 + 1$, $\text{sgn}(w) = 1$.

Lemma 3. *For $q \equiv 2$ (mod 3) and for all d in $\mathbb{F}_q$ with $d \neq 0, 1$, the function ext_d, given by (15), is well defined and surjective.*

Proof. Recall from Proposition 1 that, for $x \in \mathbb{F}_q$, we have $x \in \mathcal{X}_d$ if and only if $\chi(\Delta_x) \neq 1$, where Δ_x is given by (5). So, we have $x \in \mathcal{X}_d$ if and only if

$$\chi\left(-27\left(x^6 + 2\left(1 - 2d^3\right)x^3 + 1\right)\right) \neq 1.$$

Since $\chi(-3) = -1$, we have $x \in \mathcal{X}_d$ if and only if

$$x^6 + 2\left(1 - 2d^3\right)x^3 + 1 = w^2$$

for some element w in $\mathbb{F}_q$. Therefore, x is a point of $\mathcal{X}_d$ if and only if

$$z^2 - w^2 = 4d^3(d^3 - 1),$$

where $z = x^3 + 1 - 2d^3$. Then, by the definition of the function ext_d given by (15), for $x \in \mathcal{X}_d$, we have

$$\mathsf{ext}_d(x) = |\mathsf{num}(s)|,$$

where $s = z + w$ and $\mathsf{num}(w) \geq 0$. Clearly $\mathsf{ext}_d(x) \neq 0$, since $d \neq 0, 1$. Also, we have $\mathsf{ext}_d(x) \in \mathbb{N}_\ell$, so the function ext_d is well defined.

Next, we shall prove that ext_d is a surjective map. Let $n \in \mathbb{N}_\ell$. Then, there exist z_1, w_1 in $\mathbb{F}_q$ such that $\mathsf{num}^{-1}(n) = z_1 + w_1$ and $z_1^2 - w_1^2 = 4d^3(d^3 - 1)$. Let $s = \mathsf{num}^{-1}(\mathsf{sgn}(w_1)n)$. Then,

$$s = \mathsf{sgn}(w_1)\mathsf{num}^{-1}(n) = \mathsf{sgn}(w_1)z_1 + \mathsf{sgn}(w_1)w_1.$$

Let $z = \mathsf{sgn}(w_1)z_1$ and $w = \mathsf{sgn}(w_1)w_1$. So, we have $s = z + w$ and $\mathsf{sgn}(w) = 1$. Next, let $x = (z + 2d^3 - 1)^{1/3}$. Then, one can easily see that $\mathsf{ext}_d(x) = n$. $\square$

Remark 2. We note that the function ext_d, for $d \neq 0, 1$, is $2 : 1$ at the points of $\mathcal{X}_{2,d}$. We recall from Remark 1 that for $d \neq 0, 1$, we have $x \in \mathcal{X}_{2,d}$ if and only if $\Delta_x = 0$. From Proposition 1, we have $\#\mathcal{X}_d = \left(q + \chi(d^4 - d)\right)/2$ if $d \neq 0, 1$. By Lemma 3, the function ext_d is surjective. So, the function ext_d is $1 : 1$ at all points except at the points of $\mathcal{X}_{2,d}$. Therefore, the function ext_d is a bijection if and only if $\chi(d^4 - d) = -1$.

Remark 3. Recall the set $\mathcal{H}_{2,d}$ from (13) that is $\mathcal{H}_{2,d} = \pi_d^{-1}(\mathcal{X}_{2,d})$. From Lemma 2, we have $\mathcal{H}_{2,d} = \{P_1, P_2\}$ if $\chi(d^4 - d) = 1$, where

$$P_1 = \left((2d^3 - 1 + z)^{1/3}, \ (z - 2d^3)x^2/d\right),$$

$$P_2 = \left((2d^3 - 1 - z)^{1/3}, \ (-z - 2d^3)x^2/d\right),$$

and $z^2 = 4d^3(d^3 - 1)$ with $\mathsf{sgn}(z) = 1$.

Now, we extend the function $\mathtt{ext}_d$ to the image set $\mathcal{H}_d$ and also make it bijective by small modification.

Let $m = \#\mathcal{H}_d$. Let $\mathtt{Ext}_d$ be the function defined by

$$\mathtt{Ext}_d : \mathcal{H}_d \longrightarrow \mathbb{Z}_m$$

$$\mathtt{Ext}_d(P) = \begin{cases} 0, & \text{if } P = \mathcal{O} \\ \mathtt{ext}_d(x), & \text{if } P = (x, y), \ P \neq P_2 \\ m - 1 & \text{if } P = P_2, \end{cases} \tag{16}$$

Corollary 1. *For $q \equiv 2 \pmod 3$ and for all $d \in \mathbb{F}_q$ with $d \neq 0, 1$, the function $\mathtt{Ext}_d$, given by (16), is a bijection.*

Proof. The proof is a direct consequence of Lemma 3 and Remarks 2, 3. $\qquad\square$

5 An Injective Encoding Map

Here, we define an injective map from the set $\mathbb{Z}_m$ with

$$m = (q + \chi(d^4 - d) + 2)/2$$

into the set of $\mathbb{F}_q$-rational points of the Hessian curve H_d over $\mathbb{F}_q$.

Let $q = 2\ell + 1$. We recall the definition of the functions $\mathtt{num}$ and $\mathtt{sgn}$, see §4. Let $\mathtt{elt}$ be the injective function defined by

$$\mathtt{elt} : \mathbb{N}_\ell \longrightarrow \mathbb{F}_q^*,$$
$$\mathtt{elt}(n) = \mathtt{num}^{-1}(n).$$

In other words, the function $\mathtt{elt}$ represent uniquely each positive integer $n \leq \ell$ by an element of $\mathbb{F}_q$.

For $q \equiv 2 \pmod 3$, we define the map

$$\mathtt{i}_d : \mathbb{N}_\ell \longrightarrow \mathrm{H}_d(\mathbb{F}_q) \tag{17}$$

by $\mathtt{i}_d(n) = (x, y)$, where

$$x = duv \qquad \text{and} \qquad y = d(u + v)$$

with

$$u = -\left(1 + \frac{2(d^3 - 1)}{\mu \mathtt{elt}(n)}\right)^{1/3}, \qquad v = -\left(1 + \frac{\mu \mathtt{elt}(n)}{2d^3}\right)^{1/3},$$

$$\mu = \mathtt{sgn}\left(\frac{\mathtt{elt}(n)^2 - 4d^3(d^3 - 1)}{2\mathtt{elt}(n)}\right). \tag{18}$$

Proposition 3. *For $q \equiv 2 \pmod 3$ and for all d in $\mathbb{F}_q$ with $d \neq 0, 1$, the map $\mathtt{i}_d$, defined by (17), is well defined and injective.*

Proof. Let $n \in \mathbb{N}_\ell$ and let u, v be given by the equation (18). We note that u, v are well defined, since $q \equiv 2 \pmod{3}$. Let $x = duv$ and $y = d(u + v)$. By the definition of the map h_d, given by (7), we can see that $(x, y) = h_d(u) = h_d(v)$. So, the map $\mathtt{i}_d$ is well defined.

Next, we prove that $\mathtt{i}_d$ is an injective map. Let $\iota : \mathbb{N}_\ell \longrightarrow \mathbb{N}_\ell$, be the composite function defined by $\iota = \mathtt{ext}_d \circ \pi_d \circ \mathtt{i}_d$, where the functions $\mathtt{ext}_d$, π_d and $\mathtt{i}_d$ are given by (15), (2), and (17), respectively. We have $\pi_d(\mathtt{i}_d(n)) = x$, where $x = duv$. We note that $x \in \mathcal{X}_d$, so the function ι is well defined. Then,

$$\iota(n) = \mathtt{ext}_d(\pi_d(\mathtt{i}_d(n))) = \mathtt{ext}_d(x).$$

We have $x^6 + 2(1 - 2d^3)x^3 + 1 = w^2$, where

$$w = \left(\frac{\mathtt{elt}(n)^2 - 4d^3(d^3 - 1)}{2\mathtt{elt}(n)} \right).$$

By the equation (18), we also have $\mu = \mathtt{sgn}(w)$. So, $\mathtt{sgn}(\mu w) = 1$. Let $s = x^3 + \mu w + 1 - 2d^3$. We see that $s = \mathtt{elt}(n)/\mu$ and from equation (15), we obtain $\mathtt{ext}_d(x) = n$. Therefore, the function ι is the identity function. Hence, the map $\mathtt{i}_d$ is an injective map, which completes the proof of this proposition. □

Remark 4. We recall the set $\mathcal{H}_{2,d}$ from (13). From Lemma 2 and Remark 3 we have $\mathcal{H}_{2,d} = \{P_1, P_2\}$ if $\chi(d^4 - d) = 1$. Recall from Remark 3 that $x(P_1) = \left(2d^3 - 1 + z\right)^{1/3}$ where $z \in \mathbb{F}_q$ with $z^2 = 4d^3(d^3 - 1)$ and $\mathtt{sgn}(z) = 1$. For $n = |\mathtt{num}(z)|$, we have $\mathtt{i}_d(n) = P_1$. Furthermore, the point P_2 is not in the image set of the map $\mathtt{i}_d$. Actually, this is the only point of $\mathcal{H}_d$ which is not in the image set of $\mathtt{i}_d$.

Now, we extend the definition of the map $\mathtt{i}_d$ to the set $\mathbb{Z}_m$, where

$$m = \#\mathcal{H}_d = \left(q + 2 + \chi(d^4 - d)\right)/2.$$

Let $\mathtt{I}_d$ be the function defined by

$$\mathtt{I}_d : \mathbb{Z}_m \longrightarrow \mathtt{H}_d(\mathbb{F}_q)$$

$$\mathtt{I}_d(n) = \begin{cases} \mathcal{O}, & \text{if } n = 0, \\ \mathtt{i}_d(n), & \text{if } 1 \le n \le m - 2, \\ \mathtt{i}_d(n), & \text{if } n = m - 1, \ \chi(d^4 - d) = -1, \\ P_2, & \text{if } n = m - 1, \ \chi(d^4 - d) = 1, \end{cases} \tag{19}$$

where $P_2 = \left(\left(2d^3 - 1 + z\right)^{1/3}, \left(z - 2d^3\right)x^2/d\right)$ with $z^2 = 4d^3(d^3 - 1)$ and $\mathtt{sgn}(z) = -1$.

Corollary 2. *For $q \equiv 2 \pmod{3}$ and for all $d \in \mathbb{F}_q$ with $d \neq 0, 1$, the function $\mathtt{I}_d$, given by (19), is injective.*

Proof. The proof is a direct consequence of Proposition 3 and Remark 4. □

6   Concluding Remarks

In this paper, we gave an efficient hashing of the elements of $\mathbb{F}_q$ into the $\mathbb{F}_q$-rational points of the Hessian curve H_d. The size of the image set of this function is about $q/2$ if $d \neq 0$ and q if $d = 0$. We remark that the case $d = 0$ is corresponded to the supersingular Hessian curve.

For ordinary Hessian curves, our encoding map h_d, given by (6), is a $2 : 1$ map at all points except at one or three points, depending on the value of $\chi(d^4 - 4)$, that is $1 : 1$. So, in comparison with Icart's map, [15], our map have the uniform size 2 for the size of almost all preimages. We recall that the size of the preimages of Icart's map is varied between 1 and 4.

Moreover, we observed a bijection between the image set $h_d(\mathbb{F}_q)$, denoted by $\mathcal{H}_d$, and the set $\mathcal{X}_d \cup \{\infty\}$, given by (4). This observation leads us to extract random bits from the points in the image set $\mathcal{H}_d$ by extracting random bits from the elements of $\mathcal{X}_d$. Next, we defined an injective map from the set $\mathbb{Z}_m$ into the set of points of H_d over $\mathbb{F}_q$, where m is the size of the image set $\mathcal{H}_d$. This function can be used for several application in many cryptographic scheme and pseudorandom generators based on elliptic curves.

We note that our map h_d is not surjective. Moreover, using the general construction of the well behaved hash functions into the points of elliptic curves, studied in [7], we can obtain *indifferentiable* hash functions into the points of Hessian curves with very tight regularity bounds.

In the full version of this paper, the similar results will be presented for Hessian curve over the binary finite field $\mathbb{F}_{2^k}$. In particular, we will present an injective hashing function from the bit strings of length $k - 1$ into points on a Hessian curve over $\mathbb{F}_{2^k}$.

Acknowledgment. The author would like to thank anonymous reviewers for their useful comments.

References

1. Boneh, D., Franklin, M.K.: Identity-based encryption from the weil pairing. In: Kilian, J. (ed.) CRYPTO 2001. LNCS, vol. 2139, pp. 213–229. Springer, Heidelberg (2001)
2. Bernstein, D.J., Lange, T.: Explicit-formulas database, http://www.hyperelliptic.org/EFD/
3. Boyko, V., MacKenzie, P.D., Patel, S.: Provably secure password-authenticated key exchange using diffie-hellman. In: Preneel, B. (ed.) EUROCRYPT 2000. LNCS, vol. 1807, pp. 156–171. Springer, Heidelberg (2000)
4. Brier, E., Coron, J.-S., Icart, T., Madore, D., Randriam, H., Tibouchi, M.: Efficient indifferentiable hashing into ordinary elliptic curves. In: Rabin, T. (ed.) CRYPTO 2010. LNCS, vol. 6223, pp. 237–254. Springer, Heidelberg (2010)
5. Chudnovsky, D.V., Chudnovsky, G.V.: Sequences of numbers generated by addition in formal groups and new primality and factorization tests. Advances in Applied Mathematics 7(4), 385–434 (1986)

6. Dalen, K.: On a theorem of Stickelberger. Math. Scand. 3, 124–126 (1955)
7. Farashahi, R.R., Fouque, P.-A., Shparlinski, I., Tibouchi, M., Voloch, F.: Indifferentiable deterministic hashing to elliptic and hyperelliptic curves. Cryptology ePrint Archive, Report 2010/539 (2010), http://eprint.iacr.org/2010/539
8. Farashahi, R.R., Joye, M.: Efficient Arithmetic on Hessian Curves. In: Nguyen, P., Pointcheval, D. (eds.) PKC 2010. LNCS, vol. 6056, pp. 243–260. Springer, Heidelberg (2010)
9. Farashahi, R.R., Shparlinski, I., Voloch, F.: On hashing into elliptic curves. J. Math. Cryptology 3, 353–360 (2009)
10. Fouque, P.-A., Tibouchi, M.: Estimating the size of the image of deterministic hash functions to elliptic curves. In: Abdalla, M., Barreto, P.S.L.M. (eds.) LATIN-CRYPT 2010. LNCS, vol. 6212, pp. 81–91. Springer, Heidelberg (2010)
11. Fouque, P.-A., Tibouchi, M.: Deterministic encoding and hashing to odd hyperelliptic curves. In: Joye, M., Miyaji, A., Otsuka, A. (eds.) Pairing 2010. LNCS, vol. 6487, pp. 265–277. Springer, Heidelberg (2010)
12. Hesse, O.: Über die Elimination der Variabeln aus drei algebraischen Gleichungen vom zweiten Grade mit zwei Variabeln. Journal Für Die Reine und Angewandte Mathematik 10, 68–96 (1844)
13. Hisil, H., Carter, G., Dawson, E.: New formulæ for efficient elliptic curve arithmetic. In: Srinathan, K., Rangan, C.P., Yung, M. (eds.) INDOCRYPT 2007. LNCS, vol. 4859, pp. 138–151. Springer, Heidelberg (2007)
14. Hisil, H., Wong, K.K.-H., Carter, G., Dawson, E.: Faster group operations on elliptic curves. In: Brankovic, L., Susilo, W. (eds.) AISC 2009, vol. 98, pp. 7–19 (2009)
15. Icart, T.: How to hash into elliptic curves. In: Halevi, S. (ed.) CRYPTO 2009. LNCS, vol. 5677, pp. 303–316. Springer, Heidelberg (2009)
16. Jablon, D.P.: Strong password-only authenticated key exchange. SIGCOMM Comput. Commun. Rev. 26(5), 5–26 (1996)
17. Joye, M., Quisquater, J.-J.: Hessian elliptic curves and side-channel attacks. In: Koç, Ç.K., Naccache, D., Paar, C. (eds.) CHES 2001. LNCS, vol. 2162, pp. 402–410. Springer, Heidelberg (2001)
18. Kammerer, J.-G., Lercier, R., Renault, G.: Encoding points on hyperelliptic curves over finite fields in deterministic polynomial time. In: Joye, M., Miyaji, A., Otsuka, A. (eds.) Pairing 2010. LNCS, vol. 6487, pp. 278–297. Springer, Heidelberg (2010)
19. Lidl, R., Niederreiter, H.: Finite fields. Cambridge University Press, Cambridge (1997)
20. Shallue, A., van de Woestijne, C.: Construction of rational points on elliptic curves over finite fields. In: Hess, F., Pauli, S., Pohst, M. (eds.) ANTS 2006. LNCS, vol. 4076, pp. 510–524. Springer, Heidelberg (2006)
21. Smart, N.P.: The hessian form of an elliptic curve. In: Koç, Ç.K., Naccache, D., Paar, C. (eds.) CHES 2001. LNCS, vol. 2162, pp. 118–125. Springer, Heidelberg (2001)
22. Stickelberger, L.: Über eine neue Eigenschaft der Diskriminanten algebraischer Zahlkörper. In: Verh. 1 Internat. Math. Kongresses, Zürich, Leipzig, pp. 182–193 (1897)
23. Swan, R.G.: Factorization of Polynomials over Finite Fields. Pac. J. Math. 19, 1099–1106 (1962)
24. Ulas, M.: Rational points on certain hyperelliptic curves over finite fields. Bull. Polish Acad. Sci. Math. 55(2), 97–104 (2007)
25. Vishne, U.: Factorization of Trinomials over Galois Fields of Characteristic 2. Finite Fields and Their Applications 3, 370–377 (1997)

On Randomness Extraction in Elliptic Curves

Abdoul Aziz Ciss and Djiby Sow

École doctorale de Mathématiques et d'Informatique,
Université Cheikh Anta Diop de Dakar, Sénégal
BP: 5005, Dakar Fann
abdoul.ciss@ucad.edu.sn, sowdjibab@ucad.sn

Abstract. A deterministic extractor for an elliptic curve, that converts a uniformly random point on the curve to a random k-bit-string with a distribution close to uniform, is an important tool in cryptography. Such extractors can be used for example in key derivation functions, in key exchange protocols and to design cryptographically secure pseudorandom number generator.

In this paper, we present a simple and efficient deterministic extractor for an elliptic curve E defined over $\mathbb{F}_{q^n}$, where q is prime and n is a positive integer. Our extractor, denoted by $\mathcal{D}_k$, for a given random point P on E, outputs the k-first $\mathbb{F}_q$-coordinates of the abscissa of the point P. This extractor confirms the two conjectures stated by R. R. Farashahi and R. Pellikaan in [6] and by R. R. Farashahi, A. Sidorenko and R. Pellikaan in [7], related to the extraction of bits from coordinates of a point of an elliptic curve.

Keywords: Elliptic curves, Randomness extraction, character sums.

1 Introduction

The problem of randomness extraction from a point of an elliptic curve has several cryptographic applications. For example, it can be used in key derivation functions, in key exchange protocols and to design cryptographically secure pseudorandom number generator. For instance, by the end of Diffie-Hellman key exchange protocol [3], Alice and Bob agree on a common secret $K_{AB} \in G$, where G is a cryptographic cyclic group, which is indistinguishable from another element of G under the decisional Diffie-Hellman assumption [1]. The secret key used for encryption or authentication of data has to be indistinguishable from a uniformly random bit-string. Hence, the common secret K_{AB} cannot be directly used as a session key.

A classical solution is the use of a hash function to map an element of the group G onto a uniformly random bit-string of fixed length. However, the indistinguishability cannot be proved under the decisional Diffie-Hellman assumption. In this case, it is necessary to appeal to the Random Oracle or to other technics. Many results in this direction can be found in [4,10]. An alternative to hash function is to use a deterministic extractor when G is the group of points of an elliptic curve.

A. Nitaj and D. Pointcheval (Eds.): AFRICACRYPT 2011, LNCS 6737, pp. 290–297, 2011.

A deterministic extractor for an elliptic curve is a function that converts a uniformly random point on the curve to a random l-bit-string with a distribution close to uniform.

Several deterministic extractors for elliptic curves were proposed. One of them is Gürel's extractor [8]. This extractor, for a given point P on $E(\mathbb{F}_{q^2})$, where q is some power of an odd prime, outputs half of the bits of the abscissa of P. If the point P is taken uniformly at random, the bits extracted from P are indistinguishable from a uniformly random bit-string of the same length [8]. He proposed in the same paper an extractor for an elliptic curve defined over a prime field but this one extracts less than the half of the bits of the abscissa of a random point on the curve.

In 2007, R. R. Farashahi and R. Pellikaan [6] proposed a good deterministic extractor for (hyper)elliptic curves defined over the quadratic extension of a prime field $\mathbb{F}_{q^2}$, $q \neq 2$ and improved at the same time Gürel's extractor. In their work, they stated a conjecture on the randomness of an extractor over a curve $\mathcal{C}$ (absolutely irreducible nonsingular affine) that is defined over a field F_{q^n} (non necessary quadratic) by $y^m = f(x)$. They left the proof of this conjecture as an open problem.

In 2008, R. R. Farashahi, R. Pellikaan and A. Sidorenko [7] studied the binary case by working over a quadratic extension of binary field. In fact, they present two deterministic and efficient extractors for the binary elliptic curve $E(\mathbb{F}_{2^N})$, where $N = 2l$ and l is a positive integer. For a given point P on $E(\mathbb{F}_{2^N})$, they extract the first or the second $\mathbb{F}_{2^l}$-coefficient of the abscissa of the point P. In the paper [7], they state the corresponding of the above conjecture for binary elliptic curve defined by $y^2 + xy = f(x)$. They leave also the proof of this second conjecture as an open problem.

In this paper, we prove that these two conjectures in [6] and [7] are true for elliptic curves. To our knowledge, these two conjectures have not been resolved yet.

In fact, we propose a quite simple deterministic extractor, denoted $\mathcal{D}_k$ for the elliptic curve E defined over $\mathbb{F}_{q^n}$ (where q is a prime integer and n is an integer without restriction) by $y^2 + (a_1x + a_3)y = x^3 + a_2x^2 + a_4x + a_6$. $\mathcal{D}_k$ extract the k first $\mathbb{F}_q$-coefficients of the abscissa of the point P (where the abscissa x of P is an element of $\mathbb{F}_{q^n}$ considered as a n-dimensional vector space over $\mathbb{F}_q$).

We show that $\mathcal{D}_k$ is a good extractor for $E(\mathbb{F}_{q^n})$. Our approach is somewhat similar to the technic developed by C. Chevalier, P. Fouque, D. Pointcheval and S. Zimmer in [2] at Eurocrypt 2009, where they proposed a quite simple deterministic randomness extractor from a random Diffie-Hellman element defined over a group of points of an elliptic curve. We use also results from [13] published by D. Kohel and I. Shparlinski in 2000.

We organize the paper as follows:

Section 1: We recall some basic definitions related to collision probability, statistical distance and randomness extractors.

In section 2: we review some notations, definitions and fundamentals theorems on character sums on elliptic curves.

In section 3: we describe our new extractor which solves the two problems in [6] and [7] .

2   Preliminaries

2.1   Deterministic Extractor

Definition 1. *(Collision probability): Let S be a finite set and X be an S-valued random variable. The collision probability of X, denoted by $Col(X)$, is the probability*

$$Col(X) = \sum_{s \in S} Pr[X = s]^2.$$

If X and X' are identically distributed random variables on S, the collision probability of X is interpreted as $Col(X) = Pr[X = X']$.

Definition 2. *(Statistical distance): Let X and Y be S-valued random variables, where S is a finite set. The statistical distance $\Delta(X, Y)$ between X and Y is*

$$\Delta(X, Y) = \tfrac{1}{2} \sum_{s \in S} |Pr[X = s] - Pr[Y = s]|.$$

Let U_S be a random variable uniformly distributed on S. Then a random variable X on S is said to be δ-uniform if

$$\Delta(X, U_S) \leq \delta.$$

Lemma 1. *Let X be a random variable over a finite set S of size $|S|$ and $\epsilon = \Delta(X, U_S)$ be the statistical distance between X and U_S, the uniformly distributed random variable over S. Then,*

$$Col(X) \geq \frac{1 + 4\epsilon^2}{|S|}.$$

Proof. The proof of this lemma is given in [2].

Definition 3. *Let S and T be two finite sets. Let Ext be a function $Ext : S \longrightarrow T$. We say that Ext is a deterministic (T, δ)-extractor for S if $Ext(U_S)$ is δ-uniform on T. That is*

$$\Delta(Ext(U_S), U_T) \leq \delta.$$

For more information on extractors, see [14,15].

3   Character Sums and Elliptic Curves

In this section we recall some notions and results that we will use later.

3.1   On Character Sums

In the following, we denote by e_q the character on $\mathbb{F}_q$ such that, for all $x \in \mathbb{F}_q$

$$e_q(x) = e^{\frac{2i\pi x}{q}} \in \mathbb{C}^*.$$

and by $\Psi = \mathrm{Hom}(\mathbb{F}_{q^n}, \mathbb{C}^*)$, the group of additive characters on $\mathbb{F}_{q^n}$ that can be described by the set

$$\Psi = \{\psi, \psi(z) = e_q(\mathrm{Tr}(\alpha z)), \text{ for } \alpha \in \mathbb{F}_{q^n}\}$$

where $\mathrm{Tr}(x)$ is the trace of $x \in \mathbb{F}_{q^n}$ to $\mathbb{F}_q$ (see [13]).

Lemma 2. *For any interval I of $\mathbb{F}_{q^n}$, the bound*

$$\sum_{\psi \in \Psi} \left| \sum_{\beta \in I} \psi(\beta) \right| \leq q^n (1 + \log(q))$$

holds.

Proof. See [13] for the proof.

3.2   Elliptic Curves

Let E be an elliptic curve [9,11] over $\mathbb{F}_{q^n}$ given by the Weierstrass equation

$$y^2 + (a_1 x + a_3)y = x^3 + a_2 x^2 + a_4 x + a_6.$$

We denote by $E(\mathbb{F}_{q^n})$ the group of elements of E over $\mathbb{F}_{q^n}$. The cardinality of $E(\mathbb{F}_{q^n})$ is N, where N satisfies

$$|N - (q^n + 1)| \leq 2\sqrt{q^n}.$$

We denote by $\mathbb{F}_{q^n}[E]$ the coordinate ring of E over $\mathbb{F}_{q^n}$ and by $\mathbb{F}_{q^n}(E)$ the function field of E over $\mathbb{F}_{q^n}$. $\mathbb{F}_{q^n}[E] = \mathbb{F}_{q^n}[x, y]/(h(x, y))$, where $h(x, y) = y^2 + (a_1 x + a_3)y - x^3 - a_2 x^2 - a_4 x - a_6$ is irreducible.

We denote also by $\mathbb{F}_{q^n}(E)$ the field of fractions of $\mathbb{F}_{q^n}[E]$. For any point $P \in E(\mathbb{F}_{q^n}) - \{\infty\}$, we denote $P = (x(P), y(P))$, where $x(P)$ and $y(P)$ are the coordinates of the point P.

If $f \in \mathbb{F}_{q^n}(E)$, we denote by $\deg(f)$ its degree, that is $\sum_{i=1}^{s} n_i \deg(P_i)$ if $\sum_{i=1}^{s} n_i P_i$ is the divisor of poles of f. We denote by $\Omega = \mathrm{Hom}(E(\mathbb{F}_{q^n}), \mathbb{C}^*)$, the group of characters on $E(\mathbb{F}_{q^n})$, and by ω_0 the trivial character, that is $\omega_0(P) = 1$ for each $P \in E(\mathbb{F}_{q^n})$.

For a subgroup G of $E(\mathbb{F}_{q^n})$, we define

$$S(\omega, \psi, f, E(\mathbb{F}_{q^n})) = \sum_{P \in E(\mathbb{F}_{q^n})} \omega(P)\psi(f(P))$$

$$S(\omega, \psi, f, G) = \sum_{P \in G} \omega(P)\psi(f(P))$$

and

$$S(\psi, f, E(\mathbb{F}_{q^n})) = S(\omega_0, \psi, f, E(\mathbb{F}_{q^n})) = \sum_{P \in E(\mathbb{F}_{q^n})} \psi(f(P))$$

$$S(\psi, f, G) = S(\omega_0, \psi, f, G) = \sum_{P \in G} \psi(f(P))$$

where $\omega \in \Omega$, $\psi \in \Psi$ and $f \in \mathbb{F}_{q^n}(E)$. In particular, we will be interested in the sum with $f = x$.

In [13], D. R. Kohel and I. E. Shparlinski presented the following theorem and corollary which give a bound for $S(\omega, \psi, f, E(\mathbb{F}_{q^n}))$.

Theorem 1. *(see [13]) Let E be an elliptic curve over $\mathbb{F}_{q^n}$ and $f \in \mathbb{F}_{q^n}(E)$, $\omega \in \Omega$ and $\psi \in \Psi$ be non trivial characters. Then*

$$S(\omega, \psi, f, E(\mathbb{F}_{q^n})) \leq 2 \deg(f) \sqrt{q^n}$$

and, in particular, if $f = x$, $\deg(f) = 2$ and

$$S(\psi, f, E(\mathbb{F}_{q^n})) \leq 4\sqrt{q^n}.$$

Corollary 1. *Let E be an elliptic curve over $\mathbb{F}_{q^n}$ and G a subgroup of $E(\mathbb{F}_{q^n})$, $\omega \in \Omega$ and $\psi \in \Psi$ be non trivial characters. Then*

$$S(\omega, \psi, f, G) \leq 2 \deg(f) \sqrt{q^n}$$

and, in particular, if $f = x$, $\deg(f) = 2$ and

$$S(\psi, f, G) \leq 4\sqrt{q^n}.$$

In the following section, we use the bound of the sums $S(\omega, \psi, f, E(\mathbb{F}_{q^n}))$ to show that $\mathcal{D}_k$ is a good randomness extractor for $E(\mathbb{F}_{q^n})$.

4   Randomness Extraction in $E(\mathbb{F}_{q^n})$

Consider the finite field $\mathbb{F}_{q^n}$, where q is prime and n is a positive integer. Then $\mathbb{F}_{q^n}$ is a n-dimensional vector space over $\mathbb{F}_q$. Let $\{\alpha_1, \alpha_2, \ldots, \alpha_n\}$ be a basis of $\mathbb{F}_{q^n}$ over $\mathbb{F}_q$. That means, every element x of $\mathbb{F}_{q^n}$ can be represented in the form $x = x_1\alpha_1 + x_2\alpha_2 + \ldots + x_n\alpha_n$, where $x_i \in \mathbb{F}_{q^n}$. Let E be the elliptic curve over $\mathbb{F}_{q^n}$ defined by the Weierstrass equation

$$y^2 + (a_1 x + a_3)y = x^3 + a_2 x^2 + a_4 x + a_6.$$

The extractor $\mathcal{D}_k$, where k is a positive integer less than n, for a given point P on $E(\mathbb{F}_{q^n})$, outputs the k first $\mathbb{F}_q$-coordinates of the abscissa of the point P.

Definition 4. *Let G be a subgroup of $E(\mathbb{F}_{q^n})$ and k a positive integer less than n. The extractor $\mathcal{D}_k$ is defined as a function*

$$\mathcal{D}_k : G \longrightarrow \mathbb{F}_q^k$$

$$P = (x, y) \longmapsto (x_1, x_2, \ldots, x_k)$$

where $x \in \mathbb{F}_{q^n}$ is represented as $x = x_1\alpha_1 + x_2\alpha_2 + \ldots + x_n\alpha_n$, and $x_i \in \mathbb{F}_{q^n}$.

Theorem 2. *Let E be an elliptic curve defined over $\mathbb{F}_{q^n}$ and G a subgroup of $E(\mathbb{F}_{q^n})$. Then*

$$\Delta(\mathcal{D}_k(U_G), U_{\mathbb{F}_q^k}) \leq \frac{2\sqrt{q^{n+k}}\sqrt{1 + \log(q)}}{|G|}$$

where U_G is uniformly distributed in G and $U_{\mathbb{F}_q^k}$ is the uniform distribution in $\mathbb{F}_q^k$.

Proof. Let $f = x \in \mathbb{F}_{q^n}(E)$ and consider the sets

$$M = \{(x_{k+1}\alpha_{k+1} + x_{k+2}\alpha_{k+2} + \ldots + x_n\alpha_n), x_i \in \mathbb{F}_q\} \subset \mathbb{F}_{q^n}$$

and

$$\mathbb{A} = \{(P, Q) \in G^2, \exists m \in M : f(P) - f(Q) = m\}.$$

Since

$$\frac{1}{q^n} \sum_{\psi \in \Psi} \psi(f(P) - f(Q) - m) = 1_{(P,Q,m)}$$

where $1_{(P,Q,m)}$ is the characteristic function which is equal to 1 if $f(P) - f(Q) = m$ and 0 otherwise, we have

$$|\mathbb{A}| = \frac{1}{q^n} \sum_{P \in G} \sum_{Q \in G} \sum_{m \in M} \sum_{\psi \in \Psi} \psi(f(P) - f(Q) - m)$$

and

$$Col(\mathcal{D}_k(U_G)) = \frac{1}{|G|^2} |\mathbb{A}|$$

$$Col(\mathcal{D}_k(U_G)) = \frac{1}{|G|^2 \times q^n} \sum_{P \in G} \sum_{Q \in G} \sum_{m \in M} \sum_{\psi \in \Psi} \psi(f(P) - f(Q) - m)$$

$$= \frac{1}{|G|^2 q^n} q^{n-k}|G|^2 + \frac{1}{|G|^2 q^n} \sum_{P \in G} \sum_{Q \in G} \sum_{m \in M} \sum_{\psi \neq \psi_0} \psi(f(P) - f(Q) - m)$$

$$= \frac{1}{q^k} + \frac{1}{|G|^2 q^n} \sum_{\psi \neq \psi_0} \left(\sum_{P \in G} \psi(f(P))\right) \left(\sum_{Q \in G} \psi(-f(Q))\right) \left(\sum_{m \in M} \psi(-m)\right)$$

$$= \frac{1}{q^k} + \frac{1}{|G|^2 q^n} \sum_{\psi \neq \psi_0} S(\psi, f, G) S(\psi, -f, G) \left(\sum_{m \in M} \psi(-m)\right)$$

$$\leq \frac{1}{q^k} + \frac{R^2}{|G|^2 q^n} \sum_{\psi \neq \psi_0} \left|\sum_{m \in M} \psi(-m)\right|$$

$$\leq \frac{1}{q^k} + \frac{R^2 q^n(1 + \log(q))}{|G|^2 q^n}$$

$$\leq \frac{1}{q^k} + \frac{R^2(1 + \log(q))}{|G|^2}$$

where $R = \max_\psi(|S(\psi, f, G)|)$

By Lemma 1, we have

$$\frac{1 + 4\Delta^2(\mathcal{D}_k(U_G), U_{\mathbb{F}_q^k})}{q^k} \leq Col(\mathcal{D}_k(U_G)) \leq \frac{1}{q^k} + \frac{R^2(1 + \log(q))}{|G|^2}$$

Since $R \leq 4\sqrt{q^n}$ by Corollary 1, we have

$$\Delta(\mathcal{D}_k(U_G), U_{\mathbb{F}_q^k}) \leq \frac{R\sqrt{q^k}\sqrt{1 + \log(q)}}{2|G|} \leq \frac{2\sqrt{q^{n+k}}\sqrt{1 + \log(q)}}{|G|}$$

$\square$

The following theorem confirms the conjecture of Farashahi et al. in [6,7] in the case of elliptic curves.

Theorem 3. *Let E be an elliptic curve defined over $\mathbb{F}_{q^n}$, then*

$$\Delta(\mathcal{D}_k(U_E), U_{\mathbb{F}_q^k}) \leq \frac{c}{\sqrt{q^{n-k}}}$$

where U_E is the uniform distribution in $E(\mathbb{F}_{q^n})$ and c is a constant depending on n.

Proof. Using the fact that $||E(\mathbb{F}_{q^n})| - (q^n + 1)| \leq 2\sqrt{q^n}$, we have

$$\Delta(\mathcal{D}_k(U_E), U_{\mathbb{F}_q^k}) \leq \frac{2\sqrt{q^{n+k}}\sqrt{1 + \log(q)}}{|E(\mathbb{F}_{q^n})|} \leq \frac{2\sqrt{q^{n+k}}\sqrt{1 + \log(q)}}{q^n - 2\sqrt{q^n} + 1}$$

Put $c = \frac{2\sqrt{1 + \log(q)}}{1 - 2q^{-n/2} + q^{-n}}$ to obtain the desired result.

$\square$

Remark 1. Since for cryptographic use, q^n is very large then we have $c \approx 2\sqrt{1 + \log(q)}$. For example, for any n we can assume that $|q| \leq 1024$, then $c \leq 65$

For the binary case, as stated by Farashahi et al. in [7], we have the following theorem.

Theorem 4. *If $q = 2$ and $n \geq 11$ then*

$$\Delta(\mathcal{D}_k(U_E), U_{\mathbb{F}_2^k}) \leq \frac{3}{\sqrt{2^{n-k}}}$$

Proof. Follows from the above theorem and remarks.

This theorem confirms the second conjecture of Farashahi et al. in [7].

5   Conclusion

We constructed a simple and efficient deterministic extractor $\mathcal{D}_k$, where k is a positive integer, for the elliptic curves defined over $\mathbb{F}_{q^n}$. The extractor $\mathcal{D}_k$, for a given point P on E outputs the k-first $\mathbb{F}_q$-coordinate of the abscissa of the point P. The main part of the paper is the analysis of the extractor which shows that $\mathcal{D}_k$ is a good randomness extractor. This extractor can be used in any elliptic curve protocol.

At the same time, we resolve the two different conjectures of Farashahi and al. stated in [6] and [7].

As further work, our aim is to generalize this extractor to hyperelliptic [12] and Edwards curves [5] and also on curve $\mathcal{C}$ (absolutely irreducible nonsingular affine) that is defined over a field $\mathbb{F}_{q^n}$ by $y^m = f(x)$ as stated by Farashahi et al. in [7] .

References

1. Boneh, D.: The decision diffie-hellman problem. In: Buhler, J.P. (ed.) ANTS 1998. LNCS, vol. 1423, pp. 48–63. Springer, Heidelberg (1998)
2. Chevalier, C., Fouque, P., Pointcheval, D., Zimmer, S.: Optimal Randomness Extraction from a Diffie-Hellman Element. In: Joux, A. (ed.) EUROCRYPT 2009. LNCS, vol. 5479, pp. 572–589. Springer, Heidelberg (2009)
3. Diffie, W., Hellman, M.: New Directions in Cryptography. IEEE Transactions On Information Theory 22(6), 644–654 (1976)
4. Dodis, Y., Gennaro, R., Håstad, J., Krawczyk, H., Rabin, T.: Randomness Extraction and Key Derivation Using the CBC, Cascade and HMAC Modes. In: Franklin, M.K. (ed.) CRYPTO 2004. LNCS, vol. 3150, pp. 494–510. Springer, Heidelberg (2004)
5. Edwards, H.M.: A normal form for elliptic curves. Bulletin of the American Mathematical Society 44 48(177), 393–422 (2007), http://www.ams.org/bull/2007-44-03/S0273-0979-07-01153-6/home.html
6. Farashahi, R.R., Pellikaan, R.: The Quadratic Extension Extractor for (Hyper)elliptic Curves in Odd Characteristic. In: Carlet, C., Sunar, B. (eds.) WAIFI 2007. LNCS, vol. 4547, pp. 219–236. Springer, Heidelberg (2007)
7. Farashahi, R.R., Sidorenko, A., Pellikaan, R.: Extractors for Binary Elliptic Curves. Designs, Codes and Cryptography 94, 171–186 (2008)
8. Gürel, N.: Extracting bits from coordinates of a point of an elliptic curve, Cryptology ePrint Archive, Report 2005/324 (2005), http://eprint.iacr.org/
9. Handbook of elliptic and hyperelliptic curve cryptography. Discrete Math. Appl. (Boca Raton). Chapman Hall/CRC, Boca Raton, FL (2006)
10. Håstad, J., Impagliazzo, R., Levin, L., Luby, M.: A pseudorandom generator from any one-way function. SIAM Journal on Computing 28(4), 1364–1396 (1999)
11. Koblitz, N.: Guide to Elliptic Curve Cryptography. Springer, Heidelberg (2004)
12. Koblitz, N.: Hyperelliptic Cryptosystems. Journal of Cryptology 1, 139–150 (1989)
13. Kohel, D.R., Shparlinski, I.E.: On Exponential Sums and Group Generators for Elliptic Curves over Finite Fields. In: Bosma, W. (ed.) ANTS 2000. LNCS, vol. 1838, pp. 395–404. Springer, Heidelberg (2000)
14. Shaltiel, R.: Recent Developments in Explicit Constructions of Extractors. Bulletin of the EATCS 77, 67–95 (2002)
15. Trevisan, L., Vadhan, S.: Extracting Randomness from Samplable Distributions. In: IEEE Symposium on Foundations of Computer Science, pp. 32–42 (2000)

Fault Analysis of Grain-128 by Targeting NFSR

Sandip Karmakar and Dipanwita Roy Chowdhury

Department of Computer Science and Engineering,
Indian Institute of Technology, Kharagpur,
India

Abstract. Fault attack is one of the most efficient form of side channel attack against implementations of cryptographic algorithms. This kind of attacks have been shown to be extremely successful against stream ciphers. The eStream cipher Grain-128 has already been shown to be weak against fault attack, when faults are injected in the LFSR. In this paper, we show that Grain-128 can also be attacked by inducing faults in the NFSR. The attack requires about 56 fault injections for NFSR and a computational complexity of about 2^{21}.

Keywords: Stream Cipher, Grain-128, Side Channel Attack, Fault Attack, NFSR Fault Attack.

1 Introduction

The eStream [1] project was an effort to study and standardize stream ciphers. The final eStream portfolio lists three hardware based stream ciphers and four software based stream ciphers. Those ciphers are vulnerable against a number of side channel attacks ([9], [10], [11], [2]).

Fault attacks are one of the most efficient side channel attacks known till date. In this kind of attack, faults are injected during cipher operations. The attacker then analyzes the fault free and faulty cipher-texts or key-streams to deduce partial or full value of the secret *key*. The literature shows that both the block ciphers ([5], [6]) and stream ciphers ([9], [10], [11]) are vulnerable against fault attack. A number of recent works ([9], [10], [11]) have been carried out successfully on fault attacks against stream ciphers. Recent research shows that stream ciphers are extremely susceptible to fault attacks. Although, injecting faults in a cipher is a challenging task, most of the related research on stream ciphers work by inducing faults at only one bit position of the cipher. Methods like clock glitch, laser shots ([12], [13]) have been shown to be a practical way of inducing faults in a crypto-system.

Grain-128 [8] proposed by Martin Hell et al. is one of the three hardware based ciphers enlisted in the eStream portfolio. According to the final report on eStream project [3], Grain-128 is only the second best stream cipher in hardware domain. Till date only few cryptanalysis are reported against Grain-128. A cryptanalysis based on dynamic cube attack [7] and a fault based attack [4] are the only known weaknesses of Grain-128. The fault based attack [4] works on

A. Nitaj and D. Pointcheval (Eds.): AFRICACRYPT 2011, LNCS 6737, pp. 298–315, 2011.

inducing faults in the LFSR register of a Grain-128 implementation. It exploits the fault to obtain the full internal state of the cipher and consequently obtains the full secret *key* due to the reversibility of Grain-128 round operations. The work presented in [4] is a strong attack which employed a realistic fault model. It [4] needs an average of 24 consecutive faults and consumes couple of minutes of off-line computation to recover the secret *key* of the cipher. In [4], the authors also present a countermeasure which considers only the LFSR as a fault target. However, in this work we show that the NFSR of Grain-128 is also not protected against fault attack. Unlike [4], we inject faults in the NFSR and show that secret *key* of the cipher can be recovered. Complexity of the attack is comparable to that of [4].

In this work, we assume that faults can be injected into Grain-128 through some conventional techniques. Faults are induced at the NFSR of the cipher. We analyze Grain-128 under this fault injection. Once we have determined the fault location, internal state of the cipher at a given cycle of operation can be found out. It is seen that about 56 single bit faults can reveal the full internal NFSR state of the cipher and about 128 faults can reveal full LFSR state. Once, the full internal state of Grain-128 is known, due to reversibility of Grain-128 operation, we can obtain the full secret *key* of the cipher. The whole process requires an online computational complexity of at most 2^{21}.

This paper is organized as follows. Following this introduction, section 2 briefly discusses the specification of Grain-128. We present the fault model of our analysis in section 3. The proposed fault attack is presented in section 4. Section 5 estimates the overall complexity of the attack. We mention limitations of our attack and its possible extensions in that section, as well. Finally, section 6 concludes the paper.

2   Specification of the Grain-128 Stream Cipher

Grain-128 is a hardware based stream cipher enlisted in the final list of the eStream [1] project. We briefly describe the specification of this stream cipher here. A detailed description may be found in [8].

Grain-128 stream cipher consists of three main building blocks, namely, an NFSR, an LFSR and a nonlinear filter function, $h(x)$(Fig. 1). The contents of the NFSR are denoted by $b_i, b_{i+1}, \ldots, b_{i+127}$ and the contents of the LFSR are denoted by, $s_i, s_{i+1}, \ldots, s_{i+127}$. The update function of the LFSR is given by,

$$s_{i+128} = s_i + s_{i+7} + s_{i+38} + s_{i+70} + s_{i+81} + s_{i+96}$$

The NFSR is updated by,

$$b_{i+128} = s_i + b_i + b_{i+26} + b_{i+56} + b_{i+91} + b_{i+96} + b_{i+3}b_{i+67} + b_{i+11}b_{i+13}$$
$$+ b_{i+17}b_{i+18} + b_{i+27}b_{i+59} + b_{i+40}b_{i+48} + b_{i+61}b_{i+65} + b_{i+68}b_{i+84}$$

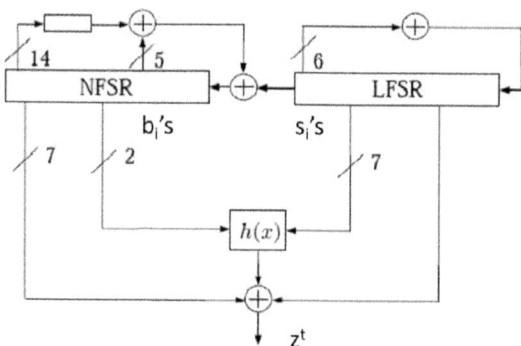

Fig. 1. Operation of Grain-128

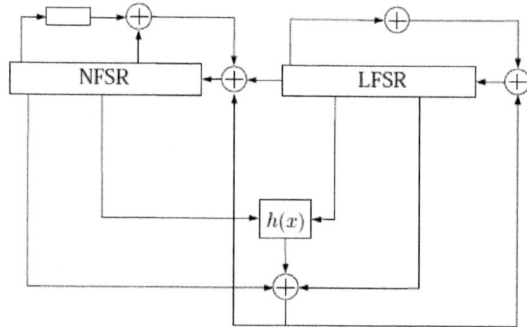

Fig. 2. Initialization of Grain-128

The NFSR and the LFSR together represent the internal state of the cipher. The nonlinear filter function h is defined with 2 input bits from the NFSR and 7 input bits from the LFSR and is described by,

$$h = b_{i+12}s_{i+8} + s_{i+13}s_{i+20} + b_{i+95}s_{i+42} + s_{i+60}s_{i+79} + b_{i+12}b_{i+95}s_{i+95}.$$

The output bit z_i is given as,

$$z_i = b_{i+2} + b_{i+15} + b_{i+36} + b_{i+45} + b_{i+64} + b_{i+73} + b_{i+89} + h + s_{i+93}$$

An *initialization* phase is carried out before the cipher generates keystream bits. The 128 bit key, $k = (k_0, k_2, \ldots, k_{127})$ and the 96 bit initialization vector $IV = (IV_0, IV_2, \ldots, IV_{95})$ are loaded in the NFSR and the LFSR respectively as, $b_i = k_i, 0 \le i \le 127$ and $s_i = IV_i, 0 \le i \le 95$, rest of the LFSR bits, $(s_{96}, s_{98}, \ldots, s_{127})$ are loaded with 1. During initialization, the cipher is run for 256 rounds without producing any keystream, and the output bit, z_i is fed back and XOR-ed with both the LFSR and the NFSR (Fig. 2).

In the following sections, we propose a fault attack on Grain-128 stream cipher. The proposed attack induces fault in the NFSR (b-bits) of the stream cipher and obtains equations of the state bits in both NFSR and LFSR using output differential.

3   Fault Analysis Model of Grain-128

In this section, we describe the fault analysis model of Grain-128 assumed in our attack. The NFSR i.e. nonlinearity of Grain-128 provides the security to the cipher. As already mentioned, an earlier work [4] has demonstrated that inducing faults in the LFSR of Grain-128 can break the cipher. In this paper, we show that even inducing faults in the NFSR can reveal both the NFSR and the LFSR bits at an instance of operation. As a result, the full internal state of Grain-128 can be found out.

3.1   Assumptions of the Fault Model

Our fault model creates faults in the NFSR. Single bit faults are injected in the NFSR and the difference of the faulty and fault-free keystreams are exploited to analyze the system. We assume the following controllability in order to perform this attack.

1. The attacker is able to induce faults at *random* positions of the NFSR of the Grain-128 implementation (hardware or software). Hence, exact fault position is not known beforehand.
2. The fault affects *exactly one* bit of the NFSR at any cycle of operation. So, the fault amounts to flipping *exactly one bit* of the NFSR of Grain-128 implementation.
3. A fault to an NFSR bit can be reproduced at any cycle of operation, once, it is created.
4. The attacker is able to determine and control the cycles of operation of the implementation, i.e., the timing of the implementation is under control of the attacker.
5. The attacker can reset the implementation to its original state.
6. The attacker can run the implementation with different IV, without changing the key. This is an reasonable assumption as IV bits are public.

Flipping exactly one bit of the NFSR is a strong assumption, but can be achieved practically by triggering laser shots through the I/O signal for hardware implementations ([12], [13]).

4   Proposed Fault Analysis of Grain-128

The fault attack on Grain-128 will induce faults at random locations of the implementation and exploit the differences in normal (z_{normal})and faulty (z_{faulty}) keystreams to obtain full internal state of the cipher (i.e. $b_0, b_1, \ldots, b_{127}, s_0, s_1,$

$\ldots, s_{127})$ at a target cycle T of operation after the initialization phase. The algorithm we present next, will obtain $b_0, b_1, \ldots, b_{127}, s_0, s_1, \ldots, s_{127}$, which is the internal state of Grain-128 after cycle T of operation following *initialization*. We will refer to this point as the *base point*. Further, we denote the output difference of faulty and fault-free keystream at iteration t after the base point by δ^t, i.e., $z^t_{normal} + z^t_{faulty} = \delta^t$, where, $+$ refers to modulo 2 addition.

Our attack will follow the following five steps.

1. Determining fault position in the NFSR.
2. Pre-computation of fault traces.
3. Determining NFSR bits, $b_0, b_1, \ldots, b_{127}$.
4. Determining LFSR bits, $s_0, s_1, \ldots, s_{127}$.
5. Invert states from cycle T to obtain the *key*.

In the following five subsections we describe the methodology carried out in the above steps.

4.1   Determining the Fault Location in the NFSR

Once, a random single bit fault is induced in the NFSR of the Grain-128 implementation, the first objective is to determine the location of this fault.

Algorithm 1. FormδPattern(f)

$N = 100000;$
for $i = 1$ **to** N **do**
    set random *key* and *IV* to Grain-128;
    run fault free for T cycles after initialization;
    induce fault at $NFSR[f]$;
    run fault free for 128 cycles;
    run faulty for 128 cycles;
    determine δ^t, $t = 0, 1, 2, \ldots, 127$;
end for
$\sigma_f = \{\};$
for $t = 0$ **to** 128 **do**
    if δ^t is 1 $\forall$ N **then**
        $\sigma_f = \sigma_f \cup \{t\};$
    end if
end for

Basic Idea: The basic idea for obtaining the location of the fault is the following observation. The output z is given by,

$$z_i = b_{i+2} + b_{i+15} + b_{i+36} + b_{i+45} + b_{i+64} + b_{i+73} + b_{i+89}$$
$$+ b_{i+12}s_{i+8} + s_{i+13}s_{i+20} + b_{i+95}s_{i+42}$$
$$+ s_{i+60}s_{i+79} + b_{i+12}b_{i+95}s_{i+95} + s_{i+93}.$$

Also, it can be noted that after the initialization phase is over, a fault induced in the NFSR *can not* propagate to the LFSR. So, a fault induced in the NFSR, according to the output equation given above will produce different δ^t depending on the fault location at cycle T for different t. For example, a fault at b_{89} *must have* $\delta^t = 1$ for $t = 0, 16, 25$ etc., if we try over a large number of *key* and *IV*. This is due to the fact that, over a large random number of *key* and/or *IV* the nonlinear b-bits will not show distinct δ^t, but the linear terms will always produce distinct δ^t. We note that, $\delta(z_i) = 1$ for linear terms, and $\delta(z_i) = b_k$ or higher degree monomial for nonlinear terms, after fault is moved to an NFSR bit, corresponding to linear or nonlinear b-bits. For the constant term we always get 1 in δ^t, but we get different δ^t for other cases, when fault is moved to nonlinear b-bits, for different key and/or IV. Now due to the positioning of the *linear terms* in z_i, we expect to obtain different patterns δ^t for different fault locations. Because of this reason, we can identify exact fault positions in the NFSR.

The $\delta^t = 1$, $(t = 0, 1, \ldots, 128)$ pattern for faults at different NFSR positions is shown in tables 3 and 4 in the appendix.

Algorithm 1 generates a pattern of δ^t for fault at location f, which generates δ^t for a large number of *random key* and *IV*. Here, σ_f stores the set of cycles for which $\delta^t = 1$ for single bit fault at location f. It is seen after execution of algorithm 1, that all fault locations give unique σ_f. Therefore, fault locations can be obtained simply by running the faulty and fault-free implementations for 128 more cycles from the instance of fault injection and matching with the above pattern table σ.

Algorithm 2 presents the procedure for determining the fault location. In algorithm 2 we vary *IV* randomly sufficient number of times till we pin-point the exact fault location. Throughout this process, *key* is kept fixed. In this algorithm, size($FaultLocation$) refers to the size of the $FaultLocation$ set, while $NumIVs$ is the number of random IVs tried for a fixed *key* to determine exact fault location (identified by, size($FaultLocation$) == 1). Until unique fault location is identified we increase number of random IVs to try by *inc*, which is taken to be 10, here.

4.2   Pre-computation of Fault Traces

In this pre-computation phase, we generate a table that stores the corrupted b-bits after t cycles of operations $(t = 0, 1, 2, \ldots, 256)$ following fault induction at location f.

Basic Idea: The basic idea is based on the observation that the b-bit positions, $0, 3, 11, 13, 17, 18, 26, 27, 40, 48, 56, 59, 61, 65, 67, 68, 84, 91, 96$ determine the feedback bit.

$$b_{i+128} = s_i + b_i + b_{i+26} + b_{i+56} + b_{i+91} + b_{i+96} + b_{i+3}b_{i+67} + b_{i+11}b_{i+13}$$
$$+ b_{i+17}b_{i+18} + b_{i+27}b_{i+59} + b_{i+40}b_{i+48} + b_{i+61}b_{i+65} + b_{i+68}b_{i+84}$$

So, a fault at those positions *may* produce a fault at the feedback bit b_{127} during the following cycle. Also, currently corrupted b-bit positions will shift in the following cycle. All other b-bits will remain uncorrupted. s_0 will not have any effect on feedback as no fault can propagate to the LFSR.

Algorithm 2. DetermineFaultlocation()

$FaultLocation \leftarrow \{\}$;
$NumIVs \leftarrow 0$;
$inc \leftarrow 10$;
while size($FaultLocation$) != 1 **do**
  $NumIVs \leftarrow NumIVs + inc$;
  for $i = 0$ **to** $NumIVs$ **do**
    initialize Grain with random IV, with that fixed key;
    form δ^t, $t = 0, 1, 2, \ldots, 127$;
  end for
  for $i = 0$ **to** 127 **do**
    $FaultLocation \leftarrow \{\}$
    if all positions of $\delta^t = 1 \ \forall \ j = 0, 1, 2, \ldots, NumIVs$ is in σ_i **then**
      $FaultLocation \leftarrow FaultLocation \cup \{i\}$
    end if
  end for
end while
return $FaultLocation$

Algorithm 3. FaultTrace(f)

$FeedbackPositions \leftarrow \{0, 3, 11, 13, 17, 18, 26, 27, 40, 48, 56, 59, 61, 65, 67, 68, 84, 91, 96\}$;
FaultTrace[0] $\leftarrow \{f\}$;
for $i = 0$ **to** 127 **do**
  $FaultTrace[i] \leftarrow \{\}$;
  for $element \in FaultTrace[i-1]$ **do**
    $FaultTrace[i] \leftarrow FaultTrace[i] \cup \{element - 1\}$
    if $element \in FeedbackPositions$ **then**
      $FaultTrace[i] \leftarrow FaultTrace[i] \cup \{127\}$
    end if
  end for
end for

Algorithm 3, stores fault traces after t cycles of fault induction at location f. After the execution of algorithm 3, we know that a fault at location f after its injection, *may* induce faults to locations $FaultTraces(f)[t]$ of the $NFSR$ after t cycles of operation. Therefore, all other locations of the $NFSR$ *will be* fault-free after t cycles of operation. Algorithm 3 is run for all possible fault locations, i.e., $0 \leq i \leq 127$. We construct a table of fault traces for all possible f, $0 \leq f \leq 127$ and t, $0 \leq t \leq 256$ using this algorithm.

4.3   Determining the $NFSR$ Bits

At this phase, we use the difference of fault-free and faulty output to obtain the $NFSR$ bit values. We use both the feedback and output bit equations for this purpose. It can be seen that, the output bit equation, z has monomials of degree higher than 1 having b-bits that also always contain s-bits ($b_{12}s_8$, $b_{95}s_{42}$

and $b_{12}b_{95}s_{95}$). So, it is not possible to single out equations involving b-bits only. Therefore, we will use this nonlinear b-bit monomials of z to obtain values of s register, once all the b-bit values are known. At this phase, instead, we use the linear b terms of z in connection with the feedback equation b_{128} to ascertain values of b-bits. In this paper, we concentrate on linear equations containing single b-bit only.

Basic Idea: The feedback equation b_{128} has 7 degree-2 monomials containing b-bits only ($b_3b_{67}, b_{11}b_{13}, b_{17}b_{18}, b_{27}b_{59}, b_{40}b_{48}, b_{61}b_{65}, b_{68}b_{84}$).

$$b_{i+128} = s_i + b_i + b_{i+26} + b_{i+56} + b_{i+91} + b_{i+96} + b_{i+3}b_{i+67} + b_{i+11}b_{i+13}$$
$$+b_{i+17}b_{i+18} + b_{i+27}b_{i+59} + b_{i+40}b_{i+48} + b_{i+61}b_{i+65} + b_{i+68}b_{i+84}$$

The idea is to move the induced fault to any of these 14 locations, i.e., we move fault to b_m and/or b_n if b_mb_n is a degree 2 monomial in the feedback function. So, if fault has not propagated to b_{128} through any other feedback taps, at T + movement cycle, the feedback difference of normal and this faulty executions will have a difference of the other bit, i.e. if fault moves to b_m, the difference will be b_n and if fault moves to b_n, the difference will be b_m. Similarly, if fault into the feedback bit comes through other linear or nonlinear taps of the feedback function as well, we will have a feedback difference containing multiple b-bits. Again this difference will be linear as the *algebraic degree* of the feedback function is, 2. Since, the least index of degree-2 b terms in the feedback function is 3, faults induced at positions ≥ 3 only can yield equations.

Next, we use the linear b terms of z to obtain equations involving linear b terms. It will be the same as the feedback difference obtained earlier. This is done by moving the feedback fault to one of the single b-bit output taps, $2, 15, 36, 45, 64, 73, 89$. Again, if at this point the fault has not corrupted the output bit in no other way than at that particular output tap, we get the value of b_m or b_n from the δ^t at that point in case of linear equations of single b-bit, i.e., we get value of a single b-bit. In case of linear equations containing multiple b-bits, we have one linear equation, but, to solve for all those b-bits we need more linear equations.

Therefore, we consult the $FaultTraces$ table twice, once at the time of feedback through degree-2 monomial and the other at the time of output through linear b terms, to construct LHS of equations. The expression obtained earlier will equal the difference of output bits (δ^t) after the movement to the linear b term. Since, the b value we obtained is actually moved from another location, the corresponding value will be the value of a b-bit at a later location. So, if we need to move the fault c cycles from the original location to effect b_m of b_{128}, we obtained b_{n+c} at the base point. This process can be carried out for each 2 degree monomials of b_{128} and each 1 degree monomial of z.

Algorithm 4 presents the method in pseudo-code for obtaining b values from fault at f.

Algorithm 5 constructs LHS of feedback linear equations, when faults are moved from f, through *movement* shifts, to $feedbacklocation\_b$ bit. The idea is that, if during *movement* steps, fault has not corrupted any other feedback

Algorithm 4. Determine$NFSR$Bits(f)

$feedBack\_b[] \leftarrow \{0, 26, 56, 91, 96, 3, 11, 13, 17, 18, 27, 40, 48, 59, 61, 65, 67, 68, 84\}$
$Double\_feedBack\_b[] \leftarrow \{3, 11, 13, 17, 18, 27, 40, 48, 59, 61, 65, 67, 68, 84\}$
$Double\_feedBack\_b\_corr[] \leftarrow \{67, 13, 11, 18, 17, 59, 48, 40, 27, 65, 61, 3, 84, 68\}$
$Single\_output\_b[] \leftarrow \{2, 15, 36, 45, 64, 73, 89\}$
$movement \leftarrow 0$
for $i = 0$ **to** $length(Double\_feedBack\_b)$ **do**
  if $f \geq Double\_feedBack\_b[i]$ **then**
    $movement \leftarrow (f - Double\_feedBack\_b[i])$
    $eqnLHS \leftarrow ConstructFeedbackDiffEqn(f, Double\_feedBack\_b[i] - f,$
    $Double\_feedBack\_b[i])$
    for $j = 0$ **to** $length(Single\_output\_b)$ **do**
      $movement \leftarrow movement + 127 - Single\_output\_b[j];$
      if $OnlyCorrupt(feedBack\_b, movement, Single\_output\_b[j], f)$
      $\&\& \ (Double\_feedBack\_b\_corr[i] + movement \leq 127)$ **then**
        obtained $eqnLHS = \delta^{movement}$
      end if
    end for
  end if
end for

Algorithm 5. ConstructFeedbackDiffEqn($f, movement, feedbacklocation$)

$linearTerms = \{\};$
for $element \in FaultTrace(f)[movement]$ **do**
  for $i = 0$ **to** $length(feedBack\_b)$ **do**
    if $element == feedBack\_b[i]$ **then**
      if $element == Double\_feedBack\_b[k]$ for some k **then**
        $linearTerms = linearTerms \cup \{Double\_feedBack\_b\_corr[k]\};$
      else
        $linearTerms = linearTerms \cup \{1\};$
      end if
    end if
  end for
end for
return XOR of $linearTerms;$

---

taps than the $feedbacklocation$ tap, we get LHS as b_m or b_n explained earlier, otherwise we need to accumulate all corresponding linear or constant terms corresponding to those taps.

The function, $OnlyCorrupt(array, movement, location, f)$ returns $true$ if only $location$ is corrupt after $movement$ cycles of operation, among the elements of $array$ for fault at f at base point. Algorithm 6 describes the procedure.

After the experiment is carried out, we could obtain 0 to 5 b-bits from single bit fault involving $single\ bit$ linear equations. The $base\ point$ fault locations and number of bits obtained from that location in single b-bit is tabulated in table 1. 125 faults at the identifiable positions can give linear equations. The single bit equations that we can obtain are, $b_3, b_4, \ldots, b_{127}$. Other 3 bits, b_0, b_1, b_2 can not be obtained. An average of $\frac{0 \times 3 + 1 \times 8 + 2 \times 23 + 3 \times 31 + 4 \times 26 + 5 \times 37}{128} = 3.40$ b-bits can be obtained from a single fault at the NFSR from equations involving single b-bit. It is seen experimentally that on an average about 56 faults are required to determine state bits, $b_0, b_1, \ldots, b_{127}$ of the NFSR, which may be explained by the pattern of obtained b-bits from faults as shown in 1. We can also reduce number of induced faults by inducing faults at consecutive cycles. So, if for example, from the fault at b_{67} at base point, we can obtain value of bit b_3. A fault at the previous cycle at b_{67} will give value of b_3 at that cycle, which is the value of b_2 at *base point*. Continuing this way, we can gather values of b-bits, b_0 to b_{127}, at the *base point*.

Algorithm 6. OnlyCorrupt(array, movement, location, f)

---

   for *element* $\in$ *FaultTrace(f)[movement]* **do**
     for $i = 0$ **to** *length(array)* **do**
       if *element* $!=$ *location* && *element* $==$ *array[i]* **then**
         return false;
       end if
     end for
   end for
   return true;

4.4   Determining the *LFSR* Bits

Once, the NFSR bits are known, the next objective is to obtain the LFSR (s) bits.

Basic Idea: The three monomials of degree more than 1 in z involving both b and s-bits are, $b_{12}s_8$, $b_{95}s_{42}$ and $b_{12}b_{95}s_{95}$.

$$z_i = b_{i+2} + b_{i+15} + b_{i+36} + b_{i+45} + b_{i+64} + b_{i+73} + b_{i+89}$$
$$+ b_{i+12}s_{i+8} + s_{i+13}s_{i+20} + b_{i+95}s_{i+42}$$
$$+ s_{i+60}s_{i+79} + b_{i+12}b_{i+95}s_{i+95} + s_{i+93}.$$

So, if the induced fault propagates to any of the locations b_{12} or b_{95} without corrupting other b-bits of z_i, we obtain an equation involving s and b-bits. This will be one equation of the form, $s_p + s_q b_r = \delta$. So, if this b_r bit is 0, we immediately have the value of the other s-bit, s_p. If however, b_r is 1, we have a linear equation in s-bits. Again, the list of corrupt b-bits can be seen by consulting *FaultTraces* table.

Algorithm 7 describes the determination algorithm for LFSR bits. The function *OnlyContains(outputPos, movement, Output_b_double_s[i], f)* checks whether due to fault at f and after *movement* cycles following the induction of fault at f, only fault passing through feedback is, *Output_b_double_s[i]*. This function is similar to the *OnlyCorrupt* function and is not listed here.

66 faults (at locations $12, 13, \ldots, 44, 95, 96, \ldots, 127$) in the NFSR gives equations following above algorithm. Of these 66 equations, 33 on an average will

Table 1. Fault location vs. NFSR Bits Obtained

Fault Location	NFSR Bits Obtained	Fault Location	NFSR Bits Obtained	Fault Location	NFSR Bits Obtained
b_0		b_{43}	$b_{41}, b_{44}, b_{45}, b_{51}, b_{75}$	b_{86}	$b_{54}, b_{70}, b_{82}, b_{102}$
b_1		b_{44}	$b_{42}, b_{45}, b_{46}, b_{52}, b_{76}$	b_{87}	$b_{55}, b_{71}, b_{83}, b_{103}$
b_2		b_{45}	$b_{43}, b_{46}, b_{47}, b_{53}, b_{77}$	b_{88}	$b_{56}, b_{72}, b_{84}, b_{104}$
b_3	b_{67}	b_{46}	$b_{44}, b_{47}, b_{48}, b_{54}, b_{78}$	b_{89}	$b_{57}, b_{73}, b_{85}, b_{105}$
b_4	b_{68}	b_{47}	$b_{45}, b_{48}, b_{49}, b_{55}, b_{79}$	b_{90}	$b_{58}, b_{74}, b_{86}, b_{106}$
b_5	b_{69}	b_{48}	$b_{40}, b_{46}, b_{49}, b_{56}, b_{80}$	b_{91}	b_{75}, b_{87}, b_{107}
b_6	b_{70}	b_{49}	$b_{41}, b_{47}, b_{50}, b_{57}, b_{81}$	b_{92}	b_{76}, b_{88}, b_{108}
b_7	b_{71}	b_{50}	$b_{42}, b_{48}, b_{51}, b_{58}, b_{82}$	b_{93}	b_{77}, b_{89}, b_{109}
b_8	b_{72}	b_{51}	$b_{43}, b_{49}, b_{52}, b_{59}, b_{83}$	b_{94}	b_{78}, b_{90}, b_{110}
b_9	b_{73}	b_{52}	$b_{44}, b_{50}, b_{53}, b_{60}, b_{84}$	b_{95}	b_{79}, b_{91}, b_{111}
b_{10}	b_{74}	b_{53}	$b_{45}, b_{51}, b_{54}, b_{61}, b_{85}$	b_{96}	b_{80}, b_{92}, b_{112}
b_{11}	b_{13}, b_{75}	b_{54}	$b_{46}, b_{52}, b_{55}, b_{62}, b_{86}$	b_{97}	b_{81}, b_{93}, b_{113}
b_{12}	b_{14}, b_{76}	b_{55}	$b_{47}, b_{53}, b_{56}, b_{63}, b_{87}$	b_{98}	b_{82}, b_{94}, b_{114}
b_{13}	b_{11}, b_{15}, b_{77}	b_{56}	b_{48}, b_{88}	b_{99}	b_{83}, b_{95}, b_{115}
b_{14}	b_{12}, b_{16}, b_{78}	b_{57}	b_{49}, b_{89}	b_{100}	b_{84}, b_{96}, b_{116}
b_{15}	b_{13}, b_{17}, b_{79}	b_{58}	b_{50}, b_{90}	b_{101}	b_{85}, b_{97}, b_{117}
b_{16}	b_{14}, b_{18}, b_{80}	b_{59}	b_{27}, b_{51}	b_{102}	b_{86}, b_{98}, b_{118}
b_{17}	$b_{15}, b_{18}, b_{19}, b_{81}$	b_{60}	b_{28}, b_{52}	b_{103}	b_{87}, b_{99}, b_{119}
b_{18}	$b_{16}, b_{17}, b_{19}, b_{20}, b_{82}$	b_{61}	b_{29}, b_{53}, b_{65}	b_{104}	b_{88}, b_{100}, b_{120}
b_{19}	$b_{17}, b_{18}, b_{20}, b_{21}, b_{83}$	b_{62}	b_{30}, b_{54}, b_{66}	b_{105}	b_{89}, b_{101}, b_{121}
b_{20}	$b_{18}, b_{19}, b_{21}, b_{22}, b_{84}$	b_{63}	b_{31}, b_{55}, b_{67}	b_{106}	b_{90}, b_{102}, b_{122}
b_{21}	$b_{19}, b_{20}, b_{22}, b_{23}, b_{85}$	b_{64}	b_{32}, b_{56}, b_{68}	b_{107}	b_{91}, b_{103}, b_{123}
b_{22}	$b_{20}, b_{21}, b_{23}, b_{24}, b_{86}$	b_{65}	b_{33}, b_{61}, b_{69}	b_{108}	b_{92}, b_{104}, b_{124}
b_{23}	$b_{21}, b_{22}, b_{24}, b_{25}, b_{87}$	b_{66}	b_{34}, b_{62}, b_{70}	b_{109}	b_{93}, b_{105}, b_{125}
b_{24}	$b_{22}, b_{23}, b_{25}, b_{26}, b_{88}$	b_{67}	$b_3, b_{35}, b_{63}, b_{71}$	b_{110}	b_{94}, b_{106}, b_{126}
b_{25}	$b_{23}, b_{24}, b_{26}, b_{27}, b_{89}$	b_{68}	$b_4, b_{36}, b_{64}, b_{84}$	b_{111}	b_{95}, b_{107}, b_{127}
b_{26}	$b_{24}, b_{27}, b_{28}, b_{90}$	b_{69}	$b_5, b_{37}, b_{65}, b_{85}$	b_{112}	b_{96}, b_{108}
b_{27}	$b_{25}, b_{28}, b_{29}, b_{59}, b_{91}$	b_{70}	$b_6, b_{38}, b_{66}, b_{86}$	b_{113}	b_{97}, b_{109}
b_{28}	$b_{26}, b_{29}, b_{30}, b_{60}, b_{92}$	b_{71}	$b_7, b_{39}, b_{67}, b_{87}$	b_{114}	b_{98}, b_{110}
b_{29}	$b_{27}, b_{30}, b_{31}, b_{61}, b_{93}$	b_{72}	$b_8, b_{40}, b_{68}, b_{88}$	b_{115}	b_{99}, b_{111}
b_{30}	$b_{28}, b_{31}, b_{32}, b_{62}, b_{94}$	b_{73}	$b_9, b_{41}, b_{69}, b_{89}$	b_{116}	b_{100}, b_{112}
b_{31}	$b_{29}, b_{32}, b_{33}, b_{63}, b_{95}$	b_{74}	$b_{10}, b_{42}, b_{70}, b_{90}$	b_{117}	b_{101}, b_{113}
b_{32}	$b_{30}, b_{33}, b_{34}, b_{64}, b_{96}$	b_{75}	$b_{11}, b_{43}, b_{71}, b_{91}$	b_{118}	b_{102}, b_{114}
b_{33}	$b_{31}, b_{34}, b_{35}, b_{65}, b_{97}$	b_{76}	$b_{12}, b_{44}, b_{72}, b_{92}$	b_{119}	b_{103}, b_{115}
b_{34}	$b_{32}, b_{35}, b_{36}, b_{66}, b_{98}$	b_{77}	$b_{13}, b_{45}, b_{73}, b_{93}$	b_{120}	b_{104}, b_{116}
b_{35}	$b_{33}, b_{36}, b_{37}, b_{67}, b_{99}$	b_{78}	$b_{14}, b_{46}, b_{74}, b_{94}$	b_{121}	b_{105}, b_{117}
b_{36}	$b_{34}, b_{37}, b_{38}, b_{68}, b_{100}$	b_{79}	$b_{15}, b_{47}, b_{75}, b_{95}$	b_{122}	b_{106}, b_{118}
b_{37}	$b_{35}, b_{38}, b_{39}, b_{69}, b_{101}$	b_{80}	$b_{16}, b_{48}, b_{76}, b_{96}$	b_{123}	b_{107}, b_{119}
b_{38}	$b_{36}, b_{39}, b_{40}, b_{70}, b_{102}$	b_{81}	$b_{17}, b_{49}, b_{77}, b_{97}$	b_{124}	b_{108}, b_{120}
b_{39}	$b_{37}, b_{40}, b_{41}, b_{71}, b_{103}$	b_{82}	$b_{18}, b_{50}, b_{78}, b_{98}$	b_{125}	b_{109}, b_{121}
b_{40}	$b_{38}, b_{41}, b_{42}, b_{48}, b_{72}$	b_{83}	$b_{19}, b_{51}, b_{79}, b_{99}$	b_{126}	b_{110}, b_{122}
b_{41}	$b_{39}, b_{42}, b_{43}, b_{49}, b_{73}$	b_{84}	$b_{52}, b_{68}, b_{80}, b_{100}$	b_{127}	b_{111}, b_{123}
b_{42}	$b_{40}, b_{43}, b_{44}, b_{50}, b_{74}$	b_{85}	$b_{53}, b_{69}, b_{81}, b_{101}$		

Algorithm 7. Determine$LFSR$Bits(f)

$Output\_b\_double\_s[] = \{12, 95\};$
$Output\_s\_double\_b[] = \{8, 42\};$
$outputPos[] = \{12, 95, 2, 15, 36, 45, 64, 73, 89\};$
$movement \leftarrow 0;$
for $i = 0$ **to** 1 **do**
   $movement \leftarrow f - Output\_b\_double\_s[i];$
   if $OnlyContains(outputPos, movement, Output\_b\_double\_s[i], f)$ &&
   $(Output\_s\_double\_b[i] + movement) <= 127$ &&
   $(Output\_b\_double\_s[1 - i] + movement) <= 127$ &&
   $(95 + movement) <= 127$ **then**
      obtained equation,
      $s_{Output\_s\_double\_b[i]+movement} + b_{Output\_b\_double\_s[1-i]+movement} \cdot s_{95+movement}$
      $= \delta^{movement}$
   end if
end for

---

involve a single s-bit and can be solved immediately. Other linear equations are to be stored till we get sufficient number of independent *linear equations*. The equations obtained from faults in the NFSR are tabulated in table 2. Since, the LFSR bits are updated according to a *linear* feedback relation,

$$s_{i+128} = s_i + s_{i+7} + s_{i+38} + s_{i+70} + s_{i+81} + s_{i+96}$$

all the s-bits at any cycle t after/before the *base point* can be written as linear combinations of the *base point* LFSR bits $s_0, s_1, \ldots, s_{127}$. So, essentially we need 128 *linearly independent* equations from faults at different cycles after/before the *base point*. Hence, we obtain equations involving LFSR bits using algorithm 7 after inducing faults at later/earlier cycles of operation. This process is continued till we obtain 128 linearly independent equations involving 128 s-bits at the base point. Hence, on an average, $(128/33) * 66 = 256$ faults need to be injected to obtain all LFSR bits, from single variable linear equations and 128 faults need to be injected in NFSR to obtain all s-bits at *base point*. 128 linearly independent equations can be solved through Gaussian elimination in time $128^3 = O(2^{21})$. Note that, most of the equations will involve only one or two s variables at *base point*, s_i as only s_{127} is updated by a *linear feedback*, while other bits get simple shifts from previous cycles.

4.5 Inverting Internal States

The earlier phases of the attack successfully obtain the value of full internal state of Grain-128 at *base point*. So, we essentially have the full internal state of Grain-128 after cycle, T, $(s_0^T, s_1^T, \ldots, s_{127}^T, b_0^T, b_1^T, \ldots, b_{127}^T)$. We describe below the procedure of obtaining *key* from this known full internal state. This technique is similar to that of [4].

Table 2. Fault location vs. LFSR, NFSR Equations Obtained

Fault Location	Equations	Fault Location	Equations
b_{12}	$s_8 + b_{95}.s_{95}$	b_{95}	$s_{42} + b_{12}.s_{95}$
b_{13}	$s_9 + b_{96}.s_{96}$	b_{96}	$s_{43} + b_{13}.s_{96}$
b_{14}	$s_{10} + b_{97}.s_{97}$	b_{97}	$s_{44} + b_{14}.s_{97}$
b_{15}	$s_{11} + b_{98}.s_{98}$	b_{98}	$s_{45} + b_{15}.s_{98}$
b_{16}	$s_{12} + b_{99}.s_{99}$	b_{99}	$s_{46} + b_{16}.s_{99}$
b_{17}	$s_{13} + b_{100}.s_{100}$	b_{100}	$s_{47} + b_{17}.s_{100}$
b_{18}	$s_{14} + b_{101}.s_{101}$	b_{101}	$s_{48} + b_{18}.s_{101}$
b_{19}	$s_{15} + b_{102}.s_{102}$	b_{102}	$s_{49} + b_{19}.s_{102}$
b_{20}	$s_{16} + b_{103}.s_{103}$	b_{103}	$s_{50} + b_{20}.s_{103}$
b_{21}	$s_{17} + b_{104}.s_{104}$	b_{104}	$s_{51} + b_{21}.s_{104}$
b_{22}	$s_{18} + b_{105}.s_{105}$	b_{105}	$s_{52} + b_{22}.s_{105}$
b_{23}	$s_{19} + b_{106}.s_{106}$	b_{106}	$s_{53} + b_{23}.s_{106}$
b_{24}	$s_{20} + b_{107}.s_{107}$	b_{107}	$s_{54} + b_{24}.s_{107}$
b_{25}	$s_{21} + b_{108}.s_{108}$	b_{108}	$s_{55} + b_{25}.s_{108}$
b_{26}	$s_{22} + b_{109}.s_{109}$	b_{109}	$s_{56} + b_{26}.s_{109}$
b_{27}	$s_{23} + b_{110}.s_{110}$	b_{110}	$s_{57} + b_{27}.s_{110}$
b_{28}	$s_{24} + b_{111}.s_{111}$	b_{111}	$s_{58} + b_{28}.s_{111}$
b_{29}	$s_{25} + b_{112}.s_{112}$	b_{112}	$s_{59} + b_{29}.s_{112}$
b_{30}	$s_{26} + b_{113}.s_{113}$	b_{113}	$s_{60} + b_{30}.s_{113}$
b_{31}	$s_{27} + b_{114}.s_{114}$	b_{114}	$s_{61} + b_{31}.s_{114}$
b_{32}	$s_{28} + b_{115}.s_{115}$	b_{115}	$s_{62} + b_{32}.s_{115}$
b_{33}	$s_{29} + b_{116}.s_{116}$	b_{116}	$s_{63} + b_{33}.s_{116}$
b_{34}	$s_{30} + b_{117}.s_{117}$	b_{117}	$s_{64} + b_{34}.s_{117}$
b_{35}	$s_{31} + b_{118}.s_{118}$	b_{118}	$s_{65} + b_{35}.s_{118}$
b_{36}	$s_{32} + b_{119}.s_{119}$	b_{119}	$s_{66} + b_{36}.s_{119}$
b_{37}	$s_{33} + b_{120}.s_{120}$	b_{120}	$s_{67} + b_{37}.s_{120}$
b_{38}	$s_{34} + b_{121}.s_{121}$	b_{121}	$s_{68} + b_{38}.s_{121}$
b_{39}	$s_{35} + b_{122}.s_{122}$	b_{122}	$s_{69} + b_{39}.s_{122}$
b_{40}	$s_{36} + b_{123}.s_{123}$	b_{123}	$s_{70} + b_{40}.s_{123}$
b_{41}	$s_{37} + b_{124}.s_{124}$	b_{124}	$s_{71} + b_{41}.s_{124}$
b_{42}	$s_{38} + b_{125}.s_{125}$	b_{125}	$s_{72} + b_{42}.s_{125}$
b_{43}	$s_{39} + b_{126}.s_{126}$	b_{126}	$s_{73} + b_{43}.s_{126}$
b_{44}	$s_{40} + b_{127}.s_{127}$	b_{127}	$s_{74} + b_{44}.s_{127}$

Step 1: When, $t > 256$, let, $(s_0^{t+1}, s_1^{t+1}, \ldots, s_{127}^{t+1}, b_0^{t+1}, b_1^{t+1}, \ldots, b_{127}^{t+1})$ be the full internal state of Grain-128 after $(t + 1)$ cycles of operation. Then, according to Grain specification (refer to section 2),

$$s_i^{t+1} = s_{i+1}^t; i = 0, 1, \ldots, 126; \tag{1}$$

$$s_{127}^{t+1} = s_0^t + s_7^t + s_{38}^t + s_{70}^t + s_{81}^t + s_{96}^t; \tag{2}$$

$$b_i^{t+1} = b_{i+1}^t; i = 0, 1, \ldots, 126; \tag{3}$$

$$
\begin{aligned}
b_{127}^{t+1} = &\; s_0^t + b_0^t + b_{26}^t + b_{56}^t + b_{91}^t + b_{96}^t \\
&+ b_3^t.b_{67}^t + b_{11}^t.b_{13}^t + b_{17}^t.b_{18}^t + b_{27}^t.b_{59}^t \\
&+ b_{40}^t.b_{48}^t + b_{61}^t.b_{65}^t + b_{68}^t.b_{84}^t;
\end{aligned} \tag{4}
$$

The above equations can be rewritten as follows.

$$s_{i+1}^t = s_i^{t+1}; i = 0, 1, \ldots, 126; \tag{5}$$

$$s_0^t = s_{127}^{t+1} + s_7^t + s_{38}^t + s_{70}^t + s_{81}^t + s_{96}^t; \tag{6}$$

$$b_{i+1}^t = b_i^{t+1}; i = 0, 1, \ldots, 126; \tag{7}$$

$$b_0^t = s_0^t + b_{127}^{t+1} + b_{26}^t + b_{56}^t + b_{91}^t + b_{96}^t$$
$$+ b_3^t . b_{67}^t + b_{11}^t . b_{13}^t + b_{17}^t . b_{18}^t + b_{27}^t . b_{59}^t$$
$$+ b_{40}^t . b_{48}^t + b_{61}^t . b_{65}^t + b_{68}^t . b_{84}^t; \tag{8}$$

Equation (5) straightaway gives the bit values of s_i^t, i.e., $(s_0^t, s_1^t, \ldots, s_{127}^t)$ except s_0^t. s_0^t can be obtained from equation (6), since all the values in RHS are known. In a similar way, b_i^t's can be obtained from equations, (7) and (8).

Step 2: When, $t <= 256$, the output bits z^t is also fed back at s_{127}^{t+1} and b_{127}^{t+1}. Now,

$$z^t = b_{26}^t + b_{26}^t + b_{26}^t + b_{26}^t + b_{26}^t + b_{26}^t +$$
$$b_{26}^t + s_{93}^t + b_{12}^t . s_8^t + s_{13}^t . s_{20}^t + b_{95}^t . b_{42}^t$$
$$+ s_{60}^t . s_{79}^t + b_{12}^t . b_{95}^t . s_{95}^t, \tag{9}$$

which can be written using variables,
$s_i^{t+1}, i = 0, 1, \ldots, 127$ and
$b_i^{t+1}, i = 0, 1, \ldots, 127$. For example, $s_{20}^t = s_{21}^{t+1}$ and $b_{26}^t = b_{27}^{t+1}$. Hence, once z^t is computed,

$$s_0^t = s_{127}^{t+1} + s_7^t + s_{38}^t + s_{70}^t + s_{81}^t + s_{96}^t + z^t. \tag{10}$$

Thus in both the cases, the previous cycles internal state can be found. Hence, after, $(t + 1)$ such inversions, we obtain in $\{b_0, b_1, \ldots, b_{127}\}$, the Key used in the encryption.

5   Complexity, Limitations and Extensions

In this section, we measure the overall complexity of our proposed attack described in the previous section. The complexity is estimated by the operations used in the analysis process. We also discuss the limitations and extensions of our attack.

1. *Fault Location Determination*: This phase requires the formation of a σ table in off-line mode and later a fault location determination method in online mode. The off-line mode requires a space overhead of $128 * 128 = 2^{14}$. It is experimentally verified over a large number of random key and IV that maximum 2^{20} Grain round operations are needed to determine exact fault location per fault following algorithm 2.

2. *Pre-computation of Fault Traces*: This phase stores pre-computed traces for all 128 faults for the following 256 cycles. Hence, space required in $128 * 256 * 128 = 2^{22}$. Time complexity of this phase is $128 * 256 = 2^{15}$ Grain round operations. This is an off-line operation.

3. *Determining NFSR Bits*: In this phase we determined NFSR bits from single bit faults at NFSR. As we obtained single variable linear equations only, almost constant computation is required to solve for these variables. Also, we only needed to store values of the obtained single bit linear equations. Hence, space complexity is also constant. We required about 56 faults to determine all NFSR bits on average.
4. *Determining LFSR Bits*: In this phase we deduced LFSR bits. Again of the three variable equations, we concentrated on equations where only single LFSR bit remains. Hence, again constant space is required to store the values. When we deduced LFSR bits by inducing faults at different cycles, we tried to obtain 128 linearly independent equations, which can be solved in time 2^{21}. However, since most of equations will be sparse, the complexity is expected to be much lower. The number of faults required at this step is at most 256.
5. *Inverting States*: This phase inverts Grain states from a known full state value. For inversion operation per cycle, we need constant computational complexity and a storage of $256 = 2^8$. Hence, for inverting till the first round, we need linear computation in terms of rounds of operation and space of 2^8.

To sum up, the total space complexity of the attack is, $O(2^{22})$, time complexity is $O(2^{21})$ and faults required to perform an attack is at most 256.

The attack may be extended to Grain-like ciphers with higher degree feedback functions and output functions. However, determining fault locations can be a challenging task if linear terms are removed from output bit expression. Higher degree feedback functions and output functions will however certainly increase the attack complexity as mostly nonlinear equations will be obtained.

In this work, we have considered linear equations involving only one unknown state bit. The attack can be improved by including other linear/nonlinear equations to reduce requirements of number of faults at the cost of more computation. Faults affecting multiple b register bits per fault injection, can be studied. This assumption is less strict compared to a single bit fault, which may be difficult to administer. Also, multi-bit faults will certainly reduce number of fault requirements. But, determination of fault positions may be difficult.

6   Conclusion

In this paper, we have described a fault analysis on the eStream finalist Grain-128. The earlier fault attack on Grain-128 induced faults at the LFSR of the implementation. In this paper, we have demonstrated that even injecting faults at the NFSR can break the cipher. The experimental result shows that about 56 faults at different cycles are needed for determining the NFSR bits and at most 256 faults at different cycles are needed to obtain the full LFSR state of the cipher at any particular time T of execution. A system of 128 linearly independent equations need to be solved to obtain all LFSR state bits. Hence, the complexity of our attack is $O(2^{21})$. Both the number of fault injections and equation solving can be carried out in practical scenario.

References

1. The eStream Project, http://www.ecrypt.eu.org/stream/
2. Agrawal, M., Karmakar, S., Saha, D., Mukhopadhyay, D.: Scan Based Side Channel Attacks on Stream Ciphers and Their Counter-Measures. In: Chowdhury, D.R., Rijmen, V., Das, A. (eds.) INDOCRYPT 2008. LNCS, vol. 5365, pp. 226–238. Springer, Heidelberg (2008)
3. Babbage, S., Canniere, C.D., Canteaut, A., Cid, C., Gilbert, H., Johansson, T., Parker, M., Preneel, B., Rijmen, V., Robshaw, M.: The eStream Portfolio, http://www.ecrypt.eu.org/stream/portfolio.pdf
4. Berzati, A., Canovas, C., Castagnos, G., Debraize, B., Goubin, L., Gouget, A., Paillier, P., Salgado, S.: Fault Analysis of Grain-128. In: IEEE International Workshop on Hardware-Oriented Security and Trust, pp. 7–14 (2009)
5. Biham, E., Shamir, A.: Differential Fault Analysis of Secret Key Cryptosystems. In: Kaliski Jr., B.S. (ed.) CRYPTO 1997. LNCS, vol. 1294, pp. 513–525. Springer, Heidelberg (1997)
6. Blomer, J., Seifert, J.-P.: Fault Based Cryptanalysis of the Advanced Encryption Standard (AES). In: Wright, R.N. (ed.) FC 2003. LNCS, vol. 2742, pp. 162–181. Springer, Heidelberg (2003)
7. Dinur, I., Shamir, A.: Breaking Grain-128 with Dynamic Cube Attacks. Cryptology ePrint Archive: Report 2010/570
8. Hell, M., Johansson, T., Meier, W.: A Stream Cipher Proposal: Grain-128. eSTREAM, ECRYPT Stream Cipher Project (2006)
9. Hoch, J.J., Shamir, A.: Fault Analysis of Stream Ciphers. In: Joye, M., Quisquater, J.-J. (eds.) CHES 2004. LNCS, vol. 3156, pp. 1–20. Springer, Heidelberg (2004)
10. Hojsk, M., Rudolf, B.: Differential Fault Analysis of Trivium. In: Nyberg, K. (ed.) FSE 2008. LNCS, vol. 5086, pp. 158–172. Springer, Heidelberg (2008)
11. Kircanski, A., Youssef, A.M.: Differential Fault Analysis of Rabbit. In: Jacobson Jr., M.J., Rijmen, V., Safavi-Naini, R. (eds.) SAC 2009. LNCS, vol. 5867, pp. 197–214. Springer, Heidelberg (2009)
12. Skorobogatov, S.P.: Optically Enhanced Position-Locked Power Analysis. In: Goubin, L., Matsui, M. (eds.) CHES 2006. LNCS, vol. 4249, pp. 61–75. Springer, Heidelberg (2006)
13. Skorobogatov, S.P., Anderson, R.J.: Optical Fault Induction Attacks. In: Kaliski Jr., B.S., Koç, Ç.K., Paar, C. (eds.) CHES 2002. LNCS, vol. 2523, pp. 2–12. Springer, Heidelberg (2003)

Appendix

Due to faults at different locations of the NFSR, we obtain $\delta^t = 1$ at various cycles of operation following fault induction. The corresponding mappings are given in tables 3 and 4.

Table 3. Fault location vs. $\delta^{t*} = 1$ (σ), Fault Locations 0 to 61

Fault Location	$t =$	Fault Location	$t =$
0		1	39,55,70,75,86,91,106,110,111,122,127
2	0,40,56,71,76,87,92,107,111,112,123,128	3	1,41,57,72,77,88,93,108,112,113,124
4	2,42,58,73,78,89,94,109	5	3,43,59,74,79,90,95,110
6	4,44,60,75,80,91,96,111	7	5,45,61,76,81,92,97,112
8	6,46,62,77,82,93,98,113	9	7,47,63,78,83,94,99,114
10	8,48,64,79,84,95,100,115	11	9,49,65,80,85,96,101,116
12	10,50,66,81,97,102	13	11,51,67,82,98,103
14	12,52,68,83	15	0,13,53,69,84
16	1,14,54,70,85	17	2,15,55,71,86
18	3,16,56,72,87	19	4,17,57,73,88
20	5,18,58,74,89	21	6,19,59,75,90
22	7,20,60,76,91	23	8,21,61,77,92
24	9,22,62,78,93	25	10,23,63,79,94
26	11,24,64,80,95	27	12,25,39,55,65,75,81,86,96
28	13,26,40,56,66,87,97	29	14,27,41,57,67,88,98
30	15,28,42,58,68,89,99	31	16,29,43,59,69,90,100
32	17,30,44,60,70,91,101	33	18,31,45,61,71,92,102
34	19,32,46,62,72,93,103	35	20,33,47,63,73,94,104
36	0,21,34,48,64,74,95,105	37	1,22,35,49,65,75,96,106
38	2,23,36,50,66,76,97,107	39	3,24,37,51,67,77,98,108
40	4,25,38,52,68,78,99,109	41	5,26,53,79
42	6,27,54,80	43	7,28,55,81
44	8,29,56,82	45	9,30,57,83
46	10,31,58,84	47	11,32,59,85
48	12,33,60,86	49	13,34,61,87
50	14,35,62,88	51	15,36,63,89
52	16,37,64,90	53	17,38,65,91
54	18,39,66,92	55	19,40,67,93
56	20,41,68,94	57	21,39,42,70,75,110
58	22,40,43,71,76,111	59	23,41,44,72,77,112
60	24,42,45,73,78	61	25,43,46,74,79

$*\delta^t$: output difference between faulty and fault-free keystreams at t^{th} instant

Table 4. Fault location vs. $\delta^{t*} = 1$ (σ), Fault Locations 62 to 127

Fault Location	$t =$	Fault Location	$t =$
62	26,44,47,80	63	27,45,48,81
64	0,28,46,49,82	65	1,29,47,50,83
66	2,30,48,51,84	67	3,31,49,52,85
68	4,32,50,53	69	5,51,54
70	6,52,55	71	7,53,56
72	8,54,57	73	0,9,55,58
74	1,10,56,59	75	2,11,57,60
76	3,12,58,61	77	4,13,59,62
78	5,14,60,63	79	6,15,61,64
80	7,16,62,65	81	8,17,63,66
82	9,18,64,67	83	10,19,65,68
84	11,20,66,69	85	12,21,67
86	13,22,68	87	14,23,69
88	15,24,70	89	0,16,25,71
90	1,17,26,72	91	2,18,27,73
92	3,19,28,39,55,70,74,75,86,91	93	4,20,29,40,56,71,75,76,87,92
94	5,21,30,41,57,72,76,77,88,93	95	6,22,31,42,58,73,77,78,89,94
96	7,23,32,43,59,74,78,79,90,95	97	8,24,39,44,55,60,75,79,80,91,96
98	9,25,40,45,56,61,76,80,81,92,97	99	10,26,41,46,57,62,77,81,82,93,98
100	11,27,42,47,58,63,78,82,83,94,99	101	12,28,43,48,59,64,79,83,84,95,100
102	13,29,44,49,60,65,80,84,85,96,101	103	14,30,45,50,61,66,81,85,86,97,102
104	15,31,46,51,62,67,82,86,87,98,103	105	16,32,47,52,63,68,83,87,88,99,104
106	17,33,48,53,64,69,84,88,89,100,105	107	18,34,49,54,65,70,85,89,90,101,106
108	19,35,50,55,66,71,86,90,91,102,107	109	20,36,51,56,67,72,87,91,92,103,108
110	21,37,52,57,68,73,88,92,93,104,109	111	22,38,53,58,69,74,89,93,94,105,110
112	23,39,54,59,70,75,90,94,95,106,111	113	24,40,55,60,71,76,91,95,96,107,112
114	25,41,56,61,72,77,92,96,97,108,113	115	26,42,57,62,73,78,93,97,98,109,114
116	27,43,58,63,74,79,94,98,99,110,115	117	28,44,59,64,75,80,95,99,100,111,116
118	29,45,60,65,76,81,96,100,101,112,117	119	30,46,61,66,77,82,97,101,102,113,118
120	31,47,62,67,78,83,98,102,103,114,119	121	32,48,63,68,79,84,99,103,104,115,120
122	33,49,64,69,80,85,100,104,105,116,121	123	34,50,65,70,81,86,101,105,106,117,122
124	35,51,66,71,82,87,102,106,107,118,123	125	36,52,67,72,83,88,103,107,108,119,124
126	37,53,68,73,84,89,104,108,109,120,125	127	38,54,69,74,85,90,105,109,110,121,126

$*\delta^{t}$: output difference between faulty and fault-free keystreams at t^{th} instant

Differential Fault Analysis of Sosemanuk

Yaser Esmaeili Salehani, Aleksandar Kircanski, and Amr Youssef

Concordia Institute for Information Systems Engineering,
Concordia University
Montreal, Quebec, H3G 1M8, Canada

Abstract. SOSEMANUK is a software-based stream cipher which supports a variable key length of either 128 or 256 bits and 128-bit initial values. It has passed all three stages of the ECRYPT stream cipher project and is a member of the eSTREAM software portfolio. In this paper, we present a fault analysis attack on SOSEMANUK. The fault model in which we analyze the cipher is the one in which the attacker is assumed to be able to fault a random inner state word but cannot control the exact location of injected faults. Our attack, which recovers the secret inner state of the cipher, requires around 6144 faults, work equivalent to around 2^{48} SOSEMANUK iterations and a storage of around $2^{38.17}$ bytes.

1 Introduction

The European Network of Excellence of Cryptology (ECRYPT) [12] stream cipher project, also known as eSTREAM [14], is a project that aimed to identify new promising stream ciphers. SOSEMANUK [4] is a fast software-oriented stream cipher that has passed all the three phases of the ECRYPT eSTREAM competition and is currently a member of the eSTREAM Profile 1 (software portfolio). It uses a 128-bit initialization vector and allows keys of either 128-bit or 256-bits, whereas the claimed security is always 128-bits. The design of SOSEMANUK (See Fig. 1) is based on the SNOW2.0 stream cipher [13] and utilizes elements of the Serpent block cipher [2]. SOSEMANUK aims to fix weaknesses of the SNOW 2.0 design and achieves better performance, notably in the ciphers initialization phase. Also, the secret inner state of SOSEMANUK is reduced when compared to SNOW 2.0 and amounts to 384 bits.

The preliminary analysis [4], conducted during the SOSEMANUK design process, includes the assessment of the cipher with respect to different cryptanalytic attacks such as correlation attacks, distinguishing attacks and algebraic attacks. Public analysis followed and SOSEMANUK was assessed in [1] by Ahmadi *et al.* where a guess-and-determine attack requiring 2^{226} operations and 2^4 keystream words was provided. Another improved guess-and-determine attack was presented by Tsunoo *et al.* in [24]. A correlation attack on SOSEMANUK was presented by Jung-Keun Lee *et al.* [20] with a computational complexity of $2^{147.88}$ and success probability 99% to recover the initial secret inner state. The data requirement for the attack was relaxed by Cho *et al.* [9]. In 2009, Lin *et al.* [21] improved the guess-and-determine attack, achieving complexity of 2^4

A. Nitaj and D. Pointcheval (Eds.): AFRICACRYPT 2011, LNCS 6737, pp. 316–331, 2011.

word keystream using 2^{192} steps. Another guess-and-determine attack with time complexity 2^{176} was recently presented by Feng et al. in Asiacrypt 2010 [15].

In this paper, we present a fault analysis attack on SOSEMANUK. The fault analysis model adopted in the paper is the one in which the attacker is assumed to be able corrupt a random inner state register in between the iterations of the cipher but the attacker has no control or knowledge over which inner state register has been corrupted. Also, the attacker is assumed to be able to reinitialize the cipher with the same key and IV arbitrary number of times. The attack recovers the secret inner state without recovering the key and requires about 6144 faults, 2^{48} operations each equivalent to one SOSEMANUK iteration and the storage of about $2^{38.17}$ bytes.

The rest of the paper is organized as follows. In the next section, we provide a brief overview of fault analysis attacks. In Section 3, relevant details of SOSEMANUK are reviewed. An overview of the proposed attack is provided in Section 4. Details of the attack are described in Section 5 and Section 6. Finally, the conclusion is given in Section 7.

2   Fault Analysis Attacks

In fault analysis attacks, the cryptanalyst applies some kind of physical influence, such as ionizing radiation, on the internal state of the cryptosystem which influence the crypto-primitive execution or memory. By carefully studying the results of computations performed under such faults, an attacker can retrieve information about the secret key. In 1996, Boneh et al. [8] introduced fault analysis by describing an attack that targets the RSA public key cryptosystem and exploits a faulty Chinese Remainder Theorem computation to factor the modulus n. Subsequently, fault analysis attacks were extended to symmetric systems such as DES [7] and later to AES [11]. Fault analysis attacks became a more serious threat after cheap and low-tech methods of applying faults were presented [23].

Fault attacks against stream ciphers were introduced by Hoch et al [16], where attacks against LILI-128 and SOBER-t32 and RC4 were described. Other stream ciphers that have been analyzed in the fault analysis model include SNOW 3G [10], Trivium [17], HC-128 [19] and Rabbit [18,5]. The number of required faults in the above attacks varies depending on the assumed fault analysis model. In general, all models follow the one given in Armknecht et al. [3], which assumes that the attacker has access to the physical device, and that the attacker is able to reset the device to the same unknown initial settings as often as needed. However, different assumptions with respect to the amount of control the attacker has over the induced faults are utilized. For example, the attacker may have control over the location of the faulted memory register, or may be able to restrict to Hamming weight of the induced faults. For instance, Biham et al. [6] assumed a model in which the attacker can choose the exact location (register) of the fault which causes RC4 to enter a special inner state and makes its recovery a trivial task. Similarly, Armknecht et al. [3] described a fault analysis attack gainst SNOW 2.0 where they assumed that the fault occurs exactly in a particular register of the cipher. On the other hand, in the fault analysis of Trivium [17], it

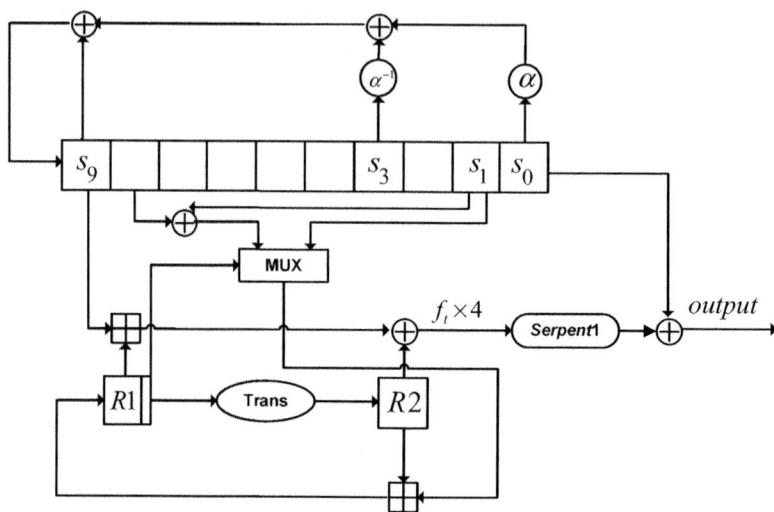

Fig. 1. Overview of the SOSEMANUK stream cipher

is assumed that the attacker has no control or knowledge over the fault position. Different assumptions also exist regarding the Hamming weight of induced faults. For instance, in [19] it is assumed that the fault causes a 1-bit flip in the inner state of the cipher, whereas in [6] it is assumed that the fault is localized in one byte of the inner state.

3   The Sosemanuk Specification

The following notation will be utilized throughout the rest of the paper:

- x^i: i-th bit of an n-bit word x
- $\boxplus, \times$: addition and multiplication modulo 2^{32}, respectively
- $\oplus$: bit-wise XOR
- $\lll$: left rotation defined on 32 bit values
- $|$: concatenation
- $X_i = f^i_{t+3}|f^i_{t+2}|f^i_{t+1}|f^i_t$: input value for i-th S-box applied in the Serpent1 function at some step t (the t value will be clear from the context). The Serpent1 function, shown in Fig. 2, is defined by 32 applications of S in the bit-slice mode, where

$$S = [8, 6, 7, 9, 3, 12, 10, 15, 13, 1, 14, 4, 0, 11, 5, 2]$$

is the S-box used in the third S-box layer of the Serpent block cipher [2].
- $'$: Sign for denoting faulty cipher registers or output. For example s'_0 will denote the LFSR register s_0 in the faulty instance of the cipher.

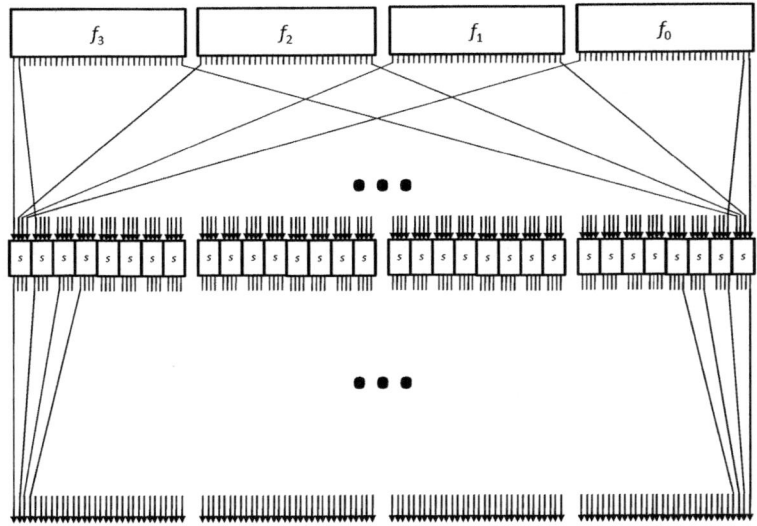

Fig. 2. The Serpent1 function

While the claimed security level of SOSEMANUK is 128 bits, it supports a variable key length of 128 or 256 bits and 128 bit initialization value. As depicted in Fig. 1, the secret inner state of SOSEMANUK consists of 12 32-bit words $(s_0, \ldots, s_9, R1, R2)$ and utilizes three main components to generate the keystream output: a linear feedback shift register (LFSR), a finite state machine (FSM) and an S-box-like function, Serpent1. To update the LFSR, the following recurrent relation is applied:

$$s_{t+10} = s_{t+9} \oplus \alpha^{-1} s_{t+3} \oplus \alpha s_t \tag{1}$$

where α is a root of the primitive polynomial $P(X) = X^4 + \beta^{23} X^3 + \beta^{245} X^2 + \beta^{48} X + \beta^{239}$ over $GF(2^8)$ and β ia a root of the primitive polynomial $Q(X) = X^8 + X^7 + X^5 + X^3 + 1$ over $GF(2)$.

The FSM update procedure is defined as follows:

$$R1_{t+1} = (R2_t \boxplus mux(lsb(R1_t), s_{t+1}, s_{t+1} \oplus s_{t+8})) \tag{2}$$

$$R2_{t+1} = (Trans(R1_t)) \tag{3}$$

where $mux(c, x, y) = \begin{cases} x \ if \ c = 0 \\ y \ if \ c = 1 \end{cases}$, $Trans(x) = (M \times x) \lll 7$ and $M = 0x54655307$.

The FSM output at each step is defined by

$$f_t = (s_{t+9} \boxplus R1_{t+1}) \oplus R2_{t+1} \tag{4}$$

The inner state right after the initialization is denoted by $(s_0, \ldots, s_9, R1_0, R2_0)$. At each step, first the FSM is updated and the f_t and s_t values are preserved in the internal buffer, then the LFSR is updated. Once every four steps, a 128-bit word is generated by

$$z_t|z_{t+1}|z_{t+2}|z_{t+3} = Serpent1(f_t|f_{t+1}|f_{t+2}|f_{t+3}) \oplus s_t|s_{t+1}|s_{t+2}|s_{t+3}. \quad (5)$$

For a more detailed description of SOSEMANUK, the reader is referred to [4].

4   The Attack Overview

In this section, we provide a high level overview of the proposed attack. According to our fault analysis model, the attacker is assumed to be able to re-initialize the cipher an arbitrary number of times. Furthermore, while we assume that each induced fault corrupts only one of the 12 inner state registers, the attacker does not know, and cannot control the position or the new value of the faulted register.

4.1   The Main Idea

The main idea of the attack can be explained as follows. In every SOSEMANUK iteration, 32 S-boxes are applied in the bit-slice mode as a part of the Serpent1 function. The first part of the attack restricts the input for each of the S-boxes by considering faults that occur at s_5 and s_4. Consider the case where the fault has been injected right after the SOSEMANUK initialization step and that it occurred in the register s_5. During the next cipher iteration in which the $z_0|z_1|z_2|z_3$ 128-bit keystream word is produced, the fault moves in the right-hand direction as the LFSR is clocked for 4 times. In particular, no faulty values participate in generation of f_0. Furthermore, since in every step, first the FSM is updated and then the f_t value is computed and finally the LFSR is clocked, f_1 and f_2 are computed without error and the fault affects only f_3. Now the non-faulty f_0, f_1, f_2 and the faulty f_3 enter the Serpent1 function. In the bit-slice mode, the Serpent1 function applies 32 S-boxes 4-bit inputs, where i-th bit comes from register f_i, $i = 0, \ldots 3$ (See Fig. 2). Thus, the input difference of all activated S-boxes will be equal to $0x8$ (1000 in binary). The attacker can then retrieve the corresponding S-box output difference and restrict the set of candidates for the S-box input-output values. When the fault occurs at register s_5, each S-box output will be faulted with probability $\frac{1}{2}$, which allows us to establish a criterion to recognize faults in register s_5. Similarly, in the case where the fault occurs at s_4, it propagates as shown in Figure 3 potentially affecting only f_2 and f_3. In other words, only the two most significant bits of every S-box input might be affected. Since a criterion for recognizing faults at s_4 can also be established, observing the output S-box differences for such faults also reduces the set of candidates for the S-box input-output values.

After the candidates for the S-box input-output values have been restricted, equation (5) is used to provide a restriction on the LFSR registers. From (1), it follows that the LFSR registers are not independent and restrictions on the LFSR registers can be coupled with the dependence of the LFSR registers to further prune the candidates for the s_t values. Finally, a guess and determine attack is used to find the rest of the inner state.

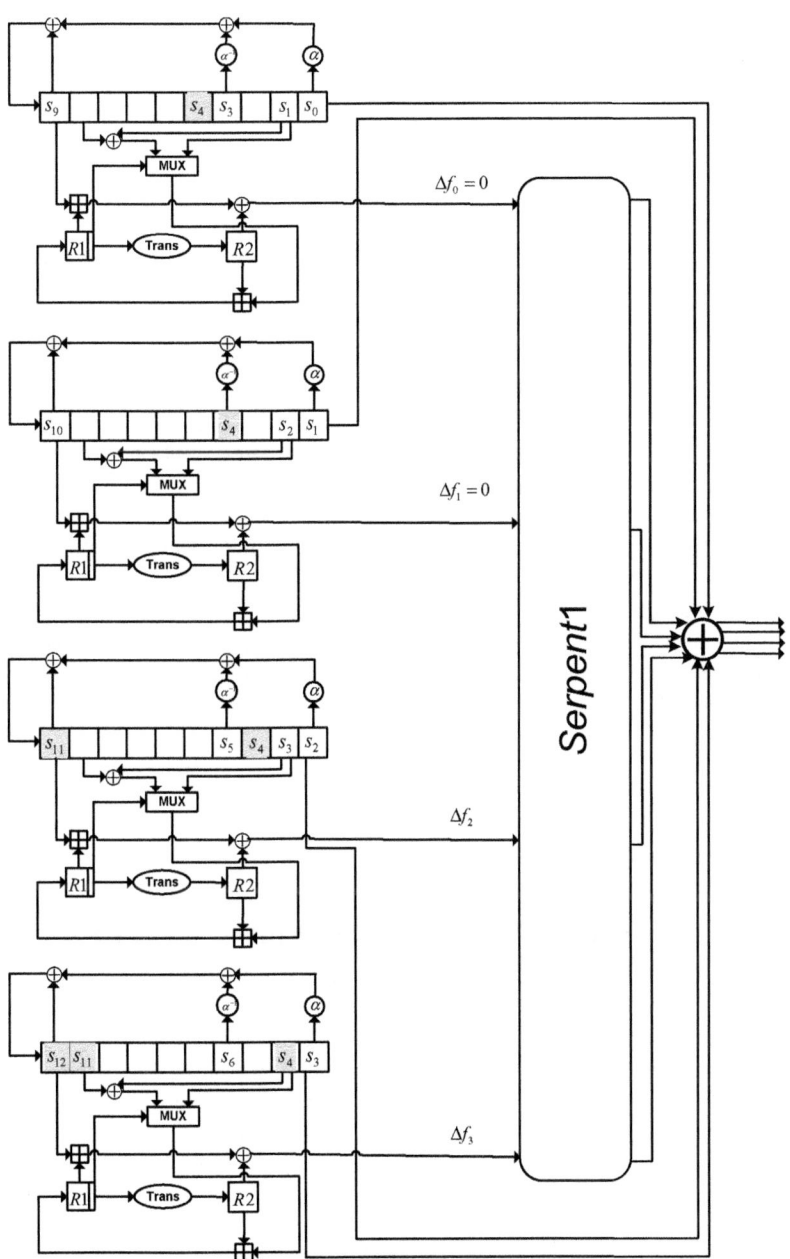

Fig. 3. The Δf values corresponding to the case where s_4 is faulted

4.2   The Steps of the Attack

The attack can be divided into two phases. The first phase collects faulty output in four different steps of the cipher execution and can be summarized as follows:

- For $l \in \{0, 1, 2, 4\}$
  - Repeat the steps below for m times
    - Reinitialize the cipher
    - Iterate for l times
    - Induce a fault, corrupting a random inner state register
    - Collect and store the keystream output word $z'_{4l} | z'_{4l+1} | z'_{4l+2} | z'_{4l+3}$

The second phase, which uses the collected information to uniquely determine the secret inner state, can be summarized as follows:

(1) Use the faulty outputs gathered in the first phase of the attack for $l \in \{0, 2, 4\}$ to reduce the number of candidates for (s_0, s_1, s_2, s_3), $(s_8, s_9, s_{10}, s_{11})$ and $(s_{16}, s_{17}, s_{18}, s_{19})$ to 2^{32} each. Then, use dependencies between the three four-plets imposed by relation (1) to further reduce the corresponding numbers of candidates (details are explained in Section 5)

(2) Similar to the previous step, using the information collected in the first phase of the attack for $l = 1$, reduce the number of candidates for (s_4, s_5, s_6, s_7) to 2^{32} (details are explained in Section 5)

(3) Apply the guess-and-determine strategy through the space reduced sets of candidates obtained by previous two steps to recover the complete inner state (details are explained in Section 6)

In the first phase of attack, data is collected for $l = 4$ and not for $l = 3$ since the LFSR registers candidate sets due to $l = 0$, $l = 2$ and $l = 4$ are correlated and allow further reduction. The reduction due to $l = 1$ is used later in the guess-and-determine attack.

5   Reducing the Number of Candidates for LFSR Registers (s_0, s_1, s_2, s_3) and $(s_8, s_9, s_{10}, s_{11})$

The starting number of candidates for the LFSR registers (s_0, s_1, s_2, s_3) and $(s_8, s_9, s_{10}, s_{11})$ is 2^{128} each. In this section, first we show how to reduce this number to 2^{32} and then, by exploiting the fact that the two register components are linked by relation (1), reduce it further to 2^{16}, each.

5.1   Recovering the S-Box Differences

Let SOSEMANUK be in state $t = 0$. From (5) and since $z_0 | z_1 | z_2 | z_3$ is accessible to the attacker, it is evident that reducing the uncertainty for $f_0 | f_1 | f_2 | f_3$ leads to reducing the uncertainty of $s_0 | s_1 | s_2 | s_3$. In this subsection, the $f_0 | f_1 | f_2 | f_3$ value is constrained by calculating the S-box input-output differences using the faulty information. Since the algorithms below are also applied to constraint $f_4 | f_5 | f_6 | f_7$,

$f_8|f_9|f_{10}|f_{11}$ and $f_{16}|f_{17}|f_{18}|f_{19}$, these algorithms are specified for general time t and will be used for $t \in \{0, 4, 8, 16\}$.

Define δ_i and Δ_i by

$$\delta_i = S(X_i \oplus \text{0x8}) \oplus S(X_i),$$
$$\Delta_i = \{S(X_i \oplus \text{0x4}) \oplus S(X_i), S(X_i \oplus \text{0xc}) \oplus S(X_i)\}$$

for every $i = 0, \ldots 31$. Algorithm 1 and Algorithm 2, described below, are used to recover δ_i and Δ_i, respectively, for each $i = 0, \ldots 31$.

In what follows, the probability distribution of the number of non-activated S-boxes in the SOSEMANUK output is analyzed. In particular, probabilities of the event that there will be more than 16 non-activated S-boxes are estimated under different assumptions about the location of the fault. For that purpose, let $0 \leq n \leq 32$ be a random variable which denotes the number of S-boxes that are *not* active in the application of the 32 S-boxes of Serpent1 in some steps of a faulty SOSEMANUK instance. Consider for example the probability that a particular S-box will not be activated given that the fault has occurred at s_0. In that case, only the 3 most significant bits of the S-box input may be corrupted. Note that, due to (5) by which the corrupted s_0 is XOR-ed to the least significant bits of each S-box, it may also happen that the difference in the S-box output caused by the S-box input cancels out. However, such a possibility has been ruled out by exhaustively checking that for each S-box input value it is not possible to cause a difference only in the least significant bit of the S-box output by any of the differences in the 3 most significant bits of the input. Thus, the probability that the particular S-box has not been activated is 2^{-3}. Now, it is clear that variable $n \sim B(2^{-3}, 32)$, i.e., n follows binomial distribution with parameters $p = 2^{-3}$ and $n = 32$. According to the binomial distribution, $P[16 \leq n \leq 31] = \sum_{i=16}^{31} \binom{32}{i} p^i (1-p)^{32-i} \approx 2^{-21}$. More generally, the distribution of n in terms of the fault position is given follows:

- $\{s_0\}$: $P[16 \leq n \leq 31] \approx 2^{-21}$ as explained above.
- $\{s_1, s_9, R1, R2\}$: all four S-box input bits may be corrupted. Hence, $n \sim B(2^{-4}, 32)$. For the fault position s_1, the possibility of cancelling out the S-box output difference has been ruled out the same way as in the case of s_0. Using the binomial distribution, it follows that $P[16 \leq n \leq 31]$ is negligible
- $\{s_8\}$: if $R1_0^0 = 0$, then, $n = 0$ with probability 1. Otherwise, all four S-box input bits may be corrupted and $n \sim B(2^{-4}, 32)$ and as for the previous case, $P[16 \leq n \leq 31]$ is negligible.
- $\{s_2, s_3\}$: only the least significant bit will certainly not be corrupted. For s_3, the cancellation of the S-box output difference is ruled out as in the case of s_0. In case of s_2, there exists one S-box input such that the S-box output difference can be cancelled out by inverting the second most significant bit $(S(1111) = S(1111 \oplus 1110) \oplus 0100)$. Approximating $n \sim B(2^{-3}, 32)$ gives $P[16 \leq n \leq 31] \approx 2^{-21}$.
- $\{s_4\}$: the most significant two bits may be corrupted, from which it follows that $n \sim B(2^{-2}, 32)$. So, $P[16 \leq n \leq 31] \approx 0.002$

- $\{s_6, s_7\}$: no S-box input bits can be corrupted and thus $n = 32$ with probability 1
- $\{s_5\}$: Only the most significant bit of every S-box input may be corrupted. Thus $n \sim B(\frac{1}{2}, 32)$ and $P[16 \leq n \leq 31] = \sum_{i=16}^{31} \binom{32}{i} \frac{1}{2^i} \frac{1}{2^{(32-i)}} = 0.569$

From the above reasoning, it follows that when the fault does not occur at s_5, $P[16 \leq n \leq 31] \approx \frac{1}{11} \times 0.02 \approx 0.0018$, where $\frac{1}{11}$ is the probability that the fault occurred at s_4, given that it did not occur at s_5. On the other hand, if the fault occurred at s_5, the probability of event $16 \leq n \leq 31$ is equal to 0.569. This analysis indicates that one can decide whether the fault occurred at s_5 or not by verifying whether $16 \leq n \leq 31$, or not, respectively.

In Algorithm 1, keystream words for which $16 \leq n \leq 31$ are considered. Namely, once such a keystream word have been found, the values of *activated* S-boxes are used to learn about the corresponding δ_i values. According to the discussion above, if the fault indeed occurred at s_5, such differences necessarily represent the S-box output difference for the input difference equal to $0x8$. To diminish the possibility of false positives (event $16 \leq n \leq 31$ takes place, but the fault does not occur at s_5), the final output difference value is taken as the most frequent difference candidate taken over different faulty keystream words at the (fixed) SOSEMANUK step in question, for which $16 \leq n \leq 31$ holds.

Algorithm 1

- Initialize 32 multisets: $Cand_1(k) = \emptyset$, $k = 0, \ldots, 31$.
- For each faulty keystream word $z'_t | z'_{t+1} | z'_{t+2} | z'_{t+3}$, such that

$$16 \leq \#\{z'^i_t | z'^i_{t+1} | z'^i_{t+2} | z'^i_{t+3} = z^i_t | z^i_{t+1} | z^i_{t+2} | z^i_{t+3} : i = 0, \ldots 31\} \leq 31 \qquad (6)$$

do:
  - For each $0 \leq k \leq 31$, if $d = z'^k_t | z'^k_{t+1} | z'^k_{t+2} | z'^k_{t+3} \oplus z^k_t | z^k_{t+1} | z^k_{t+2} | z^k_{t+3}$ is different than 0, add d to $Cand_1(k)$.
- Return the most frequent element in the multiset $Cand_1(i)$ as $\delta_i = S(X_i \oplus 0x8) \oplus S(X_i)$, for each $0 \leq i \leq 31$.

The overall number of required fault injections $m = 1536$ has been determined by incrementing m in steps of 128 and experimentally verifying that Algorithm 1 always recovers the correct $\delta_i = S(X_i \oplus 0x8) \oplus S(X_i)$, $i = 0, \ldots 31$ for 1000 randomly initialized instants of SOSEMANUK.

Algorithm 2 uses δ_i recovered by Algorithm 1 to find the sets Δ_i, $i = 0, \ldots 31$. In particular, the algorithm recognizes faulty keystream words that correspond to an error in register s_4 and then uses the S-box output differences in such keystream words to deduce Δ_i for $i = 0, \ldots 31$.

The criterion for recognizing faults in register s_4 is similar to the previously stated criterion for recognizing faults in s_5. However, instead of asking for 16 or more unactivated S-boxes, we expect to have more than 16 S-boxes which are either unactivated or with output difference equals to δ_i. Namely, let v be the number of S-boxes in one step of SOSEMANUK which are either not activated, or activated by an input difference of $0x8$. The probability of the event that one S-box is either not activated, or activated by an input difference of $0x8$ depends on the location where the fault occurred. In case the error is in register s_4, the probability in question will be $\frac{1}{2}$ since in that case only the 2 most significant bits of the S-box input may be faulted and the input difference has to among $0x0$, $0x8$, $0xc$ and $0x4$ values. Thus, if the fault is in s_4, $v \sim B(\frac{1}{2}, 32)$, and $P[16 \leq v \leq 31] = 0.569$. On the other hand, if the fault occurs at some other register, say at $R1$, all four S-box input bits may be corrupted and the probability that the input difference will be either $0x8$ or $0x0$ is significantly smaller. Again, this gives a methodology to decided whether the fault occurred at s_4 or not by counting the number of S-boxes which reacted with difference of either δ_i (using the corresponding i) or 0. Once the faults due to an error in register s_4 are recognized, finding the sets Δ_i proceeds with the following logic. When a keystream word for which the event $16 \leq v \leq 31$ took place has been found, the output S-box differences which are not due to input difference of $0x8$ or $0x0$ have to be due to difference $0xc$ or $0x4$. Again, to diminish the possibility of false positives (i.e., $16 \leq v \leq 31$ but the fault does not occur at s_4), the final output set is taken as the set with two most frequent difference candidates for the difference taken over different faulty keystream words at the SOSEMANUK step in question for which $16 \leq v \leq 31$ holds.

Algorithm 2

- Initialize 32 multisets: $Cand_{2,3}(k) = \emptyset$, $k = 0, \ldots, 31$.
- For each faulty keystream output word $z'_t|z'_{t+1}|z'_{t+2}|z'_{t+3}$, such that

$$
\begin{aligned}
16 \leq \#\{z'^i_t|z'^i_{t+1}|z'^i_{t+2}|z'^i_{t+3} = z^i_t|z^i_{t+1}|z^i_{t+2}|z^i_{t+3}|i = 0, \ldots 31\}+ \\
\#\{z'^i_t|z'^i_{t+1}|z'^i_{t+2}|z'^i_{t+3} \oplus z^i_t|z^i_{t+1}|z^i_{t+2}|z^i_{t+3} = \delta_i|i = 0, \ldots 31\} \leq 31
\end{aligned}
\tag{7}
$$

where δ_i, $0 \leq i \leq 31$ has been recovered by Algorithm 1, do:
  - For each $0 \leq k \leq 31$, add each $d = z'^k_t|z'^k_{t+1}|z'^k_{t+2}|z'^k_{t+3} \oplus z^k_t|z^k_{t+1}|z^k_{t+2}|z^k_{t+3}$ such that $d \notin \{0, \delta_k\}$ to the multiset $Cand_{2,3}(k)$.
- Return the two highest occurring elements in the multiset $Cand_{2,3}(i)$ as the required two-element set Δ_i, for each i.

For the above choice of total number of faults $m = 1536$, Algorithm 2 always succeeded in recovering the sets Δ_i, $i = 0, \ldots 31$, for 1000 randomly initialized instants of SOSEMANUK.

5.2   Restricting the Number of Candidates for the LFSR Registers

In each SOSEMANUK step, in which a 128-bit keystream word is produced, according to (5), 32 4×4 S-boxes are applied. In the previous subsection, it has been shown how to use the faulty information to deduce the S-box output differences for certain input S-box differences. Naturally, these evaluated input-output differences impose a constraint on the actual input-output values. In this subsection, the sets of possible S-box input-output values are deduced and the effect of

Table 1. Determining the S-box input-output values based on sets δ_i and Δ_i

δ_i,Δ_i	i-th S-box input	i-th S-box output
5,{8,B}	0	8
9, {2,D}	2	7
3,{B,E}	4	3
F,{4,D}	6	A
5,{D,E}	8	D
9,{4,B}	A	E
3,{8,D}	C	0
F,{2,B}	E	5
7,{A,D}	{1,5,9,D}	{6,C,1,B}
D,{6,B}	{3,7,B,F}	{9,F,4,2}

the deduced input-output S-box values constraints on the number of candidates for the LFSR registers (s_0, s_1, s_2, s_3) is presented.

Having determined the δ_i value and the two-element set Δ_i by Algorithms 1 and 2, for each $0 \leq i \leq 31$, the actual input-output values for the S-box are deduced according to Table 1. As can be noted from the table, in case the S-box input is even, the input-output value can be deduced uniquely. On the other hand, in case when the S-box input value is odd, there exist four candidates for the S-box input-output.

Assuming a uniform distribution on the S-box input values, it is expected that the attacker will deduce 64 out of 128 output bits. For the remaining 64 bits, it will be composed out of 16 4-bit values, each restricted to 4 candidates. The overall number of candidates for the 128-bit value $Serpent1(f_0|f_1|f_2|f_3)$ is then $4^{16} = 2^{32}$. Since we have

$$z_0|z_1|z_2|z_3 = Serpent1(f_0|f_1|f_2|f_3) \oplus s_0|s_1|s_2|s_3 \qquad (8)$$

and $z_0|z_1|z_2|z_3$ is known, it follows that there will be 2^{32} candidates for $s_0|s_1|s_2|s_3$.

The number of candidates for $s_4|s_5|s_6|s_7$, $s_8|s_9|s_{10}|s_{11}$ and $s_{16}|s_{17}|s_{18}|s_{19}$ can be restricted in a similar way. Namely, for that purpose, Algorithms 1 and 2 need to be applied using $z_4|z_5|z_6|z_7$, $z_8|z_9|z_{10}|z_{11}$ and $z_{16}|z_{17}|z_{18}|z_{19}$ and the faulty values obtained by the first phase of the attack described in Section 4 for $l = 1$, $l = 2$ and $l = 4$, respectively. Then, Table 1 is utilized to restrict the S-box input-output values occurring in steps $t = 1$, $t = 2$ and $t = 4$. Following the procedure explained in this section, it follows that $s_4|s_5|s_6|s_7$, $s_8|s_9|s_{10}|s_{11}$ and $s_{16}|s_{17}|s_{18}|s_{19}$ are expected to be restricted to 2^{32} candidates each.

5.3   Further Pruning of the LFSR Registers Candidates

In the previous subsection, the uncertainty for (s_0, s_1, s_2, s_3), $(s_8, s_9, s_{10}, s_{11})$ and $(s_{16}, s_{17}, s_{18}, s_{19})$ values has been reduced. In this subsection, we note that these three four-tuples of 32-bit values are not independent. Namely, according to (1), we have $s_{10} = s_9 \oplus \alpha^{-1}s_3 \oplus \alpha s_0$ and $s_{18} = s_{17} \oplus \alpha^{-1}s_{11} \oplus \alpha s_8$. These two relations are used to further prune candidates for (s_0, s_1, s_2, s_3) and $(s_8, s_9, s_{10}, s_{11})$. More precisely, after the end of the process, the attacker is left with 2^{16} candidates for

$$(f_0, f_1, f_2, f_3, s_0, s_1, s_2, s_3, f_8, f_9, f_{10}, f_{11}, s_8, s_9, s_{10}, s_{11}) \tag{9}$$

The two relations from the previous paragraph can be rewritten as

$$\alpha^{-1} s_3 \oplus \alpha s_0 = s_{10} \oplus s_9 \tag{10}$$
$$\alpha^{-1} s_{11} \oplus \alpha s_8 = s_{18} \oplus s_{17} \tag{11}$$

Before stating the candidate reduction procedure, we note that the candidates for (s_0, s_1, s_2, s_3) are specified in a way which allows listing them in a table efficiently. In particular, the candidate set for (s_0, s_1, s_2, s_3) is specified by sets B_i, $i = 0, \ldots 31$, such that $s_0^i | s_1^i | s_2^i | s_3^i \in B_i$. Then, each element of the set $B_0 \times B_1 \times \ldots \times B_{31}$ specifies one (s_0, s_1, s_2, s_3) value. The sets of candidates for $(s_8, s_9, s_{10}, s_{11})$ and $(s_{16}, s_{17}, s_{18}, s_{19})$ can be transformed to a list in the same way and this property is used in step (1) and step (5) of the procedure below.

1. List all of the (s_0, s_1, s_2, s_3) and $(s_{16}, s_{17}, s_{18}, s_{19})$ candidates and call the two generated tables T_1 and T_3, respectively. Include also the columns containing (f_0, f_1, f_2, f_3) and $(f_{16}, f_{17}, f_{18}, f_{19})$ in T_1 and T_3, respectively. Create an empty table T.
2. Extend T_1 by adding a column with the left-hand side of equation (10).
3. Extend T_3 by adding a column with the right-hand side of equation (11).
4. Sort T_1 and T_3 by columns added in steps (2) and (3).
5. For each candidate for $(s_8, s_9, s_{10}, s_{11})$
   5.1. Calculate the left-hand side of equation (11). If there does not exists an element in T_3 such that (11) holds, go to the next $(s_8, s_9, s_{10}, s_{11})$ candidate (step (5)).
   5.2. Otherwise, calculate the right-hand side of equation (10) and find rows of T_1 for which (10) holds. For each such row, add the complete row of the form (9) to table T.

To find the expected size of table T, note that it is expected that 16 bits of the T_3 table column containing $s_{18} \oplus s_{17}$ value are constant, due to the fact that 16 out of 32 S-box inputs corresponding to $(s_{16}^i, s_{17}^i, s_{18}^i, s_{19}^i)$ have been recovered uniquely by the procedure in the previous subsection. On the other hand, no constant bits are expected to exist in $\alpha^{-1} s_{11} \oplus \alpha s_8$ values due to randomization resulting from multiplying by α and α^{-1}. Thus, about 2^{16} candidates for $(s_8, s_9, s_{10}, s_{11})$, with the corresponding $(f_8, f_9, f_{10}, f_{11})$, will pass the elimination step (5.1).

In step (5.2), the remaining 2^{16} candidates are joined with T_1, which contains 2^{32} rows, according to (10). Since there exists no fixed bits in the $\alpha^{-1} s_3 \oplus \alpha s_0$ column of T_1, it is expected that around 2^{16} will be present in the output of the join step, i.e., in table T. Since both T_1 and T_3 contain 9 32-bit words in each row and table T contains 16 32-bit words in each row, the required memory space for the previous procedure is $2 \times 2^{32} \times 9 \times 4 + 2^{16} \times 16 \times 4 = 2^{38.17}$ bytes. The computational cost is equal to sorting two tables of 2^{32} rows, executing a search in a sorted table of length 2^{32} for 2^{32} times and finally executing a search for 2^{16} times in the sorted table of 2^{32} entries. By noting that sorting tables of length n takes $O(nlog(n))$ steps and that a binary search in the sorted table requires $O(log(n))$ steps, the overall cost is about $2^{32} \times 32 \times 2 + 2^{32} \times 32 + 2^{16} \times 32 = 2^{38.585}$ operations.

6 Recovering the Rest of the Inner State

In the previous subsections, we have reduced the LFSR complexity to 2^{32} candidates for (s_4, s_5, s_6, s_7) and 2^{16} candidates for the registers present in (9). In this subsection, a guess-and-determine like procedure that completes the secret inner state recovery is provided.

Let $R1_t^0$ denote the least significant bit of register $R1_t$. To recover s_4, s_5, $R1_0$ and $R2_0$, the following steps are applied:

- Pick a row from table T as a guess for (9)
- Determine s_4 from $s_4 = \alpha(\alpha s_1) \oplus \alpha(s_{10} \oplus s_{11})$ which holds due to (1) since s_1, s_{10} and s_{11} are known
- Guess $R1_0$ by fixing the register to one of the 2^{32} possible values.
- Determine:
    - $R2_0$, from $f_0 = (R1_0 \boxplus s_9) \oplus R2_0$
    - $R2_1$, from $R2_1 = Trans(R1_0)$
    - $R1_1$, from $R1_1 = R2_0 \boxplus (s_2 \oplus R1_0^0 \cdot s_9)$, which is another way to formulate (2)
    - $R2_2$, from $R2_2 = Trans(R1_1)$
    - $R1_2$, from $R1_2 = R2_1 \boxplus (s_3 \oplus R1_1^0 \cdot s_{10})$, which follows from (2)
    - $R2_3$, from $R2_3 = Trans(R1_2)$
    - $R1_3$, from $R1_3 = R2_2 \boxplus (s_4 \oplus R1_2^0 \cdot s_{11})$, which follows from (2)
    - s_{12}, from $f_3 = (R1_3 \boxplus s_{12}) \oplus R2_3$
    - s_5, from $s_{12} = s_{11} \oplus \alpha^{-1} s_5 \oplus \alpha s_2$

With a guess for (9) from the first step of the procedure above and having recovered s_4, s_5, $R1_0$ and $R2_0$, the only left unknown inner state registers are s_6 and s_7. To recover the remaining two registers, the table of 2^{32} candidates for (s_4, s_5, s_6, s_7) obtained in Section 5.2 is matched with newly found value for s_4, s_5, as follows. Consider the S-box input-output in the second iteration of SOSEMANUK, for which the input-output has not been recovered uniquely. For some $0 \le i \le 31$, $f_7^i|f_6^i|f_5^i|f_4^i$ and consequently, $S(f_7^i|f_6^i|f_5^i|f_4^i)$ can take 4 values as specified by Table 1. More precisely, rewriting (5) while isolating i-th S-box

$$z_7^i|z_6^i|z_5^i|z_4^i = S(f_7^i|f_6^i|f_5^i|f_4^i) \oplus s_7^i|s_6^i|s_5^i|s_4^i, \tag{12}$$

we have two options regarding the possible candidates. In other words, from the last two rows of Table 1, we have either

$$S(f_7^i|f_6^i|f_5^i|f_4^i) \in \{0110, 1100, 0001, 1011\} \qquad (13)$$

or

$$S(f_7^i|f_6^i|f_5^i|f_4^i) \in \{1001, 1111, 0100, 0010\}. \qquad (14)$$

Moreover, according to the procedure given in this subsection, the value of bits s_4^i, s_5^i has been determined uniquely. Since s_4^i and s_5^i are known, according to (12), the two least significant bits of $S(f_7^i|f_6^i|f_5^i|f_4^i)$ can be determined uniquely. Finally, due to the structure of sets (13) or (14), given information on the two least significant bits, all the 4 bits of $S(f_7^i|f_6^i|f_5^i|f_4^i)$ are uniquely determined. Presented reasoning uniquely determines the input-output for every S-box, from which, according to (12), s_7 and s_6 are determined uniquely, which completes the recovery of the whole secret inner state.

Now, the found secret inner state can be verified by comparing the actual SOSEMANUK output with the output produced by the recovered inner state. If a difference registered, the next guess for (9) and $R1_0$ is made and the procedure is repeated.

7   Summary and Conclusions

In this paper, a differential fault analysis attack on SOSEMANUK has been presented. The overall attack complexity can be summarized as follows:

- The average number of faults required to perform the attack is $4 \times 1536 = 6144$. These 1536 transient faults are introduced in steps $t = 0$, $t = 1$, $t = 2$ and $t = 4$. This fault injection phase requires the attacker to reinitialize the cipher for 6144 times
- The number of operations required for the attack is dominated by the guess-and-determine part of the analysis. Namely, as concluded in Section 5.3, table T has 2^{16} rows and thus there exists 2^{16} possible guesses for (9). Since register $R1_0$ is a 32-bit value, the number of guesses that need to be checked is $2^{16} \times 2^{32} = 2^{48}$. Verifying each guess according to the procedure in Section 6 is equivalent to one SOSEMANUK iteration and thus the attack requires work equivalent to around 2^{48} iterations.
- The storage amount required for the attack is equal to the size of the tables T_1, T_3 and T which amounts to $2^{38.17}$ bytes.

It should be noted that, when compared to other stream ciphers in the equivalent fault analysis model, DFA of SOSEMANUK requires a relatively smaller number of faults. For example, the DFA attack on RC4 given in [16] requires 2^{16} faults in random locations of the RC4 inner state. Another DFA attack on HC-128 [19] requires around 2^{13} faults in random locations. In future work, it will be interesting to see whether the number of faults for the DFA of SOSEMANUK and other stream ciphers can be drastically decreased in the assumed fault model.

A naive approach to prevent our attack is to use algorithm level redundancy and disable the device output if the two produced key stream values do not match. Another more efficient approach, which partially protects against fault attacks, is to add parity bits to all the inner state registers and disable the device output if any of these parity checks is violated. Efficient fault analysis resistant implementations for SOSEMANUK, as well as for other stream ciphers, need to be addressed in future research.

References

1. Ahmadi, H., Eghlidos, T., Khazaei, S.: Improved guess and determine Attack on SOSEMANUK (2006), http://www.ecrypt.eu.org/stream/sosemanukp3.html
2. Anderson, R., Biham, E., Knudsen, L.R.: Serpent: A proposal for the advanced encryption standard, NIST AES Proposal (1998)
3. Armknecht, F., Meier, W.: Fault Attacks on Combiners with Memory. In: Preneel, B., Tavares, S. (eds.) SAC 2005. LNCS, vol. 3897, pp. 36–50. Springer, Heidelberg (2006)
4. Berbain, C., Billet, O., Canteaut, A., Courtois, N., Gilbert, H., Goubin, L., Gouget, A., Granboulan, L., Lauradoux, C., Minier, M., Pornin, T., Sibert, H.: Sosemanuk, a fast software-oriented stream cipher. eSTREAM, the ECRYPT Stream Cipher Project, Report 2005/027 (2005)
5. Berzati, A., Canovas-Dumas, C., Goubin, L.: Fault Analysis of Rabbit: Toward a Secret Key Leakage. In: Roy, B., Sendrier, N. (eds.) INDOCRYPT 2009. LNCS, vol. 5922, pp. 72–87. Springer, Heidelberg (2009)
6. Biham, E., Granboulan, L., Nguyen, P.Q.: Impossible Fault Analysis of RC4 and Differential Fault Analysis of RC4. In: Gilbert, H., Handschuh, H. (eds.) FSE 2005. LNCS, vol. 3557, pp. 359–367. Springer, Heidelberg (2005)
7. Biham, E., Shamir, A.: Differential Fault Analysis of Secret Key Cryptosystems. In: Kaliski, B.S. (ed.) CRYPTO 1997. LNCS, vol. 1294, pp. 513–525. Springer, Heidelberg (1997)
8. Boneh, D., DeMillo, R.A., Lipton, R.J.: On the Importance of Checking Cryptographic Protocols for Faults. In: Fumy, W. (ed.) EUROCRYPT 1997. LNCS, vol. 1233, pp. 37–51. Springer, Heidelberg (1997)
9. Cho, J.Y., Hermelin, M.: Improved linear cryptanalysis of SOSEMANUK. In: Lee, D., Hong, S. (eds.) ICISC 2009. LNCS, vol. 5984, pp. 101–117. Springer, Heidelberg (2010)
10. Debraize, B., Corbella, I.M.: Fault analysis of the stream cipher Snow 3G. In: Workshop on Fault Diagnosis and Tolerance in Cryptography 2009, pp. 103–110 (2009)
11. Dusart, P., Letourneux, G., Vivolo, O.: Differential fault analysis on A.E.S. In: Zhou, J., Yung, M., Han, Y. (eds.) ACNS 2003. LNCS, vol. 2846, pp. 293–306. Springer, Heidelberg (2003)
12. ECRYPT, the European Network of Excellence for Cryptology, http://www.ecrypt.eu.org/ecrypt1/
13. Ekdahl, P., Johansson, T.: A New Version of the Stream Cipher SNOW. In: Nyberg, K., Heys, H.M. (eds.) SAC 2002. LNCS, vol. 2595, pp. 47–61. Springer, Heidelberg (2003)
14. eSTREAM, the ECRYPT Stream Cipher Project, http://www.ecrypt.eu.org/stream/
15. Feng, X., Liu, J., Zhou, Z., Wu, C., Feng, D.: A Byte-Based Guess and Determine Attack on SOSEMANUK. In: Abe, M. (ed.) ASIACRYPT 2010. LNCS, vol. 6477, pp. 146–157. Springer, Heidelberg (2010)

16. Hoch, J., Shamir, A.: Fault Analysis of Stream Ciphers. In: Joye, M., Quisquater, J.-J. (eds.) CHES 2004. LNCS, vol. 3156, pp. 240–253. Springer, Heidelberg (2004)
17. Hojsík, M., Rudolf, B.: Floating fault analysis of Trivium. In: Chowdhury, D.R., Rijmen, V., Das, A. (eds.) INDOCRYPT 2008. LNCS, vol. 5365, pp. 239–250. Springer, Heidelberg (2008)
18. Kircanski, A., Youssef, A.M.: Differential Fault Analysis of Rabbit. In: Jacobson Jr., M.J., Rijmen, V., Safavi-Naini, R. (eds.) SAC 2009. LNCS, vol. 5867, pp. 197–214. Springer, Heidelberg (2009)
19. Kircanski, A., Youssef, A.M.: Differential Fault Analysis of HC-128. In: Bernstein, D.J., Lange, T. (eds.) AFRICACRYPT 2010. LNCS, vol. 6055, pp. 261–278. Springer, Heidelberg (2010)
20. Lee, J.-K., Lee, D.-H., Park, S.: Cryptanalysis of sosemanuk and SNOW 2.0 using linear masks. In: Pieprzyk, J. (ed.) ASIACRYPT 2008. LNCS, vol. 5350, pp. 524–538. Springer, Heidelberg (2008)
21. Lin, D., Jie, G.: Guess and Determine Attack on SOSEMANUK. In: Proceedings of the 2009 Fifth International Conference on Information Assurance and Security, vol. 01, pp. 658–661. IEEE, Los Alamitos (2009)
22. Messerges, T.S., Dabbish, E.A., Sloan, H.R.: Examining Smart-Card Security under the Threat of Power Analysis Attacks. IEEE Trans. on Computers 51(4), 541–552 (2002)
23. Skorobogatov, S.P., Anderson, R.J.: Optical fault induction attacks. In: Kaliski Jr., B.S., Koç, Ç.K., Paar, C. (eds.) CHES 2002. LNCS, vol. 2523, pp. 2–12. Springer, Heidelberg (2003)
24. Tsunoo, Y., Saito, T., Shigeri, M., Suzaki, T., Ahmadi, H., Eghlidos, T., Khazaei, S.: Evaluation of Sosemanuk with regard to guess-and-determine attacks (2006), http://www.ecrypt.eu.org/stream/sosemanukp3.html

An Improved Differential Fault Analysis on AES-256

Sk Subidh Ali and Debdeep Mukhopadhyay

Dept. of Computer Science and Engineering
Indian Institute of Technology Kharagpur, India
{subidh,debdeep}@cse.iitkgp.ernet.in

Abstract. In this paper we present an improved differential fault attack on the Advanced Encryption Standard (AES) with 256-bit key. We show an improved attack which retrieves the AES-256 key using two pairs of fault free and faulty ciphertexts and a brute-force search of 2^{16} with a time complexity 2^{32}. The attack retrieves the secret key within approximately 45 minutes, running on desktop $Intel\ Core^{TM}2\ Duo$ processor of $3GHz$ speed. To the best of the knowledge of the authors, this is the most optimized fault attack on AES-256 among reported results requiring only two faulty ciphertexts.

Keywords: Differential Fault Analysis, Fault Attack, Advanced Encryption Standard.

1 Introduction

The modern ciphers implemented in embedded device such as smart cards, are shown to be extremely vulnerable to the fault based cryptanalysis. An attacker can deliberately induce fault into a crypto-device by means of external noise like electromagnetic radiation, voltage variation , glitch in the input clock line [3]. Then by analysing the faulty and fault free output ciphertexts she can retrieve the entire secret key of the cryptosystem. Fault attack was introduced by Boneh et al. [7] in 1997. Subsequently, a more lethal form of the attack was proposed by Adi Shamir and Biham which is known as the Differential Fault Analysis (DFA) [5]. They retrieved the secret key of DES cryptosystem by analysing the differences between the faulty and fault free ciphertexts.

In 2001, NIST introduced AES [1] as the next generation symmetric key block cipher. Since then there were many DFA attack on AES-128 [6, 9, 11]. Most efficient among them was the attack proposed by Piret and Quisquater [19]. They, for the first time showed that a DFA analysis on AES-128 is possible with only two faulty ciphertexts by injecting a fault at the eighth round input. In 2009, D. Mukhopadhyay proposed an improved version of the Piret's attack in [18], which required only one faulty ciphertext and a brute-force search of 2^{32}. The same result was also shown by Fukunaga et al. in [10]. In 2010, Michael Tunstall et al. in [21] showed that the attack on AES-128 using single faulty ciphertext can further be improved by reducing the brute-force search to 2^8

A. Nitaj and D. Pointcheval (Eds.): AFRICACRYPT 2011, LNCS 6737, pp. 332–347, 2011.
© Springer-Verlag Berlin Heidelberg 2011

from 2^{32}. Subsequently, there were two more works [2,13] proposed which made the attack proposed in [21] four times faster by reducing the time complexity of the attack to 2^{30}, which was earlier 2^{32}.

All these previous attacks only targeted AES-128. There are two more versions of AES, AES-192 and AES-256 which was subsequently analyzed by fault attacks. It was assumed that the proposed attack of Piret et al. in [19] on AES-128 can be extended to AES-192 and AES-256 with little modifications. However, later that assumption was proved to be wrong. It was only in 2009, Li et al. first proposed a DFA on AES-192 and AES-256. They were motivated by the work of M. Amir et al. [17]. The proposed attack on AES-256 was based on two different fault models which requires 6 and 3000 pairs of fault free and faulty ciphertexts. Takahashi and Fukunaga in [20] first time exploited the relations between the round keys of the key scheduling algorithm. They proposed an attack on AES-192 and AES-256. The attack on AES-192 required three pairs of correct and faulty ciphertexts and the attack on AES-256 required two pairs of correct and faulty ciphertext and two pairs of correct and faulty plaintexts. The attack was further improved by Chong Hee Kim in [14,15]. The author proposed a new attack on AES-192 and AES-256. The attack on AES-192 required two pairs of fault free and faulty ciphertexts, and the attack on AES-256 required three pairs of fault free and faulty ciphertexts. A Similar attack was proposed by Christophe Giraud et al. in [12], which reduced the AES 256-bit key space to 2^{18} choices using three faulty ciphertexts and a fault free ciphertext. The author also proposed a DFA using two faulty ciphertexts with attack complexity 2^{84} which is not in practical limit. Recently a DFA on AES-256 was proposed in [16], which required two faulty ciphertexts, but still had a high time complexity of 2^{48}.

In this paper we propose an improved DFA on AES-256. Our attack uses two pairs of correct and faulty ciphertexts. We show that the AES-256 key space reduces to 2^{16} using an attacking algorithm which has a time complexity of 2^{32}. We present experimental results to show that such an attack can be done on desktop $Intel\ Core^{TM}2\ Duo$ processor of $3GHz$ speed, in around 45 minutes.

Organization

The paper is organized as follows: In Section 2 we describe the Preliminaries to this paper. In Section 3 we describe the existing attack. In Section 4 we describe the attack improvement techniques. In Section 5 we explain the proposed attack. In Section 6 we describe some experimental results. In Section 7 we compare the work presented in this paper with the previous works, and we conclude in Section 8.

2   Preliminaries

2.1   The AES Algorithm

AES [1] is a 128-bit symmetric key block cipher which has three different versions AES-128, AES-192, and AES-256 with key length 128, 192, and 256 bits respectively. A 128-bit block is represented as a 4×4 matrix, known as the state matrix. The elements of the matrix are represented by a variable, $b_{i,j}$, where $0 \leq i,j \leq 3$ and i,j refers to the ith row and j^{th} column of the state matrix. The entire AES algorithm is a repetition of the round operation, which consist of four basic transformations namely SubBytes, ShiftRows, MixColumns and AddRoundKey. AES-128 has 10 rounds, AES-192 has 12 rounds, and AES-256 has 14 rounds. The last round of each of the three version of AES does not have MixColumns operation. The four basic transformations are described as follows:

SubBytes : It is the only non-linear transformation in AES. Each element of the state matrix is replaced by its inverse and followed by an affine mapping. All the operations are under $\mathbf{F_{2^8}}$.

ShiftRows : In this transformation the last three rows of the state matrix are circularly rotated towards left. The second row is rotated by one bytes, the third row is rotated by two bytes and the last row is rotated by three bytes.

MixColumns : It is a column level linear transformation of the state matrix. Each column of the state matrix is considered as a polynomial of degree 3 with coefficient in $\mathbf{F_{2^8}}$ and multiplied with the polynomial $\{03\}x^3 + \{01\}x^2 + \{01\}x + \{02\}$.

AddRoundKey: In this transformation the 128-bit round key is bit-wise xor-ed with the 128-bit state.

From now onwards we denote the SubBytes, ShiftRows, and MixColumns as SB, SR and MC respectively and the corresponding inverse functions as SB^{-1}, SR^{-1} and MC^{-1}.

2.2   Fault Model Used

The fault model of an attack defines the type of the fault i.e. single byte fault or multi byte fault and the location where the fault is being induced.

In this work we assume that the attacker has the ability to induce a single byte arbitrary fault in any particular round of AES. The assumption is based on the iterative implementation of AES, where the attacker can precisely calculate the timing of a particular round and induce a fault by means of a glitch in the clock input line or power supply line [10].

In the next section we describe the existing DFA on AES-256 developed by Kim [14, 15], which takes three faulty ciphertexts and uniquely determines the key.

3   Existing Fault Analysis

The existing attack [14, 15] on AES-256 took its motivation from the attacks [18] and it's improved version [21] on AES-128 . The attack requires three faulty ciphertexts: $\widehat{C_1}, \widehat{C_2}$, and $\widehat{C_3}$. The first two ciphertexts are obtained by inducing fault in between 11th and 12th round $MixColumns$ and the third ciphertext is obtained by inducing fault in between the 10th and 11th round $MixColumns$.

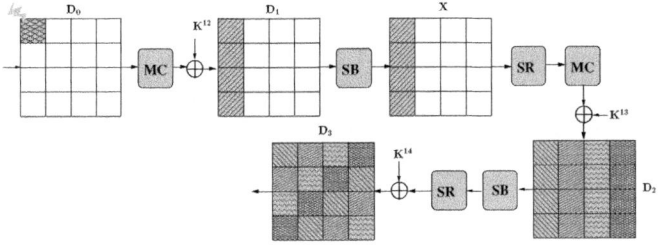

Fig. 1. Fault induced in between 11th and 12th round MixColumns

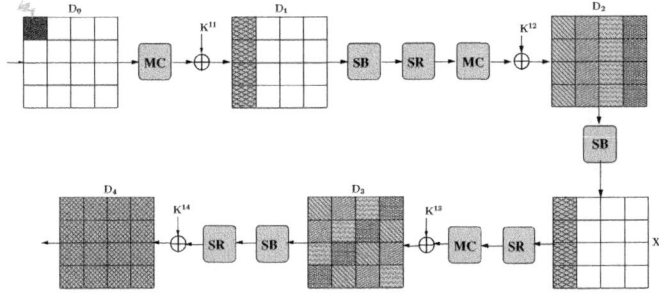

Fig. 2. Fault induced in between 10th and 11th round MixColumns

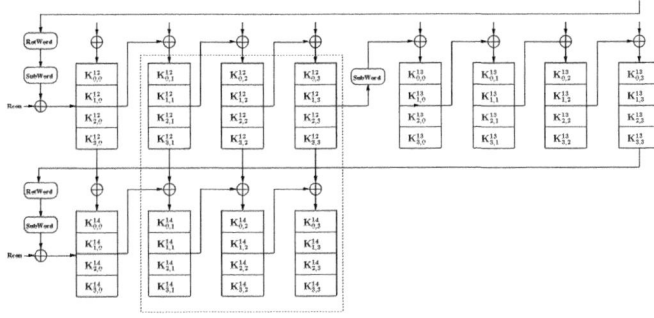

Fig. 3. AES-256 Key scheduling algorithm for last three round key K^{12}, K^{13} and K^{14}

The attack analysis can be divided into three phases. In the first phase of the attack requires two pairs of fault free and faulty ciphertexts $(C, \widehat{C_1})$ and $(C, \widehat{C_2})$ to retrieve the final round key K^{14} of the AES-256. In the second phase of the attack a third pair $(C, \widehat{C_3})$ is used to get the possible candidates of the penultimate round key K^{13}. In the final phase, the 256-bit AES key is uniquely determined.

We describe the three phases in brief.

3.1   First Phase of the Attack

The first phase of the attack is direct application of the attack proposed in [18]. The two faulty ciphertext $\widehat{C_1}$ and $\widehat{C_2}$ are used to uniquely determined the final round key K^{14}. Figure 1 shows the propagation of a single byte fault induced in between the 11th and 12th round *MixColumns*. The state matrix $D_0, D_1, D_2,$ and D_3 show the *xor* differences of corresponding faulty and fault free states. The differences in the first column of D_2 will produce the following system of equations as in [18]:

$$2F_1 = SB^{-1}(C_{0,0} \oplus K_{0,0}^{14}) \oplus SB^{-1}(\widehat{C_{1(0,0)}} \oplus K_{0,0}^{14})$$
$$F_1 = SB^{-1}(C_{1,3} \oplus K_{1,3}^{14}) \oplus SB^{-1}(\widehat{C_{1(1,3)}} \oplus K_{1,3}^{14})$$
$$F_1 = SB^{-1}(C_{2,2} \oplus K_{2,2}^{14}) \oplus SB^{-1}(\widehat{C_{1(2,2)}} \oplus K_{2,2}^{14}) \tag{1}$$
$$3F_1 = SB^{-1}(C_{3,1} \oplus K_{3,1}^{14}) \oplus SB^{-1}(\widehat{C_{1(3,1)}} \oplus K_{3,1}^{14})$$

Using this system of equations the attacker reduces the number of choices of quadruples $\langle K_{0,0}^{14}, K_{1,3}^{14}, K_{2,2}^{14}, K_{3,1}^{14} \rangle$ to 2^8 from 2^{32}. Similarly, from the other three columns of D_2 three more systems of equations are deduced, which reduce the search space of the quadruples $\langle K_{0,1}^{14}, K_{1,0}^{14}, K_{2,3}^{14}, K_{3,2}^{14} \rangle$, $\langle K_{0,2}^{14}, K_{1,1}^{14}, K_{2,0}^{14}, K_{3,3}^{14} \rangle$, and $\langle K_{0,3}^{14}, K_{1,2}^{14}, K_{2,1}^{14}, K_{3,0}^{14} \rangle$ to 2^8 choices each. Combining all four quadruple we have 2^{32} choices of K^{14}. Therefore, this technique filters 2^{32} candidates out of 2^{128} possible candidate of K^{14}. So, repeating this technique once again with another pair of fault free and faulty ciphertexts and the 2^{32} candidates of K^{14}, the attacker uniquely determines the key. Now the attacker gets the 13th round faulty and fault free output values by performing one round inverse operation with the help of the ascertained K^{14}.

In the second phase of the attack, the attacker uses the last round key K^{14} to deduce the 13th round key K^{13}.

3.2   Second Phase of the Attack

In the second phase of the attack, another pair of fault free and faulty ciphertexts $(C, \widehat{C_3})$ is used by inducing a single byte fault in between the 10th and 11th round MixColumns. Figure 2 depicts the flow of fault corresponding to the faulty ciphertext $\widehat{C_3}$. Now the differences in each columns of D_2 produce four differential equations. For example the first column produces the following set of equations:

$$2\alpha = SB^{-1}(X_{0,0}) \oplus SB^{-1}(X_{0,0} \oplus \varepsilon_{0,0})$$
$$\alpha = SB^{-1}(X_{1,0}) \oplus SB^{-1}(X_{1,0} \oplus \varepsilon_{1,3})$$
$$\alpha = SB^{-1}(X_{2,0}) \oplus SB^{-1}(X_{2,0} \oplus \varepsilon_{2,2}) \tag{2}$$
$$3\alpha = SB^{-1}(X_{3,0}) \oplus SB^{-1}(X_{3,0} \oplus \varepsilon_{3,1})$$

where X is the 13th round SubBytes output and $\varepsilon = MC^{-1}\Big(SR^{-1}\big(SB^{-1}(C \oplus K^{14})\big) \oplus SR^{-1}\big(SB^{-1}(\widehat{C_3} \oplus K^{14})\big)\Big)$. The 14th round key K^{14} and the faulty and fault free ciphertexts C and $\widehat{C_3}$ are known to the attacker. Therefore, the unknown in the system of equations (2) are the values of X. The above system of equations reduce the number of candidates of quadruple $\langle X_{0,0}, X_{1,0}, X_{2,0}, X_{3,0} \rangle$ to 2^8 from 2^{32}. Similarly, from the other three columns of D_2, three more systems of equations are deduced and subsequently the number of possible candidates of quadruples $\langle X_{0,1}, X_{1,1}, X_{2,1}, X_{3,1} \rangle$, $\langle X_{0,2}, X_{1,2}, X_{2,2}, X_{3,2} \rangle$ and $\langle X_{0,3}, X_{1,3}, X_{2,3}, X_{3,3} \rangle$ are reduced to 2^8 each. Similar equations can also be deduced from the differences in the first column of D_1 in Figure 1, which corresponds to faulty ciphertext $\widehat{C_1}$ and $\widehat{C_2}$. These equations, further reduce the possible candidates of $\langle X_{0,0}, X_{1,0}, X_{2,0}, X_{3,0} \rangle$ to one choice from 2^8 choices. Therefore, finally there are 2^{24} possible candidates of X. Each of these candidates of X is then transformed into the 13th round key K^{13} by using the relation $K^{13} = MC(SR(X)) \oplus C^{13}$, where C^{13} is 13th round output ciphertext value, which is known to the attacker from the output ciphertext and K^{14} ascertained previously.

The third phase of the attack uniquely determines the master key from one choice of K^{14} and 2^{24} choice of K^{13}.

3.3   Third Phase of the Attack

The third phase of the attack employs the key reduction technique proposed in [21]. Using the key scheduling algorithm of AES-256 the 12th round key K^{12} is deduced from K^{13} and K^{14}. Each candidate of K^{12} is tested by the four sets of equations deduced from the differences in the first column of the state matrix D_1 in Figure 2. These four equations reduce the 2^{24} possible candidates of K^{12} to one candidate. Therefore, finally there is only one candidate of K^{12}, K^{13}, and K^{14}.

3.4   Analysis

The above three phase attack reduces the number of possible 256-bit key of AES-256 to one choice. However, the attack's worst case time complexity is 2^{24}. It is when the faulty ciphertexts $\widehat{C_1}$ and $\widehat{C_2}$ are affected in the same column by the induced fault. It may be observed that the existing attack can also be done using two faulty ciphertexts, for example using faulty ciphertext C_1 and C_3. In that case the attacker can deduce 2^{32} possible candidates of K^{14} using faulty ciphertext $\widehat{C_1}$, following the method proposed in [18]. Then the attacker can apply the existing attack on each candidates of K^{14}. However, the time complexity of the attack will be $2^{32} \times 2^{24} = 2^{56}$ which is not in practical limits.

In the next section we explain two observations based on which the existing attack's time complexity can be reduced further.

4   Attack Time and Search Space Complexity Reduction Techniques

There are two main observations we discuss in this section. The first observation is in the second phase of the attack which is already used in existing attack

[14,15] as well as in the attack proposed in [12], to reduce the number of possible candidates of K^{13} to 2^{24} (or 2^{16} if the byte faults in $\widehat{C_1}$ and $\widehat{C_2}$ are induced in two different columns) from 2^{32}. However, we used the first observation with two different purposes: first for reducing the possible candidates of final round key and secondly to reduce the possible candidates of 13th round keys. The second observation is in the third phase of the attack. We observed that the time complexity of the existing attack is based on the third phase which is currently 2^{24}. This time complexity of the third phase can be reduced to 2^{16} based on the second observation. We show that these two observations lead to an improved DFA on AES-256 with two faulty ciphertexts.

In the remaining part of the section we elaborate our observations.

4.1   The First Observation

In the second phase of the attack we have four sets of equations from the differences in the four different columns of the state matrix D_2 (as depicted in Figure 2), which corresponds to the faulty ciphertexts $\widehat{C_3}$. The first column produces the set of equations (2) with unknown $\langle X_{0,0}, X_{1,0}, X_{2,0}, X_{3,0} \rangle$. Similarly, from the first column of D_1 (as depicted in Figure 1), which corresponds to faulty ciphertext $\widehat{C_1}$ we have following set of equations with same unknowns $\langle X_{0,0}, X_{1,0}, X_{2,0}, X_{3,0} \rangle$:

$$
\begin{aligned}
2\alpha' &= SB^{-1}(X_{0,0}) \oplus SB^{-1}(X_{0,0} \oplus \rho_{0,0}) \\
\alpha' &= SB^{-1}(X_{1,0}) \oplus SB^{-1}(X_{1,0} \oplus \rho_{1,3}) \\
\alpha' &= SB^{-1}(X_{2,0}) \oplus SB^{-1}(X_{2,0} \oplus \rho_{2,2}) \\
3\alpha' &= SB^{-1}(X_{3,0}) \oplus SB^{-1}(X_{3,0} \oplus \rho_{3,1})
\end{aligned}
\tag{3}
$$

where $\rho = MC^{-1}\Big(SR^{-1}\big(SB^{-1}(C \oplus K^{14})\big) \oplus SR^{-1}\big(SB^{-1}(\widehat{C_1} \oplus K^{14})\big)\Big)$. The fault free and faulty ciphertexts C and $\widehat{C_1}$ are fixed. If the final round key K^{14} is fixed then the values of ρ and ε also gets fixed. For a given value of α and α', one choice of $\langle X_{0,0}, X_{1,0}, X_{2,0}, X_{3,0} \rangle$ satisfies the two sets of equations (2) and (3) with a probability $(\frac{1}{2^8})^8 = \frac{1}{2^{64}}$. We have to consider all possible 256 values of α and α'. Therefore, the probability of satisfying both the sets of equations is $\frac{(2^8)^2}{2^{64}} = \frac{1}{2^{48}}$. There are 2^{32} candidates of $\langle X_{0,0}, X_{1,0}, X_{2,0}, X_{3,0} \rangle$ out of which $\frac{2^{32}}{2^{48}} = \frac{1}{2^{16}}$ candidate satisfy both the sets of equations. This implies that only the actual candidate of $\langle X_{0,0}, X_{1,0}, X_{2,0}, X_{3,0} \rangle$ will satisfy both the sets of equations, rest will be discarded with very high probability $(1 - \frac{1}{2^{16}})$.

However, if K^{14} is not fixed, in that case each value of K^{14} and the corresponding value of ρ and ε will have 2^{32} possible candidates of $\langle X_{0,0}, X_{1,0}, X_{2,0}, X_{3,0} \rangle$. For example say K^{14} has 2^M candidates which implies $2^M \times 2^{32} = 2^{M+32}$ candidates of K^{14} and $\langle X_{0,0}, X_{1,0}, X_{2,0}, X_{3,0} \rangle$ out of which $\frac{2^{M+32}}{2^{48}} = 2^{M-16}$ candidates satisfy both the sets of equations (2) and (3). This means, out 2^M candidates of K^{14} in an average 2^{M-16} candidates will have one choice of

$\langle X_{0,0}, X_{1,0}, X_{2,0}, X_{3,0} \rangle$ satisfying both the sets of equations (2) and (3). Therefore, the two sets of equations (2) and (3) can be used as a filter to reduce the possible candidates of K^{14} by considering only those candidates of K^{14} which returns at least one candidate of $\langle X_{0,0}, X_{1,0}, X_{2,0}, X_{3,0} \rangle$. Therefore, the first observation can be used to reduce the space complexity of the final round key K^{14}.

4.2   The Second Observation

This observation is based on the third phase of the attack as described in Section 3.3. In the third phase of the attack each of the 2^{24} possible candidates of K^{13} is converted to 12th round key K^{12}, using the key scheduling algorithm. Then three rounds of inverse operations are performed on the fault free and faulty ciphertexts C and $\widehat{C_3}$ using unique value of K^{14} and one choice of K^{13} and the corresponding candidate of K^{12} to get the differences $\{2\delta, \delta, \delta, 3\delta\}$ in the first column of D_1 as depicted in Figure 2, where δ is a non-zero arbitrary byte. Then using the relation $\{2\delta, \delta, \delta, 3\delta\}$, the number of possible candidates of K^{12} are reduced. However, this requires a huge execution overhead which is equivalent to seven round operations: one round inverse operation for getting K^{14}, two round inverse operations for getting X, one round operation for deducing K^{13} from X, and finally three round inverse operations for getting the differences at the first column of D_1. We can reduce these execution overhead by reusing the intermediate results. First, we can save the 13th round outputs while calculating K^{14} and use it in calculating X. Similarly, we can save the 12th round fault free and faulty output $SB^{-1}(X_{i,j})$ and $SB^{-1}(X_{i,j} \oplus \varepsilon_{p,q})$ while calculating X and can directly use it to get the differences in the first column of D_1 as follows:

$$
\begin{aligned}
2\delta = &SB^{-1}\big(14(SB^{-1}(X_{0,0}) \oplus K_{0,0}^{12}) \oplus 11(SB^{-1}(X_{1,0}) \oplus K_{1,0}^{12}) \\
&\oplus 13(SB^{-1}(X_{2,0}) \oplus K_{2,0}^{12}) \oplus 9(SB^{-1}(X_{3,0}) \oplus K_{3,0}^{12})\big) \\
&\oplus SB^{-1}\big(14(SB^{-1}(X_{0,0} \oplus \varepsilon_{0,0}) \oplus K_{0,0}^{12}) \oplus 11(SB^{-1}(X_{1,0} \oplus \varepsilon_{1,3}) \oplus K_{1,0}^{12}) \oplus \\
&13(SB^{-1}(X_{2,0} \oplus \varepsilon_{2,2}) \oplus K_{2,0}^{12}) \oplus 9(SB^{-1}(X_{3,0} \oplus \varepsilon_{3,1}) \oplus K_{3,0}^{12})\big)
\end{aligned}
\tag{4}
$$

$$
\begin{aligned}
\delta = &SB^{-1}\big(9(SB^{-1}(X_{0,3}) \oplus K_{0,3}^{12}) \oplus 14(SB^{-1}(X_{1,3}) \oplus K_{1,3}^{12}) \oplus \\
&11(SB^{-1}(X_{2,3}) \oplus K_{2,3}^{12}) \oplus 13(SB^{-1}(X_{3,3}) \oplus K_{3,3}^{12})\big) \\
&\oplus SB^{-1}\big(9(SB^{-1}(X_{0,3} \oplus \varepsilon_{0,3}) \oplus K_{0,3}^{12}) \oplus 14(SB^{-1}(X_{1,3} \oplus \varepsilon_{1,2}) \oplus K_{1,3}^{12}) \oplus \\
&11(SB^{-1}(X_{2,3} \oplus \varepsilon_{2,1}) \oplus K_{2,3}^{12}) \oplus 13(SB^{-1}(X_{3,3} \oplus \varepsilon_{3,0}) \oplus K_{3,3}^{12})\big)
\end{aligned}
\tag{5}
$$

$$
\begin{aligned}
\delta = &SB^{-1}\big(13(SB^{-1}(X_{0,2}) \oplus K_{0,2}^{12}) \oplus 9(SB^{-1}(X_{1,2}) \oplus K_{1,2}^{12}) \oplus \\
&14(SB^{-1}(X_{2,2}) \oplus K_{2,2}^{12}) \oplus 11(SB^{-1}(X_{3,2}) \oplus K_{3,2}^{12})\big) \\
&\oplus SB^{-1}\big(13(SB^{-1}(X_{0,2} \oplus \varepsilon_{0,2}) \oplus K_{0,2}^{12}) \oplus 9(SB^{-1}(X_{1,2} \oplus \varepsilon_{1,1}) \oplus K_{1,2}^{12}) \oplus \\
&14(SB^{-1}(X_{2,2} \oplus \varepsilon_{2,0}) \oplus K_{2,2}^{12}) \oplus 11(SB^{-1}(X_{3,2} \oplus \varepsilon_{3,3}) \oplus K_{3,2}^{12})\big)
\end{aligned}
\tag{6}
$$

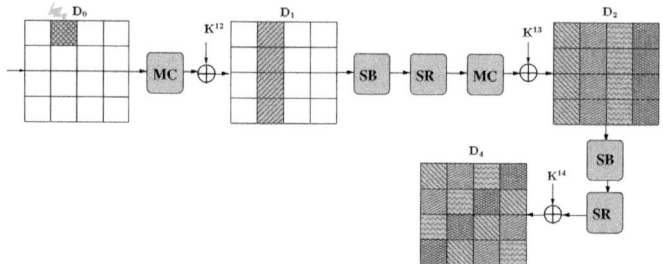

Fig. 4. Propagation of fault when the single byte fault is injected in between 11th and 12th round MixColumns

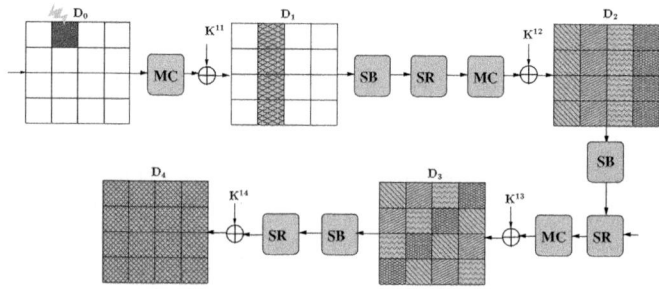

Fig. 5. Propagation of fault when the single byte fault is injected in between 10th and 11th round MixColumns

$$
\begin{aligned}
3\delta =& SB^{-1}\big(11(SB^{-1}(X_{0,1}) \oplus K_{0,1}^{12}) \oplus 13(SB^{-1}(X_{1,1}) \oplus K_{1,1}^{12}) \oplus \\
& 9(SB^{-1}(X_{2,1}) \oplus K_{2,1}^{12}) \oplus 14(SB^{-1}(X_{3,1}) \oplus K_{3,1}^{12})\big) \\
& \oplus SB^{-1}\big(11(SB^{-1}(X_{0,1} \oplus \varepsilon_{0,1}) \oplus K_{0,1}^{12}) \oplus 13(SB^{-1}(X_{1,1} \oplus \varepsilon_{1,0}) \oplus K_{1,1}^{12}) \oplus \\
& 9(SB^{-1}(X_{2,1} \oplus \varepsilon_{2,3}) \oplus K_{2,1}^{12}) \oplus 14(SB^{-1}(X_{3,1} \oplus \varepsilon_{3,2}) \oplus K_{3,1}^{12})\big)
\end{aligned} \tag{7}
$$

Each of the above equations consist of one column of X and one column of K^{12}. It may be noted that the last three columns of K^{12} are solely dependent on K^{14}. Figure 3 depicts the relation between the last three round keys K^{12}, K^{13} and K^{14} as per the AES-256 key scheduling algorithm. Therefore, now the execution overhead is reduced to almost three rounds of inverse operation which was seven rounds earlier.

Now if we observe the above four equations we can see that only the first equation required all the four columns of X, as the first column of K^{12} depends on K^{13}. The remaining three equations are independent of each others as each of them consist of one column of X and one column of K^{12} which can independently be calculated from K^{14}. Therefore, we can choose any two equations of the last three equations and reduce the corresponding X values [2]. After that we can choose the third equation to further reduce the values of X. For example we can first select equations (5) and (6) which will reduce the possible candidates of quartet pair $\langle X_{0,3}, X_{1,3}, X_{2,3}, X_{3,3} \rangle$ and $\langle X_{0,2}, X_{1,2}, X_{2,2}, X_{3,2} \rangle$ to $\frac{2^8 \times 2^8}{2^8} = 2^8$ from 2^{16}. Then we can choose the equation (7) which will finally reduce the possible choices of three quartets $\langle X_{0,1}, X_{1,1}, X_{2,1}, X_{3,1} \rangle$, $\langle X_{0,2}, X_{1,2}, X_{2,2}, X_{3,2} \rangle$ and $\langle X_{0,3}, X_{1,3}, X_{2,3}, X_{3,31} \rangle$ to $\frac{2^8 \times 2^8}{2^8} = 2^8$. After that if we choose the first equation (4), where the number of possible candidates of quartet $\langle X_{0,0}, X_{1,0}, X_{2,0}, X_{3,0} \rangle$ is 1, then the possible candidates of X reduce to $\frac{1 \times 2^8}{2^8} = 1$. Therefore, through out the third phase of the attack the time complexity remain 2^{16}. This observation serves two purpose: first it reduces the required operation from 7 rounds to 3 rounds and secondly it reduces the time complexity of the third phase of the attack to 2^{16}.

Note : It may be noted that if the fault occurs in any one of the last three columns of the state matrix, the same observation gives better result. As Figure 4 and Figure 5 show, the fault induced at the second column. In that case the number of possible candidates of the third column of X will reduce to one choice and rest of the columns possible choices remain 2^8 each. Therefore, the possible candidates of last three column will reduce to one choice by following the above technique. Finally, the time complexity will reduced to 2^8.

In the next section we propose an improved DFA on AES-256 based on observation one and two which requires two faulty ciphertexts.

5   Improved Attack on AES-256 Using Two Faulty Ciphertexts

The second observation stated above (Section 4.2) shows that the existing attack's time complexity can be reduce to 2^{16} which implies that the same attack can be done using two faulty ciphertexts with a time complexity of $2^{32} \times 2^{16} = 2^{48}$. This is shown in [16]. However, this complexity is quite high in terms of actual execution time of the attack. We implemented the attack using the optimization technique mentioned in observation two as well as using sbox difference table and found that the attack still consumes on an average 10 million CPU cycles on $Intel\ Core^{TM}2\ Duo$ processor of $3GHz$ speed for one choice of K^{14}. Therefore, 2^{32} such choices will take a huge execution time which is not feasible in terms of side-channel attacks. We proposed an improved attack using two faulty ciphertexts $\widehat{C_1}$ and $\widehat{C_2}$ with time complexity 2^{24} when the fault is induced in last three columns of the state matrix and 2^{32} when the fault is induced in the first column of the state matrix.

The faulty ciphertext $\widehat{C_1}$ is generated by inducing a single byte fault in between 11th and 12th round $MixColumns$ whereas the faulty ciphertext $\widehat{C_2}$ is generated by inducing a single byte fault in between 10th and 11th round Mix-$Columns$. The attack is divided into two phases. The first phase of the attack reduces the possible candidates of K^{14} to 2^{16} choices. In the second phase, the attack deduces the corresponding 2^{16} candidates of penultimate round key K^{13}.

In the next section we describe the first phase of the attack.

5.1   First Phase of the Proposed Attack

In the first phase of the attack we first use the faulty ciphertext $\widehat{C_1}$ which corresponds to Figure 1. Therefore, as per the Figure 1, the differences in the four columns of the state matrix D_2 produce four quartets of key bytes $\langle K_{0,0}^{14}, K_{1,3}^{14}, K_{2,2}^{14}, K_{3,1}^{14} \rangle$, $\langle K_{0,1}^{14}, K_{1,0}^{14}, K_{2,3}^{14}, K_{3,2}^{14} \rangle$, $\langle K_{0,2}^{14}, K_{1,1}^{14}, K_{2,0}^{14}, K_{3,3}^{14} \rangle$, and $\langle K_{0,3}^{14}, K_{1,2}^{14}, K_{2,1}^{14}, K_{3,0}^{14} \rangle$, each of size 2^8. Using these four quartets we first deduce the values of the four faulty bytes $\langle \rho_{0,0}, \rho_{1,3}, \rho_{2,2}, \rho_{3,1} \rangle$ at the first column of the state matrix X. Each of these four faulty bytes require one of the four quartets of key bytes. For example the first byte is given by:

$$
\begin{aligned}
\rho_{0,0} =& \big(14(SB^{-1}(C_{0,0} \oplus K_{0,0}^{14}) \oplus SB^{-1}(\widehat{C_{1(0,0)}} \oplus K_{0,0}^{14})) \oplus \\
& 11(SB^{-1}(C_{1,3} \oplus K_{1,3}^{14}) \oplus SB^{-1}(\widehat{C_{1(1,3)}} \oplus K_{1,3}^{14})) \oplus \\
& 13(SB^{-1}(C_{2,2} \oplus K_{2,2}^{14}) \oplus SB^{-1}(\widehat{C_{1(2,2)}} \oplus K_{2,2}^{14})) \oplus \\
& 9(SB^{-1}(C_{3,1} \oplus K_{3,1}^{14}) \oplus SB^{-1}(\widehat{C_{1(3,1)}} \oplus K_{3,1}^{14})))
\end{aligned}
\tag{8}
$$

If we observe the above equation (8) and the set of equations (1) carefully we can see that the equation (8) consists of only the differences $(2F_1, F_1, F_1, 3F_1)$ of the set of equations (1). Therefore, to speed up the execution we can reuse the differences from the equation (1) to calculate the values of ρ as follows:

$$
\rho_{0,0} = 14(2F_1) \oplus 11(F_1) \oplus 13(F_1) \oplus 9(3F_1)
\tag{9}
$$

Similarly, we calculate the values of the other three faulty bytes $\rho_{1,3}, \rho_{2,2}$ and $\rho_{3,1}$ of the first column of state matrix X corresponding to the faulty ciphertext $\widehat{C_1}$. It may be noted that each of these faulty bytes corresponds to one quartet of key byte of K^{14}. Using the same method we calculate the differences $\langle \epsilon_{0,0}, \epsilon_{1,3}, \epsilon_{2,2}, \epsilon_{3,1} \rangle$ at the first column of X (as depicted in Figure 2), which corresponds to the second faulty ciphertext $\widehat{C_2}$.

Now we apply the observation one as described in Section 4.1 to reduce the possible candidates of K^{14}. In order to reduce the time complexity of the first phase we rewrite the system of equations (2) and (3) as follows:

$$
2\alpha' = SB^{-1}(X_{0,0}) \oplus SB^{-1}(X_{0,0} \oplus \rho_{0,0})
\tag{10a}
$$

$$
2\alpha = SB^{-1}(X_{0,0}) \oplus SB^{-1}(X_{0,0} \oplus \varepsilon_{0,0})
\tag{10b}
$$

$$
\alpha' = SB^{-1}(X_{1,0}) \oplus SB^{-1}(X_{1,0} \oplus \rho_{1,3})
\tag{11a}
$$

$$
\alpha = SB^{-1}(X_{1,0}) \oplus SB^{-1}(X_{1,0} \oplus \varepsilon_{1,3})
\tag{11b}
$$

$$
\alpha' = SB^{-1}(X_{2,0}) \oplus SB^{-1}(X_{2,0} \oplus \rho_{2,2})
\tag{12a}
$$

$$
\alpha = SB^{-1}(X_{2,0}) \oplus SB^{-1}(X_{2,0} \oplus \varepsilon_{2,2})
\tag{12b}
$$

$$3\alpha' = SB^{-1}(X_{3,0}) \oplus SB^{-1}(X_{3,0} \oplus \rho_{3,1}) \tag{13a}$$

$$3\alpha = SB^{-1}(X_{3,0}) \oplus SB^{-1}(X_{3,0} \oplus \varepsilon_{3,1}) \tag{13b}$$

The above four pairs of equations are independent of each others because each pair of equations require one of the four quartets of K^{14}. Therefore, instead of considering all the four pairs of equations at a time we consider two pairs of equations at a time. For example we first choose the pairs of equations (10) and (11), those who satisfy these two pairs of equations are tested by the third pair of equations (12). Those who satisfy the third pairs of equations are tested by the fourth pair of equations (13). These four pairs of equations reduce the possible candidates of K^{14} to 2^{16} each having one candidate of $\langle X_{0,0}, X_{1,0}, X_{2,0}, X_{3,0} \rangle$.

Analysis. To get the values of $\langle X_{0,0}, X_{1,0}, X_{2,0}, X_{3,0} \rangle$ for a given value of α, α', ρ, and ε, we use sbox difference table. Therefore, for the two equations (10a) and (11a), we guess the values of α' for each value of the pair $(\rho_{0,0}, \rho_{1,3})$ and then we get the corresponding values of $\varepsilon_{0,0}, \varepsilon_{1,3}, X_{0,0}$, and $X_{1,0}$ and are tested by the equations (10b) and (11b). Therefore, in equation (10a) and (11a), we have $2^8 \times 2^8 \times 2^8 = 2^{24}$ possible choices of $\alpha', \rho_{0,0}$, and $\rho_{1,3}$, which is reduced to 2^{16} by the equations (10b) and (11b). Each of these 2^{16} values combined with 2^8 values of $\rho_{2,2}$ and tested by the third pair of equations (12), which is again reduced to 2^{16}. Each of these values again combined with 2^8 values of $\rho_{3,1}$ and tested by the fourth pair of equations (13), which is finally reduced to 2^{16}. Therefore, through out the process we test only 2^{24} values. Hence, the time complexity of the first phase of the attack is 2^{24}.

The total probability of above eight equations (four pairs (10),(11), (12) and (13)) is 2^{-48}. There are total 2^{32} possible candidates of K^{14}, each having 2^{32} possible candidates of $\langle X_{0,0} X_{1,0}, X_{2,0}, X_{3,0} \rangle$. Therefore, only $\frac{2^{32} \times 2^{32}}{2^{48}} = 2^{16}$ candidates will satisfy the above eight equations. Which means out of 2^{32} candidates of K^{14} only 2^{16} candidates will have one candidate of $\langle X_{0,0}, X_{1,0}, X_{2,0}, X_{3,0} \rangle$ each, rest of the 2^{16} candidates of K^{14} will produce no candidate of $\langle X_{0,0}, X_{1,0}, X_{2,0}, X_{3,0} \rangle$.

5.2   Second Phase of the Proposed Attack

In the second phase, we deduce the penultimate round key K^{13} corresponding to each of the 2^{16} candidates of K^{14} generated from the first phase of the attack. For one choice of K^{14} we first deduce the possible candidates of the last three columns of X, i.e. $\langle X_{0,1}, X_{1,1}, X_{2,1}, X_{3,1} \rangle, \langle X_{0,2}, X_{1,2}, X_{2,2}, X_{3,2} \rangle$ and $\langle X_{0,3}, X_{1,3}, X_{2,3}, X_{3,3} \rangle$, corresponding to the second faulty ciphertext $\widehat{C_2}$. As per the AES-256 key scheduling algorithm which is depicted in Figure 3, the last three columns of 12th round key K^{12} are directly deduced from the candidate of K^{14} as $K^{12}_{i,j} = K^{14}_{i,j} \oplus K^{14}_{i,j-1}$ where $0 \leq i \leq 3$ and $1 \leq j \leq 3$.

Now, we can apply the observation two (Section 4) to reduce the time complexity of the attack. We first consider equation (5) and (6) and reduce the possible candidates of $\langle X_{0,3}, X_{1,3}, X_{2,3}, X_{3,3} \rangle$, and $\langle X_{0,2}, X_{1,2}, X_{2,2}, X_{3,2} \rangle$ to 2^8

from 2^{16} choices. Then each of these candidates are combined with 2^8 candidates of $\langle X_{0,1}, X_{1,1}, X_{2,1}, X_{3,1} \rangle$ and tested by equation (7) which further reduces the possible candidates of three quartets to 2^8 and then each of these candidates of three quartets are combined with one candidate of $\langle X_{0,0}, X_{1,0}, X_{2,0}, X_{3,0} \rangle$ and tested by equation (4) which actually reduces the possible choices of four quartets of X to one choice. Therefore, for each candidates of K^{14} we get one candidate of X which corresponds to one candidate of K^{13}. Therefore, 2^{16} candidates of K^{14} will produce on an average 2^{16} candidates of K^{13}. So, finally we get 2^{16} possible pairs of candidates (K^{13}, K^{14}).

The attack procedure is summarized in Algorithm 1.

Algorithm 1. Fault Attack on AES-256 using two Faulty Ciphertexts

---

Input: $C, \widehat{C_1}, \widehat{C_2}$
Output: List of 256-bit key L_k
/* $X_{i,j} = \langle X_{0,j}, X_{1,j}, X_{2,j}, X_{3,j} \rangle$*/
/* $K_{i,j}^{12} = \langle K_{0,j}^{12}, K_{1,j}^{12}, K_{2,j}^{12}, K_{3,j}^{12} \rangle$*/
Get the 2^{16} candidates of K^{14} by applying first phase of the proposed attack
for *each candidates of K^{14}* **do**
    Guess the possible candidates of $X_{i,1}$, $X_{i,2}$, and $X_{i,3}$
    Get the values of $K_{i,1}^{12}$, $K_{i,2}^{12}$, and $K_{i,3}^{12}$ from K^{14}
    for *each candidates of $X_{i,3}$* **do**
        for *Each candidates of $X_{i,2}$* **do**
            Test equations (5) and (6)
            if *Satisfied* **then**
                for *Each candidates of $X_{i,1}$* **do**
                    Test equation (7)
                    if *Satisfied* **then**
                        for *Each candidates of $X_{i,0}$* **do**
                            Get $K_{i,0}^{12}$ from K^{14} and $X_{i,1}, X_{i,2}, X_{i,3}$
                            Test equation (4)
                            if *Satisfied* **then**
                                Get K^{13} from X
                                Get 256-bit key from AES-256 Key Scheduling algorithm
                                save the 256-bit key to L_k
                          end
                    end
                end
            end
        end
        end
    end
end

Analysis. For one candidates of K^{14} the time complexity of the second phase of the attack is 2^{16}. Therefore, for 2^{16} candidates the time complexity is 2^{32}. The probability of the four equations (4),(5),(6) and (7) is 2^{-24}. There are 2^{16} candidates of K^{14} each of which have 2^{24} possible candidates of X. Therefore, finally $\frac{2^{16} \times 2^{24}}{2^{24}} = 2^{16}$ candidates satisfy the four equations in the second phase of the attack. Hence, the entire two phase attack's complexity is 2^{32}.

Note : It may be noted that if the single byte fault induced in any one of the last three columns of the state matrix as shown in Figure 4 and Figure 5, in that case the time complexity of the second phase of the proposed attack will reduce to 2^8. This implies, over all two-phase attack time complexity will reduce to 2^{24}.

6   Experimental Results

We evaluated the program for fault analysis on several test cases where the two byte faults were induced in between 11th and 12th round *MixColumns* and in between 10th and 11th round *MixColumns* separately. On an average, on $3GHz$ *Intel Core^{TM}2 Duo* platform with $2GB$ RAM, the attack required nearly 45 minutes to reduce the key space of AES-256 to 2^{16} values. Such a byte fault is indeed practical and can be achieved on actual hardware through even less costly techniques like clock glitch [10] or voltage fluctuation [4]. We also developed a laboratory setup to induce faults in an FPGA implementation of AES using glitches in the clock input line created by an arbitrary clock generator. Furthermore, due to the note mentioned in Section 4, if the fault is induced in any one of the last three columns of the AES state matrix, the time required by the attack is even less, i.e. around 40 minutes. Over 100 tests were conducted with different random keys. Table 1 shows some of the keys which were attacked. We tested both the cases when the fault is induced in first column as well as when the fault is induced in any one of the last three columns. In both the cases, the key space is reduced to 2^{16}.

Table 1. Experimental Results

Random 256-bit Key	Fault in first column		Fault in any one of the last three columns	
	Number of Keys	Running Time (minutes)	Number of Keys	Running Time (minutes)
22615643211247530329 4a5bc2326a96 19345421476b4e2b7219 1a845d30942a	$43048 \approx 2^{15}$	45.697	$59964 \approx 2^{16}$	41.242
12325456678995279083 279465237316 17531573718516238276 32153ba5b384	$35202 \approx 2^{15}$	44.994	$52231 \approx 2^{15}$	40.426
f23246d39882375602c9 684ba2266273 17da5b421c6b2e263218 1adc642725b2	$31685 \approx 2^{15}$	43.994	$53544 \approx 2^{16}$	40.147
603deb1015ca71be2b73 aef0857d7781 1f352c073b6108d72d98 10a30914dff4	$27636 \approx 2^{15}$	43.68	$32284 \approx 2^{15}$	41.07
34322233445699778899 aa9434ca3c4d 1f352c073b6108d72d98 10a30914dff4	$37265 \approx 2^{15}$	46.103	$41527 \approx 2^{15}$	40.763

7   Comparison

The method proposed in [14, 15] requires three faulty ciphertexts and a time complexity of 2^{24}. The attack requires three faulty byte inductions, two in between 11th and 12th round *MixColumns* and one in between 10th and 11th round *MixColumns*. However, the objective of a more optimized fault attack is to make it more practical by reducing the number of faults and still keeping a practical space and time complexity. In these lines there has been recent research to develop DFA on AES-128 with reduced number of faults [18]. Recently in [16], it was mentioned that AES-256 also can be subjected to a DFA with two faulty ciphertexts with time complexity of 2^{48} as it iterates the entire attack for 2^{32} time using all the possible candidates of the final round key K^{14}, which incurs a huge attack execution time. However, ideally we would want to optimize the attack to a practical time complexity which is lesser then 2^{40}.

Table 2. Comparison with existing attack on AES-256

Reference	Fault Model	Number of Faults	Exhaustive Search	Time Complexity
[14, 15]	1 byte random fault	3	1	2^{24}
[16]	1 byte random fault	2	2^{16}	2^{48}
Our attack	1 byte random fault	2	2^{16}	2^{32}

The proposed attack requires two faulty ciphertexts with time complexity of 2^{32} and the final search space of AES-256 key is 2^{16}, which is also within practical limits. The optimization is a resultant of two improvements: first, reduction of possible key space of K^{14} to 2^{16} values, with a time complexity of 2^{24}, as opposed to 2^{32} values in [16]. Secondly, using acceleration methods to compute 2^{16} corresponding values of K^{13} for 2^{16} possible values of K^{14} using a time complexity of 2^{32} as opposed to 2^{48} values in [16]. It may also be noted that when the fault is induced in any one of the last three columns, our attack time complexity reduce to 2^{24} as opposed to 2^{40} in [16]. In short, our attack reduces the search space of K^{10} to 2^{16} from 2^{32} at the beginning of the attack, so that the rest of the attack is iterated for 2^{16} times. Where as in case of attack in [16], almost the entire attack is repeated for all the possible 2^{32} candidates of K^{10}, which increases the attack time complexity. The summary of the comparison is given in Table 2.

8 Conclusions

In this paper we proposed an improved differential fault attack on AES-256 using two faulty ciphertexts with time complexity of 2^{32}. The final search space of AES-256 key is reduced to 2^{16}. We present extensive simulation results on the proposed DFA to demonstrate that the attack is indeed successful within practical time limits. To the best of our knowledge, the present attack improves existing differential fault analysis of AES-256 by reducing the time complexity of the attack from 2^{48} to 2^{32} using only two faulty ciphertexts.

References

1. National Institute of Standards and Technology, Advanced Encryption Standard, NIST FIPS PUB 197 (2001)
2. Ali, S., Mukhopadhyay, D.: Acceleration of Differential Fault Analysis of the Advanced Encryption Standard Using Single Fault. Cryptology ePrint Archive, Report 2010/451 (2010), http://eprint.iacr.org/
3. Bar-El, H., Choukri, H., Naccache, D., Tunstall, M., Whelan, C.: The Sorcerers Apprentice Guide to Fault Attacks. Cryptology ePrint Archive, Report 2004/100 (2004), http://eprint.iacr.org/
4. Barenghi, A., Bertoni, G., Parrinello, E., Pelosi, G.: Low Voltage Fault Attacks on the RSA Cryptosystem. In: Breveglieri, et al. (eds.) [8], pp. 23–31

5. Biham, E., Shamir, A.: Differential Fault Analysis of Secret Key Cryptosystems. In: Kaliski Jr., B.S. (ed.) CRYPTO 1997. LNCS, vol. 1294, pp. 513–525. Springer, Heidelberg (1997)
6. Blömer, J., Seifert, J.-P.: Fault Based Cryptanalysis of the Advanced Encryption Standard (AES). In: Wright, R.N. (ed.) FC 2003. LNCS, vol. 2742, pp. 162–181. Springer, Heidelberg (2003)
7. Boneh, D., DeMillo, R.A., Lipton, R.J.: On the Importance of Checking Cryptographic Protocols for Faults (Extended Abstract). In: Fumy, W. (ed.) EUROCRYPT 1997. LNCS, vol. 1233, pp. 37–51. Springer, Heidelberg (1997)
8. Breveglieri, L., Gueron, S., Koren, I., Naccache, D., Seifert, J.-P. (eds.): Sixth International Workshop on Fault Diagnosis and Tolerance in Cryptography, FDTC 2009, Lausanne, Switzerland. IEEE Computer Society, Los Alamitos (September 2009)
9. Dusart, P., Letourneux, G., Vivolo, O.: Differential Fault Analysis on A.E.S. Cryptology ePrint Archive, Report 2003/010 (2003), http://eprint.iacr.org/
10. Fukunaga, T., Takahashi, J.: Practical Fault Attack on a Cryptographic LSI with ISO/IEC 18033-3 Block Ciphers. In: Breveglieri, et al. (eds.) [8], pp. 84–92
11. Giraud, C.: DFA on AES. Cryptology ePrint Archive, Report 2003/008 (2003), http://eprint.iacr.org/
12. Giraud, C., Thillard, A.: Piret and Quisquater's DFA on AES Revisited. Cryptology ePrint Archive, Report 2010/440 (2010), http://eprint.iacr.org/
13. Gomisawa, S., Li, Y., Takahashi, J., Fukunaga, T., Sasaki, Y., Sakiyama, K., Ohta, K.: Efficient Differential Fault Analysis for AES. Cryptology ePrint Archive, Report 2010/336 (2010), http://eprint.iacr.org/
14. Kim, C.H.: Differential fault analysis against AES-192 and AES-256 with minimal faults. Slides of the presentation at FDTC 2010 (2010), http://sites.uclouvain.be/security/download/slides/Kim-2010-fdtc-slides.pdf
15. Kim, C.H.: Differential Fault Analysis against AES-192 and AES-256 with Minimal Faults. In: FDTC, pp. 3–9 (2010)
16. Li, Y., Gomisawa, S., Sakiyama, K., Ohta, K.: An Information Theoretic Perspective on the Differential Fault Analysis against AES. Cryptology ePrint Archive, Report 2010/032 (2010), http://eprint.iacr.org/
17. Moradi, A., Shalmani, M.T.M., Salmasizadeh, M.: A Generalized Method of Differential Fault Attack Against AES Cryptosystem. In: Goubin, L., Matsui, M. (eds.) CHES 2006. LNCS, vol. 4249, pp. 91–100. Springer, Heidelberg (2006)
18. Mukhopadhyay, D.: An Improved Fault Based Attack of the Advanced Encryption Standard. In: Preneel, B. (ed.) AFRICACRYPT 2009. LNCS, vol. 5580, pp. 421–434. Springer, Heidelberg (2009)
19. Piret, G., Quisquater, J.-J.: A Differential Fault Attack Technique against SPN Structures, with Application to the AES and KHAZAD. In: Walter, C.D., Koç, Ç.K., Paar, C. (eds.) CHES 2003. LNCS, vol. 2779, pp. 77–88. Springer, Heidelberg (2003)
20. Takahashi, J., Fukunaga, T.: Differential Fault Analysis on AES with 192 and 256-Bit Keys. Cryptology ePrint Archive, Report 2010/023 (2010), http://eprint.iacr.org/
21. Tunstall, M., Mukhopadhyay, D.: Differential Fault Analysis of the Advanced Encryption Standard using a Single Fault. Cryptology ePrint Archive, Report 2009/575 (2009), http://eprint.iacr.org/

Benaloh's Dense Probabilistic Encryption Revisited*

Laurent Fousse[1], Pascal Lafourcade[2], and Mohamed Alnuaimi[3]

[1] Université Grenoble 1, CNRS, Laboratoire Jean Kuntzmann, France
Laurent.Fousse@imag.fr
[2] Université Grenoble 1, CNRS, Verimag, France
Pascal.Lafourcade@imag.fr
[3] Global Communication & Software Systems, United Arab Emirates
mohamed.alnuaimi@nkc.ae

Abstract. In 1994, Josh Benaloh proposed a probabilistic homomorphic encryption scheme, enhancing the poor expansion factor provided by Goldwasser and Micali's scheme. Since then, numerous papers have taken advantage of Benaloh's homomorphic encryption function, including voting schemes, private multi-party trust computation, non-interactive verifiable secret sharing, online poker. In this paper we show that the original description of the scheme is *incorrect*, because it can result in ambiguous decryption of ciphertexts. Then we show on several applications that a bad choice in the key generation phase of Benaloh's scheme has a real impact on the behaviour of the application. For instance in an e-voting protocol, it can inverse the result of an election. Our main contribution is a corrected description of the scheme (we provide a complete proof of correctness). Moreover we also compute the probability of failure of the original scheme. Finally we show how to formulate the security of the corrected scheme in a generic setting suitable for several homomorphic encryptions.

Keywords: public-key encryption, probabilistic encryption, homomorphic encryption scheme, Benaloh's scheme.

1 Introduction

An encryption scheme is homomorphic when it preserves some algebraic structure (usually group, sometimes ring) between the cleartext space and the ciphertext space, allowing computations on data encrypted with the same key. Examples of such encryptions are RSA [37] or ElGamal [19] which have the property that $\mathcal{E}(m_1) \times \mathcal{E}(m_2) = \mathcal{E}(m_1 \times m_2)$. In 1982 Goldwasser-Micali [25] introduced an encryption scheme with the different property $\mathcal{E}(b_1) \times \mathcal{E}(b_2) = \mathcal{E}(b_1 \oplus b_2)$. Several homomorphic encryption schemes have followed: Benaloh [3], Naccache and Stern [32], Okamoto and Uchiyama [33], Paillier [34] and its generalization proposed by Damgård and Jurik [17], Sander, Young and Yung [40], Boneh

---

* This work was supported by ANR SeSur AVOTE.

A. Nitaj and D. Pointcheval (Eds.): AFRICACRYPT 2011, LNCS 6737, pp. 348–362, 2011.
© Springer-Verlag Berlin Heidelberg 2011

et al [6]. All these schemes are partially homomorphic, meaning they allow homomorphic computation of only one operation (either addition or multiplication) on plaintexts. A cryptosystem allowing for homomorphic computation of two operations is called fully homomorphic. In 2009, Craig Gentry [21] found the first fully homomorphic encryption scheme, using lattice-based cryptography. However his scheme, while revolutionary, is not really practical and several recent works focus on concrete realizations of a fully homomorphic encryption scheme [41,45,22,23]. Practitioners rely therefore on already existing partially homomorphic encryption. A survey of such cryptosystems can be found in [7] for non specialists, or in [2] with a complexity analysis. In [36], Rappe considers homomorphic cryptosystems and their applications, such as multiparty computation [12,29,18,16], electronic voting [4,9,39,38,10,3,11,15,13,28], key exchange using a server [44], non-interactive zero-knowledge [14], e-auction [1,43,8], non-interactive verifiable secret sharing [10], and others [27,26,20,31].

Motivations and contributions: In 1994, Benaloh [3] proposed a homomorphic encryption which has a better expansion factor than Goldwasser-Micali's scheme [25]. This leads to a more practical scheme which has found several applications, such as voting schemes [4,38,10], private multi-party trust computation [12,29,18], non-interactive verifiable secret sharing [10], online poker [26]. Given all these applications of Benaloh's scheme, we were surprised to discover that its key generation process may in some cases lead to an ambiguous encryption.

Our first contribution is to show that the original scheme proposed by Benaloh in [3] does not give a unique decryption for all ciphertexts. We exhibit a simple example and characterize when this can happen and how to produce such counter-examples. The problem comes from the condition in public key generation: the original condition is not strong enough and allows to generate such keys that will compute ambiguous ciphertexts for some plaintexts.

Our second contribution is to describe how this error in key generation can have dramatic consequences in the applications of Benaloh's scheme. In each case we briefly explain how the application works on a simple example and show that a wrong key generation can have important consequences. In the case of the e-voting protocol it can change the result of an election; for private multi-party trust computation it can completely modify the computed trust value.

Our last contribution is a new condition (suitable for implementations) for the key generation which avoids such problems. We also compute the probability of failure of the original scheme, in order to understand why nobody discovered the problem before us. Moreover we discuss some schemes related to Benaloh's encryption. We also put the semantic security of the corrected encryption in the context of Kristian Gjøsteen's work [24]. Indeed revisited Benaloh's scheme can be seen as an instance of the general framework proposed for homomorphic cryptosystem based on subgroup membership problem.

Outline: In Section 2 we recall the original Benaloh scheme. In Section 3 we give a small example of parameters following the initial description and where we have ambiguous decryption. In the next section, we discuss the (possibly serious) consequences of the problem we discovered in some applications. In Section 5 we give a corrected description of the scheme, with a proof of correctness. Then in Section 6, we analyze the probability of choosing incorrect parameters in the initial scheme. In Section 7 we discuss some schemes related to Benaloh's scheme. Finally before concluding, a semantic security analysis of the corrected scheme is given in Section 8.

2   Original Description of Benaloh's Scheme

Benaloh's "Dense Probabilistic Encryption" [3] describes a homomorphic encryption scheme with a significant improvement in terms of expansion factor compared to Goldwasser-Micali [25]. For the same security parameter (the size of the RSA modulus n), the ciphertext is in both cases an integer mod n, but the cleartext in Benaloh's scheme is an integer mod r for some parameter r depending on the key, whereas the cleartext in Goldwasser-Micali is only a bit. When computing the expansion factor for random keys, we found that it is most of the times close to 2 while it is $\lceil \log_2(n) \rceil$ for Goldwasser-Micali. We now recall the three steps of the original scheme given in Benaloh's paper [3].

Key Generation: The public and private key are generated as follows:

- Choose a block size r and two large primes p and q such that:
    - r divides $(p-1)$.
    - r and $(p-1)/r$ are relatively prime.
    - r and $q-1$ are relatively prime.
    - $n = pq$.
- Select $y \in (\mathbb{Z}_n)^* = \{x \in \mathbb{Z}_n : \gcd(x,n) = 1\}$ such that

$$y^{\varphi/r} \neq 1 \bmod n \tag{1}$$

  where φ denotes $(p-1)(q-1)$.

The public key is (y, r, n), and the private key is the two primes p and q.

Encryption: If m is an element in $\mathbb{Z}_r$ and u a random number in $(\mathbb{Z}_n)^*$ then we compute the randomized encryption of m using the following formula:

$$E_r(m) = \{y^m u^r \bmod n : u \in (\mathbb{Z}_n)^*\}.$$

It is easily verified that:

$$E_r(m_1) \times E_r(m_2) = E_r(m_1 + m_2).$$

Decryption: We first notice that for any m, u we have:

$$(y^m u^r)^{(p-1)(q-1)/r} = y^{m(p-1)(q-1)/r} u^{(p-1)(q-1)} = y^{m(p-1)(q-1)/r} \quad \bmod n.$$

Since $m < r$ and $y^{(p-1)(q-1)/r} \neq 1 \mod n$, Benaloh concludes that $m = 0 \mod r$ if and only if $(y^m u^r)^{(p-1)(q-1)/r} = 1 \mod n$. So if $z = y^m u^r \mod n$ is an encryption of m, given the secret key (p, q) we can determine whether $m = 0 \mod r$. If r is small, we can decrypt z by doing an exhaustive search of the smallest non-negative integer m such that $(y^{-m} z \mod n) \in E_r(0)$. By precomputing values and using the baby-step giant-step algorithm it is possible to perform the decryption in time $O(\sqrt{r})$. Finally if r is smooth we can use classical index-calculus techniques. More details about these optimization of decryption are discussed in the original paper [3].

We remark that there is a balance to find between three parameters in this cryptosystem:

- ease of decryption, which requires that r is a product of small prime powers,
- a small expansion factor, defined as the ratio between the size of the cipher-texts and the size of the cleartexts. Because p and q have the same size and $r \mid p - 1$, this expansion factor is at least 2,
- strength of the private key, meaning that n should be hard to factorize. In the context of the P-1 factorization method [35], a large smooth factor of $p - 1$ is a definite weakness.

We notice that the cryptosystem proposed by Naccache-Stern [32] four years after Benaloh's scheme and based on the same approach addresses this issue and does not produce ambiguous encryption.

3   A Small Counter-Example

We start by picking a secret key $n = pq = 241 \times 179 = 43139$, for which we can set $r = 15$. Algorithm 1 may be used to compute the maximal suitable value of the r parameter if you start by picking p and q at random, but a smaller and smoother value may be used instead, for an easier decryption.

Algorithm 1. Compute r from p and q.

$r \leftarrow p - 1$;
while $\gcd(q - 1, r) \neq 1$ **do**
    $r \leftarrow r / \gcd(r, q - 1)$;
end while

We verify that $r = 15$ divides $p - 1 = 240 = 16 \times 15$, r and $(p-1)/r = 16$ are relatively prime, $r = 15 = 3 \times 5$ and $q - 1 = 178 = 2 \times 89$ are coprime. Assume we pick $y = 27$, then $\gcd(y, n) = 1$ and $y^{(p-1)(q-1)/r} = 40097 \neq 1 \mod n$ so according to Benaloh's key generation procedure all the original conditions are satisfied.

By definition, $y^1 12^r = 24187 \mod n$ is a valid encryption of $m_1 = 1$, while $y^6 4^r = 24187 \mod n$ is also a valid encryption of $m_2 = 6$. In fact we can verify that with this choice of y, the true cleartext space is now $\mathbb{Z}_5$ instead of $\mathbb{Z}_{15}$ (hence the ambiguity in decryption): first notice that in $\mathbb{Z}_p$, $y^5 = 27^5 = 8 = 41^{15} = 41^r$.

This means that a valid encryption of 5 is also a valid encryption of 0. For any message m, the set of encryptions of m is the same as the set of encryptions of $m + 5$, hence the collapse in message space size. The fact that the message space size does not collapse further can be checked by brute force with this small set of parameters.

For this specific choice of p and q, there are $\frac{r-1}{r}\varphi(n) = 39872$ possible values of y according to the original paper, but 17088 of them would lead to an ambiguity in decryption (that's a ratio of 3/7), decreasing the cleartext space to either $\mathbb{Z}_3$ or $\mathbb{Z}_5$. Details are provided in Section 6.

4   Applications

In this section, we present some applications which explicitly use Benaloh's encryption scheme. We analyze the consequences of using a bad y parameter produced during the key generation for each application.

4.1   Receipt-Free Elections

In [4], Benaloh and Tuinstra propose an application of homomorphic encryption for designing new receipt-free secret-ballot elections. They describe two protocols which use a homomorphic encryption scheme and verify a list of properties. They also give in the appendix of the paper a precise description of an encryption scheme which satisfies their properties. Its relation with [3] is given in Section 7.

The new voting protocol uses the fact that the encryption is homomorphic and probabilistic. If we have two candidates Nicolas and Ségolène then the system associates for instance the ballot 0 for Nicolas and the ballot 1 for Ségolène. The main idea is that the server collects the m authenticated encrypted ballots $\{v_i\}_k$ corresponding to the choices v_i of the m voters. Then the server performs the multiplication of the ciphertexts to sum the votes and decrypts the product once to obtain the result. The number obtained corresponds to the number of votes n_S for Ségolène and the difference $m - n_S$ gives the number of votes for Nicolas.

We construct a basic application of the first protocol proposed in [4] and based on the example described in Section 3. In this example we consider only 12 voters. Suppose when the encryption is correctly done the final result is $\{11\}_k$. It means that after decryption Ségolène has 11 votes and Nicolas has 1 vote. But if as we explain in Section 3 instead of computing the result 11 mod 15 we are taking the result modulo 5, then we obtain a result of 11 mod 5 = 1. This time the server concludes that Nicolas obtains 11 votes and Ségolène only 1. This example clearly shows that the flaw in the parameters generation process can have important consequences.

4.2   Private Multi-party Trust Computation

In [18], Dolev *et al* give a multiple private key protocol for private multi-party computation of a trust value: an initiating user wants to know the (possibly weighted) average trust the network of nodes has in some user. In a first phase of the protocol, each of the n nodes splits its trust value t in $n-1$ shares (s_i) such that

$$t = s_1 + s_2 + \ldots + s_{n-1} \bmod r.$$

Here r is a common modulus chosen large enough with respect to the maximum possible global trust value, and in order to ensure the privacy of its trust value the shares should be taken as random number mod r, except for the last one. The shares are then sent encrypted (using Benaloh's scheme) to each other user, to be later recombined. If we assume that one of the users has chosen a faulty value for his public parameter y, then his contribution to the recombined value will be computed mod r' instead of mod r for some divisor r' of r. As an extreme example, assume

- that the queried user is a newcomer, untrusted by anyone (hence the private value of t for every node is 0),
- that the true recombined value contributed by the faulty user should have been $r-1$,
- that $r' = r/3$.

Due to his miscalculation, the faulty node will contribute the value $r'-1$ instead of -1, causing the apparent calculated trust value to be quite high (about $1/3$ of the maximum possible trust value, instead of 0). This can have dramatic consequences if the trust value is used later on to grant access to some resource. These assumptions are not entirely unlikely: remember that $r = 3^k$ is an explicitly suggested choice of parameter of the cryptosystem (chosen for instance in [29]) in which we will find that the failure probability (ρ) is close to $1/3$ and faulty nodes occur with high probability even with moderate-sized networks (see Section 6). We also note that the description from [3] is given *in extenso*, with its incorrect condition. One reason for choosing Benaloh's cryptosystem in this application is because the cleartext space can be common among several private keys, a feature unfortunately not achieved *e.g.* by Paillier's cryptosystem [34] but also possible with Naccache-Stern's [32].

4.3   Secure Cards Dealing

Another application of this encryption scheme is given in [26]: securely dealing cards in poker (or similar games). Here again the author gives the complete description of the original scheme, with a choice of parameter $r = 53$ (which is prime). Because r is prime, this application does not suffer from the flaw explained here, but this choice of a prime number is done for reasons purely internal to the cards dealing protocol, namely testing the equality of dealt cards.

Given two ciphertext $E(m_1)$ and $E(m_2)$, the players need to test if $m_1 = m_2$ without revealing anything more about the cards m_1 and m_2. The protocol is as follows:

1. Let $m = m_1 - m_2$, each player can compute $E(m) = E(m_1)/E(m_2)$ because of the homomorphic property of the encryption.

2. Each player P_i secretly picks a value $0 < \alpha_i < 53$, computes $E(m)^{\alpha_i}$ and discloses it to everyone.
3. Each player can compute $\prod_i E(m)^{\alpha_i} = E(m)^{\alpha}$ with $\alpha = \sum_i \alpha_i$. The players jointly decrypt $E(m)^{\alpha}$ to get the value $m\alpha \bmod r$.

Now because for each player the value of α is unknown and random, if $m\alpha \neq 0 \bmod r$ then the players learn nothing about m. Otherwise they conclude that the cards are equal.

We claim that this protocol fails to account for two problems:

- there is no guarantee that $\alpha \neq 0 \bmod r$. When this happens, two distinct cards will be incorrectly considered equal. One possible fix is to repeat the protocol to decrease the probability of false positive to an acceptable level.
- knowing the value of $E(m)$ and $E(m)^{\alpha_i}$, it is easy to recover α_i because of the small search space for α_i. This means the protocol leaks information when $m_1 \neq m_2$. The fix here is to multiply by some random encryption of 0.

It should be noted that these problems are unrelated to the incorrect parameter generation flaw discussed in this paper.

5   Corrected Version of Benaloh's Scheme

Let g be a generator of the group $(\mathbb{Z}_p)^*$, and since y is coprime with n, let α be the value in $\mathbb{Z}_{p-1}$ such that $y = g^{\alpha} \bmod p$. We will now state in Theorem 1 our main contribution:

Theorem 1. *The following properties are equivalent:*

a) α *and* r *are coprime;*
b) *decryption works unambiguously;*
c) *for all prime factors* s *of* r, *we have* $y^{(\varphi/s)} \neq 1 \bmod n$.

Of course property (b) is what we expect of the scheme, while (a) is useful to analyze the proportion of invalid y's and (c) is more efficient to verify in practice than (a), especially considering that in order to decrypt efficiently the factorization of r is assumed to be known. In the following proof we interpret statement (b) to mean that two different cleartexts cannot be encrypted to the same value:

$$\forall m_1, m_2 \in \mathbb{Z}_r, \forall u_1, u_2 \in (\mathbb{Z}_n)^*, \quad y^{m_1} u_1^r = y^{m_2} u_2^r \bmod n \Rightarrow m_1 = m_2 \bmod r.$$

Another way to interpret (b) is that, for a given $z \bmod n$, there is at most one value $m \bmod r$ such that $y^{-m} z$ is an r-th power mod n. In fact these two interpretations are equivalent (the proof is easy and omitted here).

Proof. We prove first (a) $\Leftrightarrow$ (b) then we show (a) $\Leftrightarrow$ (c).

- We start by showing (a) $\Rightarrow$ (b). Assume two messages m_1 and m_2 are encrypted to the same element using nonce u_1 and u_2:

$$y^{m_1} u_1^r = y^{m_2} u_2^r \bmod n.$$

Reducing mod p we get:

$$g^{\alpha(m_1 - m_2)} = (u_2/u_1)^r \bmod p$$

and using the fact that g is a generator of $(\mathbb{Z}_p)^*$, there exists some β such that

$$g^{\alpha(m_1 - m_2)} = g^{\beta r} \bmod p$$

which in turns implies

$$\alpha(m_1 - m_2) = \beta r \bmod p - 1.$$

By construction r divides $(p-1)$, we can further reduce mod r and get

$$\alpha(m_1 - m_2) = 0 \bmod r$$

and since r and α are coprime, we can deduce $m_1 = m_2 \bmod r$, which means that decryption works unambiguously since the cleartexts are defined mod r.

- We now prove (b) $\Rightarrow$ (a). Assume α and r are not coprime and let $s = \gcd(\alpha, r)$, $r = sr'$, $\alpha = s\alpha'$. Then

$$y^{r'} = g^{\alpha r'} \bmod p$$
$$= (g^{\alpha'})^r \bmod p.$$

Since r and $q-1$ are coprime, every invertible number mod q is an r-th power. Therefore $y^{r'}$ is an r-th power mod n and is a valid encryption of 0 as well as a valid encryption of r'.

- We now prove that (a) $\Rightarrow$ (c). Assume that there exists some prime factor s of r such that

$$y^{(\varphi/s)} = 1 \bmod n.$$

As above, by reducing mod p and using the generator g of $(\mathbb{Z}_p)^*$ we get

$$\alpha \frac{\varphi}{s} = 0 \bmod p - 1.$$

So

$$\alpha \frac{\varphi}{s} = (p-1) \frac{\alpha(q-1)}{s}$$

is a multiple of $p-1$ and s divides $\alpha(q-1)$. Since s does not divide $q-1$, s divides α and α and r are not coprime.

– We now prove (c) $\Rightarrow$ (a). Assume α and r are not coprime and denote by s some common prime factor. Then

$$y^{(\varphi/s)} = g^{\alpha\varphi/s} \bmod p$$
$$= g^{(\alpha/s)\varphi} \bmod p = 1 \bmod p.$$

And by construction of r, $s \nmid q - 1$ so $y^{(\varphi/s)} = 1 \bmod q$. $\square$

Notice than in the example of Section 3 we have $y^{(p-1)(q-1)/3} = 1 \bmod n$ so condition (c) is not satisfied. We claimed that the real ciphertext space is now $\mathbb{Z}_5$, and we gave a precise analysis of the cleartext space reduction at the end of Section 6.

6   Probability of Failure of Benaloh's Scheme

We now estimate the probability of failure in the scheme as originally described. For this we need to count the numbers y that satisfy Equation (1) in Section 2 and not property (c) of Theorem 1. We call these values of y "faulty".

Lemma 1. *Equation (1) is equivalent to the statement: $r \nmid \alpha$.*

Proof. Assume that r divides α: $\alpha = r\alpha'$. So

$$y^{\varphi/r} = g^{\alpha\varphi/r} \bmod p$$
$$= (g^{\alpha'})^{\varphi} \bmod p$$
$$= 1 \bmod p.$$

Since r divides $p - 1$, $y^{\varphi/r} = 1 \bmod q$ hence $y^{\varphi/r} = 1 \bmod n$.
    Conversely, if $y^{\varphi/r} = 1 \bmod n$, then

$$g^{\alpha\varphi/r} = 1 \bmod p$$
$$\alpha\frac{\varphi}{r} = 0 \bmod p - 1.$$

Since r divides $p - 1$ and is coprime with $\frac{\varphi}{r}$ (by definition), we have $r \mid \alpha$. $\square$

Since picking $y \in (\mathbb{Z}_p)^*$ at random is the same when seen mod p as picking $\alpha \in \{0, \ldots, p - 2\}$ at random, we can therefore conclude that the proportion ρ of faulty y's is exactly the proportion of non-invertible numbers mod r among the non-zero mod r. So $\rho = 1 - \frac{\varphi(r)}{r-1}$. We notice that this proportion depends on r only, and it is non-zero when r is not a prime. Since decryption in Benaloh's scheme is essentially solving a discrete logarithm in the subgroup of $(\mathbb{Z}_p)^*$ of order r, the original scheme recommends to use r as a product of small primes' powers, which tends to increase ρ. In fact, denoting by (p_i) the prime divisors of r we have:

$$\rho = 1 - \frac{\varphi(r)}{r-1}$$

$$= 1 - \frac{r}{r-1} \frac{\varphi(r)}{r}$$

$$= 1 - \frac{r}{r-1} \prod_i \frac{p_i - 1}{p_i}$$

$$\approx 1 - \prod_i \frac{p_i - 1}{p_i}$$

which shows that the situation where decryption is easy also increases the proportion of invalid y's when using the initial description of the encryption scheme.

As a practical example, assume we pick two 512 bits primes p and q as

$p = 2 \times (3 \times 5 \times 7 \times 11 \times 13) \times p' + 1$

$p' = 44648045054753903095484598728624196228702516885089555\backslash$
      $50373744969820904563106012220339722753851711735853811\backslash$
      $3914691524677018107022404660225439441679953592$

$q = 10055855947456947824680518748654384595609524365444299\backslash$
      $50332926710827913230225551602326014057236251775707677\backslash$
      $5238936398645381403154121089599274598252367545682799.$

Then

$$\gcd(q-1, p-1) = 2$$

$$r = (3 \times 5 \times 7 \times 11 \times 13) \times p'$$

$$\rho = 1 - \frac{r}{r-1} \times \frac{2}{3} \times \frac{4}{5} \times \frac{6}{7} \times \frac{10}{11} \times \frac{12}{13} \times \frac{p'}{p'-1}$$

$$\rho > 61\%.$$

This example was constructed quite easily: first we take p' of suitable size, and multiply its value until $p = k \times p' + 1$ is prime. Then we generate random primes q of suitable size until the condition $\gcd(p-1, q-1) = 2$ is verified; it took less than a second on a current laptop using Sage [42].

Putting it all together, we can also characterize the faulty values of y, together with the actual value r' of the cleartext space size (compared to the expected value r):

Lemma 2. *Let $u = \gcd(\alpha, r)$. Then $r' = \frac{r}{u}$. Moreover if $r' \neq r$, this faulty value of y goes undetected by the initial condition as long as $u \neq r$.*

The proof of the first implication in Theorem 1 is easily extended to a proof of the first point of this lemma, while the second point is a mere rephrasing of the previous lemma.

This result can be used to craft counter-examples as we did in Section 3: for a valid value y of the parameter and u a proper divisor of r, the value $y' = y^u \bmod n$ is an undetected faulty value with actual cleartext space size $r' = r/u$. It can also be used to determine precisely, for every proper divisor r' of r the probability of picking an undetected faulty parameter y of actual cleartext space size r'. Such an extensive study was not deemed necessary in the examples of Section 4, but it confirms that ambiguous parameters can happen more frequently than expected.

7   Related Schemes

We briefly discuss in this section some schemes related to that of [3].

In [4], Benaloh and Tuinstra describe a cryptosystem which closely resembles that of [3], but the conditions given on r are less strict. Let us recall briefly the parameters of the cryptosystem as described in [4]:

- $r \mid p - 1$ but $r^2 \nmid p - 1$.
- $r \nmid q - 1$.
- y is coprime with n and $y^{(p-1)(q-1)/r} \neq 1 \bmod n$.

It is clear that $r^2 \nmid p - 1$ is weaker than $\gcd((p - 1)/r, r) = 1$, and that $r \nmid q - 1$ is weaker than $\gcd(q - 1, r) = 1$. Therefore any set of parameters satisfying [3] are also valid parameters as defined in [4].

Unfortunately the condition imposed on y is the same and still insufficient, and finding counter-examples is again a matter of picking α not coprime with r. Our theorem still stands for this cryptosystem if you replace condition (c) by the following condition:

$$\text{For all prime factors } s \text{ of } r, \text{ we have } y^{(p-1)/s} \neq 1 \bmod p. \tag{2}$$

Going back in time, the scheme of Goldwasser and Micali [25] can be seen as a precursor of [4] with a fixed choice of $r = 2$. The choice of y in [25] as a quadratic non-residue mod n is clearly an equivalent formulation of condition (2).

Before [3] and [4], the scheme was defined by Benaloh in [5], with the parameter r being a prime. In this case our condition (c) is the same as the one proposed by Benaloh, and the scheme in this thesis is indeed correct. The main difference between the different versions proposed afterwards and this one is that it is not required for r to be prime, which leads in some cases to ambiguous ciphers. This remark clearly shows that all details are important in cryptography and that the problem we discovered is subtle because even Benaloh himself did not notice it.

Finally the scheme proposed by Naccache and Stern [32] is quite close to the one proposed in [5] but with a parameterization of p and q. It makes decryption correct, efficient, and leaves the expansion factor as an explicit function of the desired security level with respect to methods of factoring taking advantage of this specific form of n, like the $P - 1$ method [35] (the expansion is essentially the added size of the big cofactors of $p - 1$ and $q - 1$). If we drop this requirement that

$p-1$ and $q-1$ have big cofactors, their scheme becomes a corrected generalization of Benaloh's, so application writers should probably use Naccache-Stern's scheme directly. We note that a modulus size of 768 bits was considered secure at the time, a fact disproved twelve years later [30] only!

8   Semantic Security of the Corrected Scheme

In [24], Kristian Gjøsteen formulates the security of several homomorphic encryption schemes in a common setting and relates the semantic security of the schemes to a generic problem (the Decisional Subgroup Membership Problem) which we recall here:

Problem 1 (DSMP). Let G be an abelian group with subgroups K, H such that $G = KH$ and $K \cap H = \{1\}$. The *Decisional Subgroup Membership Problem* is to decide whether a given $g \in G$ is in K or not.

The cryptosystems by Goldwasser-Micali, Naccache-Stern, Okamoto-Uchiyama and Paillier respectively are shown to fit in this setting, with a proper definition for G (the ciphertexts space), H (coding the cleartexts) and K (the "cloak" space used to randomize encryptions). For example for Paillier's encryption, the ciphertext space is $G = (\mathbb{Z}_{n^2})^* \simeq (\mathbb{Z}_n)^* \times \mathbb{Z}_n$, the cleartexts coding subgroup H is the subgroup of order n (generated by $g = 1 + n$) and K is the set of invertible n-th powers mod n^2. This is consistent with the probabilistic encryption function
$$E_u(m) = (1 + n)^m u^n \bmod n^2.$$

It can be verified quite easily that the following choices make the corrected version of Benaloh's scheme fit in this setting:

- $G = (\mathbb{Z}_n)^*$
- H the cyclic subgroup of order r of G
- K the set of invertible r-th powers in G
- the public element y must generate H.

Using the result in [24], the semantic security of our corrected scheme is therefore equivalent to the DSMP for K, that is, being able to distinguish r-th powers modulo n.

Although several homomorphic encryption schemes are analyzed in [24], Benaloh's is not. Our correction ensures that the last condition is met, otherwise y could generate a strict subgroup of the intended group H.

9   Conclusion

We have shown that the original definition of Benaloh's homomorphic encryption does not give sufficient conditions in the choice of public key to get an unambiguous encryption scheme. We also explain on some examples what can be the consequences of the use of the original Benaloh scheme. Our discussion on the probability of choosing an incorrect public key shows that this probability is non negligible for parameters where decryption is efficient: for example using the suggested value of the form $r = 3^k$, this probability is already close to $1/3$. Our main contribution is to propose a necessary and sufficient condition which fixes the scheme. In fact, it is surprising this result was not found before, considering the number of applications built on the homomorphic property of Benaloh's scheme. This strongly suggests this scheme was rarely implemented or even worse, implementations were rarely well tested.

References

1. Abe, M., Suzuki, K.: $M+1$-st price auction using homomorphic encryption. In: Naccache, D., Paillier, P. (eds.) PKC 2002. LNCS, vol. 2274, pp. 115–124. Springer, Heidelberg (2002)
2. Akinwande, M.: Advances in Homomorphic Cryptosystems. Journal of Universal Computer Science 15(3), 506–522 (2009)
3. Benaloh, J.: Dense Probabilistic Encryption. In: Proceedings of the Workshop on Selected Areas of Cryptography, pp. 120–128 (1994)
4. Benaloh, J., Tuinstra, D.: Receipt-free Secret-Ballot Elections (extended abstract). In: STOC 1994: Proceedings of the Twenty-sixth Annual ACM Symposium on Theory of Computing, pp. 544–553. ACM, New York (1994)
5. Benaloh, J.D.C.: Verifiable Secret-Ballot Elections. PhD thesis, Yale University, New Haven, CT, USA (1987)
6. Boneh, D., Goh, E.-J., Nissim, K.: Evaluating 2-dnf formulas on ciphertexts. In: Kilian, J. (ed.) TCC 2005. LNCS, vol. 3378, pp. 325–341. Springer, Heidelberg (2005)
7. Fontaine, C., Galand, F.: A Survey of Homomorphic Encryption for Nonspecialists. In: EURASIP Journal on Information Security. Hindawi Publishing Corporation (2007)
8. Chen, X., Lee, B., Kim, K.: Receipt-free electronic auction schemes using homomorphic encryption. In: Lim, J.-I., Lee, D.-H. (eds.) ICISC 2003. LNCS, vol. 2971, pp. 259–273. Springer, Heidelberg (2004)
9. Cohen, J.D., Fischer, M.J.: A robust and verifiable cryptographically secure election scheme (extended abstract). In: 26th Annual Symposium on Foundations of Computer Science, Portland, Oregon, USA, October 21-23, pp. 372–382. IEEE, Los Alamitos (1985)
10. Benaloh, J.C.: Secret Sharing Homomorphisms: Keeping Shares of a Secret Secret. In: Odlyzko, A.M. (ed.) CRYPTO 1986. LNCS, vol. 263, pp. 251–260. Springer, Heidelberg (1987)
11. Cramer, R., Gennaro, R., Schoenmakers, B.: A secure and optimally efficient multi-authority election scheme. In: Proc. International Conference on the Theory and Application of Cryptographic Techniques (EUROCRYPT '97), Konstanz, Germany. lncs, vol. 1233, pp. 103–118. Springer, Heidelberg (1997)
12. Cramer, R., Damgård, I.B., Nielsen, J.B.: Multiparty computation from threshold homomorphic encryption. In: Pfitzmann, B. (ed.) EUROCRYPT 2001. LNCS, vol. 2045, pp. 280–299. Springer, Heidelberg (2001)

13. Cramer, R., Franklin, M.K., Schoenmakers, B., Yung, M.: Multi-authority secret-ballot elections with linear work. In: Maurer, U.M. (ed.) EUROCRYPT 1996. LNCS, vol. 1070, pp. 72–83. Springer, Heidelberg (1996)

14. Damgård, I., Fazio, N., Nicolosi, A.: Non-interactive zero-knowledge from homomorphic encryption. In: Halevi, S., Rabin, T. (eds.) TCC 2006. LNCS, vol. 3876, pp. 41–59. Springer, Heidelberg (2006)

15. Damgård, I., Jurik, M., Nielsen, J.B.: A generalization of paillier's public-key system with applications to electronic voting. Int. J. Inf. Sec. 9(6), 371–385 (2010)

16. Damgård, I., Nielsen, J.B.: Universally composable efficient multiparty computation from threshold homomorphic encryption. In: Boneh, D. (ed.) CRYPTO 2003. LNCS, vol. 2729, pp. 247–264. Springer, Heidelberg (2003)

17. Damgård, I., Jurik, M.: A Generalisation, a Simplification and Some Applications of Paillier's Probabilistic Public-Key System. In: Kim, K.-c. (ed.) PKC 2001. LNCS, vol. 1992, pp. 119–136. Springer, Heidelberg (2001)

18. Dolev, S., Gilboa, N., Kopeetsky, M.: Computing Multi-Party Trust Privately: in $O(n)$ time units sending one (possibly large) message at a time. In: SAC 2010: Proceedings of the 2010 ACM Symposium on Applied Computing, pp. 1460–1465. ACM, New York (2010)

19. El Gamal, T.: A public key cryptosystem and a signature scheme based on discrete logarithms. In: Blakely, G.R., Chaum, D. (eds.) CRYPTO 1984. LNCS, vol. 196, pp. 10–18. Springer, Heidelberg (1985)

20. Freedman, M.J., Nissim, K., Pinkas, B.: Efficient private matching and set intersection. In: Cachin, C., Camenisch, J.L. (eds.) EUROCRYPT 2004. LNCS, vol. 3027, pp. 1–19. Springer, Heidelberg (2004)

21. Gentry, C.: Fully homomorphic encryption using ideal lattices. In: Mitzenmacher, M. (ed.) Proceedings of the 41st Annual ACM Symposium on Theory of Computing, STOC 2009, Bethesda, MD, USA, May 31 - June 2, pp. 169–178. ACM Press, New York (2009)

22. Gentry, C.: Toward basing fully homomorphic encryption on worst-case hardness. In: Rabin, T. (ed.) CRYPTO 2010. LNCS, vol. 6223, pp. 116–137. Springer, Heidelberg (2010)

23. Gentry, C., Halevi, S., Vaikuntanathan, V.: i-hop homomorphic encryption and rerandomizable yao circuits. In: Rabin, T. (ed.) CRYPTO 2010. LNCS, vol. 6223, pp. 155–172. Springer, Heidelberg (2010)

24. Gjøsteen, K.: Homomorphic cryptosystems based on subgroup membership problems. In: Dawson, E., Vaudenay, S. (eds.) Mycrypt 2005. LNCS, vol. 3715, pp. 314–327. Springer, Heidelberg (2005), http://dx.doi.org/10.1007/11554868_22

25. Goldwasser, S., Micali, S.: Probabilistic Encryption and How to Play Mental Poker Keeping Secret All Partial Information. In: STOC, pp. 365–377 (1982)

26. Golle, P.: Dealing Cards in Poker Games. In: Proc. of ITCC 2005 E-Gaming Track (2005)

27. Groth, J.: A verifiable secret shuffle of homomorphic encryptions. J. Cryptology 23(4), 546–579 (2010)

28. Hirt, M., Sako, K.: Efficient receipt-free voting based on homomorphic encryption. In: Preneel, B. (ed.) EUROCRYPT 2000. LNCS, vol. 1807, pp. 539–556. Springer, Heidelberg (2000)

29. Jha, S., Kruger, L., McDaniel, P.: Privacy preserving clustering. In: di Vimercati, S.d.C., Syverson, P.F., Gollmann, D. (eds.) ESORICS 2005. LNCS, vol. 3679, pp. 397–417. Springer, Heidelberg (2005)

30. Kleinjung, T., Aoki, K., Franke, J., Lenstra, A.K., Thomé, E., Gaudry, P., Montgomery, P.L., Osvik, D.A., Riele, H.T., Timofeev, A., Zimmermann, P.: Factorization of a 768-bit RSA modulus (2010)
31. Lipmaa, H.: Verifiable homomorphic oblivious transfer and private equality test. In: Laih, C.-S. (ed.) ASIACRYPT 2003. LNCS, vol. 2894, pp. 416–433. Springer, Heidelberg (2003)
32. Naccache, D., Stern, J.: A New Public Key Cryptosystem Based on Higher Residues. In: ACM Conference on Computer and Communications Security, pp. 59–66 (1998)
33. Okamoto, T., Uchiyama, S.: A new public-key cryptosystem as secure as factoring (Lecture Notes in Computer Science). In: Nyberg, K. (ed.) EUROCRYPT 1998. LNCS, vol. 1403, pp. 308–318. Springer, Heidelberg (1998)
34. Paillier, P.: Public-Key Cryptosystems Based on Composite Degree Residuosity Classes. In: Stern, J. (ed.) EUROCRYPT 1999. LNCS, vol. 1592, pp. 223–238. Springer, Heidelberg (1999)
35. Pollard, J.M.: Theorems on Factorization and Primality Testing. Mathematical Proceedings of the Cambridge Philosophical Society 76(03), 521–528 (1974), doi:10.1017/S0305004100049252
36. Rappe, D.K.: Homomorphic Cryptosystems and their Applications. Cryptology ePrint Archive, Report 2006/001 (2006), http://eprint.iacr.org/
37. Rivest, R.L., Shamir, A., Adleman, L.: A method for obtaining digital signatures and public-key cryptosystems. Commun. ACM 21, 120–126 (1978)
38. Ruiz, A., Villar, J.L.: Publicly Verifiable Secret Sharing from Paillier's Cryptosystem. In: Wolf, C., Lucks, S., Yau, P.-W. (eds.) WEWoRC. LNI, vol. 74, pp. 98–108. GI (2005)
39. Sako, K., Kilian, J.: Secure Voting Using Partially Compatible Homomorphisms. In: Desmedt, Y.G. (ed.) CRYPTO 1994. LNCS, vol. 839, pp. 411–424. Springer, Heidelberg (1994)
40. Sander, T., Young, A., Yung, M.: Non-Interactive CryptoComputing for NC^1. In: FOCS, pp. 554–567 (1999)
41. Smart, N.P., Vercauteren, F.: Fully homomorphic encryption with relatively small key and ciphertext sizes. In: Nguyen, P.Q., Pointcheval, D. (eds.) PKC 2010. LNCS, vol. 6056, pp. 420–443. Springer, Heidelberg (2010)
42. Stein, W.A., et al.: Sage Mathematics Software (Version 4.5.1). The Sage Development Team (2010), http://www.sagemath.org
43. Suzuki, K., Yokoo, M.: Secure generalized vickrey auction using homomorphic encryption. In: Wright, R.N. (ed.) FC 2003. LNCS, vol. 2742, pp. 239–249. Springer, Heidelberg (2003)
44. Tatebayashi, M., Matsuzaki, N., Newman Jr., D.B.: Key distribution protocol for digital mobile communication systems. In: Brassard, G. (ed.) CRYPTO 1989. LNCS, vol. 435, pp. 324–334. Springer, Heidelberg (1990)
45. van Dijk, M., Gentry, C., Halevi, S., Vaikuntanathan, V.: Fully homomorphic encryption over the integers. In: Gilbert, H. (ed.) EUROCRYPT 2010. LNCS, vol. 6110, pp. 24–43. Springer, Heidelberg (2010)

On the Security of the Winternitz One-Time Signature Scheme

Johannes Buchmann, Erik Dahmen, Sarah Ereth,
Andreas Hülsing*, and Markus Rückert**

Technische Universität Darmstadt
{buchmann,dahmen,huelsing,rueckert}@cdc.informatik.tu-darmstadt.de,
ereth@mais.informatik.tu-darmstadt.de

Abstract. We show that the Winternitz one-time signature scheme is existentially unforgeable under adaptive chosen message attacks when instantiated with a family of pseudo random functions. Compared to previous results, which require a collision resistant hash function, our result provides significantly smaller signatures at the same security level. We also consider security in the strong sense and show that the Winternitz one-time signature scheme is strongly unforgeable assuming additional properties of the pseudo random function. In this context we formally define several key-based security notions for function families and investigate their relation to pseudorandomness. All our reductions are exact and in the standard model and can directly be used to estimate the output length of the hash function required to meet a certain security level.

Keywords: Hash-based signatures, post-quantum signatures, pseudorandom functions, security reductions.

1   Introduction

Digital signatures are ubiquitous in our computer dominated society. They are basic building blocks of eGovernment and eCommerce. They are used to guarantee the integrity and authenticity of software updates and enable secure Internet connections. The security of currently used signature schemes – RSA and ECDSA – relies on the hardness of certain number theoretic problems, whereas the actual hardness of these problems remains unclear. In 1994 Shor presented a quantum algorithm that can be used to solve the factorization and discrete logarithm problems in polynomial time, thus completely breaking RSA and ECDSA [24]. Given the importance of digital signatures, the search for alternative signature schemes that resist attacks arising from algorithmic and technological advances is an important research goal.

* Supported by grant no. BU 630/19-1 of the German Research Foundation (www.dfg.de).
** Supported by CASED (www.cased.de).

A. Nitaj and D. Pointcheval (Eds.): AFRICACRYPT 2011, LNCS 6737, pp. 363–378, 2011.

One promising alternative are hash-based signatures. Their sole security requirement is the existence of hash function families with certain properties. Current research suggests, that the security of hash-based signatures will not be significantly harmed by quantum computer supported attacks [13]. Another benefit of hash-based signature schemes is that they are provably secure in the standard model [7,8,9,14]. A hash-based signature scheme or Merkle signature scheme (MSS) consists of the combination of a one-time signature scheme (OTS) to sign the data and Merkle's tree authentication scheme [18] which reduces the authenticity of many one-time verification keys to the authenticity of a single public key. Examples for one-time signature schemes are the Lamport-Diffie OTS [15], the Merkle OTS [18], the Winternitz OTS [18,9], the Bleichenbacher-Maurer OTS [3], the BiBa OTS [19] and HORS [21]. The Winternitz OTS (W-OTS) is most suitable for combining it with Merkle's tree authentication scheme because of the small verification key size and the flexible trade-off between signature size and signature generation time. Further it is possible to compute the corresponding verification key given a W-OTS signature. So a MSS signature does not need to contain the verification key. This is not the case for all of the above mentioned schemes besides the Bleichenbacher-Maurer OTS but it reduces the MSS signature size significantly. Hence efficient variants of the Merkle signature scheme rely on W-OTS [5]. W-OTS is also used for authentication in sensor networks [17].

The size of a Winternitz signature is roughly mn/w bits and signing roughly requires $2^w m/w$ hash operations, where m is the bit length of the hash value to be signed, n is the output length of the hash function used in the scheme, and w is the Winternitz parameter determining the trade-off between signature size and signature generation time. In [9,14], the authors provide security reductions for graph based one-time signature schemes, a general class of OTS which includes W-OTS. Due to the generality of graph based OTS, these security reductions require the used hash function to be collision resistant. Collision resistance is one of the strongest security notions of hash functions and admits effective generic attacks using the birthday paradox. Following these reductions, to achieve b bits of security one must use $n = 2b$ and $m = 2b$ which yields W-OTS signatures of size roughly $4b^2/w$ bits.

Our results. In this paper we show that weaker assumptions are sufficient for the security of W-OTS. We show that W-OTS is existentially unforgeable under adaptive chosen message attacks [12] when instantiated with a family of pseudorandom functions (PRF). Since the PRF property is not affected by birthday attacks, hash functions with shorter output length can be used which in turn reduces the signature size. This result is especially meaningful because the main issue with hash-based signatures is the signature size. Also, it has been shown that PRF exist if one way functions (OWF) exist [25,16,11] and further, that OWF exist if secure digital signature schemes exist [23]. So our result shows that a secure instance of W-OTS exists, as long as there exists any secure signature scheme. For collision resistant hash function families it is unknown if their existence can be based on the existence of OWF.

We also consider unforgeability in the strong sense by reducing the strong unforgeability of W-OTS to the intractability of finding *key collisions* (given x, find k, k' such that $k \neq k'$ and $f_k(x) = f_{k'}(x)$) or *second keys* (given x and key k, find k' such that $k \neq k'$ and $f_k(x) = f_{k'}(x)$). The notion of key collision resistance was used before by the authors of [20] in the security analysis of the TESLA protocol. In [10], the author uses this notion as property of pseudorandom function tribe ensembles to construct a committing and key-hiding private-key encryption scheme. The authors of [6] provide a construction for perfectly one-way functions assuming key collision resistance. We provide a thorough treatment of these key based notions and pseudo randomness. We define them formally and investigate implications and separations among them.

Our results are exact and in the standard model. Such reductions are of enormous practical value compared to asymptotic results or the random oracle model. Exact reductions allow the security level of the scheme to be estimated for fixed security parameters. The standard model uses only security notions which can be efficiently realized in practice. Exact reductions are also of theoretical interest, because they indicate the quality of a reduction and allow an easy comparison of the hardness of the problems.

Notation. Throughout the paper we stick to the following notation. We use n as the main security parameter. Efficient algorithms require only polynomial time and space in n. The statement $x \xleftarrow{\$} X$ means x is chosen uniformly at random from X. The concatenation of strings is done via $||$. We also write log for $\log_2$. During the paper we measure the runtime of an algorithm in terms of the number of evaluations of the function family used.

Organization. We prove the existential unforgeability of W-OTS using pseudorandom functions in Section 2. We prove the strong unforgeability of W-OTS using second key resistant or key collision resistant functions in Section 3. We examine implications and separations between the introduced security notions in Section 4. We interpret our results and provide concluding remarks in Section 5.

2   Existential Unforgeability of the Winternitz One-Time Signature Scheme

In this section we prove that the Winternitz one-time signature scheme (W-OTS) is existentially unforgeable under adaptive chosen message attacks (EU-CMA) when instantiated with a family of pseudo-random functions. We begin by reviewing W-OTS and introduce a little tweak required by the reduction. Then we introduce the required security notions. Finally we state the reduction and use it to estimate the security level.

2.1   The Winternitz One-Time Signature Scheme

The Winternitz one-time signature scheme was first mentioned in [18] as a generalization of Merkle's OTS also proposed in [18]. A complete description can be found in [9]. The core idea of W-OTS is to iteratively apply a function on a secret input, whereas the number of iterations depends on the message to be signed. The used functions are members of the function family

$$F(n) = \{f_k : \{0,1\}^n \rightarrow \{0,1\}^n | k \in \{0,1\}^n\} \tag{1}$$

parameterized by key $k \in \{0,1\}^n$ and the security parameter n. For our purposes iteratively applying a function is defined as follows. We use the output of the function f_k as *key* for the next iteration. The function is always evaluated on the same input x. This is in contrast to the original construction, where the output of the function is used as input for the next iteration and the key remains fixed. We use the notation $f_k^i(x)$ to denote that the function is iterated i times on input x using key k for the first iteration and the output of the function as key for the next iteration, e.g. $f_k^2(x) = f_{f_k(x)}(x)$ and $f_k^0(x) = x$.

In the following, we only describe the generation of signatures for m-bit messages. The generalization to arbitrary sized messages is straight forward by utilizing a collision resistant hash function.

Key pair generation (Algorithm Kg). First we choose the Winternitz parameter $w \in \mathbb{N}, w > 1$, defining the compression level. Next we choose a random value $x \xleftarrow{\$} \{0,1\}^n$. The signature key consists of ℓ bit strings of length n chosen uniformly with the random distribution,

$$\mathsf{sk} = (\mathsf{sk}_1, \ldots, \mathsf{sk}_\ell) \xleftarrow{\$} \{0,1\}^{(n,\ell)},$$

where ℓ is computed as follows.

$$\ell_1 = \left\lceil \frac{m}{\log(w)} \right\rceil, \ell_2 = \left\lfloor \frac{\log(\ell_1(w-1))}{\log(w)} \right\rfloor + 1, \ell = \ell_1 + \ell_2.$$

The verification key is computed using functions from the family $F(n)$. The bit strings in the signature key are used as key for the function f and the function is iterated $w - 1$ times on input x.

$$\mathsf{pk} = (\mathsf{pk}_0, \mathsf{pk}_1, \ldots, \mathsf{pk}_\ell) = (x, f_{\mathsf{sk}_1}^{w-1}(x), \ldots, f_{\mathsf{sk}_\ell}^{w-1}(x))$$

Signature generation (Algorithm Sign.) We describe how to sign an m-bit message $M = (M_1, \ldots, M_{\ell_1})$ given in base-w representation, i.e. $M_i \in \{0, \ldots, w-1\}$ for $i = 1, \ldots, \ell_1$. We begin by computing the checksum

$$C = \sum_{i=1}^{\ell_1} (w - 1 - M_i) \tag{2}$$

and represent it to base w as $C = (C_1, \ldots, C_{\ell_2})$. The length of the base-w representation of C is at most ℓ_2 since $C \le \ell_1(w-1)$. Then we set $B = (b_1, \ldots, b_\ell) = M \parallel C$. The signature of message M is computed as

$$\sigma = (\sigma_1, \ldots, \sigma_\ell) = (f_{\mathsf{sk}_1}^{b_1}(x), \ldots, f_{\mathsf{sk}_\ell}^{b_\ell}(x)). \tag{3}$$

Signature verification (Algorithm Vf.) The verifier first computes the base-w string $B = (b_1, \ldots, b_\ell)$ as described above. Then he checks whether

$$(f_{\sigma_1}^{w-1-b_1}(\mathsf{pk}_0), \ldots, f_{\sigma_\ell}^{w-1-b_\ell}(\mathsf{pk}_0)) \stackrel{?}{=} (\mathsf{pk}_1, \ldots, \mathsf{pk}_\ell). \tag{4}$$

The signature is accepted iff the comparison holds.

2.2 Security Notions for Signature Schemes and Function Families

We begin by reviewing the standard definition of digital signature schemes and the security notion existential unforgeability under adaptive chosen message attacks (EU-CMA) [12]. We then define two security notions for function families required for our reduction. The first is the well known pseudo-randomness property. The second is *key one-wayness* which states that it is hard to find a key k such that the function f_k maps a given input x to a given output y. We also state two lemmas about these notions which will be useful for the reduction of W-OTS.

Definition 1 (Digital signature schemes). *A digital signature scheme* Sig $=$ (Kg, Sign, Vf) *is a triple of PPT algorithms:*

- Kg(1^n) *on input of a security parameter 1^n outputs a private signing key* sk *and a public verification key* pk;
- Sign(sk, M) *outputs a signature σ under* sk *for the message M;*
- Vf(pk, σ, M) *outputs 1 iff σ is a valid signature on M under* pk.

Definition 2 (Existential unforgeability (EU-CMA)). *EU-CMA is defined by the following experiment.*

Experiment $\mathsf{Exp}_{A,\mathsf{Sig}}^{EU\text{-}CMA}(n)$
  (sk, pk) $\leftarrow$ Kg(1^n)
  $(M^\star, \sigma^\star) \leftarrow A^{\mathsf{Sign(sk,\cdot)}}(\mathsf{pk})$
  Let $\{(M_i, \sigma_i)\}_1^{q_{\mathsf{Sign}}}$ *be the query-answer pairs of* Sign(sk, $\cdot$).
  Return 1 iff Vf(pk, $M^\star$, $\sigma^\star$) $= 1$ *and* $M^\star \notin \{M_i\}_1^{q_{\mathsf{Sign}}}$.

Sig *is (t, ϵ, q)-existentially unforgeable if there is no t-time adversary that succeeds with probability $\geq \epsilon$ after making $\leq q$ signature oracle queries.*

A $(t, \epsilon, 1)$-EU-CMA secure signature scheme is called one-time signature scheme.

Definition 3 (Pseudorandom functions (PRF)). *A family of functions $F(n)$ is pseudorandom, if no efficient algorithm* Dis *is able to distinguish a randomly chosen function $f_k \in F(n)$ from a randomly chosen function from the set $G(n)$ of all functions with same domain and range as $F(n)$. The formal definition is taken from [2].* Dis *gets access to an oracle* Box($\cdot$) *implementing a function randomly chosen from $F(n)$ or $G(n)$ in a black box manner. The distinguisher may adaptively query* Box($\cdot$) *as often as he likes. Finally, the distinguisher outputs 1 if he thinks that* Box *models a function from $F(n)$ and 0 otherwise.*

Let $F(n)$ be a family of functions as in (1) and $G(n) = \{g : \{0,1\}^n \to \{0,1\}^n\}$ the family of all functions with domain and range $\{0,1\}^n$. We call $F(n)$ (t, ϵ)-PRF, if the advantage

$$\mathrm{Adv}^{\mathrm{PRF}}_{F(n)}(\mathrm{Dis}) = \left| \Pr[\mathrm{Box} \xleftarrow{\$} F(n) : \mathrm{Dis}^{\mathrm{Box}(\cdot)} = 1] \right.$$

$$\left. - \Pr[\mathrm{Box} \xleftarrow{\$} G(n) : \mathrm{Dis}^{\mathrm{Box}(\cdot)} = 1] \right| \quad (5)$$

of any distinguisher Dis that runs in time t is at most ϵ.

Definition 4 (Key one-wayness (KOW)). *Let $F(n)$ be a family of functions as in (1). We call $F(n)$ (t, ϵ)-KOW, if the success probability*

$$\mathrm{Adv}^{\mathrm{KOW}}_{\mathsf{A}} = \Pr[(x, k) \xleftarrow{\$} \{0,1\}^n \times \{0,1\}^n, y \leftarrow f_k(x),$$

$$k' \longleftarrow \mathsf{A}(x, y) : y = f_{k'}(x)] \quad (6)$$

of any adversary A that runs in time t is at most ϵ.

Please recall, that the time t is counted in terms of evaluations of f. We assume, that a call to Box takes the same time as an evaluation of f. The *security level* or *bit security* b the family $F(n)$ or a signature scheme Sig provides against attacks on the respective notion is computed as $b = \log(t/\epsilon)$.

A key collision of $F(n)$ is defined as a pair of distinct keys (k, k') such that $f_k(x) = f_{k'}(x)$ holds for some $x \in \{0,1\}^n$. We define an upper (κ) and lower (κ') bound on the number of key collisions that occur in the family $F(n)$.

Definition 5. *The upper bound κ is defined as follows: For each pair (x, k), there exist at most $\kappa - 1$ different keys $k_1, \ldots, k_{\kappa-1}$, which are also different from k, such that $f_k(x) = f_{k_i}(x)$ for $i = 1, \ldots, \kappa - 1$. Equivalently we define the lower bound κ': For each pair (x, k), there exist at least $\kappa' - 1$ different keys $k_1, \ldots, k_{\kappa'-1}$, which are also different from k, such that $f_k(x) = f_{k_i}(x)$ for $i = 1, \ldots, \kappa' - 1$.*

The values κ and κ' restrict the number of different images y some preimage x can be mapped to by functions in $F(n)$, i.e.

$$\frac{2^n}{\kappa} \leq \left| \{f_k(x) : k \in \{0,1\}^n\} \right| \leq \frac{2^n}{\kappa'} \quad (7)$$

for all $x \in \{0,1\}^n$. Also, given $y \xleftarrow{\$} \{0,1\}^n$ the probability that there exists a key k and preimage x such that $f_k(x) = y$ holds is at least $1/\kappa$.

The following lemma describes an interesting relation between the security level of pseudorandom functions and the value κ defined above.

Lemma 1. *Let $F(n)$ be (t, ϵ)-PRF with security level $b = \log(t/\epsilon)$ and κ as in Definition 5. Then $\kappa \leq 2^{n-b} + 1$.*

Proof. Assume $\kappa > 2^{n-b} + 1$ and let (x, y) be a pair where there exist κ keys mapping x to y. The distinguisher Dis queries Box with x. If $\text{Box}(x) = y$ then Dis returns 1 and 0 otherwise. Clearly Dis runs in time $t' = 1$. Further we have $\Pr[\text{Box} \xleftarrow{\$} F(n) : \text{Dis}^{\text{Box}(\cdot)} = 1] = \kappa/2^n > 2^{-b} + 2^{-n}$ and $\Pr[\text{Box} \xleftarrow{\$} G : \text{Dis}^{\text{Box}(\cdot)} = 1] = 2^{-n}$ and therefore $\epsilon' = \text{Adv}_{F(n)}^{\text{PRF}}(\text{Dis}) > 2^{-b}$ which is a contradiction. $\qquad\square$

The following lemma states that the KOW property is implied by the PRF property. In other words, an efficient attacker against the KOW property leads to an efficient distinguisher.

Proposition 1 (PRF $\Rightarrow$ KOW). *Let $F(n)$ be (t, ϵ)-PRF. Then $F(n)$ is $(t - 2, \epsilon/(1/\kappa - 1/2^n))$-KOW.*

Proof. Assume there exists an adversary $\text{A}_{\text{KOW}}(x, y)$ who finds a key k satisfying $y = f_k(x)$ in time t_{KOW} with probability ϵ_{KOW}. Then we can construct a distinguisher Dis using A_{KOW} the following way: Dis queries $\text{Box}(\cdot)$ with $x \in \{0,1\}^n$. After receiving the answer y, Dis runs $\text{A}_{\text{KOW}}(x, y)$ to obtain key k. Then Dis queries Box with a second value $x' \in \{0,1\}^n$. If $\text{Box}(x') = f_k(x') = y'$ Dis returns 1 and 0 otherwise. In case $\text{Box} \xleftarrow{\$} F(n)$, the probability that A_{KOW} outputs a key k such that $f_k(x) = y$ holds is ϵ_{KOW}. The probability that $f_k(x') = y'$ holds is at least $1/\kappa$, because at least one of the κ functions in $F(n)$ mapping x to y also maps x' to y'. In case $\text{Box} \xleftarrow{\$} G(n)$, the probability that A_{KOW} outputs a key k such that $f_k(x) = y$ holds is at most ϵ_{KOW}. The probability that $f_k(x') = y'$ holds is $1/2^n$, because from the $2^{n(2^n - 1)}$ functions in G mapping x to y, only $2^{n(2^n - 2)}$ also map x' to y'. In summary we get $\epsilon \geq \text{Adv}_{F(n)}^{\text{PRF}}(\text{Dis}) \geq \epsilon_{\text{KOW}} (1/\kappa - 1/2^n)$. $\qquad\square$

2.3 Security Reduction

We now state the main result of this section.

Theorem 1. *Let $F(n)$ be a family of functions as in Equation (1) and κ as in Definition 5. If $F(n)$ is $(t_{\text{PRF}}, \epsilon_{\text{PRF}})$-PRF then W-OTS is $(t, \epsilon, 1)$ EU-CMA with*

$$t = t_{\text{PRF}} - t_{\text{Kg}} - t_{\text{Vf}} - 2 \tag{8}$$

$$\epsilon \leq \epsilon_{\text{PRF}} \ell^2 w^2 \kappa^{w-1} \frac{1}{\left(\frac{1}{\kappa} - \frac{1}{2^n}\right)} \tag{9}$$

Proof. The proof works as follows: First we use a forger for W-OTS to construct an adversary on the key one wayness of $F(n)$. This adversary is then used to construct a distinguisher using Proposition 1. Algorithm 1 shows how a forger $\text{For}^{\text{Sign}(\text{sk}, \cdot)}(\text{pk})$ for W-OTS can be used to construct an adversary A_{KOW} on the key one-wayness of $F(n)$. The signing oracle Sign is simulated by the adversary.

The goal of the adversary A_{KOW} is to produce a key k' such that $f_{k'}(x) = y$ for x, y provided as input. A_{KOW} begins by generating a regular W-OTS signature

---

Algorithm 1. A_{KOW}

Input: Security parameters n, m, Winternitz parameter w, description of $F(n)$, KOW
challenge (x, y) as in Definition 4
Output: k', such that $f_{k'}(x) = y$ or fail

1. generate W-OTS signature key sk
2. choose indices $\alpha \in \{1, ..., \ell\}, \beta \in \{1, ..., w-1\}$ uniformly at random
3. compute verification key as $pk_0 = x$, $pk_i = f_{sk_i}^{w-1}(x)$ for $i = 1, ..., l, i \neq \alpha$ and
   $pk_\alpha = f_y^{w-1-\beta}(x)$
4. run $For^{Sign(sk, \cdot)}(pk)$
5. **when** $For^{Sign(sk, \cdot)}(pk)$ queries Sign with message M **then** compute $B = (b_1, ..., b_\ell)$
6. **if** $b_\alpha < \beta$ **return** fail
7. generate signature σ of M and respond to $For^{Sign(sk, \cdot)}(pk)$
8. **when** $For^{Sign(sk, \cdot)}(pk)$ returns valid (σ', M') **then** compute $B' = (b'_1, ..., b'_\ell)$
9. **if** $b'_\alpha \geq \beta$ **return** fail
10. compute $k' \leftarrow f_{\sigma'_\alpha}^{\beta - 1 - b'_\alpha}(x)$
11. **if** $f_{k'}(x) \neq y$ **return** fail
12. **return** k'

---

key pair and choosing random positions α and β (Lines 1,2). Then he computes
the W-OTS verification key using value x. The bit string at position α in the
verification key (pk_α) is computed by inserting y at position β in the hash chain
used to compute pk_α (Line 3). Next, A_{KOW} calls the forger and waits for it to
ask an oracle query. The forgers query can only be answered if $b_\alpha \geq \beta$ holds,
because A_{KOW} doesn't know the first β entries in the corresponding hash chain
(Line 6). The forgery produced by the forger is only meaningful to A_{KOW} if
$b'_\alpha < \beta$ holds (Line 9). Only then the bit string σ_α in the forged signature
might yield a key k' such that $y = f_{k'}(x)$ holds (Lines 10,11). We now compute
the success probability of A_{KOW}. W.l.o.g we assume that the forger queries the
signing oracle. The probability of $b_\alpha \geq \beta$ in Line 6 is at least $(\ell w)^{-1}$. This
is because of the checksum which guarantees that not all of the b_i are zero
simultaneously. The probability that the forger succeeds in Line 8 is at least ϵ
by definition. This probability holds under the condition that the verification
key pk computed in Line 3 resembles a regular verification key which is the case
if there exists a key k such that $f_k^\beta(x) = y$. This happens with probability at
least $1/\kappa^\beta$ according to Definition 5. The probability of $b'_\alpha < \beta$ in Line 9 is at
least $(\ell w)^{-1}$. This is because of $M \neq M'$ and the checksum which guarantees
that $b_i > b'_i$ for some $i \in \{1, ..., \ell\}$. The probability that $y = f_{k'}(x)$ holds in
Line 11 is at least $1/\kappa^{w-1-\beta}$. This is because there exist κ^{w-1} keys mapping
x to pk_α after $w - 1$ iterations and only κ^β of these keys map x to y after β
iterations.

In summary we have $\epsilon_{KOW} \geq \epsilon/(\ell^2 w^2 \kappa^\beta \kappa^{w-1-\beta})$ and $t_{KOW} = t + t_{Kg} +$
t_{Vf} as the time for the signature query is already taken into account at the
runtime of the forger. Combining this with Proposition 1 yields $\epsilon_{PRF} \geq \epsilon(1/\kappa - 1/2^n)/(\ell^2 w^2 \kappa^{w-1})$ and $t_{PRF} = t + t_{Kg} + t_{Vf} + 2$ which concludes the proof. □

2.4   Security Level

We now compute the security level of W-OTS for the case that only generic attacks against the PRF property of the function family $F(n)$ exist.

Corollary 1. *Let* $b = \log(t/\epsilon)$ *denote the security level and use* ℓw *as upper bound for* t_{Kg} *and* t_{Vf}, *respectively. Let* $F(n)$ *be* $(2^{n-1-\log \kappa}, 1/2(1/\kappa - 1/2^n))$-*PRF with* $\kappa = 2$. *Then the security level of W-OTS is*

$$b \geq n - w - 1 - 2\log(\ell w) \tag{10}$$

Proof. We use a $(t_{PRF}, \epsilon_{PRF})$-PRF family $F(n)$ and assume that the best attack on the pseudorandomness of $F(n)$ is a brute-force key recovery attack. An attacker that searches through $t_{KOW} = 2^{n-1-\log \kappa}$ keys has success probability $\epsilon_{KOW} = 1/2$ for recovering the correct key. By Proposition 1 this yields an $t_{PRF} = 2^{n-1-\log \kappa} + 2, \epsilon_{PRF} = 1/2(1/\kappa - 1/2^n)$ distinguisher for the pseudorandomness of $F(n)$. The security level of the PRF property of $F(n)$ in presence of this distinguisher is $b = n$ which in turn implies $\kappa \leq 2$ according to Lemma 1. The security level of W-OTS using $F(n)$ is computed as follows

$$2^b = \frac{t}{\epsilon} \geq \frac{t_{PRF} - t_{Kg} - t_{Vf} - 2}{\epsilon_{PRF}\ell^2 w^2 \kappa^{w-1}}\left(\frac{1}{\kappa} - \frac{1}{2^n}\right)$$

$$\geq \frac{2^{n-\log \kappa} - 4\ell w}{\ell^2 w^2 \kappa^{w-1}}$$

$$\geq 2^{n-w-2\log(\ell w)} - \frac{4}{\ell w 2^{w-1}}$$

Since $4/(\ell w 2^{w-2}) \leq 2^{n-w-1-2\log(\ell w)}$ for all reasonable choices of w and m we finally obtain $b \geq n - w - 1 - 2\log(\ell w)$ as security level of W-OTS.   □

3   Strong Unforgeability of the Winternitz One-Time Signature Scheme

While the reduction of the last section shows that W-OTS is EU-CMA assuming a standard security notion for hash functions, it does not provide security in the strong sense. This is accomplished by two reductions presented in this section. We show that W-OTS is strongly unforgeable under adaptive chosen message attacks (SU-CMA), if the used function family is either *second key resistant* or *key collision resistant*. The difference between EU-CMA and SU-CMA is, that in SU-CMA the adversary also wins if he returns a new signature for an already queried message. While these reductions provide stronger security guarantees, they do not rely on standard security notions of hash functions. One is therefore confronted with a trade-off between security and requirements on the hash function. Again we begin by introducing the required security notions and then continue with the reductions and the computation of the security levels.

3.1 Security Notions for Signature Schemes and Function Families II

We begin by reviewing the definition of strong unforgeability under adaptive chosen message attacks. Then, we define two security notions for function families required for our reductions. The first is *second key resistance* which states that given key k and preimage x, it is hard to find a key $k' \neq k$ such that $f_k(x) = f_{k'}(x)$. The second is *key collision resistance* which states that given preimage x, it is hard to find two distinct keys k, k' such that $f_k(x) = f_{k'}(x)$.

Definition 6 (Strong unforgeability (SU-CMA)). *SU-CMA is defined by the following experiment.*

Experiment $\mathsf{Exp}_{\mathsf{A,Sig}}^{\mathsf{SU\text{-}CMA}}(n)$
  $(\mathsf{sk}, \mathsf{pk}) \leftarrow \mathsf{Kg}(1^n)$
  $(M^*, \sigma^*) \leftarrow \mathsf{A}^{\mathsf{Sign}(\mathsf{sk}, \cdot)}(\mathsf{pk})$
  Let $\{(M_i, \sigma_i)\}_1^{q_{\mathsf{Sign}}}$ *be the query-answer pairs of* $\mathsf{Sign}(\mathsf{sk}, \cdot)$.
  Return 1 iff $\mathsf{Vf}(\mathsf{pk}, M^*, \sigma^*) = 1$ *and* $(M^*, \sigma^*) \notin \{(M_i, \sigma_i)\}_1^{q_{\mathsf{Sign}}}$.

The signature scheme Sig *is* (t, ϵ, q)-*SU-CMA if there is no t-time adversary that succeeds with probability $\geq \epsilon$ after making $\leq q$ signature oracle queries.*

Definition 7 (Second key resistance (SKR)). *Let $F(n)$ be a family of functions as in (1). We call $F(n)$ (t, ϵ)-SKR, if the success probability*

$$\mathsf{Adv}_{\mathsf{A}}^{\mathsf{SKR}} = \Pr[(x, k) \xleftarrow{\$} \{0,1\}^n \times \{0,1\}^n,$$
$$k' \leftarrow \mathsf{A}(x, k) : k' \neq k, f_{k'}(x) = f_k(x)] \quad (11)$$

of any adversary A *that runs in time t is at most ϵ.*

Definition 8 (Key collision resistance (KCR)). *Let $F(n)$ be a a family of functions as in (1). We call $F(n)$ (t, ϵ)-KCR, if the success probability*

$$\mathsf{Adv}_{\mathsf{A}}^{\mathsf{KCR}} = \Pr[x \xleftarrow{\$} \{0,1\}^n, (k, k') \leftarrow \mathsf{A}(x) :$$
$$k \neq k', f_k(x) = f_{k'}(x)] \quad (12)$$

of any adversary A *that runs in time t is at most ϵ.*

Proposition 2 (SKR $\Rightarrow$ KOW). *Let $F(n)$ be (t, ϵ)-SKR with $\kappa' > 1$. Then $F(n)$ is $(t - 1, \epsilon/(1 - 1/\kappa'))$-KOW.*

Proof. Towards contradiction, let us assume a successful adversary A that breaks KOW for $F(n)$. We show how to use A as a black-box in an algorithm $\mathcal{B}$ to break SKR. On input (x, k) from the SKR experiment, the algorithm $\mathcal{B}$ computes $y \leftarrow f_k(x)$ and runs $\mathsf{A}(x, y)$. The subroutine returns k' such that $f_k(x) = f_{k'}(x)$ with probability at least ϵ. Then, $\mathcal{B}$ returns k'. Since $\kappa'(F(n)) > 1$, the algorithm A returns a key that is different from k with probability at least $1 - 1/\kappa' \geq 1/2$. Thus, $\mathcal{B}$ is successful with probability $\epsilon(1 - 1/\kappa')$. $\kappa' > 1$ is required to guarantee that a different key actually exists. $\qquad\square$

3.2   Security Reductions

We now state the main result of this section.

Theorem 2. *Let $F(n)$ be a family of functions as in Equation (1) and κ, κ' as in Definition 5.*
a) If $F(n)$ is $(t_{\text{SKR}}, \epsilon_{\text{SKR}})$-SKR then W-OTS is $(t, \epsilon, 1)$ SU-CMA with

$$t \geq t_{\text{SKR}} - t_{\text{Kg}} - t_{\text{Vf}} - 1 \tag{13}$$

$$\epsilon \leq \epsilon_{\text{SKR}} \ell^2 w^2 \kappa^{w-2} \frac{\kappa'}{\kappa' - 1} \tag{14}$$

b) If $F(n)$ is $(t_{\text{KCR}}, \epsilon_{\text{KCR}})$-KCR then W-OTS is $(t, \epsilon, 1)$ SU-CMA with

$$t \geq t_{\text{KCR}} - t_{\text{Kg}} - t_{\text{Vf}} \tag{15}$$

$$\epsilon \leq \epsilon_{\text{KCR}} \frac{\kappa'}{\kappa' - 1} \tag{16}$$

The proof of this theorem can be found in the full version[4].

3.3   Security Level

We now compute the security level of W-OTS for the case that only generic attacks against the SKR or KCR property of the function family $F(n)$ exist.

Note, that in case of $\kappa = 1$ it is impossible to find two signatures for the same message by construction. Therefore W-OTS is SU-CMA secure if it is EU-CMA secure and $\kappa = 1$. For the computation of the security level in this section we therefore assume $\kappa, \kappa' \geq 2$, such that there exists at least one key collision for each preimage.

Corollary 2. *Let $b = \log(t/\epsilon)$ denote the security level and use ℓw as upper bound for t_{Kg} and t_{Vf}, respectively.*
a) Let $F(n)$ be $(2^{n-1-\log \kappa} + 1, (\kappa' - 1)/(2\kappa'))$-SKR and $(t_{\text{PRF}}, \epsilon_{\text{PRF}})$-PRF with $\log(t_{\text{PRF}}/\epsilon_{\text{PRF}}) = n$ and $\kappa' = \kappa = 2$. Then the security level of W-OTS is

$$b \geq n - w - 2\log(\ell w) \tag{17}$$

b) Let $F(n)$ be $(2^{(n-\log \kappa')/2}, 1/2)$-KCR and $(t_{\text{PRF}}, \epsilon_{\text{PRF}})$-PRF with $\log(t_{\text{PRF}}/\epsilon_{\text{PRF}}) = n$ and $\kappa' = \kappa = 2$. Then the security level of W-OTS is

$$b \geq (n-1)/2 - 1 \tag{18}$$

Proof. a) We use a $(t_{\text{SKR}}, \epsilon_{\text{SKR}})$-SKR family $F(n)$ and assume that the best attack on the second key resistance of $F(n)$ is a brute-force key recovery attack. An attacker that searches through $t_{\text{KOW}} = 2^{n-1-\log \kappa}$ keys has success probability $\epsilon_{\text{KOW}} = 1/2$ for recovering the correct key. By Proposition 2 this yields an

$$t_{\text{SKR}} = 2^{n-1-\log \kappa} + 1, \epsilon_{\text{SKR}} = \frac{1}{2} \cdot \frac{\kappa' - 1}{\kappa'}$$

adversary on the second key resistance of $F(n)$. The security level of the SKR property of $F(n)$ in presence of this adversary is $b = n - \log(\kappa - 1)$, assuming $\kappa = \kappa'$. We further assume that $F(n)$ is $(t_{\mathrm{PRF}}, \epsilon_{\mathrm{PRF}})$-PRF with $\log(t_{\mathrm{PRF}}/\epsilon_{\mathrm{PRF}}) = n$. This justifies using $\kappa' = \kappa = 2$ since $\kappa' \geq 2$ is required to ensure that second keys actually exist. The security level of W-OTS is computed as follows

$$
\begin{aligned}
2^b = \frac{t}{\epsilon} &\geq \frac{t_{\mathrm{SKR}} - t_{\mathrm{Kg}} - t_{\mathrm{Vf}} - 1}{\epsilon_{\mathrm{SKR}} \ell^2 w^2 \kappa^{w-2}} \cdot \frac{\kappa' - 1}{\kappa'} \\
&= \frac{2^{n-\log \kappa} - 4\ell w}{\ell^2 w^2 \kappa^{w-2}} \cdot \frac{\kappa' - 1}{\kappa'} \cdot \frac{\kappa}{\kappa - 1} \\
&\geq 2^{n-w+1-2\log(\ell w)} - \frac{4}{\ell w 2^{w-2}}
\end{aligned}
$$

Since $4/(\ell w 2^{w-2}) \leq 2^{n-w-2\log(\ell w)}$ for all reasonable choices of w and m we finally obtain $b \geq n - w - 2\log(\ell w)$ as security level of W-OTS.

b) We use a $(t_{\mathrm{KCR}}, \epsilon_{\mathrm{KCR}})$-KCR family $F(n)$ and assume that the best attack on the key collision resistance of $F(n)$ is a birthday attack, i.e. an adversary that searches through $t_{\mathrm{KCR}} = 2^{(n-\log \kappa')/2}$ keys has success probability $\epsilon_{\mathrm{KCR}} = 1/2$ for finding a key collision. The security level of the KCR property of $F(n)$ in presence of this adversary is $b = (n - \log \kappa')/2 - 1$. Again we assume that $F(n)$ is $(t_{\mathrm{PRF}}, \epsilon_{\mathrm{PRF}})$-PRF with $\log(t_{\mathrm{SKR}}/\epsilon_{\mathrm{SKR}}) = n$ and use $\kappa' = \kappa = 2$. The security level of W-OTS is computed as follows

$$
2^b = \frac{t}{\epsilon} \geq \frac{t_{\mathrm{KCR}} - t_{\mathrm{Kg}} - t_{\mathrm{Vf}}}{\epsilon_{\mathrm{KCR}}} \cdot \frac{\kappa' - 1}{\kappa'} \geq 2^{(n-1)/2} - 2\ell w
$$

Since $2\ell w \leq 2^{(n-1)/2-1}$ for reasonable choices of w and m we finally obtain $b \geq (n-1)/2 - 1$ as security level of W-OTS.

4 Relation between Security Notions

In this section we complete the analysis of implications and separations between key one-wayness (KOW), second key resistance (SKR), key collision resistance (KCR), and pseudorandomness (PRF) started with Propositions 1 and 2, whereas the suspected separation PRF $\not\Rightarrow$ SKR is left as an open problem. The proofs of this section can be found in the full version [4]. Figure 1 summarizes our findings.

Proposition 3 (KOW $\not\Rightarrow$ PRF). *Let $g : \{0,1\}^n \to \{0,1\}^n$ be a one-way function. Then there exists a family $F(n)$ that is KOW but not PRF.*

Proposition 4 (KOW $\not\Rightarrow$ SKR). *Let $F(n)$ be (t, ϵ)-KOW. Then, there is a family $F'(n)$ that is $(t, 2\epsilon)$-KOW but not SKR.*

Proposition 5 (KOW $\not\Rightarrow$ KCR). *Let $F(n)$ be (t, ϵ)-KOW. Then, there is a family $F'(n)$ of functions that is $(t, \epsilon + 2/2^n)$-KOW but not KCR.*

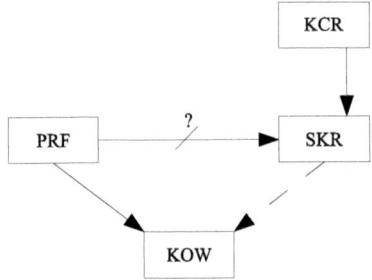

Fig. 1. Implications among PRF, KOW, SKR, and KCR. A straight arrow $A \to B$ means that property A implies property B and a dashed line means that the implication is conditional. When there is no arrow, it means that we show a separation. The suspected separation between PRF and SKR is an open problem.

Proposition 6 (KCR $\Rightarrow$ SKR). *Let $F(n)$ be (t, ϵ)-KCR. Then $F(n)$ is (t, ϵ)-SKR.*

Proposition 7 (SKR $\not\Rightarrow$ KCR). *Let $F(n)$ be (t, ϵ)-SKR. Then, there is a family $F'(n)$ of functions that is $(t, \epsilon + 2/2^n)$-SKR but not KCR.*

Proposition 8 (PRF $\not\Rightarrow$ KCR). *Let $F(n)$ be (t, ϵ)-PRF. Then, there is a family $F'(n)$ of functions that is $(t, \epsilon + 2/2^n)$-PRF but not KCR.*

The following corollaries can be proven in analogy to Proposition 3.

Corollary 3 (SKR $\not\Rightarrow$ PRF). *If second preimage resistant functions exist, there is a family $F(n)$ that is SKR but not PRF.*

Corollary 4 (KCR $\not\Rightarrow$ PRF). *If collision resistant functions exist, there is a family $F(n)$ that is KCR but not PRF.*

5 Conclusion

We have provided three security reductions for W-OTS. The first one shows that W-OTS provides a security level of at least $n - w - 1 - 2\log(\ell w)$, if the security level of the PRF property of the used function family is at least n. When using $n = 128$ and $w = 16$ the security level of W-OTS is at least 91 while the size of a signature is 560 Bytes. The more conservative approach of using $n = 160$ yields a security level of at least 129, which guarantees long-term security but results in larger signatures of 860 Bytes. This reduction is especially appealing because it only assumes a standard security notion of hash functions. SHA-1 and SHA-2 being PRFs is required when using them in the HMAC construction and SHA-3 will be specifically designed to be a PRF. Furthermore, this reduction also works for the special class of pseudorandom permutations (PRP). PRP is the standard model for block ciphers, so it is possible to replace the hash function family with a block cipher. As a block cipher with n bit keys is normally assumed to provide n bit security against distinguishing attacks this justifies our assumption of $\kappa \leq 2$ given Lemma 1. Since several of today's CPUs are equipped with an AES co-processor, this might also lead significant speed-ups in practice.

However, this reduction does not guarantee strong unforgeability, except in case of $\kappa = 1$ meaning that no key collisions exist. If no key collisions exist, each message has a unique signature and the scheme is trivially SU-CMA when it is EU-CMA. Showing SU-CMA in general requires that the underlying functions are either SKR or KCR. This has been shown in the second and third reduction. The security level of W-OTS is at least $n - w - 1 - 2\log(\ell w)$ if the security level of the SKR property of the used PRF is at least $n - \log(\kappa - 1)$. When using KCR, the security level of W-OTS is at least $(n-1)/2 - 1$ if the security level of the KCR property of the used PRF is at least $(n - \log \kappa)/2 - 1$. We remark that the last reduction also works with the original Winternitz construction using a family of collision resistant hash functions. In other words, W-OTS is SU-CMA if the used function is collision resistant. However, using a PRF with additional KCR property has the benefit that an exact value for the maximum number κ of key collisions that occur within the family is known. This is required for the estimation of the exact security level.

As a by-product we have defined three key-based security notions for function families: key one-wayness (KOW), second key resistance (SKR), and key collision resistance (KCR). We have analyzed implications and separations among these properties and pseudorandomness. Although, these relations have not been analyzed before, they support the common intuition. In fact, key-based and non-key-based notions share an analoguous hierarchy of implications and separations with respect to preimage resistance, second preimage resistance, and collision resistance. We refer the reader to [22] for a discussion on non-key-based notions.

We would like to point out that KCR functions f_k can easily be obtained from collision resistant functions g_k by defining $f_k(x) = g_x(k)$. If we require f to inherit the PRF property of g, we have to assume that the compression function of g is dual-PRF, meaning that it is a PRF regardless of which input it is keyed with. This is also a requirement of the security proof of HMAC [1]. SKR functions can be constructed equivalently while the KOW property is immediately implied by the PRF property. While we have shown the separation of PRF and KCR, we leave the suspected separation of PRF and SKR as an open problem. Moreover, we have studied the relation between the security level of a PRF and the maximum number of key collisions that can occur.

References

1. Bellare, M.: New proofs for nmac and hmac: Security without collision-resistance. In: Dwork, C. (ed.) CRYPTO 2006. LNCS, vol. 4117, pp. 602–619. Springer, Heidelberg (2006)
2. Bellare, M., Kilian, J., Rogaway, P.: The security of the cipher block chaining message authentication code. Journal of Computer and System Sciences 61(3), 362–399 (2000)

3. Bleichenbacher, D., Maurer, U.M.: Directed acyclic graphs, one-way functions and digital signatures. In: Desmedt, Y.G. (ed.) CRYPTO 1994. LNCS, vol. 839, pp. 75–82. Springer, Heidelberg (1994)

4. Buchmann, J., Dahmen, E., Ereth, S., Hülsing, A., Rückert, M.: On the security of the winternitz one-time signature scheme. Cryptology ePrint Archive, Report 2011/191 (2011), http://eprint.iacr.org/

5. Buchmann, J., Dahmen, E., Klintsevich, E., Okeya, K., Vuillaume, C.: Merkle signatures with virtually unlimited signature capacity. In: Katz, J., Yung, M. (eds.) ACNS 2007. LNCS, vol. 4521, pp. 31–45. Springer, Heidelberg (2007)

6. Canetti, R., Micciancio, D., Reingold, O.: Perfectly one-way probabilistic hash functions (preliminary version). In: STOC, pp. 131–140 (1998)

7. Coronado García, L.C.: On the security and the efficiency of the merkle signature scheme. Technical Report 2005/192, Cryptology ePrint Archive (2005), Available at http://eprint.iacr.org/2005/192/

8. Dahmen, E., Okeya, K., Takagi, T., Vuillaume, C.: Digital signatures out of second-preimage resistant hash functions. In: Buchmann, J., Ding, J. (eds.) PQCrypto 2008. LNCS, vol. 5299, pp. 109–123. Springer, Heidelberg (2008)

9. Dods, C., Smart, N., Stam, M.: Hash based digital signature schemes. In: Smart, N.P. (ed.) Cryptography and Coding 2005. LNCS, vol. 3796, pp. 96–115. Springer, Heidelberg (2005)

10. Fischlin, M.: Pseudorandom function tribe ensembles based on one-way permutations: Improvements and applications. In: Stern, J. (ed.) EUROCRYPT 1999. LNCS, vol. 1592, pp. 432–445. Springer, Heidelberg (1999)

11. Goldreich, O., Goldwasser, S., Micali, S.: How to construct random functions. J. ACM 33(4), 792–807 (1986)

12. Goldwasser, S., Micali, S., Rivest, R.L.: A digital signature scheme secure against adaptive chosen-message attacks. SIAM J. Comput. 17(2), 281–308 (1988)

13. Grover, L.K.: A fast quantum mechanical algorithm for database search. In: Proceedings of the Twenty-Eighth Annual Symposium on the Theory of Computing, pp. 212–219. ACM Press, New York (1996)

14. Hevia, A., Micciancio, D.: The provable security of graph-based one-time signatures and extensions to algebraic signature schemes. In: Zheng, Y. (ed.) ASIACRYPT 2002. LNCS, vol. 2501, pp. 379–396. Springer, Heidelberg (2002)

15. Lamport, L.: Constructing digital signatures from a one way function. Technical Report SRI-CSL-98, SRI International Computer Science Laboratory (1979)

16. Levin, L.: One way functions and pseudorandom generators. Combinatorica 7, 357–363 (1987)

17. Luk, M., Perrig, A., Whillock, B.: Seven cardinal properties of sensor network broadcast authentication. In: ACM Workshop on Security of Ad Hoc and Sensor Networks, SASN (2006)

18. Merkle, R.C.: A certified digital signature. In: Brassard, G. (ed.) CRYPTO 1989. LNCS, vol. 435, pp. 218–238. Springer, Heidelberg (1990)

19. Perrig, A.: The biba one-time signature and broadcast authentication protocol. In: ACM Conference on Computer and Communications Security, pp. 28–37 (2001)

20. Perrig, A., Canetti, R., Tygar, J.D., Song, D.: Efficient authentication and signing of multicast streams over lossy channels. In: IEEE Symposium on Security and Privacy, pp. 56–73 (2000)

21. Reyzin, L., Reyzin, N.: Better than biBa: Short one-time signatures with fast signing and verifying. In: Batten, L.M., Seberry, J. (eds.) ACISP 2002. LNCS, vol. 2384, pp. 1–47. Springer, Heidelberg (2002)

22. Rogaway, P., Shrimpton, T.: Cryptographic hash-function basics: Definitions, implications, and separations for preimage resistance, second-preimage resistance, and collision resistance. In: Roy, B., Meier, W. (eds.) FSE 2004. LNCS, vol. 3017, pp. 371–388. Springer, Heidelberg (2004)
23. Rompel, J.: One-way functions are necessary and sufficient for secure signatures. In: STOC 1990: Proceedings of the twenty-second annual ACM symposium on Theory of computing, pp. 387–394. ACM Press, New York (1990)
24. Shor, P.W.: Algorithms for quantum computation: Discrete logarithms and factoring. In: Proceedings of the 35th Annual IEEE Symposium on Foundations of Computer Science (FOCS 1994), pp. 124–134. IEEE Computer Society Press, Los Alamitos (1994)
25. Yao, A.C.: Theory and application of trapdoor functions. Annual IEEE Symposium on Foundations of Computer Science 0, 80–91 (1982)

Efficient Zero-Knowledge Proofs

Jens Groth

UCL, London, UK

Abstract. A zero-knowledge proof is a two-party protocol that enables a prover to convince a verifier of the truth of a statement without revealing anything else. Zero-knowledge proofs are widely used in cryptography to guarantee that parties are acting correctly without revealing their private information.

Interestingly, it is possible to make highly efficient zero-knowledge proofs where the amount of communication is much smaller than the size of the statement. We will in this talk discuss practical communication-efficient zero-knowledge proofs.

A. Nitaj and D. Pointcheval (Eds.): AFRICACRYPT 2011, LNCS 6737, p. 379, 2011.

Some Key Techniques on Pairing Vector Spaces

Tatsuaki Okamoto[1] and Katsuyuki Takashima[2]

[1] NTT, 3-9-11 Midori-cho, Musashino-shi, Tokyo 180-8585, Japan
okamoto.tatsuaki@lab.ntt.co.jp
[2] Mitsubishi Electric, 5-1-1 Ofuna, Kamakura, Kanagawa 247-8501, Japan
Takashima.Katsuyuki@aj.MitsubishiElectric.co.jp

Abstract. Recently we have introduced a new concept on bilinear pairing groups, *dual pairing vector spaces (DPVS)*. Although we have already enjoyed the merits of DPVS in our results [1,2,3,4,5], we here explain them more explicitly, especially some key techniques on DPVS.

We firstly briefly explain DPVS constructed on symmetric pairing groups $(q, \mathbb{G}, \mathbb{G}_T, G, e)$, where q is a prime, $\mathbb{G}$ and $\mathbb{G}_T$ are cyclic groups of order q, G is a generator of $\mathbb{G}$, $e : \mathbb{G} \times \mathbb{G} \to \mathbb{G}_T$ is a non-degenerate bilinear pairing operation, and $e(G, G) \neq 1$. Here we denote the group operation of $\mathbb{G}$ by addition and $\mathbb{G}_T$ by multiplication, respectively. Note that this construction also works on *asymmetric* pairing groups.

Vector space $\mathbb{V}$: $\mathbb{V} := \overbrace{\mathbb{G} \times \cdots \times \mathbb{G}}^{N}$, whose element is expressed by N-dimensional vector, $\boldsymbol{x} := (x_1 G, \ldots, x_N G)$ $(x_i \in \mathbb{F}_q$ for $i = 1, \ldots, N)$.

Canonical base $\mathbb{A}$: $\mathbb{A} := (\boldsymbol{a}_1, \ldots, \boldsymbol{a}_N)$ of $\mathbb{V}$, where $\boldsymbol{a}_1 := (G, 0, \ldots, 0), \boldsymbol{a}_2 := (0, G, 0, \ldots, 0), \ldots, \boldsymbol{a}_N := (0, \ldots, 0, G)$.

Pairing operation: $e(\boldsymbol{x}, \boldsymbol{y}) := \prod_{i=1}^{N} e(x_i G, y_i G) = e(G, G)^{\sum_{i=1}^{N} x_i y_i} = e(G, G)^{\overrightarrow{x} \cdot \overrightarrow{y}} \in \mathbb{G}_T$, where $\boldsymbol{x} := (x_1 G, \ldots, x_N G) = x_1 \boldsymbol{a}_1 + \cdots + x_N \boldsymbol{a}_N \in \mathbb{V}$, $\boldsymbol{y} := (y_1 G, \ldots, y_N G) = y_1 \boldsymbol{a}_1 + \cdots + y_N \boldsymbol{a}_N \in \mathbb{V}$, $\overrightarrow{x} := (x_1, \ldots, x_N)$ and $\overrightarrow{y} := (y_1, \ldots, y_N)$. Here, $\boldsymbol{x}$ and $\boldsymbol{y}$ can be expressed by coefficient vector over basis $\mathbb{A}$ such that $(x_1, \ldots, x_N)_{\mathbb{A}} = (\overrightarrow{x})_{\mathbb{A}} := \boldsymbol{x}$ and $(y_1, \ldots, y_N)_{\mathbb{A}} = (\overrightarrow{y})_{\mathbb{A}} := \boldsymbol{y}$.

Base change: Canonical basis $\mathbb{A}$ is changed to basis $\mathbb{B} := (\boldsymbol{b}_1, \ldots, \boldsymbol{b}_N)$ of $\mathbb{V}$ using a uniformly chosen (regular) linear transformation, $X := (\chi_{i,j}) \xleftarrow{\mathsf{U}} GL(N, \mathbb{F}_q)$, such that $\boldsymbol{b}_i = \sum_{j=1}^{N} \chi_{i,j} \boldsymbol{a}_j$, $(i = 1, \ldots, N)$. $\mathbb{A}$ is also changed to basis $\mathbb{B}^* := (\boldsymbol{b}_1^*, \ldots, \boldsymbol{b}_N^*)$ of $\mathbb{V}$, such that $(\vartheta_{i,j}) := (X^T)^{-1}$, $\boldsymbol{b}_i^* = \sum_{j=1}^{N} \vartheta_{i,j} \boldsymbol{a}_j$, $(i = 1, \ldots, N)$. We see that $e(\boldsymbol{b}_i, \boldsymbol{b}_j^*) = e(G, G)^{\delta_{i,j}}$, $(\delta_{i,j} = 1$ if $i = j$, and $\delta_{i,j} = 0$ if $i \neq j)$ i.e., $\mathbb{B}$ and $\mathbb{B}^*$ are dual orthonormal bases of $\mathbb{V}$.

Here, $\boldsymbol{x} := x_1 \boldsymbol{b}_1 + \cdots + x_N \boldsymbol{b}_N \in \mathbb{V}$ and $\boldsymbol{y} := y_1 \boldsymbol{b}_1^* + \cdots + y_N \boldsymbol{b}_N^* \in \mathbb{V}$ can be expressed by coefficient vectors over $\mathbb{B}$ and $\mathbb{B}^*$ such that $(x_1, \ldots, x_N)_{\mathbb{B}} = (\overrightarrow{x})_{\mathbb{B}} := \boldsymbol{x}$ and $(y_1, \ldots, y_N)_{\mathbb{B}^*} = (\overrightarrow{y})_{\mathbb{B}^*} := \boldsymbol{y}$, and $e(\boldsymbol{x}, \boldsymbol{y}) = e(G, G)^{\sum_{i=1}^{N} x_i y_i} = e(G, G)^{\overrightarrow{x} \cdot \overrightarrow{y}} \in \mathbb{G}_T$.

Intractable problem: One of the most natural decisional problems in this approach is the decisional subspace problem [2]. It is to tell $\boldsymbol{v} := v_{N_2+1} \boldsymbol{b}_{N_2+1} +$

A. Nitaj and D. Pointcheval (Eds.): AFRICACRYPT 2011, LNCS 6737, pp. 380–382, 2011.

$\cdots + v_{N_1} \boldsymbol{b}_{N_1}$ $(= (0,\ldots,0,v_{N_2+1},\ldots,v_{N_1})_\mathbb{B})$, from $\boldsymbol{u} := v_1\boldsymbol{b}_1 + \cdots + v_{N_1}\boldsymbol{b}_{N_1}$ $(= (v_1,\ldots,v_{N_1})_\mathbb{B})$, where $(v_1,\ldots,v_{N_1}) \xleftarrow{\mathsf{U}} \mathbb{F}_q^{N_1}$ and $N_2 + 1 < N_1$.

Trapdoor: Although the decisional subspace problem is assumed to be intractable, it can be efficiently solved by using some *trapdoor*, from top level to lower levels. The top level trapdoor is X, which can decompose $\boldsymbol{u}$ to $\boldsymbol{v}$, and a lower level is $\boldsymbol{t}^* \in \mathsf{span}\langle \boldsymbol{b}_1^*,\ldots,\boldsymbol{b}_{N_2}^* \rangle$, where we can tell $\boldsymbol{v}$ from $\boldsymbol{u}$ using $\boldsymbol{t}^*$ since $e(\boldsymbol{v},\boldsymbol{t}^*) = 1$ and $e(\boldsymbol{u},\boldsymbol{t}^*) \neq 1$ with high probability.

Higher dimensional vector treatment of bilinear pairing groups have been already employed in literature especially in the areas of IBE, ABE and BE. For example, in a typical vector treatment, two vector forms of $P := (g^{x_1},\ldots,g^{x_n})$ and $Q := (g^{y_1},\ldots,g^{y_n})$ are set and pairing for P and Q is operated as $e(P,Q) := \prod_{i=1}^{n} e(g^{x_i},g^{y_i})$. Such treatment can be rephrased in this approach such that $P = x_1\boldsymbol{a}_1 + \cdots + x_n\boldsymbol{a}_n$ $(= (x_1,\ldots,x_n)_\mathbb{A})$, and $Q = y_1\boldsymbol{a}_1 + \cdots + y_n\boldsymbol{a}_n$ $(= (y_1,\ldots,y_n)_\mathbb{A})$ over canonical basis $\mathbb{A}$. The major drawback of this approach is the easily *decomposable* property over $\mathbb{A}$ (i.e., the decisional subspace problem is easily solved). That is, it is easy to decompose $x_i\boldsymbol{a}_i = (1,\ldots,1,g^{x_i},1,\ldots,1)$ from $P := x_1\boldsymbol{a}_1 + \cdots x_n\boldsymbol{a}_n = (g^{x_1},\ldots,g^{x_n})$.

In contrast, our approach, DPVS, employs basis $\mathbb{B}$, which is linearly transformed from $\mathbb{A}$ using a secret random matrix $X \in \mathbb{F}_q^{n\times n}$. A remarkable property over $\mathbb{B}$ is that it seems hard to decompose $x_i\boldsymbol{b}_i$ from $P' := x_1\boldsymbol{b}_1 + \cdots x_n\boldsymbol{b}_n$ (and the decisional subspace problem seems intractable). In addition, the secret matrix X (and the dual orthonormal basis $\mathbb{B}^*$ of $\mathbb{V}$) can be used as a source of the trapdoors to the decomposability (and distinguishability for the decisional subspace problem through the pairing operation over $\mathbb{B}$ and $\mathbb{B}^*$ as mentioned above). The hard decomposability (and indistinguishability) and its trapdoors are ones of the key tricks in our approach.

Composite order pairing groups are often employed with similar tricks such as hard decomposability (and indistinguishability) of a composite order group to the prime order subgroups and its trapdoors through factoring.

The DPVS approach has, however, the following several advantages over the composite order pairing group approach.

Efficiency. In the DPVS approach, the construction is based on prime order pairing groups and more efficient than that on composite order pairing groups.

Flexibility. In the DPVS approach it is easy to realize a higher (e.g., 1000 or 10000) dimensional space, while it is hard to extend it to such a higher dimensional space in the composite order pairing groups approach (e.g., using composite $n = p_1 \cdots p_{10000}$).

Public Parameters. In some setting, the parameters of pairing groups should be publicly set up. In the DPVS approach, such a setting is easy, e.g., it can be from public or standard documents, since the parameters are on prime order pairing groups and there is no trapdoor. In contrast, in the composite order pairing groups approach, a *trusted party* should generate the parameters of composite order pairing groups since there is a trapdoor, where if the party is corrupted (or the trapdoor is compromised), the system should be totally broken down.

Hierarchical Trapdoors. The trapdoors in the DPVS approach are hierarchical, from the top level to lower levels. The top level trapdoor is X, the next top level is $\mathbb{B}^*$, and there are variously lower level trapdoors such as $t^* \in \text{span}\langle b_1^*, \ldots, b_{N_2}^* \rangle$, mentioned above. There are many applications of the hierarchical trapdoors. The trapdoor of the composite order pairing groups approach is much simpler and there is no such hierarchical trapdoor, only prime factorization of n or prime order subgroup generators,

Information Theoretic Techniques. The most important advantage of the DPVS approach over the composite order pairing groups approach is that it has information theoretic properties or techniques. As mentioned above, there are dual orthonormal bases $(\mathbb{B}, \mathbb{B}^*)$, where $\mathbb{B}$ is basically a public key and $\mathbb{B}^*$ is a secret key. In our approach, however, we often use a part of $\mathbb{B}$, $\widehat{\mathbb{B}}$, instead of the whole of $\mathbb{B}$, as a public key, and the remaining part of $\mathbb{B}$ is information theoretically secret. That is, even an infinite power adversary has no idea on the secret part of $\mathbb{B}$. We have essentially employed this information theoretic property in [1,3,4,5], while there is no such information theoretic property in the composite order pairing groups approach since an infinite power adversary can obtain the whole trapdoor, factorization of composite n.

References

1. Lewko, A., Okamoto, T., Sahai, A., Takashima, K., Waters, B.: Fully secure functional encryption: Attribute-based encryption and (Hierarchical) inner product encryption. In: Gilbert, H. (ed.) EUROCRYPT 2010. LNCS, vol. 6110, pp. 62–91. Springer, Heidelberg (2010)
2. Okamoto, T., Takashima, K.: Homomorphic encryption and signatures from vector decomposition. In: Galbraith, S.D., Paterson, K.G. (eds.) Pairing 2008. LNCS, vol. 5209, pp. 57–74. Springer, Heidelberg (2008)
3. Okamoto, T., Takashima, K.: Hierarchical predicate encryption for inner-products. In: Matsui, M. (ed.) ASIACRYPT 2009. LNCS, vol. 5912, pp. 214–231. Springer, Heidelberg (2009)
4. Okamoto, T., Takashima, K.: Fully secure functional encryption with general relations from the decisional linear assumption. In: Rabin, T. (ed.) CRYPTO 2010. LNCS, vol. 6223, pp. 191–208. Springer, Heidelberg (2010), Full version is available at http://eprint.iacr.org/2010/563
5. Okamoto, T., Takashima, K.: Efficient attribute-based signatures for non-monotone predicates in the standard model. In: Catalano, D., Fazio, N., Gennaro, R., Nicolosi, A. (eds.) PKC 2011. LNCS, vol. 6571, pp. 35–52. Springer, Heidelberg (2011)

The NIST SHA-3 Competition: A Perspective on the Final Year

Bart Preneel

Katholieke Universiteit Leuven and IBBT
Dept. Electrical Engineering-ESAT/COSIC,
Kasteelpark Arenberg 10 Bus 2446, B-3001 Leuven, Belgium
bart.preneel@esat.kuleuven.be

Abstract. Cryptographic hash functions map input strings of arbitrary length to fixed length output strings. They are expected to satisfy several security properties that include preimage resistance, second preimage resistance, and collision resistance. The free availability of efficient software-oriented hash functions such as MD4, MD5 and SHA-1 has resulted in a very broad deployment of hash functions, way beyond their initial design purposes. In spite of the importance for applications, until 2005 the amount of theoretical research and cryptanalysis invested in this topic was rather limited. Moreover, cryptanalysts had been winning the battle from designers: about 4 of every 5 designs were broken. In 2004 Wang et al. made a breakthrough in the cryptanalysis of MD4, MD5 and SHA-1. Around the same time, serious shortcomings were identified in the theoretical foundations of existing designs. In response to this hash function crisis, in the last five years a substantial number of papers has been published with theoretical results and novel designs. Moreover, NIST announced in November 2007 the start of the SHA-3 competition, with as goal to select a new hash function family by 2012. We present a brief outline of the state of the art of hash functions in the last year of the competition and attempt to identify the lessons learned and some open research problems.

1 Background

Cryptographic hash functions first appeared in the cryptographic literature in the 1976 seminal paper of Diffie and Hellman on public-key cryptography [8]. Today, hash functions are used in a broad range of applications: to compute a short unique identifier of a string (e.g. for a digital signature), as one-way function to hide a string (e.g. for password protection), to commit to a string in a protocol, for key derivation and for entropy extraction. In addition, they have been deployed to instantiate random oracles and as building block for other cryptographic primitives.

Most of the first hash function designs were broken very quickly; in the late 1980s there was a clear understanding that there was a need for more secure and more efficient hash functions. The first theoretical result was the construction

A. Nitaj and D. Pointcheval (Eds.): AFRICACRYPT 2011, LNCS 6737, pp. 383–386, 2011.

of a collision-resistance hash function based on a collision-resistant compression function, proposed independently by Damgård [7] and Merkle [15] in 1989. Around the same time, the first cryptographic algorithms were proposed that were intended to be fast in software; the hash functions MD4 [19] and MD5 [20] fall in this category. Both functions were picked up quickly by application developers as they were ten times faster than DES; in addition they were not patent-encumbered and they posed less export problems than an encryption algorithm such as DES. As a consequence, hash functions were also used to construct MAC algorithms (e.g., HMAC as analyzed by Bellare et al. [4,3]) and even block ciphers and stream ciphers.

During the 1990s, a growing number of hash functions were proposed [18], but unfortunately very few of these designs have withstood cryptanalysis. Notable results were obtained by Dobbertin, who found collisions for MD4 in 1995 [9] and collisions for the compression function of MD5 in 1996 [10]. Very few theoretical results were available in the area. At the same time however, MD5 and SHA-1, the latter introduced in 1995 by NIST (National Institute for Standards and Technology, US) [12], were deployed in an ever growing number of applications, resulting in the name "Swiss army knifes" of cryptography.

In 2004, Wang et al. made substantial progress on the cryptanalysis of the MD4 family: by introducing a sophisticated variant of differential cryptanalysis they found collisions for MD4 by hand and for MD5 in a few minutes [22]. They managed to reduce the cost of collisions for SHA-1 by three orders of magnitude [21], which undermined the confidence in this widely used standard. As a consequence, the interest in hash functions surged: many new theoretical results were obtained, new designs were proposed and the cryptanalytic techniques of Wang et al. were further developed. Today RIPEMD-160 [11] seems to be one of the few older 160-bit hash functions for which no shortcut attacks are known. NIST introduced in 2002 the SHA-2 family of hash functions [13] with as goal to match the security levels provided by 3-DES and AES (output results of 224 to 512 bits). There is a concern that the attacks of Wang et al. would also apply to these functions, which have design principles that are quite similar to those of SHA-1; however, it should be pointed out that the more complex diffusion and the nonlinear message expansion of SHA-2 have held up against the current attack techniques.

2   The SHA-3 Competition

In November 2007, NIST announced that it would organize an open competition to select the SHA-3 algorithm [16]. In October 2008, 64 candidates were submitted; 51 of these were selected for the first round and in July 2009, 14 were admitted to the second round. In December 2010, NIST has announced 5 finalists: Blake, Grøstl, JH, Keccak, and Skein. The final winner will be selected by mid 2012.

Some preliminary conclusions can be drawn. A first observation is that during the SHA-3 competition many new designs have broken and many of the (strong) designs been tweaked; this clearly shows that designing a secure hash function is very delicate. The largest design innovation is the introduction by Bertoni et al. [5] of sponge functions, that are very different from the Merkle-Damgård design; the idea of a sponge function is not to start from a strong compression function, but to use a larger intermediate state and to obtain security from the iteration. Keccak [6] is an instantiation of a sponge function, while JH is a generalization of a sponge function that has been studied under the name parazoa [2]. The most powerful attack that has emerged right before and during the competition has been the rebound attack [14]; it has been applied successfully to many designs (or to reduced-round versions). The five finalists represent a large diversity: JH and Keccak use small S-boxes or Boolean functions only, Grøstl uses an 8-bit S-box as found in AES, while Blake and Skein use ARX (addition/rotation/xor) operations on larger words of 32/64 bits. From a theoretical perspective, substantial progress has been made with security reductions, but major gaps still remain as explained in [1]. The performance of all finalists is very good; Keccack seems to offer the best hardware performance, while Blake and Skein (that use CPU arithmetic) have some advantage in software on high end CPUs.

3   Conclusions

Based on the five finalists, it seems safe to predict that SHA-3 will be a robust and efficient hash function. The design itself will be very different from SHA-2, and it will likely co-exist for an extended period with SHA-2. One can expect that NIST will standardize a tree mode for hash functions to obtain improved performance on multi-core processors (see [7,17] and several SHA-3 submissions). For the long term, we face the challenging problem to design an efficient hash function for which the security can be reduced to a mathematical problem that is elegant and for which we have a convincing security reduction.

References

1. Andreeva, E., Mennink, B., Preneel, B.: Security reductions of the second round SHA-3 candidates. In: Burmester, M., Tsudik, G., Magliveras, S., Ilić, I. (eds.) ISC 2010. LNCS, vol. 6531, pp. 39–53. Springer, Heidelberg (2011)
2. Andreeva, E., Mennink, B., Preneel, B.: The parazoa family: generalizing the sponge hash functions. Cryptology ePrint Archive: Report 2011/028, 14 January (2011)
3. Bellare, M.: New proofs for NMAC and HMAC: security without collision resistance. In: Dwork, C. (ed.) CRYPTO 2006. LNCS, vol. 4117, Springer, Heidelberg (2006)
4. Bellare, M., Canetti, R., Krawczyk, H.: Keying hash functions for message authentication. In: Koblitz, N. (ed.) CRYPTO 1996. LNCS, vol. 1109, pp. 1–15. Springer, Heidelberg (1996)
5. Bertoni, G., Daemen, J., Peeters, M., Van Assche, G.: On the indifferentiability of the sponge construction. In: Smart, N.P. (ed.) EUROCRYPT 2008. LNCS, vol. 4965, pp. 181–197. Springer, Heidelberg (2008)

6. Bertoni, G., Daemen, J., Peeters, M., Van Assche, G.: The KECCAK sponge function family (2009), submission to the NIST SHA-3 competition
7. Damgård, I.B.: A design principle for hash functions. In: Brassard, G. (ed.) CRYPTO 1989. LNCS, vol. 435, pp. 416–427. Springer, Heidelberg (1990)
8. Diffie, W., Hellman, M.E.: New directions in cryptography. IEEE Trans. Information Theory 22(6), 644–654 (1976)
9. Dobbertin, H.: Cryptanalysis of MD4. J. Cryptology 11, 253–271 (1998); See also in Gollmann, D. (ed.) FSE 1996. LNCS, vol. 1039, pp. 53–69. Springer, Heidelberg (1996)
10. Dobbertin, H.: The status of MD5 after a recent attack. CryptoBytes 2, 1–6 (1996)
11. Dobbertin, H., Bosselaers, A., Preneel, B.: RIPEMD-160: a strengthened version of RIPEMD. In: Gollmann, D. (ed.) FSE 1996. LNCS, vol. 1039, pp. 71–82. Springer, Heidelberg (1996)
12. FIPS 180-1, Secure Hash Standard. Federal Information Processing Standard (FIPS), Publication 180-1, National Institute of Standards and Technology, US Department of Commerce, Washington D.C., April 17 (1995)
13. FIPS 180-2, Secure Hash Standard. Federal Information Processing Standard (FIPS), Publication 180-2, National Institute of Standards and Technology, US Department of Commerce, Washington D.C., August 26 (2002) (Change notice 1 published on December 1, 2003)
14. Lamberger, M., Mendel, F., Rechberger, C., Rijmen, V., Schläffer, M.: Rebound distinguishers: Results on the full Whirlpool compression function. In: Matsui, M. (ed.) ASIACRYPT 2009. LNCS, vol. 5912, pp. 126–143. Springer, Heidelberg (2009)
15. Merkle, R.C.: One way hash functions and DES. In: Brassard, G. (ed.) CRYPTO 1989. LNCS, vol. 435, pp. 428–446. Springer, Heidelberg (1990)
16. NIST SHA-3 Competition, http://csrc.nist.gov/groups/ST/hash/
17. Pal, P., Sarkar, P.: PARSHA-256 – A new parallelizable hash function and a multi-threaded implementation. In: Johansson, T. (ed.) FSE 2003. LNCS, vol. 2887, pp. 347–361. Springer, Heidelberg (2003)
18. Preneel, B.: Analysis and design of cryptographic hash functions Doctoral Dissertation, Katholieke Universiteit Leuven (1993)
19. Rivest, R.L.: The MD4 message digest algorithm. In: Menezes, A., Vanstone, S.A. (eds.) CRYPTO 1990. LNCS, vol. 537, pp. 303–311. Springer, Heidelberg (1991)
20. Rivest, R.L.: The MD5 message-digest algorithm. Request for Comments (RFC) 1321, Internet Activities Board, Internet Privacy Task Force (April 1992)
21. Wang, X., Yin, Y.L., Yu, H.: Finding collisions in the full SHA-1. In: Shoup, V. (ed.) CRYPTO 2005. LNCS, vol. 3621, pp. 1–16. Springer, Heidelberg (2005)
22. Wang, X., Yu, H.: How to break MD5 and other hash functions. In: Cramer, R. (ed.) EUROCRYPT 2005. LNCS, vol. 3494, pp. 19–35. Springer, Heidelberg (2005)

Author Index